Eurodélices

DINE WITH
EUROPE'S MASTER CHEFS

Eurodélices

DINE WITH EUROPE'S MASTER CHEFS

APPETIZERS
MAIN DISHES
DESSERTS

KÖNEMANN

Acknowledgements

We would like to thank all those people, restaurants and companies whose invaluable help made this book possible.

Skill ratings of the recipes:

★   easy
★★   medium
★★★ difficult

This book and the information contained herein has been researched and compiled with the greatest of care. However, content errors cannot be completely ruled out. Changes in the field of catering are at all times possible. The Master Chefs' places of work and their gourmet guide ratings are especially prone to constant change. The publisher cannot therefore accept any responsibility whatsoever for information concerning either the recipes or the chefs and pastry chefs listed in this book.

Photos: Studio Lucien Loeb, Maren Detering

© for the original edition: Fabien Bellahsen and Daniel Rouche

Title of the German edition: *Eurodélices — Europas Meisterköche bitten zu Tisch*
ISBN-10: 3-8331-1052-X
ISBN-13: 978-3-8331-1052-8

© 2004 for the English edition:
Tandem Verlag GmbH
KÖNEMANN is a trademark and an imprint of Tandem Verlag GmbH

Translation into English:
Cold Appetizers: Tobias Kommerell / CPM, Cambridge
Hot Appetizers: Regina Bailey / CPM, Cambridge
Fish & Seafood: Translate-A-Book, a division of Transedition Limited, Oxford
Meat & Poultry: Translate-A-Book, a division of Transedition Limited, Oxford
Desserts: Fiona Hulse / CPM, Cambridge
Pastries: Fiona Hulse / CPM, Cambridge

Project management: Isabel Weiler
Editing: Claudia Boss-Teichmann

Printed in China

ISBN-10: 3-8331-1158-5
ISBN-13: 978-3-8331-1158-7

10 9 8 7 6 5 4 3 2
X IX VIII VII VI V IV III II

Contents

Foreword

"Eurodélices" brings a selection of European haute cuisine right into your kitchen. More than 100 professional chefs, many of them recipients of multiple awards and distinctions, associated with renowned restaurants in 15 countries throughout Europe, joined forces to create this unique book. Here they divulge their best and their favorite recipes for unsurpassed hot and cold appetizers, fish and meat entrées, desserts, and pastry specialties.

The collection contains more than 350 recipes on over 830 pages and is not only an essential guide for gourmet cooks, but also an absorbing document of European culture that goes far beyond short-lived culinary trends. In a fascinating way, Eurodélices explores the common roots of the different "arts of cooking" that have developed in various geographic locations, as well as their abundant variety.

For eating is much more than the fulfillment of a basic bodily need; cooking is often elevated to the level of an art, especially in association with parties and celebrations of all kinds, in private life and in the public sphere. Young couples plan their futures over a special dinner at an elegant restaurant, partners gather at table to launch new business ventures, heads of state are wined and dined. Every conceivable celebration involves food, from weddings to funerals, from intimacies shared over coffee and cake to Sunday dinners to Passover and Thanksgiving feasts.

We often have our first contact with the cultures of other lands, whether nearby or across an ocean, through their food. Precisely because the various contributing chefs are rooted in their distinct traditions, some flavors and combinations will be new to readers from other parts of the world, and occasionally ingredients are called for that may be unfamiliar or even difficult to locate. The texts accompanying each recipe help elucidate and, wherever possible, suggest substitutes for ingredients that are not readily available everywhere. A glossary is also included to explain terms that may not be obvious, listing some ingredients.

Because precision is often crucial to the success of recipes of this caliber, a few words regarding measurements and conversions are in order. In Europe, it is customary to use metric units of liquid volume or weight, that is, milliliters or grams. Every household has a kitchen scale and solid ingredients are weighed, rather than measured by volume. Converting milliliters to fluid cups and grams to ounces is straightforward, if not always neat. More problematic are ingredients given in grams that North Americans measure by volume, in tablespoons and cups. Throughout the book, the original metric measurement follows the North American equivalent. The conversions are painstakingly accurate up to 100 ml and 100 g (which necessitates some awkward-looking amounts). Thereafter, they are more neatly, and thus less accurately, rounded off. As with all recipes, measurements are approximate for many ingredients, and a wide variety of factors ranging from temperature and humidity to accuracy of kitchen implements to the way food is sold will affect the amount actually used. If the reader wants to recreate the recipes as given, however, the use of a kitchen scale is strongly recommended.

The unique collection of around 350 recipes contained in Eurodélices aims to excite its readers' curiosity. Classic dishes, which have been enjoyed for generations and thus form the foundations of modern cookery, are liberally presented. But there are also new and surprising pleasures, familiar foods prepared in novel ways, as well as culinary delights composed of ingredients from far away places that we experience for the first time. Allow yourself to be inspired by the European master chefs to try and, perhaps, try again.

Cold Appetizers

Preparation time: 20 minutes
Cooking time: 10 minutes
Difficulty: ★

Serves four

For the soup:
$^1/_2$ lb to 1 lb / 250 g to 500 g salted cod
2 lbs / 1 kg potatoes
3 sprigs of thyme
half a bunch of parsley
5 cloves of garlic
2 cups / 500 ml olive oil

For the broth:
2 leeks
2 onions
half a bunch of parsley

For the garnish:
1 red pepper
1 green pepper
1 tomato

This soup is like a play for five actors taking very different roles – salted cod, potato, parsley, olive oil, and garlic – which, together, make an excellent soup that is delicious either hot or chilled. It can thus be enjoyed all year round, though our chef considers winter the most appropriate season for serving this particular fish.

Salted cod is a favorite among the Basque fishermen in Spain, who prepare the fish right on the boat by preserving it in salt brine before handing it over to their wives, who know hundreds of ways of preparing it. Salted cod is also regarded as a delicacy in other parts of Spain, as well as in Portugal, Norway, and France. For this soup, you need a salted cod that has been marinated in salt for at least six months, which is why it needs to be soaked in water for a few days before it can be used. Large fillets should be cut into strips first, which makes preparation much easier later on.

Garlic and olive oil, typical Basque ingredients, feature strongly in this recipe. Our chef always recommends the use of fresh garlic, though if its flavor seems too strong, you may substitute the lighter-flavored pickled garlic. Or, if for some reason you want to do without garlic completely, you can compensate by increasing the amount of olive oil you use.

1. Soak the salted cod in water for 36 hours before preparing it, changing the water every eight hours. Reserve the water for the broth, to which leeks, onions, and parsley are added.

2. Place the salted cod, potatoes, parsley, and thyme in a saucepan. Pour in the strained fish stock and simmer for about 15 minutes. Save an attractive-looking piece of cod for the garnish.

# of Salted Cod

3. Cut the garlic into strips. In a non-stick frying pan, fry until brown in a little olive oil and then add to the soup. Remove the seeds from the tomato, clean and dice the green and red peppers, then dice the tomato and the piece of fish saved for the garnish.

4. When the soup has been cooked, purée in a blender or food processor and season to taste. Place a tablespoon of the diced vegetables and cod garnish in the middle of a deep plate and pour the soup around it. This soup may be eaten hot, warm, or chilled.

Preparation time: *15 minutes*
Difficulty: ★

Serves four

For the salad:
half a bunch of basil
half a bunch of chervil
half a bunch of chives
half a bunch of garden cress
   (or, if unavailable, substitute watercress)
half a bunch of fennel
half a bunch of flat-leafed parsley
half a bunch of pimpernel (the leaves of a type
   of primrose)

half a bunch of cilantro
half a bunch of spinach
half a bunch of arugula
a few borage flowers (if available, or substitute
   nasturtiums or violets)

For the dressing:
$^7/_8$ cup / 220 ml extra virgin olive oil
1 clove of garlic
half a bunch of basil
salt to taste

Most aromatic herbs are Mediterranean in origin. Their therapeutic properties have been well known since antiquity, and during Roman times they made the transition from medicine to cuisine. Even today we can enjoy their variety and full flavor without any further ingredients, as chef Jean Bardet proves with this herbal feast.

We have spicy and aromatic parsley and garden cress, whose sharp flavor becomes surprisingly mild when chopped, and chervil with its complex scent, which quickly evaporates. You will substantially enhance this dish's visual impact if you use the freshest herbs available; your palate will be all the more pleased as well. You can, of course, add seasonal herbs according to taste. The edible flowers are an interesting addition, brightening up the dish with their luminous colors. Borage, a

European flower that blooms from May to September, sometimes at altitudes of more than five thousand feet, has lovely blue, white, and red flowers, of which the best should be picked for this recipe. But if these are unavailable, you might substitute the hotter-colored nasturtiums, or violets.

In order to underline the marvelous spicy flavor of the fresh herbs and complement the vivid green of this salad, only extra virgin olive oil, with its lovely green color, should be used. "Extra vergine" olive oil (as it is known in France), which is less than one year old, has a distinctive flavor that melds extremely well in this Provençal recipe.

1. Clean one garlic clove and the basil and chop finely, mix into the olive oil.

2. Strip the leaves off the remaining herbs and toss in cold water. Let drip-dry before putting them into the salad spinner to get rid of any remaining water.

Fresh Herbs

3. If necessary, dry the herbs even further on kitchen towelling. Mix with part of the dressing.

4. Place a ring of borage flowers on a plate. Place a portion of salad in the middle and garnish with a few more borage flowers. Sprinkle with dressing.

Preparation time: 15 minutes
Cooking time: 7 minutes
Difficulty: ★

Serves four
1¼ lbs / 600 g Baccalà (fresh cod)
scant ¾ lb / 350 g potatoes
4 plum tomatoes
4 sundried tomatoes
4 basil leaves
¾ cup / 180 ml extra virgin olive oil
¼ cup / 60 ml lemon juice
1 tbsp tapenade (olive paste)
3–4 black olives
salt, pepper to taste

The Provençal writer Alphonse Daudet caught the spirit of the cod's popularity and its numerous styles of preparation by coining the phrase "cod evenings," referring to regular events held at a famous Parisian café. Many contemporary chefs continue to use cod in their creations and thus help to maintain the gastronomic importance of this fish, which lives in the Atlantic Ocean, the English Channel, and the North Sea.

Like their German colleagues, French fishermen distinguish between fresh and dried cod. Cod is particularly easy to catch when the fish converge toward the open sea for reproduction. In Italy, cod dried gently in the air is referred to as "baccalà," based on the Spanish term for it, "bacalao." This salad, created by Giuseppina Beglia, should be eaten at once as it can not be stored. The salad can also be prepared with extremely fresh

monkfish or with sliced freshwater trout, providing these fish have been pre-boiled a little to make their flesh tender.

"Tapenade" is a typical Provençal accompaniment, which conveys close links to neighboring Italy. First-class, tangy ingredients are needed to produce a fine tapenade: olive oil, capers, black olives, and anchovies are pressed according to traditional methods in an olive wood press. Sundried tomatoes are prepared in a very simple manner: they are exposed to the summer sun for a few weeks. They can, of course, also be bought in the shops already dried, and as a last resort you can dry them yourself in the oven. To soften them for eating, they are soaked in a bowl full of hot water and olive oil for a half an hour, then drained.

1. Skin the cod and remove the bones. Wash and quarter the potatoes. Place the potatoes in boiling salted water and add the cod two or three minutes later. Simmer for five minutes.

2. Place the fish on a plate and carefully cut into chunks with a tablespoon. Finely chop the sundried tomatoes and basil leaves.

Salad

3. Put a tablespoon of tapenade into a bowl, then add four tablespoons of lemon juice. Add salt and pepper, then stir in the olive oil. Blanch and skin the plum tomatoes and set them aside.

4. On a plate, place the potato pieces in a star shape. Place the cod slices in the center of the plate, on top of the inside of the star, and garnish with the chopped tomatoes and basil. Pour over a little sauce, sprinkle with freshly ground pepper and decorate with plum tomato strips and black olive pieces.

Artichoke and Lobster

Preparation time: 30 minutes
Cooking time: 30 minutes
Difficulty: ★★

Serves four

2 lobsters, either European blue or Northern,
    1¼ lbs / 600 g each
8 artichokes
fish stock
juice of 1 lemon
2 tbsp flour
2 cups / 500 g cream

½ cup / 125 ml mustard vinaigrette
2 tsp peanut oil
2 sheets of gelatin
salt, pepper to taste

For the green sauce:
1 cup mayonnaise (see basic recipes p. 802)
half a bunch of tarragon
half a bunch of chervil
half a bunch of flat-leafed parsley
half a bunch of basil
half a bunch of spinach

The inhabitants of coastal areas, lobsters can grow up to 30 inches / 76 cm long. Nature has equipped them with two large claws for good reason: one claw is used to pulverize, the other to catch prey. Both also represent a danger for the cook, so they must be tied with string, or plugged with small pieces of wood and tied with rubber bands, before being cooked. For this recipe, it is not so crucial whether you use a male or female lobster since it will only be boiled for a short time, and coral (roe) is not called for.

In centuries past, the artichoke (originally from Sicily) was believed to have not only therapeutic, but also aphrodisiac proporties – which often resulted in women being forbidden from consuming it. But the French Queen Catherine of Medici, who favored them for just that reason, wholeheartedly encouraged the cultivation of this vegetable. Thanks to her, the artichoke eventually enjoyed substantial popularity at the royal court by the end of the sixteenth century, and became increasingly popular in France.

Most artichoke varieties reach full maturity in May and June. Choose large, fleshy artichokes with rough, green leaves that sit heavily in your hand. They should be boiled in water to which a little lemon juice has been added; add a little flour to the water as well to prevent the artichokes from oxidizing and losing their color. Once out of the pot, the latter is, alas, unavoidable unless they are eaten almost immediately.

The artichoke hearts are prepared with olive oil and herbs, ingredients that provide a link to the green sauce – an ideal sauce for shellfish whose color may be intensified by adding more spinach. The aromatic herbs should all be very fresh, otherwise one may overpower the others. Mix them in the order they're listed in the recipe.

1. Ahead of time, soak the gelatin in cold water. Separate the artichoke hearts from the globes by twisting them; rub with lemon. Put about two inches of water into a glass and add the peanut oil and flour; mix. Add lemon juice and a pinch of salt; transfer to a saucepan; add enough water to cover the artichoke hearts, and boil for ten minutes. Leave the hearts to cool in the liquid. Using a very sharp knife, cut four hearts into twelve slices.

2. Finely dice two of the remaining hearts (yielding approximately ¾ cup / 150 g). In a food processor, chop the remaining hearts and the top leaves, then pass through a fine-meshed sieve. Thicken the resulting purée with the gelatin, which has previously been soaked in cold water. Whip the cream until stiff and fold into the mixture. Season to taste; let chill.

Layers in a Green Sauce

3. Drop the lobsters into boiling fish stock; boil for five minutes and simmer for another ten minutes. Drain, then plunge lobsters into cold water. When cool, extract the lobster meat, discarding the stomach, internal vein, coral (roe) and tomalley or liver. Cut one tail into medallions and dice the other. Retain some of the chervil for the garnish, and blanch all the herbs. Rinse with cold water and work into a purée; mix the mayonnaise into the purée.

4. Mix together the diced lobster and diced artichokes. Pour green sauce onto the plates. Place one artichoke base in the center, and then cover it with a ring of artichoke purée piped through a pastry bag. Add the diced lobster and artichoke. Repeat this procedure five or six times, finishing with an artichoke base on top. Add a few drops of mustard vinaigrette. Decorate with lobster medallions, a small section of the claw, and chervil leaves.

Connaught

Preparation time: 3 hours
Cooking time: 1 hour, 15 minutes
Marinating time: 24 hours
Cooking time: 24 hours
Difficulty: ★★★

Serves twelve

2 wild ducks (of the light-fleshed variety
   or, if unavailable, 2 pheasants)
2 lbs / 1 kg pork shoulder
scant 1 lb / 400 g fatty belly of pork
   (use pancetta)
$^3/_8$ cup / 75 ml port

2 tbsp Cognac
1 tbsp / 10 ml rum
$^1/_4$ lb / 100 g goose liver (foie gras)
4 button mushrooms
2 cups / 500 ml duck stock
1 tbsp salt
fresh-ground black pepper to taste
1 tsp mixture of four herbs
1 tsp baking soda
$^1/_4$ cup / 50 g sliced truffles
3 sheets of gelatin
2 tbsp / 30 g pistachios
half a bunch of thyme
1 bay leaf

Wild duck, such as canvasback or mallard, is rich in potassium and phosphorus and is highly prized by gourmets and hunters alike. It has also been the symbol of Chinese cooking for four thousand years.

This terrine is particularly suitable for ducks with very white flesh, such as the ducks from Nantes in France. Pheasants, another popular game bird, can be used instead, but, as the meat is a bit drier, it needs to be mixed with pork. In the case of this dish, whether one is using duck or pheasant, the choicer parts of pork, for example the shoulder, should be used.

According to chef Michel Bourdin's directions, making this terrine will take the better part of three days, and baking can only begin on the third day. Ten minutes before baking is complete, the lid of the terrine should be removed to allow a thin and aromatic crust to develop. Once the terrine has been removed from the oven, a small glass (about $^1/_2$ / 125 ml) of rum should be poured over it. Or, if pheasant has been used, pour over an herbal liqueur. Then the most difficult part begins: slowly pressing the terrine as it cools, in order to build up the natural aspic it contains.

This dish develops its full flavor after sitting for a week, but it should never be kept for longer than three weeks, as the quality of the aspic will deteriorate. The original version of this terrine can be found on the menu of the eminent Connaught in London, an undisputed highlight amongst the restaurants of the British capital.

1. Soak the gelatin in cold water ahead of time. Remove the bones and tendons from the ducks, then slice the meat into $^3/_8$ in / 1 cm strips wide. Marinate the meat for 24 hours in a mixture of port, Cognac, salt, and pepper. Separate the pork meat from the bone, put $^7/_8$ lb / 450 g of lean pork aside, and make a stock with the duck bones, pork bones, and spices. Strain through a fine-meshed sieve. Place the bones in fresh water and cook until reduced to half a cup of aspic.

2. Run the lean pork and the pork belly through the meat grinder using a coarse blade; do the same with the marinated duck meat on a medium blade. Mix the soaked gelatin with the duck stock. Soak the four-herb mixture in alcohol; add salt, pepper, and baking soda. Prepare a stuffing with the duck stock, the aspic, the sliced truffles, and the ground meat. Chill and let the flavors blend for 24 hours.

Terrine

3. Cut the goose liver and mushrooms into $^3/_8$ in / 1 cm strips wide. At the bottom of the terrine form, place a layer of meat stuffing, then alternate strips of duck meat, liver, and mushrooms. Place a second layer of stuffing on this, then sprinkle with the pistachios. Cover with the remaining stuffing. Add thyme and bay leaf; cover.

4. In a bain-marie, bake for 50 minutes at 375 °F / 175 °C. Remove cover and increase heat to 400 °F / 200 °C; bake for 10 to 15 minutes without cover. Remove from the oven, pour a little rum over it, and set aside to cool. Cover with an adequately sized board and place on top a weight heavy enough to apply pressure without breaking the terrine. Store. Serve sliced, garnished with diced aspic.

Lobster Salad

Preparation time: 45 minutes
Cooking time: 25 minutes
Difficulty: ★

Serves four

4 European lobsters, or, if unavailable,
  Northern lobsters, a bit over ³/₄ lb each, and
  female if possible
4 Granny Smith apples
1 head radicchio
1 head green frisée lettuce
1 head red frisée lettuce
¹/₄ / 50 g cup roasted pine nuts

³/₄ cup / 200 ml peanut oil
¹/₂ cup / 125 ml red wine vinegar
2 cups / 500 ml white wine
1 gallon plus one cup / 4 l water
a pinch of curry powder
half a bunch of thyme
1 bay leaf
salt, pepper to taste

For the mustard mayonnaise:
yolks of 4 eggs
¹/₂ cup / 100 ml wine vinegar
1 cup / 250 ml peanut oil
1 tsp / 5 g prepared Dijon mustard
salt, pepper to taste

Usually, two lobster varieties are considered for cooking: the European or blue lobster from Brittany or Norway, and the Northern lobster from Canada and northern New England. The European lobster is more popular in France as it is considered to have a more delicate flavor. Buying more small live lobsters as opposed to a couple of large ones is recommended, as the larger the lobster, the tougher, usually, the meat.

The lobsters can be prepared a few hours in advance. They need to boil in the broth for only a few minutes. Once they have been removed from the pot, let the cooking liquid cool off and put the lobsters back to keep them moist and juicy. When the meat is extracted, the roe, or coral, of the female lobster should be taken out, dried, and then retained, as it is an invaluable ingredient for many kinds of sauces.

The lobster tail, which should be very crisp, is an ideal partner for the tangy, slightly acidic apple slices. Granny Smith apples were first grown in Australia and are now widely cultivated in France; they are in season from October to April and have white flesh underneath characteristically shiny, light-green skin.

The mayonnaise called for here will be modified by adding to it a bit of the lobsters' cooking broth, some mustard, and a pinch of curry, which needs to be carefully measured and added at the very last moment.

For a slightly less expensive version of this dish, use crab or langoustines instead of lobsters.

1. In a stockpot, prepare a broth of white wine, water, herbs, salt and pepper. Bring to a rolling boil and cook the lobsters for fifteen minutes in the broth. When done, add cold water to slow the cooking process, and leave the lobsters to cool in the broth. For the mayonnaise: add salt and pepper to the egg yolks; add mustard. Whisk vigorously, adding the vinegar and, bit by bit, the oil. Set aside for later.

2. Roast the pine nuts in a pre-heated oven at between 375 and 400 °F / 190 and 200 °C until light brown, or in a frying pan on a high heat on the stovetop for between three and four minutes. Wash the salad greens and dry thoroughly; season with salt, pepper, vinegar, and oil, and add the pine nuts. Place the salad decoratively in the center of the plate.

with Green Apples

3. Take the lobsters out of the broth, halve, and set aside the legs and shells for decoration. Cut the tails lengthwise into thin slices. Reserve the roe for future uses (see, for instance, the recipe on page 40). Quarter the apples and cut these as well into thin slices.

4. Stir two tablespoons of cooking broth into just under five-eights of a cup of mayonnaise. Taste, then add a pinch of curry. Dip each lobster slice into the mayonnaise and place on a plate, always alternating with an apple slice. Decorate with the shell and legs.

Preparation time: 20 minutes
Cooling time: 24 hours
Difficulty: ★

Serves four

1 lb / 500 g sardines
8 young leek stalks
1 large Granny Smith, Melrose, or Cameo
   apple
1 lemon
$^1/_4$ cup / 50 ml heavy cream
$^1/_3$ cup / 80 ml whole milk
$1^1/_3$ tbsp / 20 ml olive oil
salt, pepper to taste

For the garnish:
4 sprigs of dill
2 tbsp / 30 g poppy seeds
1 tsp / 5 g paprika
salt, pepper to taste

Normandy has natural treasures, lively fishing villages and large agricultural farms aplenty, and our chef, Michel Bruneau, takes special interest in creating recipes that use the ingredients from this area. We all know and love the famous Normandy butter and cream, but the region also produces fabulous cheeses and apples in an endless range of flavors and colors.

This refreshing appetizer is prepared with fillets of sardines (or anchovies), if possible bought straight from the fishing boat. The marinated sardines, however, should be eaten a day after being prepared, for the ingredients will need twenty-four hours' chilling to meld and deliver their unique flavor, and only then will the dish have developed its finesse. The sardines should be small, firm, and have shiny eyes, and their flesh

should be a bit fatty. The way their innards are arranged makes gutting very easy. The choice of apples is more difficult: should one opt for the very aromatic, originally American (now cultivated in New Zealand) Melrose or similar Cameo, or the more acidic, originally Australian (now also American) Granny Smith? In any case, whatever kind of apple is chosen, it must be very fresh and crisp.

If you have trouble inverting the marinade right onto a plate, you can try to separate it from the container by very carefully running a knife around the rim, making sure not to break its contents. The completed dish is then graced with sprigs of fresh dill or other seasonal herbs, small leeks, olive oil, poppy seeds, lemon zest, and paprika.

1. Gut, fillet and wash the sardines. Peel a lemon and squeeze the juice into a glass. Cut the lemon peel into fine strips; blanch. Peel the apples and cut into thin round slices; with a serrated-edged, circular cutter, cut out disks that are $2^1/_2$ inches / 65 mm in diameter from the apple slices. Spice and sprinkle with lemon juice.

2. Marinade the sardine fillets in salt, pepper, and half of the lemon juice for about 15 minutes. Whisk the double or heavy cream and whole milk into a light whipped cream; add the rest of the lemon juice.

Fresh Sardines

3. Trim the young leeks and wash. Blanch briefly and set aside. Take four circular forms of around 2¹/₂ inches / 65 mm in diameter and one-and-a-half inches high. Place an apple disc at the bottom of each form, then line the sides of the form with a marinated sardine fillet.

4. Continue to fill the forms with layers of cream, then apple, then cream, and finally, sardine. Chill for about 24 hours. Invert each one carefully onto a plate, place two leeks on the side, sprinkle with olive oil. Garnish with lemon zest, dill, poppy seeds, and paprika.

Crayfish and Caviar

Preparation time: 45 minutes
Cooking time: 45 minutes
Difficulty: ★

Serves four

24 crayfish
2¹/₂ oz / 75 g Ossetra caviar
20 green asparagus stalks
1 leek
1 onion
1 potato
scant 1 quart-chicken stock

1 cup / 250 ml whipping cream
scant ¹/₂ cup / 100 g butter
¹/₄ tsp / 1 g ground nutmeg
salt, pepper to taste

It could be called a crayfish revolution: initially caught exclusively in rivers, from where they have all but disappeared, these freshwater crustaceans are today farmed on a large scale, with excellent results. Crayfish farms can be found in Australia and, in the U.S., in Louisiana, where the variety *procambarus clarki*, better known simply as red crayfish, is farmed. Before preparation you must remove the intestinal vein that runs down a crayfish's back, as its bitter taste would impair the crustacean's otherwise fine flavor. The stomach, which is attached to the vein, should be removed at this point as well.

Today, sturgeons are found almost exclusively in the Caspian Sea, which severely limits the number of countries that can produce caviar. These wonderful "pearls of the sea" were mentioned as early as the sixteenth century by the French writer François Rabelais. For this recipe, chef Jan Buytaert recommends Ossetra caviar, which many people prefer to Beluga. Its coarse grains will mix well with the cream.

The asparagus tips should be steamed *al dente*, so that their firmness provides a nice contrast to the smooth cream; the asparagus stalks, however, should be poached. To achieve good results buy only very firm, green asparagus.

This cold appetizer is the ideal opener for a summer dinner. If you prefer, you may substitute thin strips of lobster for the crayfish.

1. Coarsely chop the leek and onion, and peel the potato. Peel the asparagus and halve into tips and stalks. Set aside the tips and sauté the stalks with the leek and onion in butter. Add the chicken stock and the whole potato; simmer for 45 minutes.

2. Steam the asparagus tips in a steamer. In a blender or food processor, blend two-thirds of the cream with the leek, onion, potato, and asparagus stalks to make the asparagus cream. Adjust its flavor with salt and pepper. Reserve the stock for the crayfish, adding some nutmeg to the liquid and then letting it cool before cooking again.

in Asparagus Cream

3. Boil the crayfish in the nutmeg-infused stock for four to five minutes, depending on size, let cool, and then remove the shells. Mix two-thirds of the asparagus cream with the remaining third of the cream and blend in the caviar.

4. Distribute the caviar-asparagus cream on the plates. Place a few tepid asparagus tips on each plate, and set the crayfish on top. Garnish with a crayfish head. Serve immediately.

Preparation time: *45 minutes*
Cooking time: *45 minutes*
Difficulty: ★★

Serves four

2¹/₄ lbs / 1 kg zucchini
2 lbs / 850 g tomatoes
3 onions
6 cloves garlic
1 bunch of watercress
1¹/₂ lbs / 675 g eggplant
4 green peppers

4 red peppers
12 eggs
salt, pepper to taste

If desired, for an alternative garnish:
¹/₄ lb / 125 g mixed lettuces, such as mesclun
    and arugula
2 tbsp / 30 ml red wine vinegar
3 tbsp / 45 ml virgin olive oil
salt, pepper to taste

The word "piper," (pronounced "peeper"), from which the name of this dish is derived, is the term for peppers used by the inhabitants of the Béarn region in southwestern France. The many different versions of this Basque dish vary from region to region, and, depending on how hearty the ingredients added are, it can be served as an appetizer or a main course. In this recipe, the color red predominates, but our inventive chef Jacques Cagnas adds even more colors, extending the palette with the green watercress purée and a yellow omelette. To achieve an intensive red for this dish, use only very ripe and fleshy tomatoes, ideally Mediterranean varieties. The red-green-yellow color aspect of the dish is reminiscent of the flags of many French-speaking African countries.

In Europe, watercress has always been credited with having blood-cleansing properties. Due to its tangy and sharp flavor, it has developed widespread popularity. It grows in water and will wither as soon as it is taken out of its natural habitat. The most successful watercress breeders can be found in the Essonne area just outside Paris, where growers trade their precious goods at large cress markets every Easter.

Nature should determine the choice of what other vegetables are used: according to season, choose either medium-sized eggplants or red and green peppers.

1. In a blender, purée the watercress and set aside; then do the same with enough tomatoes (probably four) to make about ¹/₂ cup / 125 ml of purée. Dice and strain the remaining tomatoes. Into three separate bowls, beat four eggs apiece. Blend the puréed cress into one, and the puréed tomato into the second. The eggs in the third bowl should be left plain. Season with salt and pepper and then prepare three flat omelettes.

2. Once the omelettes have cooled, use a circular cutting tool to cut out four slices of about 3 in / 75 mm in diameter from each omelette. Place each slice on a separate plate and set aside.

Piperade

3. Dice the garlic and remaining vegetables; sauté each vegetable separately for about 15 minutes or until brown; mix together and set aside to cool.

4. In the bottom of a 3 in / 75 mm (about 1½ in / 40 mm in height) circular form, place one cut-out omelette slice. On it place about a tablespoon of the diced and cooked vegetables, then lay down another slice of omelette in a different color, top with another layer of vegetables, and finish with an omelette of the third color. Invert onto the center of a plate. Decorate with the watercress purée, the diced vegetables, and the tomato purée. Or, garnish with dressed lettuces.

Scottish Salmon

Preparation time: 30 minutes
Cooking time: 5 minutes
Difficulty: ★

Serves four

⁵/₈ lb / 300 g smoked salmon
1 lemon
4 sprigs of dill

For the lemon cream sauce:
¹/₂ cup / 100 ml heavy cream
juice of 1 lemon
salt, pepper to taste

For the oat cakes:
¹/₄ cup / 50 g ground oats
¹/₄ cup / 50 g oats
1¹/₂ tbsp / 115 g lard
water to moisten
1 tsp / 3 g dry yeast
pinch of salt

Our chef Stewart Cameron devised this recipe on a trip to Japan. The rose is a symbol of England, the oat cake is symbolic for Scotland, and the simple presentation is Japanese in flavor.

Scottish salmon usually comes from the River Tay, where it can be caught all year round, as opposed to most other rivers where catching salmon is a seasonal affair. For this recipe, a chef might choose a large salmon (about 10 lb / 5 kg), then marinate it overnight in sea salt to make it tender, and then smoke it. Everybody has their own private trick for curing salmon: Cameron, for example, uses salmon rubbed down with wood chips from the whisky barrels that originally stored

sherry imported from Spain. In other words, the recipe can be as complicated or simplified as you want. For the private cook it is best to just buy a large piece of smoked salmon, about ⁵/₈ lb / 300 g. Making the "roses" may appear a little difficult at first: before you fold the first triangle, you must wrap several triangles around its base and make them stick together. It is all made easier because salmon is, of course, rather oily.

The oat cake dough should not be too moist before it is put in the oven. Or, if you don't like the taste or consistency of oat cakes, you can substitute brioche, toasted bread, or brown bread.

1. With a very sharp knife, cut the salmon into very thin slices.

2. Halve each slice lengthwise to get strips of around 2 in / 5 cm in width. Cut each strip into relatively even-sided triangles.

Rose on Oat Cake

3. Form the triangles into "roses," beginning in the middle and working your way out. To prepare the lemon cream sauce, carefully stir the lemon juice into the cream. Taste and, if necessary, add more lemon, then set aside to chill. Peel the other lemon, quarter, and remove any remaining pith or skin.

4. To make the oat cakes, mix all the oat cake ingredients in a bowl with enough tepid water to lightly moisten; roll out the dough very thinly on a pastry board or a cold marble slab and cut with a circular cutter. Place the dough discs on a baking tray and bake for five minutes at 355 °F / 180 °C. To serve, place an oat cake on each plate, place a salmon rose on top, and garnish with sprigs of dill, lemon pieces, and a dollop of lemon cream.

Preparation time: 50 minutes
Cooking time: 30 minutes
Marinating time: 1 hour, 30 minutes
Cooling time: 2 hours
Difficulty: ★★

Serves four

7/8 lb fresh tuna (bonito if available)
4 medium-sized eggplants, or
6 Italian or baby eggplants
2 tomatoes
1 lemon
1 small cucumber
1 red pepper
1 green pepper
4 zucchini flowers

1 clove garlic
1 dozen shelled or blanched almonds
4 basil leaves
2 sprigs flat-leafed parsley

2 sprigs thyme
1 dozen red olives
1/2 cup / 125 ml cold-pressed olive oil
salt, pepper to taste

For the gazpacho:
1 clove garlic
1 onion
1 cucumber
1 red pepper
1 green pepper
6 tomatoes
6 sprigs flat-leafed parsley
6 mint leaves
1/2 cup / 125 ml cold-pressed olive oil
2 tbsp / 30 ml sherry vinegar
salt, fresh-ground pepper to taste

This delicious recipe, which combines marinated tuna and chilled gazpacho, is typically Spanish. An ideal variety of tuna for the dish is the small, flavorful bonito. The flavor of the grilled and marinated eggplant complements the fish perfectly and makes this dish a feast for the palate.

The whole tuna should be a fine, fresh specimen with striped skin, weighing about 6–8 lb / 3–4 kg. The tender and flavorful meat will be cut into twelve medallions. When preparing and grilling these, care must be taken not to let them dry out, as the flesh will fray. Marinating the tuna in olive oil beforehand will ensure that the fish remains moist, making it easier to grill.

The eggplants are the perfect side vegetable, particularly if they are of the smaller Italian or baby variety, which retain most of their juices when grilled. Grilled and then cut into strips, the eggplant will retain its flavor and firmness.

The gazpacho that chef Francis Chauveau presents here should be left to infuse in olive oil for at least an hour so that its flavor can develop fully. This chilled soup can also be sprinkled with lightly crushed star anise, and served with socca, or chickpea pancakes, an old Niçoise recipe.

1. Finely chop the garlic. Grill the eggplants whole and unpeeled. After letting them cool, halve lengthwise, carefully separate the flesh from the skin, and cut into thin strips. Marinate the strips with the garlic in olive oil for one and a half hours.

2. For the gazpacho, wash the peppers, halve, and discard the seeds. Cut the peppers, tomato, onion and cucumber into large chunks, finely chop the garlic and add mint and parsley. Season with vinegar, olive oil, salt and pepper; refrigerate for two hours. Stir well and then strain. Peel the almonds; briefly sauté the basil leaves and zucchini flowers over low heat, just until they wilt.

with Gazpacho

3. Cut the tuna into twelve medallions. Marinate these in olive oil, thyme, and lemon juice for half an hour. Grill each medallion for a minute on each side. Grill the remaining peppers, peel under cold running water, and discard the seeds. Peel the second tomato and, if desired, cut the peel into the form of flower petals. Cut the olives into slivers. Trim the leaves off the parsley sprigs.

4. To serve, place the eggplant strips in the center of the plate. Place the tuna medallions on top, along with zucchini flowers and basil leaves and, if you made them, the petals of tomato skin. Pour a little gazpacho around the eggplant and tuna; garnish with vegetable chunks, almonds, olive slivers, and parsley leaves. Serve the remaining chilled gazpacho in an accompanying bowl.

Mackerel Strips

Preparation time: 30 minutes
Marinating time: 24 hours
Difficulty: ★

Serves four

4 large mackerels
1 red pepper
1 lemon
herb and spice mixture
1 bay leaf
half a bunch of chives
half a bunch of tarragon

half a bunch of parsley
$^1/_2$ cup / 125 ml olive oil
coarse sea salt
fresh-ground pepper
4 basil leaves

The mackerel, a distant cousin of the tuna, is a fast-swimming, spindle-shaped fish with an instantly recognizable steel-blue back. It does not like to be lonely, always appearing in large groups. This schooling instinct makes it easy for fishermen to catch them, even without bait, in rather small nets. Occasionally, when a huge school of mackerel has been caught in the nets, it has been known to drag the fishing boats along for a ride. Its firm, medium-fat flesh is suitable for all kinds of preparations.

To check a mackerel's freshness, look for bright red gills and luminous colors along the skin. This is particularly important since this recipe requires mackerels that have just been caught: they are served raw after having marinated for twenty-four hours. Cutting them into thin strips may present the only difficult part of preparation, but this task can be made easier by chilling the fish for a few hours in the freezer to firm up the flesh.

1. Gut each mackerel, separating the back from the belly and removing the bones with pincers. Marinate in sea salt in the refrigerator for 24 hours.

2. The following morning, wipe the fillets clean, making sure to remove all traces of salt; cut into even strips 4 in / 10 cm long; chill.

à la Sète

3. Cut the chilled fillets into even smaller pieces, about 2 in / 5 cm long. Crush the chives, tarragon, and parsley with a mortar and pestle. Finely chop the red pepper.

4. In a large metal bowl mix the fresh herbs, herb and spice mix, bay leaf, pepper, and chopped peppers; add olive oil and lemon juice. To serve, place the mackerel strips on the plate in a fan shape, covering the entire surface. Dress with the herbs and vegetable sauce; garnish with basil leaves.

Fried Duck Liver

Preparation time: 30 minutes
Cooking time: 15 minutes
Difficulty: ★★

Serves four

1¹/₄ lbs / 600 g duck liver
1 bunch of white asparagus
1 bunch of green asparagus
a few chervil leaves
3 tbsp / 45 g lard
¹/₂ cup / 250 g fresh cranberries
half a bunch of chives (optional)

For the vinaigrette:
1 cup / 250 ml olive oil
generous 1¹/₂ cups / 400 ml vinegar
salt, pepper to taste

In antiquity, the Gauls introduced the Romans to the concept of foie gras. According to the Gaul recipe, ducks and geese destined for the delicacy were force-fed succulent figs; their livers would then be preserved in a mixture of honey and milk, which caused the organs to bloat and develop a delicate, oily film.

Whether from a goose or a duck, the liver should be very fresh, smooth and well-lobed, with an even color ranging somewhere between yellow and white. Too thick a liver may lose all its fat when frying. It is increasingly common these days to find raw livers available in markets, but note that these will last only a week in the refrigerator before the gall seeps out and renders the entire organ bitter.

Since scallops of consistent width and shape are called for here, the chefs Bernard and Jean Couseau recommend using a very thin knife. For easier cutting, warm the blade in hot water just before use.

You may experiment with the two different asparagus colors, choosing, for example, violet and white stalks instead of green and white, but the bottom line should always be quality. The stalks should be rough and stiff, the tips very straight; they should be cooked, appropriately, in an asparagus cooker or a similarly tall saucepan, and steamed or boiled in an upright position with the tips up. Since the top half of the spears will be used for decoration, it is essential that the tips in particular retain their color.

Serve this dish warm – not hot – to better feature the delicate flavor of the duck liver.

1. Cut the duck liver into even slices, ³/₈ in / 1 cm thick.

2. Peel the asparagus; boil each bunch separately in salted water for ten minutes. Rinse with cold water and set aside.

with Asparagus Tips

3. Sprinkle the duck liver scallops with salt and fry in lard, browning each side for about three minutes; set aside. Prepare the vinaigrette.

4. To serve, arrange the asparagus tips in a fan-shape on half of each plate, alternating colors. Brush with vinaigrette. On the other half of the plate, arrange the duck liver. Garnish with chervil, cranberries, and, if desired, chive sprigs.

Carpaccio of Monkfish

Preparation time: 30 minutes, with some preparations made in advance
Smoking time: 36 hours
Marinating time: 3 hours
Difficulty: ★

Serves four

1 lb / 450 g monkfish tail, filleted
1/2 lb / 250 g sea snails
1 tomato
1 shallot

1 lemon
4 lbs / 2 kg sea salt
scant 1/2 cup / 100 ml olive oil
2 tbsp / 30 g green peppercorns
2 tbsp / 30 g pink peppercorns
1 bouquet garni
half a bunch of fresh tarragon
half a bunch of fresh chervil
half a bunch of fresh chives
salt, pepper to taste

Originally made with beef, the nineteenth-century innovation known as *carpaccio* has many imitators, and this *carpaccio* of monkfish created by Richard Coutanceau is definitely one of the best.

Though the recipe calls for monkfish – a fish increasingly used in a variety of dishes – it is not always readily available. If this is the case, you can substitute monkfish with sea bass, which is another fish well-suited for *carpaccio*. In any case, the fish must be marinated in sea salt for a few hours to firm up the flesh without impairing its tenderness. As preparation takes quite a while, it is advisable to start a few days in advance. The biggest challenge for this dish, however, will be cutting the monkfish into very thin slices and then gently flattening them in order to conform to the definition of a *carpaccio*.

The snails, with their very crisp flesh, provide a good contrast for the monkfish. After being cooked in an aromatic, salted broth, they must be extracted from their shells with a needle, a task that requires some patience and a calm hand. Their soft ends are their most delicious part, earning this section praise from culinary experts, who like to call it the snail's own foie gras.

1. If it has not been skinned already, skin the monkfish fillet. Dab it with olive oil to moisten, and marinate in sea salt for one hour. Rinse with water; let rest for 12 hours. Then place in a smoking oven for 36 hours (a procedure known as hot-smoking).

2. Scrub the snails, removing their opercula, and soak for three hours in frequently changed, salted water. Rinse several times. To cook, blanch in a broth seasoned with salt, a few peppercorns, and the bouquet garni for three to four minutes. Let drip dry, then use a needle to scoop them out of their shells.

with Snail Salad

3. Peel the tomato, discard the seeds, and dice; crush the peppercorns; chop the chervil and shallot. Prepare a dressing for the snails made of lemon juice and olive oil, adding chopped tarragon, crushed pink and green peppercorns, some of the diced tomatoes, chopped chervil, and a pinch of salt, and finally, the chives and chopped shallot. Set aside some of the dressing.

4. To serve, slice the monkfish fillet into extremely fine, even slices and arrange on the plate like the petals of a flower. Season with the same dressing used for the snails. In the center of this "flower," place a small heap of the snail salad. Garnish with chervil leaves and chopped tomato.

Preparation time: 30 minutes
Cooking time: 15 minutes
Difficulty: ★★

Serves four

3 dozen large oysters
1/4 cup / 50 ml cream, whipped
1/4 lb / 100 g spinach
1/4 lb / 100 g leeks
1/8 lb / 50 g carrots
6 shallots
1 1/2 cups / 370 ml dry white wine

3/4 cup / 200 ml wine vinegar
1/4 cup / 50 ml olive oil
1/2 cup / 125 ml crème fraîche
1/4 lb / 100 g butter
pinch of saffron thread
coarse sea salt
salt, pepper to taste

For the dressing:
1/2 cup / 125 ml olive oil
salt, pepper to taste

Chef Jean Crotet had the idea of using the small portions of different sauces that were left over; thus was this oyster recipe conceived. A delectable appetizer, it consists of a delicate mixture of vegetables with warm and cold oysters.

The recipe requires fresh oysters with a wavy shell, as thick and fleshy as possible. Oysters from Normandy, with their strong iodine taste, are perfect, especially the heavy "special" oysters with their excellent aroma; if these are unavailable, look for any curly-shelled variety of the flavorful Atlantic oyster. These high-quality molluscs should be carefully simmered at a maximum of 100 °F / 40 °C, otherwise their flavor will literally evaporate. Some fine oysters will simply not survive any cooking; they are eaten raw.

The vegetables, including the shallots, need to be as fresh as possible. They will be mixed with an olive oil-based dressing and dry white wine to make a smooth cream. Instead of white wine, champagne may also be used: its flavor will further the link between vegetables and oysters.

A little trick for the presentation: generously sprinkle the plates with coarse sea salt first and place the oysters on the salt. This way the shells will not wobble, making it easier not to spill the sauce when you pour it in. On no account should this dish be reheated as the taste of the oysters will be irrevocably altered. Instead, this dish should be eaten immediately upon serving.

1. Open the oysters and carefully shell them; save the sea water inside the shell. Wash well and place in a casserole with the sea water; infuse at a gentle simmer over low heat for three minutes; set aside.

2. Cook a quarter of the shallots in vinegar; set aside half of those and let cool, then mix them with whipped cream, salt and pepper. To the other half of the cooked shallots add olive oil, salt, and pepper to make what is in fact a warm dressing. Cook the remaining shallots in wine. Divide this batch in half as well, adding crème fraîche and saffron to one half and bringing it to a boil; season. To the other half, add butter and whisk constantly.

Oyster Platter

3. Wash the spinach, discard the stalks and quickly blanch the leaves until they wilt. Julienne the leeks and carrots and blanch for five minutes.

4. To serve, sprinkle each plate with a ring or a bed of coarse sea salt. Place nine oyster shells on each. Fill as follows: three shells with spinach under saffron sauce, three with leeks under butter sauce, three with julienned carrots in the warm dressing. Heat the oysters briefly in the oven and place them in the shells as well.

Gazpacho

Preparation time: 20 minutes
Cooking time: 2 hours
Difficulty: ★

Serves four

10 tomatoes
1 cucumber
1 bunch of celery
1 zucchini
1 red pepper
1/2 green pepper
1 shallot

1 egg yolk
generous 4 tbsp / 60 g black olive tapenade
5/8 lb / 300 g fromage frais (from sheep's milk)
2 tbsp / 30 ml heavy cream
2 tbsp / 30 ml olive oil
1 drop of Tabasco
4 good basil leaves
half a bunch of chives
salt, pepper to taste
1 cup / 250 g ice cubes

Elegantly served with a bit of stuffing, this dish features a slightly modified version of the traditional gazpacho in order to provide an appetizer suitable for a more substantial meal. Chef Michel Del Burgo has created this recipe in his kitchen at the Hôtel de l'Europe in Avignon, France, which makes it, therefore, an ideal participant in a collection of European delicacies.

Although gazpacho is a simple dish in Spain, where it originated, it can nonetheless be prepared with special ingredients. Our chef includes, for example, French fromage frais (or unripened cheese) made from sheep's milk, which blends well with the tomatoes. There are many varieties of this kind of fromage frais available, including brousse, cachat, and tomme fraîche. If sheep's milk fromage frais is not available, fromage frais made from cow's or goat's milk may be used. Del Burgo also

prefers small, very aromatic, sun-ripened tomatoes, since they lend the necessarily full-bodied flavor to the soup. Select firm, full tomatoes that are a deep, vibrant red.

Preparing gazpacho presents one basic problem: binding the liquid, which rarely forms a smooth emulsion with the tomato pulp alone. Furthermore, the amount of juices the tomatoes release can render the gazpacho too thin. In order to achieve an even emulsion, Michel Del Burgo recommends binding the sauce with egg yolk.

The other vegetables featured here underscore the tomato flavor: the cucumber, for example, is marinated in salt to make it more digestible. The olive tapenade gives the gazpacho a tangy touch.

1. To prepare the gazpacho, dice half the red pepper and chop the shallot; in a blender or food processor mix them with the olive oil and egg yolk. Chop five tomatoes; add them to the mixture. Add Tabasco to taste; blend with enough ice cubes to make a fine puree and continue blending until the liquid has emulsifies.

2. Peel and seed one of the remaining tomatoes. Cut them, as well as the remaining red pepper, the cucumber, green pepper, zucchini, and celery into small chunks. Briefly blanch the green peppers, zucchini and celery. Peel the other four tomatoes, cut off their tops, hollow them out, and bake in the oven for 15 minutes at 250 °F / 120 °C.

with Tapenade

3. Drain any excess liquid from the fromage frais and mix with the cream into a creamy, rich emulsion. Chop the chives; add with salt and pepper to the mixture. Pour four-fifths of it into a bowl, add the olive tapenade, and whisk into a smooth paste.

4. Thoroughly mix the chopped vegetables together. Finely chop the basil. Season the vegetables with salt, pepper and the basil; stuff the tomatoes with this mixture. To serve, place one stuffed tomato in the center of each shallow bowl; replace the top of each tomato. Surround this centerpiece with the creamy gazpacho, and garnish with basil leaves and a small mound of leftover vegtables.

Salad Cocktail with

Preparation time: 30 minutes
Cooking time: 3 minutes
Difficulty: ★

Serves four
20 scallops
16 tomatoes
1 bunch of dill
1 cup / 250 ml olive oil

For the salad:
choose any of the following:
1 head bibb or boston lettuce
1 bunch of lollo rosso
1 bunch of lamb's lettuce
1 head radicchio

4 endives
1 bunch of frisée
1 bunch of oak leaf lettuce

For the cream vinaigrette:
$^1/_2$ cup / 125 ml red wine vinegar
1 cup / 250 ml olive oil
$^3/_4$ cup / 200 ml cream
salt, fresh-ground pepper to taste

For the sherry vinaigrette:
$^1/_4$ cup / 60 ml sherry vinegar
$^1/_2$ cup / 125 ml peanut oil
$^3/_4$ cup / 175 ml cold-pressed olive oil
salt, fresh-ground pepper to taste

In France, lettuce comes in endless varieties, with nicknames like "Queen of May," "Pride of Nantes," or "Capucin beard." Originally regarded as an appetizer and served without any other ingredients, green salads have advanced to become the diverse and tasty dishes they are today, served with a seemingly endless variety of sauces and seasonings. They need to be well mixed with their dressing for the flavors to be fully expressed.

Here, the salad bed for the scallops includes lettuce, lamb's lettuce, and frisée, as well as some other distinctive varieties: as going to the market with such a diverse shopping list may not be everyone's cup of tea, there are alternatives. For instance

one can purchase ready-mixed salads at the market that will include at least some of the lettuces listed above.

The scallops add finesse to this appetizer. The best scallops for this purpose, ideally, are very fresh and medium-sized, with tightly closed shells – in other words, still alive. The scallops and their coral (roe) are washed and then carefully fried. Scallops are, incidentally, the symbol of the pilgrims of Santiago de Compostela. Correctly preparing the scallops will ensure that their iodine-rich taste will harmonize wonderfully with the crispy salad and the two vinaigrettes.

1. Shell the scallops. Remove the whiskers; wash the scallops and the coral (roe) quickly and thoroughly. Leave to dry on kitchen towels. Marinate in olive oil sprinkled with dill for at least 15 minutes.

2. To prepare the cream vinaigrette, in a bowl mix olive oil and red wine vinegar and add a pinch of salt. Fold in the cream; adjust seasoning to taste. To prepare the sherry vinaigrette; mix the sherry vinegar, peanut oil, olive oil, salt, and pepper.

Warm Scallops and Dill

3. Dress the lettuces with the cream vinaigrette. Into a hot frying pan, sprinkle a pinch of salt; fry the scallops and the coral for a maximum of one minute on each side.

4. Score the tomatoes in a cross; submerge in boiling water for one to two minutes. As soon as the skin begins to peel off, rinse with cold water, then peel. Quarter, cut into strips, then dice. Place the diced tomatoes in the sherry vinaigrette and whisk to coat thoroughly. To serve, heap the salad cocktail in the middle of a plate; ring with an alternating arrangement of scallops and scoops of chopped tomato; decorate with a generous sprinkling of dill sprigs.

Lobster with Apple

Preparation time: 25 minutes
Cooking time: 10 minutes
Difficulty: ✫

Serves four

2 1¹/₂ lb / 700 g lobsters
2 Golden Delicious apples
2 tomatoes
¹/₄ lb / 100 g fine green beans
³/₄ lb / 400 g mixed lettuce
¹/₄ lb / 100 g lamb's lettuce
¹/₂ cup / 100 ml olive oil
¹/₂ cup / 100 ml red wine vinegar
salt, pepper to taste

For the curry vinaigrette:
3 tbsp / 40 g curry powder
1 cup / 250 g tomato puree
¹/₄ of an apple
2 egg yolks
2 tsp / 10 g mustard
scant 1 cup oil
scant 1 cup crème fraîche
2 tbsp / 200 ml lemon juice
2 tbsp / 200 ml vinegar
salt, pepper to taste

Claude Dupont describes this starter as a "méli-mélo," which translates roughly as a hodge-podge with a little bit of everything. But with its harmonious mix of colors, tastes, and textures, the dish does not resemble anything so unplanned. Dupont is probably also referring to the freestyle method with which he created this refreshing composition of shellfish, fruit, and vegetables.

Choose fresh, healthy, live lobsters. When extracting the meat in a fresh lobster, it will be well attached to the shell. Lobster meat is lean, tender and spicy – and in this dish, those qualities are well underscored. If at all possible, seek out blue lobsters from Brittany, or a North American variety such as the Maine lobster. To cook, peg and bind the claws and bring a large stockpot of broth to a rolling boil before immersing the lobsters head-first. Boil for eight minutes and then leave in the broth to cool off, a process that ensures that the meat will remain tender.

The balance of flavors in this recipe depends on the correct dosage of curry powder; its exotic perfume is the leading flavor in the vinaigrette. There are many different varieties of curry powder, which is really a mixture of many individual spices: ginger, cumin, coriander, turmeric, and other ingredients. They may be mixed to form a powder, or at times can be found as a paste. Too much curry powder would most certainly kill the delicate flavor of the lobster, whose subtle taste is easily drowned out. That is why for this recipe – as in all recipes, really – careful application of spices takes top priority.

1. Prepare the vinaigrette: grate the apple quarter and pass the tomato purée through a sieve; whisk two egg yolks with the mustard, oil, vinegar, salt, and pepper. Add the curry powder, the grated apple and the sieved tomato purée. Fold in the crème fraîche and lemon juice. Set aside to rest for 15 minutes, then pass through a sieve.

2. Cook the lobsters briefly in broth and leave immersed in the liquid to cool. Halve the lobsters and extract the flesh (tails, claws, and legs) from the shell. Set aside any coral (roe) for later use. Dress the mixed lettuces with salt, pepper, olive oil, and vinegar.

and a Light Curry Sauce

3. Peel tomato strips for decoration; blanch the green beans. Garnish the plate with an arching ring of these tomato strips and the green beans. Arrange a rosette of lamb's lettuce, and press it down to stay within a circular form. Chop one and a half Golden Delicious apples and dress with a little of the curry vinaigrette.

4. Dress the lamb's lettuce. Fill the circular form with chopped apple, then a layer of mixed lettuce, and finally place a few slices of lobster meat and one or two claws on top. Dress with the curry vinaigrette; garnish with a sprig of herb.

Venison Tartlets with Goose Liver,

Preparation time: 1 hour, 30 minutes
Cooking time: 8 minutes
Cooling time: 2 hours
Difficulty: ★★

Serves four

For the tartlets:
¹/₂ lb / 240 g saddle of venison
generous ¹/₄ lb / 150 g goose liver
1 sheet of gelatin
1 carrot
¹/₂ bulb celeriac
1 tbsp / 10 ml Sauternes
1 tbsp Cognac
¹/₂ cup / 125 ml meat juice (to be retained from
   the venison)
¹/₂ cup / 125 ml whipping cream

salt, fresh-ground pepper to taste

For the jelly:
1 cup / 250 ml venison broth
1¹/₂ sheets of gelatin

For the marinated white cabbage:
¹/₂ lb / 200 g white cabbage
¹/₂ cup / 100 ml grapeseed oil
¹/₂ cup / 100 ml white wine vinegar
¹/₂ tsp / 10 g sugar
a pinch of ground cumin
salt, pepper to taste

For the sauce:
¹/₄ lb / 250 g chanterelles
1 shallot
1 cup / 250 ml meat juice (to be retained)
¹/₄ cup / 60 ml raspberry vinegar
half a bunch of chervil

In the heart of the dark forests of Württemberg in southwest Germany is an elegant hotel and restaurant. Located in an old hunting lodge on grounds belonging to the Prince of Hohenlohe-Öhringen, it is home for our talented chef, Lothar Eiermann. As he puts it, to be a chef there is to be in the center of "game heaven": the forests are so plentiful with deer and other forest animals that the preparation of game has become his speciality. This recipe is Eiermann's homage to Prince Kraft-Alexander, the present proprietor of the hotel.

Chef Eiermann has an ideal delivery system: animals are delivered whole to his kitchen almost directly from the forest. Provided with every part, he can let his creativity run free to conceive unforgettable recipes. The end of summer is the only time the supply is slightly less plentiful: then, Eiermann has to make do with deer that have fed entirely on fresh herbs, which requires him to wait a few days before preparing the meat. But

this seems like a minor detraction from a veritable cornucopia of game.

This appetizer is based on a boneless saddle of venison from which the tendons have also been removed. The most difficult aspect of the preparation involves the jelly, which is made by first blanching the chopped bones, then cooking them until they reduce down to a thick aspic.

The venison tartlets are accompanied by cabbage, the result of the chef's frequent experiments with both red and white varieties – eventually, he opted for the white. This is the same unassuming white cabbage used in the Alsatian speciality, sauerkraut. The raspberry vinegar, which the chef settled on after some unsuccessful tries with sherry vinegar, provides an ideal link between venison and goose liver pâté.

1. To make the goose liver mousse, reduce the venison gravy by half, cool, and then puree with the washed goose liver in the blender. Soak the gelatin in the Sauternes, then fold into the puree. Mix a third of the whipping cream with the liver puree; fold in the rest with a spatula. Adjust seasoning to taste and add the cognac.

2. Separate the venison from the bones; briefly fry on all sides; set aside to cool. Peel the carrot and celeriac, cut into strips of approximately 2 in / 5 cm high and ¹/₄ in / 1 cm thick; blanch in salted water. Rinse with cold water; set aside to drip dry. Take four circular forms and vertically line their inside walls with alternating strips of carrot and celeriac. Chop the white cabbage; marinate in the ingredients listed above.

White Cabbage, and Chanterelles

3. Fill the circular forms up to a $^1/_4$ in / 1 cm from the top with the goose liver mousse. For the sauce, fry the chopped shallot until brown, add some raspberry vinegar, then add venison gravy; reduce over low heat.

4. Cut the saddle of venison into thin slices. Lay in a rosette shape on top of the goose liver mousse still in the forms. Mix the game broth with the gelatin and pour over the tartlets; set the tartlets to chill. Drip-dry the cabbage and lightly fry until brown. Sweat the chanterelles. Garnish the plate with the cabbage and chanterelles. Add the sauce at the last moment, and decorate with chervil leaves.

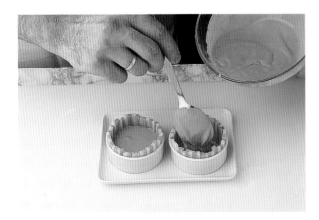

Young Herring

Preparation time: 20 minutes
Cooking time: 30 minutes
Difficulty: ✳

Serves four

4 young marinated herrings
4 round potatoes
1 onion
1 tsp / 5 g mustard
1 cup / 250 ml dry white wine
1 cup / 250 ml soy oil
sea salt, pepper to taste

In the Netherlands, the arrival of young herrings at the beginning of May is a similar event to the arrival of the Beaujolais nouveau in France. In the eighteenth century, the season was marked by a traditional fishing race, involving scores of fishermen – numbering in the thousands. The aim of the race was to be the first to present Her Majesty with the "Queen's herring." The young herrings, caught by the netloads, would be cured while still on the boat: according to the method developed by a certain Willem Benkleszoon, the fish would promptly be put into barrels to marinate in salt. The commodity was considered a veritable treasure: the barrels of pressed and salted herrings fetched high prices. At one public auction, a barrel reportedly fetched some 35,000 gilders (approximately US$18,000).

Normally, herring is served with sliced onion, cucumber, and white bread (particularly in Amsterdam), and eaten with the fingers. In this recipe, created specially for Eurodélices, the herring is served with potatoes instead. If at all possible, seek out the Dutch variety of potato known as Opperdoezer Ronde, a unique and completely round variety that grows in sulphur-rich soil, is harvested by hand, ripens in a mere nine weeks, and remains very firm during cooking. However, the variety is somewhat rare outside the Netherlands, and may take some serious sleuthing. If not, some suitable alternatives might be new potatoes or Katahdin round whites.

Unfortunately, there are few substitutes for the incomparable North Sea herring, which should have a red center bone and be of adequate size – about 8 in / 20 cm in length. A rather substantial dish, this fish and potato starter is ideal for winter, and confirms the Dutch version of a traditional American saying: "A herring a day keeps the doctor away."

1. Mix together the white wine, oil, and mustard in a blender. Immerse a few onion rings into this vinaigrette and leave to marinate.

2. Gut and fillet the herrings, remove the bones and use a circular cutter to cut rounds 1 in / 2.5 cm in diameter.

with Round Potatoes

3. *Peel the potatoes, boil (but take care not to overcook) and cut into the same circles as the herrings.*

4. *To serve, arrange the potato circles in a ring around the plate, each with a herring circle on top. Garnish with the marinated onion rings and dress with the vinaigrette.*

Crab Vegetables with

Preparation time: 1 hour
Cooking time: 20 minutes
Difficulty: ★★

Serves four

1 crab (approximately 6 lbs / 3 kg)
1 lb / 500 g leeks
1 lb / 500 g potatoes (such as Roseval or
    round white)
12 cherry tomatoes
juice of 2 limes
1/2 cup / 125 ml heavy cream

2 oz / 50 g lobster coral (cooked)
2 cups / 500 ml olive oil
scant 4 pints / 2 l vegetable broth
3 sprigs of flowering thyme (to yield
    1 tbsp / 15 g)
1 bunch of chives
1 bunch of dill
salt, pepper to taste

With its massive front claws and broad body, the Atlantic crab has one of the highest meat contents of all crab varieties. This peaceful crustacean, often seeming to be taking a siesta on the ocean floor, is easy prey for the fishermen of the English Channel and the Mediterranean, where it is caught in large numbers. It is available all year round, and has close relatives in the United States. Buy heavy, live crabs, and preferably female ones, since they contain coral. Crabs are cooked in broth so that their flesh remains tender. For easy extraction of the flesh, buy crabs that weigh at least two pounds (one kilogram); if you cannot find a crab weighing six pounds (three kilograms), buy two or three to equal that weight. Conveniently, the lobster coral called for in this receipe can be left over from lobsters used for another dish; it should be cooked.

The Roseval potato, a European variety, is harvested in the autumn and has pink or red skin and yellow, very dense flesh. It is preferably boiled whole, but is just as tasty in chunks. You can, of course, use a different variety, so long as it is not too starchy, as will be some varieties of Idaho (or russet potatoes) grown primarily for baking. Instead, look for round whites or reds, or Yukon Gold. For an extra dash of color, you might also try one of the red-fleshed potatoes, such as the huckleberry. Both the potatoes and leeks should be cooked *al dente*.

Prepare the accompanying dressing with olive oil only, as not only does it have superior digestive properties, but its delicate flavor imparts a Mediterranean subtlety to this appetizer. Chef Louis Grondard stresses using only cold-pressed olive oil, whose fine aroma is enhanced by the lime juice. Limes, incidentally, are very popular in Japanese and Mexican cuisine: both use lime juice as a marinade base for raw seafood.

This appetizer should, ideally, be consumed at once, although it can be stored for up to forty-eight hours.

1. Cut the leeks into rectangles and the potatoes into cubes. Cook separately in salted water and then rinse with cold water to arrest the cooking process. Both should still be quite crisp and firm after cooking. Mix the two vegetables. Fry the washed cherry tomatoes with thyme flowers over low heat in olive oil; chill.

2. Chop the chives. Bind the leeks and potatoes with a tablespoon of heavy cream in a bowl; season. Cook the crabs in broth and then extract the meat. Season the meat with olive oil, some of the chives, salt, and pepper.

Olive Oil and Limes

3. Place four circular forms (about 4 in / 10 cm in diameter) on aluminum foil and fill halfway with vegetables. Place the cooked crab meat on top, stir in a little heavy cream, sprinkle with lobster coral and chopped chives, and chill. Prepare a dressing with olive oil, lime juice, salt, and pepper.

4. Place the crab and vegetables in the middle of the plate. Arrange cherry tomatoes, the crab meat, and the claws in an alternating circle surrounding the crab and vegetable mixture. Sprinkle with the dressing and the rest of the chopped chives. Garnish with sprigs of dill, and serve chilled.

Preparation time:	1 hour
Cooking time:	20 minutes
Cooling time:	1 hour (optional)
Difficulty:	★★

Serves four

4 spider crabs, 1¼ lbs / 600 g each
2 spider crabs, 2 lbs / 1 kg each
5 crabs, 1½–2 lbs / 700 g–1 kg each
1 squid, ½ lb / 250 g
½ lb / 250 g fresh seaweed, or ⅛ lb / 75 g
   dried seaweed

10 tomatoes
8 cloves of garlic
1 lemon
yolks of 2 eggs
½ cup / 125 ml olive oil
¼ cup / 50 ml wine vinegar
1¼ gallon / 5 l water
1 bouquet garni
1 oz / 30 g salmon roe
¾ oz / 20 g Sevruga caviar
1 bunch of basil
2 tbsp / 20 g coarse sea salt
1 tbsp / 10 g white pepper

Despite its hard shell, the spider crab has a very tender and delicate taste. It compensates for its gauche appearance by hiding behind algae and rocky outcroppings. The largest specimens, which have claw spans of up to ten feet (three meters), live on the coast of Japan; the next biggest, about half that size, can dive down a hundred and fifty feet (forty-five meters) and live predominantly on the south coast of England. For this appetizer, chef Phillipe Groult recommends well-developed spider crabs weighing between one and a quarter and two pounds (six hundred grams and one kilogram), preferably from the coast of Brittany, if you have access to them. Always buy live crabs, and cook them within twenty-four hours, keeping them refrigerated until then.

After being steamed or cooked in broth for fifteen minutes, the crabmeat and coral have to be carefully extracted from the shell. The spider crab contains so much cartilage that the consistency and flavor of this dish needs to be refined; for this purpose, add squid, as well as the meat from king or blue crabs, particularly the claw meat. The spider crab coral can be used to make a traditional sauce that will blend quite well with any shellfish.

If indeed you are able to obtain female spider crabs (which you can recognize by a jagged ridge across the inside of its shell), this appetizer can be nicely ornamented with their own roe, set in the "lid" of the spider crab's shell. Spider crab roe is even more decorative than caviar or salmon roe. The crab is served on a bed of seaweed; if only male spider crabs are available, they can be served with fresh herbs.

1. Wash and scrub the spider crabs, cook in broth for 15 minutes; cook the other crabs for 20 minutes. Extract the meat from the small spider crabs without removing the legs, and then extract the meat from the remaining crabs (removing the claws and legs, but retaining whole claws from two crabs for garnish). Set the coral aside, pass it through a sieve, make an aïoli (two egg yolks whisked with crushed garlic and olive oil into a mayonnaise); blend the coral into it.

2. Chop three garlic cloves, peel and seed the tomatoes, gently fry together in olive oil. Add salt and pepper. Clean the squid and cut into thin strips (if possible freeze for an hour first to make it firmer); heat in the tomato liquid for five minutes.

Spider Crab

3. Mix together the squid, crab meat, and spider crab meat. Add all of the basil leaves and two-thirds of the aïoli. Using a cutter, cut a circle a bit under 3 in / 7.5 cm in diameter out of the shells of the four small spider crabs. Then remove this "lid."

4. Rinse the seaweed well; blanch in boiling water for two minutes, then rinse in cold water. To serve, stuff the spider crabs with the meat and aïoli mixture through the hole in their shell. Decorate with crab shells, salmon roe, and caviar. Serve on a bed of seaweed, and, if desired, fill the lids with crab eggs, brushing them with olive oil.

Tripe Salad with Goose

Preparation time: 30 minutes
Cooking time: 1 hour 30 minutes
Difficulty: ★★

Serves four

1 generous lb / 450 g tripe
$^5/_8$ lb / 300 g goose liver
$^5/_8$ lb / 300 g fava beans
1 onion
1 carrot
1 celery stick
1 clove of garlic
1 shallot
4 quail eggs
2 eggs

1 tbsp / 20 g hot mustard
1 tbsp / 20 g mild mustard
$^1/_2$ cup / 125 ml olive oil
2 cups / 500 ml white wine (Reisling)
1 tbsp / 45 ml balsamic vinegar
$^5/_8$ lb / 300 g breadcrumbs
3 tbsp flour
2 cups / 500 g mixed lettuces (Bibb and red leaf), or mesclun
1 bunch of chervil
1 bunch of thyme
$^1/_4$ cup / 60 g bay leaves
salt, pepper to taste

Tripe and goose liver are both very popular in Alsaçe, a region in northeastern France on the German border. The combination of tripe and a Riesling sauce has gained a reputation across the Alsatian border for good reason: it's fabulous. The dry but fruity Riesling, an Alsatian wine, is indispensable as a base for sauces, in particular with sautéed potatoes. It is somewhat remarkable that the Alsatian recipe for tripe has remained intact, uninfluenced by French cuisine: the Alsaçe region still retains its own strong character.

Tripe are the mixed trimmings from a cow's stomach that are carefully cleaned and blanched by the butcher. They should nonetheless be boiled in broth for an hour before preparation to impart some flavor into them. Normally they are prepared the day before and then left to chill in the refrigerator in their cooking broth. The small rectangles get coated with breadcrumbs and fried, with care taken to respect the indicated frying time, as excessive browning of the breadcrumbs will render them bitter.

The goose liver lends a certain softness to this dish. While not crucial, it provides a welcome contrast to the crispy tripe. The vinaigrette should be fairly sharp so as not to be dominated by the tripe's strong flavor.

If fava beans are available – your best chance for fresh, in-season favas is the summertime – choose ones whose pods are smooth, since the older the bean, the more the pod will bulge. Or substitute them with green beans or lentils. This dish is served at room temperature.

1. Blanch the tripe and boil for one hour. Cut into twelve 1 in / 2.5 cm squares and roll in flour, egg, and then breadcrumbs. Cut the remaining tripe into strips and simmer once more in the white wine and broth with egg white for 30 minutes; drain. Retain some cooking liquid.

2. In a blender or food processor, blend the shallot, wine, balsamic vinegar, salt, pepper, hot and mild mustards, a little cooking liquid from the tripe, and olive oil for a few seconds. Blanch the fava beans in salt water, rinse with ice water, and extract the beans from the pods. If the beans themselves have a tough skin on them, blanch or rub this off to reveal the tender bean.

Liver and Fava Beans

3. Cut the goose liver into four slices (they should be about $^1/_8$ lb / 60 g each). Fry with the tripe squares in peanut oil for two to three minutes on each side. Fry the quail eggs sunny-side up. Heat the tripe strips and fava beans in the vinaigrette.

4. To serve, arrange the lettuce in a circle in the middle of the plate. Place the warm beans and tripe strips on top, then add three breaded tripe squares, then the fried goose liver. Top with a fried quail's egg. Garnish with chervil leaves.

Preparation time: 30 minutes
Cooking time: 30 minutes
Cooling time: 24 hours
Difficulty: ★★

Serves four

2 lobsters, a generous 1 lb / 1 kg each
1 cucumber
8 tomatoes
$^1/_2$ red pepper
1 leek stalk
$^5/_8$ lb / 300 g onions
1 clove of garlic
3 slices of bread, crust removed
3 basil leaves

pinch of cumin
pinch of coriander
$^3/_4$ cup / 200 ml olive oil
$^1/_2$ cup / 100 ml red wine vinegar
1 cup / 250 ml cream
2 cups / 500 ml lobster soup
    (see basic recipes p. 802)
salt, pepper to taste

For the garnish:
1 red pepper
1 green pepper
1 cucumber
3 slices white bread
1 cup / 250 ml olive oil
half a bunch of basil leaves

Gazpacho was created in Seville, in southern Spain. Spanish farmers prepared this refreshing dish right in the fields, using a mortar to crush cucumbers, tomatoes, and onions into a pulpy liquid that they would pour into a clay pot, binding it with breadcrumbs and seasoning it with garlic and olive oil. The whole process, from clay pot to seasoning, imparted a fresh and particular flavor to the dish. Here, chef Michel Haquin uses the same original ingredients, but adds lobster to give it a marine nuance.

The cucumber has been known for more than three thousand years; today, it is particularly appreciated by diet-conscious consumers. Thanks to them, the cucumber – member of the pumpkin family – has become popular again, after having been

rejected for a long time for tasting too bitter. These days we appreciate its beneficial properties, from its few calories to the large amount of water it contains, which of course is important for the gazpacho. But all the vegetables going into the gazpacho must be ripe and juicy.

If you happen to be out of fish stock you can also stretch the lobster soup with water, as the lobster flavor is very strong. This does not necessarily apply to all shellfish, but does to shrimp, crayfish, and langoustines as well; they would, incidentally, be a fine alternative to lobster in this recipe.

Gazpacho is an appetizer that is served chilled; some like to serve it as an intermediate course instead of a *digestif*.

1. Chop all the vegetables; peel and chop the garlic; chop the basil leaves. Stir in the basil leaves and the garlic. Cook the lobster quickly; extract the lobster meat from the shells. Add the claws and tails into the broth and prepare the lobster soup.

2. Add the red wine vinegar, olive oil, cumin, and coriander to the vegetable mixture. Season with salt and pepper. Remove the crust from the bread and retain for later; blend the bread with the other ingredients and leave the mixture to rest for 24 hours.

Gazpacho

3. *After the 24-hour rest period, use a hand-held blender to mix well. Take about a quart of the gazpacho, and mix with the lobster soup. Adjust seasoning to taste, mix once more, add the cream and mix one last time; chill.*

4. *Peel the peppers and the cucumber, chop separately. Cut the retained breadcrust into small chunks and fry until brown in a little olive oil. Serve the gazpacho chilled in a deep plate, accompanied by separate small bowls of garnish. Set the lobster meat in the gazpacho; decorate with basil leaves.*

Cool Tomato Broth with

Preparation time: 45 minutes, plus 24 hours for straining
Cooking time: 3 minutes
Difficulty: ★

Serves four

2$^1/_2$ lbs / 1$^1/_4$ kg tomatoes
1 bunch of basil (to yield $^1/_8$ lb / 50 g)
1 bunch of chervil (to yield a scant $^1/_4$ lb / 100 g)
1 bunch of smooth parsley
3 sprigs thyme

1 clove of garlic
1 shallot
$^1/_2$ cup / 125 ml white wine
coarse sea salt to taste

For the vegetables:
2 carrots
4 tomatoes
2 zucchini
1 celeriac
$^1/_2$ lb / 250 g fresh fava beans
$^1/_2$ lb / 250 g small peas

This tomato broth can be served as an appetizer or as a digestive treat after the main course. It is simple to prepare and very refreshing. Make sure you buy very ripe, red, and tasty tomatoes, such as the Roma variety, which is sold on the stem – a sure indicator of ripeness. Romas have firm flesh and the sweet flavor that this dish requires. Nineteenth-century England considered the tomato, a member of the nightshade family, a toxic vegetable, and hygiene laws required any cook to boil them for three hours before consumption. Certainly, our knowledge of nature's products has improved since then, and the preparation of this dish is a little quicker than that, if one disregards the draining time.

The tomato broth requires some spicing up – enter the aromatic herbs, such as fresh basil, smooth parsley, and chervil. If you wish, add dill, fennel, and chives as well to this bouquet garni.

Crushed with your very own hands, the tomatoes only gradually release their juices, so they need to be strained through a muslin cloth for twenty-four hours. Use a muslin that is not too finely woven, so that a little of the flesh also passes through. The vegetables need to be cooked *al dente* so they retain their vitamins. If for some reason you can't obtain fresh fava beans, follow the instructions in previous recipes on dealing with dried ones.

1. Wash the tomatoes, remove the stems, and place the tomatoes in a bowl. Add the chopped herbs, shallot, and garlic as well as the wine and seasoning.

2. Squash the tomatoes by pressing them between your fingers until they are transformed into a pulp.

Chervil and Vegetables

3. Place the squashed mixture into a muslin cloth over a container and leave to strain for 24 hours.

4. For the vegetable garnish, peel and finely chop the vegetables. Skin the beans; remove the peas from the pods; cook the vegetables with the beans, and then the peas. Drain the tomato liquid; pour a portion into a soup bowl or cup, add the vegetable garnish and chervil leaves. Serve cold.

Salad of Sea Bream

Preparation time: 20 minutes
Cooking time: 30 minutes
Marinating/Pickling time: 2 hours total
Difficulty: ✶

Serves four

1 2 lb / 1 kg sea bream
2 lb / 1 kg coarse sea salt
scant $^1/_2$ lb / 200 g green beans
1 bunch of radishes
scant $^1/_2$ cup / 25 g lettuce
2 tbsp / 30 ml olive oil
4 potato skins (see below)

For the marinade:
scant quart / 1 l white wine vinegar
$^5/_8$ cup / 150 g sugar

For the vegetable sauce:
1 small head lettuce
1 cucumber
1 green or red tomato
1 lemon
half a bunch of basil leaves
$^1/_4$ cup / 60 ml extra virgin olive oil
salt, pepper to taste

The sea bream, which lives on the rocky ocean floor, is mainly caught in the Atlantic and the Mediterranean. Its rather fat, firm and white flesh is very high in iodine.

Being particularly fond of marinated fish, our chef, Alfonso Iaccarino, wholeheartedly recommends this delicate salad. Instead of being cooked, the fish is first pickled in coarse sea salt and then marinated in white wine vinegar, giving it a distinctive flavor. How long the fish is marinated for depends on the thickness of the fillets: calculate about one hour per two pounds (one kilogram) of fish meat but err, if at all, on the side of underdoing it. The fillet should remain firm underneath the exterior layer. If no sea bream is available or if it is not to your taste, you can substitute it with a small perch.

The vegetable sauce is dominated by the cucumber, a vegetable known since antiquity (see page 56 for more information) but never really appreciated. Its bitterness can be neutralized by pickling the cucumber in honey or – as in this recipe – rolling it in salt and leaving it to infuse for ten minutes. You can then add it to the sauce along with a slightly acidic green tomato.

If you would like to vary the color of the sauce a bit, try adding beets, celery or carrots as well.

1. Clean and fillet the sea bream, and pickle in coarse sea salt for one hour; afterwards, rinse thoroughly in cold water. Prepare a marinade with vinegar and sugar and immerse the fillets in it; leave for one hour, regularly basting the fillets with the liquid.

2. Remove the fillets from the marinade and cut into thin slices. Chill for one hour.

with Vegetable Sauce

3. Wash the green beans and cook al dente. Julienne the beans and radishes into thin strips.

4. To make the potato cups, scrub the potatoes well; hollow out into thin shells; deep-fry in hot oil until crisp. To make the vegetable sauce, chop the lettuce, cucumber, basil and tomato in a blender. Add olive oil and salt. Heap some mixed lettuce in the middle of the plate, season, and place a few fish slices on top. Surround with the julienne of beans and radish. Serve with the sauce poured into an edible potato cup placed on top of the fish slices.

Smoked Breast of Duck

Preparation time: 30 minutes
Cooking time: 10 minutes
Pickling time: 24 hours (optional)
Cooling time: 24 hours
Difficulty: ★★

Serves four

2 breasts of duck
2 tbsp / 30 g dry black tea leaves
1 tbsp / 15 g hoisin sauce (ready-made)

For the vegetables:
8 fresh baby corn
10 cherry tomatoes
$^3/_8$ lb / 80 g snow peas

For the salt brine:
Salt for pickling (2 tsp / 10 g per 1 lb)

For the miso vinaigrette:
1 tbsp / 15 g white miso (see below)
1 tbsp / 15 ml vegetable oil
1 tbsp / 15 ml rice vinegar
2 tbsp / 30 ml broth

For the garnish:
half a bunch of smooth parsley
half a bunch of curly parsley
half a bunch of chervil

In days gone by, food was smoked in order to preserve it; now the process is primarily used to impart flavor. Here, chef André Jaeger demonstrates how this method can transform a breast of duck.

Smoking with tea is practiced in China to this day (with whole leaves, not broken ones). It lends a delicious flavor to the meat. The black tea sold in wooden crates is particularly suitable for this purpose, as its aroma is very strong. You don't need a smokehouse to do it: you can smoke the meat by placing it on a perforated rack in a covered frying pan, or make your own makeshift smokehouse from wood scraps. For better smoking, the duck breasts should be pickled in a salt brine for twenty-four hours to make the meat more tender. After smoking the breasts should be brushed with hoisin sauce, which consists of

fermented and perfumed soybeans with spices and is available in many Asian markets and health-food stores. The combination of hoisin sauce and duck meat might seem a little strange at first to a Western palette, but in fact it is a perfect match. After preparation, the meat should be left to rest so it becomes even more tender; it is then cut into slices with a pointed knife.

Miso, a paste made of fermented soybeans, comes in two basic varieties: red miso has a stronger flavor; white a milder one. For this recipe, the delicate, pale color of the white miso vinaigrette constrasts well with the hearty color of the duck, but, on the other hand, if your tastes run to the stronger flavor, use red miso instead.

1. Rub the duck breasts with salt; refrigerate for 24 hours. Then pour the dry tea leaves into a frying pan, place a flat sieve or perforated lid on top, place the salted breast on that, and cover.

2. Heat on the stove top until the tea leaves start smoking, and maintain the heat for 15 to 20 minutes. When smoke appears from the meat, reduce the heat so the duck will not cook prematurely.

with Vegetables and Miso

3. Cross-hatch the skin of the duck breasts every ¹/₄ in / ¹/₂ cm or so. In a skillet, heat the oil over high heat and fry the meat for five minutes each side, skin side down first. Leave to rest for ten minutes. Brush the meat with hoisin sauce and slice with a sharp knife.

4. To make the miso vinaigrette, mix all ingredients with the miso paste and stir. Wash the vegetables; quarter the cherry tomatoes and cut the corn into ¹/₂ in / 1 cm slices. To serve, arrange the vegetables on the plates in mounds, pour over the vinaigrette, and place the duck breasts on top. Decorate with herbs.

Dough Cornucopia

Preparation time: 45 minutes
Cooking time: 30 minutes
Difficulty: ★★

Serves four

2 crabs, 1½ lb / 800 g each
4 flat rounds of dough, or puff pastry dough
  (see below)
2 grapefruit
1 orange

1 lemon
1 shallot
1½ tbsp / 20 g sesame seeds
⅞ cup / 200 g whipping cream
1 cup / 250 ml vegetable oil
¼ lb / 125 g butter
1 bunch of chives
half a bunch of chervil
half a bunch of tarragon
1 cup / 250 g mixed lettuce leaves
salt, pepper to taste

These cones stuffed with crab are irresistible. They look like little horns of plenty containing a special and delicious treasure, in this case crab meat. The flat dough discs we propose here are made from a Tunisian dough, by now popular and quite common all over Europe. The dough, made with flour, water, salt, and soy oil, is extremely versatile and can be worked into all sorts of shapes. It must be stored in a dry place, particularly if making it in advance. If you can not get this kind of dough, you can use ordinary puff pastry dough instead. Whichever dough you use, it has to be rolled into thin rounds to form the cones.

Around the globe, there is a veritable plethora of crabs: green, blue, red, and brown. These shellfish have an underdeveloped tail that disappears underneath the back shell, unlike the lobster or langoustine crayfish. Sometimes described by the French as "sleepers" because they hardly move, crabs are particularly tasty from April to July. Choose female crabs, as they have better developed shells and come with tasty crab roe, or coral. They should be very fresh – ideally, bought live.

To cook, the crabs are immersed in boiling water; the cooking time begins once the water comes to a boil again. It is important that the crab is left to cool in the cooking liquid so that the meat remains tender. Then take it out and cover with a moist cloth. Ideally, keep the crab in a warm place.

You could also use chopped tuna for this recipe (even freshly boiled and subsequently frozen tuna); instead of the grapefruit, you could substitute ripe avocados cut in quarters.

1. Plunge the crabs into fast boiling water and cook for 25 minutes. Afterwards, leave to infuse in the cooking liquid. Crack the shells and use a spoon to extract the meat. Prepare the dressing with oil, the juice of half a lemon and the shallot, which has already been cut into rounds.

2. Cut a circle 8–10 in / 20–25 cm in diameter out of cardboard and fasten into a cone; use as the form for four cones, wrapping them with aluminum foil.

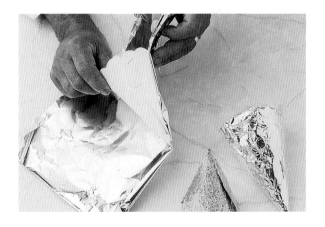

with Crab Filling

3. Clarify the butter. Cut out the wafer-thin dough into enough of a disc to roll into four cones over the foil-covered forms. Sprinkle with sesame seeds and brush with clarified butter; bake at 355 °F / 180 °C for four to five minutes.

4. Mix the crab meat with the cream, chopped chives, orange zest, salt, and pepper. Fill the cones with this. To serve, place on on a plate with grapefruit slivers arranged on one side and the dressed salad leaves on the other. Garnish with tarragon and chervil.

Preparation time: 45 minutes
Cooking time: 45 minutes
Cooling time: 30 minutes
Difficulty: ★★

Serves four

4 potatoes
2 leeks
³/₄ cup / 200 ml cream
³/₄ cup / 200 ml clear broth
generous cup / 300 ml chicken broth

To clarify the soup:
scant ¹/₈ lb / 40 g ground beef
1 tomato

2 leeks (to yield 2 tbsp / 20 g chopped)
2 carrots (to yield 2 tbsp / 20 g chopped)
¹/₂ celeriac (to yield 2 tbsp / 20 g chopped)
white of 1 egg
¹/₂ sheet of gelatin
3 ice cubes

For the vegetable garnish:
1 small zucchini
1 small carrot
1 turnip
half a bunch of chervil

For the meat garnish:
¹/₄ lb / 125 g chicken breast
scant ¹/₄ lb / 100 g cooked goose liver

The Alsace region has, thanks to its agriculture, rivers, and large game population, always considered food and drink one of its prime concerns and passions. And while Alsatian cuisine is certainly known for its famous choucroute, it is far from limited to it: chefs around the world regard its cuisine as one of the most creative, with countless recipes to be inspired by.

Our chef, Émile Jung, provides proof, as if proof was ever required, of this creativity with his Alsation soup platter, which has as a centerpiece a potato and leek puree. Leeks have been popular in antiquity, considered a symbol of strength and courage: Pharaoh Cheops rewarded leeks to his most courageous soldiers, and Emperor Nero consumed them to increase his vocal power. Harvested in spring, fall and winter, leeks in France are mainly cultivated in Normandy and Brittany. This recipe calls for only the sweet-tasting white of the leek.

Choose waxy potatoes for this dish to go with the leeks. The potato is deeply rooted in Alsatian tradition, having served its people well during times of war and famine: the Alsace region has been threatened time and again by its neighbors on both sides of the Rhine.

Preparation and seasoning requires some attention, though a few tips may make it easier: add ice cubes when clarifying the soup to prevent the egg white from stiffening, and make sure the aspic remains relatively runny (rather than letting it achieve its classic, firm consistency) so that it simply melts in the mouth and retains its delicate aroma.

1. To clarify the soup, chop all ingredients into coarse chunks and mix with the egg white. Stir in the ice cubes. Add clear broth and chicken broth bit by bit, constantly stirring. Retain a little of the liquid for the aspic.

2. Cook the soup for 20 minutes over medium heat, constantly stirring and then strain.

Soup Platter

3. Peel, wash, and dice the potatoes and cook with a scant ¹/₂ cup / 20 ml of the cleaned and chopped leeks. In a food processor or blender, prepare a puree from the leeks, potatoes, clear broth, and chicken broth, adding cream. Place in the middle of the plate with the aid of a 2 in / 5 cm in diameter circular form.

4. Gently cook the chicken breast in its own juices. Dice it, as well as the cooked goose liver, and arrange in a ring around the puree. Pour the slightly jellied broth (not yet an aspic) around the puree. Garnish with small carrot, turnip, and zucchini balls, and chervil leaves.

Duck's Liver Tar

Preparation time: 1 hour
Cooking time: 5 minutes
Cooling time: 12 hours
Difficulty: ★★★

Serves eight

1 duck's liver, 1¼ lb / 600 g
scant ½ cup / 100 g slivered almonds
1 cup / 250 ml cream
½ tbsp / 7 g starch
1¼ cups / 300 ml clear broth
³⁄₈ cup / 100 ml sweet muscat wine (see
    below)
scant ¼ cup / 50 ml cognac
4 sheets of gelatin
salt, fresh-ground white pepper to taste

For the confit of grapes:
1 lb / 500 g green seedless grapes
⅛ lb / 50 g sugar
2 cloves
half a lemon
2 sheets of gelatin
³⁄₈ cup / 100 ml white wine

For the génoise:
(see basic recipes p. 801)

Chef Dieter Kaufmann, is the man behind the Traube restaurant – renowned throughout Germany for its passion for excellent wines. Kaufmann has a wine cellar with more than thirty thousand bottles, among them great French crus (Romanée-Conti, Yquem, Lafite and Pétrus) as well as top German wines, used in some of Kaufmann's recipes.

This appetizer was initially conceived as a proper pudding, with a layer of génoise (a versatile, spongy cake), and a sweet, almost caramelized wine aspic; it was modified for the birthday celebration of a close friend and then finally included on the restaurant's menu.

Duck liver contains less fat than goose liver, making it more appropriate for this dish. It is imperative that the filling is prepared at the right temperature, or the liver will become bitter. The cream is carefully folded into the mousse, which will be layered over the filling. Both layers need to be equal in height and balanced in flavor in order to achieve the desired effect.

Prepare the grapes ahead of time so you can then focus on the tart. If possible, Kaufmann recommends the excellent Chasselas grapes, which can keep in the refrigerator for more than a week; otherwise, look for a succulent, firm, green seedless variety that is ripe, but not overly so, unless you are preparing them the same day.

1. Chill half of the duck liver; strain the remaining portion and chill as well. Heat ³⁄₈ cup / 100 ml of clear broth with a scant ¼ cup / 50 ml of the muscat wine and the cognac, remove from the heat and carefully fold into the strained duck liver. Do not allow the liver to become too warm. Line the base of a circular cake form (about 4–6 in / 10–15 cm in diameter) with a thin layer of génoise and pour the duck liver filling into the form. Chill for 20 minutes.

2. To prepare the mousse, heat another ³⁄₈ cup / 100 ml of clear broth and bind with the starch. Cut the remaining half of the duck liver into thin slices, add to the broth, and melt slightly. Puree in the blender and then strain. Add four pre-soaked gelatin sheets. Chill for 15–20 minutes.

with a Confit of Grapes

3. Whip the cream until half-stiff and carefully fold into the basic mousse mixture. Season with salt and pepper according to taste. Pour on top of the génoise in the cake form to make the second layer. Chill for 12 hours. To make the grape aspic, heat the rest of the clear broth with a pre-soaked sheet of gelatin, add a ¼ cup / 125 ml of muscat wine, and leave to cool. Glaze the tart with this aspic.

4. For the confit of grapes (which can be made ahead of time), mix the lemon juice, the remaining white wine, and cloves. Soak a gelatin sheet. Peel the grapes, remove any seeds and marinate in the wine-juice mixture. Make a caramel mixture from 2 tbsp of sugar and pour the grape marinade over it. Add a pre-soaked gelatin sheet and remove from the heat instantly. Remove the tart from the form and coat the outside with slivered almonds.

Preparation time: 25 minutes
Cooking time: 5 minutes
Difficulty: ★

Serves four

scant ¹/₂ lb / 200 g whitefish roe
⁷/₈ lb / 400 g potatoes
¹/₄ cup / 60 ml crème fraîche
1 red onion (to yield ¹/₄ cup / 60 g chopped)
¹/₂ lb / 125 g butter
1 lemon
1 bunch of chives
salt, pepper to taste

Usually, fish roe is considered a luxury, used to decorate little canapés, embellish festive dishes, or add elegance to a meal. But, in Sweden, it is a popular and common ingredient, which is why it appears in this recipe. The dish, conceived by Örjan Klein, was inspired by the Russian blini the sturgeon roe having been replaced by whitefish roe, and the blini by the potato cake.

Whitefish has become increasingly rare. Not only does it have a unique, delicious taste, but its scales are distilled into an essence with which glass pearls are coated to give them the lustre of real pearls. In Sweden, the fish is called *lörja*, and is chiefly caught in the Baltic Sea.

The best whitefish roe comes from the fishing port of Kalix in northern Sweden, close to the Finnish border. When the roe is prepared, every egg is separated from the skin and cured with salt. The resulting salty flavor has a strong iodine element, and its color – yellow or red – is extremely bright (avoid gray roe). Although its flavor is more delicate than salmon or trout roe, the latter can be used alternatively.

1. Wash and peel the potatoes. Slice thinly; cut the slices into very fine strips.

2. Press the potato strips well so that all the water oozes out (try sandwiching the strips between two boards, using a light book to weigh down the top one). Chop the red onion and chives.

with Potato Cake

3. Form the potato strips into little cakes and sauté them in a frying pan that is, ideally, the same size as the cakes, if not much bigger, in order to keep the cakes' shape.

4. To serve, place a potato cake in the middle of each plate and dollop the whitefish roe, onion, and chives into separate mounds. Garnish with a sliver of lemon. Accompany the dish with a separate pot of bowl of crème fraîche.

Vegetable Terrine with

Preparation time: 1 hour
Cooking time: 2 hours, 30 minutes

Cooling time: 3 hours
Difficulty: ★★

Serves eight

4 fennel bulbs
5 zucchini
5 eggplants
4 lb / 2 kg tomatoes
2 red peppers
1 clove of garlic
7 sheets of gelatin
1 scant quart / 1 l olive oil
1 cup / 250 g pastis

1 bunch of thyme
salt, pepper to taste

For the mustard puree:
1 artichoke
1 carrot
1 onion
1 clove of garlic
2 large button mushrooms
1 1/2 tbsp / 15 g mustard
scant 1/2 cup / 125 ml white wine
1/2 cup / 125 ml olive oil
1 cup / 250 ml milk
a pinch of coarse sea salt

Serve with: bread
chèvre (goat's milk cream cheese)

To garnish:
dill
chives

Terrines come in countless varieties, and have many admirers. A terrine might be filled with meat, fish, or simply vegetables, its aspic sweet or sour, its accompaniment a puree or a salad.

In the sixteenth century, people began listing all vegetables with edible leaves, stems, or bulbs, that did not have to be prepared with sugar. The list soon included three hundred vegetables, all with their own history and methods of preparation.

Choose fennel, zucchini, and eggplants that are very firm and unblemished. They will be steamed in a blend of their own juices and olive oil, imparting a Mediterranean aroma. Keep the vegetables *al dente* to contrast with the soft tomatoes.

Buy ripe and firm tomatoes and, above all, buy plenty of them: you will need around four pounds (two kilograms) raw to yield one-and-a-quarter pounds (six hundred grams) pickled. It is a good idea to prepare these the day before. They are well-seasoned before being placed on a baking tray and baked in the oven. If you like garlic, add it to the tomatoes, but be sure to blanch the garlic cloves in milk twice before cooking them into a paste, otherwise their flavor will be too overwhelming.

This appetizer should be served with a slice of country bread and fresh chèvre, or goat's milk cream cheese, sprinkled with dill and chives.

1. Discard the rough outer fennel layers and peel apart the inner layers. Peel and seed the peppers and chop. Gently fry the fennel in olive oil and add a little salt. Add a little pastis and cook for 20 minutes. Place the peppers in hot olive oil and gently fry for 20 minutes.

2. Cut the zucchini and eggplants in wide strips but discard the eggplant's seeded core. Gently fry in olive oil, add salt and pepper, and continue to gently fry for 15 minutes. Marinate the tomatoes in olive oil, garlic, thyme, salt, and pepper. Leave to infuse for two and a half hours in a low-oven – about 180 °F / 80 °C.

a Sweet Mustard Puree

3. To prepare the mustard puree, chop the artichoke hearts, carrot, onion, mushrooms, and garlic (which has been blanched in milk twice) into medium-sized chunks. Heat some olive oil, add the vegetables, and heat for ten minutes; with the heat still going, add the white wine, mustard, and a pinch of coarse sea salt. Cover with aluminum foil and cook gently for another 15 minutes. Puree in a blender or food processor.

4. Pre-soak the gelatin. Line the terrine form with foil or plastic wrap than can withstand high temperatures and fill, in layers, the eggplants, zucchini, fennel, peppers, fennel, zucchini, and then eggplants again, placing a layer of marinated tomatoes and a sheet of gelatin between each layer. Close the terrine form and cook in a bain-marie for 20 minutes at 350 °F / 180 °C. Serve in slices, accompanied by a spoonful of the mustard puree and a dollop of the chèvre.

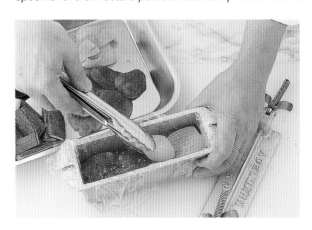

Oxtail Balls

Preparation time: 1 hour
Cooking time: 4 hours
Difficulty: ★★★

Serves four

half an oxtail
2 slices of goose liver pâté
4 tomatoes
1 celeriac
1 carrot
1 small leek
1 onion stuck with 3 cloves

1 tbsp / 15 g concentrated tomato paste
1 tbsp / 15 g poppy seeds
2 sprigs of thyme
1 bay leaf
half a bunch of flat-leafed parsley
1 1/4 cups / 300 ml red wine
scant quart / 1 l beef broth
1/2 cup / 125 ml sherry vinegar
3/8 cup / 100 ml walnut oil
fat for frying
salt, pepper to taste

Oxtail is not regarded too highly, although it is inexpensive, very tasty, and has a sublime consistency. Its upper portion bears the most delicious meat. Our chef, Étienne Krebs, recommends the tail from a young ox; when he makes this recipe, he looks for an ox of the Simmental breed from the Swiss region of Waadt. The oxtail has to cook for a long time, around four hours, over a very low heat, in order to draw out all the flavor and make it easier to separate the meat from the bone. Since only the meat will be consumed, it requires a bit of patience to discard all the fat and nerve tissue.

To make the celeriac ravioli you will need even, thin slices of celeriac: a slicing machine works well for this task; slice the celeriac as if you were slicing a ham. The celeriac itself should not be fibrous but firm and fresh. In Switzerland, the best

varieties are Alba or Mentor, if they have been cultivated traditionally; otherwise, get one in season (September through May) that is relatively free of knobs or blemishes. The celeriac flavor is the ideal accompaniment for the goose liver pâté, as quite a few recipes can attest to.

The choice of pâté depends on the consistency and the subtle differences of the slightly sweet flavors involved: a marinade of Madeira and sugar is a perfect contrast to the poppy seed crust that will coat the pâté.

Instead of the oxtail, you can make this dish with calf's tail; instead of ravioli, you might trying serving it with a julienne of deep-fried onions.

1. Quarter the tomatoes. Salt and pepper the oxtail on all sides. Place in a pan lined with tomatoes and spices, add wine, salt, and pepper, stir, and cook for four hours over very low heat. Peel the celeriac, slice extremely thin, and boil in broth for one to two minutes. Using a circular cutter, cut out 24 circles of about 3 in / 5 cm in diameter from the celeriac slices.

2. Let the oxtail cool a little, strain the meat juice, and reduce to an aspic. Separate the meat from the bone, discard the fat and nerve tissue, and dice into small chunks. Chop the vegetables finely. Mix the meat with parsley and add the vegetables, tomato paste, vinegar and 4 tbsp / 60 ml of reduced meat broth. Mix well and season to taste.

with Celeriac Ravioli

3. Place this filling on 12 of the celeriac slices and cover with the other 12 slices to make them look like ravioli. Then prepare the sauce: put a large portion of the remaining celeriac, vinegar, walnut oil, and a little meat broth in a blender or food processor and puree thoroughly. Fry about a ¼ cup / 50 g of the celeriac julienne and set aside.

4. Halve the liver pâté slices, form four balls, and roll with the palm of your hand in a mixture of celeriac julienne and poppy seeds. To serve, place three celeriac ravioli in the middle of each plate, place one ball of the liver pâté on top, and garnish with sauce.

Breton Terrine of

Preparation time: 40 minutes
Cooking time: 20 minutes
Cooling time: 12 hours
Difficulty: ★★

Serves four

2 lobsters, 1¼ lb / 600 g each
broth (for the lobster)
2 onions
1 bunch of leeks (⅞ lb / 375 g)
scant ½ lb / 200 g red peppers
⅛ lb / 50 g green beans

generous ¼ lb / 125 g spinach
1 bunch of carrots
1 cup / 250 ml olive oil
salt, pepper to taste

For the tomato sauce:
½ lb / 250 g tomatoes
2 tbsp / 25 g tomato paste
two dashes of Tabasco
2 tbsp / 30 ml vinegar
½ cup / 125 ml olive oil
a pinch of salt

Although the preparation of this appetizer is a little time-consuming, it does have some tempting advantages: you can modify the recipe according to season, using whatever vegetable is available and suitable, and the terrine will keep in the refrigerator for a few days.

The outside leaves of the leeks are particularly pretty, and their fiber is very beneficial for digestion. Paradoxically, leek is consumed more during the winter than the summer, though this vegetable does not like to be exposed to frost at all. The leek belongs to the family of lilies, along with its cousins, onion and garlic. Remove the green sprout so the leek tastes less bitter. And, when preparing the terrine, make sure the individual layers of vegetables are even and season every layer. For full effect, the lobster tail is placed in the center.

Finally, the terrine must be pressed down with a weight and set to cool for twelve hours, after which point it will have set enough to be cut into three-quarter-inch (two centimeter) slices that are served on a delicate tomato sauce. The tomatoes are, depending on the season, more or less juicy, so you should puree them in any case to obtain a smooth and even mixture.

1. Tie the leeks together in a bundle and boil in salted water for 8–10 minutes; rinse in cold water. Cook the onions, carrots, green beans, and spinach in the same cooking liquid; afterwards, very briefly dip into ice water. Line the terrine with plastic wrap, then halve the leeks and line the terrine with the leaves.

2. Plunge the lobster into broth that has reached a rolling boil. Peel the red pepper, cut into thin strips, and fry briefly in olive oil. Halve the carrots; line the corners of the terrine with the carrot pieces.

obster with Tomato Sauce

3. Continue to fill the terrine with the various layers of green beans, chopped onions, spinach, and peppers, then add the lobster tail before layering another series of vegetables.

4. Close the terrine with the overlapping leek leaves and plastic wrap. Place the terrine dish into another dish and press with a 10 lb / 5 kg weight; chill in the refrigerator for 12 hours. To prepare the sauce, chop the tomatoes in the blender, add the other ingredients, and puree into a fine thick sauce. Serve a slice of terrine on a bed of sauce; garnish with herbs.

Shrimps and Cookec

Preparation time: 40 minutes
Cooking time: 20 minutes
Difficulty: ★★

Serves four

generous ³/₄ lb / 400 g shrimps (raw or cooked)
2 cups / 500 g salt (¹/₂ cup / 125 g per ¹/₂ gallon / 1 l of liquid)
1–2 tomatoes
¹/₂ red pepper
1 cup / 250 g lettuce leaves
1 shallot
2 tbsp / 15 ml mayonnaise (see basic recipes p. 802)
1 baguette
a dash of Tabasco

salt, pepper to taste
1 sprig of dill

For the spicy oil:
¹/₂ cup / 125 ml sesame oil

5 green peppercorns
half a bunch each: parsley, tarragon, basil, dill
half a clove of garlic

For the vegetables:
half a head of cauliflower
half a bunch of carrots
half a bunch of parsnips
1 parsley root (see below)
1 small zucchini
2 saffron threads
1 clove of garlic
1 sprig of dill flowers

For the saffron cream:
¹/₂ cup / 125 ml whipping cream
1 saffron thread
1 bunch of flowering dill

Our Chef, Erwin Lauterbach, has created a colorful recipe from an array of vegetables that complement each other perfectly, dominated by the dill flowers, which are much tastier than the leaves normally used in cooking. Available from mid-August to the end of October, they are perfect with lamb, seafood, and, of course, fish.

The shrimp, which can be bought uncooked or cooked, should – if they were bought uncooked – be boiled for about two minutes in salty water. Their size is not as important a consideration as their flavor – after all, there are more than three thousand varieties of crustaceans, from the small gray shrimp to the enormous sea crab. According to season or preference, you can substitute crab, crayfish or lobster for shrimps as well.

The mélange of vegetables is the dominant force of this dish. Chef Lauterbach combines a wide range, including parsnips, carrots, cauliflower, fennel, celery, and parsley root – a vegetable not always found in the United States, which is also known as Hamburg parsley. Parsley root is tan and somewhat carrot-shaped, with a spray of bright green, feathery leaves attached. If you can find it, its sweet, distinctive taste will certainly enhance this dish.

The intriguing saffron cream, unusual for Denmark, lends further contrast. To refine the dish even more, add a subtle sprinkling of cinnamon to the mayonnaise as well.

1. Clean the vegetables and simmer in salted water along with a sprig of dill flowers, a garlic clove, and saffron. After cooking, set the vegetables on a kitchen towel and chill. Cook the shrimps in their shells with a sprig of dill, and then shell them. Peel and seed the tomato and chop, along with the red pepper, into small cubes.

2. To prepare the spicy oil, put sesame oil, peppercorns, garlic, and herbs into a blender; mix well. Slit the baguette lengthwise and slice into four quarters; apply the spicy oil generously on each slice and grill in a frying pan until crisp.

Dill-vegetables

3. Finely chop the shallot. Mix the mayonnaise with a dash of Tabasco and the chopped shallot; chop all the vegetables and thoroughly mix with the mayonnaise. To make the saffron cream, add saffron and dill flowers to the cream and reduce by half. Strain and season to taste.

4. To serve, place a tall (2–3 in / 5–7 cm) and slender circular form on each plate, and layer as follows: first half the vegetables, then half the shrimps, then the remaining vegetables. Press firmly. Add a layer of the tomato-pepper mixture, then remove the form. Arrange the remaining shrimps, the grilled bread and the saffron cream on the plate. Garnish with lettuce leaves.

Puff Pastry Tart with

Preparation time: 40 minutes
Cooking time: 15 minutes
Marinating time: 24 hours
Difficulty: ★

Serves four

1¼ lb / 600 g tuna
3–4 lb / 400 g puff pastry dough
  (see basic recipes p. 803)
1¾ lbs / 800 g tomatoes
6 cloves of garlic
4¼ cups / 1 l olive oil
1 bunch of basil
half a bunch of thyme
2 bay leaves
salt, peppercorns

In the eighteenth century, an enormous earthquake shook Lisbon, Portugal, taking many lives and decimating the area's marine life. The tuna, which had been a resident since antiquity, disappeared from the Portuguese waters. Today, the (almost) undefeatable swimmer is still found in abundance in the Bay of Biscay and the Mediterranean, where it is considered a delicacy.

Choose fresh red tuna, available from April through November. The firmer the fish, the fresher; for this recipe, in which the tuna is served half-raw, the fish should be extremely fresh. When planning to make this dish, bear in mind the twenty-four hours the fish needs to marinate, since it will take that long for the meat to absorb the flavor of the herbs. And, as our chef,

Dominique Le Stanc, points out, tuna meat tends to dry out rather quickly, so it should never be overcooked. Here the cooking procedure is borrowed from Japan: the tuna is picked up with a fork (or cooking chopsticks) and quickly passed through an open flame, imparting an agreeably smoky flavor.

The puff pastry slices forming the base of the tart should not be baked for too long, as overcooking can lend a bitterness to the pastry's taste. Our chef recommends you cut out the dough after it has been baked, rather than before, to achieve slices that match in size.

This simple appetizer, served at room temperature, is ideal for summer.

1. A day in advance, marinate the tuna in olive oil, bay leaf, thyme (about two sprigs), garlic, and peppercorns. If you prefer, prepare the puff pastry dough in advance as well, as it can chill up to 24 hours before using.

2. Roll out the dough. Cut out four 8 in / 18 cm circles, score with a fork, and chill for 20 minutes. Bake in the oven for 10–12 minutes (take it out before it begins to brown) at 400 °F / 210 °C.

Tuna, Tomatoes and Basil

3. Peel and seed the tomatoes, chop, and cook in olive oil, salt and pepper. While the tomatoes are cooking, swiftly pass the marinated tuna fillets through an open flame to sear them and impart a smoky flavor.

4. Add the herbs and a little oil from the marinade to the well-reduced tomatoes. Brush the puff pastry base generously with the tepid tomato mixture, and then cover with a layer of thin tuna slices arranged in a flat rosette. Brush with a little oil from the marinade to give the tuna a shiny film; garnish with basil leaves, and serve warm.

Suckling Pig in Aspic

Preparation time: 20 minutes
Cooking time: 2 hours
Cooling time: 24 hours
Difficulty: ★★

Serves four

shoulder and neck of suckling pig
5 carrots
1 leek
$1/2$ celeriac
2 onions
1 gelatin envelope
1 bunch of thyme
1 bay leaf
1 bunch of flat-leafed parsley

1 tbsp cloves
$2^{1}/_{2}$ cups white wine
1 cup mixed lettuce
salt, pepper to taste

For the vinaigrette:
1 leek
1 shallot
1 tomato
1 tbsp capers
2 tbsp white wine vinegar
$1/4$ cup peanut oil
$1/2$ tsp mustard
1 bunch of tarragon
salt, pepper to taste

This appetizer from chef Léa Linster is an example of the cuisine of Luxemburg, and reflects the country's Franco-German history. Based on suckling pig accompanied by an array of other ingredients, the aspic presents all of its contents, from meat to vegetables to herbs, as if you are looking at them in a shop window.

Give yourself ample time to prepare this dish, as it will take a while before all the piglet's meat comes off the bone. Since it comes off not in large, attractive pieces but in small chunks, it will take a little patience to find the choice pieces to use in this recipe. The dish's success depends on the aspic reaching a firm consistency. While a quick and easy preparation, the cooking

method nevertheless prohibits one from cooking the presoaked gelatin envelopes along with the other ingredients, as they would impair the flavor. It is, however, fine to cook the pig together with a knuckle of veal, which releases its own natural jelly into the broth-this would, as Chef Linster assures us, also produce a good, firm aspic.

The aspic's flavor should be subtle enough that it does not dominate the flavor of the meat; the same applies to the leek vinaigrette. Served on its own, suckling pig in aspic is a delicious appetizer, and served with sautéed potatoes it is a hearty main course suitable for all seasons.

1. If your butcher has not already done so, carve the suckling pig, separating the shoulder from the neck. Bring the meat to a boil in the wine before covering with water and continuing to cook until the meat is clearly softening and coming away from the bone. After cooking, take out the carrots and let the meat dry in the air as it cools. Carefully separate the meat from the bones and cut into chunks. Strain the cooking liquid and add the gelatin envelopes.

2. Cut the carrots into strips and chop the parsley. Fill a terrine form with layers of meat, carrot strips, chopped parsley, another layer of meat, and then another layer of each ingredient in the same order until all are used up. Cover with the cooking liquid and chill for twenty-four hours.

with Leek Vinaigrette

3. For the vinaigrette, beat mustard, vinegar, salt, tomato, and pepper with a whisk. Add peanut oil. Chop the vegetables and tarragon and add, along with the capers, to the vinaigrette.

4. To serve, slice the aspic and place one slice on each plate, with a pool of vinaigrette poured around it; serve with a small portion of mixed lettuce.

Rabbit and Celeriac

Preparation time: 1 hour
Cooking time: 45 minutes
Cooling time: 12 hours
Difficulty: ★★

Serves eight

1 lb / 500 g rabbit meat
⁵/₈ lb / 300 g duck liver
1 lb / 500 g celeriac
2¹/₂ sheets of gelatin
1 cup / 250 ml mead (honey wine)
2¹/₂ / 750 ml cups chicken stock
1 lemon

For the aspic's aromatic garnish:
2¹/₂ cups / 750 ml chicken stock
1 carrot
1 onion
1 leek stalk
1 bouquet garni

For the side salad:
2 cups / 200 g mixed lettuce
¹/₂ cup / 100 g sprouts, such as sunflower or mung bean
¹/₂ cup / 100 ml vinaigrette

Honey has always been universally known for its healing properties; the bees that collected it were revered in antiquity. According to Greek mythology, mead – essentially the fermented essence of honey – was the preferred beverage of the gods on Mount Olympus, and they even allowed mere mortals to share this natural delight. Often available in shops that sell herbs and honey, mead here lends the aspic flavor and subtlety without dominating its own character.

For this recipe, created by Chef Régis Marcon, the quality of the rabbit is key: if possible, buy a free-range breeding rabbit from a farm. The bones and trimmings can be used for making the jelly, and the ribs should be cooked and retained for decoration. If you prefer, you can substitute chicken for rabbit, but make sure it is free-range chicken, as its quality will match that of the rabbit it replaces.

As for the terrine, we recommend you prepare it the day before so it can chill and set overnight. The final result will be a triangular slice, so, if you do not have a triangular form, make one by adding slanted, foil-wrapped cardboard along the sides of the terrine pan. Making a faultless terrine will require your full attention. One hint: carefully cut the celeriac and duck liver into proper rectangles so that the terrine will be perfectly lined up.

1. Cut the rabbit meat into chunks and set the ribs aside. Into a saucepan filled with cold water, put the meat along with the aromatic garnish for the aspic. Bring to a boil, then reduce the heat and leave to simmer for 45 minutes. Heat the chicken stock and add the sheets of gelatin. Once the stock has cooled, add the mead.

2. Peel the celeriac and cut into even ¹/₈ in / 3 cm slices. Cook the slices in salted water laced with lemon juice for three to four minutes, making sure they remain crisp; afterwards, place in a single layer of paper towels to dry.

Terrine with Honey Wine

3. Line a triangular terrine that has been covered with foil with the celeriac rectangles, then with the liver rectangles. Pour over the aspic and chill for one hour, then fill the terrine with rabbit meat and cover with aspic. Cover and chill for 12 hours.

4. To serve, sauté the seasoned rabbit ribs for three to four minutes. Invert the terrine and slice into 1¼ in / 3 cm thick slices with a knife frequently dipped in hot water. Stand on a plate alongside a trio of ribs. Dress the salad with vinaigrette and serve on the side.

Potato-truffle

Preparation time: 35 minutes
Cooking time: 6–8 minutes
Difficulty: ★★

Serves twelve

4 lbs / 2 kg potatoes
5 oz / 150 g truffles
generous 3 cups / 800 ml truffle juice
  (see below)
¹/₂ cup / 100 ml reduced veal stock
¹/₄ lb / 125 g mushrooms (optional)
salt, pepper to taste

The combination of the common potato with the noble truffle, presented here by our Chef, Guy Martin, provides for an intriguing and surprising culinary experience. Were one cooking this in a European kitchen, the ideal potato for this recipe would be the B. F. 15 or Bintje, but in a North American kitchen, there are many other varieties that will work, such as the newly popular Yukon Gold. Essentially, you should opt for a waxy potato that remains firms after cooking; as it is a crucial component in building the terrine, it will ensure that the terrine remains firm and that all the layers remain in place. The potatoes should be cut into slices of the same thickness as the truffle slices.

The truffle, a member of the large mushroom family sometimes referred to as the "black pearl of the kitchen," can be found in numerous varieties at French speciality markets in Carpentras, d'Aups, or Cahors. Nearly all of its forms are imported, including the top-notch black truffle. Searching for truffles has recently become a little easier with the introduction of specially trained truffle hounds, who are easier to keep than truffle pigs (though they must be trained not to devour the truffles the instant they find them!). Chef Martin recommends the black Périgord truffles above all others; when ripe in winter, they can weigh up to one or two ounces (twenty-five or fifty grams).

A light weighing-down and a sufficient amount of time spent chilling will give the terrine a chance to become firm. Slice the terrine with an electric knife in order to maintain the visual feature of the thinly sliced truffles and potatoes, as the fast-moving knife will not disturb the terrine's contents.

To make a less expensive version of this dish, replace the truffles with salmon or anchovy fillets, and season them alternately with pesto and basil.

1. Peel and wash the potatoes. Using a slicer, slice them lengthwise into extremely thin slices. Season with salt and pepper and then steam them in either a steamer or a pressure cooker.

2. Cut the truffles into thin slices using the same slicer.

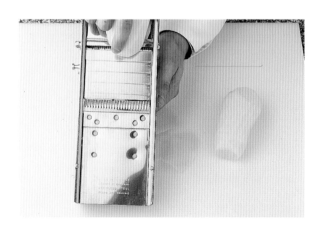

Terrine

3. Line the terrine form with moistened plastic wrap and layer with two levels of potatoes to every one level of truffles, continuing to fill the terrine form with alternating layers until all the ingredients are used up.

4. Reduce the veal stock and truffle juice to an aspic and pour over the terrine. Press lightly and set in the refrigerator to chill for several hours. To serve, slice with an electric kitchen knife and arrange on a plate. If desired, garnish with crisp-fried mushrooms.

Scorpion Fish with Tapenade and

Preparation time: 1 hour
Cooking time: 8 minutes
Marinating time: 48 hours
Difficulty: ★★

Serves four

2 scorpion fish, 2 lb / 1 kg each
1 avocado
4 rice-flour wrappers (see below)
4 cherry tomatoes
2 tbsp / 20 ml vermouth
salt, pepper to taste

For the marinade:
³/₄ cup / 200 ml olive oil
2 cloves of garlic
2 coriander corns
3 sprigs of thyme
2 sprigs of basil
1 sprig of rosemary
1 sprig of sage

For the tapenade:
generous ¹/₈ lb / 80 g olives
¹/₂ oz / 10 g capers
³/₈ cup / 80 ml olive oil
1 tsp / 5 ml balsamic vinegar
salt, pepper to taste

Chef Dieter Müller of Germany is constantly looking to stretch his culinary horizons; one way he accomplishes this is to incorporate the traditional products from different regions into new recipes. Raised in a family of gourmets, Müller is quite familiar with the countries of the Mediterranean, and he often extends his repertoire with regional specialities from the region.

Scorpion fish, or rockfish, is an integral part of the bouillabaisse, that icon of French seafood tradition, and of the Provençal fish soup. The former was originally cooked right on the beach by fishermen, who used the fish unsuitable for the market, such as the large-headed, ungainly-looking scorpion fish. For this recipe you will need a relatively large scorpion fish with firm flesh. If none is available, look for another sub-species of rockfish, since there are many. It will be marinated in olive oil before being cooked.

Dieter Müller discovered rice-flour wrappers in Asia, where they are often used to wrap a whole range of dumplings and spring rolls; baked, they will provide the forms for the avocado mousse. Although avocado has a high fat content, it blends well with all kinds of flavors and is therefore very popular; it is also extremely easy to prepare. Choose a ripe but not yet brown fruit from California, Israel, or the Antilles.

The tapenade is, of course, typical of Provence, and will create a delicate aroma, conveying the Mediterranean, to the delight of your guests.

1. Wash, clean, and fillet the scorpion fish; remove the bones and skin. Wash the fillets and leave to dry on a kitchen towel. Marinate in olive oil for 24 hours, after which the fish should be seasoned, wrapped in basil and sage leaves, and finally wrapped and then rolled up in layers of plastic wrap and then aluminum foil.

2. Leave the fillets to infuse for ten minutes in water at 155 °F / 65 °C. Remove from the saucepan and set aside to cool. For the tapenade, remove the olive pits, chop the olives very finely, and mix with the other ingredients. Place in an air-tight container and set aside for the next day.

Avocado Mousse in Rice Leaves

3. Cut the rice-flour wrappers into small squares-about 4 x 4 in / 8 x 8 cm, form into little containers by shaping them around a cork, and bake in the oven for five minutes. Mix the avocado with the vermouth, salt, and lemon juice until it becomes a light mousse. Fill the rice-flour wrappers with the avocado mousse using a pastry bag with a star-shaped nozzle.

4. Cut the scorpion fish fillets into medallions that are $3/8$ in / 1 cm thick. Place a small bouquet of salad leaves and two medallions on a plate and garnish with tapenade. Place a rice leaf filled with the avocado mousse on one side, and cherry tomato on the other. Sprinkle with olive oil.

Mediterranean Salad

Preparation time: 30 minutes
Cooking time: 8 minutes
Difficulty: ★

Serves four

12–16 jumbo shrimps
12 cockles
20 clams, winkles, or other seasonal mollusks
$^1/_2$ lb / 250 g mixed lettuce
$^1/_4$ lb / 120 g green beans
$^1/_2$ lb / 250 g button mushrooms

2 tomatoes
1 stick of celery
1 orange (see below)
1 tsp / 5 g sesame seeds (see below)

For the vinaigrette:
$^1/_4$ cup / 60 ml sweet wine vinegar
$^1/_2$ cup / 125 ml cold-pressed olive oil
1 tbsp / 15 g mustard
salt, pepper to taste

This seafood salad, typical of the seafood-based Catalan cuisine, is a marvellous summer appetizer. Featuring jumbo shrimps, which are very popular in Spain and often served as an appetizer, it also reflects the Catalan facility for salads. Coming in endless varieties, the cuisine's summery salads provide chefs with countless opportunities to stretch their creativity.

The Spanish are particularly fond of the algae-nuanced taste of extremely fresh jumbo shrimps. In fact, the shrimps are often served with their heads intact; evidence of how fresh they are, since the head is like a freshness-gauge. If the head is colored black, then do not attempt to eat the shrimp. Frozen, the shrimps come only as tails. In order to preserve their excellent flavor, the delicious crustacean should ideally be steamed or boiled in a broth of sea water.

The molluscs underscore the iodine flavor of the jumbo shrimps, and the marine aspect of the dish. You can certainly use other shellfish for this dish, such as crayfish or langoustines. Cockles, though not as popular in the United States as Europe, as generally tasty, as are other molluscs such as winkles. With all shellfish, placing them while still alive in sea water for a couple of days can help them get rid of the sand in their shells, since they will be able to move around as they normally would, only without picking up more sand.

1. Wash the lettuce. Cook the green beans al dente. Peel and chop the celery and the tomatoes. Clean the mushrooms and cut into thin strips.

2. Prepare the vinaigrette and mix with the vegetables in a salad bowl. Cut the orange peel to yield thin strips of orange zest; marinate.

# of Jumbo Shrimp

3. Clean the jumbo shrimps, discarding the intestinal vein, but do not remove the head. Steam them until their shells are bright red. Clean the cockles, clams, and other shellfish well, and soak in water.

4. Roast the sesame seeds for a few minutes, either in a dry frying pan on the stove top or in the oven, or in a toaster. In a frying pan over a high flame, heat the cockles, clams, and other shellfish with a little unpeeled garlic for two minutes. To serve, place the mixed lettuce on the plates, add the vegetables, and dress with vinaigrette. Sprinkle with the roasted sesame seeds and marinated orange zest strips. Arrange the seafood on the plate.

Salad with Roasted

Preparation time: 30 minutes
Cooking time: 30 minutes
Difficulty: ★

Serves four

4 whole quails
1/4 lb / 120 g Puy lentils
1/8 lb / 50 g young spinach leaves
1 bouquet garni
1 bunch of chives

For the lentil dressing:
2 tomatoes
1 shallot
1 tsp / 5 g Dijon mustard
1 tsp / 5 ml sherry vinegar
1 tbsp / 15 ml peanut oil
1 tbsp / 15 g chopped chives
salt, fresh-ground pepper to taste
coarse sea salt

Here, we present a salad created by Chef Pierre Orsi that is based on roasted quail. This low-fat bird has come to play a different role in cuisine than in the past, when it was hunted from April through October and considered almost an everyday ingredient in cooking. Today, there are far fewer wild populations, but the number of quail being farm-raised has increased.

Quail meat is often fried on a skewer, but there are many other preparation methods. The firm, light-colored flesh is ideal for smoking, and the different kinds of wood used for smoking impart an array of strong and unusual flavors to the meat. Or, if you prefer, you can substitute the smoking process with a little

extra frying time, which will impart the birds with a similarly deepened flavor.

For this recipe we use the most famous green lentils of all, the Puy lentil from Le Puy in central France, which grows in volcanic soil and is a source of much French culinary pride. Puys should never be overcooked, just blanched and cooked very slowly so they retain their crisp consistency. Season sparingly with a mild mustard. The young spinach leaves called for in this recipe are washed and dried thoroughly; their fresh character combines well with the quail.

1. Chop the shallot and chives. Blanch the lentils and gently cook with the bouquet garni for 30 minutes; set aside to drain. Season with oil, sherry vinegar, chopped shallot, salt, and freshly ground pepper. Blanch, peel, and then chop the tomatoes. At the last moment, add a teaspoonful of Dijon mustard to the lentils and chopped chives along with the chopped tomatoes.

2. Flambé the quail, halve, and remove the bones. Fry gently for 30 minutes in a casserole, skin side down. Towards the end of the cooking time, season the quail on all sides; fry on a higher flame on both sides until the skin turns a golden brown.

Quail and Puy Lentils

3. Wash the spinach well and select the best, most intact leaves. Slice the quail fillets and mix with the meat from the legs.

4. To serve, warm four plates. Arrange a semi-circle of spinach leaves in a petal pattern on each plate, and mound the lentils over the spinach stems. Surround with quail pieces and slices. Sprinkle with freshly ground pepper and a few grains of coarse sea salt, and garnish with remaining chopped chives.

Cream of Chicken Soup with

Preparation time: 30 minutes
Cooking time: 1 hour, 30 minutes
Difficulty: ★★

Serves four

For the cream of chicken soup:
1 chicken, about 3 lb / 1½ kg
1 gallon / 2 l water
3 carrots
1 bunch of celeriac greens
1 onion
4 cloves

1 clove of garlic
1 bouquet garni
2 tbsp / 30 g flour
2 tbsp / 30 g butter
1 cup / 250 ml whipping cream
salt, pepper to taste

For the whisked egg whites:
8 egg whites
1 bunch of watercress
salt to taste

In France, whisked egg-whites are normally served with custard as a pudding. In days gone by they were prepared with biscuits or dry brioche dipped in liqueur and accompanied by fresh berries. Our chef, Georges Paineau, has created instead a soup with whisked egg whites that are salted. This is, perhaps, an unusual concept, but nonetheless it works very successfully in combination with cream of chicken soup.

Start by preparing a nice large and meaty chicken that forms the main component of the broth's taste, underscored by the other ingredients added in careful doses. The roux for the soup should not contain too much flour, as the soup will then become too thick. If by accident you add too much, however, just compensate by adding a bit more cream or chicken stock.

The egg whites must be whisked briskly to make them stiff enough; salt is added to make the firm froth more durable. The watercress – a green that is rich in both iodine and vitamin C – adds a lovely pastel green color and a tangy note to the egg whites. Almost all of the watercress available in Europe is produced in France and the United Kingdom, particularly in Scotland. In the United States, it is available year round. Choose small-leafed watercress, which is much more flavorful. Wild watercress would be ideal since it has an intensely sharp taste, but it is difficult to find. In any event, the cress must be folded into the whisked egg whites very carefully to prevent them from losing their firmness and collapsing. A last tip: poach the whisked egg whites in water at a maximum of 175 °F / 80 °C, to prevent the egg white from spoiling.

1. Peel the onion and garlic. Gut and prepare the chicken; put into a saucepan filled with cold water, add carrots, the celeriac greens, onion, cloves, garlic, and bouquet garni and bring to a boil. Cook for one hour, then remove the chicken from the cooking liquid and cut the meat into fine strips; set aside.

2. Make a roux with 2 tbsp / 30 g each of butter and flour, and pour the chicken stock into it. Cook for 20 minutes. Stir in the cream and continue to cook for ten more minutes. Strain and set aside to cool.

Watercress and Whisked Egg White

3. Strip the watercress stalks of the leaves, wash the leaves, and drain well. Beat the egg whites until very stiff, adding a little salt during whisking. Carefully fold in the watercress leaves.

4. Scoop out portions of the whisked egg white and poach for one and half minutes on each side in water no hotter than 175 °F / 80 °C. Drain. To serve, arrange the strips of chicken meat on four plates, adjust the seasoning of the soup, and pour over the meat. Add two or three scoops of whisked egg white to each plate.

Salad of Duck Fille

Preparation time: 1 hour
Cooking time: 10 minutes
Difficulty: ★

Serves four

2 breasts of duck
1 orange
half a bunch of watercress
2 tbsp / 30 g butter
1 tsp / 5 g coriander seeds
salt, pepper to taste

For the pear salad with pine nuts:
2 ripe green pears
scant $^{1}/_{2}$ cup / 100 g pine nuts
1 tbsp / 15 ml sherry vinegar
3 tbsp / 45 ml peanut oil

For the julienne:
1 carrot
1 celery stick

The Chinese are credited with raising ducks, and the bird was already a popular meat in antiquity: the Romans particularly enjoyed duck brain and breast. In feudal times duck was traditionally served for Christmas. In the late nineteenth century, four ducks on a ship from Peking to Long Island gave the latter region its own indigenous species. Today there are many subspecies, all of which can be traced back to either the mallard or the muscovy, and the popularity of duck is widespread.

The breast is the choicest part: the breast of ducks raised for making foie gras is particularly full and meaty. The French used to cook the duck breast for hours and then preserve it; contemporary recipes may even call for the duck breast to be smoked. For this dish, the breast is fried skin side down first, so the meat can draw all the fat, and then only briefly fried on the other side. The meat is then set aside to sit before it is sliced, a step that keeps the meat tender.

As they are just the slightest bit acidic, green pears are an ideal accompaniment for substantial and hearty dishes such as this one. Make sure to sprinkle the chopped pears immediately with lemon juice to prevent their turning brown. This lovely fruit salad with pine nuts is dressed with sherry vinegar, whose subtle aroma – not unlike that of Madeira – underlines the pear's flavor. Depending on the season, you may garnish this dish with watercress, coriander, blueberries, or pomegranate seeds.

1. Peel and finely chop the pears; mix with the pine nuts. Prepare a vinaigrette with sherry vinegar and peanut oil; dress the pears with three-fourths of the vinaigrette.

2. Fry the duck breasts in butter – skin side down first and then the other side briefly – but only until rare; leave to rest for a short while and then slice against the direction of the grain.

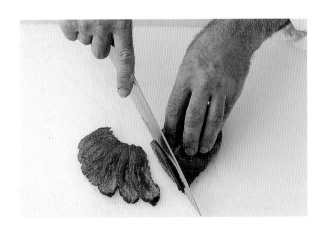

with Pears and Sherry

3. Prepare a julienne of carrots and celery and then blanch the vegetables. Prepare a little zest of orange the same way.

4. Moisten the meat with the remaining vinaigrette. To serve, place the pear salad in the center of the plate and sprinkle with some of the julienne of carrots and celery. Lay the duck slices around the mound of pears. Garnish with the blanched julienne of the zest of orange, and place a few watercress leaves with coriander seeds in-between the meat slices.

Crayfish and Snowpeas

Preparation time: 1 hour
Cooking time: 1 hour 15 minutes
Difficulty: ★★

Serves four

16 crayfish
3¹/₂ oz / 100 g Périgord truffles
2 lb / 1 kg snowpeas

For the crayfish stock:
crayfish claws and shells
half a bunch each of fennel, leeks
¹/₄ bulb of celeriac (to yield scant
  ¹/₂ cup / 100 g chopped)
2 shallots
¹/₂ clove of garlic
1 tbsp / 15 g tomato paste

1 sprig each of tarragon, thyme
1 tsp / 5 g sugar
³/₄ cup / 200 ml white wine
¹/₈ lb / 50 g butter
salt, pepper to taste

For the broth:
¹/₂ cup / 100 ml vinegar
generous cup / 300 ml dry white wine
7 pints / 3 l of water
1 bunch of dill
half a bay leaf
10 crushed peppercorns
1 leek, 1 onion
¹/₄ celeriac bulb
1 tsp / 5 g sugar

For the vinaigrette:
¹/₂ cup / 100 ml each truffle juice, light veal
  stock
1 tbsp / 15 ml each fruit vinegar, balsamic
  vinegar, olive oil
1 tbsp / 15 ml grapeseed oil

Crayfish have been very popular since the Middle Ages. During the nineteenth century they became so fashionable that they were consumed in vast quantities; after the Belle Epoque, however, they became rare and expensive. The wild crayfish has all but disappeared from most areas now, the most famous being a crayfish with red legs that was caught in summer and fall. Ideally, choose live crayfish. For this recipe you need crayfish that weigh at least two ounces (sixty five grams) and no more than a scant quarter-pound (one hundred and fifteen grams). As usual you must remove the intestines before preparation. Cook the crayfish at the last minute so they do not have a chance to dry out.

Snowpeas, known as "mange-touts" in France because one can eat the whole snowpea, are ripe in May and June. Originally the snowpea was imported to France from Italy in the seventeenth century. There are countless varieties of the vegetable – for example, there is one with light-colored pods and one with violet flowers, and there is also a kind that does not contain threads and is thus referred to as the "gourmet pea." Choose thick, bright-green pods without blemishes, and, for this recipe, remove the threads that run along their top line.

Made even more elegant by Chef Horst Petermann's including Périgord (black) truffles, this is an ideal summer appetizer, ideally suited to complement meat dishes such as veal.

1. For the crayfish stock: sweat the chopped vegetables in a little butter for two to three minutes, then add the crayfish claws and crushed shells, all the spices and the tomato paste. Cook this mixture for another two or three minutes before adding the white wine, then covering with water. Simmer for 30–40 minutes, and add salt and pepper to taste. Strain and then reduce to 4 tbsp / 60 ml of crayfish stock.

2. Wash the snowpeas, remove the threads, and cook very briefly in salted water. Set aside on a kitchen towel to air-dry and cool. Bring the broth to a boil with all ingredients, and leave to infuse for one hour. Cook the crayfish for two minutes in the broth, then discard the heads and shells.

with a Truffle Vinaigrette

3. With a long-bladed knife, chop the truffles as finely as possible. To prepare the vinaigrette, pour the veal stock into a casserole, add half of the chopped truffles, reduce by half, and set aside to cool. Add the other half of the chopped truffles and remaining ingredients, and mix well. Bring to a boil once more and simmer for one hour. Add the crayfish, cook for two or three minutes, and leave to cool.

4. To serve, arrange the snowpeas in a star shape on each plate, sprinkling with a little vinaigrette. Place the crayfish in the center of the star and sprinkle with the remaining truffle vinaigrette. Pour the crayfish stock in a ring around the outside of the snowpea star.

Preparation time: 45 minutes
Cooking time: 15 minutes
Difficulty: ★

Serves four

8 crayfish
$^1/_2$ lb / 240 g fillet of salmon (lake) trout
generous $^1/_2$ lb / 260 g tomatoes
1 cucumber
$^1/_2$ red pepper
1 onion
1 clove of garlic
2 tbs / 30 g bread crumbs

2 tbsp / 30 ml olive oil
1 tbsp / 15 ml vinegar
1 drop of Tabasco
salt, pepper to taste

To garnish:
$^1/_2$ green pepper
$^1/_2$ red pepper
$^1/_2$ yellow pepper
3 tomatoes
4 sprigs salicornia (see below)
4 sprigs flat-leafed parsley
half a bunch of chives

Although he is Swiss, our chef, Roland Pierroz, was inspired by Andalusian tradition when he devised this recipe. The dish's originality lies in the combination of crayfish and lake trout (*salmo trutta lacustris*), a large trout whose diet of shellfish turns its flesh pink and thus becomes known as a salmon trout.

But there is, actually, a link to Roland Pierroz's homeland: the lake or salmon trout is very common to Switzerland's Alpine lakes, where, thriving in the high altitude's cold waters, it grows quite large. If cooked over low heat for only a short time the pink and tender flesh tastes delicious, and retains its color.

Unfortunately, crayfish are rarely caught in the wild, having all but disappeared from rivers; the crayfish sold today are usually farm-raised.

For the gazpacho, Roland Pierroz recommends using shapely, round peppers of different colors with smooth and shiny skins. Salicornia, a type of edible, coastal plant called a samphire, is also sometimes called glasswort or sea bean; its spiky green leaves bear the hint of the sea in their salty taste, particularly when salicornia is at its peak season in the summer. The gazpacho should be served chilled but should not be frozen, otherwise the careful blending of ingredients will be lost when the mixture disintegrates back into its individual components.

1. Peel the tomatoes, retaining three for decoration. Halve the remaining tomatoes, hollow them out, and chop up the pulp. Wash the red pepper, remove the seeds and the pith. Peel the onion and cucumber, seed the cucumber; chop both.

2. In a blender or food processor puree all the vegetables. Add the bread crumbs and olive oil and blend once more. Stir in the vinegar, salt, pepper, garlic and a dash of Tabasco. Strain and chill.

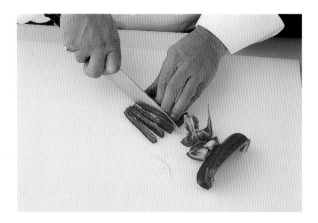

with Crayfish

3. In a stainless steel saucepan, bring salted water to a boil. Cook the crayfish in the water for one minute, remove them from the saucepan, shell them, and then place the meat in a little cooking liquid; set aside. Steam the trout fillets for three minutes: they should remain slightly pink inside. Wash the green and yellow peppers, remove the stalks, seeds and pith.

4. Chop the peppers and the three retained tomatoes into separate piles. Wash the salicornia, drain, and keep cool. To serve, pour the gazpacho into a deep plate and add one piece of trout fillet and two crayfish tails. Decorate with crayfish shells and a sprig of parsley and sprinkle with the chopped peppers, tomatoes, and chives.

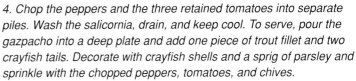

Preparation time: 1 hour
Cooking time: 10 minutes
Difficulty: ★★

Serves four

16 small squid (measuring 3–4 in/8–10 cm)
8 langoustines
2 tomatoes
1 red pepper
1 eggplant
8 baby zucchini
1 onion

$^1/_2$ cup / 125 ml olive oil
1 bunch of chives

For the vinaigrette:
1 lemon
$^3/_4$ cup / 200 ml olive oil
$^1/_2$ cup / 125 ml walnut oil
2 tsp / 10 ml soy sauce
1 bunch of chives
1 sprig of basil
salt, fresh-ground pepper to taste

Ratatouille, of which this appetizer is a variation, is a Provençal dish. Essentially, it comprises a vegetable ragout that is cooked very slowly in olive oil and seasoned with Provençal herbs. There are as many recipes for ratatouille in Provence as there are chefs, and the ingredients vary significantly from recipe to recipe.

There is one thing, however, common to all versions of ratatouille: the ingredients are always fried separately before they are mixed together to be slowly cooked into an even, smooth vegetable mixture. Soft-fleshed zucchini are the exception: they must be blanched in boiling water and then immediately rinsed with cold water. Our chefs, the Pourcel brothers, prepare their ratatouille following these traditional steps and then add their signature, which is a cluster of delicious langoustines.

In this appetizer, the squid is actually filled with the ratatouille; in Sète, southern France, the squid are usually filled with cured sausage. The former is an ideal preparation method, as filling the squid with ratatouille will ensure that the squid does not become too dry and, furthermore, it provides a nice accompaniment for the langoustines.

Related to the octopus and differing mainly in size, squid is available in many types. For this recipe, we use sepiola, caught in large numbers in the Mediterranean, though if none are available, choose any smallish variety that seems fresh (with unclouded eyes, and an ocean smell). The squid is fried for only a short period of time, and the filling, as well, is not cooked for too long, as that would rob it of its intense flavor.

1. Peel all the vegetables and chop finely, discarding the core of the zucchini. Fry all the vegetables but the zucchini in separate batches in a non-stick frying pan. Shell the langoustines, discard the intestines, then chop finely. Mix all the vegetables together for the ratatouille. Prepare the vinaigrette.

2. Gut the squid, wash thoroughly under running water, and set aside. Blanch the heads and then chop them finely before adding them to the ratatouille.

Squid

3. Use a pastry bag to fill the squid with the ratatouille; close using a wooden toothpick. Heat gently in olive oil for ten minutes or until brown; season and bake in a hot oven to brown if necessary. Slice the zucchini into long, thin slices (use a slicer or the slicing side of a food grater for the best results), cook in salted water and then immediately rinse with cold water.

4. Sauté the zucchini in butter, season, and set aside. Retain the liquid released by the squid during cooking and stir into the vinaigrette. To serve, place the zucchini in the middle of the plate and surround with three stuffed squid. Sprinkle with the vinaigrette and garnish with chives.

Preparation time: 1 hour
Cooking time: 45 minutes
Difficulty: ✶

Serves four

1 lb / 500 g fillet of beef
half a bunch of celery
1 clove of garlic
2 tbsp / 30 ml cold-pressed olive oil
1 tbsp / 15 ml light olive oil
$^{1}/_{2}$ tsp / 3 g salt
1 tsp / 5 g crushed peppercorns

For the garnish:
$^{1}/_{4}$ lb / 100 g arugula
$^{1}/_{4}$ lb / 100 g parmesan

For the vinaigrette:
$^{1}/_{4}$ cup / 50 ml cold-pressed olive oil
$^{1}/_{4}$ cup / 50 ml white truffle oil
$^{1}/_{4}$ cup / 50 ml balsamic vinegar
$^{1}/_{4}$ cup / 50 ml beef gravy
salt, black pepper to taste

For this dish our chef, Paul Rankin, recommends Scottish beef: Angus beef from Aberdeen, to be more precise. Angus cattle spend their days grazing on healthy fields and the selection process is very strict indeed, so the meat's excellent quality is assured. Feel free to use other top-quality beef if Angus is not available: there are a number of breeds in the United States, particularly recently, that are raised free-range, and prime cuts (the highest quality of meat), once the province of only select butchers, are now available in many different markets.

This recipe is based on the tenderloin or short loin cut, a fillet of beef muscle that runs alongside the backbone. Fry the fillet for a minute on each side over very high heat to cook it rare, which, according to British tradition, means very brown and crisp on the outside, and quite tender and pink on the inside. This can be achieved by heating a frying pan (preferably grid-

dled) over an extremely high heat and, when it is really hot, frying the meat and seasoning it while frying.

Chef Rankin's recipe was inspired by the Italian *carpaccio*, and contains a range of transalpine products, such as white truffle oil from the Piedmont region, balsamic vinegar from Modena, and Parmesan from the Reggiano region. All these ingredients should be of the highest quality and be dispensed exactly in the quantities indicated.

Instead of fillet of beef, you can also use other cuts, such as rumpsteak or short loin; whichever cut of beef you decide to use, do not trim the fat off before frying as it will help the meat retain its flavor and juices during the cooking process. If you want to try further modifications, try using venison or, more simply, grilled chicken for a different culinary slant.

1. Wash the fillet and halve lengthwise, seasoning with crushed peppercorns and oil. Fry in a very hot frying pan for one minute each side until dark brown on the outside but still rare on the inside. Set aside to cool at room temperature until tepid.

2. Peel the celery and cut into medium-sized chunks; add to salted water. Bring to a boil with a whole, unpeeled clove of garlic and leave to simmer until the celery is cooked. Remove from the heat, add olive oil and black pepper, and leave to infuse for at least one hour.

Celery and Truffle Oil

3. Shortly before serving, cut the fillet into slices around a ¼ in / ½ cm thick. Carefully whisk the ingredients of the vinaigrette in a bowl. Wash the arugula and discard any yellowing or decaying leaves. Shave the Parmesan to yield about 2–3 tbsp / 30 g.

4. To serve, arrange the salad in layers on four plates: the beef fillet first, and then the celery, arugula, and Parmesan, until all ingredients have been used up. Generously pour the vinaigrette over the salad and serve immediately.

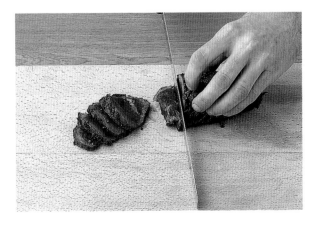

Preparation time: 1 hour
Cooking time: 20 minutes
Cooling time: 2 hours
Marinating time: 6 hours
Difficulty: ★★

Serves four

2 saddles of rabbit, a scant
  ³/₄ lb / 350 g each
¹/₂ lb / 250 g crushed rabbit bones
4 small artichokes
2 shallots

¹/₄ lb / 100 g mixed lettuce, such as mesclun
white of 2 eggs
2 sheets of gelatin
2 cups / 500 ml white wine (Chinon blanc)
³/₄ cup / 200 ml vinaigrette
1 bunch of rosemary
1 bunch of chervil leaves
salt, pepper to taste

During the Middle Ages, wild rabbit was hunted in France whenever game was rare; today it has taken on a slightly higher status. Breeders now offer a variety of domesticated species. It is best to choose young rabbits that have been raised on a farm, since the animal will carry a seal of quality. Preparation should not begin until at least forty-eight hours have passed since the animal was slaughtered, as meat well hung will be much more tender.

The saddle, a particularly good piece of rabbit meat, is located directly above the leg. This round section should be loosely tied with string before being marinated for about six hours. Towards the end of the cooking time the vegetables are added to the rabbit and cooked for another two minutes; the broth is then clarified with whisked egg whites and finally strained. The liquid is left to cool and set, which results in a lovely, clear aspic.

Of the other ingredients, all are essential. The artichoke hearts will provide an intriguing contrast to the meat and aspic. Before slicing their bases, they should be thoroughly chilled. The rosemary is an indispensable partner for rabbit and most other meat dishes. Mesclun, often comprised of young lettuces once found in wild meadows, strikes an interesting note in a dish of a meat once hunted in the same such meadows. And finally, the white wine (our chef is a Chinon blanc aficionado) lends a perfect balance to the rabbit and the aspic.

1. Chop the shallot and divide the rosemary into sprigs. Wash the rabbit saddle, tie with string, and place in a casserole or large saucepan, along with the crushed bones, 4 sprigs of rosemary, and the chopped shallot. Cover with white wine, sprinkle with salt, and simmer for 20 minutes. Remove from the heat.

2. Soak the gelatin in cold water, add to the rabbit cooking liquid (from which the rabbit and bones have been removed and set aside), and then strain the liquid through a muslin cloth. Strip and clean the artichokes; slice and cook the artichoke hearts, and leave to cool.

White Wine Aspic

3. Untie the rabbit meat, pour the aspic over the meat and chill. Season the artichoke hearts and the mixed lettuce separately with vinaigrette.

4. Cut the jellied meat into medallions. To serve, place a mound of sliced artichoke heart in the center of the plate on a broad bed of mesclun and surround with an arrangement of rabbit medallions. Garnish with chervil leaves and sprinkle with diced aspic.

Salad of Lobster and

Preparation time:	30 minutes
Cooking time:	10 minutes
Difficulty:	★★

Serves four

1 dozen scallops
2 lobsters, generous ³/₄ lb / 400 g each
1 cup / 200 g mixed lettuce

For the lobster broth:
1 onion
1 carrot
1 stalk of leek stalk
1 stick of celery
1 sprig of thyme
1 bay leaf

1 lemon
salt, pepper to taste

For the leek vinaigrette with truffles:
1 small leek
2 shallots
¹/₂ oz / 10 g truffles
1–2 tbsp / 20 ml truffle juice
2¹/₂ tbsp / 40 ml sherry vinegar
¹/₃ cup / 80 ml peanut oil
salt, pepper to taste

To garnish:
half a bunch of parsley
half a bunch of chervil
half a bunch of chives

The combination of lobster and scallops is a classic, and it is served as part of the most elegant meals. As our chef, Michel Rochedy, will attest, only the freshest seafood of the highest quality, professionally prepared, will do.

Whether it comes from Canada or Brittany, lobster (after being plunged head-first into already boiling cooking liquid) must never be left in the cooking pot for too long, as it takes only eight minutes to destroy the wonderful flavor that helps to justify its high market value. Apart from lemon juice or perhaps a dash of white wine, you might consider adding a little seaweed to the cooking liquid to emphasize the iodine flavor of the lobster. For a slightly different-flavored variation, the lobster can be substituted with langoustines.

Although termed a cold appetizer, this salad should actually be served warm. Its flavor is further refined with chopped truffles and truffle juice. In order to facilitate serving, Chef Rochedy recommends you brush the lobster and scallops with oil and put them under the grill for just a minute or so. He also suggests that you gently heat the vinaigrette.

If you want to add another component to complete the composition, the salad could be served with a few thin slices of perch or sturgeon.

1. Prepare the lobster broth. Bring to a boil and cook the lobster for five minutes, then take the lobster out of the broth and shell. Shuck the scallops and clean them thoroughly.

2. Cut the scallops into slices and arrange these in a rosette shape on a non-stick tray or a circular form. Place half a lobster in the middle of each rosette. Select the best leaves from the mixed lettuce and wash them thoroughly; let them air-dry.

Scallops with Truffles

3. For the vinaigrette, finely chop the shallots, place in a hot frying pan, pour sherry vinegar over and reduce the liquid. Chop the truffles, reserving about a dozen slices for garnish. Add peanut oil, truffle juice, and half a tablespoon of chopped truffles. Chop the leek finely. Warm the vinaigrette and season to taste with salt and pepper. Add the leek.

4. Toss the lettuce with the vinaigrette in a roomy bowl. Preheat the over to 395 °F / 200 °C and heat the lobster-scallop rosettes for two minutes. To serve, heap a little salad in the middle of each plate, and careully set the rosette on top. Sprinkle with the truffle-laced vinaigrette. Decorate with chopped chives, chervil leaves, and truffle slices.

Steamed King Prawns with

Preparation time: 2 hours, 30 minutes
Cooking time: 40 minutes
Difficulty: ✱

Serves four

16 king (or large) prawns
1 pig's trotter
3 bunches of green asparagus
1 bunch of baby carrots
1 shallot

1 onion
1 bunch of parsley
$^1/_8$ lb / 50 g butter
1 quart / 1 l veal stock
2 cups / 500 ml port
1 cup / 250 ml olive oil
salt, pepper to taste

To garnish:
1 lb / 450 g small onions
1 bunch of arugula

Tangy and spicy arugula has been popular since the Romans; its flavor has been described as reminiscent both of dried fruit and wild radish leaves. Called rocket in Europe – *rocchetta* in Italian and *roquette* in French – it belongs to the mustard family, and came to the Mediterranean from southern and central Europe. Its pungent intensity combines well with the strong flavor of the giant prawns, who are able to "tame" the arugula's sharp flavor enough to balance it.

The prawns most Europeans know come from the Mediterranean: deep pink in color, they have flesh that tastes different from that of shrimps and are smaller than langoustines. Their fleshy tail is very firm and quite flavorful, and shelling them can be a bit tricky. The crusteacean can be prepared in many different ways: cooked briefly in boiling water, grilled, steamed, or in true Catalan fashion, fried with garlic and parsley.

Small green asparagus (you need thirty-two spears for this dish) is the perfect partner for king prawns. Wild asparagus, which is sometimes still found in the forests, would be ideal. The woody stalks should be trimmed off and the tips cooked very briefly so they remain crisp. Unfortunately, in Europe, small green asparagus is usually available for only about four weeks a year, beginning in mid-June, and mostly in southern regions. Hothouse asparagus, however, is available year round, and, due to regional farming, the growing season in the United States has been extended from February into the summertime. But, if for some reason you cannot get your hands on green asparagus, young leeks could be an interesting alternative.

1. Cook the pig's trotter with a carrot and an onion for two hours. Take out the trotter and add a sliced carrot and parsley to the water, bring to a boil and cook the prawns for three to four minutes in that liquid. Trim the meat off of the trotter bone and chop into small dice. Melt the small onions for about 30 minutes in olive oil over low heat.

2. Cook the remaining carrots al dente. Peel and trim the asparagus, cook in boiling water, and immediately rinse in cold water. Melt a little butter in a frying pan, add olive oil, and gently fry the asparagus and carrots.

Pig's Trotter and Asparagus

3. Shell the prawns and remove their intestinal veins. Chop the shallot. Fry the shallot with port in a frying pan and reduce, then add the veal stock and the diced meat.

4. Reduce once more, remove the meat from the heat and fold in the remaining butter. To serve, arrange the meat and stock decoratively on the plates. Dress the arugula, place in the center of the plates, and arrange the prawns around it. Garnish with baby carrots and melted onions.

Tomato-eggplant Terrine

Preparation time: 10 minutes
Chilling time: 2 hours
Cooking time: 4 minutes
Difficulty: ☆

Serves four

3 small eggplants
1¹/₄ lbs / 600 g tomatoes
1 cup / 100 ml extra virgin olive oil
³/₄ cup / 200 g vegetable aspic
1 bunch of flowering basil
salt, pepper to taste

This cold appetizer from chef Nadia Santini, with its fresh ingredients such as tomatoes, eggplant, and basil, will be particularly welcome in summer. Ripe and tasty tomatoes are crucial for its success. Choose tomatoes that are deep red. Once scorned superstitiously as a poisonous fruit, it was then adopted in earnest by the French, who call them "love apples," as do the Italians, who gave them the name *pomodoro*. To maintain the integrity of the tomato's delicate pulp, it should not be blanched. Instead, though it is, alas, a little harder to peel raw tomatoes with a knife, it is worth it, since this way consistency and intense flavor will not be impaired at all.

The eggplants should be long rather than round, as they will be used in long strips to line the terrine. Long eggplants also contain fewer seeds and are easier to cut into even strips that will not split or break during baking. When lining the terrine with the eggplant, the strips should not only overlap beyond the edge of the terrine, but they should also overlap each other for increased stability.

Basil blossoms and the extra virgin oil lend this dish a refined touch. Extra virgin olive oil, still produced using traditional methods, neutralizes the tomatoes' natural acidity and slightly emulsifies the terrine. Olive oil is an indispensable ingredient in Italian cooking, and comes in many grades; the extra-virgin kind is called "green gold" by the Italians.

1. Peel the eggplants and slice lengthwise. Heat half of the olive oil in a non-stick frying pan and fry the eggplant strips in batches (since they won't all fit in the pan). Season and leave to dry on a kitchen cloth.

2. Line a terrine form with the eggplant strips; they must overlap each other as well as lay over the edge of the terrine. Peel the tomatoes with a sharp knife, discard the juice and seeds. Bring water to a boil in a casserole and dissolve the vegetable aspic in it.

with Basil Blossoms

3. Fill the terrine form with the tomatoes. Add the aspic and close the terrine with the overlapping eggplant. Separate the edges of the terrine slightly with a spoon so the jelly is distributed evenly throughout. Chill for two hours.

4. Remove the terrine from the refrigerator. Invert and cut into $^1/_2$ in / 1 cm slices. To serve, place a slice in the middle of each plate, surround with a light pool of olive oil and garnish with basil flowers.

Preparation time: 20 minutes
Cooking time: 25 minutes
Difficulty: ★

Serves four

4 crabs, 1¼ lb / 600 g each
2 eggs
2 gherkin pickles
2 tsp / 10 ml whiskey
1 tsp / 10 g custard
1 bunch of flat-leafed parsley
1 pimento
salt to taste

For the crab broth:
1 onion stuck with cloves
¼ cup / 50 ml white wine
1 bunch of parsley
1 tsp / 5 g peppercorns
salt to taste

Fishing forms an integral part of Portuguese life, as Portugal's coastline is some 340 miles / 547 kilometers long with waters that yield prime quality fish and seafood in abundance. It is therefore not surprising that a large part of Portuguese cuisine is dedicated to seafood, and that the Portuguese know many methods for preparing the myriad crab varieties that populate Portugal's coast.

Like all crab species, the common crab is essentially a ten-legged shellfish with an underdeveloped tail. It is characterized by the lovely color of its meat when fried, by the oval shape of its shell, and by the enormous front claws, the meat of which is a particular delicacy. In reality the crab leads a very dull life, just sitting on the ocean floor and waiting for its prey, hardly bothering to move at all. When the prey is close enough, the crab throws itself upon the unsuspecting creature, having, usu-

ally, a distinct advantage on account of its weight and the large claws. The largest crabs, at home in French and British coastal waters, can be as heavy as twelve pounds / six kilograms. This recipe, from Chef Maria Santos Gomes, calls for much smaller fare.

Our chef is particularly partial to the rich, creamy area directly beneath the lower shell, and to the coral-rich ovaries in a female crab, which are used to form the basis of many sauces because of their subtle flavor. The crab meat is complemented by the tart pickle, which the British have been producing since the seventeenth century. You can make pickle yourself and store it for up to three months, or look for high-quality examples at your market. The mélange of flavors in this appetizer is rounded out with a dash of whisky.

1. Cook the crab for around 25 minutes in salted water along with the peppercorns, parsley, the onion stuck with cloves, and the white wine. Leave to cool in the cooking liquid. Afterwards, remove the legs and shell. Retain the front claws for decoration.

2. Extract the crab meat and the coral, chop, and mix with the creamy substance from the crab belly.

Stuffed Crab

3. Hard-boil the eggs. Add the pickles, whiskey, custard, pimento, and half a chopped hard-boiled egg. Adjust seasoning to taste.

4. Mix everything carefully. Fill the crab shells with this mixture and garnish with the remaining chopped hard-boiled egg and a center strip of parsley. Arrange on the plates with the front claws on either side.

Shrimp Dolmas with a

Preparation time: 15 minutes
Cooking time: 15 minutes
Difficulty: ★★

Serves four

24 vine leaves
$1/2$ / 100 g cup short-grain rice
20 shrimp
8 crayfish (optional)
2 egg yolks
1 tbsp / 15 g butter
$1/4$ cup / 50 ml cream

2 cups / 500 ml fish broth
$1/4$ cup / 50 ml ouzo
$1/2$ cup / 100 ml white wine
$1/2$ cup / 100 ml vegetable oil
half a bunch of dill
juice of 1 lemon
salt, pepper to taste

For the filling:
2 carrots (to yield $1/4$ cup/ 50 g)
2 zucchini (to yield $1/4$ cup / 50 g)
2 leeks (to yield $1/4$ cup / 50 g)
1 onion (to yield $1/4$ cup / 50 g chopped)

Vine leaves are a traditional ingredient of Greek cuisine. But they are so easy to prepare that they have become popular all over Europe. A vine leaf filling based on rice can be varied almost infinitely if a few basic rules are observed. If fresh, the vine leaves should first be blanched in boiling salt water to make them flexible. If no fresh vine leaves are available, choose some that have been marinated in salt brine: these will have to be thoroughly soaked in water before they can be used. Cover the dolmas with a plate during cooking to prevent them splitting, an action caused by the expansion of the rice grains inside. Use light colored short-grain rice, as it will cook quickly.

The individual ingredients of the filling should be cooked separately, as all require different cooking times; for example, if you cooked the shrimps with the rice they would wind up overcooked, the meat tough. Therefore the filling should only be mixed at the end, immediately after the shrimps have cooked just long enough to become soft. There is a tried and true trick for rolling the dolmas: fold the edges of the vine leaf inwards, holding the filling down with your fingers while rolling up the leaf lengthwise, as if you were hand-rolling a cigarette.

The aniseed flavor of Greece's national drink, ouzo, underscores the shrimps' aroma and rounds off the balance of flavors in this appetizer. And, if you have a surplus of crayfish, use two of them on each plate as a garnish, as pictured here.

1. Blanch the vine leaves in salted water. Sweat the chopped vegetables for the filling in butter. Add the rice and (chopped) dill, mix gently, and add salt to taste. Pour over the fish broth, bring to a boil, and leave to simmer. Dice eight shrimps, briefly fry in butter, add the white wine, mix with the rice and finally stir in half of the ouzo.

2. To make the dolmas, drop a tablespoon of filling onto each vine leaf and roll up the leaf. Line the base of a casserole with vine leaves, place the dolmas in the casserole, and cover with vine leaves.

Butter, Lemon and Ouzo Sauce

3. Add a little broth, oil and the remaining ouzo. Cover with a plate (to prevent the vine leaves from splitting) and cook for about ten minutes.

4. To prepare the sauce, reduce the fish broth, add cream and lemon juice, and reduce further. Remove from the heat, add the egg yolks and fold in the butter. Strain, add chopped dill and a dash of ouzo, and adjust seasoning to taste. Pour the sauce on the plates, arrange the dolmas, and garnish with julienned zucchini, sprigs of dill, and, if you prefer, two cooked crayfish per plate.

Herb Fritters with

Preparation time: *1 hour*
Cooking time: *15 minutes*
Cooling time: *12 hours*
Difficulty: ★

Serves four
scant ¼ cup / 100 g nettles
scant ¼ cup / 100 g sugar
scant ¼ cup / 100 g dextrose (see below)
2 cups / 500 ml water
juice of one lemon

For the batter:
1 cup / 250 g cornstarch
scant 1 cup / 200 ml water

1 egg (separated into yolk and white)

For the herbs and flowers:
8 baby carrots
4 sprigs of fennel
8 sprigs of carrot greens
1 dozen violets
4 tulips
4 sprigs of thyme
4 sprigs of red sage
4 sprigs of green sage
4 sprigs of lovage
4 sprigs of lemon balm
4 sprigs of flat-leafed parsley
½ cup / 125 ml sunflower oil

Our Belgian chef, Roger Souvereyns, would like to use this recipe to introduce the reader to the use of some unexpected plants. Most of these grow in ordinary gardens, but are generally (and mistakenly) regarded as inedible, though their therapeutic value is undisputed. Do take care in the selection of individual plants, though, and make sure you find out where they are from; some plants, particularly flowers, may have been treated with artificial colors and preservatives so they look more appealing to the uneducated buyer. Taste everything before preparing it, to make sure it does not have any undesired aftertaste – an indication of artificial additives.

There are many herbs suitable for making fritters, from the usual ones, such as basil and parsley, to the more unusual ones,

such as lemon balm and lovage – an herb originally from Persia that has blood-cleansing properties.

Wear gloves when you collect the nettles, then cook and drain them. The nettle is, incidentally, often used in European sauces and soups, and has many healing properties. Even the burning nettle sap, though it seriously irritates our skin at the slightest contact, is known to act as a circulation booster. If you are not partial to nettles, or if none are available, you can use tarragon or sage instead, using the same preparation methods.

1. Mix the water, sugar, dextrose, nettles, and lemon juice. Bring to a boil and take off the heat; set aside to cool and infuse for 12 hours. Strain and freeze. Once set, use a fork to loosen the mixture until crumbly, and then form into scoops with a spoon.

2. Separate the egg into yolk and white. Mix the egg yolk with the cornstarch, add water, and mix well. Whisk the egg white until stiff and carefully fold in with a spatula.

Nettle Dumplings

3. Wash and drain the herbs well. Heat the sunflower oil in a saucepan over medium heat. When it is hot, dip the herbs in the batter and deep-fry until slightly brown. Remove from the oil and leave to drain dry on absorbent paper towels.

4. Arrange the herbs and flowers as well as the nettle dumplings on the plate and serve immediately.

Chicken Salad with

Preparation time: 45 minutes
Cooking time: 20 minutes
Difficulty: ★★

Serves four

4 chicken breasts
16 langoustines (between ¹/₈ and ¹/₄ lb /
  80–100 g each)
1 tbsp / 10 g curry powder
4 cherry tomatoes
1 bunch of spinach (to yield 12 leaves)
1 bunch of lamb's lettuce (to yield 12 leaves)

4 button mushrooms
4 baby pumpkins
1 carrot
1 cucumber (to yield a scant ¹/₄ lb / 100 g)
1 lemon
2 tbsp / 30 ml whipping cream
2 tbsp / 30 ml olive oil
2 sprigs of chervil
1 quart / 1 l broth
salt, fresh-ground pepper to taste

The combination of poultry and crustaceans lends this appetizers its unusual aspect. The fine-grained curry powder used to flavor it comes from India via the British, who first brought it to Europe. The exact composition of curry powder varies enormously: the basic spices usually found in all curry powders are cumin, nutmeg, and turmeric, but some also contain cloves, cayenne pepper, and ginger. Use curry quite sparingly, as too much curry will render the other ingredients bitter.

Our chef, Émile Tabourdiau, recommends you buy free-range chicken; their breast meat comes easily off the bone before it is steamed. The breasts contain less fat than the legs and are easier to prepare. To cook them without rendering them too tough, the breasts are wrapped in plastic wrap or cloth.

If you can find them, the relatively large Breton langoustines are ideal for the filling. They should be cooked in broth for only a very short time, otherwise their flesh disintegrates. You can use prawns or shrimps instead, but they are not quite so decorative as the langoustines.

Choose whole spinach leaves without tears or fissures; they are blanched in boiling water and immediately afterwards rinsed in cold water. Their flavor and color aptly complements the delicate aspect of the langoustine filling.

Cut the chicken breast open far enough for easy filling. To add a further visual feature, roll the spinach leaves into tiny balls and place them with the filling into the chicken breasts.

1. Cook the langoustines in a spicy broth, leave to cool and shell, but reserve four whole langoustines for the presentation. Blanch the spinach leaves, rinse with cold water, and drain on a kitchen cloth. Bend the four langoustines retained for decoration so they are arching backwards, and stick the front claws into the shell to hold the langoustine in position.

2. Skin the chicken breasts and cut each piece of meat open with a knife to make a pocket. Peel and hollow out the cherry tomatoes. Chop the peeled cucumber finely, season with cream and chervil; fill the cherry tomatoes with the cucumber.

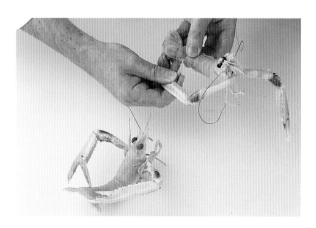

Curried Langoustines

3. Powder the langoustines with curry; season the chicken breasts, and fill with spinach and langoustines. Wrap in plastic wrap and steam for eight to twelve minutes. Once cooked, remove from the saucepan and set aside to cool in the plastic wrap.

4. Blanch the baby pumpkins, hollow them out, and fill with carrot balls and meat from the langoustines' claws. Slice the mushrooms thinly and sprinkle with olive oil and lemon juice. To serve, place a langoustine on each plate, surrounded by a fan-shaped arrangement of chicken medallions. Garnish with lamb's lettuce and the filled baby pumpkins and cherry tomatoes.

Preparation time: 15 minutes
Difficulty: ★

Serves four

generous ³/₄ lb / 400 g rump steak
¹/₈ lb / 50 g aged Parmesan
2 oz / 50 g Périgord truffles

1 bunch of portulaca (see below)
1 bunch of arugula
1 lemon
¹/₄ cup / 50 ml sherry vinegar
³/₈ cup / 75 ml walnut oil
³/₈ cup / 75 ml peanut oil
salt, pepper to taste

Carpaccio is the Italian term for raw, wafer-thin slices of beef fillet. This delicious appetizer exists in many versions, as many fine ingredients are suitable for this kind of preparation. There are *carpaccios* of duck meat, salmon or sea bream (check the Index in this volume for many of these variations). Here, our Chef, Dominique Toulousy, presents a traditional *carpaccio*, but he has seasoned it in his own distinctive way.

The truffle season starts in January and ends in March. The black truffles from Périgord have slightly fissured skin and white marbled flesh, the density of which should be checked before purchase. You should also marinate the truffles in vinaigrette before preparation so they can lend their flavor to the vinaigrette.

It is difficult to find a harder and drier cheese than aged Parmesan, whose tangy flavor is incomparable. Parmigiano Reggiano is the most famous of all Parmesans; the *Grana padano* variety from the Po valley is also delicious. (Look for the name stamped on the rind to find out what kind of Parmesan it is.) To slice this very hard cheese wafer-thin in keeping with the carpaccio theme, it is recommended that you use a slicer or an extremely sharp knife.

Portulaca, extremely rare in American markets, is a type of purslane, a sturdy plant that originated in India. It is a rather fatty green, whose leaves are usually used in salads and soups. The best variety has large, slightly sticky leaves and is sometimes called gold portulaca, or gold purslane. The crunchy leaves of this plant form the ideal partner for the beef and Parmesan in this appetizer; if you can't find any, substitute a robust-flavored green of your choice.

1. Wash the salads thoroughly under running water. Slice one-half of the truffles thinly and cut the other half into fine strips.

2. Prepare the vinaigrette. Dissolve the spices in sherry vinegar, then stir in the walnut and peanut oils. Add all of the truffles. Leave to infuse for at least one hour.

Beef with Aged Parmesan

3. Cut the rump steak into paper-thin slices just before serving.

4. Lace the vinaigrette with lemon juice; salt and pepper the meat, sprinkle with vinaigrette. Dress the salads and arrange on the plates along with the meat slices. Garnish with the remaining truffle slices and strips and wafers of aged Parmesan.

Brandade of Coc

Preparation time: *1 hour*
Cooking time: *45 minutes*
Difficulty: ★★

Serves four

2 lbs / 900 g fresh cod fillets
1 onion, 1 leek
1/4 cup / 50 ml cream
1 pint / 500 ml water

For the vinaigrette:
white of 1 egg
3 tbsp / 40 g mustard
1 tbsp / 15 ml red wine vinegar
1 tbsp / 16 ml custard
7/8 cup / 200 ml peanut oil
1/2 tbsp / 5 g salt and pepper

For the Basque sauce:
2 lbs / 1 kg tomatoes
2 onions
1 green pepper
1/4 cup / 50 ml each white wine, stock

1 tbsp / 15 g concentrated tomato paste
2 tbsp / 30 ml olive oil
salt, pepper to taste

For the spicy sauce:
1/2 cup / 120 ml vinaigrette
generous 1 cup / 300 ml Basque sauce

For the purée:
scant 1/2 lb / 200 g potatoes
2 cloves of garlic

For the brandade:
3 sheets of gelatin
5/8 cup / 150 ml cream
7/8 cup / 200 ml cooking liquid
3/8 cup / 30 ml olive oil
salt, pepper to taste

The traditional Provençal brandade is based on cod, cream, milk, garlic and olive; pounded together, it forms a delicious puree. This version, from Chef Gilles Tournadre, serves some of the same purpose, as it provides an ideal opportunity to use up the parts of the cod that are usually discarded: the underside, tail fillet, and other trimmings. In northern France, cod has many names, such as *doguette* or *moulou*; it is very popular in Normandy, where cod recipes abound. The ports of Dieppe and Fécamp are important cod suppliers.

Here, cod is enhanced in the traditional manner, with cream, and then cooked with leek like a soup. The resulting slightly sweet flavor provides a fitting contrast to the Basque sauce, which is stirred into the vinaigrette to lend an extra spicy note. Basque sauce can be served with other fish as well, such as

tuna, particularly the Bonito type. There are also chicken dishes, clear soups and some potato dishes that can carry the description *à la Basque*, having been prepared with tomatoes, peppers and raw Bayonne ham (from, naturally, Bayonne, France).

Chef Tournadre points out that combining the cod-potato mixture with the Basque sauce requires great care and attention, as you need to wind up with a smooth and even mixture. For this purpose, Tournadre prefers using French cream from Isigny, which carries the classification *appellation d'origine contrôlée* – a label of honor, meaning its production is carefully regulated by the French government – and which is high in pasteurized lactic fats.

1. For the Basque sauce, sweat the chopped onions and pepper in olive oil. Quarter the tomatoes. Pour over white wine and add the tomatoes, the tomato paste and the stock. After cooking, puree in the blender or food processor.

2. Prepare the vinaigrette. Cook the cod with a chopped onion, the bulb of the leek and the cream in water. Bring to a boil and then simmer with the lid closed for five minutes. Remove from the heat and leave the cod to cool in the cooking liquid.

with a Basque Sauce

3. For the spicy sauce, mix the vinaigrette with the Basque sauce. Prepare a potato puree with two cloves of garlic. Soak the gelatin.

4. Leave the cod to drain. To make the brandade, mix the gelatin with almost 1 cup / 250 ml of the cooking liquid. Blend everything with the puree and stir in olive oil. Leave to cool and fold in the cream. To serve, place two scoops of the brandade on each plate and decoratively surround with the spicy sauce.

Preparation time: 20 minutes
Cooking time: 1 hour 45 minutes
Difficulty: ★

Serves four

2 breasts of duck
scant ¼ lb / 100 g Parmesan
salt, pepper to taste

For the dressing:
1 small can of truffle juice
2 limes
⅞ cup / 200 ml olive oil

For the garnish:
3 Belgian endives
1 bunch of lamb's lettuce
2 tbsp / 30 g mustard

In this recipe, beef – the classic ingredient for a *carpaccio* – is replaced with duck breasts. Served with the endive, this cold appetizer will please the diet-conscious as well as the discriminating palate.

Belgian endives were introduced in Brussels towards the end of the nineteenth century. The success of this vegetable with many names – called *witloof* in the Flemish part of Belgium, *chicon* in the French part, and *endive* in France – continues to this day. Low in calories and unique in texture as well as taste, Belgian endive combines well with most lettuces, even the more tangy varieties such as lamb's lettuce or watercress. Choose Belgian endives that are still firmly shut and very white, and avoid those whose leaves have frayed brown around the edges.

Before washing, the outer leaves should be discarded; before serving, the inner core should also be discarded as it tastes rather bitter. For this appetizer the endive is chopped finely and then dressed with truffle juice and prepared mustard. The dressing should be made with walnut oil, as it is an ideal partner for endives.

Regarding the duck breasts, these should come from very fresh and fleshy ducks with a thick layer of fat under their skin, which further enhances the meat. Before slicing the breasts wafer-thin, put the meat in the freezer for a while (about one hour and forty-five minutes) as this will make slicing them easier.

1. Place the duck breasts in the freezer for about 1 hour and 45 minutes to firm up, then cut into wafer-thin slices using a sharp knife or an electric carving knife.

2. Finely chop the endives and mix with mustard. Place a small mound of endives on every plate.

Duck Breast

3. Arrange the duck breast meat in a fan shape around the endive.

4. Prepare the dressing with truffle juice, olive oil, and lemon juice. Sprinkle the breasts with the dressing, place a ring of washed and drained lamb's lettuce leaves around the mound of endive, and garnish with grated Parmesan.

Preparation time: 30 minutes
Marinating time: 48 hours
Cooking time: 8 minutes
Difficulty: ✶

Serves four

$^5/_8$ lb / 300 g spaghetti
1 oz / 50 g dried porcini mushrooms
$^1/_4$ cup / 50 g black olives
$3^1/_2$ oz / 100 g can of tuna packed in oil
$^1/_8$ lb / 50 g marinated beef tongue

$^1/_2$ cup / 100 ml olive oil
zest of half an orange
$^1/_4$ bunch of basil (to yield 1 tsp chopped)
salt, pepper to taste

To garnish:
1 zucchini

All efforts by the French gastronomic establishment could not prevent Italy from remaining the chief exporter of pasta. With more than two hundred pasta varieties, the Italians have shown how the most traditional, hand-wrought processes can be successfully converted into a successful industry.

Spaghetti – the name is derived from the Italian word for string – is, of course, well-known the world over. Until recently it was indelibly associated with the classic Bolognese sauce, but there are other, more unusual methods of preparation, as this recipe helps to prove. Everyone should know by now, but for the benefit of Chef Luisa Valazza we'll mention it nonetheless: spaghetti should be cooked *molto al dente* in water laced with olive oil, and should only be cooked at the very last minute before serving.

Chef Valazza's spaghetti salad is served with chopped marinated porcini mushrooms and tuna in oil. The marinated beef tongue lends the dish that extra note, with an acidity that provides a sublime contrast to the tuna and pasta. For this Piedmontese specialty, the tongue must be marinated in a heady mixture of wine, herbs, garlic, and onions for two days; it should be turned seven times during this process. If you would prefer not to use tongue, you can use cooked ham instead; expect, of course, a slightly different, less hearty flavor. As an alternative to marinated porcini mushrooms you can use fresh mushrooms.

Incidentally, Chef Valazza has created this appetizer to incorporate ingredients from all over Italy: oranges from Sicily, tongue from Piedmont, olives from Liguria and spaghetti, originally, from Naples.

1. Two days ahead of time, wash the beef tongue well; marinate in the herbed wine mixture described above. One day ahead of time, soak the dried porcini mushrooms in hot water to soften, then marinate overnight in vinegar. On cooking day, cut the marinated tongue of beef into fine strips. It must be stored in the refrigerator, and added to the salad only moments before serving.

2. Halve the olives, remove the pits; crumble the tuna and thinly slice the mushrooms. Cut the orange zest into very fine strips and blanch.

Spaghetti Salad

3. Cook the spaghetti al dente; rinse immediately in cold running water, drain and toss with olive oil in a salad bowl.

4. Mix all ingredients, then add salt and pepper to taste. Arrange on the plates and garnish with zucchini strips and basil leaves.

Bellevue Lobster with

Preparation time: 15 minutes
Cooking time: 20 minutes
Difficulty: ★

Serves four

2 1 lb / 500 g lobsters
2 artichokes
1 head of broccoli
2 celery sticks
half an onion
¹/₄ cup / 50 ml peanut oil
juice of one lemon

¹/₂ tsp flour
8 sprigs of chives
half a bunch of chervil (to yield 1 tbsp / 15 g
    chopped)
salt, pepper to taste

For the mayonnaise:
2 egg yolks
1 tsp / 5 g mustard
4 tsp / 20 ml white vinegar
¹/₄ cup / 50 ml vegetable oil
salt, pepper to taste

Lobster is considered the king of the Brittany coast, but unfortunately, these days, it is rare in the region. One of the most famous lobster dishes is Bellevue lobster, which Madame de Pompadour is supposed to have served King Louis XV at his Bellevue residence near Meudon.

For this recipe, our chef, Freddy Van Decasserie, recommends putting in the effort to find female blue Brittany lobsters, as the females contain more meat than the males. Tie their claws with string and peg them, as they might still be active. Cook the lobster quickly in a broth refined with seaweed. The most humane method is to wait until the cooking stock has come to a rolling boil, and then plunge the lobsters in head first.

The mayonnaise should be made exactly to the instructions given by our chef; the olive oil, in particular, has to be added very slowly – dribbled in a continuous, thin line as you are stirring constantly. Otherwise, the sauce could curdle.

The visual impact of the lobster is emphasized by the various greens of the vegetables: chervil, watercress (if desired), artichoke hearts, and broccoli. The latter, a cousin of the cauliflower, not only looks good but also contains many nutrients. You can use the leaves as well as the flowers.

1. Prepare the broth for the lobster using half an onion and celery. Start cold, and immerse the lobster once the broth has come to a rolling boil. Cook for eight minutes over high heat. Then, leave the lobster in the broth to cool; the lobster will thus impart more flavor to the broth.

2. Halve the lobster lengthwise, beginning at the head. Roll up the tail so it will not be squashed during cutting. Extract the claw flesh and set two or three legs aside for decoration; cut the meat into medallions.

Chervil Vinaigrette

3. Prepare the mayonnaise with two egg yolks, a pinch of salt, pepper, mustard and vinegar. Add the olive oil in a very thin stream, stirring constantly. Put one tablespoon of mayonnaise, $1/4$ cup / 50 ml of water and the chervil leaves in a blender or food processor. Mix well and gradually stir in the peanut oil until it is fully blended.

4. Clean and trim the artichokes down to the hearts. Simmer the artichoke hearts for 15 minutes in water with the lemon juice and a pinch of flour; then quarter. Cook the broccoli al dente (you can steam it just as quickly) and rinse with cold water immediately after cooking. Arrange the ensemble on the plates in a decorative fashion, garnishing with sprigs of chives and lobster legs. Serve chilled.

Pigeon and Goose Live

Preparation time: 1 hour 30 minutes
Cooking time: 1 hour 5 minutes
Difficulty: ★★★

Serves four

2 large Bresse pigeons (see below)
3½ oz / 100 g canned goose liver
4 lbs / 2 kg goose fat
4 carrots
4 turnips
8 radishes
¼ lb / 50 g young peas
¼ lb / 50 g green beans
1 1 oz / 20 g truffle
1 tbsp / 10 g spice mix
generous 1 cup / 300 ml truffle oil
1 cup / 250 ml olive oil

juice of half a lemon
sugar, salt, pepper to taste

For the aspic:
pigeon carcasses
1 carrot
1 onion
half a bunch of celery
1 bouquet garni
1½ tbsp / 20 g concentrated tomato paste
1 sheet of gelatin

For clarifying:
3 egg whites
1 carrot
1 leek (leaf only)
4 star anise

In France, breeding pigeons used to be the privilege of aristocratic judges, and during the *ancien régime* pigeons could only be found on the dinner tables of the rich. Today, breeding pigeons can be purchased all year round, unlike wild pigeons. The best time to buy fresh-killed pigeons is in June and July.

Our chef, Geert Van Hecke of Belgium, has devised this recipe around pigeons from Bresse in France, which measure in the neighborhood of a half a pound (two hundred and fifty grams) and have, according to Van Hecke, meat that is more dense and more tender than that of most other pigeons. This subtlety strikes a perfect balance with the marinated goose liver and the crunchy, young vegetables. Of course, markets differ consider-

ably in different countries, so in any event, look for succulent, mature pigeons, rather than the smaller squabs.

To lend the aspic the intense aroma it requires, star anise is added; the star anise flowers have healing properties. The herb got its name from its slightly aniseed flavor, although it is not related to the proper anise at all. It is also frequently an ingredient in the five-spice mix often used in Asian cooking, which also usually contains cloves, cassia (Chinese cinnamon bark), fennel, and fagara (or szechuan pepper).

1. Soak the gelatin ahead of time. Prepare a stock with the pigeon carcasses along with the bouquet garni, the tomato paste, and chopped carrot, onion, and celery stick. Cook for one hour, strain and add the pre-soaked gelatin. Clarify the stock with egg white, star anise, the green part of a leek and a chopped carrot.

2. Glaze the base of the four plates with this aspic. Season the goose liver with salt, pepper, and spice mix. Cook for a half an hour in goose fat at 155 °F / 80 °C, then set aside to cool for one hour.

3. Fry the pigeon meat rare; slice. Cut the goose liver and truffles into thin slices.

4. Clean and chop the vegetables and gently cook in olive oil with a pinch of sugar, salt, and pepper for a half an hour. Mix the cooked vegetables with the truffle oil and the juice of half a lemon. On the plates, arrange a row of alternating truffles and pigeon meat slices in the middle, with the goose liver slices on either side. Garnish with the vegetables.

Lukewarm Squid with

Preparation time:	30 minutes
Cooking time:	20 minutes
Infusing time:	24 hours
Difficulty:	★★

Serves four

2 lbs / 1 kg small squid
1 quart / 1 l chicken broth
2 tbsp / 30 g butter
1 sprig thyme

For the vegetables:

scant $^3/_8$ lb / 150 g parsnips
scant $^3/_8$ lb / 150 g heliantus tuberosus
 (a variety of tuberose)

scant $^3/_8$ lb / 150 g chervil (the bulbs only)
scant $^3/_8$ lb / 150 g parsley root
scant $^3/_8$ lb / 150 g fennel root

For the vinaigrette:

$^1/_2$ cup / 100 ml wine vinegar
$^1/_2$ cup / 100 ml balsamic vinegar
$^3/_4$ cup / 200 ml olive oil
$^1/_2$ cup / 100 ml soy sauce
$^1/_4$ tsp chili sauce
$^1/_4$ tsp Tabasco
1 chopped anchovy
1 onion
1 clove of garlic
1 shallot
$^1/_4$ lb / 50 g fresh ginger root
1 bunch each of: mint, lemon balm, and thyme
salt, fresh-ground pepper to taste

Not far from the Versailles restaurant Trois Marches where Chef Gérard Vié holds court, the royal gardeners used to cultivate many fruit and vegetable varieties that are only rarely used today. Chef Vié's appetizer is dedicated to these rare vegetables.

Parsnips are members of the family of umbelliferous plants, and they are very similar to the carrot; thus the Romans gave both of them the same name: *pastinaca*. Parsnips, however, are white, and have a very intense aromatic flavor. There are many different parsnip varieties, from round ones to the longer types. Other root vegetables used here are the parsley root, similar in taste to celeriac, and the fennel root, which the Romans consumed both raw and cooked and, finally, the stunted chervil bulbs, with their white and sweet pulp.

The small squid are prepared in two stages, both of which require only very brief frying so the meat does not have a chance to dry out. The soy vinaigrette will finally be sprinkled onto the squid. Of the herbs, onion, ginger, and shallot for the vinaigrette, when all are chopped they should yield about one heaping cupful. You should prepare the vinaigrette the day before, as it will need twenty-four hours to infuse.

1. Prepare the vinaigrette and leave to infuse for 24 hours. Wash the squid, drain and cut into thin slices. Retain the ink.

2. Peel the vegetables, cut into sticks and cook each as a separate batch in chicken broth. Keep warm.

Vegetables and Herbs

3. Dress the vegetable sticks with part of the vinaigrette; strain the remaining vinaigrette and retain the oily liquid. Season the squid and briefly pan-fry half with part of the vinaigrette oil.

4. Fry the remaining squid with the remaining vinaigrette-oil, add the ink and gently cook for three to four minutes. Place a bed of vegetables in the middle of each plate, arrange the ink-stained squid in a ring around the vegetables; place the white squid on top of the vegetables. Decorate the rest of the plate with vegetable sticks in a radiating wheel, much like the spokes of wagons used at Versailles in the days of the royal gardens.

Preparation time: *30 minutes*
Difficulty: ☆

Serves four

16 large (sea) scallops
2 oz / 50 g Beluga caviar
2 oz / 50 g salmon roe
¼ cup / 60 g crème fraîche
1 bunch of chives
24 dandelion leaves (only the tips
    will be used)
juice of half a lemon
salt, fresh-ground pepper to taste

For the lemon marinade:
half a bunch of lemon balm
juice of half a lemon
juice of half a lime
⅝ cup / 150 ml olive oil
a pinch of sugar
1 tsp / 5 g sea salt

A real connoisseur of scallops, our chef, Harald Wohlfahrt, has them flown in from Ireland or Scotland to transform them into a *carpaccio* and tartare. The cold waters of the Irish Sea in particular provide the perfect breeding ground for many scallop varieties, which are caught from November through March.

The scallop has had many names, depending on period and region; the French call it large pelerine or Jacob's comb. Despite depictions dating from the Middle Ages, St. Jacob never carried the scallop that eventually became his symbol. Rather, it was the pilgrims of Santiago de Compostela who used the scallop as a plate, due to its shape; eventually it became the emblem of their union.

You will need very fresh (that is, live) scallops that are still firmly shut. They always contain a little sea water and are quite difficult to open. Clean the inside of all unnecessary bits and begin preparation.

Lemon balm, originally from the Far East, has conquered Mediterranean cuisine. Here it is responsible for giving the marinade its strong flavor, combined with chives and dandelion, whose young leaves are slightly bitter. Lemon balm is often used instead of lemons because it has a similar taste but a less aggressive aroma. Finally, the caviar lends this dish an oily, salty, elegant note.

1. For the marinade, coarsely chop the lemon balm and mix with olive oil, lemon juice, and lime juice. Add sea salt and a pinch of sugar and leave to infuse for 24 hours.

2. Extract the flesh from the scallop shells, remove the exterior mucous, clean in ice water and drain on paper towels. Finely chop half of the scallops.

Tartare of Scallops

3. Season this tartare with half of the chives (finely chopped), a little marinade, salt, and pepper. Mix with half of the salmon roe. Mix the crème fraîche with the remaining salmon roe and a third of the caviar and season with lemon juice. Cut the remaining scallops into thin slices and distribute on the plates. Sprinkle with a little marinade.

4. Form the tartare into balls or dollops and place on top of the carpaccio; garnish with dandelion leaves and chives. Pour caviar sauce around the carpaccio and place the remaining caviar in the middle; garnish with chopped chives and marinade, and serve immediately.

Preparation time: 30 minutes
Cooking time: 20 minutes
Difficulty: ★

Serves four

8 baby carrots
4 baby turnips
4 small potatoes
4 spring onions
4 small artichokes
1 large leek
2 bunches of broccoli

For the horseradish sauce:
$^1/_4$ lb / 50 g horseradish root (to yield 1 tbsp grated)
1 shallot
3 eggs
juice of one lemon
1 tbsp / 15 g mustard
$^3/_4$ cup / 200 ml whipping cream
salt, pepper to taste

For the Béchamel sauce:
1 pint / 500 ml of milk
2 tbsp / 20 g butter
2 tbsp / 20 g all-purpose flour
a pinch of salt

This cold appetizer is meant to symbolize the variety of a vegetable garden – *alla giardiniera* simply means a dish that features chopped vegetables, usually ones fresh from the garden. Our chef, Armando Zanetti, a vegetable and garden lover, has enhanced this traditional recipe with a spicy horseradish sauce that replaces the usual mayonnaise.

Our chef uses hard-boiled egg yolk because it is more digestible than raw. Cream is also an important ingredient; it contains less fat than olive oil. And the fresh horseradish, laced with a dash of white wine, completes the picture. The horseradish root must only be grated at the last moment, otherwise it

will become stale. Never use a horseradish root that is no longer fresh or has seedlings sprouting from it – these aging versions are so bitter they will destroy the sauce. It is best to cook the vegetables in stainless steel pots, as the neutral, clean metal helps to keep them fresh. You can compose the "vegetable garden" to your own taste with seasonal vegetables – in summer a mélange of raw and crunchy vegetables, in winter a mixture of heartier, cooked ones. Whatever vegetables you use, it is the sauce that will lend this dish its special character.

One last note: choose waxy potatoes for this dish, and do not over- or undercook them.

1. Wash the vegetables and chop decoratively. Divide the leek into four pieces and the broccoli into four florets. Peel the spring onions and trim, leaving 1 in / 2$^1/_2$ cm of green.

2. Cook each vegetable (except the potatoes) al dente, in its own batch of boiling salted water. The potatoes should be cooked normally.

Horseradish Sauce

3. For the Béchamel sauce, heat the butter and flour together. Leave to cool, then add the boiling milk. Bring to a boil and set aside. For the horseradish sauce, hard-boil the eggs, chop the shallot, and grate the horseradish root to yield one tablespoon. Mix three hard-boiled egg yolks with a tablespoon of mustard and then add the shallot, grated horseradish, and the Béchamel sauce.

4. Mix the horseradish sauce for two to three minutes, stirring in the lemon juice and cream. To serve, pool the sauce onto the plates, and decoratively arrange the vegetables.

Hot Appetizers

Preparation time: 30 minutes
Cooking time: 20 minutes
Difficulty: ★

Serves four

2 lb / 1 kg green beans
1 cauliflower
2 lb / 1 kg artichokes
2 lb / 1 kg fava beans
2 lb / 1 kg fresh peas
2 lb / 1 kg fresh porcini mushrooms

2 cloves of garlic
1 bunch of green asparagus
1 bunch of white asparagus
2 slices raw ham (or Prosciutto)
$^1/_2$ cup / 125 ml vegetable oil
$^1/_2$ cup / 125 g flour
1 cup / 250 ml meat broth
  (such as veal or beef)
salt, pepper to taste

Easily digestible and therefore, in Europe, considered ideally suited for business dinners, this dish reminds our chef, Hilario Arbelaitz, of his mother; it was she who introduced him to the pleasures of cooking at an early age. When preparing this dish, the distinct aromas of each of the ingredients must be preserved. Each will in turn enhance the other, allowing these garden vegetables and wild mushrooms to meld in a most harmonious way.

Porcini, predominantly found in the Basque region, lends this vegetable dish a rustic flavor – a very interesting contrast to the vegetables cooked *al dente*. If no fresh porcini can be found, substitute the more commonly available dried version, which should be soaked in hot water about twenty minutes to soften. Or, alternatively, one could also substitute fresh chanterelles. Regarding the vegetables, since no two of these spring vegetables call for the same cooking time, they must all be pre-

pared separately. The exact composition of vegetables, according to Chef Arbelaitz, is not of any great consequence. What is important is that the main components are peas, green beans, white beans, asparagus, and porcini. Around this central theme you may create your own composition according to what is freshest in the market, as well as your whim and taste. Ideally, the various vegetables chosen should be very fresh, and direct from the garden if possible.

The mushrooms, which tend to toughen up if overcooked and lose their flavor if left to sit for too long, should not be prepared until the last minute. The raw Serrano ham from Spain puts the finishing touch to this dish; if unavailable, one may substitute prosciutto.

If you are preparing this appetizer out of season, spinach and cabbage (use sparingly) may be added.

1. Wash all the vegetables and peel if necessary. Follow the different cooking times meticulously: green beans – eight minutes, cauliflower – ten minutes, artichokes – fifteen minutes, fava beans – three minutes, peas – five minutes, green asparagus – four minutes, white asparagus – ten minutes.

2. Cut the ham into thin strips, fry in oil, add a little flour and fry until crisp.

Porcini Mushrooms

3. Cut the vegetables into 1 in / 2 cm pieces; clean the artichoke down to the heart and cut into pieces as well. Add the vegetables and a little broth to the cooking ham. If fresh, clean the mushrooms with a damp cloth or sponge (not under running water, which will saturate them). If dried, rinse, then soak for 20 minutes in hot water.

4. Slice the mushrooms, fry them in a pan with oil and add them to the vegetable mixture. Slice the garlic; fry in oil until golden brown and add to the vegetables as well. Serve piping hot, garnished, if you wish, with sprigs of chive and chervil leaves.

Preparation time: 1 hour, 30 minutes
Cooking time: 1 hour
Soaking time: 24 hours
Difficulty: ★★

Serves four

generous $\frac{1}{2}$ lb / 250 g cod, salted
8 red peppers (see below)
1 onion
3 cloves of garlic
scant $\frac{1}{4}$ cup / 50 g fresh bread crumbs
$\frac{2}{3}$ cup / 150 ml olive oil

$\frac{2}{3}$ cup / 150 ml cream
1 egg
3 sprigs of parsley
a pinch of sugar

On the Spanish side of the Pyrennees mountains, peppers are very popular, especially the so-called Piquillo from the area of Pampelune in Navarra. This is a very fleshy variety that is very hard to find elsewhere. Harvested in September, it is cleaned by hand and then grilled; if it is washed under running water it loses many essential qualities. If desired, this dish can work as a side dish accompanying an entrée instead of an appetizer, with peppers as the main component of the course. Among the peppers you may substitute for the Spanish Piquillos are sweet red bell peppers, or fresh pimientos.

Peppers go particularly well with the strong flavor of cod, which the Spaniards love presenting in a thick sauce made richer with the addition of bread crumbs. Chef Firmin Arrambide recommends serving the sauce separately, as he asserts that this will make the dish more easily digestible.

Cooking is kept to a minimum here to retain the ingredients' freshness: the red peppers, only cooked very briefly, thus do not lose their lovely, bright red color, while the cod stuffing is also cooked for a very short time to prevent it from drying out. The addition of garlic and onion lend the cod a certain lightness of flavor, and make it easily digestible.

This recipe for stuffed peppers served in their own sauce may, of course, also be used with other ingredients. Crab stuffing, minced poultry, or lamb stuffing, or even a delicious potato puree with garlic, for instance, are perfect complements and may be prepared the same way. Likewise, most mushrooms and herbs complement the peppers harmoniously. Indeed, this appetizer may take on innumerable variations.

1. One day ahead, soak the salt cod in water for 24 hours. The next day, to prepare the dish, skewer the eight peppers onto a fork and place them on the grill until their skins turn black. Rinse under cold water, skin, and remove the stems and seeds. Pour olive oil over the peeled peppers, salt them on both sides, and bake in the oven for 15 minutes at 355 °F / 180 °C. Set aside to cool.

2. Peel the onions and cut into strips. Chop the garlic and fry together with the onions in 1 tbsp plus 1 tsp of olive oil, then cook over a low heat for 15 minutes. In the meantime, flake the cod and carefully remove the bones. Add the fish to the onions and garlic and fry for one minute. Take the pan off the heat and add the bread crumbs to bind the stuffing.

Stuffed with Cod

3. Cut 1 in / 2¹/₂ cm off the wide end of each pepper. Cook these small pieces in ²/₃ cup / 150 ml of cream for 15 minutes, then puree in a blender or food processor and run through a sieve. Season with salt and a pinch of sugar.

4. Use a pastry bag to fill the peppers. Dust with flour and turn in a beaten egg. Fry briefly in a pan with five tablespoons of olive oil. To serve, cover the base of a serving platter with half the pepper sauce, and pour the rest into a gravy boat. Arrange the peppers in the sauce on the platter, and garnish with parsley.

Preparation time: 1 hour
Cooking time: 10 minutes
Difficulty: ★★

Serves four

For the pasta dough:
generous 1 cup / 250 g fine-ground flour
8 egg yolks
a pinch of salt

For the prawn sauce:
1 dozen large prawns
4 zucchini (to yield 3½ oz / 100 g)

4 zucchini flowers
4 tomatoes
1 shallot
generous ³/₈ cup / 100 ml extra virgin olive oil
salt, pepper, hot chili powder to taste

The invention of pasta has been claimed by many cultures, in particular the Italians and the Chinese; still others maintain that they had invented their own version of pasta by the Middle Ages, if not earlier. Regardless of the debate, it is, however, a fact that pasta already adorned Italian menus in the Renaissance period, and that as early as the 15th century noodles were being produced in Naples for commercial distribution and consumption.

This gourmet's treasure deserves as much praise as there are variations – and, considering the inventiveness of great chefs, there will continue to be a host of new creations. The secret of the dough is its admirable simplicity, a basic combination of just water and flour, sometimes with eggs, often with colorings from beets, spinach, or squid, for example. If you prepare the pasta dough in advance, cover it with a damp cloth and keep it in the refrigerator to prevent it from drying out. Then, as our

chef, Giuseppina Beglia advises, roll it out just before you cook it, so the dough is supple and easy to work.

Zucchini nowadays is available all year round. Its skin, with a slightly rough surface and bright green, freckled appearance, should not show any brown marks, as the vegetable is so tender that a bruise will ruin its flavor. The smaller the zucchini, the more tender and flavorful. And if they are are cooked only briefly, their flesh will remain pleasingly *al dente*.

Chef Beglia used the Italian gamberoni for this recipe, a large pink prawn that is found in the gulf of San Remo. Since the availablity of these in the United States is, of course, up to chance, substitute them with any other variety of large prawn, so long as the shellfish are fresh. It is advisable, though laborious, to shell the prawns before preparing them, in order to infuse the flesh with the aroma of the other ingredients.

1. Heap the flour onto a pastry board or marble slab on a solid, flat table, add a pinch of salt and the eggs, and knead well until the dough is soft and elastic. Cover and set aside for an hour, then roll out thinly.

2. Cut the rolled-out dough into approximately 2 in / 5 cm squares and roll these up diagonally over a pencil to make the tubes.

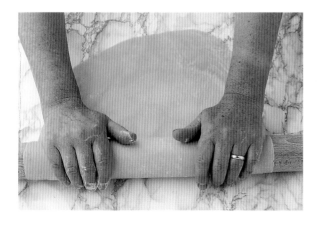

Tubes with Prawns

3. Chop the shallot, dice the zucchini and tomatoes, and shell the prawns. Heat olive oil in a frying pan, add the chopped shallots and diced zucchini and sauté for five minutes. Add the shelled prawns, the diced tomatoes, and zucchini flowers, and season with salt and hot chili powder.

4. Fry all the ingredients for another five minutes, set aside, and keep warm. Cook the pasta rolls in salted water for five minutes, drain, mix with the prawns and vegetables, arrange on plates, and serve immediately.

Risotto with Zucchini

Preparation time: 15 minutes
Cooking time: 20 minutes
Difficulty: ★★

Serves four

4 zucchini flowers
³/₄ cup / 180 g rice (such as Carnaroli or Arborio)
20 mussels (such as vongole or blue)
4 red prawns
4 zucchini (to yield generous 3¹/₂ oz / 100 g)
4 tomatoes

1 small leek
1 white onion
2 shallots
1 clove of garlic
generous 1 cup / 250 ml dry white wine
generous 2 cups / 500 ml chicken stock
³/₄ cup / 200 ml extra virgin olive oil
¹/₈ lb Parmesan cheese (to yield scant ¹/₄ cup / 50 g grated)
scant ¹/₈ lb / 50 g butter
1 bunch of parsley
1 sprig of rosemary
salt, pepper to taste

Traditionally, risotto (in Italian the word means "little rice") is mixed with hot stock, fried in fat with chopped onions and then cooked in broth. These days, it is also enriched with numerous ingredients such as seafood, poultry liver, mushrooms, vegetables, or cheese.

In this recipe, as Giuseppina Beglia advises, do not deviate from the instructions when you prepare the rice, or it will not come out with the right consistency. Use a white short-grained variety, like Arborio, or the Italian variety Carnaroli – which Chef Beglia prefers. Do not wash the rice, as the water will rinse the vital starch away. Instead, stir it carefully with a wooden spoon. Once fried with onion and plenty of olive oil, the rice should not be cooked for more than twenty minutes. Towards the end, when the rice is nearly done, add butter and grated Parmesan and cook the mixture over a low heat for a few more minutes.

For the ragout of mussels and prawns, only very fresh seafood should be used. The vongole Chef Beglia prefers for this recipe is a type of mussel predominantly found in the Mediterranean. However, the market may not offer this variety: instead, try substituting cockles or small clams. The only purpose of the white wine in this recipe is to lend the dish a slightly tart flavor, offsetting the presence of the shellfish. It should therefore be used sparingly.

The zucchini flowers are served raw, stuffed with the risotto. Thus large, strong and fleshy flowers should be selected, the male ones being better suited for stuffing although they are certainly more delicate to handle. And bear in mind that the petals wilt very fast, even when covered with a damp cloth, so this part of the preparation should be done quickly, and, if possible, without any interruptions. This warm appetizer, according to Chef Beglia, is particularly popular in the summertime.

1. *Chop the onion, shallots, leek, and zucchini, and sauté in a generous pool of olive oil in a deep pot or sauté pan over a low heat for 5–10 minutes. Add the rice, stir with a wooden spoon, and cook for another 3–4 minutes. Add the white wine and cook until the liquid has been absorbed. Grate the Parmesan cheese.*

2. *Add a cup of hot chicken stock and braise the rice over a high heat while stirring continuously, adding a little more chicken stock gradually. Five minutes before the rice is cooked, bind it with butter and grated Parmesan cheese. Chop the garlic and finely dice the tomatoes.*

Flowers and Mussel Ragout

3. In a frying pan lightly pooled with olive oil, place a sprig of rosemary and chopped garlic. Wash the mussels and prawns carefully and shell the tails of the prawns; add into the pan. As soon as the mussels open, add the finely diced tomatoes. Chop the parsley.

4. Pour in the white wine, season, and sprinkle with chopped parsley at the last minute. To serve, after having removed its leaves and stem, fill the calyx of the zucchini flower with risotto. Arrange on plates and garnish with mussel and prawn ragout.

Cream Soup with

Preparation time: 30 minutes
Cooking time: 40 minutes
Difficulty: ★★

Serves four

4 lb 4 oz / 2 kg mussels
4 lb 4 oz / 2 kg Mediterranean fish, such as
   rockfish, stingray, sea eel, sea robin
   (also known as gurnard)
4 leeks (to yield $^5/_8$ cup / 150 g)
generous 1$^1/_2$ lb / 750 g tomatoes
4 onions (to yield $^5/_8$ cup / 150 g)
1 clove of garlic
2 shallots

3$^1/_2$ tbsp / 50 g butter
$^1/_8$ lb / 50 g Swiss cheese (to yield scant $^1/_8$ lb /
   50 g grated)
1 baguette
1$^1/_4$ cups / 300 ml crème fraîche
$^1/_2$ cup / 125 ml olive oil
generous 2 cups / 500 ml sweet white wine
scant $^1/_4$ cup / 50 ml pastis (aniseed liqueur)
half a bunch of parsley
$^1/_2$ bunch fresh fennel (to yield 1 oz / 30 g)
1 bay leaf
1 sprig of thyme
a pinch of saffron filaments
salt, pepper to taste

Whatever else you might think about it, inattentiveness can sometimes leads to surprising results. One day, our chef, the usually meticulous Christian Bouvarel, accidentally added mussels to his usually fish-laden bouillabaisse, and thus inadvertently invented this recipe. It was so successful that it is now a regular item on the menu of Paul Bocuse's restaurant.

Naturally, the quality of the mussels is crucial. The common blue mussel, with its tasty, wonderful orange-yellow flesh, is best suited for this dish. Famous all over the world, the blue mussel is cultivated to keep it free of sand; when arriving at market, it is usually already de-sanded and filtered, thanks to the experience of generations of its farmers. For Chef Bouvarel this is the only type of mussel worth considering, be it from Spain or from the Netherlands, for this reason. Nevertheless, strain the stock once the mussels are cooked and have opened.

(Do not, of course, cook the mussels for too long.) Cook the soup gently over a low heat and round off the flavor by adding crème fraîche.

The Mediterranean fish required for this recipe are basically the same as for a conventional bouillabaisse (if one can call any form of this dish conventional). If you can not find rockfish (also known as scorpion fish), substitute any other fish that catch your eye, such as rosefish or sea bass. The subtle mixture of saffron and pastis, together with a heavy white wine – actually Pouilly-Fuissée in the original recipe – lends the dish a heady, unforgettable presence that will most likely leave no one unmoved. Saffron, incidentally, an aromatic spice that has enjoyed great popularity since the Middle Ages, was first brought to France by Savoyan merchants and has since mainly been grown there in the Rhône valley.

1. Chop the shallots and parsley. Cook the mussels in white wine with the chopped shallots, parsley and 3 tbsp / 50 g of butter until they open. Set aside a few of the cooked mussels for decoration and shell the rest. Gut and scale the fish and chop into large pieces.

2. Chop the onions and cut the leeks into thin strips. Heat the olive oil, add the onions and the saffron filaments, as well as the strips of leek. Steam over a low heat for five minutes.

Mussels and Saffron

3. Chop the tomatoes. To the same pot, add aniseed liqueur, then a little water, wine, mussel stock, fish, tomatoes, and all of the herbs. Cook for 40 minutes and season to taste. Pass the ingredients through a fine sieve to puree the fish as much as possible, then bring to a boil again.

4. Lastly, add the crème fraîche, cook for another two minutes, and pour into a tureen. Grate the cheese and toast the baguette. The grated cheese and the toasted, sliced baguette spread with olive oil and garlic are served separately. Serve the creamy soup with the mussels in soup plates and decorate with the mussels in their shells. Garnish, if desired, with parsley.

Lasagna

Preparation time: 3 hours
Cooking time: 20 minutes
Difficulty: ★★★

Serves four

4 sea perch filets (see below)

For the dough:
generous 1 lb / 500 g flour
4 egg yolks
2 eggs

1 bunch of spinach
2 tbsp / 10 ml squid ink
¹/₄ cup / 50 g tomato paste
salt

For the basil butter:
generous 2 cups / 500 ml water
1 bunch of basil
1 tbsp / 15 ml roast juice
7 tbsp / 100 g butter

When quizzed on the source for his culinary philosophy, our chef, Carlo Brovelli, tells this story. His uncle went on a trip around the world, and returned with the most important secrets of cooking. These, he passed on to his nephew: treat the products used with respect, follow the cooking times meticulously, and pay attention not only to the role the different flavors play, but how they work together when combined.

Thus is introduced Chef Brovelli's lasagna appetizer, which stands out both because of its inventive dough, and because it combines the principles mentioned above. Pasta ribbons are dyed with the natural essences of squid ink, tomatoes, and spinach and the dish encapsulates all of the chef's skills into a delight for eye and palate. Depending on one's whim and taste, the dough may of course also be dyed with other ingredients to achieve other colors, such as beets or yellow bell peppers.

Naturally, a multitude of lasagna recipes exist in Italy. The most well-known is probably *lasagna alla Bolognese* – that is, with a rich, meaty, tomato and vegetable sauce, but *lasagna al pesto* (with basil) or *lasagna verdi* (with a green sauce) are also very popular. In this case our chef garnishes his lasagna with a fillet of sea perch that has been steamed only briefly so that it does not lose its flavor. This Mediterranean version of the fish is actually an ordinary perch – unlike the genuine sea perch from the North Sea, which is most often used for smoked fillets. If you cannot obtain a Mediterranean perch, substitute sea bass, for instance, or a similar fish.

Reference should also be made to the butter spiced with basil: this aromatic herb thrives in the southern Italian sun. Not surprisingly, the symbol of this sun, *il sole*, adorns the sign of our chef's century-old restaurant, which is situated on one of the most romantic roads in Lombardy.

1. Cook the roast juice with five basil leaves in two cups of water. Reduce to one cup, mix, and strain. Add the remaining chopped basil leaves and butter, whip, and keep warm.

2. Prepare the lasagna dough with flour, eggs, and 4 egg yolks. Puree the spinach. Separate the dough into four equal portions; knead squid ink into the first, tomato paste into the second, spinach puree into the third, and leave the fourth portion uncolored. Keep all under a damp cloth for one hour, then roll out in thin layers. Carefully cut these into long, ribbon-shaped strips.

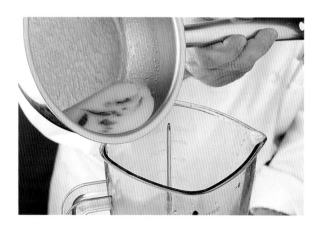

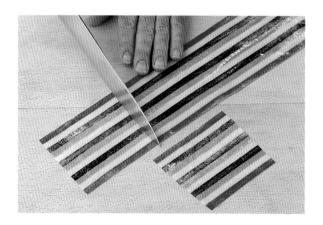

del Sole

3. Place these colorful strips next to each other, adhere together with the remaining egg yolk, cook in salted water, and spread out on a cloth. Season the sea perch filets and steam for three minutes; keep warm.

4. Place a colorful lasagna sheet onto each plate, lay a piece of sea perch fillet on top, pour on the basil butter and cover with another sheet of lasagna. Serve immediately.

Ravioli with Fresh

Preparation time: 1 hour
Cooking time: 8 minutes
Difficulty: ★

Serves four

For the ravioli dough:
generous 1 cup / 250 g semolina flour
1 tbsp / 15 ml oil
3 egg yolks
1 egg
generous $\frac{1}{2}$ lb / 250 g spinach
salt to taste

For the filling:
2 zucchini
1 red pepper
1 fennel bulb
1 celery heart
1 bunch mustard greens (7 oz / 200 g)
7 oz / 200 g Ricotta
$\frac{1}{2}$ cup / 120 g butter
1 bunch of basil
salt, pepper to taste

Particularly in this culinarily adventurous age, when classics are being constantly reinterpreted, there is nothing to prevent a skilled chef from flouting old traditions and filling ravioli with something other than the customary meat, fish or cheese. From Chef Carlo Brovelli, then, comes this suggestion, a vegetarian ravioli filled with a masterly mixture of vegetables cooked *al dente*, balanced by the famous Ricotta cheese.

Spinach, dried well beforehand, lends the dough its green tint. The "starry sky" pattern of the dough – albeit a semolina sky, dotted with green stars, can also be achieved by using Swiss chard leaves. Parsley is not recommended, as it will tint the dough too intensely.

Be careful to adhere strictly to the prescribed cooking instructions of each vegetable, since the individual flavor of each one must be preserved. And, as Chef Brovelli emphasizes, by no means should one give in to the temptation to use any other vegetables, as this would complicate the recipe unecessarily. One exception, however, are mustard greens, which may certainly be added to this exclusive mixture if you so desire.

Ricotta, a cheese made from cow's or sheep's milk, does not melt when cooked, a characteristic that makes it ideal for fillings, as well as antipasti and pasta dishes. It also adds a strong flavor to the vegetable filling. It should be bought particularly fresh, as it tends to adopt a bitter aftertaste quite quickly – and sometimes gets a bit watery after sitting for a long time – which would spoil the recipe. Chef Brovelli recommends diluting in the blender or food processor with a little milk so it may meld more easily with the vegetable filling.

1. Blanch and chop the spinach. Prepare the ravioli dough with the ingredients indicated and mix it with a portion of the blanched and chopped spinach. Set aside the dough to rest in a damp cloth for an hour and a half, then roll out thinly and cut into wide strips.

2. Cut the zucchini into $\frac{1}{2}$ in / 1 cm wide strips, dice, and cook until al dente. Do the same with the other vegetables. Drain everything well and refrigerate.

Vegetable Filling

3. Melt the butter. If using mustard greens, wash and chop them. Mix with the chilled and diced vegetables and the Ricotta cheese, season, and add in melted butter.

4. Cut the dough strips into squares, baste one half with an egg yolk. Prepare the ravioli, spooning a portion of the filling onto each square and covering with another square. Cook in salted water for two minutes, and then arrange four or five on each plate in the shape of a flower. To serve, place one spoonful of diced vegetables in the center of each plate, pour melted butter over, and sprinkle with chopped basil leaves.

Poached Eggs

Preparation time: 30 minutes
Chilling time: 3 hours
Cooking time: 10 minutes
Difficulty: ★

Serves four

8 eggs
6 egg yolks
scant $^7/_8$ lb / 400 g hop shoots (or substitute
   soybean or mung bean sprouts)
generous 2 cups / 500 ml cream

generous 1 cup / 250 ml pale lager beer
   (Saint-Feuillien from Belgium, if available)
scant $^1/_4$ cup / 50 ml white whine vinegar
1 tbsp / 15 g mild prepared mustard
1 bunch of chervil
salt, pepper to taste

Eggs have the virtually unchallenged position of being utilized in every realm of cooking, from appetizer to dessert. Sweet or savory, they contribute to innumerable gastronomic masterpieces. One of the great egg-producing countries in Europe is Belgium, with a production figure of more than three billion eggs a year. The nutritional value of eggs is extraordinary; the egg is practically the only natural product containing vitamin D as well as vitamins A, E and K, thus providing exceptionally balanced and nourishing nutrition.

Eggs, importantly, should always be consumed fresh. One way to test their freshness is to put them in cold water. A fresh egg lies horizontally at the bottom of the bowl, whereas a less fresh one stands up vertically, or even floats to the surface. For the preparation of poached eggs, extremely fresh eggs are naturally required. These should be refrigerated beforehand for a

few hours, so that the egg white coagulates better when cooked. Trim any irregular edges before serving.

Hop shoots are an interesting Belgian specialty, unfortunately only available from mid-March to the end of April, and rare in the United States. They are said to have medicinal healing powers; the French poet Rabelais swore by their aphrodisiac effect. The best shoots are firm and crisp. They have to be washed several times under running water, since they grow underground. If hop shoots are not available, they may be substituted with soybean or mung bean sprouts, though since quite delicate, these can be cooked only for about a minute.

Saint-Feuillien beer, a pale lager, is very common in Belgium and harmonizes well with the hop shoots. If it is unavailable, other beers, preferably pale lagers, may be used for the sauce.

1. Wash the hop shoots well and remove the hard part of the shoots. Reduce $^2/_3$ cup / 150 ml of beer in a pot by a quarter. Add cream, bring to a boil again, and season with salt and pepper. Add the drained hop shoots, cook for another five minutes, then take them out and set the liquid aside. If using soybean or mung bean sprouts, cook for only one minute.

2. Bring $^1/_2$ cup / 100 ml of water and a $^1/_4$ cup / 50 ml of vinegar to a boil in a pot. In the meantime, crack eight eggs into eight small bowls. Gently slide one egg after the other into the boiling vinegar water. Cook them for two minutes; then take out and set aside in lukewarm water.

n Beer Sauce

3. In a bowl, blend six egg yolks with 7 tbsp / 100 ml of pale lager, beat until frothy, and then whisk briskly over a low heat until a creamy sauce develops. Add the stock from the hop shoots and 1 tsp / 5 g of mustard, and season with salt and pepper. Pass the sauce through a sieve.

4. To serve, arrange the hop sprouts on the plate in the shape of a nest. Dry the poached eggs and trim off the rough edges. Place one egg on each nest, pour the sauce around it, and garnish with chervil leaves.

Tomato Tarts in Olive

Preparation time: 1 hour
Baking time: 15 minutes
Difficulty: ★

Serves four

14 oz / 400 g puff pastry
  (see basic recipes p. 803)
5¹/₂ lb / 2¹/₂ kg tomatoes
3 sprigs of lavender
4 oz / 100 g fresh mozzarella
generous ³/₈ cup / 100 ml olive oil
salt, pepper to taste

For the decoration:
4 small cherry tomatoes
half a bunch of chives

In the past, olive oil was not as lauded as it is now, said to raise one's cholesterol levels and contain too much fat. Nutritionists, if they recommended it at all, did so only reluctantly. But these days, pure, extra-virgin olive oil is highly touted, and enjoys the reputation of being one of the sun's true gifts. Master chefs like Ducasse and Troisgros are especially partial to it; this appetizer, from Chef Alain Burnel, celebrates it well.

French master chefs get their oil from Maussane-les-Alpilles, a little village near Baux-de-Provence in the magnificent Provence district in the south of France. The region's oil mills are famous all over the world. Each process – from selecting the olives to the actual milling – is repeated four times, carried out with utmost care according to the old Provençal traditions. Following these time-tested methods, this area produces a most extraordinary olive oil with a delicate flavor.

But olive oil alone is not enough; the tomatoes selected have to be firm, not too watery, very fresh, and, of course, very tasty. The so-called Roma tomatoes combine all these qualities, particularly during the sunny months of July and August when they are in season. Otherwise, use vine-ripened globe or beef-steak tomatoes. After the tomatoes are peeled they should be dried thoroughly before being marinated in olive oil – from Maussane, if at all possible, according to our chef.

Lavender lends the olive oil an authentic Provençal touch, evoking an image of the huge lavender fields that stretch like a mauve carpet all the way to the horizon. In this recipe, the lavender sprigs (with their flowers) are marinated in olive oil and placed in the sun; if one is lucky enough to live in a sunny region, forty-eight hours are usually enough.

1. Peel and seed the tomatoes. Dry well, cut out rounds, and dry again with paper towels. Bake in a 430 °F / 220 °C oven for 12 minutes.

2. Pour olive oil over the tomatoes, salt them, and set them aside to cool. Slice the fresh Mozzarella into strips. Marinate the lavender in olive oil and leave to steep.

Oil and Lavender

3. Fill small baking molds with one layer of tomatoes, one layer of Mozzarella, another layer of tomatoes, and so on. Roll out the puff pastry and cut it to fit the baking molds.

4. Cover the filled baking molds with puff pastry and bake for 15 minutes. Cool and turn over onto the plates. Sprinkle a few drops of olive oil and a few lavender flowers around the tart, and garnish it with chive sprigs and a cherry tomato centerpiece. Serve at room temperature.

Loch Fyne Mussels

Preparation time: 35 minutes
Cooking time: 10 minutes
Chilling time: approximately 1 hour
Difficulty: ★★

Serves four

3 lb / 1½ kg mussels (see below)

For the salmon filling
14 oz / 400 g salmon fillet
1 shallot
2 large egg whites
generous 1 cup / 250 ml cream

1 oz / 15 ml cognac (or brandy)
a pinch of cayenne pepper
salt, pepper to taste

For the sauce:
4 tsp / 20 g Keta caviar (see below)
4 tsp / 20 g butter
generous 1 cup / 250 ml cream
⅔ cup / 150 ml mussel juice
2 tbsp / 30 ml white wine
quarter bunch of chives (to yield 1 tbsp / 15 g chopped)
1 shallot
salt, pepper to taste

Our chef Stewart Cameron, from Scotland, bases this appetizer on the renowned mussels farmed in the Loch Fyne area on Scotland's west coast. Loch Fyne is one of those rare examples of a haven for saltwater and freshwater fish alike, and this recipe, combining salmon roe and mussels, reflects that quality. As opposed to the larger versions of the mollusc from Spain or the Mediterranean Bouchot mussels, here Chef Cameron calls for medium-sized mussels. And in honor of the old adage that a good mussel is either open or closed, these are opened, filled, and then tied shut to cook. Finally, they are served open, adorned with globes of salmon roe.

The trick in this recipe lies in filling the mussel shells as full as possible. For this reason, remove the thin membrane-like skin inside the shells before spooning in the filling. You have probably never tied up a mussel to keep it closed before, but without this precautionary measure the recipe can not be prepared correctly. As the filling should not be too stiff, it is important not to add too much egg white.

Keta caviar is a cured salmon roe imported from Norway. Though Chef Cameron often uses it as an integral component of his recipes, here it is actually used only for decoration. Since its flavor goes so well with the other ingredients, you can certainly be generous when you sprinkle it over the mussels.

As far as any substitutions or additions, Chef Cameron relates that, after many failed attempts at using oysters in this recipe, he must advise against it. Other than that, any variations in the combination making up the filling are welcome, even if it is only to enjoy more fully the multitude of both saltwater and freshwater delicacies from Loch Fyne.

1. To prepare the filling, chop the shallot. Combine the salmon with cognac, chopped shallot, egg whites, and cayenne pepper; puree. Refrigerate for approximately 15 minutes, add cream, and refrigerate once more.

2. Wash the mussels thoroughly and cook them briefly over a high heat until they open up. Shell and set aside the flesh. Fill half the mussel shells with the salmon filling.

with Salmon Filling

3. Place the mussel flesh back into the shells, on top of the filling. Close both halves of the shells and tie them up. Poach the mussels for about five minutes, as this will be enough to cook the filling.

4. Remove the strings and the top half of the shell, and arrange the filled mussels in a star pattern on each plate. For the sauce, sauté a teaspoon of chopped shallots in butter, add the white wine, and reduce to half the amount. Then add the mussel juice and reduce once more. Stir in the cream and strain. Sprinkle with chopped chives and Keta caviar.

Preparation time: 2 hours
Cooking time: 20 minutes
Difficulty: ★★

Serves four

For the ravioli dough:
1¼ cups / 300 g flour
3 eggs
half a bunch of spinach
 (to yield generous 1 oz / 40 g)

For the sauce:
1 eggplant
2 zucchini

generous ³/₈ cup / 100 ml cream
generous ³/₈ cup / 100 g butter
half a bunch of thyme
salt to taste

For the filling:
scant ½ lb / 200 g fish (such as halibut, sole,
 cod)
3½ oz / 100 g Ricotta
1 shallot
½ cup / 120 ml white wine
½ tbsp / 10 g butter
half a bunch of parsley
salt, pepper to taste

There exist innumerable Italian pasta dishes, many of which have whimsical, memorable names. A mixture of green spinach-dyed noodles and golden-yellow egg noodles, for instance, is called *paglia e fieno*, or hay and straw. In the case of this appetizer from our inventive chef Marco Cavalucci, green and yellow ravioli are shaped like half-moons, thus aptly named *mezzeluna*. Adapted by our chef to the taste of the time, this traditional recipe has conquered a widespread public.

Ricotta, a fresh sheep's milk cheese of remarkable versatility, provides an ideal addition to the filling made of Adriatic fish. Raw or cooked, it works well in a wide array of combinations, from salads to appetizers, from main courses to desserts.

As Chef Cavalucci emphasizes, the choice of fish must never be left to chance: whatever is used and in whatever combina-

tion, be it halibut, sole, or cod, for instance, it should all hail from the same maritime region and have certain common qualities. The delicate character and fine structure of the three fish mentioned means they will work well together, and harmonize perfectly with the spices used here. You could, of course, also use ocean perch or monkfish, but under no circumstances should you use salmon or goatfish, as their flavor is too strong for this appetizer.

The vegetable sauce, laced with thyme, lends the dish a certain lightness. If you wish, substitute other ingredients for the zucchini and eggplant, such as yellow peppers, boletus mushrooms, or even lentils. Let the old kitchen adage, "It should look good, taste good, and be easy to digest," guide you.

1. Chop the shallot and parsley. Clean and cut the fish into pieces; steam in butter with the chopped shallots. Add white wine and reduce. Add the parsley and set aside to cool. Set a small portion aside for garnishing. Stir in Ricotta, salt and pepper, and puree the mixture in a blender or food processor. Blanch and chop the spinach.

2. Prepare the ravioli dough and dye some of it with the spinach. Allow to sit for an hour. Roll out the dough and cut out small rounds. Spoon the fish filling onto these, fold in half, and shape into half-moons.

Vegetables and Thyme

3. Dice the eggplant and zucchini finely, season with salt and thyme, and fry in 3$^1\!/_2$ tbsp / 50 g of butter. Keep half warm, add the cream to the other half, and cook until done.

4. Cook the ravioli in salted water (until al dente), drain, and add the remaining butter. Puree and strain the cooked vegetables. Pour this sauce onto pre-warmed plates. Arrange the ravioli on top in the shape of a flower, alternating between green and yellow half-moons. Place the pieces of fish and the rest of the diced vegetables in the center as a garnish.

Sheep's Milk Cheese Raviol

Preparation time: 1 hour 15 minutes
Cooking time: 40 minutes
Difficulty: ★★

Serves four

For the pepper cream:
2 yellow peppers
1 shallot
scant ¼ cup / 50 ml cream
2 tbsp / 30 g butter
salt to taste

For the filling:
7 oz / 200 g Ricotta
7 oz / 200 g aged sheep's milk cheese
2 egg yolks
½ tsp / 3 g grated nutmeg
1 bunch of parsley
salt, pepper to taste

For the ravioli dough:
1¼ cups / 300 g flour
3 eggs

For the decoration:
1 red pepper

Once again, credit is due to Marco Cavalucci, for reminding us that filled pasta comes in countless varieties, the only limits being the chef's creativity. Certainly, the art of preparing ravioli allows the imagination to go unfettered, and yet requires extraordinary culinary skills.

Chef Cavalucci provides a typical Italian example, here using two different kinds of sheep's milk cheese that are equally popular on the peninsula. One is Ricotta, a two- to three-day-old sheep's milk cheese from the Emilia-Romagna region, recognizable by its smooth consistency. The other one is a classic cheese made from curdled sheep's milk, which matures for several months, if not for over a year, by which point it assumes a considerably stronger character. These two cheeses harmonize very well, provided the latter has not exceeded its maturity and, as a result, exudes too strong an aroma. Ravioli

may of course also be prepared with other types of sheep's milk cheese, even with *pecorino di fossa* – its name referring to its three-month-long maturation process, which takes place in a hole in the ground. The variety of flavors, which may all be combined with each other, thus provide innumerable options for ravioli fillings.

On the other hand, however, one should take into account the mildness of the peppers, for the contrast between this vegetable's sweet flavor and the filling's strong taste is what will render this recipe a solid success. Among all the different color varieties of the sweet bell pepper, our chef recommends choosing the yellow variety, which is tender and juicy with a glossy, smooth skin.

1. To prepare the yellow pepper cream, chop the shallot and then fry it in butter. Finely dice the peppers, then add to the shallot with some water and salt; cook until soft. Puree in the blender or food processor, then strain and add the cream. Cook again until the sauce is smooth and creamy, then let it sit in a warm place.

2. Melt the different types of cheese in a double boiler and then stir in the other ingredients.

with Yellow Pepper Cream

3. Prepare the ravioli dough from flour and eggs, form into a ball, and set aside to rest for one hour. Roll out the dough into two sheets of similar size. Place little balls of the filling onto the one sheet and cover with the other. Cut into traditional square ravioli with a pastry cutter, then cook in plenty of water. Cut the red pepper into long, fine strips.

4. Briefly fry the ravioli and the strips of red pepper in butter. Cover the center of the pre-warmed plates with the pepper cream, arrange the ravioli on top, and decorate with the red pepper strips.

Scampi Risotto with Boletus

Preparation time: 30 minutes
Cooking time: 45 minutes
Difficulty: ☆

Serves four

12 prawns, scant $^1/_8$ lb / 50g each
scant $^7/_8$ cup / 200 g Italian Arborio rice
$10^1/_2$ oz / 300 g fresh boletus mushrooms
4 violet artichokes
1 large onion (to yield generous $^1/_8$ cup /
    40 g chopped)
1 oz / 30 g Provence black truffles
scant $^1/_4$ cup / 50 ml truffle juice
1 cup / 250 ml extra virgin olive oil

4 whole, large leaves of basil
$^1/_4$ cup / 50 g butter
$^1/_4$ lb / 50 g Parmesan cheese
salt, fresh-ground pepper to taste

For the scampi stock:
1 carrot (to yield generous 1 oz /
    40 g chopped)
1 onion (to yield 1 generous 1 oz /
    40 g chopped)
1 celery stalk (to yield generous 1 oz /
    40 g chopped)
1 clove of garlic
1 sprig of thyme
$^2/_3$ cup / 150 ml white wine

Here, courtesy of Chef Francis Chauveau, we are introduced to various specialties – truffles from Provence in the south of France, risotto from Italy, and scampi from the Mediterranean – combined to make a Mediterranean treasure.

Risotto alla milanaise is famous all over the world. It is traditionally prepared from a variety of rice, Nano Vialone, that is renowned south of the Alps, but unfortunately very difficult to find in shops. Carnaroli, on the other hand, another popular type, is more common; even more common still is Arborio, now a fixture in American gourmet shops. The latter is what Chauveau has chosen.

Since Arborio rice's thick grains contain a high starch content, the rice should not be washed before it is cooked. Instead it is fried in olive oil with chopped onions, and then dark brown, light-veined truffles – mashed with a fork ahead of time – are added. While cooking the rice, add scampi stock (made from prawns) regularly to prevent the rice from drying out: Chef Chauveau recommends crushing the prawn heads before cooking to lend the stock even more flavor. Should prawns be unavailable, use langoustines or northern lobsters. To ensure the dish's creamy consistency, the rice should be stirred gently with a wooden spoon. The result will be a gorgeous risotto in which the boletus mushrooms act like a soft counterpoint to the shrimp's firmer flesh.

1. Mash the truffles with a fork to soften them. Chop the onions. Fry with the rice in olive oil until golden, then add the mashed truffles and braise. For the scampi stock, shell the prawn tails, cut lengthwise into two pieces, and remove the guts. Crush the heads and fry together with the vegetable mixture mentioned above. Add a dash of white wine and water, cook for 30 minutes and strain.

2. Pour the scampi stock over the rice. Cook for 18 minutes, repeatedly adding a little stock while stirring gently with a wooden spoon. Add the truffle juice and, if necessary, more stock. Stir in butter and a little olive oil to render the rice soft and creamy.

Mushrooms and Truffle Essence

3. Remove the leaves of the artichokes, cut the hearts and stems into slices. Clean the boletus mushrooms and slice as well. Fry the artichokes and mushrooms separately. Cut four long, pointed strips from a chunk of Parmesan cheese. Strip leaves off the basil, and fry the basil leaves in oil. Fry the scampi briefly, but over a high heat.

4. To serve, spread a layer of risotto over the entire plate, then arrange the boletus and artichokes on top. Heap the scampi in the center, and decorate with cheese strips and basil leaves.

Green Asparagus with

Preparation time:	20 minutes
Cooking time:	10 minutes
Difficulty:	☆

Serves four

3 bunches green, white, or violet asparagus
  (to yield 32 good spears)
¼ cup / 60 g coarse salt (to add to the cooking
  water)
2 fresh, firm eggplants (to yield ⅝ lb / 300 g
  chopped)
⅛ cup / 30 g coarse salt (to add to the cooking
  water)

To season the eggplants:
1 tbsp / 30 ml olive oil
1 clove of garlic
half a bunch of dill or fennel
2 oz / 60 g black olives

For the sauce:
⅓ cup / 80 g butter
scant ¼ cup / 50 ml water
1 tsp / 5 g green aniseed
juice and grated peel of 1 lemon
½ cup / 125 ml olive oil
salt, pepper to taste

This appetizer, from Chef Jacques Chibois, combines three gastronomic specialties from the area surrounding Cannes in the south of France – asparagus, eggplants, and black olives. The combined colors of these ingredients will appeal to the eye as much as their blending flavors please the palate.

Chef Chibois recommends green or white asparagus – particularly the violet type, with tips that have blushed purple from being exposed to the sun for a few hours, giving them a slightly stronger flavor. If you must store the asparagus for a few days before preparing the dish, Chibois advocates wrapping it in a damp cloth and refrigerating it in a horizontal position. It will be cooked in water to which coarse sea salt has been added: this salt contains more iodine, which will keep the spears tender and supple. The best eggplants to use are firm with a smooth, shiny skin; they should also be as young as possible (and therefore of a smaller size and with fewer seeds) to reduce the amount of time they need to be cooked. The olives, of course, should be small and juicy: look for the so-called Nice olives, which have to be blanched to rid them of the brine in which they are preserved, but which have a superior, redolent flavor.

Take care when preparing the butter sauce, as, being very delicate, it can easily curdle if labored over for too long. Finally, this recipe would be incomplete without making reference to the green aniseed (not to be mistaken for star anise) employed here, whose subtle, typically southern flavor plays an important role in this appetizer.

1. Peel the asparagus, tie into bundles, and cut the bottoms to the same length. Add coarse salt and asparagus to boiling water and cook, uncovered, for ten minutes. Rinse with hot water and keep warm.

2. Skin the eggplants and cut them into cubes of approximately ½ in / 1 cm. Cut the skin into thin strips, cook in salted water, and immediately rinse under cold water to stop the cooking process. Soak the eggplant cubes in water for 15 minutes, then cook in boiling water for five minutes; rinse under cold water and drain for an hour.

Olives and Aniseed

3. Place the cubed eggplant in a non-stick frying pan with olive oil, garlic, salt, pepper, and half the black olives, and brown briefly. Seed the other half of the olives, cut into eighths, and blanch twice.

4. Boil up the aniseed in water, add butter and olive oil as well as grated lemon peel, a dash of lemon juice, salt and pepper. Lastly, add the other half of the olives to the sauce. Arrange the eggplants, sprinkled with lemon juice to keep their color, on the plates, place asparagus on top, and pour the sauce over. Decorate with olives and small sprigs of dill.

Anchovy

Preparation time: 45 minutes
Cooking time: 20 minutes
Difficulty: ★★

Serves four

1 lb / 450 g fresh anchovies (approximately 80 fish)
8 medium-sized potatoes
20 large tomatoes
2 large onions
1 bouquet garni
generous 1 oz / 40 g black olives

2 tsp / 10 ml sherry vinegar
1/2 cup / 125 ml olive oil
half a bunch of chives (to yield 2 tbsp chopped)
1 bunch of basil
salt, pepper to taste

For the dressing:
1/2 cup / 125 ml olive oil
4 tsp / 20 ml lemon juice
4 large pieces of cod liver
salt, pepper to taste

Chef Michel Del Burgo, representing the French region of Languedoc-Roussillon, once prepared an enormous anchovy gâteau at an official reception in Barcelona. The recipe is set out here, albeit in much smaller proportions, and provides a rare opportunity to appreciate the delicate, unforgettable flavor of fresh anchovies.

The Europeans know only one type of anchovy, as a true anchovy hails from the Mediterranean region, while there are countless other fishes labeled anchovies that are not, in fact, the real thing. Anchovies, which belong to the herring family, travel in the summer months in big shoals, swimming just beneath the surface of the sea. They spend the winter breeding at the bottom of the ocean. The fishermen of the Mediterranean lure them at night with their searchlights and catch them by

their thousands in fine-meshed trawling nets. The harbor of Sete, a particularly rich site for the fish, is the main center for the anchovy trade.

When fresh, anchovies are roughly four to five inches (ten to fifteen centimeters) long, with shiny eyes and stiff and fragile bodies. Once the head is removed, filleting and removing the relatively big bones is easy. For this recipe, which centers around an olive oil and lemon juice dressing, cod liver is an important ingredient. If the liver is well prepared and passed through a sieve, it will make a delicious, even, creamy sauce. For the base of the tarts, slightly floury potatoes (such as Idaho) are just as suitable as new potatoes. And, if fresh anchovies are unavailable, small sardines will do as well, although their flavor is not quite as pronounced.

1. Gut and clean the anchovies as described above and wash thoroughly. Arrange on a stainless steel plate in a rosette, using a ring of approximately 5 in / 15 cm in diameter. Skin, seed, and coarsely chop the tomatoes. Chop the onions finely and fry in olive oil. Add the tomatoes and bouquet garni, season, and reduce the liquid a little.

2. Cook and peel the potatoes. Mash with a fork to form the bases of the tarts. Add a little olive oil, sherry vinegar, salt, pepper, and chopped chives. Warm this mixture in a bowl. Seed the black olives and chop into small pieces.

Tarts

3. For the vinaigrette, mix olive oil and lemon juice. Mash the cod liver pieces with a fork, add the sauce, season, and pass through a fine sieve. Add the olive pieces and the chopped basil leaves to the tomatoes and season to taste.

4. Use the same rings as for the anchovy rosettes and spoon in a $^1/_2$ in / 1 cm thick layer of potatoes, followed by an equally thick layer of tomatoes. In the meantime, bake the anchovy rosettes under the grill and place them on top of the tarts with the help of a spatula. Serve decorated with chives and basil leaves, and dribbled with the sauce.

Lamb Sweetbreads

Preparation time: 1 hour
Cooking time: 10 minutes
Difficulty: ★★

Serves four

generous 1 lb / 500 g lamb sweetbreads
1 bunch of young carrots
1 bunch of green asparagus (to yield
  12 spears)
6 purple artichokes
1 zucchini
2³/₄ oz / 80 g young peas
3¹/₂ oz / 100 g small, fresh fava beans
1 bunch of chives
juice of 1 lemon
¹/₈ cup / 25 g flour

For the vinaigrette:
3 shallots (to yield scant ¹/₃ cup / 80 g)
generous 1 cup / 250 ml balsamic vinegar
generous ³/₈ cup / 100 ml olive oil

For the veal broth:
generous ¹/₂ lb / 250 g veal (soup bone, etc.)
1 tomato
2 carrots
2 onions
1 bouquet garni
²/₃ cup / 150 ml white wine
¹/₃ cup / 80 ml port
¹/₄ cup / 50 g butter
half a bunch of chervil
half a bunch of chives
salt, pepper to taste

Chef Michel Del Burgo was in Flamanville in northern France when he discovered the exquisite flavor of lamb sweetbreads, although his homeland, the Basque region, has a similar specialty called *atxuria*. In both cases the sweetbreads are from lamb that are quite young – no older than nine or ten weeks, and no heavier than twenty or twenty-two pounds (a generous kilo).

Offal should always be prepared and consumed immediately. The sweetbreads are first placed into ice-cold water and then cleaned thoroughly. Before being fried briefly over a high heat, the thin skin surrounding them must be removed.

The vegetables chosen for this dish are well-known and loved amongst the Basques, from the fava beans (known in Europe as broad beans), to the artichokes. Fava beans in particular are a Basque favorite, used in soups and ragouts or as a raw ingredient in salads.

Always make sure all the vegetables are fresh and, whenever possible, cook them only until *al dente*. This applies above all to the peas, which ought to be prepared first. Chef Del Burgo always finds fresh vegetables in the markets of his hometown of Carcassonne. But increasing varieties of fresh vegetables are generally available at any time of the year, and sometimes there is even a surprising selection of new types of produce.

1. Remove the artichoke leaves and partially sever the stems. Sprinkle the hearts with lemon juice, cover, and cook in salted water with a little lemon juice and flour. Remove the fine hairs (the choke) after cooking. Peel the carrots and retain the greens. Cook all the vegetables separately in salted water, then leave to cool.

2. For the veal broth, brown the meat pieces, add the bouquet garni and the vegetables, then pour on the white wine and port. Reduce the liquid, add water and cook; pass through a fine sieve. For the vinaigrette, sauté the shallots in olive oil, add the balsamic vinegar, reduce, add the veal broth and reduce again.

with Fresh Vegetables

3. Blanch the sweetbreads and set aside to cool, then pan-fry in butter and oil until golden brown. Chop shallots and chives. Add the chopped shallots, a little broth, olive oil, the chives, chervil leaves and the juice of a lemon to the reduced vinaigrette and season.

4. Heat the vegetables in butter again, adding the fava beans and peas at the last minute. Serve the vegetable mixture with the sweetbreads on plates, sprinkled with vinaigrette and garnished with fresh herbs.

Scrambled Eggs in Waffle Pastry

Preparation time: 20 minutes
Cooking time: 5–7 minutes
Difficulty: ★

Serves four

8 eggs
2 sea urchins
generous 1oz / 40 g truffles
4 tsp / 20 g butter
1/3 cup / 80 ml heavy cream
3 sprigs of chervil (to yield 1 tsp / 5 g chopped)
6 sheets phyllo dough, or 3/4 lb / 350 g puff
   pastry (see basic recipes)
pepper to taste

For the sea urchin sauce:
1 tsp / 5 g sea urchin flesh
2 tsp / 10 g butter
generous 3/8 cup / 100 ml cream
juice of 1 lemon
1/2 bunch cilantro

For the tomato puree:
5 1/4 oz / 150 g tomatoes
1 bouquet garni
2 shallots
2 cloves of garlic
salt, pepper to garlic

During the open season for sea urchins from early May to the end of August, sophisticated dishes often appear on menus in Japan, Europe, and the United States to take advantage of this marine delicacy. To balance their extremely pronounced iodine flavor, sea urchins are here served with scrambled eggs and truffles; the concoction, from Chef Phillippe Dorange, will certainly delight your guests.

There are three types of edible sea urchins available: green, black, and purple. The latter should be given preference. This type lives on the bottom of the sea at a depth of some one hundred yards (one hundred meters), and is caught in cast-out fishing nets that are weighted down to comb the seabed as they drag across it. The only edible part of a sea urchin is the flesh inside the shell, where five "tongues" form a star shape around the very complex mouth opening. These so-called tongues are actually sex organs, and within them are contained minute, delicious eggs. After a complicated metamorphosis the eggs produce a new sea urchin, a miniature version of the adult. Since, as it has been proven, sea urchins can breed only in their natural environment, there are no farmed sea urchins for sale, and they remain a delicacy. When purchasing them, black, shiny spikes clinging tightly to the shell are the safest indication of freshness.

Never prepare scrambled eggs in a hurry, as any chef will tell you, or they will become tough. Instead, stir them gently with a wooden spoon and add the heavy cream right at the last minute. Use only very fresh eggs to obtain an even, creamy consistency.

1. Crack the eggs into a bowl. Chop the truffles, mix with the eggs, and set aside. Open the sea urchin, take the eggs out, and preserve the liquid. Wash the shells.

2. To prepare the sauce, pour the sea urchin liquid into a saucepan, add a dash of lemon juice, a little butter, and chopped, fresh cilantro. Heat up and bind with the eggs of the sea urchins. Whip with a whisk and pass through a sieve. Fold in the whipped cream. Prepare the tomato puree in a blender or food processor with the above ingredients.

with Sea Urchins and Truffles

3. Using a wooden spoon, prepare the scrambled eggs in a pan in melted butter. Season with salt and pepper, add heavy cream right at the end, and remove the mixture from the stove.

4. Spoon the scrambled eggs either into the sea urchin shells or into phyllo or puff pastry molds. Place the lukewarm eggs of the sea urchins on top. Spread a tablespoon of tomato puree in the center of each soup plate, arrange the shells or pastry molds on top and pour the sauce around them. Decorate with chopped truffles and chervil leaves.

Leipziger Medley

Preparation time: 30 minutes
Soaking time (optional): three hours
Cooking time: 30 minutes
Difficulty: ★★

Serves four

12 river crayfish
generous ¹/₂ lb / 250 g veal sweetbread
5¹/₄ oz / 150 g fresh morel mushrooms
generous 2 lbs / 1 kg spring vegetables
   (such as spring leeks, peas, carrots,
green and white asparagus, rutabaga,
   kohlrabi, celery stalks)
7 oz / 200 g butter
1 bouquet garni
1 tsp / 5 g nutmeg

salt, pepper to taste
4 puff pastry cookies
   (see basic recipes p. 803)

For the crayfish sauce (to yield ³/₄ cup / 200 ml):
crayfish carcasses
generous 1 cup / 250 ml chicken broth
4 tsp / 20 ml white wine
2 tsp / 10 ml brandy
2 tbsp / 30 ml cream
2 tsp / 10 ml grape seed oil
2 shallots
4 tsp / 20 g butter
4 tsp / 20 g tomato puree
1 bay leaf
1 clove
4 peppercorns
salt, pepper to taste

For the champagne sauce (to yield ³/₄ cup /
   200 ml):
(see basic recipes p. 806)

This recipe might well go down in German history, created by Chef Lothar Eiermann on October 3, 1990, when Germany became unified once again. The original title, *Leipziger Allerlei*, refers to a recipe from post-war Leipzig in the former German Democratic Republic, when even vegetables like carrots, asparagus, and peas were hard to come by. According to vague records, the original recipe also contained, somewhat surprisingly, veal sweetbreads and crayfish. Thus, here is our chef's own new version of this post-war recipe.

As Eiermann insists, veal sweetbreads, crayfish, and morels do not tolerate being substituted, so immediately set aside any intention to substitute one or another of these with more common produce. Also, the success of this recipe depends on the quality of the veal sweetbreads, which should, if at all possible, come from very young (preferably suckling) calves only. These should be no bigger than a man's fist and have an even color without blemishes or bruising. If still containing blood, they should be placed in cold water for a few hours and then cooked in one piece. Since the skin covering the sweetbread acts as a protection against excessive heat exposure, Eiermann recommends removing it only after cooking. Finally, follow the instructions carefully when preparing the crayfish sauce.

1. Clean the veal sweetbreads, and cook in seasoned water until pink. For the champagne sauce, add shallot, bay leaf, and pepper to the sweetbread stock and reduce to half the amount. Stir in cream and reduce again. Strain through a cloth, add Noilly (vermouth) and bring to a boil again. Stir in crème fraîche and butter. Lastly add champagne and season. Clean the morels and blanch with the vegetables.

2. Fry the crayfish carcasses over a high heat, add shallots, bay leaf, clove and pepper and fry again. Stir in the tomato puree and flambé with brandy. Add white wine and broth and reduce to half the volume. Finally stir in the cream and strain everything through a cloth. Whip up with butter and season to taste.

with Vegetables

3. Skin and slice the veal sweetbread, dust with flour, and fry in a bit of butter until golden brown. Sauté the morels, salt them lightly and mix with the bouquet garni.

4. Sauté the crayfish tails in butter. Proceed similarly with the various types of vegetables, then add the crayfish sauce. Cover the plates with the light sauce. Arrange vegetables, sweetbread, crayfish, and morels on top and decorate with a puff pastry cookie.

Preparation time: 45 minutes
Cooking time: 40 minutes
Difficulty: ★★★

Serves four

2 dozen mussels
1 pollack
1 large potatoe (such as Idaho or Yukon Gold)
6 cloves of garlic
6 egg yolks
generous $^3/_8$ cup / 100 ml olive oil
$^1/_2$ lb 250 g puff pastry (see basic recipes)
salt, pepper to taste

For the fish stock:
2 lb / 1 kg fish bones
2 onions
6 cloves of garlic
2 shallots
3 leeks (to yield generous 3 oz / 100 g of the white section)
3 celery stalks
peel of 2 oranges
scant $1^1/_2$ cups / 350 ml dry white wine
$^1/_4$ lb / 50 g butter
half a bunch of thyme
1 bay leaf
half a bunch of smooth-leaved parsley
pepper to taste

Here, Dutch chef Constant Fonk transforms the classic fish soup into a simple, yet inventive appetizer, where potatoes, a Dutch staple, substitute for bread croutons. Small puff pastry biscuits decorate the finished dish and provide a pleasant contrast to the melt-in-the-mouth fish tarts.

The success of this recipe depends to a large extent on the refined flavors of the fish stock, and on how long the pollack is cooked in it. If pollack is unavailable, other whitefish like monkfish or ocean perch are good alternatives. The mussels serve as an accompaniment: if possible search for Holland's so-called Zeeland mussels, which are the typical species of the local mussel production, and are presently experiencing a huge boom in the export business. Since they are relatively big, they are thus a bit more difficult to handle. But, on the other hand,

Dutch mussel farmers ensure that they are sand-free. French Bouchot mussels are also excellent in this dish, but they first have to be cleaned in salted water for an hour and a half. If you prefer, substitute these imported versions for a native North American mussel; just make sure you clean the shellfish thoroughly.

The potato must be thinly sliced and blanched before it is used for the tarts. As Chef Fonk relates, the tart molds he used were originally used for spice cookies, a specialty with jam filling that was predominantly baked in convents.

This appetizer must be served very hot. It will impress the gourmet with its pleasant presentation as well as its superb flavor.

1. Soak and clean the fish bones, soften in butter, and add white wine. Reduce the liquid, then pour on water again. Add the ingredients for the fish stock and cook for 25 minutes. Pass through a sieve and poach the pollack in this stock.

2. Boil the potato. Prepare the aïoli sauce in a blender, starting with the egg yolks, then adding five teaspoons of boiled potato, six crushed cloves of garlic, and olive oil. Bind the fish stock with half of this sauce. Open the mussels, place one piece of mussel flesh into each half, fill with aïoli sauce and grill in the oven.

Mussels and Sauce

3. Cut the raw potato into thin slices and blanch. Cover the base of the tart molds with a slice of potato and fill three-quarters full with the cooked pollack flesh.

4. Fill up the molds with the aïoli sauce and slide under a hot grill for three minutes. Prepare the puff pastry if you have not already done so. Shape the puff pastry into crescent moons and bake in the oven for 20 minutes, initially at 390 °F / 200 °C, later reducing the heat to 355 °F / 180 °C, until golden brown. Serve the tarts, as pictured, in deep plates in a pool of sauce with the mussels and a puff pastry

Black Salsify with

Preparation time: 45 minutes
Soaking time: 12 hours
Cooking time: 1 hour, 30 minutes
Difficulty: ★

Serves four

8.8 lb / 4 kg black salsify
7 oz / 200 g black radish
1 lemon
one dozen fresh walnuts
1 tbsp / 15 g paprika

scant ¹/₂ cup / 120 g flour
scant 1 cup / 200 ml olive oil
quarter bunch of marjoram
salt to taste

For the hollandaise sauce:
(see basic recipes p. 801)

Our chef, Phillippe Groult, enjoys crusading against culinary prejudices. Here he fights for the black salsify. This quite unappetizing-looking vegetable, also known as oyster root in the United States, makes an excellent accompaniment to meat dishes. The smoother the surface and firmer the flesh of these highly absorbent roots, the greater the freshness. For this appetizer, choose salsify that is about as thick as a thumb, as any thinner and it would not prepare well.

Opinions vary as to how long salsify should be cooked for. At any rate, it is first soaked in cold water with two heaping tablespoons (thirty grams) of flour and some lemon juice for one hour. Smaller pieces will require a shorter cooking period.

Fresh walnuts, here soaked overnight before being cooked, are available from October until March. Their flavor goes very well with black radish, which is very popular in Eastern Europe but virtually scorned (for no good reason) in the west. This bulbous root vegetable is high in vitamin C and as easy to prepare as carrots. Red radishes are easier to get hold of, particularly in the U.S., and may be used instead.

This dish is always accompanied by a hollandaise sauce enriched with unsweetened almond milk cream, which rounds off the flavor of the salsify. The paprika, on the other hand, moderates the sharpness of the radish. This appetizer should be served lukewarm.

1. The night before, soak the walnuts, still in their shells, in sugar water. The day of preparation, begin by washing the salsify under running water, peel, and cut into 5 in / 12 cm pieces. Soak in water with one teaspoon of flour per cup, and add the juice of one lemon. Bring to a boil. Cook accordingly: salsify with a diameter of approximately ¹/₂ in / 1 cm needs to be cooked for one hour and ten minutes; thicker salsify should be cooked for slightly longer.

2. Whip up the hollandaise sauce over a low heat with egg yolks and four ladles of water. Warm the butter, gradually stir into the sauce, season, and add cayenne pepper and four drops of almond milk.

Fresh Walnuts

3. Drain the salsify on a cloth, dip in olive oil, and dust the ends of the spears with paprika. Shell the pre-soaked nuts. Peel the black radish, slice thinly and place in cold water.

4. Pour 3 tbsp / 45 g of hollandaise sauce onto each plate and arrange the salsify in an attractive pattern on top. Decorate with three radish slices and three walnuts per plate, dust with paprika, and scatter a few marjoram leaves over the arrangement.

Paul Heathcote's

Preparation time: 1 hour 30 minutes
Soaking time: 12 hours
Cooking time: 3 hours, 45 minutes
Difficulty: ★★★

Serves four

1 lb / 450 g veal (or lamb) sweetbreads
1³/₄ cups / 450 ml pig's blood
sausage skin (enough for about 20 sausage slices)
2 large potatoes
1 onion
8 cocktail onions

scant ¹/₄ cup / 50 g dried Navy beans (or dried black-eyed peas)
4 carrots (to yield scant ¹/₄ cup / 50 g cut)
scant ¹/₄ cup / 50 g oats
scant ¹/₄ cup / 50 g raisins
generous 1 cup / 250 ml light veal broth
generous ³/₈ cup / 100 ml white grape vinegar
¹/₂ cup / 125 ml olive oil
scant ¹/₂ lb / 200 g butter
1 sprig of rosemary
1 sprig of thyme
3 bay leaves
salt, pepper

Paul Heathcote, of England, created this very personal version of black pudding at the request of a French restaurant in the Champagne region. They had originally envisaged a recipe based on caviar, truffles or foie gras. Many a famous British chef has since included this recipe on his menu, and its success remains unrivalled.

Chef Heathcote deviates from the old tradition of mixing fat cubes into the black pudding, substituting them with raisins marinated in vinegar. Fresh yet slightly congealed pig's blood is ideal for the preparation of this dish. It requires concentration and care, as the blood must not boil, but should curdle, in a double boiler. Heat the water in the double boiler to exactly 180 °F / 82 °C to attain the required 167 °F / 75 °C in the sausage itself. In Britain, oats and black pudding are old friends.

The various flavors of these ingredients are harmoniously enhanced by thyme and rosemary and especially by the bay leaves, which are crushed to develop a stronger aroma.

Veal sweetbreads, fresh and in immaculate condition, take the lead role – fried in a pan to sweat out as much juice as possible. Lamb sweetbreads may be used as an alternative.

For the mashed potatoes, we use a floury, and thus absorbent, type of potato. Of some one thousand different types possible, our chef recommends the Maris Piper, which is very popular in Britain, though there are certainly other varieties available in the U.S. that will work as well. For the beans, substitute black-eyed peas if Navy beans are unavailable; either variety will have to be soaked and then pre-cooked.

1. The night before, soak the dried beans in a large pot of cold water. On the day of preparation, slow-cook the rinsed beans for three hours. Blanch the sweetbreads in boiling water for one minute. Remove the skin membrane. Chop the sweetbread and fry the pieces in olive oil until golden brown. Marinate the raisins and a bay leaf in enough vinegar for it to be totally absorbed. Steam the raisins over a low heat without caramelizing them; the vinegar in them should evaporate.

2. Heat the pig's blood in a double boiler, stirring continually, until it curdles. Pick thyme and rosemary leaves off the sprigs. Mix all the ingredients indicated (onion, oats, veal sweetbread, raisins and herbs) with the blood and season to taste.

Black Pudding

3. Fill sausage skins with this mixture and poach in a double boiler at exactly 180 °F / 82 °C for 40 minutes. Cook the beans as well as the carrots and the cocktail onions in veal broth with crushed bay leaves for half an hour. Take out some of the vegetables and pass the rest through a sieve.

4. Cook the potatoes in their jackets, then skin and mash them with a fork. Add butter, salt, and pepper. To serve, slice the cooled blood sausages, fry in olive oil, and place on top of the mashed potatoes. Reheat the retained vegetables in the sauce and spoon around the mashed potatoes.

"Klippfisk'

Preparation time: 30 minutes
Soaking time: 48 hours
Cooking time: 10 minutes
Difficulty: ★★

Serves four

generous $^1/_2$ lb / 250 g dried salt cod
7 oz / 200 g potatoes
1 packet of brek pastry (see below)
1 clove of garlic
$^3/_4$ cup / 200 ml olive oil
generous $^3/_8$ cup / 100 ml whole milk

$^1/_4$ cup / 50 g melted butter
1 bunch of basil
salt, cayenne pepper to taste

For the sauce and the garnish:
1 green pepper
4 large tomatoes
1 clove of garlic
2 onions
1 dozen black olives
generous $^3/_8$ cup / 100 ml olive oil
generous $^3/_8$ cup / 100 ml fish stock

Dried cod pickled in coarse salt is not only popular in Norway but all over Europe, especially in Spain and Portugal, which actually import a large portion of what Scandinavia produces. Our recipe for crisp fish tarts with bacalao sauce (*bacalao* is the Spanish term for dried and salted cod) unites connoisseurs from both Nordic and southern European countries. Cod is mainly found in the cold waters of the North Atlantic; in winter, fishermen catch it in large fish traps in the Norwegian fjords. The big commercial trawlers, carrying up to a thousand tons (tonnes) of fish, are naturally operating on a totally different scale.

Our chef Eyvind Hellstrøm is an expert in his field. He prefers to use air-dried cod, which contains more moisture and has therefore a smoother texture, and to retain its flavor he processes the fish puree as soon as it is cooked. Fish, potatoes, and milk blend well when they are all the same temperature. This mixture, with basil added, is shaped into small tarts and wrapped in brek or puff pastry, as desired; the former is a Tunisian specialty that has found its way into many other cuisines, as its delicate, flaky layers are ideal for many different dishes. Puff pastry, on the other hand, will give the tarts a slightly heavier feel. The spicy olive puree lends this dish a Mediterranean touch, and brings out the full flavor of the fish.

Bacalao sauce originates from Spain: this delicious blend of olive oil, onions, garlic, and tomatoes with a little added cod and piquant spices will certainly delight your guests. And, if you prefer, try using salted stringray instead, which, despite its smoother flesh and higher gelatin content, is similar in flavor and may be prepared the same way.

1. Steep the dried cod for 48 hours. Peel the garlic, blanch three times, puree, and set aside for the fish filling. Poach 5$^1/_4$ oz / 150 g of dried cod in milk, peel and cook the potatoes, and blend everything with the garlic puree. Season with salt and cayenne pepper.

2. Spread out layers of brek pastry or puff pastry rolled paper-thin (see basic recipes to prepare), place some fish mixture and a basil leaf on top, fold up and shape into little parcels.

3. Fry the parcels in butter and olive oil until golden brown. Blanch the pepper, skin; slice the tomatoes. Chop the onion finely and sauté in olive oil. Make a puree of black olives, garlic, and olive oil.

4. To prepare the bacalao sauce, sauté onions, tomatoes, and garlic in olive oil. Add the fish stock and the remaining 3¹/₂ oz / 100 g dried cod and reduce the liquid. Puree and season to taste. Serve three to a plate, ringed with sauce and garnished with garlic, olive paste, basil leaves, and tomato.

Garlic Soup with

Preparation time: 30 minutes
Cooking time: 20 minutes
Difficulty: ★

Serves four

generous 1 lb / 500 g small blue mussels
generous 1 lb / 500 g fresh garlic
generous 1 lb / 500 g potatoes
1 bunch of fresh sage
generous ³/₈ cup / 100 ml extra-virgin olive oil
generous 1 cup / 250 ml white wine

generous 3 cups / 750 ml whole milk
salt, pepper

In the ancient world, the healing powers of garlic were well known. In those days it was used to rid the body of parasites and ward off infections and colds, but it was also said to be hard to digest. Today, garlic is grown in Europe on a large scale predominantly in southern Italy and in the southwest of France, mainly cultivated in Saint-Clar in the Gers region. Although normally used as a flavoring, to spice sauces and meat, fish, or poultry dishes, garlic plays the leading role in this recipe.

When garlic is prepared together with potatoes and milk, it is easier to digest. Chef Alfonso Iaccarino, who grows his garlic, amongst other crops, on his own farm, suggests using young, fresh garlic of medium size that is harvested from May to September and that is not excessively strong in taste.

Very fresh garlic should dry for a few days before being used. It dries best in plaits, (and is sold that way in Saint-Clar) and hung in an airy room at the right temperature. Old garlic, on the other hand, often absorbs an earthy taste, and is not recommended; kept in the refrigerator for too long, even fresh garlic will lose some of its flavor.

So-called winter potatoes, such as round whites or Yukon gold, are best suited to ensure the creamy consistency of the soup, as they are well-suited to boiling. To round off their flavor, you can use rosemary, marjoram, or sage, which also serves as a lovely garnish. Despite its bitter aftertaste, sage is widely used in the whole Mediterranean region for its spicy aroma.

1. Peel and dice the potatoes. Sauté with the garlic over a low heat.

2. Cover the potatoes with a mixture of white wine and whole milk and bring to a boil.

Sage and Mussels

3. Cook the potatoes over a low heat for 20 minutes, then blend and strain. Season to taste and keep warm.

4. Wash the mussels, steam them, and shell. Serve the soup in deep plates, sink mussels into the liquid, and garnish with fresh herbs, such as sage, rosemary, or marjoram.

Goatfish in Pastry Coats with

Preparation time: 45 minutes
Cooking time: 20 minutes
Difficulty: ☆

Serves four

2 goatfish
1 packet of brek pastry sheets or ½ lb / 250 g
  puff pastry dough (see basic recipes)
2 globe tomatoes
1 large tomato (to yield 1 tbsp / 15 g tomato
  puree)
1 red pepper
1 green pepper
1 yellow pepper

1 egg yolk
4 cloves of garlic
2 shallots
4 leaves of green lettuce
3½ oz / 100 g green olives
4 tbsp / 50 g rice
2 tbsp / 30 ml champagne vinegar
3 tbsp / 50 ml olive oil
1 tbsp / 15 g white sugar
1 tbsp / 15 g grated ginger
1 tbsp / 15 g tapioca starch
generous ⅜ cup / 100 ml chicken stock
salt, pepper

According to our chef, André Jaeger, it is said that there is no better goatfish (otherwise known as red barbel or red mullet) than the goatfish from Bandol, a little fishing harbour on the French Mediterranean coast that also happens to be home to a wonderful wine. But, as Jaeger notes, the goatfish found in Norway and off the Canadian coast, and even in Switzerland, are also highly esteemed.

Goatfish in general seem to be the subject of frequent debate, and the editors do not want to get involved in the argument of whether red barbels caught in rocky waters are better than those living on muddy seabeds. The latter, however, are red-brown and their flavor is less distinct. Whether from rocky waters or muddy seabeds, goatfish are often used in the famous bouillabaisse. Tender and fragile, they must be handled with great care, in particular when they are filleted and freed from their masses of bones.

Do not cook goatfish for more than seven minutes or it may lose its tender flavor. Aware of this, our chef wraps his in a coat made of either Tunisian brek pastry dough, or puff pastry, to protect them against the oven's strong heat. And he lays the fillets skin side up inside the pastry to provide even more protection.

Since Chef Jaeger has spent much time in Asia, it is not surprising that his sweet pepper sauce conveys a strong eastern influence that Europeans might not be accustomed to, with ginger root and tapioca starch. Other ingredients used in the recipe, however, will be more common to a western palate, from the egg yolk used to seal the pastry sheets together to the nice big lettuce leaves with strong ribs used as an inner wrapper for this fish.

1. First cook the rice and wash the lettuce. Fillet the goatfish and carefully remove all the bones. Spread out the brek sheets or roll out the puff pastry into very thin layers. Place a lettuce leaf and a tablespoon of rice onto each square.

2. Salt the fillets and place them, skin side up, on top of the rice. Brush the pastry edges with egg yolk and seal. Bake in the oven at 480 °F / 250 °C for seven minutes.

Asian Sweet Pepper Sauce

3. *Quarter the peppers, remove the middle section and seeds, peel the rest and cut into $^1/_4$ in / $^1/_2$ cm wide strips. Peel the garlic and the shallots, cut into small slices and blanch in boiling water. Heat olive oil in a frying pan, add peppers, garlic and shallots and fry over a high heat. Puree one tomato.*

4. *Stir the tomato puree into the mixture, and leave to steep. Skin, seed, and chop the other tomatoes. Add these to the pan, pour on the chicken stock, cover, and braise over a low heat for five minutes. Seed and halve the olives and add them to the pan. Blend the tapioca starch with vinegar and add as well. Season with ground ginger, sugar, and salt.*

Oxtail Soup with

Preparation time: 25 minutes
Chilling time: 12 hours
Cooking time: 50 minutes
Difficulty: ★★

Serves four

2²/₃ oz / 80 g black truffles
7 oz / 200 g beef (to be minced)
14 oz / 400 g beef cheek
14 oz / 400 g oxtail
5 carrots (to yield 7 oz / 200 g))
3 onions (to yield 3¹/₂ oz / 100 g))

1 leek stalk
1 celery stalk
2 tbsp / 30 ml sherry vinegar
4 tbsp / 65 ml truffle juice
1 generous lb / 500 g puff pastry
  (see basic recipes p. 803)
3 egg yolks
generous ³/₈ cup / 100 g butter
quarter bunch of thyme
1 bay leaf
quarter bunch of parsley
salt, pepper to taste

This venerable soup has been on the menu of Paul Bocuse's famous restaurant in Collongnes-au-Mont-d'Or since 1975, and it is still greeted with great enthusiasm. Here, Chef Roger Jaloux presents its preparation.

Contrary to what some believe, the size of a truffle has actually no influence on its quality. The most famous truffles are found around Aups in Provence and in the Ardèche region. Collecting truffles can be a difficult undertaking: the pigs trained to dig out truffles, so-called "truffle pigs," also enjoy eating them; the dogs who sometimes take their place have been known to dig too enthusiastically; rain is another factor. There are even merchants, like the preeminent Messrs Dumont and Guyon, who have specialized exclusively in truffles; they have been supplying the world's top restaurants for more than twenty years. If you want to buy truffles yourself, beware of street vendors, and never buy truffles that have not been thoroughly cleaned: often the dirt clinging to them can weigh more than the truffles. Truffles are best preserved in an air-tight container with uncooked rice to absorb the moisture. As a bonus, when the rice is cooked, it will have absorbed the rich aroma of the truffles.

Puff pastry should never be baked for more than twenty minutes. Chef Jaloux recommends that the pastry and the soup be prepared a day ahead of time, and stored in a cool place overnight. This precautionary measure gives the pastry a firmer structure, and prevents it from collapsing in the oven or possibly sinking into the soup.

The soup itself does not require great cooking skills. Beef cheek and oxtail ensure its delicious flavor. For some reason that is incomprehensible to the editors, this refined delicacy is also called, rather rustically, a "shepherd's soup."

1. One day ahead of time, prepare the puff pastry; let it chill overnight; you may also want to prepare the soup a day ahead as well. Begin preparing the appetizer by cleaning the truffles thoroughly and slicing them thinly.

2. Cook broth from the beef and oxtail pieces (for 20 minutes). At the same time dice the vegetables and fry them in butter. Then dice the cooked meat finely.

Puff Pastry Hat

3. Spoon the cooled meat and the fried vegetables into soup bowls and mix. Place one tablespoon of truffles on top.

4. Fill the soup bowls with broth and season. Cover with a sheet of puff pastry, brush with egg yolk, and bake in the oven at 390 °F / 200 °C for 20 minutes.

Maultaschen with Rabbi

Preparation time: 1 hour 30 minutes
Cooking time: 15 minutes
Difficulty: ★★

Serves four

backs of 2 rabbits, including kidneys and liver
heads of 2 rabbits
5$\frac{1}{4}$ oz / 150 g vegetable brunoise of celery,
   carrots, leeks
2 shallots
generous $\frac{3}{8}$ cup / 100 ml rabbit or vegetable
   stock
$\frac{1}{4}$ cup / 50 ml vegetable oil
$\frac{1}{4}$ cup / 50 g butter
half a bunch of thyme

half a bunch of rosemary
salt, pepper to taste

For the carrot sauce:
7 oz / 200 g carrots
leaves from the carrot tops
2 shallots
$\frac{3}{4}$ cup / 200 ml rabbit or vegetable stock
$\frac{1}{4}$ cup / 50 g crème fraîche
$\frac{1}{4}$ cup / 50 g butter
scant $\frac{1}{4}$ cup / 50 ml white wine

For the pasta dough:
3 small eggs
generous 1 cup / 250 g flour
pinch of salt

In southern Germany, people love *Maultaschen*: pasta pockets that look like giant ravioli with open edges. This very filling dish originating from Swabia is most often served with a broth or with mixed salads. The version presented here by Chef Dieter Kaufmann is lighter and easier to digest. The rabbit meat used is low in fat and calories, but high in protein. Free-range rabbits fed on barley and other grains are ideal for this purpose. When you select a rabbit, make sure its legs are still soft to the touch, as this is an indication of freshness.

With a chef's sense of humor, the carrots in this dish are served with a nod to the famous Bugs Bunny cartoons. Young fresh carrots are ideal; they go very well with this dish and are available throughout the year. The Mediterranean herbs suggested by Dieter Kaufmann should only be used in moderation so as not to mask the vegetables' own flavors.

Instead of decorating with carrot leaves, you may of course garnish with other vegetables or herbs, such as leeks, chervil, or smooth-leaved parsley. It is mainly the color contrast that is important, so feel free to experiment. Finally, note that this dish is not only suitable as an appetizer, but could also liven up a family supper.

1. Prepare the pasta dough ahead of time. To prepare the dish, begin by finely cutting the vegetables for the brunoise, and chopping the shallots. Fillet the rabbit backs and fry the meat in butter along with the kidneys and livers. Add the rabbit heads, with 5$\frac{1}{4}$ oz / 150 g of finely cut vegetables and chopped shallots. Add a dash of the stock and cook for 15 minutes. Remove the rabbit brains and tongues.

2. Roll out the previously prepared pasta dough into sheets. Decorate half of them with carrot greens or other herbs, cut them into rectangles, cook in rapidly boiling salted water and rinse under cold water to stop the cooking process.

Meat in Carrot Butter

3. To prepare the carrot sauce, sauté chopped shallots and diced carrots in butter. Add the crème fraîche and the stock and cook for about ten minutes. Then mix and strain. Mix the white wine and the carrot greens with the sauce.

4. Cut each of the rabbit fillets into three pieces. Place one pasta rectangle onto each plate, top with rabbit meat, a piece of tongue, brains, kidney, and liver, sprinkle with stock, cover with another sheet of pasta and surround with the carrot sauce.

Preparation time: 25 minutes
Cooking time: 5 minutes
Difficulty: ☆

Serves four

1 bunch of stinging nettles (without flowers)
4 quail eggs
4 cups / 1 l chicken broth
half a bunch of chives (to yield 4 tbsp / 80 g chopped)
a pinch of aniseed powder
a pinch of fennel powder
salt, pepper to taste

For the roux:
1 tbsp / 15 g flour
1 tbsp / 15 g butter

Chef Örjan Klein, from Sweden, fashioned this dish to remind his guests that stinging nettles have a high iron content and are good for one's health. He was raised on this understanding, since his grandmother Hildur used to take him along when she went to collect stinging nettles for her delicious soup. Collecting these nettles is quite a complicated affair, and gloves are a must. But our chef is partial to this stinging nettle soup, and claims it is well worth the trouble. So, come early spring, he treats his guests to this delight. The appetizer has become so popular that the daily consumption amounts to more than three gallons (some fifteen liters), which of course, necessitates a whole army of people to gather the nettles, and many pairs of gloves.

In the past soups were the obligatory first course of each meal. In Sweden yellow pea soup was particularly popular. This filling soup, prepared with pork and bacon, was always served on a Thursday evening since, according to Catholic tradition, Friday was a day of abstinence from meat. It did not take long for the students of Uppsala, Sweden's oldest university, to invent their own version with hot punch.

For this recipe, one needs small, young nettles without flowers; once the plants have flowered they no longer have the same flavor. The vitamin content is also dependent on the cooking time. Stinging nettles should therefore be blanched for only two to three minutes. They are then chopped and added to the soup just before it is served. A quail egg looks very good as a decoration, but a small chicken egg or even a few salmon eggs will do as well.

1. Wash and blanch the nettles, rinse them under cold water, chop, and set aside.

2. Boil the chicken broth and bind with the roux while stirring with a whisk to obtain an evenly combined mixture.

Stinging Nettle Soup

3. Stir in aniseed powder and fennel powder and season to taste. Cook the quail eggs for five to six minutes.

4. Add the stinging nettles to the soup. Mix and serve in soup plates. Decorate with a quail egg and chopped chives, and serve immediately to retain the green color.

Chopped Calf's

Preparation time: 1 hour
Soaking time: 24 hours
Cooking time: 1 hour 15 minutes
Difficulty: ★ ★

Serves four

2 dozen large Belon oysters
2 shallots
4 slices of white bread
1 bunch of smooth-leaved parsley
coarse salt

For the calf's head:
generous 1 lb / 500 g calf's head
scant 1/8 lb / 50 g lean belly bacon
3 carrots (to yield 3½ oz / 100 g cut)
1 onion (to yield 1 oz / 30 g chopped)
2 cloves of garlic
1 bouquet garni
generous 2 cups / 500 ml red wine
generous 2 cups / 500 ml veal broth
2 tbsp / 30 g butter
coarse salt, pepper to taste

At three to four years old, oysters are fully matured and suitable for consumption; in some cultures, such as the ancient Greeks, even their shells were used, ground into a powder to make a love potion. Interestingly enough, the word has some etymological coincidences, as the Latin word for oyster, *ostrea*, is not at all related to the similar-sounding Greek word that refers to a pottery tool. However, some experts point out that the pottery tool has a similar shape to an oyster shell.

Oysters are generally consumed raw, but even cooked they have an ever-increasing following, since their tender and tasty flesh can certainly withstand heating. Of all the different types of oysters offered, the so-called Belon are the ones our Dutch chef, Robert Kranenborg, prefers for this recipe. They are farmed on the banks of the Belon River in the southern part of Brittany, and are now being cultivated in the United States as

well. It is of utmost importance that the temperature never exceeds 98.6° F / 37 °C when oysters are heated, requiring the use of a good thermometer.

As Chef Kranenborg relates, in his country, calf's head is very popular. One dish, called *Kalbspolet*, is a stew made from a calf's head and brightened with lettuce leaves and peas. The recipe presented here will delight many a guest. And, though it goes without saying, we will say it anyway: only use an absolutely fresh calf's head that has been steeped in water for a full day ahead. The same applies to veal knuckles, which may, if desired, substitute the calf's head.

One last bit of advice – a heavy, sun-blessed red wine, a Côtes-du-Rhône perhaps, is excellent for the sauce.

1. Steep the calf's head in water for 24 hours, then blanch, leave to cool, and cut into big chunks. Sauté the carrots, onions, garlic and diced bacon in a pot with butter. Add the calf's head and the bouquet garni and season with a pinch of coarse salt. Add a dash of red wine and fill the pot with veal broth.

2. Cover the pot with baking paper and bake in the oven at 320° F / 160 °C for an hour and 15 minutes. Remove the chunks of calf's head and refrigerate them. Strain the stock. Cut the chilled calf's head into small cubes. Chop parsley and shallots finely. Open the oysters and filter the juice. Poach the oysters briefly over a low heat and keep warm in a cloth.

Head with Oysters

3. Reduce the juice of the oysters. Add a little stock from the calf's head, bring to a boil and whip with butter until creamy. Cut the white bread slices into small cubes and fry in melted butter to make croutons.

4. Arrange the cleaned oyster shells on a bed of coarse salt and heat up in the oven. Place the oysters in the shells, spoon the meat cubes with shallots and parsley over them, pour some sauce over, and sprinkle with bread croutons.

Burgundy Snails with

Preparation time: 20 minutes
Cooking time: 5 minutes
Difficulty: ☆

Serves four

4 eggs
4 dozen snails
3½ oz / 100 g spinach
4½ oz / 125 g button mushrooms
3½ oz / 100 g cocktail onions
4 shallots
5¼ oz / 150 g belly bacon, salted

scant ⅞ cup / 200 g butter
generous 2 cups / 500 ml water
generous ⅜ cup / 100 ml red wine
generous ⅜ cup / 100 ml vinegar
1 bunch of chervil
salt, pepper to taste

For the red wine sauce:
4 cups / 1 l red wine
generous 2 cups / 500 ml veal broth
12 red shallots
1 tbsp / 15 g butter

Imagine you are in the heart of the Bourgogne (or Burgundy), facing the ingredients for an appetizer by Chef Jacques Lameloise. In front of you are the famous snails from that region as well as other typical ingredients, like onions, bacon, and button mushrooms. The age-old recipe for eggs poached in red wine is one of the many types of *meurette*, a specialty of the Bourgogne – essentially meaning a dish cooked in red wine, and deriving from the Old French.

This method of preparation is said to be derived from an old seafarers' custom, in which eggs were cooked in hot, spiced red wine. Chef Lameloise suggests poaching them simply in a mixture of water, vinegar, and red wine; the red wine sauce should be prepared separately. Although the original recipe demands red wine for poaching, there is nothing and nobody to stop you from using white wine.

As with any poached dish, the eggs used should be absolutely fresh and of high quality. Do not add salt to the water, as it will react badly with the albumen contained in the egg white, and the egg will not be able to coagulate properly. As a matter of interest, the highest egg consumption in Europe goes to the Spaniards and the French, who hold the record of 270 eggs per inhabitant.

Regarding the snails, if you wish you can use living snails and prepare them at home, but that will require a great deal of patience. First, they must be cleaned in vinegar water and cooked twice, once in water and once in broth; the time involved in this has discouraged many an amateur. Fortunately, there are ready-to-serve snails for sale. Avoid any snail substitutions, however.

1. Finely chop the shallots and cook them with a quart / 1 l of red wine in a pot; reduce the liquid to three-quarters of its original amount. Add the veal broth and reduce again to half the volume. One should allow 1 tbsp / 15 ml of sauce per person, which will be whipped up with butter at the end.

2. Cut the belly bacon into strips and blanch. Cook the cocktail onions in water and then fry everything in butter. Cut the button mushrooms into fine slices and fry them in butter as well. Place the raw, well-washed spinach directly into the butter and steam. Proceed similarly with the snails and add more chopped shallots.

Eggs in Red Wine

3. Mix water, vinegar, and 7 tbsp / 100 ml of red wine in a pot and bring to a boil. In this mixture, which should only be allwed to simmer, bubbling lightly, poach the eggs for 3–4 minutes as usual, then take them out and drain them on kitchen paper.

4. To serve, place one egg on a bed of spinach on each plate. Surround with an assortment of snails, cocktail onions, mushrooms, and bacon, sprinkle the sauce on top, and decorate with chervil leaves.

Cuttlefish Risotto with

Preparation time: 30 minutes
Cooking time: 17 minutes
Difficulty: ★

Serves four

scant ³/₄ cup / 160 g Arborio rice
1¹/₄ lb / 600 g dwarf cuttlefish (or small squid, or octopus)
7 oz / 200 g tomatoes
4 tsp / 20 ml olive oil
2¹/₂ cups / 600 ml clear chicken stock
1¹/₄ cups / 300 g butter

7 oz / 200 g Parmesan
half a bunch of basil
salt, pepper to taste

There are more than fifty different ways to prepare risotto (*little rice*), which is actually a specialty of the city of Venice and its surrounding area; the dish is common throughout Northern Italy, stretching all the way to Lombardy and beyond. The rice used must, of course, be Italian, preferably coarse-grain Arborio, a starchy rice that triples in volume when it is cooked, making a tender, smooth risotto. During the entire cooking time it must be stirred gently (an Italian might say you should stir it with love), and with a wooden spoon only. If you add a little butter as you are frying it, it will be even creamier. Be careful not to let it turn brown.

Dwarf cuttlefish, which belong to the squid family, are highly popular components of Mediterraean and Asian cooking. They resemble both their relatives the octopus and the squid, but they are only two or three inches (four or six centimeters) long. When attacked, they also hide in a cloud of ink. These small creatures are now gaining ground in European gastronomy, possibly due to the fact that they are so easy to prepare, and – given the vogue for lighter fare – are low in calories and fat.

Our chef, Dominique Le Stanc, recommends cleaning and preparing the cuttlefish the night before, since this task requires both time and concentration. Firstly they should be skinned, then the body is cut in half lengthwise and cleaned thoroughly in clear water to remove any dirt or other impurities.

Every Easter, the citizens of the town of Aigues-Mortes in the Camargue in the south of France prepare a famous specialty from such seafood.

1. Sauté the rice in heated butter in a large pot.

2. Add clear chicken stock. Simmer over a low heat and repeatedly add a little broth, which the rice must absorb.

Tomatoes and Basil

3. As soon as the rice is cooked and quite smooth, add more butter and bind with grated Parmesan cheese.

4. Prepare the cuttlefish as described above, sauté briefly in olive oil together with skinned, coarsely chopped tomatoes and basil. Serve the rice in mounds in the center of each plate, arrange the cuttlefish, tomato, and basil mixture on top, pour on the remaining juice from the pan, and sprinkle with a few drops of olive oil over all.

Crumbed Calf's Brains with

Preparation time: 1 hour, 20 minutes
Cooking time: 15 minutes
Difficulty: ★★

Serves four

4 calf's brain pieces
generous 1/2 lb / 250 g chanterelles
6 shiitake mushrooms
1 generous oz / 40 g fresh fava beans
1 generous oz / 40 g soybean sprouts
generous 3/8 cup / 100 ml vinegar
1 tbsp / 30 ml soy sauce
2/3 cup / 150 ml beef broth
2/3 cup / 150 ml veal broth
1 head of curly lettuce

1 bunch of chervil
1 sprig of thyme
6 bay leaves
1 tsp / 5 g coriander seeds
salt, pepper to taste

For the breading:
1 egg
scant 1/4 cup / 50 g flour
scant 1/4 cup / 50 g fresh bread crumbs
2 tbsp / 30 g prepared mustard

For the vinaigrette:
5/8 cup / 150 ml balsamic vinegar
generous 3/8 cup / 100 ml grape seed oil
salt, pepper to taste

Despite numerous attempts to make brains more popular, some people are still prejudiced against this ingredient, although it is one of the most delicious types of offal. Brains are rich in vitamins, phosphorus, and proteins and should actually win over many a gourmet. If they are prepared in bread crumbs, as in this recipe, brains are a true delicacy – nice and crisp on the outside, and wonderfully tender inside.

In Europe, the soy plant has only been known for some two hundred years. We are thus lagging about five thousand years behind Asian cuisine, which has made use of this nutritious and tasty plant since the beginning of recorded time. Initially, soy was used in Europe to produce oil or margarine, and it was not until after World War I that the soy plant was fully acknowledged as a vegetable. You can use the light crunchy sprouts of this plant; wash them thoroughly and do not cook them for too long (barely more than a minute or two), otherwise they go limp and quickly lose their flavor.

Chef Michel Libotte adds a harmonious touch by serving the calf's brains in a mixture of chanterelles and shiitake, the Chinese mushrooms that grow on trees (and are rich in vitamins). Although fava beans. which as a matter of fact belong to the same plant family as the soy beans, were well known in the antique world, neither the Egyptians, nor the Greeks, nor the Romans were particularly fond of them. Only Christianity welcomed this type of pulse. In some Mediterranean countries the fava bean (or broad bean as it is also called) is the symbol of the feast of the Three Magi. It is said that Charlemagne loved these beans above all. For this recipe, according to Chef Libotte, choose very young fava beans, which are more easily digestible.

1. Steep the brains in cold salted water for an hour and a half, then remove skin, veins, and any blood stains. Poach the brains in salted vinegar water with thyme and bay leaves for 12 minutes. Scoop off the foam. Leave the brains in the stock to cool. Cut lengthwise into slices, season with salt and pepper, brush with mustard, and coat with bread crumbs.

2. Clean the chanterelles, rinse them two or three times in clear water and pat dry. Fry briefly over a high heat and remove from the pan. Add beef and veal broth to the juice remaining in the pan and cook until the liquid has boiled down. Add the whole coriander seeds, put the chanterelles back into the pan again, sauté for a few minutes and add butter.

Chanterelles and Fava beans

3. Fry the breaded brain pieces on both sides for 3–4 minutes. Prepare the vinaigrette from balsamic vinegar, grape seed oil, salt, and pepper. Add chopped chervil leaves to the chanterelles.

4. Slice the shiitake and sauté. Add the soybean sprouts, the blanched fava beans and a dash of soy sauce. Mix in the curly lettuce and season with the vinaigrette. Arrange the brain pieces on plates, place some lukewarm salad in the center, add the chanterelles, and dribble with a little sauce.

Green Bean Soup with

Preparation time: 40 minutes
Cooking time: 45 minutes
Difficulty: ☆

Serves four

generous 1 lb / 500 g fresh green beans
7 oz / 200 g belly bacon, smoked
4 smoked sausages
1 bulb celeriac
1 large leek stalk

1 onion
5¼ oz / 150 g potatoes
1 clove of garlic
generous 2 tbsp / 40 g sour cream
1 bunch of parsley
salt, pepper to taste

For the roux:
⅛ cup / 25 g butter
⅛ cup / 25 g flour
⅛ cup / 25 ml vegetable broth

With this bean soup (or *bouneschlupp*) we find ourselves right in the middle of Luxemburgian tradition. This dish, as presented here by Chef Léa Linster, is prepared all year round – in season with fresh beans, out of season with canned or frozen beans. The numerous ingredients almost make this soup a main dish; in fact, the gastronomy in the Grand Duchy generally offers very filling meals. All the tasty ingredients used for this recipe are, of course, very fresh.

Modern methods of cultivation have produced stringless beans and done away with the efforts and bother of pulling these strings out. At the same time the beans have become more tasty and tender. The other vegetables do not require any special preparation. The celeriac (or celery root) should be firm and heavy, the leeks fresh and crisp. Charlotte potatoes are the most suitable, since they do not disintegrate while cooking; if these are not available, substitute any firm-fleshed early potato.

High-quality streaky bacon with an equal amount of fat and lean meat will not get too dry or too greasy. Use hearty boiled sausages, which should be quite fatty, as are all pork products from Luxemburg. Smoked ham is particularly popular there, and rightfully so. However, if only because of your health, you do not have to be over-generous with these ingredients: their flavors will be strong enough.

1. Wash, peel, and chop the vegetables indicated and cook them in salted water.

2. Chop a clove of garlic, add to the bacon, and cook for 30 minutes. Lastly add the potatoes and cook for another 15 minutes.

Smoked Bacon and Sausage

3. Make a roux from the butter, flour, and a little vegetable broth. Use this to bind the soup; season with salt and pepper. Cook the sausages in boiling water for 20 minutes.

4. Cut the bacon into strips and the sausages into slices. Ladle the soup into plates, add the meat, pour a teaspoon of sour cream in the middle and serve sprinkled with parsley.

Cheese Terrine with

Preparation time: 30 minutes
Marinating time: 12 hours
Cooking time: 1 hour, 15 minutes
Difficulty: ★★

Serves twelve

1¼ lb / 600 g Beaufort cheese (see below)
6 artichokes
40 thin slices pancetta (or 10 thin slices
    prociutto or other ham)
1 tbsp / 15 g flour
juice of 1 lemon

12 whole eggs
6 egg yolks
generous 1 cup / 250 ml whole milk
generous ³/₈ cup / 100 ml white wine
generous 1 cup / 250 ml cream
generous ³/₈ cup / 100 ml vinegar
1 head lamb's lettuce

For the mustard sauce:
generous 2 tbsp / 40 g prepared mustard
1¼ cups / 300 ml veal broth

The renown gastronome and writer Maurice-Edmond Sailland (1872–1956), who took the name Curnonsky as his pen name, described Beaufort as the prince among the cheeses, and the king among the Gruyère cheeses. Guy Martin, our chef, gets great pleasure out of using this cheese: particularly when it comes from Savoy. With its nutty flavor, this variety was rightfully awarded the title "alpine cheese," because it is made from the milk of the beautifully dappled cows that graze in the high mountain regions of the Alps. A round of Beaufort cheese, which can weigh up to one hundred and thirty pounds (sixty kilos), matures for six months, during which time its consistency turns dense and firm. It does not have any holes, only a few random cracks, or "threads." As an alternative to Beaufort, Guy Martin suggests Emmental cheese, which has a similar consistency, though not quite as remarkable a taste.

Chef Martin recommends preparing this terrine with pancetta, a fat-streaked bacon that has been smoked the same way for decades, according to tradition. If pancetta is unavailable, other types of European ham are also suitable, such as prosciutto from San Daniele or Parma. This area in northern Italy has special connections with Savoy in France, established in the days when spice merchants from the Orient traveled through these high mountainous regions. Savoy has thus always been a connecting link between France and Italy. High-quality Spanish hams like serrano, iberico or pata negra will also go very well with this dish.

The different flavors of this dish are well balanced and will harmonize well with a side accompaniment of poached fresh eggs, doused in mustard sauce and sprinked with parsley.

1. Cut the Beaufort cheese into ¹/₂ in / 1 cm thick cubes, add white wine and leave to marinate overnight. Clean the artichokes and strip down to the hearts, which should be cooked in a mixture of water, flour, lemon juice, and salt. Line the terrine mold with the thin slices of Pancetta.

2. Crack six egg yolks into a bowl, add cream and milk, blend with a whisk and add the drained, marinated cheese. Poach the 12 eggs in boiling water (four eggs at a time) with 7 tbsp / 100 ml of vinegar – approximately 2¹/₂ tbsp / 40 ml of vinegar per batch of four eggs.

Ham and Artichokes

3. Cover the base of the terrine mold with a third of the Beaufort and a little cheese and cream mixture. In the meantime, cook 2¹/₂ tbsp / 40 g of mustard with 1¹/₄ cups / 300 ml of veal broth for the mustard sauce. Trim the artichoke hearts into squares.

4. Fill the mold with a layer each of artichoke hearts and then cheese mixture. Cover with aluminum foil. Bake in the oven at 300 °F / 155 °C for one hour and 15 minutes; leave to cool for about 15–20 minutes. To serve, place on each plate one slice of lukewarm terrine, with a poached egg resting on a bed of lamb's lettuce next to it. Sprinkle mustard sauce over the egg and around the terrine.

Portugese Fish

Preparation time: 15 minutes
Cooking time: 30 minutes
Difficulty: ★★

Serves four

1³/₄ lb / 800 g hardshell clams, such as
    littleneck, cherrystone, or butter clams
1 large onion
2 cloves of garlic
juice of 1 lemon
3 slices of white bread
1 tbsp / 15 g butter
generous ³/₈ cup / 100 ml olive oil

scant ¹/₄ cup / 50 ml white wine
2 tbsp / 30 g corn meal
2 egg yolks
1 bunch of fresh cilantro

For the fish stock:
 heads and bones from tuna, bluefish, grouper,
    or similar sea fish
1 leek stalk
1 celery stalk
1 bunch of parsley
4 black peppercorns
salt to taste

The clam belongs to the family of the bivalves, which has more than five hundred species. One of its nicknames is the Venus shell, a name that it owes to the Roman goddess of love who, as legend has it, emerged from the sea in such a shell. Bulhão Pato, Portugal's most famous gastronome in the 19th century, introduced this mollusc to his people, and since then, its flavor and its tender flesh have enjoyed great popularity. Witness, for example, this appetizer from Chef Maria Ligia Medeiros.

Clams can be eaten alive or cooked, cold or warm, without ever losing their flavor. In this recipe they are presented in a tasty soup with fresh herbs. Parsley, celery, and especially

cilantro (fresh coriander) are widely used in Portugal. It is the taste of cilantro that dominates all the other flavors and lends this dish its typical character, which should not be overshadowed by the other ingredients.

If necessary, this fish soup can be prepared in advance. You can then simply bind it with an egg yolk before serving, but do not bring it to a boil a second time. In this case the cilantro should also be added at the last moment, otherwise it will lose too much of its flavor. The bread croutons should be served separately, so that guests can help themselves. The croutons provide a delightful contrast to the creamy smooth soup.

1. Wash the clams carefully, rinse them at least two or three times, cook them in white wine until they open, and take out. Add fish heads and bones, leeks, celery, parsley, peppercorns, and salt to the broth. Bring to a boil again, then pass through a sieve.

2. In a fairly large saucepan, sauté the onion and the chopped garlic in olive oil over a low heat for ten minutes, then add the fish stock.

Soup with Clams

3. Make a roux of cornmeal and cold water, stir into the soup, and bring to a boil again.

4. Blend egg yolk, lemon juice, and the chopped cilantro in a bowl. Take the soup off the stove; add the cilantro mixture to bind the soup. To make the croutons, dice the bread slices and fry in butter until golden brown. Place a bit of clam flesh on the center of each plate and serve the soup immediately, with the croutons in a separate bowl.

Fricassee of Snails and

Preparation time: 1 hour
Cooking time: 2 hours, 30 minutes
Difficulty: ★★★

Serves four

40 snails
half a small calf's head
1 veal trotter
2 tomatoes, 1 carrot, 1 leek, 1 onion
quarter of a celeriac bulb
1 shallot
2 cloves of garlic
$^1/_2$ cup / 125 g fresh bread crumbs
scant $^1/_4$ cup / 50 ml olive oil
generous 2 tbsp / 30 g Parmesan, grated

1 bay leaf
4 sprigs each of thyme, rosemary, sage leaves
1 bunch of borage flowers
leaves from 1 head of celery

1 clove
half a bunch of parsley
4 sprigs each of chives, fresh marjoram
salt, 10 black peppercorns

For the vegetables:
1 large bunch of spinach (to yield scant $^7/_8$ lb / 400 g)
2 potatoes (such as Bintje or Yukon gold)
1 shallot
scant $^1/_4$ cup / 50 g butter
$^1/_2$ cup / 125 ml olive oil

For the sauce:
scant $^7/_8$ cup / 200 ml stock made from the calf's head
1 cup / 250 ml Banyuls red wine
1 tbsp / 15 g butter

True gastronomes are not interested in borders. This dish, from Chef Dieter Müller, provides a good example. The calf's head is a traditional ingredient from Germany (predominantly from Baden-Württemberg), the potato cake, known as a *rösti*, is from Switzerland, the snail fricassee is done in the Burgundy (or Bourgogne) style, the Banyuls is made from the black Grenache grapes of Catalonia and, last but not least, the olive oil hails from Italy. What else does one need to build a united Europe?

Our chef suggests using Roman snails that are very similar to the ones found in Burgundy – known, naturally, as Burgundy snails, or vineyard snails, and fed a diet of grape leaves. Since the flavor of Roman snails is not very strong, Chef Müller adds the tender meat of a calf's head, though good sweetbread would also be ideal. This tender ragout provides an interesting contrast to the crisp *rösti* cakes made from raw potatoes. Our chef recommends Bintje potatoes, as they are not floury and do not disintegrate when they are fried; otherwise, try Yukon gold potatoes.

The garnish for this complex appetizer is not exactly easy, considering that it includes fried veal trotter, borage flowers, and fresh marjoram. The herbs intensify the flavor of the fricassee and the wine from Banyuls adds a finishing touch. A product of the medieval art of winemaking, this wine only develops its aroma with time. In the past it was only available in the Banyuls region; today it is a must in every good European wine cellar.

1. Clean the calf's head and the veal trotter and cook together with the carrot, leek, and celeriac. Take the calf's head out after an hour and leave the trotter to cook for another hour. Cut the meat of the calf's head into small cubes and refrigerate. Bone the veal trotter and cut into 2 in / 5–6 cm strips.

2. Arrange the veal trotter strips on baking paper in the shape of a grid and refrigerate. Later, fry this grid in olive oil. (This task requires a lot of patience.) To prepare the sauce, mix the wine and the veal broth and thicken until it has a syrupy consistency. Take off the heat and stir in butter. Then pass through a sieve and season.

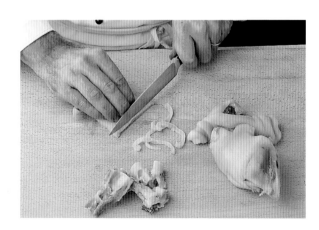

Calf's Head in Banyuls

3. Heat oil and a little butter in a non-stick frying pan rubbed with garlic. Add the snails, the diced meat from the calf's head, and the chopped shallot, and fry for 3–4 minutes. Then add the sauce, the diced tomatoes, herbs, and bread crumbs; season to taste. Cook the spinach and toss it in butter with chopped shallot.

4. Prepare the rösti from thinly cut raw potato strips and fry in a pan with olive oil. Serve the rösti on plates, spoon some spinach over, and lastly dish up the ragout. Sprinkle with grated Parmesan and briefly bake au gratin. Decorate with the borage flowers and the grid made from the veal trotter. Place a snail, in its shell, on the side.

Fisherman's Style

Preparation time: 40 minutes
Cooking time: 30 minutes
Difficulty: ★★

Serves four

8 big langoustines
1 lobster, 1 lb / 500 g
$^5/_8$ lb / 300 g baby octopus or small squid
  (with ink)
$^5/_8$ lb / 300 g clams and cockles
$3^1/_2$ oz / 100 g rice
1 green pepper
2 onions
3 cloves of garlic

1 bunch of parsley
1 quart / 1 l olive oil
salt, pepper to taste

For the fish stock (to yield $2^1/_2$ cups / 600 ml):
1 sea robin
1 bunch of fresh savory
a pinch of saffron threads

For the lobster broth:
2 carrots
2 onions (stuck with cloves)
2 stalks of celery
1 bay leaf

This Catalan specialty was originally – and, to some extent, remains – a fisherman's dish. As rice was the only provision taken on board, all the other ingredients were caught fresh there and then. Even if this simple dish as presented by our chef, Jean-Louis Neichel, has been converted into a gastronomic delicacy, one should not forget the rough life these fishermen had to live (and still do). Victor Hugo once said: "Poor people, they have to leave at night heading into the darkness, into uncertainty. Hard work, everything is cold, everything is black, no glimmer of light."

Among a crew of eight on a small fishing cutter the task of preparing the soup always falls on one, who, for safety reasons does not bake or fry the fish, but rather crushes it and cooks it with the rice (or with thin noodles). Spanish tradition demands round-grain rice cooked in stock that is repeatedly added to. As a result, the rice is unlikely to stick together.

Octopus or squid ink is used to dye the stew a most unusual black color; either will also harmonizes with the various other flavors from the sea. If you prefer to avoid the messy task of handling the ink sacs, you can get the ink in a can instead.

Chef Neichel recommends preparing the fish stock with a small sea robin (known in Europe as a gurnard), a saltwater fish that, incidentally, makes a croaking noise as it swims near the surface. Unwashed and unscaled, this fish is cooked in water with saffron and fresh savory. After cooking, all ingredients are crushed and passed through a fine sieve.

1. Prepare the fish stock ahead of time. To begin preparing the dish, chop the onions and green pepper. Wash and rinse the octopus or squid well and reserve the ink. Fry the vegetables and the octopus or squid in a covered pan with olive oil, for 15 minutes. Cook the lobster in vegetable broth with onions, carrots, celery, and a bay leaf.

2. Sauté the garlic and chopped parsley in olive oil. Add watered-down ink and rice and mix well. Gradually stir in the fish stock.

Seafood Pot

3. Wash the clams and cockles, add to the pot with the octopus or squid, and season. Cook for 15 minutes. Midway through the cooking time season to taste, if necessary.

4. Crush some of the fried garlic with parsley and a few drops of olive oil. Add to the clams and cockles, cover and set aside. Fry the langoustine tails, shell the lobster, and cut into slices. Serve the seafood and rice mixture on soup plates, decorated with lobster slices and langoustine tails.

Oysters on a Bed of Leeks

Preparation time: 30 minutes
Cooking time: 10 minutes
Difficulty: ★

Serves four

4 dozen oysters (preferably Belon)
3 leeks
juice of 1 lemon
$^3/_4$ cup / 200g butter
1 tbsp / 15 g poppy seeds
salt, fresh-ground pepper to taste

Today we eat only the seeds of the poppy, whereas in the past the leaves of this plant were consumed like spinach. In certain regions of Asia, people use poppy seed oil or *huile d'oeilette*. The pharmaceutical application of the poppy is as well known as the fact that it is refined into opium. Poppy seeds are mainly used in bakeries but also to spice hearty dishes, like this appetizer for example, where warm oysters constitute the main ingredient. Poppy seeds become more aromatic if they are roasted in the oven for a few minutes.

For this recipe you should choose the oysters from Brittany known as Belon; they are now cultivated in the United States as well. Also known as *huitres creuses*, their shells may have a deep green color, and their succulent, firm flesh develops a distinct flavor from growing in deep water. (To test the freshness of an oyster, touch its edge with the tip of a knife. If the oyster is alive, it will immediately withdraw.)

It took a while to convince the fans of raw oysters that these delicacies may also be enjoyed when warm. However, if oysters are not cooked long enough, they lack texture, and if they are cooked for too long, they turn tough and rubbery. The same or a similar rule applies to leeks, which should neither be served half-done nor be overcooked. The success obviously depends on the right timing.

Our chef, Paul Pauvert, would be quite happy to substitute the oysters with sole fillets, which also harmonize very well with the poppy seeds.

1. Open the oysters, remove their shells, and strain and reserve their juice. Poach them for a few minutes in their own juice and drain. Roast the poppy seeds lightly in the oven.

2. Slice the leeks diagonally across the stalk, into diamonds. Sauté in $3^1/_2$ tbsp / 50 g of butter. Add 1 tbsp / 15 ml of oyster stock and slowly reduce the heat. Season with pepper and simmer over a low heat for five minutes.

with Poppy Seed Butter

3. Set the leeks aside. Make a butter sauce from the remaining portion of butter, the reduced oyster stock, and the juice of a lemon.

4. Finally, add the poppy seeds and a pinch of fresh-ground pepper. Serve the leeks on plates and arrange the oysters in rosettes on top. Cover with butter sauce and serve hot.

Artichokes Filled with

Preparation time: 1 hour
Cooking time: 30 minutes
Difficulty: ★

Serves four

4 artichokes
3½ oz / 100 g chévre
4 tomatoes
juice of 1 lemon
generous 1 lb / 500 g baking potatoes
 (such as Idaho)
2 anchovy fillets (preserved in brine)
scant ⅛ lb / 50 g black olives
1 tsp / 5 g coriander
1 tsp / 5 g peppercorns
1 bunch of basil

1 bunch of thyme
1 bay leaf
1 clove of garlic

2 egg yolks
scant ¼ cup / 50 ml whole milk
scant ¼ cup / 50 ml cream
generous ⅜ cup / 100 ml olive oil
4 tsp / 20 g fresh butter
salt, pepper to taste

For the parsley juice:
¾ cup / 200 ml vegetable or poultry broth
1 bunch of smooth-leaved parsley
1 bunch of young spinach (to yield scant ⅛ lb /
 50 g leaves)
half a bunch of chervil
3 cloves of garlic (to yield 1 tbsp /
 15 g chopped)
2 tbsp / 30 g cold butter
salt, fresh-ground pepper to taste

The artichoke, a remote relative of the thistle, was only introduced to the kitchen fairly recently, after a most honorable career as a diuretic in the medical field. Only during the Renaissance period, after a remarkable introduction to the court, did it become popular on royal dinner tables. Here, in a dish presented by our chef, Horst Petermann, it assumes a starring role.

There are two major artichoke families: the southern type, a small purple artichoke or *poivrade* grown in Italy and in Provence and often consumed raw, and one from Brittany or from the north, which is cooked in boiling water. The large green artichoke from Laon and in particular the blunt-nosed one from Brittany recommended for this recipe belong to the second category. Before you prepare the artichoke, it is important to twist off the stem with a quick movement, pulling out,

at the same time, a number of tough, fibrous strings reaching right into the heart of the artichoke (otherwise known as the choke).

France boasts a great variety of chèvres, or goat's milk cheeses, partly matured in ashes, and available in various degrees of maturity. Only six of these have a controlled designation of origin. With great zeal, manufacturers monitor their refined quality, and the improvements become evident in the texture and flavor. For this appetizer, choose a small cheese that has only ripened for two weeks and still has a soft consistency.

The anchovies preserved in brine must be thoroughly rinsed in water or milk to weaken their salty taste. Use the more aromatic smooth-leaved parsley instead of the curly parsley to give the sauce a stronger flavor.

1. Remove the artichoke leaves. Twist off the stem. Cut out the artichoke hearts, trim them to pleasing, round shapes and sprinkle with lemon.

2. To cook the artichoke hearts, cover peppercorns, bay leaf, crushed coriander, thyme, and finely sliced garlic with water. Add 3½ tbsp / 50 ml of olive oil. Add the hearts and cook over a low heat for about 20 minutes. Remove the strings (chokes) of the artichokes.

Olives and Chévre

3. Blanch, skin, and chop the tomatoes. Seed the olives and chop. Dice the goat's milk cheese. Desalinate the anchovy fillets in cold water for ten minutes. Chop the basil. Mix these ingredients with 3½ tbsp / 50 ml olive oil and spread onto the artichoke hearts. Prepare the mashed potatoes with the milk and season to taste.

4. Cover the filled hearts with a tablespoon of mashed potato until they look like small hemispheres. Blend the egg yolk with the cream, use to brush the mashed potato and brown under the grill. Heat the vegetable broth, add chopped herbs and spinach and bring to a boil. Puree and pass through a sieve. Whip up with butter. Arrange on plates, served with parsley juice.

Preparation time: 45 minutes
Cooking time: 20 minutes
Difficulty: ★★

Serves four

For the lasagna sheets
scant 3/8 lb / 200 g fresh spinach
2 3/8 cups / 700 g durum wheat flour
2 eggs

For the filling:
3 1/2 oz / 100 g Séré cheese (Ricotta or Sérac)
2 red peppers (to yield 4 tsp / 20 g chopped)

2 yellow peppers (to yield 4 tsp / 20 g chopped)
2 green peppers (to yield 4 tsp / 20 g chopped)
1 eggplant
1 egg
1/2 cup / 125 ml olive oil
salt, fresh-ground pepper to taste

For the decoration:
1/8 cup / 25 ml extra-virgin olive oil
4 olives
2 cloves of garlic
2 basil leaves
1/4 lb / 50 g Parmesan cheese

This Mediterranean recipe, with its fragrances of olive oil and basil, is certainly attributable to Roland Pierroz' Italian ancestors and, though he is based in Switzerland, it has little to do with Swiss cooking. "Niçoise" refers to the tortelloni filling based on eggplants, peppers, and olives: the combination has been a part of the cuisine of the old county of Nice since long before it became part of France, in 1860.

Start with the preparation of a very smooth dough, dyed with spinach, and roll it out very thinly with a rolling pin. It should be made of gluten-rich Italian or Canadian durum wheat, which produces the tastiest noodles you could wish for. After rolling out the dough you should wind up with twelve, five-inch (twelve centimeter) squares.

These tortelloni go particularly well with vegetables from the Mediterraean region, like eggplants. Choose a medium-sized

eggplant with a smooth and very shiny skin. The peppers are an essential component; they give the filling color and a soft consistency, as does the olive oil, which also evokes the magical scent of Mediterranean cuisine. Our chef, bringing in some of his Swiss influences as well, includes Séré in his recipe, a white Swiss cheese of Latin origin (the name is derived from the word *serum*, i.e. "whey"), which has the right consistency to bind the filling.

A few changes are allowed so long as they fit the recipe's Mediterranean flair – tomatoes and zucchini, for example, are also suitable for the filling. Filled Italian pasta dishes, of which there are innumerable variations, offer constant opportunities for imagination and innovation.

1. To prepare the dough, wash, cook, and chop the spinach; mix with the flour and eggs. Cut the Parmesan cheese thinly using a slicer. Chop the basil. Peel, slice, and fry the garlic. Drain on paper towels.

2. Dice the eggplant and green, red, and yellow peppers. Boil briefly in salted water, making sure that they remain firm. Drain and sauté briefly in olive oil. Drain on paper towels. Roll out the dough to make 12 sheets, about 5 in / 12 cm on each side.

Niçoise

3. Whip up the egg. Bring a pot of water to a boil. Pass the egg through a sieve to set in the water. Strain the contents of the pot once more. Combine the egg in the sieve with the vegetables and the cheese and season. Place a tablespoon of this mixture onto the lasagna squares.

4. Fold the squares into triangles. Stick the rims together and adjust. Steam the tortelloni until done. Slowly heat 5 tbsp / 75 ml olive oil with the basil in a saucepan. Arrange the tortelloni in the center of the plate. Sprinkle with basil oil and Parmesan; decorate with olives and fried garlic.

Zucchini Flowers

Preparation time: 14 minutes
Cooking time: 15 minutes
Difficulty: ★★

Serves four

1¹/₃ lbs / 650 g clams
one dozen baby zucchini with flowers intact
2 tomatoes
1 large zucchini
generous 1 oz / 40 g truffles
1 egg yolk

1–2 tbsp / 30 ml wine
³/₄ cup / 200 ml cream
³/₄ cup / 200 ml olive oil
¹/₄ cup / 60g * butter
1 bunch of basil
salt, fresh-ground pepper to taste

This symbol of abundance and fertilly in the Orient is ubiquitous in home gardens, where it sometimes grows to enormous proportions. But the tastiest zucchini are smaller ones, and the most well-known variety among all of them, in France, is the *Diamant*. According to our French chefs, Jacques and Larent Pourcel, this type outshines all the others, with its lack of seeds and refined flavor. And, the chefs point out, there are many ways of preparing this vegetable, using any number of different sauces or cooking methods.

Judging by the impression one gets in the south of France, zucchini flowers are a common and popular dish. The baby zucchini itself, while very small, becomes all the tastier when the wide-open and well-developed flower is filled. Of course, these small zucchini have to be harvested at the right moment and processed as soon as possible. To open up the flower, blow into it gently. Remove the pistil, blanch the flowers quickly, and immediately dip them in ice water to keep them from going limp. Filling the flowers of this young vegetable is not all that easy and will probably require an extra set of hands, as well as a lot of practice.

To accompany the zucchini, our chef recommends seafood, which requires hardly any preparation apart from serving. If the clams, or *clovisses*, are nice and fresh, they will meet any expectations, particularly if they come from Sète, the Mediterranean harbor where these bivalves are mainly caught. *Clovissère*, derived from *clovisse*, is the name of a fishing device used to comb the bed of the lagoons of Languedoc-Roussillon. Especially in summer, this dish is an ideal combination of fruit from the sea and from the garden. If these clams are not available in American fish markets, subsitute them with any variety of high-quality, hardshell clams.

1. Carefully remove the pistils of the zucchini flowers. Cut off the zucchini stems. Blanch in boiling water for 15 seconds. Leave to cool and cut in half lengthwise. Set the cut-off halves aside.

2. Cook the cut-off zucchini halves and the chopped zucchini for the filling, reduce the cream and set aside. Cook the clams in wine until they open, then take them off the stove. Shell and rinse them and add them to the wine again. When the zucchini have cooked for a few minutes, take them off the heat and combine them with the egg yolk and the reduced cream.

with Clam Filling

3. Skin and dice the tomatoes. Clean and peel the truffles and cut them into fine strips. Add half the clams and season. Fill this stuffing into the zucchini flowers; a pastry bag could be used.

4. Place the zucchini in an ovenproof dish. Pour a little water and the olive oil over the bottom and season. Cover with aluminum foil and bake at 355 °F / 180 °C for 25 minutes. Add the remaining clams and season. Mix butter and truffle peels into the zucchini stock. Serve the zucchini sprinkled with the sauce, and decorated with truffle strips, tomatoes and fresh herbs.

Warm Salad with

Preparation time: 1 hour
Soaking time: 24 hours
Cooking time: 15 minutes
Difficulty: ★

Serves four

1¼ lbs / 600 g monkfish tail
1 large potato
½ lb / 250 g mixed lettuce leaves, such as
   Bibb lettuce, raddichio, or mesclun
1 egg

generous ⅜ cup / 100 g flour
3 cups / 750 ml oil or lard for deep-frying
2 tbsp / 30 ml vinaigrette
salt, freshly ground white pepper to taste

For the mustard sauce:
¾ cup / 175 ml heavy cream
2 tbsp / 30 g coarse prepared mustard

This way of preparing fish is very common in Great Britain. It proves how easy it is to combine very economical ingredients to make a tasty and cleverly designed dish. The contrast between the creamy salad and the crisp French fries and deep-fried fish is particularly delicious.

By the choice of monkfish you can tell where our chef, the Irish Paul Rankin, comes from. The two main types of monkfish caught in Irish waters are the common monkfish (*lophius piscatorius*) and the red monkfish (*lophius budegassa*). Their strong flavor and fleshy consistency have made them both popular. If you steam the monkfish pieces before you deep-fry them, they will retain their succulent texture.

The Irishman's much-loved (and at times, much depended upon) potato is a component of innumerable recipes in Ireland. Maris Piper potatoes are ideal for crisp French fries, but Stella or Apollo are very suitable too. To make them lighter, Paul Rankin leaves the cut potatoes in cold water for twenty-four hours where they lose a considerable amount of their starch. They turn wonderfully crisp if you deep-fry them slowly.

Representing a British tradition, this appetizer can be enjoyed anywhere and at any time, possibly with a hot cup of tea.

1. Set aside 2 tbsp / 30 ml of heavy cream, bring the rest to a boil. Simmer for a minute until it has thickened slightly. Take off the stove and add mustard. Peel the potato and cut it into matchstick-thick strips. Place them in cold water for an hour to lose their starch.

2. Cut the tail of the monkfish into ½ in / 1 cm thick pieces. Blend the egg and the remaining heavy cream and use to coat the fish pieces. Then cover them thoroughly with flour until all the egg and cream mixture has been absorbed.

'Fish and Chips"

3. Deep-fry the monkfish pieces at 375 °F / 90 °C for three minutes. Take out and drain on paper towels. Season with salt and pepper. Then prepare the French fries in the same manner.

4. Just before serving, dip the lettuce leaves into the vinaigrette and distribute them on four plates. Arrange the French fries and the monkfish pieces on top of the salad. Finally, add a touch of mustard sauce.

Fricassee of Snails anc

Preparation time: 40 minutes
Cooking time: 10 minutes
Difficulty: ★★

Serves four

2 dozen small squid
32 snails
1 dozen sea cucumbers
1 blood sausage
7 oz / 200 g small onions

For the sofrito:
generous 1 lb / 500 g ripe tomatoes
2.2 lbs / 1 kg onions
sugar, salt

For the sauce:
tentacles from the squid
generous 2 cups / 500 ml vegetable broth
  composed of leeks, parsley, leafy lettuce,
  and 1 shallot
a pinch of saffron
1/2 cup / 125 ml olive oil from the first pressing

For the decoration:
1 bunch of chervil
1 bunch of chives
1 bunch of parsley
1 bunch of basil
1 tbsp / 15 g gray salt
2 tbsp/ 30 g almonds (if desired)

The restuarant *El Racó de Can Fabes*, where Chef Santi Santamaria presides, is situated in a favorable spot at the foot of the mountains only a few miles from the Mediterranean. It is thus predestined for this combination of snails and squid, which represent, on a plate, the classic union of land and sea. The ingredients combined here are presented on a base of simple *sofrito*, a traditional Catalan side dish made with tomatoes and onions.

The ingredients are not hard to come by. The small gray snails you find in masses on a rainy Sunday morning are just right. These *bouer*, as their fans call them, are plentiful on both side of the Pyrenees (though, in the United States, you may have to improvise).

The squid, on the other hand, have to be selected carefully, preferably towards the end of summer, when they're in season. If

you want to fish them yourself, try to avoid the use of a trawl net and rather catch them a *la potera* (fishing rod with a special hook), like Santi Santamaria does to avoid damaging them. If you obtain them in the more ordinary way, buying them from a fish market, you may also buy *chipirones*, the small squid that the Spaniards love and eat as *tapas* at all hours of the day and night. As an alternative, look for dwarf squid, which are similar.

You might also discover the sea cucumber while you're there, a marine animal also known as a sea slug whose iodine flavor complements this crunchy appetizer. Contrary to its appearance, this creature has a tough skin covered with mobile tentacles.

1. Clean the squid. Sever the tentacles. Cut the tentacles into pieces and fry in a pan until golden brown and set aside for the sauce.

2. Remove the cooked snails from their shells. In a non-stick pan, fry the small onions and the squid separately. When they are nearly done, add the snails. For the sofrito, slice the onions finely, brown in oil and add chopped tomatoes. Steam, then reduce the liquid in the oven. Season to taste with salt and sugar.

Squid with Sofrito

3. For the sauce, add the chopped shallot, the other vegetables and the saffron to the browned tentacles. Add vegetable stock and reduce by 20%. Leave to steep for five minutes for everything to take on color. Mix with olive oil from the first pressing and season to taste.

4. Fry the blood sausage slices in a pan. Halve the sea cucumber (after having cleaned the extremities), sauté in a pan and add to the squid mixture. Serve the squid and the sea cucumber in the center of the plate. Arrange the snails and a small heap of sofrito around them. Decorate with herbs.

Poached Eggs with Goose

Preparation time: 5 minutes
Cooking time: 20 minutes
Difficulty: ★★

Serves four

4 eggs
3¹/₂ oz / 100 g goose liver (foie gras)
1 white truffle
1 shallot
scant ¹/₄ cup / 50 g butter
¹/₂ cup / 125 ml port
¹/₂ cup / 125 ml chicken broth

generous ³/₈ cup / 100 ml crème fraîche
vinegar
salt, pepper to taste

In season from late September to January, white truffles are most delicious. They are found in Piemont, Italy in the area of Alba, the name meaning *the white one*. The wines from that region, Dolcetto and Barolo (the latter is "the king of wines," according to our chef, Ezio Santin), are famous all over Europe. Unlike the black truffle, the white truffle exudes its aroma even before it is cooked. Get to know it through this superb, traditional recipe presented by Chef Santin who has prepared it for years, and this can guarantee its success.

Select very fresh grade A eggs with a uniform weight of about two ounces (sixty grams) each. Larger eggs, Santin reminds us, are of course not necessarily fresher or better. Poach them in unsalted water with a little added vinegar, making sure that the water merely simmers to prevent the egg white from spreading too much.

The sauce is prepared from a goose liver and butter mixture, and must not be spiced excessively, since very strongly flavored ingredients may conceal and thus inevitably destroy the truffle aroma. Before the foie gras is added, the port wine serving as a base for the gravy needs to be reduced and the shallots must be totally cooked away. It goes without saying that a high-quality port should be used, despite the fact that it plays only a secondary role here.

The presentation of this appetizer requires a little care. For an even appearance, the eggs should be turned over and covered with sauce in all sides.

1. Place a knob of butter in a frying pan and add the chopped shallot. Pour on the port and reduce by three-quarters. Then add the chicken broth and crème fraîche.

2. Bring to a boil again and reduce by half Take off the stove and blend the chopped liver and the butter in a food processor. Season to taste and keep warm in a double boiler.

Liver and White Truffle

3. Poach the eggs in boiling unsalted water with a little added vinegar. Drain on a cloth and trim into shape.

4. Serve the poached eggs on plates, pour the goose liver sauce over and sprinkle with thinly sliced white truffle flakes.

Small Potato Gnocch

Preparation time: 10 minutes
Cooking time: 25 minutes
Difficulty: ★★

Serves four

1¼ lbs / 600 g Bintje potatoes
1½ lbs / 750 g small boletus
2 cloves of garlic
half a bunch of parsley (to yield 1 tbsp / 15 g
   chopped)
5 sprigs of thyme
scant ½ cup / 110 g flour

⅛ lb / 25 g Parmesan
2 tbsp / 30 g butter
4 tbsp / 60 ml extra-virgin olive oil
2 tbsp / 30 ml chicken or vegetable broth
salt, pepper to taste

Gnocchi (Italian for "dumplings") are prepared in very different ways. Their first reference in literature was made by the writer Vincenzo Corrado in his *Cuisinier galant* in the early 19th century. That was the time when the potato, that had previously been fairly unknown as a food item in Italy, began to be consumed. The fact that gnocchi are made of durum wheat semolina in Rome and of cornmeal around Venice proves that cooks have a large degree of freedom when preparing this world-renowned dish. Gnocchi, it seems, can take a hundred delicious forms.

Our chef suggests cooking the unpeeled potatoes in salted water to retain their consistency. He recommends certain types that stay firm when cooked, like the potato from Bologna or the prolific Bintje potato from the Netherlands, which is available at markets all year round. If these are unavailable, just choose potatoes that are firm and fresh, such as Yukon Gold

and round whites. When cooking, make sure the potatoes do not fall apart, otherwise you will not be able to process them.

The combination of these ingredients with fresh boletus will allow hardly any alternatives. If worse comes to worse, the boletus could be substituted with morels, provided they are fresh (and prepare yourself for a lengthy cleaning process). This recipe demands softer and more aromatic ingredients than the dried morels normally used for sauces.

The ingredients for the gnocchi should be very simple. Do not use eggs, which could make the dough tough and chewy. Indenting the gnocchi by means of a fork follows the traditional presentation. Our chef, Ezio Santin, has admitted that at least twice a week he and his staff enjoy gnocchi with tomato sauce – their way of relaxing away from the busy schedule of the kitchen.

1. Cook the potatoes in salted water. Clean a boletus, dice it finely and sauté it in a non-stick pan in 2 tbsp / 30 ml oil with a clove of garlic and a sprig of thyme. Put the potatoes through the grinder. Mix the diced hot mushrooms, flour, and grated Parmesan with the warm potato paste. Combine well and add salt.

2. Make long rolls the thickness of a finger and cut into about 1 in / 2 cm pieces. Use the back of a fork to make indentations.

with Mushrooms

3. Cut the remaining well-cleaned mushrooms into large chunks and place them on a damp cloth. Then fry them in a pan with 2 tbsp / 30 ml of oil and a clove of garlic. Add parsley and salt and gradually pour the stock over. Set the mushrooms aside.

4. Cook the gnocchi uncovered in a big pot of salted water for 3–5 minutes. Drain in a strainer and then reheat in the pan with the mushroom sauce finished off with a knob of butter. Serve on very hot plates and decorate with a sprig of thyme.

Saffron Risotto

Preparation time: 10 minutes
Soaking time: 4–5 hours
                      (for the saffron)
Cooking time: 15 minutes
Difficulty: ★

Serves four

generous 1 cup / 250 g Arborio rice
  (see below)
¹/₄ lb / 125 g goose liver (foie gras)
1 pinch saffron threads

1 small onion
³/₄ cup / 200 ml beef broth
scant ¹/₄ cup / 50 g butter
¹/₂ tsp / 5 ml balsamic vinegar
half a bunch of rosemary
salt, pepper to taste

Saffron originally served as a pigment, was used extensively for the different greens of the frescos and stained glass windows when the *duomo* was built, a great Milanese cathedral that is still one of the most impressive buildings of Christianity. Legend has it that this risotto had its origin in a comment made by a master glazier to his apprentice working with saffron on the site of the cathedral: "You could even manage to use this for cooking!"

If one is to believe a story passed on for generations, and related here by our chef, Nadia Santini, this dish was served at the wedding of the daughter of Master Valery of Flanders. From then on the golden yellow risotto became popular in the whole of northern Italy and was particularly enjoyed in Milan by the artists of the Scala and high society. One must not forget that the climate of sun and rain had a positive influence on rice cultivation and that, as a result, there is a multitude of rice dishes from northern Italy.

To prepare this dish, you should try to choose a type of rice that is characteristic of this region, such as *vialone nano*, which is cooked *mantecato* or until *al dente*, to make it more easily digestible. If this is unavailable, choose a robust-grained Arborio. Coloring with saffron is easier if you soak the saffron threads for about four or five hours in advance. As an alternative to the goose liver slices our chef suggests artichoke hearts, or finely sliced mushrooms.

1. Fry the small, finely chopped onion in butter until golden.

2. Add the rice and stir it with the onion for 2–3 minutes so that the butter nicely moistens the rice. Pour on very hot beef stock, ladle by ladle, as it is absorbed by the rice.

with Goose Liver

3. Add saffron (previously soaked in cold water for four to five hours until almost red) to the par-cooked rice. If necessary, add a little more beef stock until the rice is cooked al dente.

4. Cut the goose liver into pieces and fry in a non-stick pan. Remove and set aside. Add balsamic vinegar and chopped rosemary to the contents of the pan. Heap a tablespoon of risotto onto each plate and arrange the liver on top, garnished, if you wish, with saffron threads.

Tomato Soup

Preparation time: 15 minutes
Cooking time: 1 hour, 30 minutes
Difficulty: ★

Serves four

5 vine-ripened tomatoes in season
1 green chili pepper
1 onion
2 cloves of garlic
1 bunch of parsley
4 eggs

4 slices country bread (or white bread)
2 tbsp / 30 ml light grape vinegar
2 tbsp / 30 ml oil
1 tbsp / 15 g butter
salt, pepper to taste

The Portuguese seafarers not only played a central role in the discovery of unexplored sea routes, but also brought from distant countries fruit, vegetables, and spices that were integrated into European cooking. Vasco da Gama from the province of Alentejo, for example, discovered the Cape of Good Hope in 1497 and thus promoted the trade in spices and fruit with all the authority of a viceroy of Portuguese India.

The tomato came to Europe from the New World. The numerous different names it was given (golden apple, love apple, paradise apple) prove that it enjoyed extraordinary popularity and, like many foods, was thought to have powers that went beyond just nutrition. It has remained an ingredient of innumerable sauces and meals. In the province of Alentejo in southern Portugal, farmers live predominantly on tomatoes and country bread as well as goat's or sheep's milk cheese. Apart from country bread, cornmeal bread is also very popular in Portugal.

Only ripe, fleshy, and tasty tomatoes ripened under the afternoon sun are suitable for this soup. So, as our chef Maria Santos Gomes advises, it is far better to save making this soup until it can be made in season. In other words, ignore the tomatoes offered all year round no matter how red they are, for nothing can replace a tomato's natural ripening in full sun. Cook these fully ripened tomatoes of the season very slowly with a green pepper or, better still, a pinch of sugar if you want to conceal their slightly acid flavor.

1. Skin and seed the tomatoes. Slice the onion and green chili. Chop garlic and parsley. Place everything into a saucepan.

2. Add oil, butter, pepper, and salt to the vegetables. Braise over a low heat.

Alentejo

3. Pour 2 tbsp / 30 ml unsalted grape vinegar into a pot three-quarters full of water. Bring to a boil. Add the eggs and poach for 3–4 minutes. Then dip them into cold water straight away, drain and trim the edges.

4. To serve, place a slice of bread in each soup plate. Top with a poached egg and ladle the boiling tomato soup around it.

Preparation time: 30 minutes
Cooking time: 15 minutes
Difficulty: ★

Serves four

4 sheets phyllo dough (or puff pastry –
  see basic recipes)
30 mussels
4 langoustines
scant ⁷/₈ lb / 400 g sea bass
4 asparagus tips
⁵/₈ lb / 300 g carrots
scant ⁷/₁₆ lb / 200 g onions
¹/₈ lb / 60 g leeks
scant ⁷/₁₆ lb / 200 g zucchini
generous ³/₈ cup / 100 ml white wine

scant ¹/₄ cup cognac (or brandy) / 50 ml
generous ³/₈ cup / 100 ml vegetable oil
2 cloves of garlic
8 tsp / 40 g butter
salt, pepper to taste

For the sauce:
2 tomatoes
1 clove of garlic
1 bouquet garni
scant ¹/₄ cup / 50 g butter
scant ³/₄ cup / 200 ml crème fraîche
scant ¹/₄ cup / 50 ml olive oil
generous ³/₈ cup / 100 ml white wine
1 tbsp / 15 g tomato paste
salt, pepper to taste

The Aegean Sea, center of Greek mythology, could well be described as a maze of remote islands and bays, were it not for fear of insulting the peoples of the antique world. Aeacus in his desperation, waiting for his son to return, drowned himself in its waters, and Icarus, flying too close to the sun, also fell to his death into the Aegean. Today, with its variety of scarce fish and crustaceans, the Aegean Sea is worthy of being protected. It is a true treasure chest, with products that therefore deserve being being presented in a "purse," at least in Nikolaos Sarantos' opinion. He adjusted the traditional recipe to use seafood instead of lamb. Phyllo dough, prepared exclusively from flour, water, and salt, has been part of Greek cuisine for centuries, and no culinary fashion has ever been able to diminish its success. In Greek shops you may be able to buy it ready-made; if unavailable, replace it with puff pastry. If you brush the phyllo layers with butter and oil, they will turn golden brown in the oven.

The contents of this "purse" should include sea bass or a similar fish, such as ocean perch, but stay away from fatty fish. The fish must be fried in a pan, separately from the langoustines, before it is flambéed with alcohol. The other ingredient that our chef recommends is the white, extraordinarily sweet onion from the island of Cephalonie (the largest of the Ionian Islands) which gives the brunoise of finely cut vegetables a perfect consistency. Fortunately, the United States has its own version of a sweet onion in the Vidalia variety, primarily grown in the southern states.

1. Shell the langoustines and dice them as well as the fish. Sauté with the chopped garlic and half an onion, add white wine and then steam. Set aside sixteen mussels in their shells, and open the rest. Cut the vegetables into fine strips and blanch. Sauté half an onion with salt and pepper in butter and add cognac. Combine the ingredients to make the filling.

2. For the "purses," butter the phyllo sheets and place some filling in the middle. Close the sheets to make pouches and tie them up with blanched and cooled leeks. Brown in the oven at 340 °F / 170 °C for about ten minutes. Blanch the asparagus tips and leave them to steep in butter until done.

Aegean Sea

3. For the sauce, sauté the carcasses of the langoustines with some finely chopped onion, garlic and carrot. Add the tomatoes and pour wine and the mussel water over the mixture. Add a tablespoon of tomato paste and the bouquet garni. Reduce and pass through a sieve. Add crème fraîche and reduce again. Add butter.

4. To serve, place a "purse" in the center of each plate, sprinkle with sauce, and decorate with mussels, asparagus tips, and carrots.

Noodles with Boletus Filling

Preparation time: 30 minutes
Setting time: 1 hour
Cooking time: 40 minutes
Difficulty: ★★★

Serves four

For the noodle dough:
8 egg yolks
generous 2 cups / 500 g flour
4 tsp / 20 ml olive oil, salt

For the mushroom filling:
generous 1lb / 500 g boletus
2 shallots each, 1 clove of garlic
1 sprig of parsley
2 tbsp / 30 ml poultry stock, veal stock
salt, pepper to taste

For the frothy Gruyère sauce:
scant ¹/₈ lb / 50 g Gruyère
2 tsp / 10 g Parmesan
3 egg yolks
1 bay leaf, 2 sprigs of thyme, 1 clove of garlic

²/₃ cup / 150 ml cream, 4 tsp / 20 ml whipping cream
¹/₂ tsp / 5 g nutmeg
salt, pepper to taste

For the boletus juice:
5¹/₄ oz / 150 g boletus, 2 dried morels
5¹/₄ oz / 150 g button mushrooms
3¹/₂ oz / 100 g vegetables for roasting
2 tbsp / 30 g butter
scant ¹/₄ cup / 50 ml olive oil
generous ³/₈ cup / 100 ml white wine or champagne
1 clove of garlic, a pinch of coriander, 1 bay
 leaf, 2 sprigs each of thyme, parsley
salt, pepper to taste

To garnish:
8 boletus caps
4 tsp / 20 g Parmesan, parsley

Our chef, Fritz Schilling, once had to improvise an original composition with a noodle base for the editors of another cookbook. Inspired by the idea of a snail shell, he cut long noodles and rolled them around a suitable filling in the shape of a spiral. The concept allowed him to focus attention on the boletus, which he is most partial to. The recipe developed into a great classic, and he is now presenting it to us.

Irrespective of whether you use boletus from Bordeaux or any other region, wild mushrooms should not be washed in water but cleaned carefully with a brush. This also applies to other types of mushrooms, like the funnel-shaped chanterelles with their irregular edges, the meadow mushrooms, and many others. If you dry the noodles on a kitchen towel as soon as they are cooked and leave them to cool, they will stick better to

the cold filling, provided the filling is not too fluid. The success of this recipe depends to a large extent on the right temperature and the right consistency of both the noodles and the filling.

The frothy Gruyère sauce is a most interesting and tasty creation that definitely leaves scope for further variations, such as adding Emmental cheese or Comté. Even Normandy and Brittany produce excellent Gruyère which can definitely bear comparison with the products of where the cheese originated-the region of Gruyère in the Swiss canton of Fribourg. For the whipped cream use liquid cream with a 32 percent fat content (basic whipping cream) and whip it at a temperature of over 41 °F until thick but not firm.

1. Knead all the ingredients indicated into a noodle dough and leave to rest for an hour. Roll out thinly with a rolling pin and cut into 1 x 20 in / 2 x 50 cm long strips. Cook in salted water, leave to cool and dry on a cloth.

2. For the mushroom filling, chop the boletus, brown them and add the chopped shallots, the veal stock, garlic, and herbs. Reduce the liquid for a few minutes. When cool, spread onto the noodles and roll up the dough into a spiral. Place in an ovenproof dish lined with buttered baking paper and add 2 tbsp / 30 ml poultry stock. Scatter Parmesan over and bake au gratin.

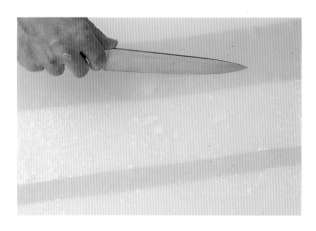

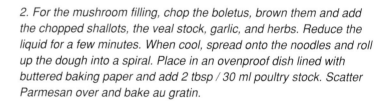

in Frothy Gruyère Sauce

3. To make the frothy Gruyère sauce, bring ²/₃ cup / 150 ml of cream to a boil and add garlic, bay leaf, thyme, and grated nutmeg; leave to steep for 5–6 minutes. Add the egg yolks and whip to a froth in a double boiler. Add grated Gruyère and Parmesan and melt in the hot froth. Pass through a sieve and complete with whipped cream.

4. For the boletus juice, sauté mushrooms and vegetables in olive oil, add herbs and white wine and season with salt and pepper. Pass through a fine sieve after two minutes. Reduce the juice a little and blend with butter. Serve decorated with the two contrasting sauces, small fried boletus caps, Parmesan, and parsley.

Preparation time: 20 minutes
Cooking time: 20 minutes
Difficulty: ★★

Serves four

$^1/_8$ lb / 60 g Cheddar cheese
$^1/_8$ lb / 60 g blue cheese
1 bunch of asparagus (to yield 12 tips)
2 tomatoes
1 shallot
4 eggs
$^1/_4$ cup / 50 g grated Parmesan cheese

scant $^7/_8$ cup / 200 ml cream
generous 1 cup / 250 g butter
1 cup / 250 ml dry white wine
generous 2 cups / 500 ml poultry stock
1 bunch of chives
1 bunch of chervil
salt, pepper to taste

For the Béchamel sauce:
scant $^1/_4$ cup / 50 g butter
scant $^1/_4$ cup / 50 g flour
generous 3 cups / 750 ml whole milk

An "accident" often results in the most creative recipes – in the case of our chefs, Rudolf Sodamim and Jonathan Wicks, that is what happened one day in the *Queen Elizabeth II* kitchens. The chefs forgot their soufflés were baking in the oven, and the only way to rescue them was with a hastily prepared Béchamel sauce. However, the guests were not quite as punctual as they should have been, so the chefs had to put the soufflés back into the oven. That was when they noticed that they could, in fact, be baked twice. In front of all the guests, they were then lifted out of their molds and served covered with butter and asparagus. This creation subsequently became a classic.

As a basis for the soufflés, our chefs recommend Cheddar, a typically English cheese that originated some time in the 16th century, during the reign of Queen Elizabeth I. The little village in Somerset from which it came, situated at the mouth of

the picturesque Cheddar Gorge, is certainly less well-known than the yellowish cylindrical or rectangular cheese. Although it is firmly pressed, the cheese is still soft to the touch. Legend has it that Queen Victoria was presented with an impressive thousand pound (five hundred kilo) Cheddar on her wedding in 1840. But you will certainly not need that much to appreciate this slightly fatty cheese, with its pronounced, distinctive flavor.

For harmony, add some soft blue cheese, which the English are particularly partial to without producing it themselves. The Bleu d'Auvergne, Bleu de Bresse or Bleu de Causses would be suitable. The cook will finally decide, of course, but according to our chefs even a Boursin with garlic will guarantee an exciting moment.

1. In a saucepan make a roux from butter and flour. Carefully add the boiling milk.

2. Grate the Cheddar and chop the blue cheese. Add the egg yolks (retaining the egg whites), the Cheddar and the blue cheese to the Béchamel sauce. Whip the egg whites until stiff and fold in gently.

Cheese Soufflé

3. Grease four small soufflé molds and sprinkle with Parmesan. Spoon the mixture into the molds and cook in a double boiler in a hot oven for 8–12 minutes. In a stockpot cook the chopped shallot and the white wine and reduce. Add the poultry stock and the cream and reduce by two-thirds. Stir small pats of butter into the cream over a low heat.

4. Season the sauce to taste and pass through a fine sieve. Slide the soufflés back into the oven until they have puffed up nicely. Dip the tomatoes into boiling water, skin and seed them. Add chives, asparagus, and the diced tomatoes to the sauce. Lift the soufflés out of their molds, serve on plates and sprinkle with the sauce. Decorate with chervil leaves.

Fried Belgian Endive

Preparation time: 30 minutes
Cooking time: 15 minutes
Difficulty: ★

Serves four

3 Belgian endives
½ lb / 250 g raw goose liver (foie gras)
2 tsp / 10 g butter
1 tbsp / 15 g black truffle
1 tsp / 5 g sugar
1 tsp / 5 g grated nutmeg

1 tsp / 5 ml sherry vinegar
1 tbsp / 15 ml olive oil
salt, fresh-ground pepper to taste

"I am a great friend of chicory," admits our chef, Roger Souvereyns, who has had this recipe on his menu since his 40th birthday. For Roger Souvereyns chicory is a vegetable that lends itself continually to new gastronomic variations, and it has accompanied him throughout his career as a chef. In this case, he is using a close relative of chicory – the Brussels, or Belgian endive (called *chicon* or *witloof* in Belgium), which is popular for its bitter substances and its digestive qualities.

Interestingly, the antique Greeks referred to Belgian endive as "friend of the liver," which might have inspired this combination with foie gras. Very low in calories and with a water content of ninety-five percent, it is a frequent component in health-conscious diets. In our recipe, the fine endive leaves are cooked over a high heat so that the water evaporates. They

should never be kept in the water they were cooked in, or they will acquire a bitter taste. Caramelize them by cautiously adding sugar and keep them warm at an adequate temperature until they are served.

In principle, a raw goose liver has no fat. Cut it carefully into very thin slices to allow these to warm by conduction from merely touching the warm chicory leaves. The also finely cut truffles serve to intensify the flavor of the foie gras.

This recipe is exclusively designed for the endive, and Roger Souvereyns refuses to substitute his beloved vegetable with anything else.

1. Cut the endives into fine strips of 1¼ in / 3 cm. Wash well and dry.

2. Fry the endive strips in oil and butter over a high heat for two minutes. Season with nutmeg, salt, pepper, and sugar. Leave to caramelize and add sherry vinegar.

with Foie Gras

3. Add the finely cut truffles and braise for ten seconds.

4. Spoon the chicory onto the center of the pre-warmed plates. Place the paper-thin liver slices on top to be warmed by the chicory. Season with a little fresh-ground pepper.

Preparation time: 15 minutes
Soaking time: 12–24 hours
Cooking time: 1 hour, 30 minutes
Difficulty: ★

Serves four

20 prawns
⅝ lb / 300 g dried chickpeas
4 nasturtium flowers
1 onion
1 bunch of chives
scant ¼ cup / 50 ml white wine

½ cup / 125 ml olive oil
½ cup / 125 ml sherry vinegar
½ cup / 125 g flour
salt, pepper to taste

For the green pepper sauce:
2 green peppers
half an onion
scant ¼ cup / 50 ml white wine
scant ¼ cup / 50 ml fish stock
¼ cup / 50 ml extra-virgin olive oil from
   first pressing
salt, pepper to taste

In Spain the chickpea is an indispensable component of a very popular stew called *cocido*. The best type, according to Chef Pedro Subijana, is grown in the little village of Fuente Saucedo close to Zamora. In the old days people used to retain the left-over chickpeas from lunch and fry them for supper. Our chef applies a similar method.

Chickpeas need to be soaked for a whole night and then cooked for a long time until their indigestible skins are shed. Only then are they fried in sufficient olive oil to cover them. The prawns are only lightly grilled. The best Mediterranean prawns are caught in Andalusia – unfortunately they are also wasted, used as bait for salmon fishing in England.

The nasturtium flower serves two purposes in this recipe. The decorative flower lends the dish a Japanese flair, and its piquant and peppery taste emphasizes the flavor of the chick-pea puree. Its taste reminds one a bit of red radish, cress, and capers, and it is most often marinated in vinegar to increase this effect. The Germans call this plant "capuchin cress," a name it owes to its calyx, which resembles the shape of a Capuchin monk's hood. With this flower, Chef Subijana wants to honor his father who, a chef himself, was very fond of this plant.

1. Soak the chickpeas overnight. Heat the chopped onion in a pan, dust with flour and sauté. Add some wine and chickpeas. Cover with water, add salt and cook for 90 minutes. Take out some of the stock for the vinaigrette and add vinegar, salt and pepper. Pass through a sieve.

2. Prepare a chickpea puree in a food processor with part of the peas and the stock. Drain the remaining chickpeas and fry them in hot oil.

Fried Chickpeas

3. Shell the prawns just before cooking them, leaving the last ring of the shell (including the tail) on. Remove the guts and season with salt, pepper, and olive oil. Place in the pan under the grill and cook gently.

4. Seed the peppers, cut into large strips and fry in oil. Add the finely cut onion midway during the cooking process. Pour the oil off and combine the mixture with wine and fish stock. Pass through a sieve, season to taste and add a dash of olive oil. Spoon some chickpea puree onto the plates, garnish each with a nasturtium flower and arrange the prawns decoratively.

Gramigna with Mild Bacon

Preparation time: 30 minutes
Cooking time: 40 minutes
Difficulty: ★

Serves four

For 7 oz / 200 g green "gramigna":
2 eggs
1²/₃ cups / 400 g flour
3¹/₂ oz / 100 g spinach
7 oz / 400 g mild bacon
generous ³/₈ cup / 100 g Parmesan
generous 1 cup / 250 ml balsamic vinegar

¹/₂ cup / 125 ml olive oil
salt, pepper to taste

For 7 oz / 200 g yellow "gramigna":
2 eggs
1²/₃ cups / 400 g flour

Originally this meal was prepared with couch grass, a wild-growing herb that gave the bacon a tangy flavor further emphasized by the balsamic vinegar. Following the century-old culinary traditions, the grass is still used for the fresh pasta that Italians are particularly partial to. As our chef, Romano Tamani attests, *gramigna*, in whatever color, is a fine alternative to tagliatelli, especially in appetizers.

It would certainly be ideal if you could prepare the two-tone *gramigna* yourself, possibly with the help of a special noodle machine that pushes the dough through a grid and produces spaghetti-like threads. If you do not own such a machine you may use ready-made spaghetti (though make sure it is imported, or at least from durum wheat), and break them carefully into small pieces.

Aceto balsamico, the indispensable balsamic vinegar used everywhere in Italy and far beyond Italy's borders, lends this dish its typical character. The Italian town of Modena, where it originated, looks back onto a long tradition. Since the Italian Renaissance, unfermented Trebbiano grapes have been processed into a particularly valuable vinegar that has to mature for up to ten years in specially constructed small vats in order to develop its incomparable aroma. A bottle labeled *aceto balsamico tradizionale di Modena* guarantees its origin and its traditional method of production. The particularly high price is also indicative of the exclusivity of this product used in cold and warm dishes. Here, its prominent flavor seasons the fried bacon, which is one of the other main components of this dish.

1. Dice the mild bacon finely. Prepare the dough to make the gramigna. For the yellow gramigna, blend eggs and flour. For the green gramigna, add the cooked, drained, and chopped spinach to the eggs and the flour. Put both doughs through the noodle machine and cut into small pieces.

2. Fry the finely diced bacon in a pan with very hot olive oil for a few seconds.

and Balsamic Vinegar

3. Season with salt, add the balsamic vinegar and braise until the liquid has boiled down completely.

4. Cook the noodles in a big pot of water, drain and combine with the bacon. Sprinkle with grated Parmesan cheese.

Preparation time: 30 minutes
Cooking time: 1 hour, 40 minutes
Difficulty: ★

Serves four

7 oz / 200 g rabbit meat
generous $^1/_8$ lb / 70 g bacon
2 oz / 50 g tomato
$^1/_2$ lb / 250 g assorted vegetables for roasting
 (celery, carrots, shallots)
1 cup / 250 ml white wine
generous $^3/_8$ cup / 100 ml beef bouillon

5$^1/_4$ oz / 150 g Parmesan
2 bay leaves
2 sprigs of rosemary
$^1/_4$ cup / 50 ml oil
1 tbsp / 15 g butter
salt to taste

For the macaroni (generous 1 cup / 250 g):
1$^2/_3$ cups / 400 g flour
3 eggs

What would Italian cooking be without pasta? This dish, normally served as an appetizer, is closely linked to the traditions of the neighboring regions of Lombardy and Emilia-Romagna. It is, moreover, a very balanced appetizer incorporating equal amounts of pasta, vegetables, meat, and cheese.

Italians are particularly fond of rabbit meat. They consume more than eight pounds per inhabitant per year and thus take first place worldwide. Try to find firm meat without an excessive amount of fat, dice it finely and cook until light pink. There is, in fact, a more economical version of this recipe, without meat but with plenty of vegetables to obtain the required amount of liquid.

Traditionally, noodles are prepared by hand. It is common to make use of very specific instruments to refine presentation.

For instance, macaroni are shaped into little pipes by means of a small wooden rod, a "pettine," and a grooved board is used for the even pattern of finely crossed grooves on the outside of the noodles. Other instruments applied are, for example, the "chitarra," a wooden frame with metal strings, or the ravioli board.

To round this dish off, our chef, Romano Tamani, recommends a cheese from the Po region, the Grano Padano Parmesan, which he prefers to its classic competitor, the Parmigiano Reggiano from the south. However, if chef Tamani's favorite is unavailable, you may substitute it with the latter.

1. Chop carrots, celery, and shallots very finely. For the macaroni, knead flour and eggs into a dough, roll it out and cut into rectangles. Roll these over the pettine, (a little wooden rod), shape into macaroni and decorate by rolling them over a grooved board.

2. In a pan with olive oil, sauté the diced bacon and the vegetable mixture consisting of carrots, celery, and shallots.

Rabbit Sauce

3. Cut the rabbit meat into small pieces. Add the tomato and the small rabbit pieces, then bay leaves, rosemary, wine and bouillon. Braise for 90 minutes until the liquid is slightly reduced and thickened.

4. Cook the macaroni until al dente. Rinse under cold water, drain and season with the sauce and the grated Parmesan cheese. Serve on pre-heated plates, garnished with fresh herbs.

Sardine Fritters with

Preparation time: 1 hour
Cooking time: 30 minutes
Difficulty: ★

Serves four

12 sardines
4 zucchini flowers
4 celery leaves
2 red peppers
1 onion
scant ¼ cup / 50 ml olive oil
5 quarts / 5 l peanut oil

4 sprigs of basil
4 sprigs of sage
4 sprigs of cilantro
4 sprigs of smooth parsley
salt, pepper to taste

For the batter:
generous ⅓ cup / 85 g flour
generous ⅓ cup / 85 g cornstarch
3 tsp / 15 g baking powder
generous 1 cup / 250 ml warm water
scant ¼ cup / 50 ml olive oil
fine salt to taste

Fritters are served in various ways, savory or sweet, as appetizers or desserts. They are available in all kinds of shapes and are loved for their lightness as well as for the contrast between the crisp dough and the juicy, succulent contents.

The basic principle of fritter-making is simple. You dip a small piece of vegetable, meat or fish into the batter, and then deep-fry it. Apart from batter you may also use choux pastry or even a yeast dough, though this will need time to rise.

Our chef, Laurent Tarridec, chose a light batter in which to dip the sardines and herbs. As he notes, when you coat frozen food with a batter and then deep-fry it, it experiences a strong thermal shock, and the fritters puff up in weird and wonderful shapes.

Chef Tarridec has his origins in Brittany, but his heart belongs to the Mediterranean. In his opinion, sardines from the Atlantic coast, from Douarnenez or Saint-Gilles-Croix-de-Vie, are just as good as those from Marseilles, Sète or any other harbor of the Midi where they are caught with the aid of lantern lights at night. Most inappropriately, this classic fish with its shiny skin and its moderately fat flesh is squeezed into cans, a complete contradiction of its incomparable quality when fresh.

Serve this dish hot and garnished with parsley. Instead of sardines, fritters may also hide other secrets, like langoustine or cod fillet pieces.

1. Make a well in a mixture of flour, cornstarch, baking powder, and salt and gradually pour in water and olive oil. Blend all these ingredients well. Leave this batter to rest for half an hour.

2. Gut and de-head the sardines. Remove the backbone above the stomach with a filleting knife. Wash and dry the sardines as well as the herbs.

Aromatic Herbs

3. Peel and chop the onion and sauté in olive oil. Add the washed, seeded, and diced peppers. Simmer, covered, for half an hour. Puree in a food processor and keep warm.

4. Dip the sardines celery leaves, zucchini flowers, and the herbs into the fritter batter. Drain and deep-fry separately in hot peanut oil at 320 °F / 160 °C. Drain on paper towels and add salt. Serve three fritters on each plate with a few herbs, garnished with a generous tablespoon of pepper puree and parsley.

Skate Salad with Lentils

Preparation time: 50 minutes
Cooking time: 35 minutes
Difficulty: ★

Serves four

4 skate fillets, approximately ⅝ lb / 300 g)
7 oz / 200 g lentils

For the bouillon:
1 bouquet garni
1 carrot,
1 onion
¼ cup / 60 ml white wine
1 tbsp / 15 g coarse salt

For the garnish:
1 carrot
1 zucchini
1 onion
1 celery stalk

For the vinaigrette:
⅓ cup / 80 ml olive oil
scant ¼ cup / 50 ml sherry vinegar
¾ cup / 200 ml poultry stock
1 bunch of chives
1 pinch of curry powder
1 bunch of chervil
1 tbsp / 15 g mustard

It is time to discard those awful memories of a tepid mush of tasteless lentils stuck together in a gooey lump. We are not in a canteen, and the exquisite Ponote lentils that our chef recommends are a totally different story. (Ponote is also the name given to the inhabitants of Puy-en-Velay, a select area for growing green lentils.) The dreaded sessions around the kitchen table sorting out lentils are also a thing of the past, since the little stones have long disappeared. In other words, there is no valid reason to look down on the main ingredient in this delectable warm appetizer, with juicy vegetables that contrast well with the tender flesh of the ray.

"The lentil represents both tradition and modernity. It enchants us with its authenticity and simplicity yet sets no limits to imagination," proclaimed Michel Troisgros, the master chef from Roanne, in celebration of the lentil from Puy. This variety of lentil boasts a controlled designation of origin and therefore presents itself as a lentil *de luxe*.

To cook the lentils, put them on the stove in cold water and make sure they remain *al dente*. Unlike dried beans, they do not have to be soaked ahead of time. The best accompaniment for them is the skate, also known as a stingray, with its sweet-tasting, somewhat scallop-like flavor. Put the skate on the stove in cold water and take it off when the water has reached boiling point. The salad dressing for the dish, with the pure aroma of sherry vinegar, lends a special character. If you like strong seasoning, you could add horseradish or galangal root for an added bite.

1. Make a bouillon from the ingredients indicated, add the skate fillets, and cook for 12 minutes. Leave to cool in the stock, drain, and set aside to dry on a cloth. Remove the skin and the fat (the black part on the flesh) of the skate.

2. Cook the lentils the classic way for 30 minutes. Mix the ingredients for the vinaigrette.

in Sherry Vinaigrette

3. Dice the carrot, zucchini, onion, and celery stalk finely.

4. Sauté the diced vegetables in butter, add the cooked and rinsed lentils, the poultry stock, and the vinaigrette. Arrange the ray fillets on the plates and scatter the vinaigrette with the lentils evenly around them. Decorate with chervil leaves or sprigs of chives.

Pennette with

Preparation time: 20 minutes
Cooking time: 8 minutes
Difficulty: ✭

Serves four

scant $^7/_8$ lb / 400 g fresh or dried pennette
tomato sauce from fresh tomatoes (if desired)
1 garlic clove
4 tomatoes
1 shallot

1 anchovy fillet
1 tsp / 5 g capers, chopped
1 tsp / 5g black olives,
1 tsp / 5g chili pepper
1 bunch of basil
$^1/_4$ cup / 50 ml olive oil
$^1/_4$ lb / 50 g Parmesan cheese
salt, pepper to taste

Preparing pasta without turning it into an unappetizing mush requires a fair amount of skill. To avoid a temperature shock that could have disastrous effects (for one, it could ruin the consistency), do not submerge the cooked and drained noodles in cold water to stop the cooking process. And, if you serve the noodles in a sauce, thin it with a few tablespoons of the noodle water before you stir them in. These are helpful tricks for this very subtle recipe with its rich flavors that will, if prepared right, undoubtedly delight your guests.

The noodles chosen here are pennette, or small penne rigate. Their shape is inspired by the larger macaroni cut at an angle. There are medium-sized penne as well (mezze penne), which are relatively common.

The success of this recipe depends to a large extent on the quality of the tomatoes, a fruit of American origin that was introduced to Europe in the 16th century via Naples and Genoa. In our recipe, this "golden apple" accompanies typical Mediterranean ingredients, the amount and combination of which is left up to your personal preference. This kind of option is what causes debates in the Valazza family: Mr. Valazza enjoys this dish with red peppers, whereas Mrs. Valazza insists on Parmesan. In this case, domestic peace is restored by accepting variety as the rule. Our chef, Luisa Valazza, recommends the tasty black olives from Liguria, but green olives may be used as an alternative. The fine aroma of basil, however, is indispensable.

1. Chop the black olives, chili pepper, garlic, and shallot; slice the anchovy. Heat the olive oil in a pan and sauté the chopped garlic, shallot, anchovies, capers, the black olives, and chili pepper.

2. Then add the sauce made of fresh tomatoes (essentially pureeing garlic and fresh tomatoes before adding them to the mélange). Cook for a few minutes, while stirring.

Mediterranean Flavors

3. Cook the pennette in boiling salted water until al dente, drain, and set aside. Dip the tomatoes briefly into boiling water, leave to cool, cut the tops off and hollow them out.

4. Fry the pennette in the sauce. Add a 1 tbsp / 15 g of Parmesan and 1 tbsp / 15 g of chopped basil. Fill the tomatoes with pennette and sauce, arrange on plates, and sprinkle with the tomato sauce.

Eggplant Cakes

Preparation time: 10 minutes
Cooking time: 10 minutes
Difficulty: ★★

Serves four

3¹/₂ oz / 100 g bonito tuna (or yellowback, skipjack, or bluefin tuna)
3¹/₂ oz / 100 g salmon trout
1 eggplant
3¹/₂ oz / 100 g carrots
3¹/₂ oz / 100 g spinach

3¹/₂ oz / 100 g green beans
⁷/₈ cup / 200 g flour
1 bunch of smooth-leaved parsley
1 tbsp / 15 g oil
4 tsp / 20 ml cream
¹/₈ cup / 30 ml whole milk
1 tsp / 5 g nutmeg
salt, pepper to taste

The bonito, a large type of tuna, lives mostly in warm waters, and is found in the Mediterranean, the Atlantic, and the North Sea. Its flesh, with characteristic white stripes, is perhaps slightly fatty, but very tender. Bonito and bluefin tuna have much in common, and are also prepared similarly. The salmon trout, which accompanies the bonito in this inventive appetizer from Chef Freddy Van Decasserie, is at its best from April to June; the fish is actually a trout that has matured on a seafood diet, which colors its flesh. This light pink flesh is a delicacy and must always be prepared when very fresh. A firm round belly and a very stiff body with shiny scales are indications of its freshness.

Although eggplants are available all year round, their flavor is best in summer. Choose medium-sized unblemished specimens with a very shiny dark skin, as large eggplants often have too many seeds. If you dip the slices into milk, then coat them with flour and gently tap off any excess, they will turn out tender and succulent.

The vegetables should provide some color variety to intensify the visual impression of this appetizer. Choose anything you like, except early green peas with their soft green hue. Add a little water and cream to the spinach and carrot purees to give them a creamier texture.

You can build the pyramid form of this without any difficulty if you first cut the fish into very thin slices. Baked on the grill, bonito and salmon trout retain their succulent consistency and freshness.

1. Cut the eggplant into ¹/₄ in / ¹/₂ cm rounds. Season with salt and pepper. Dip the slices into milk and coat them with flour. Fry in oil over a high heat for two minutes on each side.

2. Steam and dice the carrots finely. Proceed similarly with the beans. Blanch the spinach, chop finely and heat with 4 tsp / 20 ml cream and a pinch each of salt and nutmeg. Use part of the spinach and the carrots to make a puree.

Fisherman's Style

3. Clean the salmon trout and the bonito carefully. Fillet them and remove the bones. Cut both fish into thin, even slices.

4. Slide the fish slices briefly onto the grill. Then, build a pyramid of eggplant slices covered with salmon trout and bonito. Place them in alternate layers on top of each other with vegetables in-between. Spoon a green and orange ring of spinach and carrot puree around the pyramid, and garnish with parsley leaves.

Ragout of Caramelized

Preparation time: *4 hours*
Soaking time: *12 hours*
Cooking time: *2 hours*
Difficulty: ★★

Serves four

1 calf's tongue
1 piece of calf's head (about 2.2 lbs / 1 kg)
1 veal sweetbread
2 veal knuckles, boned
2 carrots
2 onions
1 celery stalk
1 quart / 1 l veal stock

1 quart / 1 l red Banyuls
1 quart / 1 l red wine
1 cup / 250 ml port
scant ¼ cup / 50 ml oil
1 bouquet garni
salt, pepper to taste

For the garnish:
20 asparagus tips
3½ oz / 100 g fava beans
1 bunch of young carrots
1 bunch of young turnips
1 bunch of cocktail onions
1 bunch of chervil

In the 17th and 18th centuries, offal was very popular. Calf's head, for example, was prepared in many different ways, some considered fit for a king. With the traditions of those days in mind, our chef, Gérard Vié, presents a most original warm appetizer based on various calf's innards. You can even save it for several days if your guests, against all odds, leave any leftovers.

When you buy offal, both red and white, make sure it is very fresh and in immaculate condition and prepare it straight away. Soak it first for quite a long time to remove the unavoidable bloodstains and marks. Owing to this procedure, this recipe requires a number of steps that should be spread out over two to three days. With regard to the veal sweetbread, the most del-

icate part of the offal, take a few precautionary measures into account. Remove any yellowish fibers, any traces of blood or other tissue, and use only the very white, odorless meat.

Choose tender young vegetables to accompany this ragout. Prepare them individually, according to their requirements, and as late as possible to preserve their full flavor. This refers particularly to the fava beans, which have to be skinned beforehand, particularly if they are older beans with their indigestible white skins. Prepare a few more than planned; you will find that you will be continually tempted to sample them. Banyuls, with its high sugar content, is ideal for caramelizing. The wine will lend the dish a superb flavor.

1. Soak all the offal in cold water overnight to rid it of any traces of blood. Then blanch it and leave it to cool. Drain and clean it, and cut the meat into cubes.

2. To cook the meat in Banyuls, heat all the offal pieces in oil first and add the finely cut carrots, celery, and onions and the bouquet garni.

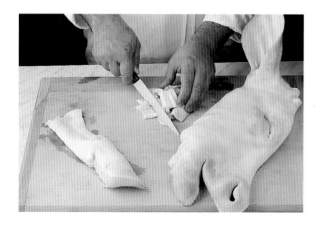

Offal with Banyuls

3. Brown and spoon out the fat, then add port and Banyuls. Boil down and add the remaining red wine. Reduce again, add the veal stock and cook over a low heat for an hour and a half.

4. Cook the vegetables individually in salted water, then braise them together in a pan with the offal stock. Remove the offal pieces, strain the liquid, and reduce to a creamy sauce. Add the offal pieces again. Serve on deep plates and sprinkle with chives. Garnish with vegetables, and serve very hot.

Preparation time: 20 minutes
Cooking time: 2 hours,
30 minutes
Difficulty: ★★★

Serves four

14 oz / 400 g egg noodle dough (see below),
  or noodles as desired
generous 1 lb / 500 g rabbit meat
5 oz / 150 g sheep's milk cheese
1 cup / 250 ml vegetable brunoise from celery,
  carrot, onions (see below)

2 cups / 500 ml chicken stock
5 spinach leaves
2 cloves of garlic
1 tomato
1 sprig of rosemary
3 sage leaves
2 bay leaves
1 small chili pepper
1 bunch of chervil
generous 3/8 cup / 100 ml red wine
1/2 cup / 125 ml extra-virgin olive oil
salt, black pepper to taste

Rabbit meat has been used in numerous dishes since time immemorial. This recipe, from Chef Gianfranco Vissani, is based on culinary traditions that have been passed on right through the whole history of the Italian peninsula. The very prominent flavor of the rabbit meat (preferably a young male specimen) will certainly delight your guests. To make sure that the rabbit is fresh when you buy it, check that its fur is shiny and its paws are still covered with hairs. Do not leave it to hang, as rabbit meat goes off quickly. Or, if you are not keen on game, you might want to use poultry instead of rabbit.

The central component of this recipe is the noodle dough prepared with eggs. Use at least forteen egg yolks for this recipe.

If our chef has his way you will have to use no fewer than thirty egg yolks for two pounds (one kilo) of flour. If this far exceeds the amount you require, you can keep what is left over and use it for lasagna, tagliatelle, ravioli, tortellini, spaghetti or any other traditional noodle recipes at a later stage. As an alternative, you can, of course, also use dry noodles. The freshness of the spinach is of utmost importance, since the structure of the leaves used to line the mold determines the appearance and the success of the whole dish.

1. Heat olive oil in a pan and add the brunoise, the chopped garlic, sage, bay leaves, rosemary, and chili pepper and braise for ten minutes. For the rabbit ragout, dice the rabbit meat and brown lightly in oil.

2. Add a dash of red wine and cook over a low heat for two hours. To prepare the sauce, mix some chopped tomato with the olive oil and thin with a ladle of poultry bouillon. Puree the mixture in the blender and then pass through a sieve. Add to the rabbit ragout.

Rabbit Sauce

3. Before the rabbit ragout has totally boiled down, add the rabbit stock prepared from the rabbit bones and take off the stove. Line small pâté molds with raw spinach leaves. Cook the noodles, drain them, place them in a pan, add rabbit ragout and mix with a fork.

4. Fill the molds with noodles, cover with grated sheep's milk cheese and bake in the oven for five minutes. Turn the pappardelle out of their molds, arrange them on plates and spoon sauce around them. Decorate with tomato cubes and chervil leaves.

Polenta

Preparation time: 30 minutes
Cooking time: 30 minutes
Difficulty: ★★

Serves four

7oz / 200 g sheep's milk ricotta
7oz / 200 g fresh anchovies
4 tsp / 20 g white cocktail onions
1³/₄ oz / 50 g garlic
half a chili pepper
2 tbsp / 30 ml olive oil
1 bay leaf
salt, black pepper to taste

For the polenta:
⁵/₈ lb / 300 g cornmeal
3¹/₄ cups / 800 ml mineral water
scant ¹/₈ lb / 50 g sheep's milk cheese
¹/₂ tsp olive oil
salt, pepper to taste

Traditionally, polenta is a porridge made of fine-grain corn semolina, which, according to historical records, was already a staple food in pre-Columbian civilization. The corn fritters were so popular that cornmeal was called "golden rain" on account of its fascinating beautiful color. Chef Gianfranco Vissani here presents a dish that was originally designed for pork ragout, but is now prepared with onions and anchovies in keeping with Sicilian tradition.

You should use small fresh anchovies with firm and shiny bodies that are easy to clean. As soon as the head is removed, you should be able to take out the backbone without any difficulty. Outside the main fishing grounds in Spain, Italy or the French Midi, fresh anchovies are extremely hard to find.

It is an Italian custom to invite friends for the preparation of a polenta: they are then enlisted in helping to stir the flour slowly into the boiling water. The polenta must be liquid and creamy and not have any lumps. It must also be served as soon as it is cooked, which requires last-minute preparation. The same applies to the mixture of anchovies and onions. The anchovies can be substituted with tomatoes and garlic, but that is a matter of taste and personal choice.

Ricotta, available in any good cheese shop, is a very versatile sheep's milk cheese with a surprisingly light consistency. In this recipe, as Vissani insists, it should not be replaced by any other cheese.

1. Add a drop of olive oil, the grated sheep's milk cheese, and salt and pepper to the mineral water. Bring to a boil. Add the cornmeal and cook over a low heat for 20 minutes, stirring it with a wooden spatula. Sauté the cocktail onions with chopped garlic, bay leaf, and the half of a chili pepper in a pan with oil and brown lightly.

2. Clean and wash the anchovies, cut them into small cubes and combine them with the onions. Cook for a maximum of two minutes and take off the stove.

with Ricotta

3. Spread a ¹/₂ in / 1 cm thick layer of cooked polenta in an ovenproof dish. Place the onion and anchovy mixture on top, and sprinkle with the oil of that mixture.

4. Scatter the diced ricotta and the rest of the grated sheep's milk cheese over the polenta. Slide under the grill for a few minutes. Take it out, sprinkle with fresh grated garlic, and serve hot.

Red Beets in Beer Batte

Preparation time: 20 minutes
Cooking time: 40 minutes
Difficulty: ✴

Serves four

1¹/₄ lbs / 600 g small red beets
scant ¹/₄ cup / 50 ml tarragon vinegar
pinch of caraway seeds
1 bunch of parsley
salt to taste

For the batter:
⁵/₈ lb / 300 g flour
scant 5 tbsp / 70 g butter

3 eggs, separated
1¹/₄ cups / 300 ml pale lager beer
2 pinches of salt

For the horseradish sauce:
1 fresh horseradish root
1 shallot
generous 2 cups / 500 ml white wine
scant ¹/₄ cup / 50 ml Noilly Prat (vermouth)
1¹/₄ cups / 300 ml vegetable stock
⁵/₈ cup / 150 g butter
¹/₄ cup / 60 ml cream
salt, pepper to taste

The bulk of German red beets are produced in Bavaria. In this recipe, which could have been invented by dedicated followers of vegetarian cooking, our chef, Heinz Winkler, makes use of all the possibilities inherent in this remarkable vegetable. Rich in sugar, calcium, and iron, it was once the issue in a fight between the Greeks and the Romans, who could not agree on where it originally came from. Whatever the case may have been, the Europeans welcomed the red beets with great enthusiasm. The French eat them raw or cooked in salads, the English fill them, the Norwegians serve them with herrings, the Russians make them into soup, and the Americans boil them and slice them into thin rounds.

There are four types of beets: round, flat, half-long and long ones. Heinz Winkler recommends the small, fairly young beets, which hide their fleshy roots under large green leaves.

Tarragon vinegar lends them a delicious aroma and the art only lies in covering them in sufficient batter to conceal a surprise for your guests.

The batter will turn pleasantly crisp when deep-fried if you add some butter to it and leave it to stand for a while. Grate the fresh horseradish just before you stir it into the sauce, otherwise it will lose the sharp flavor that gives this dish that extra something.

Some gourmets will probably frown at this "sweet adventure" which – though delicious – might be a little too imaginative for their taste. You may use alternatives like asparagus or salsify for this recipe, but in that case the horseradish sauce must be left out.

1. For the deep-fry batter, blend egg yolks and beer in a bowl. Melt the butter in a pan and add to the batter. Add salt, whip the egg whites and carefully fold into the mixture. Leave the batter to stand at room temperature for 30 minutes.

2. For the horseradish sauce, chop the shallot, add to a saucepan with wine and Noilly Prat and bring to a boil. Add the vegetable stock, reduce to a third of its original volume, and stir in butter and seasoning. Clean, peel, and grate the horseradish. Reheat the sauce, stir, and fold in 1 tbsp / 15 g of horseradish as well as some whipped cream.

with Horseradish Sauce

3. Clean the red beets and bring to a boil in a pot with water, tarragon vinegar, salt, and caraway seeds. Cook over a medium heat for 35–40 minutes. Drain, rinse under cold water and peel. Heat oil in a deep-fat fryer to 320 °F / 160 °C, roll the red beets in flour, dip them into batter and deep-fry them for one to two minutes.

4. Lift the "doughnuts" out with a skimmer and dry them on paper towels. Deep-fry the parsley for decoration. Pour the horseradish sauce onto the plates and arrange the deep-fried red beets and parsley on top.

Pike Dumplings

Preparation time: 1 hour, 30 minutes
Chilling time: 1 hour
Cooking time: 30 minutes
Difficulty: ★★

Serves four

12 large crayfish
3 each leeks, carrots, stalks of celery
1–2 tbsp / 20 g coarse salt
1 quart / 1 l fish stock

For the pike filling:
5$\frac{1}{4}$ oz / 150 g pike fillet
1 egg white
generous $\frac{3}{8}$ cup / 100 ml cream
salt, pepper to taste
juice of 1 lemon

generous $\frac{3}{8}$ cup / 100 ml whipping cream

For the sauce:
crayfish carcasses
2 tbsp / 30 ml vegetable oil

2 shallots (to yield $\frac{1}{4}$ cup / 60 g diced)
1 oz / 30 g each diced carrot, celery, fennel, tomato.
2 coriander seeds, 2 peppercorns
1 bunch of fresh dill
1$\frac{1}{4}$ cups / 300 ml Riesling (wine)
generous $\frac{3}{8}$ cup / 100 ml Noilly Prat (vermouth)
2$\frac{1}{2}$ tbsp / 40 ml port
4 tsp / 20 ml cognac
generous 1 cup / 250 ml fish stock
generous 1 cup / 250 ml cream
juice of 1 lemon
6 tbsp / 80 g butter

For the garnish:
1 carrot, 1 leek, 1 stalk of celery
scant $\frac{1}{8}$ lb / 50 g snowpeas

The German *knödel* and the French *quenelles*, both meaning dumplings, basically differ only in shape and are generally made from similar ingredients, such as minced meat, fish, or vegetables. Whether French or German, the mixture is then bound with eggs and poached, often in broth.

In this recipe the pike takes the lead role, accompanied by vegetables cut into diamond-shaped pieces – you should wind up with a quarter of a pound (one hundred and twenty grams) when all is cut. Considered a superb eating fish, pike is easily recognizable by its hammer-shaped mouth and light, silvery belly. This predatory fish makes its home in freshwater, and is extremely clever, adapting to the color of its surroundings and camouflaging itself to better surprise its chosen prey. In lakes with lush vegetation the pike has a greenish color, whereas it is

yellower in brackish water. If you want to serve a pike whole choose a medium-sized one of a maximum of six pounds (three kilos) to make sure it will retain its tenderness and flavor when cooked. For our recipe, larger pikes are recommended, since their fillets are more suitable for the preparation of dumplings (and pike is the fish customarily used in *quenelles*). Removing the bones with which the pike has very generously been endowed by nature requires a lot of patience.

The sauce is easy to prepare if all the numerous ingredients are available and of good quality. This frothy cream with its Mediterranean herbs (fennel, coriander) and subtle flavors (Riesling, Noilly Prat, port, and brandy) will doubtlessly delight your guests. So long as they are fresh, the origin and type of the crayfish is of no major importance.

1. For the pike filling Dice the pike fillets and season with salt and pepper. Refrigerate for an hour, then blend in a food processor with egg white and cream to make a smooth filling. Season to taste, add a few drops of lemon juice, strain and refrigerate. Cook the crayfish and the vegetables in salted water for four minutes, reserving the crayfish shells. Cut the vegetables into diamonds, blanch and rinse under cold water.

2. For the crayfish sauce sauté the crayfish shells in oil, add vegetables, spices, and, dill. Add white wine, vermouth, port and cognac and reduce. Pour the fish stock over and reduce to a third. Add the cream and cook over a low heat for ten minutes. Season to taste, strain and add the juice of a lemon.

with Crayfish

3. Heat the crayfish sauce and add the crayfish and vegetables. Stir in the butter.

4. Fold the whipped cream into the cooled pike filling. Heat the slightly salted fish stock. Form 12 pike dumplings with a tablespoon and poach them for 12–14 minutes. Place the dumplings onto the plates, garnish with crayfish and vegetables and sprigs of dill and pour the sauce over the whole arrangement.

Minestrone with

Preparation time: 15 minutes
Soaking time: 12 hours
Cooking time: 2 hours,
30 minutes
Difficulty: ★

Serves four

5/8 lb / 300 g borlotti beans, dried
5/8 lb / 300 g potatoes
5/8 lb / 300 g onions
2 cloves of garlic

3½ oz / 100 g Parma ham (the end piece)
2 tbsp / 30 g butter
¼ lb / 50 g Parmesan
½ cup / 125 ml olive oil
1 bundle of sage
1 zucchini
1 bunch of parsley
salt, pepper to taste

Aside from the summer months, this dish is never taken off the menu of the Vecchia Lanterna, Armando Zanetti's restaurant in Turin. Its preparation has been strongly influenced by traditions that can be traced back to the 14th century in the Piemont region. Minestrone is a simple, economical, and nourishing dish that can claim popularity among all social strata. Some of the restaurant's most famous regular customers (politicians, actors, journalists) order it the minute they come through the front doors.

Minestrone (Italian for "big soup") is basically a soup made of a mixture of different coarsely chopped vegetables such as carrots, potatoes, and celery, the combination varying depending on the chef and the region. It is often prepared with noodles or rice. Thus, as Zanetti encourages, choose the ingredients as

whim directs you: add large amounts of beans or fried boletus, like our chef's grandmother used to do, or cook it with pieces of bacon or ham like a Sunday soup from the old days, or do both. In this recipe, our chef processes the ham into small dumplings to add them to the minestrone. Parma ham, being both tasty and lean, is well suited for this purpose.

It is no coincidence that our chef recommends borlotti beans, as they have regional significance for him, being grown in the Italian province of Belluno. They are light red and slightly speckled and their taste is evocative of chestnuts. But if they are unavailable, substitute pinto beans, small kidney beans, or even adzuki beans instead. If you substitute Parma ham with pork or veal knuckle, the soup can be served as an appetizer, and the knuckle with the beans as a main dish.

1. Soak the beans overnight in lukewarm water. The next day, bring to a boil with the potatoes and the Parma ham. Top up with water and add salt.

2. Sauté the garlic and the tied-up sage in a pan with olive oil and butter.

Beans Piemont Style

3. Peel and slice the onions, add to the pan with garlic and sage bundle and braise.

4. Stir everything into the beans and cook over a low heat for about two and a half hours. Serve in soup plates with milled pepper, chopped parsley, and a tablespoon of olive oil, and decorate with zucchini strips. Add a little grated Parmesan on top, or serve on the side for your guest, to use as they desire.

Preparation time: 20 minutes
Cooking time: 30 minutes
Difficulty: ✼

Serves four

For the savarin:
scant $1/8$ lb / 50 g durum wheat semolina
generous 2 cups / 500 ml whole milk
1 egg
generous 2 tbsp / 30 g Parmesan (grated)
4 tsp / 20 g butter
a pinch of salt

For the artichokes:
2 artichokes
scant $1/4$ cup / 50 g butter
1 bunch of parsley
salt, pepper to taste

For the fonduta:
$1 1/4$ cups / 300 ml milk
7 oz / 200 g Emmental cheese
5 tsp / 25 g butter
5 tsp / 25 g flour
2 egg yolks
salt, pepper to taste

The Italian *fonduta* is the counterpart of the cheese fondue. In Piemont it is called *fondua* and made of Fontina, a rich semi-soft cooking cheese made from full-cream cow's milk that is similar to Raclette. The *fonduta* is always bound with an egg yolk and seasoned with pepper, unlike similar cheeses in Switzerland or the French mountainous regions.

If you are unable to get hold of Fontina, our chef recommends using Raclette cheese with butter added to make it into a nice and smoothly bound paste. However, if you find the cheese too fatty, just add a little water to give the *fonduta* the right consistency. Emmental, available almost anywhere in Europe (it is even produced in Brittany) and in many North American markets, generally also complies with all the requirements of

this recipe. The gentle touch of Parmesan, however, or preferably even Parmesan Grano Padano, is irreplaceable for rounding off this small semolina cake.

The savarin in this recipe is exclusively prepared of durum wheat semolina – couscous semolina is unsuitable. If possible, use a savarin mold that is suitable for an attractive presentation of a rice accompaniment. The sliced artichokes may be replaced by forest mushrooms, boletus or topinambur.

This appetizer can be served on its own or with meat in sauce and allows for numerous variations, such as the addition of sliced white truffles, a popular Piemont specialty.

1. To prepare the savarin, bring the milk to a boil, add butter and salt, sprinkle in the semolina and stir with a whisk for a minute. Cook for 15 minutes. Take off the stove and stir in egg yolk and grated Parmesan.

2. Butter four molds, fill to the rim with the semolina mixture and refrigerate.

Artichokes and Fonduta

3. Prepare the artichoke hearts and cut them into thin slices. Heat the butter and add the artichoke hearts, chopped parsley, salt and pepper. Braise over a low heat for about 15 minutes.

4. For the fonduta, heat the butter with the flour. Add the milk, bring to a boil and stir in the Emmental cheese. When the cream is even and smooth add the egg yolks, salt, as well as pepper if desired. Cover the base of the plates with fonduta, place the semolina savarin in the middle, and heap the fried artichokes on top.

Marmitako

Preparation time: 45 minutes
Cooking time: 50 minutes
Difficulty: ★

Serves four

3 lbs / 1¹/₂ kg bonito tuna (saving the head
    and tail for the fish stock)
3 lbs / 1¹/₂ kg potatoes
6 tomatoes
3 red onions
6 green chili peppers
5 dried red peppers

generous ³/₈ cup / 100 ml oil
salt, pepper to taste

The term *marmitako* refers both to the container used for the preparation of this Basque specialty and to the dish itself – a tasty combination of bonito, onions, potatoes, and red peppers. Its origin goes back to the first fishermen from Bermeo, a well-known harbor on the Bay of Biscay that is famous for its sea pike and bonito fishing. These tough fishermen who went out to sea for days on end had no choice but prepare their catch with the only vegetables they could preserve.

The bonito tuna is a red-fleshed fish, a relative of the white tuna; they both belong to the family of osseous fish. The best kind does not grow large and is caught in the vast Cantabrique. Wherever it is a rarity or unavailable, it can be substituted with any other type of tuna to obtain a similar result. Other fish with a relatively high fat content like salmon are also suitable for this dish.

Our chef, Alberto Zuluaga, cautions that this dish is not exactly simple. The red peppers of the Basque region are sometimes difficult to preserve, as they contain more water than the usual Andalusian peppers. It is also not easy to remove the skin from the flesh required for the preparation of this dish. Make sure the onion does not caramelize when it is grilled. Also, the potatoes should remain firm when cooked to prevent the marmitako from turning into mush.

1. Immerse the five dried red peppers into boiling water and blanch three times, rinse well, and remove the skin. In the meantime make a fish stock from the head and the tail of the bonito.

2. Sauté the chopped red onions in a pot over a high heat until golden brown. Sauté the tomatoes and the flesh of the red peppers separately in oil. Cook over a low heat for 30 minutes and puree in a blender.

with Bonito

3. Add the chopped chili peppers and the diced potatoes to the fried onions. Stir well. Pass the fish stock through a sieve and add to the pot to just cover the potatoes. Season with salt.

4. As soon as the potatoes are cooked, add three small ladles of pepper and tomato puree as well as the diced bonito. Combine well and cook for 3–4 minutes. Season to taste, and serve on pre-warmed soup plates.

Fish &
Seafood

Preparation time: 2 hours
Cooking time: 5 minutes
Difficulty: ☆

Serves 4

28 clams, such as littlenecks
2 oz/50 g shiitake mushrooms
4 baby zucchini

2 lychees
⅓ cup/50 g corn kernels, fresh or frozen
2 leaves gelatin, or 4 tsp powdered gelatin
6½ tbsp/100 ml chicken stock
a little olive oil

For the lemon thyme butter:
3½ tbsp/50g butter
1 sprig of lemon thyme

Catalonia may well be several thousand miles from China, but this hasn't stopped Fernando Adría from drawing inspiration from oriental cuisine in the preparation of fresh clams. He also makes clever use of the specialties of his native region, by combining the clams with chicken stock, thus offering a fresh approach with familiar ingredients.

Although clams are plentiful throughout the Mediterranean, Adría maintains that the best clams in Europe come from Galicia in northwestern Spain, with its Atlantic coastline. His preference is not for the largest sort, but for the pale-shelled variety weighing between 1–1¾ oz/30–50 g each, which he cooks quickly over high heat. As soon as the clams open they are shucked, cooled and glazed with a mixture of their own juices and the

gelatin – the gelatin being crucial to the success of this *chaud-froid*.

The influence of Chinese cooking can be seen chiefly in the finely sliced vegetables, with the stark contrast between the tender baby zucchini and crunchy corn dominating. Shiitake mushrooms should be used if possible, but may be replaced by other wild varieties such as cèpes, horns of plenty or chanterelles.

This recipe may be made with other shellfish, our chef recommending, for example, mussels. These abound on the rocks of the Spanish Costa Brava, and he uses them from time to time with great success.

1. Plunge the clams into a pot of water over high heat for 2 minutes until they open. Immediately remove them from their shells with a knife, taking care not to damage them. Reduce the cooking water to ¾ cup/175 ml. Soften the gelatine in a little cold water and add to the cooking water. Refrigerate until syrupy.

2. When completely cool, place the clams on a rack and glaze with the jellied liquid. Next, prepare the lemon thyme butter sauce: Infuse the thyme in 6½ tbsp/100 ml of boiling water. Boil this liquid down to 2 tbsp and pass through a strainer. Over low heat, whisk in the butter.

Chop Suey

3. Peel the lychees and reserve. Cut the zucchini into thin rounds and slice the mushrooms finely, then sauté in a little olive oil over low heat until both are tender. Add the lychees and the corn with the chicken stock and cook for 1 minute.

4. Arrange the vegetables in the center of the dish, pouring the lemon thyme butter sauce all around. Top with the clams just before serving.

Preparation time: 30 minutes
Cooking time: 15 minutes
Difficulty: ★★★

Serves 4

3¼ lb/1½ kg small cuttlefish (or squid) with their ink
1 onion
1 green bell pepper
1½ cups/300 g peeled, roughly chopped tomatoes
a little oil
flat-leaf parsley
salt and freshly ground pepper

For the sauce:
cuttlefish or squid ink
¾ cup/200 ml fish stock
6½ tbsp/100 ml white wine
2 onions
salt and freshly ground pepper
a little oil

The Basques have always had a soft spot for the *chipiron* or small cuttlefish. No bar would consider its selection of *pinxos* (the Basque term for *tapas*) complete without a plate of these small cephalopods in their own ink (*en su tinta*). From 10 a.m. onwards, before their pre-lunch aperitif, San Sebastián bar-goers can enjoy the first freshly caught cuttlefish or squid, prepared simply, expertly and deliciously in the traditional manner.

As a child, Hilario Arbelaitz would often go fishing with his father. Today, in memory of these past adventures, he recommends that you seek out little *chipirones*, which he far prefers to the larger type fished along the North American coasts. The varieties found close to the coast,

rather than further out to sea, are more tender, and thus superbly suited to our purposes.

Whichever sort you choose, it is the body sac of the cuttlefish that is used for this recipe. The ink sac is reserved to color the sauce; if necessary, however, the ink available in little plastic envelopes from fishmongers may be used with equal success.

Most people quickly become firm devotees of Basque cooking, particularly of the varied seafood *tapas*– anchovies, mussels, squid, cuttlefish and octopus. If you enjoy this cuttlefish tartlet, you'll almost certainly be tempted to penetrate the mysteries of Basque cuisine yet further. A world of delicious tastes awaits you!

1. Clean the cuttlefish, reserving the ink for the sauce. Using a metal cutter, stamp out 28 coin-sized pieces from some of the cuttlefish and refrigerate.

2. Cut the remaining cuttlefish into ⅜ in/1 cm dice. Soften the finely chopped onion and green bell pepper in some oil; add the diced cuttlefish and sauté briefly, taking care not to overcook. Set aside. In a separate pan, cook the chopped tomato.

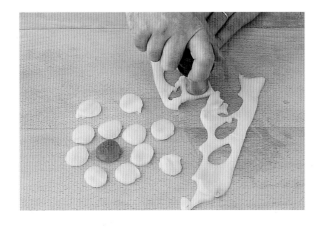

Tartlets

3. For the sauce, slice the two onions into thin rings and gently sauté in a little oil until golden. Add the white wine, ink, and fish stock and reduce slightly. Purée the sauce, then put through a fine strainer and adjust the seasoning.

4. Sauté the cuttlefish discs in a little oil; season with salt and pepper. Pour some sauce onto the center of each plate. Place a metal ring on top and spoon in the cuttlefish and onion mixture. Top with the cuttlefish rounds. Spoon the cooked tomato into the center and garnish with parsley.

Pike with

Preparation time: 10 minutes
Cooking time: 15 minutes
Difficulty: ★★

Serves 4

4½ lb/2 kg pike
32 crayfish
3½ tbsp/50 ml olive oil

For the sauce:
2 shallots
4 tsp/20 ml cognac
3½ tbsp/50 ml dry white wine
1 cup/250 ml cream
2 sprigs of fresh tarragon
salt and coarsely ground pepper

The pike, a skillful predator, lives in the lower reaches and backwaters of rivers and in large ponds, but also frequently penetrates high up into the trout zone. It is also raised in small ponds. Before the French Revolution, pike from the breeding ponds of the Louvre Palace graced the table of King Louis XIV.

The firm, white flesh of the pike is extremely fine, but it contains a great many bones, some of which are well hidden and can only be removed with the aid of tweezers. Our chef recommends specimens weighing 4¼ lb–6½ lb/2–3 kg, which he thinks contain fewer bones.

After being immersed in water for about one minute, the fish may be filleted with ease. In this recipe, steaming ensures that the fillets stay nice and tender as well as

cooking through completely. As pike generally has a reputation for being pleasant but bland, the fish is served here with a rather spicy sauce.

Before the crayfish are cooked, the intestine should be removed by pulling out the center fin of the tail.

We recommend that you strain the sauce through a piece of cheesecloth after it is made, then through a fine strainer after it has settled. Whip it gently just before serving, to achieve an even lighter and more appetizing consistency.

The recipe may be prepared with other fine-fleshed freshwater fish instead of pike – or the fish may be left out entirely and replaced by additional crayfish.

1. Fillet the pike and cut it into 4 portions. Season with salt. Wrap each piece in plastic wrap and steam at 160 °F/70 °C.

2. Devein the crayfish and cook in smoking hot olive oil until they turn red.

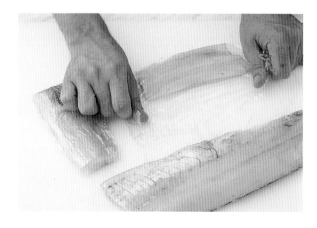

Crayfish

3. Flambé the crayfish with the cognac, then place in a hot oven for 3 minutes. Remove the meat from 16 of the crayfish tails. Reserve 4 whole crayfish for garnish. Break up the shells and remaining crayfish with a pestle or in a food processor. Return to the pan.

4. Add the lightly browned diced shallots and the coarsely ground pepper. Sweat for 2 minutes, then pour in the white wine and reduce by half. Add the cream and tarragon. Cook down to a creamy consistency and season to taste. Strain the sauce. Mask the pike fillets with this sauce, and garnish each portion with 4 crayfish tails and a whole crayfish, and a little blanched tarragon.

Swordfish Ragou

Preparation time: 15 minutes
Cooking time: 15 minutes
Difficulty: ☆

Serves 4

14 oz/400 g swordfish
2 medium eggplants
2 sweet, ripe tomatoes
2 cloves garlic

½ cup extra virgin olive oil
1 sprig of rosemary
2 sprigs of parsley
salt, coarse sea salt, freshly ground pepper
a little white wine

The swordfish, whose scientific name is *Xiphias gladius*, gets its common name from its characteristically long, spearlike upper jaw. This powerful fish, which is 13–16 feet/4–5 meters long, is caught in the Atlantic and the Mediterranean. Fortunately, it is seldom sold live, but almost always cut up into steaks.

The delicate taste of this fish is reminiscent of veal. When shopping, look for shiny, pink flesh. It is important to cook swordfish gently, because its delicate, delicious flavor is quickly spoiled by heavy-handed treatment. Cooks like to enhance its taste by sprinkling it with *fleur de sel* (see page 172), as this salt also improves the texture and prevents the flesh from falling apart easily. If this is unavailable, use coarse sea salt.

The eggplant accompaniment is especially recommended in summer. Choose fresh, glossy, unbruised fruit with dark purple skin, firm flesh and few seeds. Steer clear of overly large specimens, which may be mealy in texture and lose flavor when cooked.

This ragout can be prepared easily and quickly, substituting other firm-fleshed fish such as monkfish, if wished. Whatever fish you use, be sure to serve it nice and hot.

1. Slice the eggplant into rounds a scant ¼ in/½ cm thick and place on a large colander or baking rack. Salt, and let drain for 2 hours. Pat dry thoroughly and broil for 5 minutes on each side. Keep warm.. Cut the fish into cubes.

2. Heat the olive oil, 1 finely chopped garlic clove and the rosemary in a pan. When the oil is hot, add the fish cubes, and season with sea salt and coarsely ground pepper. Let brown for 5 minutes.

with Broiled Eggplant

3. Next, add the peeled, seeded and finely diced tomatoes and cook for 5 minutes.

4. Deglaze with white wine and season with the remaining garlic and the chopped parsley, mixing well to combine. Place 3 eggplant slices on each plate, spoon over the seasoned swordfish cubes and drizzle with olive oil.

Preparation time: 1 hour 30 minutes
Cooking time: 1 hour 30 minutes
Difficulty: ★★★

Serves 12

8 lb 12 oz/4 kg salmon
7 oz/200 g salmon flesh (can be from trimmings), puréed
7 oz/200 g shallots
generous 1 lb/500 g onions
1¼ lb/600 g button mushrooms
3½ oz/100 g wild mushrooms (such as morels or chanterelles)
1¼ cups/300 ml white wine
1⅔ cups/400 ml fish stock
5 oz/150 g shellfish *salpicon* (see glossary)
5 oz/150 g scallop *salpicon* (in season only)
1½ cups/150 g wild rice (cooked weight)

5 oz/150 g basmati rice (cooked weight)
1 oz/30 g *fines herbes*, parsley
8 eggs, hard-boiled
6 cups/1½ l crème fraîche

For the sauce:
¾ cup/200 ml Noilly Prat (French dry vermouth)
¾ cup/200 ml white wine
the salmon braising liquid
6½ tbsp/100 ml jellied meat stock or glace de viande
7 oz/200 g shallots
2¼ lb/1 kg butter
1 tsp/10 g freshly ground pepper

Crêpe batter (see basic recipes p. 800)
Brioche dough (see basic recipes p. 799)

Marie Antoine Carême achieved fame as a court chef in the late 18th and early 19th century. This koulibiac, which he created to mark his culinary debut at the court of the Russian czar, is a testament to the cosmopolitan nature of his cooking. Originally, it was prepared with ingredients including sturgeon marrow (the valuable vesiga) or poultry. The foremost aim of the koulibiac is to retain the flavor of its individual ingredients. Recipes for more modest variants of this dish also exist, containing cabbage and other vegetables.

Preparation should be approached methodically. The brioche dough should be made the day before.

The koulibiac is baked in an oven heated initially to 400 °F / 200 °C, then lowered to 350 °F / 180 °C. We also recommend that you prepare the garnish a day in advance, saving the assembly for the following day. Only then will you deal with the famous Scottish salmon, now raised in Scotland's crystal clear lochs.

The koulibiac should be brought piping hot straight from the oven to the table. You could also keep it overnight, however, and serve it cold the following day; a little lobster aspic and a cucumber salad with chives would make tasty accompaniments.

1. Line a braising dish with sliced shallots, chopped button mushrooms and parsley sprigs. Pour in the white wine and fish stock. Place the boned, skinned salmon fillets in the dish and season. Cover with aluminum foil and braise in a 350 °F/180 °C oven. Prepare a crêpe batter, adding the finely chopped herbs, and prepare six 7–in/18–cm crêpes.

2. Blanch the sliced button mushrooms and onions; cool and drain. Using the salmon flesh, prepare a rather firm stuffing. Add the other filling ingredients (parsley, onions, wild mushrooms and rice), using the rice to bind the mixture. Correct the seasoning. Slice the hard-boiled eggs into rounds. Prepare the brioche dough.

Koulibiac

3. Roll out the brioche dough and transfer to a greased baking sheet; cover with the crêpes. Spread ⅓ of the filling into a rectangle the size of the salmon in the center. Place a fillet on top and cover with another third of the filling. Top with the egg slices. Place the second fillet on top and cover with the remaining filling. Fold over the brioche and seal. Bake at 400 °F/200 °C for 30 minutes; reduce the heat to 350 °F/180 °C and continue baking for another 20–30 minutes.

4. Combine the Noilly Prat, braising liquid, jellied meat stock and the finely chopped shallots in a saucepan and boil down to a syrupy consistency. Remove from the heat and whisk in the cubed butter. Correct the seasoning. Pass the sauce through a fine strainer and add the shellfish salpicon and scallop salpicon, if using.

Light Pike

Preparation time: 1 hour
Cooking time: 30 minutes
Difficulty: ★★

Serves 4

16 crayfish
7 oz/200 g mushrooms
3 cups/750 ml *sauce américaine*
(see basic recipes p. 804)
1 bunch of chives

For the filling:
4½ oz/125 g pike flesh
4½ oz/125 g pike-perch flesh or substitute
scallops
2 egg whites
1 egg
½ cup/125 g butter, softened
¾ cup/200 ml heavy cream
salt and freshly ground white pepper

Quenelles or dumplings were once the specialty of the traditional cafés of Lyon, where families on their Sunday outings would sit down together for a meal. Christian Bouvarel has fond memories of these special occasions of his childhood and of the ice-cold lemonade that inevitably accompanied the delicious food. In those days he would also set off with his friends to catch crayfish in the nearby rivers, which his mother would then serve with the delicious dumplings.

Although a typical Lyonnais specialty, quenelles are derived – etymologically, at least – from the German *Knödel* or dumpling. Quenelles are usually made from

fish, for example, carp or pike, which must be very fresh. Christian Bouvarel is of the opinion that the flavor of the pike should be toned down for this dish by adding pike-perch or scallops to the dumpling mixture.

Lastly, it should be mentioned that traditional quenelles contain a flour-based panada, which Christian Bouvarel prefers to leave out to ensure a lighter texture. Molding the dumplings with the aid of a spoon is admittedly a slightly tricky task. Don't give up, though – it gets easier after the first few botched attempts, and remember that Lyon wasn't built in a day either!

1. Fillet and bone the fish. Refrigerate until needed.

2. To make the quenelle mixture, process the fish flesh, salt and pepper in a food processor. Add the whole egg and egg whites, followed by the well-chilled heavy cream; do not over-process. Lastly, add the softened butter. Press through a sieve, then transfer the mixture to a bowl over ice cubes for 1 hour.

Quenelles

3. To form and cook the dumplings, bring some salted water to a boil. Mold the dumplings (3 per person) using 2 tablespoons and poach for 10 minutes without boiling, turning them once. Drain on a kitchen towel.

4. Meanwhile, trim, peel and slice the mushrooms and sauté them in butter. Devein the crayfish, cook in simmering water and remove the tails from their shells. Arrange 3 quenelles and 4 crayfish on each plate and serve hot, with sauce américaine (see p. 57).

Fillet of Sole witl

Preparation time:	45 minutes
Cooking time:	15 minutes
Difficulty:	★★★

Serves 4

3 Dover soles, filleted (yields 12 fillets)
1 lobster (1¼ lb/600 g)
1 oz/25 g truffle paste
1½ cups/360 ml thickened lobster stock
(1 oz/25 g cornstarch per 4 cups/1 l)

⅓ cup/80 ml heavy cream
4 tsp/20 ml Madeira
celery leaves for garnishing
salt and freshly ground pepper

A good protein-provider like all other fish, Dover sole has always held a particular attraction for gourmets, who constantly invent superb recipes for it, some with the odd flash of genius. The fillets of this oval flatfish are easy to work with, and its firm white flesh is unusually delicate. Year-round availability is ensured by the great number of areas in which it is fished.

Choose soles weighing a generous pound/500 g each for this recipe. The skin of the fish, which must be shiny and tough, will peel away with a strong tug. To help you roll up the fillets attractively, we recommend that you use plastic or aluminum cylinders, which are also useful for other recipes. The lovely word *salpicon* supposedly derives from the Spanish *picar*, "to chop," preceded by a prefix referring to salt. In any case, here it means a variety of finely diced ingredients made into a ragout or stew, used among other things to fill puff pastry cushions.

The lobster stock takes time to prepare (3–4 hours), in other words considerably longer than the few minutes required to cook the lobster. Ideally, a sufficient quantity of stock should be prepared the day before, so as to have it on hand for other purposes.

1. Gently press the sole fillets flat. Lightly grease 12 cylinders measuring 1–1¼ in/3 cm in diameter and roll the fillets around them with the skin side inwards. Place the fillets in a pot with a steaming rack and steam for 3 minutes over boiling water.

2. Bring the lobster stock to a boil and stir in the cornstarch, which has been mixed in a little cold water. Boil for several minutes. Meanwhile, heat the oil to 300 °F /150 °C. Select a few of the best celery leaves and deep-fry. Drain on paper towels.

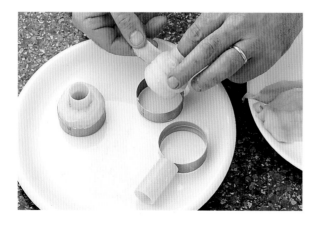

Lobster *Salpicon*

3. Cook the lobster for 7–8 minutes in boiling water. Shell the lobster, finely dice the tail meat and reserve the claw meat for garnish. Boil down the truffle paste with the Madeira and cream until you have a thickened sauce. Fold in the diced lobster meat. Adjust the seasoning and keep warm.

4. Place the sole fillets on a warmed serving plate and stuff with the lobster mixture, using a demi-tasse spoon. Pass the thickened stock through a fine strainer and pour onto the plates. Arrange the fillets in a triangle and garnish with the tips of the shelled lobster claws.

Bourride

Preparation time: 45 minutes
Cooking time: 25 minutes
Difficulty: ★★★

Serves 4

2 lb 3 oz/1 kg baby turbot
2 lb 3 oz/1 kg John Dory
12 oz/350 g sole
1 lb 5 oz/600 g monkfish fillet
1 lb 5 oz/600 g sea bream
1 baguette (for the croutons)
salt and freshly ground pepper

For the vegetable accompaniment:
4 carrots
4 baby turnips

the white part of 4 young leeks
8 pearl onions
2 tomatoes

1 green and 1 red bell pepper
4 leaves of basil, chives
1 rib celery, chervil, tarragon
6½ tbsp/100 ml white wine
1 cup/250 ml vegetable stock
1 pinch of saffron strands
1 tbsp extra virgin olive oil

For the sauce:
1 small boiled potato
3 tbsp olive oil
juice of ½ lemon
4 cloves of garlic
1 tbsp tomato paste
1 egg yolk
salt, cayenne pepper and freshly ground black pepper

The port of Sète in the south of France has its own version of this fish soup, which Michel Bruneau discovered during a stay in the town. He was so impressed that he renamed his restaurant, until then known as *Au bon accueil* ("The warm welcome") after the dish.

This dish, here cooked "à la Bruneau", honors the traditions of the south of France while incorporating raw materials from Normandy: leeks and carrots, local fish and potatoes for the garlic sauce. The assortment of fish on which *bourride* is based contains one "fine" fish (turbot, brill or John Dory), one flat fish (Dover sole, dab or lemon sole), one fatty fish (sea bream, tuna or mackerel), and, depending on the market, the most recently delivered fish,

say monkfish. Since no one fish should dominate in terms of taste, it may be necessary to reduce the amount of one or the other fish on account of its stronger flavor.

While the saffron should be used sparingly, you may be more lavish with chervil and tarragon. The most difficult part of this recipe is the cooking times for the vegetables and fish, which must be prepared at the last moment in the order given.

Rub the croutons, made from a fresh baguette, with garlic. The shoot in the center of the clove should be removed to make the garlic more digestible. When fried in hot oil, the croutons will not absorb so much fat.

1. Heat the oil in a large saucepan and gently sweat the vegetables, which have all been cut into ¼ in/½ cm chunks. Pour in the white wine and the vegetable stock. Cook, covered, for 10 minutes. Add the saffron, whole basil leaves and chives. Season with salt and pepper and simmer for a further five minutes.

2. Prepare the sauce: Pound the garlic cloves and the boiled potato in a mortar, then add the egg yolk, salt and pepper. Add the olive oil in a thin stream, stirring constantly. Finally, add the tomato paste and the juice of ½ lemon. Transfer to a saucepan.

3. Cut each fish into 4 equal-sized pieces, and season both sides with salt and pepper. Cook the fish on top of the boiling vegetables in the following sequence: monkfish, 5 minutes; sole, turbot and John Dory, 4 minutes; sea bream, 3 minutes. Cook, covered, without turning the fish.

4. Over a low heat, add 3 tbsp of the cooking liquid to the garlic mixture, which should not boil again under any circumstances. Serve the fish and vegetables in very shallow bowls, accompanied by croutons that have been rubbed with garlic, then fried in olive oil. Pass the sauce separately in a sauceboat.

A Little Provença

Preparation time: 2 hours
Cooking time: 50 minutes
Difficulty: ★★★

Serves 4

3¼ lb/1½ kg assorted fish: (red) scorpion fish, John Dory, red mullet, gurnard, conger eel, wrasse
2¼ lb/1 kg rock fish
2 tomatoes
1 fennel bulb

3 small potatoes
2 onions
6 cloves garlic
1 leek
1 baguette
saffron threads
2 egg yolks
6½ tbsp/100 ml olive oil
freshly grated Parmesan cheese
sprigs of parsley
cayenne pepper
salt and freshly grated pepper

Every family in the south of France has its own recipe for bouillabaisse, with a few common denominators: scorpion fish, red scorpion fish, gurnard, conger eel and red mullet. Few of these ever show up in American markets, but you can make a delicious fish soup using local fishes.

Alain Burnel recommends a handful of small rock fish as a basic ingredient, to give the soup body and flavor. The problem, however, is getting them, unless you live near a Mediterranean fishing port. The soup base must be reduced before the larger fish are cooked in it, so it is best to prepare it the day before and to deal with the fish shortly before serving: the plumpest ones such as the conger eel and scorpion fish first, and the more delicate ones like the red mullet last.

To merit its nickname of "golden soup," bouillabaisse must be enriched with saffron, a delight to both the eyes and palate. Harvest conditions have not changed since the time of the Crusades: 150,000 crocus flowers must be hand-picked to yield just one kilo (2.2 lbs) of the threads, which explains why it is the world's most expensive spice. You may take it for granted that cheap saffron has been adulterated, usually with annato or safflower – very effective food colorings that lack the subtle flavor of the real thing.

1. Scale, gut and clean all the fish. Cut the larger ones into pieces, leaving the small ones whole. Slice the baguette on the diagonal. Rub these croutons with garlic and put to one side.

2. Heat the oil in a saucepan until very hot, then start the soup off with the small fish, a bouquet of herbs, the onions and the white part of a leek, finely sliced, the 2 tomatoes, peeled, seeded and finely chopped, the garlic, saffron and fennel. Cook for 30 minutes and put through a food mill.

Bouillabaisse

3. Cook the 3 potatoes in this soup. Remove, peel, and pound in a mortar with the egg yolks; gradually add the olive oil. Reserve this rouille.

4. Cook the remaining fish in the soup for 10 minutes, starting with the largest, then adding the other fish in descending order of size. Season to taste with salt and cayenne pepper. Serve in a covered soup tureen, garnished with chopped parsley. Pass the grated Parmesan, rouille and garlic croutons separately.

Cod in Dark Beer

Preparation time: 45 minutes
Cooking time: 15 minutes
Difficulty: ★

Serves 4

1¼ lb/600 g cod
generous 1 lb/500 g hop shoots
1 lemon
2 egg yolks

2½ oz/75 g fresh white bread crumbs
1 cup/250 g butter
½ cup/120 ml Belgian *Koninck* beer (or other dark beer)
1 cup/250 ml fish stock
1 tsp fresh brewer's yeast (not active dry yeast)
salt and freshly ground pepper

While somewhat humbler than the "noble" fish such as European turbot or Dover sole, fish of the cod family (including haddock, pollack and whiting) nevertheless are very popular fish. Fresh cod is readily available, and lends itself well to an enormous variety of dishes.

Jan Buytaert prepares cod in the Flemish style, with the dark Belgian *Koninck* beer he so loves, and which he holds up as an example of the versatility of beer in cooking. This heady dark brew would have gone down well at the 16th century Flemish *kermis*, or fair, with its tipsy, red-cheeked villagers, as portrayed in the paintings of the Brueghels. If

you cannot get hold of *Koninck* with its many subtle nuances, the recipe may be made with any other dark beer.

The second crucial factor for the sauce is the butter. Use fresh, premium unsalted butter with plenty of flavor.

No less typically Belgian than the beer are the hop shoots. Popular since the 19th century for their high sugar content, they are traditionally compared to asparagus; many people actually prefer them. In any case, this unusual vegetable, whose harvest time is dubbed the "fifth season" by its Belgian fans, certainly repays closer acquaintance.

1. Cut the cod into 4 portions of about 5 oz/150 g each. Reserve the bones and trimmings and make into a stock. Place the cod on a baking sheet that you have buttered and sprinkled with salt and pepper, and cook in a preheated 375 °F/190 °C oven for 5–8 minutes, or until half-done.

2. Carefully clean the hop shoots and cook in the fish stock, which has been seasoned with the juice of half a lemon. Remove the shoots and keep warm.

with Hop Shoots

3. Add the beer to the hop-cooking liquid and reduce by half. Add the yeast and whisk in some butter. Pass through a fine strainer and correct the seasoning. Mix the bread crumbs with a little butter, forming into thin "cakes." In a double boiler, whisk the 2 egg yolks together with 2 tbsp water until foamy. Remove from the heat, then whisk in the remaining clarified butter to make a sabayon. Season.

4. Mound some hop shoots in the center of 4 buttered plates. Top with a piece of cod and a breadcrumb "cake." Bake briefly in the oven, until the fish is cooked through and the bread crumbs are golden brown. Pour some of the beer sauce around the fish, and spoon a bit of the sabayon on top before serving.

Stuffed Velvet Swimming

Preparation time: 1 hour 15 minutes
Cooking time: 35 minutes
Difficulty: ★★

Serves 4

20 large velvet swimming crabs

For the stuffing:
9 oz/250 g crab meat (from a large edible crab)
½ ripe mango

½ cup/125 ml béchamel sauce
1 tbsp fresh basil
1 tsp reduced *sauce américaine*
(see basic recipes p. 804)
1¾ oz/50 g Parmesan, freshly grated

For the sauce:
¾ cup/200 ml highly seasoned *sauce américaine* (carrots, onions, white wine, lobster stock)
1 tbsp/15 g butter
1 tbsp finely chopped chives
1 tbsp finely diced, peeled tomato

Among the 5,000 or so known species of true crabs, the velvet swimming crab is a fine example of the subclass of swimming crabs. It is distinguished by a flattened fifth pair of legs located just above its abdomen, which serve as flippers when it moves around. Unlike most of the other members of its class, therefore, this crustacean is relatively nimble and swims chiefly in very deep water, which is extremely useful for escaping from its enemies.

From a culinary viewpoint, however, it is very good value, has quite fine, delicate meat and can be made into excellent bisques, mousses or stuffings. Jacques Cagna has a novel way with it, filling the shell with a stuffing made from the meat of the large crab, while using the flesh of the swimming crabs as a main ingredient in the *sauce américaine*.

The disciples of Prosper Montagné still persist in calling the highly seasoned *sauce américaine sauce armoricaine* ("Armorican sauce"), despite the fact that none of the ingredients are even remotely reminiscent of Brittany. Here, Jacques Cagna offers us a new taste experience by also adding some finely diced mango, whose mellowness counterbalances the piquancy of the other ingredients. Our chef recommends a mango ripe enough not to be fibrous, but still firm.

1. Make the stuffing: Prepare a béchamel sauce out of butter, flour and milk. Peel the mango and cut into tiny dice. Chop the basil leaves. Mix together all the stuffing ingredients.

2. Cook the swimming crabs quickly in a court bouillon. Extract the flesh from their shells and reserve for the sauce américaine. Wash the reserved shells, fill with the stuffing and cover with grated Parmesan.

Crabs with Dried Tomatoes

3. To prepare the sauce américaine, sauté the reserved crab meat in a little olive oil. Add the diced carrot and onion and brown slightly. Deglaze with white wine, then reduce. Add the lobster stock and cook for 10 minutes.

4. To finish the sauce, pass through a fine strainer, reduce by half, whisk in the butter and add the chopped chives and the peeled, finely diced tomato. Season and keep warm. For each serving, spoon sauce over the bottom of a shallow bowl, place 5 swimming crabs on top and brown briefly under a very hot broiler.

Grilled Sea Bass with

Preparation time: 1 hour
Cooking time: 30 minutes
Difficulty: ★★

Serves 4

2 small sea bass (about 2 lbs/1 kg each), filleted, or 4 4–6 oz/125–175 g fillets
24 baby carrots
24 baby turnips
12 baby zucchini
12 cherry tomatoes
8 star anise
1 tbsp butter

For the court bouillon:
⅔ cup/150 ml olive oil
1 tbsp white wine vinegar
1 tbsp cider vinegar
2 tsp lemon juice
½ tbsp/15 g honey
1 pinch/2 g saffron threads
1 tbsp/5 g coriander seeds
¼ cup, loosely packed /5 g flat-leaf parsley
½ tbsp/5 g black peppercorns
1 bay leaf
salt and freshly ground pepper
sprigs of fresh dill to garnish

The fish known in France as *bar* or *loup de mer* ("seawolf") goes by the name of "sea bass" in English-speaking countries. In the territorial waters of the United Kingdom this fish occurs in its largest numbers off the Scottish coast, not all that far from the Turnberry Hotel, over whose kitchens Stewart Cameron presides. Our chef is thus certain of obtaining the freshest specimens for his grill, just a few yards away from where they are landed.

In Scotland, sea bass are a lovely blue-gray color and can weigh between 8¾ lb–11 lb/4–5 kg. Stewart Cameron, however, prefers medium-sized specimens of about 5 lb/2.5 kg. The flesh of the sea bass is especially delicate-tasting, but quite different fish such as mackerel or cod may be substituted in this recipe, in which case the approach preparation of the vegetables rather than of the fish is of prime importance.

The beauty and elegance of this dish are enhanced by the use of small vegetables, which also absorb the subtle flavors of the court bouillon better and more quickly. It is important to stick rigorously to the quantities given for the court bouillon ingredients, so that the seasonings do not overwhelm the individual flavors of the vegetables. An excess of vinegar would also spoil the delightful taste of this dish. This recipe offers a chance for the turnip to shine. This humble root vegetable, long neglected, has experienced a much-deserved increase in popularity over the last few years.

1. Place all of the ingredients for the court bouillon in a saucepan and simmer very gently over a low heat for 3–4 minutes.

2. Wash and trim all the vegetables, peeling the turnips and carrots. Cook each separately in the court bouillon until al dente, then place in a shallow bowl.

Poached Baby Vegetables

3. Trim the fish fillets and remove any remaining bones; score the skin decoratively. Brush with a little butter. Pan-fry the fish in some butter for 5 minutes; the skin should be crisp. Reheat the vegetables in the court bouillon.

4. Whisk the butter into the hot court bouillon, then strain the mixture. Place a sea bass fillet in the center of each plate, surround with the vegetables, pour over the sauce and garnish with the star anise and the sprigs of dill.

Dover Sole Fillets with

Preparation time: 30 minutes
Cooking time: 10 minutes
Difficulty: ✶

Serves 4

4 sole
7 oz/200 g spinach
3½ oz/100 g truffles
salt

For the rosemary oil:
1 sprig of rosemary
6½ tbsp/100 ml extra virgin olive oil
1 tbsp Dijon mustard
juice of 1 lemon
salt and freshly ground pepper

Rosemary, you will surely agree, is both a delightful-tasting and delightful-sounding herb (*rosmarino* in Italian). It plays a key role in many Italian recipes: in marinades, salads, terrines, ratatouilles and braised vegetables. Caution is advised, however, since rosemary has a very strong flavor that could overpower the other ingredients if not used with discretion.

That would be a particular pity here for the julienne of black truffles that grow chiefly in Umbria and the Marches. Once, and only once, our chef tried replacing them with stronger-flavored white truffles. An open conflict ensued, with both the rosemary and white truffles vying to gain the upper hand, rather than blending harmoniously.

The starring role in this recipe naturally goes to the Dover sole. In order to preserve their freshness they should be filleted at the last minute. These fillets are also lovely garnished with pomegranate seeds, whose translucent ruby color and tart flavor are a delight to both eye and palate.

A crispy note is furnished by the deep-fried spinach, whose light texture provides a superb foil for the delicate fish. A comparable effect could be achieved with Swiss chard. Our chef leaves it to the imagination of the individual cook to adapt this simple and tasty recipe encapsulating the charm of traditional Emilia-Romagna.

1. To prepare the rosemary oil, finely chop the rosemary and combine well in a bowl with the mustard, lemon juice, salt and oil.

2. Carefully pull off the skin from both sides of the sole, then fillet the fish. Steam the fillets.

Rosemary on Crispy Spinach

3. Rinse and dry the spinach leaves. Deep-fry in hot oil, drain on paper towels and season.

4. Arrange the fried spinach in the center of 4 heated plates. Place the sole fillets on top. Pour over the rosemary oil and sprinkle with the julienned truffle.

Spiny Lobste

Preparation time: 15 minutes
Cooking time: 10 minutes
Difficulty: ☆

Serves 4

4 spiny lobsters (generous 1 lb/500 g each)
8 black and 8 green olives
½ lemon
3½ tbsp/50 g butter
4 tsp chicken stock
¼ cup/4 tbsp *sauce américaine*
(see basic recipes p. 804)
2 tbsp olive oil
additional olives for garnish

For the vegetable garnish:
7 oz/200 g fennel
1 tbsp olive oil
a few dill sprigs
salt and freshly ground pepper

For the court bouillon:
1 carrot
1 onion
a little vinegar
thyme, bay leaf, flat-leaf parsley
salt and black peppercorns

Jacques Chibois' favorite kind of lobster remains the Mediterranean pink spiny (or rock) lobster, rarer than its ubiquitous red cousin, the common spiny lobster. Like all other crustaceans, the spiny lobster moves about with difficulty on the rocks, making it easy to catch. If you are not lucky enough to catch your own, choose a live one from a lobster tank weighing 1–1¼ lb/500–600 g, preferably a female, as its eggs can be used in the sauce. The flesh of the rock lobster is more delicate than that of the American lobster and must be cooked gently or it will become tough. Seasonings should also be used with discretion, so as not to mask its flavor.

In the Provençal manner, Jacques Chibois teams up green and black olives with this Mediterranean crustacean; the combined flavors will instantly transport you to the south of France. Do not forget to blanch the black olives five times, to rid them of their bitter taste.

Fennel makes a pleasant accompaniment for the lobster. The white bulbs, which should be quite firm, are rich in vitamin C and are known for their digestive properties. Once upon a time, this highly edible plant was used to frighten away witches and evil spirits.

If you are unable to find any spiny lobster to your taste, you may also make this recipe with American lobster, langoustines, or large shrimp.

1. Cut the fennel into tiny dice and the olives into thin julienne (blanch 5 times). Cook the fennel in boiling salted water until tender – it should not be at all fibrous. Refresh and drain the fennel. When ready to serve, heat in a pan with a little olive oil, salt and pepper.

2. Cook the lobsters in the court bouillon for 5 minutes. Shell them, reserving the legs and heads with their antennae; halve the heads lengthwise. Cut the lobster tails into rounds.

with Olives

3. Heat the lobster meat together with the chicken stock and the sauce américaine; season with salt and pepper to taste. Finish the sauce by whisking in the butter, olive oil and the julienned olives.

4. Pit the additional olives and thread them onto the reserved lobster legs. Arrange the fennel in the center of a shallow bowl and top with the lobster meat, placing the legs and head at the edge. Mask with the sauce and garnish with the dill sprigs.

Cod witł

Preparation time: 30 minutes
Cooking time: 30 minutes
Difficulty: ☆

Serves 4

1 small cod, about 2 lb 10 oz/1.2 kg, or 4 cod
fillets, 6 oz/175 g each
2 medium-sized tomatoes
1 red bell pepper
3½ tbsp/50 ml lemon juice

⅔ cup/150 ml extra virgin olive oil
5 tsp/25 g butter
chives
tarragon
basil
scant 2½ oz/70 g coarse salt
salt and freshly ground pepper

The Atlantic cod or *Gadus morhua* enjoys great popularity all over the western world, in both its fresh and dried forms. The Portuguese claim a thousand different ways of cooking salt cod alone, and recipes for the fresh fish also abound. On the other side of the Atlantic, in Newfoundland, cod fishing is considered a great maritime adventure, inspiring literature such as the 20th-century French novelist Roger Vercel's *Jean Villemeur*.

In order to preserve this fish, caught in cold, distant waters, European sailors used to salt it themselves on the fishing boats. It then formed the bulk of their diet during the sea crossing. Now that cod-fishing boats are veritable floating refrigerated factories, salting is no longer necessary, but the tradition is still carried on.

Choose a fleshy fish, preferably with yellow skin; use only the "loin" part of the fillets, reserving the belly for later use, in a *brandade*, for example. Serge Courville recommends marinating the fish fillets in coarse salt for 24 hours in order to firm them up nicely. They should be brushed with butter before cooking to impart an attractive color.

The *sauce vierge* or "virgin sauce" takes its name from the extra virgin olive oil, appreciated nowadays for its health-giving properties as well as its incomparable taste. Produced chiefly in the northern Mediterranean countries of Greece, Italy, Spain and France, it has the lowest acidity of any oil (1%).

1. Fillet and skin the cod. Carefully separate the "loin" fillets from the belly flesh, and remove all remaining bones.

2. Wash the fillets, pat dry and cut into individual-sized portions. Place in a bowl, sprinkle with coarse salt and refrigerate for 24 hours.

Sauce Vièrge

3. Peel and seed the tomatoes and cut into small dice. Wrap the red bell pepper in aluminum foil and bake in a hot oven, then peel and finely dice the bell pepper. Place the tomatoes, red bell pepper, chopped herbs, olive oil and lemon juice in a small saucepan; season and keep warm over low heat.

4. Pat the fish dry, then brush with butter and place in a heated nonstick pan. Cook the fillets until nicely colored on one side, then turn them over and cook until golden brown on top and opaque in the center. Ladle some sauce onto each plate and place the fish on top.

Grilled Wild Salmon

Preparation time: *30 minutes*
Cooking time: *10 minutes*
Difficulty: ★★

Serves 4

One 2¼ lb/1 kg wild salmon, or 4 salmon
steaks
9 tbsp/140 g butter
¾ cup/200 ml oil
salt and freshly ground pepper

For the béarnaise sauce:
4 egg yolks
2 shallots
3½ tbsp/50 ml vinegar
2 tbsp water
10 tbsp/150 g butter, clarified
1 bunch each of tarragon and flat-leaf parsley
⅓ oz/10 g coarsely ground black pepper

For the garnish:
2 medium zucchini
2 medium carrots
8 small potatoes

Few fish enjoy such a high reputation as the salmon. This sea fish that swims upstream to spawn, leaping over all barriers with brio, never fails to stir the hearts of nature-lovers or the taste buds of gourmets, who have delighted in its tasty pink flesh for centuries. Rich in vitamin A, salmon is one of the most coveted species of fish – especially wild salmon, leaner than its farmed cousins.

Unfortunately, wild Atlantic salmon is increasingly rare in European waters, and the Adour river in the southwest of France, where our chef used to find beautiful fish, is no exception. Poaching and water pollution must share the blame, as no law of nature could prevent the salmon, driven by instinct, from swimming upstream to spawn. Moreover, it is not universally known that once they have

spawned, Atlantic salmon swimming back downstream to the sea have lost most of their body mass, and only a sojourn in sea water can rejuvenate them.

Salmon cut into steaks stays tender when cooked, and the cooking process can be more easily monitored than when the fish is whole. The steaks are done when the flesh near the bone is pink. This dish should be served piping hot; do not reheat.

Béarnaise sauce, scented with tarragon, is the ideal accompaniment for grilled fish and enhances the salmon without masking its true flavor. It is important to prepare the béarnaise just before serving, ideally in a double-boiler, so that the temperature can be regulated.

1. Clean the fish. If using a freshly caugt fish, gut it and remove the fins, working from tail to head. Carefully wash the salmon under clear running water and drain on paper towels. Cut into steaks of equal thickness.

2. Peel the carrots and potatoes and cut these and the zucchini into olive shapes. Heat some oil in another pan and toss the vegetables until crisp-tender. For the sauce, combine the chopped shallots, chopped tarragon, coarsely ground pepper and vinegar in a heavy braising pan and reduce until almost all of the liquid has evaporated.

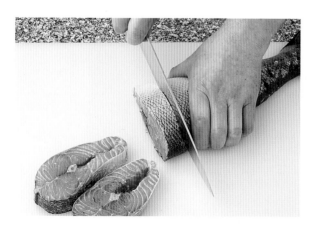

with Béarnaise Sauce

3. Add the egg yolks and water to the reduction and whisk in a double boiler until the mixture falls from the whisk in a thick ribbon. Now add the clarified butter in a thin, steady stream, whisking vigorously all the while. Pass the sauce through a strainer lined with cheesecloth. Salt to taste and add the tarragon and the finely chopped parsley. Set the béarnaise sauce aside in a warm place.

4. Marinate the salmon steaks for several minutes in the olive oil and 8 tsp/40 g clarified butter, turning 2 or 3 times. Meanwhile, steam the vegetables until the potatoes are cooked and the carrots and zucchini are crisp-tender; keep warm. In a stovetop grill pan, grill the salmon over moderately high heat for 1 minute on each side, until medium-rare, or to taste. Arrange the vegetables in a flower shape next to the salmon and serve the béarnaise sauce separately.

Sea Bass with Crispy

Preparation time: 30 minutes
Cooking time: 10 minutes
Difficulty: ★★

Serves 4

One 4½ lb/2 kg sea bass, or
4 7–8 oz/200–250 g sea bass fillets
2 ripe, red tomatoes
3½ oz/100 g fresh chanterelles
4 cloves garlic
½ shallot

4 sprigs of fresh thyme
1 bay leaf
generous 5 oz/150g fresh basil
3½ tbsp/50 g clarified butter
¾ cup/180 g butter
3½ tbsp/50 ml olive oil
3½ tbsp/50 ml fish stock
4 sprigs of fresh thyme
1 pinch *fleur de sel*
salt and freshly ground pepper

According to some sources, basil came originally from India, where a decoction of the leaves was used both as a remedy and condiment. Basil is very popular in Itlay and France, particularly Provence, and is the basis of the famous pesto and pistou, the garlic enriched sauces that originated there.

Nowadays, fresh basil is available everywhere. Naturally, it lasts longer if bought as a potted plant. Basil is the ideal accompaniment for tomatoes, and it harmonizes beautifully with garlic, thyme and bay leaf, all of which add their fragrance and flavor of Provence to this dish.

The sea bass, native to the coasts of France, is known as *loup de mer* ("sea wolf") in the Mediterranean and *loubine* around La Rochelle in the Bay of Biscay. This fish can reach lengths of up to 40 in/1 m. In addition to its impressive size, this member of the *Serranidae* family boasts lean, vitamin-rich flesh. Sea bass should always be absolutely fresh: stiff, with clear, bulging eyes and shiny scales.

Richard Coutanceau prepares the flavored oil a week in advance. To make it, place a clove of garlic in a little olive oil, add ¾ cup/200 ml peanut oil, some thyme and a bay leaf, and set aside to steep.

1. Skin and halve the tomatoes; squeeze gently to remove the seeds and excess liquid. Place in a baking dish, pour over some oil flavored with garlic, thyme, and bay leaf and bake for 40 minutes at 190 °F/90 °C. Clean the sea bass and cut into 4 fillets.

2. Blanch a generous 5 oz/150 g basil. Refresh quickly in cold running water, dry thoroughly and transfer to a blender. With the motor running, add 3½ tbsp/50 ml olive oil. Season with salt and pepper. Bring 3½ tbsp/50 ml fish stock to a boil and whisk in 10 tbsp/150 g butter.

Skin in a Basil Sauce

3. Add enough fish stock to the basil paste to achieve a pouring consistency. Sauté 3½ oz/100g chanterelles in a little oil, adding ½ finely sliced shallot toward the end of cooking.

4. Score the skin of the fish in a lattice pattern. Add 2 tbsp/30 g clarified butter and the remaining thyme to a nonstick pan. Cook the fish fillets, skin side down, for 7 minutes without turning. Place ½ tomato on each of 4 heated plates and top with a crispy sea bass fillet. Sprinkle with the fleur de sel and thin shreds of basil. Pour the sauce around the fish.

Scallop Cakes

Preparation time: 30 minutes
Cooking time: 15 minutes
Difficulty: ★★

Serves 4

20 sea scallops
6 heads of Belgian endive
4 shallots

juice of ½ lemon
1 pinch of saffron threads
1 pinch of sugar
4½ tbsp/100 g sesame seeds
3½ tbsp/50 g butter
⅔ cup/150 ml cream
3 cups/750 ml dry white wine
3½ tbsp/50 ml oil
salt, freshly ground pepper, dry pink
peppercorns

With a little imagination you can conjure up a delicious dish from almost any ingredient – even from scallops accidentally squashed on the way home from fishing. This mishap served Jean Crotet as the inspiration for a recipe in which chopped scallop meat is transformed into appetizing patties.

Whole, top-quality scallops may of course also be used. Buy dry-packed or, better, live scallops. If you can find these, first remove the coral (the reddish-orange roe sac) from the white meat, since the liquid it contains could increase the likelihood of the patties falling apart.

The farm-style preparation of the Belgian endive, which is sliced into thin strips, gives this seafood dish a rustic touch. Take care not to cook the leaves for too long.

The use of sesame, with its Arabian Nights associations, gives this dish a subtle Asian note. This blends successfully with the flavor of the scallops, particularly when enhanced by a little vermouth, which gives body to the white wine in the sauce.

If by misfortune you do not enjoy the taste of cooked Belgian endive, you can replace it with roughly shredded cabbage sautéed in butter.

1. Slice the Belgian endive into strips, then place in a pot with the butter, sugar, salt, pepper and juice of ½ lemon. Cook over high heat for 5–6 minutes, stirring frequently to bind the butter.

2. Remove the reddish orange coral (roe sac) from the white scallop meat, then chop the scallops by hand. Season with salt and pepper, then form into patties about 4 in/10 cm across. Smooth the patties and sprinkle with sesame seeds.

with Sesame Seeds

3. Reduce the white wine and the finely sliced shallots; add the cream and saffron. Season and set aside.

4. Heat the oil in a nonstick pan. Place the scallop cakes in the skillet sesame-seed-side down. Cook for 3-4 minutes over low heat until golden, then turn and briefly cook the other side. Arrange the cooked endive in the center of the plate, top with a scallop patty and pour the sauce all around. Sprinkle with a few crushed pink peppercorns.

Braised Turbot witł

Preparation time: 45 minutes
Cooking time: 30 minutes
Difficulty: ★

Serves 4

One 4½ lb/2 kg turbot
1 bunch of green asparagus
1 bunch of large golden grapes, such as muscat grapes

2 shallots
2 medium leeks
4 medium carrots
6½ tbsp/100 g butter
1 cup/250 ml *crème fraîche*
2 cups/500 ml muscadet
chervil
salt and freshly ground pepper

Originating in the south and southwest of France, an *estouffade* is a dish that is slowly stewed in a lidded pot, preserving intact the taste of all of the ingredients used in it, whether vegetables, meat or fish. In this recipe, we use European turbot, which can be recognized by its clear eyes and shiny skin.

The turbot lives on sandy sea beds in cold waters and can weigh up to 11–13 lb/5–6 kg. It is primarily caught at night with the *palangre*, a line equipped with sinkers and hooks. Popular since ancient times, there are a wealth of recipes for this splendid fish. However, turbot is very delicate and must be cooked carefully.

The accompaniment of early vegetables mounded in the center of the plate is dominated by the asparagus tips. Select small, firm specimens. The remaining vegetables are chosen according to what is in season and tastes best. The important thing is to cook them together with the turbot in muscadet. The fine bouquet of this wine is the pride of the Nantes countryside.

This dish owes its originality in part to the grapes, which should have a slightly musky taste. Once peeled, they should be slowly steamed, or cooked for a few seconds in the microwave. This unusual garnish lends a freshness to the entire dish and will not fail to delight your guests.

1. Fillet and skin the turbot. Carefully remove all bones from the fish. Cut the fillets into large cubes.

2. Cook the asparagus tips in boiling salted water. Refresh at once. Cut 1 leek into 2 in long/4–6 cm long pieces, then into thin slices. Using a very small melon-baller, cut the carrots into tiny balls, or cut into small dice. Peel the grapes, cut up small and steam for several minutes.

Muscadet and Early Vegetables

3. Peel the shallots, finely dice and sweat them in butter. Blanch the leek and the carrots and add to the shallots. Salt and pepper the turbot chunks and add these to the pot. Briefly sweat the vegetables and fish and pour over the muscadet to cover. Bring to a boil and remove from the heat at once. Cover and leave for 5 minutes.

4. Remove the turbot and keep warm. Reduce some of the vegetable-wine mixture until the liquid has evaporated, then purée in a blender. Add the crème fraîche. Reduce to a velvety consistency and correct the seasoning. Whisk the butter into the sauce. Arrange the remaining vegetables and grapes in the center of the plate. Surround with the chunks of turbot and pour some sauce all around.

Broiled Sea Bass with Mozzarell.

Preparation time: 1 hour
Cooking time: 50 minutes
Difficulty: ★★★

Serves 4

One 1¼ lb/600 g sea bass
5½ oz/160 g fresh mozzarella
3 tbsp/60 g basil
1 tbsp/20 g each chervil, tarragon, parsley
2½ tbsp/40 ml olive oil
a few celery leaves for garnishing

For the fish stock:
generous 1 lb/500 g fish bones
1 celery rib

1 small onion
1 medium leek, white part only
1 cup/250 ml white wine
1 bouquet garni
3½ tbsp/50 ml olive oil

For the vegetable mixture:
½ cup/20 g each diced carrot, cauliflower, turnip, celery root, new potatoes, peas, zucchini, mushrooms
6 large cloves garlic
4 cups/1 l fish stock
5 tbsp/75 g basil
10 tbsp/150 g butter
6½ tbsp/100 ml olive oil

Teaming sea bass fillets with a herbed mozzarella topping constitute a delicious and unusual treatment for the highly prized fish as well as for the supple young cheese, which is more frequently eaten uncooked in its native Italy.

Sea bass has firm, white flesh, to which this topping adds a fine note of flavor. The fish should be handled very carefully and boned completely: Its thick bones could spoil the fillets as well as the dining ppleasure of your guests. The skin of fillets should be scored in several places in order to prevent curling during cooking.

If bought packed in liquid, mozzarella should be drained before being puréed along with olive oil, salt, garlic and basil. The resulting delicate green mixture is spread on the pan-fried fillets, which are broiled briefly just before serving to crisp the topping. Philippe Dorange confesses to a weakness for basil, and admits to sometimes preparing a variation on this recipe with that herb alone. Basil is also the main flavoring for the vegetable accompaniment, basil and olive oil being whisked into the vegetable juices at the last moment to make a *pistou*.

1. Cut the vegetables for the accompaniment into ⅛ in/3 mm dice. Prepare the fish stock: soak the fish bones in cold water, then sweat in oil with the finely sliced celery, onions and leek. Moisten with the white wine and add sufficient water to cover the bones. Add the bouquet garni, lightly season with coarse salt and cook for 20 minutes. Strain.

2. Sweat all the vegetables in butter without allowing them to color. Pour over the fish stock and adjust seasoning. Cook for about 30 minutes. Keep warm; add basil and olive oil.

3. Purée the mozzarella with the remaining basil, chervil, tarragon and parsley in a food processor. Spread the mixture on a baking tray and set aside . Cut into 3 x 1-in/8 x 3-cm rectangles.

4. Clean and fillet the sea bass, leaving the skin on. Cut into 5 oz/150 g pieces and pan-fry skin side down in olive oil. Top with the soft mozzarella mixture, and pass under the broiler to glaze just before serving on a bed of the vegetables, garnished with the celery leaves.

Whiting with Scallop

Preparation time: 30 minutes
Cooking time: 5 minutes
Difficulty: ★

Serves 4

2 whitings weighing a generous 1 lb/500 g
each
8 sea scallops
2 tomatoes
2 shallots

1 lemon
1 sprig of thyme
6½ tbsp/100 g butter
1 cup/250 ml dry red wine (preferably
Pomerol or other Bordeaux)
6½ tbsp/100 ml veal stock
6½ tbsp/100 ml fish stock
chives, chopped
salt and freshly ground pepper

In the 18th century, powdered wigs were all the fashion, and the wigmakers, not surprisingly, were generally covered in powder themselves – like a whiting which has been dredged in flour before frying. This, at least, is the explanation given by the French poet Chateaubriand for the fact that all representatives of this profession in his day were called *merlans* or "whitings" themselves, a term later applied by extension to all hairdressers in general in the wake of the novel *Hôtel du Nord* by the French writer Eugène Dabit.

Apart from its literary career, the whiting is a modest but thoroughly decent fish from the same family as pollack and cod. It lives in cold waters and has beautiful silvery blue, scaly skin. Available year-round, its inexpensive,

nutritious flesh is suitable for many attractive preparations.

As an example, its scales can be "reconstructed" from sea scallops carefully cut into thin rounds. The scallops must be very fresh – live, if possible – and are ranged along the length of the whiting fillet like scales. The dish is then cooked quickly, so that the scallops do not dry out and the flavor of the fish is completely preserved.

Claude Dupont is a great advocate of Pomerol, a popular Bordeaux produced in the growing region between Libourne and Saint Émilion. The sauce, based on veal and fish stock, should only be made from a fine wine with a perfect bouquet.

1. Clean the scallops and soak in plenty of water for at least 2 minutes. Clean and fillet the whiting, taking care to remove all of the small bones. Place the fillets in a buttered ovenproof dish and season with salt and pepper. Cut the scallops into thin slices.

2. Arrange the scallop slices side by side and slightly overlapping on the fish fillets, like scales. Moisten with fish stock, bring to a boil, then transfer to the oven and continue to poach for a further 3 minutes.

'Scales" in Pomerol

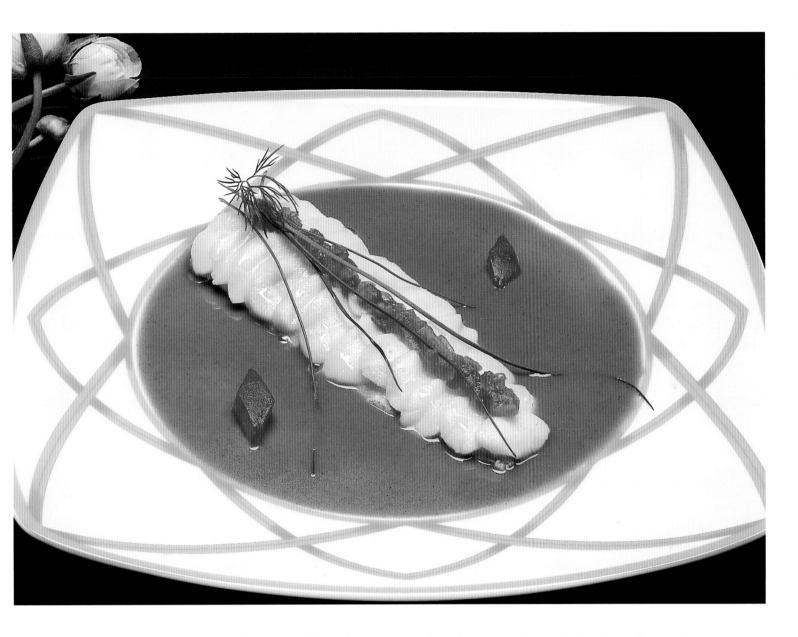

3. Place the chopped shallots and the thyme in a pan, moisten with red wine and reduce by a quarter. Add the veal stock and the liquid in which the whiting were poached. Reduce by half. Remove from heat and whisk in the butter bit by bit.

4. Correct the seasoning, add a few drops of lemon juice and put through a fine strainer. Arrange the whiting fillets on 4 plates, pour the hot sauce all around and place some peeled, roughly chopped tomatoes down the middle of the fish. Garnish with chives.

Preparation time: 10 minutes
Cooking time: 20 minutes
Difficulty: ★★

Serves 4

14 oz/400 g brill fillets
6 oz/180 g mushrooms
2 heads of Belgian endive
lemon thyme
4 tsp/20 g butter
6½ tbsp/100 ml white wine
sugar, salt and freshly ground pepper

For the orange butter:
juice of 1 orange and 1 lemon
zest of ½ orange
2 tbsp/30 g sugar
1 tbsp water
⅓ cup/80 g butter
3½ tbsp/50 ml jellied fish stock
2 tsp/10 ml champagne
2 tsp/10 ml vodka

For the onions:
12 pearl onions
1 cup/250 ml dry red wine
½ cup/125 ml dry port wine
⅓ bay leaf
1 sprig of thyme

Brill is one of the very best flatfish. Its delicious, supple-textured white flesh yields fine fillets and fires the imagination of the cook, here inspiring our chef to create a composition in the form of a rose.

The roses are not difficult to assemble. Since each fillet has both a thinner and a thicker portion, we recommend that you place the thinner strips in the center and the thicker ones on the outside when rolling them up. The steam will cause the individual parts of the rose to adhere to one another, making it easier to handle.

The vegetable accompaniment should achieve a balance between the acidity of the orange, the bitter taste of the Belgian endive and the sweetness of the pearl onions. The citrus juices are boiled down to concentrate their flavors, spiked with a dash of vodka, then softened with a little sugar and the addition of butter towards the end. Taste the sauce during preparation, if necessary correcting the seasoning to achieve the desired tartness before finally whisking in the champagne.

Although it is possible to substitute turbot for brill in this recipe, it is far less economical to use and is not easy to manipulate into the rose shapes. There is no substitute for the Belgian endive, but it can be extended by adding a few leeks, sliced and cooked until tender.

1. Prepare the brill rosettes by slicing the fillets lengthwise into 4 thin strips and rolling them up and assembling into rose shapes. Place on buttered waxed paper and steam over some white wine until opaque. Decorate with sprigs of lemon thyme.

2. Separate the leaves of the Belgian endive and slice the mushrooms. Braise the endive in butter and sprinkle with a little sugar. Add the mushrooms and deglaze with white wine. Simmer for 3–4 minutes, reducing the liquid.

Braised Belgian Endive

3. Prepare the orange butter by reducing the orange and lemon juice by half. Add the sugar, a little water, the orange zest and vodka, and bring to a boil. Simmer for several minutes. Stir in the fish stock and whisk in the butter. Add the champagne.

4. Combine the pearl onions, red wine and port in a saucepan and bring to a boil. Skim, season and reduce to a syrupy consistency. Arrange the endive leaves in the shape of a star on the heated plates, place the brill rosettes in the center, pour the orange butter between the endive leaves and garnish with the glazed onions.

Navarin of Crab

Preparation time: 30 minutes
Cooking time: 1 hour
Difficulty: ★★

Serves 4

4 large live crabs weighing 1¼–1¾ lb/
600–800 g each
white wine or vinegar

For the sauce:
3½ fl oz/100 g shrimp stock
1 tsp tomato paste
3½ tbsp/50 g butter
¾ cup/200 ml light cream
¾ cup/200 ml *vin jaune* from the Jura
1 sprig of tarragon
1 basil leaf

1 sprig of thyme
½ bay leaf
sea salt
cayenne pepper
white peppercorns

Vegetable garnish:
1 turnip
1 medium zucchini
1 medium carrot
3½ oz/100 g celery root

For the seasoning mixture:
1 oz/30 g green part of leek
1½ oz/45 g red carrot powder
½ medium shallot
a few sprigs of parsley

The French are absolutely nuts about crabs, and growing Gallic demand for this crustacean is largely met by imports from Great Britain. Most of the meat of these large crabs is found in their claws, and the creamy substance has an exquisite taste.

Constant Fonk recommends live crabs weighing 1¼–1¾ lb/600–800 g each. They are cooked in boiling water with salt and some white wine or vinegar for 15 minutes. Once the crab meat is removed, the shell must be cleaned carefully, as it will be filled with the vegetable and crab meat mixture. This can be done in advance to distribute the workload before serving.

It is asserted without any formal proof that the term

navarin derives from the battle of Navarino in 1827, in which Turkish and Egyptian naval forces opposed a British, French and Russian fleet. The large number of different uniforms was the model for the various vegetables of the accompaniment. Each vegetable must be cooked separately in order to retain its own true taste and a bit of bite.

The *vin jaune* ("yellow wine"), which is used to deglaze the seasoning mixture, is a product of the Jura region of France whose fine quality and long aging period make it ideal for this dish. It contains less alcohol than dry sherry, of which its flavor is reminiscent, and its elegance will delight your guests.

1. Pare the vegetables (turnip, zucchini, carrot, celery root) into little olive shapes and cook each kind separately in salted water. Boil the crabs in water with coarse salt and wine or vinegar for 15 minutes. Remove the meat and creamy substance from the bodies and reserve the shells, claws and legs.

2. Sweat the seasoning mixture, thyme and ½ bay leaf in 3½ tbsp/50 g butter. Add the tomato paste and deglaze with the vin jaune. Moisten with the shrimp stock (or fish stock) and the cream, and add the tarragon, basil and white peppercorns. Cook for 20 minutes.

with *Vin Jaune*

3. Bind with the creamy substance from the crab and put through a fine strainer. Season to taste with sea salt and cayenne pepper.

4. Add the decoratively cut vegetables and the crab meat to the sauce and warm through. Arrange the crab claws and legs attractively on the plates. Fill the shells with the navarin and place on top of the legs.

Lobster Fricassée with

Preparation time: 30 minutes
Cooking time: 20 minutes
Difficulty: ★★

Serves 4

4 lobsters (generous 1 lb/500 g each)
1 Savoy cabbage
3 tbsp/20 g mixed white, black and green
peppercorns and allspice berries

4 tbsp/60 g fresh ginger root
13 tbsp/200 g butter
6½ tbsp/100 ml olive oil
2 cups/500 ml lobster stock
chervil leaves
salt

Ginger, once a speciality from India and highly prized in Asian cuisines, has been known in Europe since the Middle Ages. Gray ginger is larger and more aromatic than white ginger, but either can be used in this recipe.

The lobster, preferably a female with tender, tasty flesh, should be bought live. According to its size, it should be parboiled for 1–2 minutes before plunging it in ice-cold water to cool. When cooked, lobsters are bright red, which has earned them the nickname of "cardinal of the seas." Our chef serves it here with Savoy cabbage, an attractive vegetable that has helped European peasants survive many

a famine. In rural areas it is known as the "doctor of the poor," as its high vitamin and sugar content coupled with its low price contributed decisively to the balanced diet of the less well-off. Choose a cabbage that feels quite heavy for its size and cook it right after cutting it up, since cut cabbage does not keep well. Remember that leafy vegetables reduce considerably in volume during cooking.

The addition of the different varieties of pepper and the allspice berries, whose strong taste reinforces that of the ginger, provides the ideal finish to this sprightly dish.

1. Clean and wash the cabbage. Remove the leaves, then blanch and refresh. Cut into scant ½ in/1 cm wide strips and braise in butter until crisp-tender. Boil the lobster in salted water for 1 minute, then plunge into ice-cold water. Peel the ginger, cut into tiny dice and blanch three times.

2. Shell the lobsters, reserving the coral. Cut the tail lengthwise into three. Crush the shells, reserving the heads for the garnish. Make a stock from the shells. Sauté the lobster pieces for 2–3 minutes in olive oil, then drain.

Pepper and Ginger

3. Pour the fat out of the sauté pan, deglaze with lobster stock and reduce by three-quarters. Add the butter a piece at a time. Place the contents of the pan together with the coral in the blender. Blend for 1 minute, then correct the seasoning.

4. Return the sauce to the sauté pan, add the sliced lobster, blanched ginger, and crushed peppercorns and allspice berries, and bring briefly to a boil. Spoon the cabbage onto the plates, top with the lobster meat, place the head upright on top and coat with the sauce. Garnish with chervil leaves.

Whiting with

Preparation time: 30 minutes
Cooking time: 16 minutes
Difficulty: ✳

Serves 4

Four 1¼ lb/600 g whitings (purchased ungutted or gutted through the gills)
2¼ lb/1 kg carrots
8 new scallions

5 oz/150 g slab bacon
2 tbsp/40 g honey
3 tbsp/20 g cumin seed
1 tbsp /25 g Chinese five-spice powder
5 basil leaves
2 sprigs of dill
2 sprigs of flat-leaf parsley
9 tbsp/140 g butter
salt and freshly ground pepper

Whiting is unjustly snubbed by many chefs, despite the fine texture and digestibility of its appetizing white flesh. This fish of the cod family, which abounds along the coasts of Europe and particularly in the Atlantic, certainly deserves better.

Whiting is a very fragile fish, which loses its scales if handled roughly. Choose a whole, glossy, firm fish, and treat it gently while preparing it. Be sure to remove the skin on the belly, which is dark and bitter, and which distinguishes this fish from the blue whiting.

Care is also required when cooking whiting, since exceeding the recommended cooking time could have disastrous consequences. This is why poaching or steaming, which are so difficult to monitor, are unsuitable for this fish. Philippe Groult recommends searing the whitings over high heat, taking care not to let them fall apart. This recipe is also eminently suitable for mackerel, small sea bass, or sardines.

The five-spice mixture and the deep-fried herbs make a very pleasant foil for the tender flesh of the fish.

1. Make an incision along the backbone of each whiting; remove the backbone, cutting it off at the head and tail; remove the entrails and rinse and dry. Cut off the gills and remove the small bones of the fish with tweezers.

2. Score the skin of the fish in a criss-cross pattern and sprinkle with the five-spice powder. Smear with a little butter and pan-fry over high heat for 7 minutes, turning once after 4 minutes.

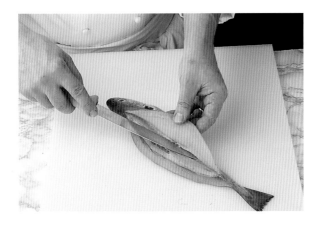

Caramelized Carrots

3. Slice the carrots on the diagonal and place in a saucepan with the butter, honey, cumin seed and a pinch of salt. Add water to come halfway up the carrots. Cook for 16 minutes, then add the parsley and dill.

4. Finely slice the scallions and stew in a little butter. Cut the bacon into thin strips, and add to the onions; cook until it renders its fat. Spoon the onion mixture onto an oval platter, arrange the carrots decoratively on top, top with the whiting and sprinkle with deep-fried herbs.

Pan-fried Monkfish

Preparation time: 30 minutes
Cooking time: 30 minutes
Difficulty: ☆

Serves 4

One 5½ lb/2½ kg monkfish tail
16 cloves garlic, unpeeled
7 oz/200 g piece smoked bacon, cut into strips
generous 1 lb/500 g fresh spinach

2 shallots, chopped
6½ tbsp/100 g butter
¾ cup/200 ml *crème fraîche*
¾ cup/200 ml brown veal stock
1 tbsp extra-virgin olive oil
4 tbsp balsamic vinegar
a little flour
salt and freshly ground pepper

Monkfish tail offers dense, lean flesh and has no bones save for the large central bone. In this recipe, the tail is first pan-fried for about 10 minutes before being baked in a hot oven on the bone, which intensifies the flavor of the fish.

Connoisseurs of the weird and wonderful will be interested to learn that this fish has a very tasty, vitamin-packed liver that can be justly compared with foie gras.

Garlic is the ideal accompaniment for this dish. Highly esteemed in ancient times (to the extent that it was given as payment to the workers who built the Egyptian pyramids), garlic is known for its tonic effect on the circulatory system. When buying, check that the cloves feel firm and plump. Do not peel them before cooking: this gives them a smoother, subtler flavor. Garlic cooked in its skin becomes creamy on the inside while the skin toughens. You need only press the skin to squeeze out the pulp.

The bacon, cut into thickish strips, also "melts" gently when cooked, infusing the other ingredients with its flavor. If you cannot find a monkfish tail, this recipe is also suitable for other fine-fleshed fish, such as baby turbot or salmon.

1. Season the monkfish with salt and pepper and dredge in flour. Heat 1 tbsp olive oil in a pan and sauté the fish on both sides until golden brown.

2. Halfway through the cooking time, add the unpeeled garlic cloves and the bacon strips. Finish cooking in a hot oven (400 °F/200 °C) for 10–15 minutes.

with Garlic and Bacon

3. Transfer the monkfish to a serving platter and garnish with the bacon and garlic cloves. To prepare the sauce, add the 2 chopped shallots to the pan and deglaze with the vinegar, then moisten with the brown veal stock.

4. Add the crème fraîche, reduce, and whisk in the cold butter. Serve with the blanched fresh spinach.

Salmon "Tournedos" with a

Preparation time: 30 minutes
Cooking time: 10 minutes
Difficulty: ★

Serves 4

4 salmon steaks (4½ oz/125 g each)
7 oz/200 g spinach
1 bunch of watercress
1 bunch of chives

2 sprigs of parsley
1¾ oz/50 g piece smoked bacon
3½ tbsp/50 g butter
1 cup/250 ml cream
2 cups/500 ml fish stock
salt and freshly ground pepper

For many gourmets, the salmon remains the finest fish – rich in protein and omega-3 fatty acids, fairly low in calories and boasting a superb flavor. It is important to know where your fish comes from, since (quite apart from differences between Atlantic and Pacific salmon) Norwegian salmon has a milder flavor than its Scottish cousin. In addition, a distinction should be drawn between wild and farmed salmon. Here, Michel Haquin shows his colors and uses the excellent farmed salmon from his native Belgium.

Although there must be a thousand different ways to prepare this versatile fish, there is at least one constant: the fish must be absolutely fresh, firm and glossy, with clear, slightly bulging eyes. The steaks are cut from the fleshiest part of the salmon, near the head; take care not to overcook them, as you wish to retain their color and tenderness. Next – and Haquin is adamant on this score – the little layer of fat between the skin and flesh must be scraped off so that it does not spoil the flavor of the "tournedos."

Watercress is featured to good effect in the herb sauce. Like spinach, it has an assertive flavor and should be used in moderation.

Fresh pasta or attractively pared potatoes are suitable accompaniments for this springtime dish, which should be served piping hot.

1. Remove the central bone from each salmon steak without separating the 2 fillets. Roll up like a "tournedos" and tie with string.

2. Wash and drain the watercress, chives, spinach and parsley. Chop coarsely with a hand-held blender or knife and set aside. Reduce the cream with the fish stock to coating consistency and pour this mixture over the chopped herbs. Purée with a hand-held blender, pass through a fine strainer and reduce again to a creamy consistency. Whisk in the butter.

Chive Cream Sauce and Bacon

3. Cut the bacon into strips and blanch; pan-fry until crisp and set aside. Season the salmon with salt and pepper and brown in butter in a hot pan for 2 minutes on each side. Drain on paper towels.

4. Remove the string from the "tournedos" and pull off the skin. Using a knife, scrape off the thin layer of fat between the skin and flesh. Spoon some hot sauce onto each plate, place the salmon in the center and sprinkle with the bacon strips. Serve piping hot.

Cod Fille

Preparation time: 1 hour
Cooking time: 15 minutes
Difficulty: ★★

Serves 4

Four 5 oz/150 g cod fillets
30 mussels, cooked
12 lettuce leaves
¼ cup/25 g capers
¼ cup/25 g cornichons
1 oz/25 g onions
1 oz/25 g parsley, chopped
1 cup/250 ml vegetable stock

½ tsp heavy cream
2 tbsp/30 g butter
juice of 1 lemon
salt and freshly ground pepper

For the herb and breadcrumb topping:
½ cup/50 g white bread crumbs
1 oz/25 g parsley
1 sprig of thyme
1 sprig of rosemary
1 clove garlic
3½ tbsp/50 ml olive oil
1 pinch of salt

In this recipe, cod fillets are coated with a bread crumb and herb mixture, and the result is a cut above the traditional British fish and chips. Cod fishing is very important to the English, who employ enormous trawlers that can gather in up to 30 tons of fish per hour.

Choose nice, thick cod fillets, which will not fall apart during cooking. Cod is known for its white, delicate flesh, but its taste is not always particularly marked. For this reason, a strong accompaniment based on capers and cornichons is used in addition to the herb and breadcrumb topping. The thyme and rosemary play a similar role in the crumb coating.

Paul Heathcote finds that the best mussels chosen to accompany the cod are the large specimens cultivated on vertical ropes in the Thau lagoon in the south of France. Other mussels can be used as well. You might also wish to substitute scallops for a more sophisticated result, or a mixture of mussels and oysters, which would allow you to incorporate the oyster liquor in the dish.

1. In a food processor, blend the dry ingredients for the herb and bread-crumb topping, then add the olive oil a little at a time.

2. Broil the cod fillets until the flesh is opaque and flaky but not quite cooked through. Season with salt, pepper and lemon juice. Top the fish with the herb mixture. Dice the onions and cook for 10 minutes in a little water; drain.

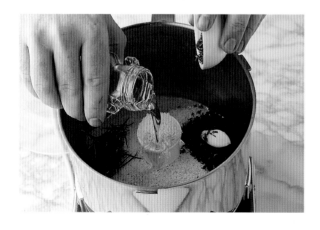

with Mussels

3. Bring the vegetable stock to a rolling boil. Dice the cornichons and add to the stock, along with the capers, chopped parsley and onions. Pour in the cream, whisk in the butter and add the cooked, shelled mussels, which have been seasoned with salt and lemon juice.

4. In the meantime, blanch the lettuce in boiling salted water and place 3 leaves in the center of each plate. Just before serving, broil the herb-topped fillets until golden brown. Dish up the fish and pour the sauce all around.

Preparation time: 30 minutes
Cooking time: 10 minutes
Difficulty: ★

Serves 4

4 medium potatoes
2 potatoes for the chips
1 bunch of young dandelion greens
1 bunch of dill
1 bunch of arugula, 1 small head escarole
1 tbsp *crème fraîche*
3½ tbsp/50 g butter
salt and freshly ground black pepper

For the gravad lax:
1¼ lb/600 g fresh salmon (for four 5 oz/150 g fillets)
¾ cup plus 1 tbsp/200 g sugar
1 bunch of dill, chopped
6½ tbsp/100 ml cognac
7 tbsp/100 g salt, coarsely crushed peppercorns
For the mustard sauce:
2 tbsp Meaux or similarly coarse-grained mustard
1 tsp dark soy sauce
1 tsp light soy sauce
1 tsp mustard seeds
1 tbsp **demi-glace** or reduced veal stock
juice of 1 lemon
1 shallot, chopped
1 tbsp sherry vinegar

Dill and marinated raw salmon are a marriage made in heaven. The highly aromatic herb never fails to flatter, rather than overpower, its delicate, subtly flavored companion. The amount of dill in the marinade should therefore give no cause for concern, as this particular partnership is based on complementarity rather than competition.

The marinade containing both sugar and salt is typically Scandinavian, and can preserve the fish for up to 10 days. In this recipe the salmon is marinated for at least 48 hours.

The *gravad lax* is cooked very briefly, on the skin-side only, leaving the flesh itself very rare. If you wish to do like the Norwegians, you can eat the salmon cold, in thin strips on toast, with mustard sauce. In the Nordic countries, everyone knows this centuries-old dish; and it enjoys the same high reputation that fresh salmon does. Norway, incidentally, plays an important role in salmon farming, being responsible for 70 percent of the world production of this fish.

The marinade may be improved by adding a mixture of fresh fennel and crushed aniseed and coriander.

1. Place the salmon fillet on a platter and sprinkle with all the marinade ingredients. Pour over the cognac and marinate for 48 hours. Bake 4 potatoes in the oven, halve lengthwise and scoop out the flesh, leaving the skins intact. Use a vegetable mandoline to cut the other two potatoes into chips, and fry these in clarified butter.

2. Mash the scooped-out potato with the butter and crème fraîche and season with salt and pepper. Fill the potato shells and keep warm. Cut the salmon into four 5 oz/150 g pieces.

Gravad Lax

3. Grill the gravad lax on the skin side only, leaving the flesh very rare. Clean the salad ingredients (dandelion, dill, arugula and escarole) and make the mustard sauce by combining the appropriate ingredients.

4. Place a piece of salmon on each plate, remove the skin, and garnish the fish with a small mound of salad, a potato boat studded with chips, and the crisp salmon skin. Pour the sauce all around.

Scorpion-fish Ragout with

Preparation time: 40 minutes
Cooking time: 1 hour
Difficulty: ★★

Serves 4

One 2¼ lb/1 kg scorpion fish
2¼ lb ripe tomatoes
1 green bell pepper
2 leeks
⅔ cup/150 ml white wine

6½ tbsp/100 ml extra-virgin olive oil
a few leaves chervil
salt and freshly ground pepper

For the pasta dough:
¾ cup plus 1 tbsp/400 g flour
4 egg yolks
1 tbsp olive oil
2 tbsp water
pinch of salt

Paccheri are one of the countless varieties of pasta consumed in record quantities in Italy. Alfonso Iaccarino has fond memories of his Neapolitan childhood, in which these noodles were a particular favorite. There is a reason why they are made into tube shapes: the sauce is meant to fill as well as cover them.

Gragnano, a little town on the Sorrento peninsula on the Gulf of Naples, is home to a museum of pasta, among other curiosities. And what better tribute could there be to the deep-rooted tradition of pasta making?

The other main ingredient in this recipe is the scorpion fish, an essential component of *bouillabaisse* and renowned for its firm flesh. Both the highly prized small brown scorpion fish and the more common large red scorpion fish live in rocky sea beds, feeding on small crustaceans. Don't forget that the head of the fish, which contains a good quantity of flesh, is crucial for the consistency of the ragout. Incidentally, the tastiest morsel of the scorpion fish is deemed to be the so-called "king's piece": the cheek.

To make the most of the flavors and colors of the fresh fish and the green bell pepper, Alfonso Iaccarino strongly recommends that you prepare this ragout at the very last moment.

1. To prepare the sauce, finely chop the leeks in a food processor or with a knife, and sweat with the fish head in olive oil. Deglaze with the white wine. Add the quartered tomatoes, and cook for about 1 hour. Pass through a fine strainer.

2. Place the green bell pepper under a hot broiler until black and blistered all over. Peel and cut into very thin strips. To prepare the pasta, place the flour on a work surface, making a well in the center; gradually incorporate the other ingredients into the flour, kneading through thoroughly. Rest the dough for 1 hour. Roll out thinly, cut into rectangles and form into tube shapes.

Paccheri di Gragnano Pasta

3. Fillet the scorpion fish and cut the flesh into cubes. Place the green bell pepper strips, chopped chervil, sauce and fish cubes in a pan and cook for about 10 minutes.

4. Cook the paccheri in plenty of boiling salted water until al dente. Mix the noodles with the sauce and the fish and serve.

Pikeperch Strips on *Rösti*

Preparation time: 45 minutes
Cooking time: 20 minutes
Difficulty: ✶

Serves 4

1 pikeperch (1¾ lb/800 g)
2 potatoes
1¾ oz/50 g soybean sprouts
3½ oz cucumber (1¾ oz in small sticks,
1¾ oz in cubes)
1 tbsp capers
1 tbsp shallot
6½ tbsp/100 g butter

pinch of Chinese five-spice powder
chives
salt and freshly ground pepper

For the sesame-cream sauce:
3½ oz/100 g white of leek
1 shallot
6½ tbsp/100 g butter
¾ cup/200 ml *crème fraîche*
¾ cup/200 ml chicken stock
6½ tbsp/100 ml white wine
6½ tbsp/100 ml Noilly Prat (French dry
vermouth)
3½ tbsp/50 ml sesame oil
salt and freshly ground pepper

Rösti is a typically Swiss dish originally eaten by farmers and manual laborers at breakfast to fortify themselves for the forthcoming day's work. It consists of potatoes boiled in their skins, shredded when cold, and formed into little pancakes that are fried quickly. Main crop, rather than new, potatoes are used because the latter do not contain enough starch. In the past, a little lard was added to make the *rösti* more substantial; nowadays, however, this is a lighter dish which Swiss chefs serve alongside bratwurst or the ever-popular Zurich-style veal.

Pikeperch contains very few bones, which makes it easier to prepare than some other fish. Like all other fish, it must, of course, be absolutely fresh, and should be scaled and gutted in the usual way. Then it needs to be cut into even-sized pieces thick enough to stand up to the cooking process.

If you wish to give this dish an Asian touch, as André Jaeger usually does, you may replace the Noilly Prat with *shaoxing*, a Chinese wine with a taste slightly reminiscent of sherry. The *shaoxing* lends character to the nutty tasting sesame cream. The soybean sprouts are used for much the same reason. This everyday food of the Orient has long been popular in Western cuisnes.

1. Finely chop the leek and shallot. Sweat in the butter, then deglaze with the white wine and Noilly Prat. Reduce by half. Add the crème fraîche and chicken stock. Season and reduce once more by half. Add the sesame oil at the last minute and purée in a blender.

2. Boil the potatoes in their skins. When cool, peel and grate. Form into small cakes. Fillet the pikeperch, remove the skin and any remaining bones and cut the fish into ½ in/1 cm slices. Finely chop the capers and shallot. Season with a little salt and the Chinese five-spice mixture, and let stand for a few minutes.

with a Sesame-cream Sauce

3. Fry the 4 small rösti pancakes in oil and butter until golden brown and crisp. In another pan, heat a little butter until it foams, then add the capers, shallot, chopped soybean sprouts and the cucumber sticks.

4. Add the pikeperch strips and sauté for 1 minute. Spoon some sesame-cream sauce onto each plate, top with a rösti pancake and arrange the fish on top. Sprinkle over the finely diced cucumber and the chopped chives.

Preparation time: 40 minutes
Cooking time: 10 minutes
Difficulty: ☆

Serves 4

One 1¼ lb/600 g pikeperch
5½ oz/160 g soft carp roe (milt of the male carp)
9 oz/260 g white of leek

11 oz/320 g shiitake mushrooms
juice of ½ lemon
oil
1 shallot
4½ tbsp butter, clarified
2½ tbsp/40 ml strong reduced veal stock
flour
salt and freshly ground pepper

The pikeperch or zander is found both in North America and Europe, including in Alsace. A close cousin of the perch and pike and the North American walleye, this voracious predator hunts by night, which makes catching it a hit-and-miss affair. If luck is on your side, you will be rewarded with beautiful soft white fillets that make very good eating.

The carp also abounds in Alsatian rivers and lakes. This fish was highly prized in the Middle Ages, appearing on royal tables in the form of pâtés. In the 19th century, Brillat-Savarin was mad about its soft roe, which he used to garnish omelets. The soft roe is absent during the spawning season from April to June. This creamy food must stay soft when cooked; it should be pan-fried just until golden brown. If you cannot get hold of soft carp roe, which is considered to be an Alsatian specialty, this recipe may also be prepared with monkfish or cod liver, whose fine qualities often go unrecognized.

Use only the white part of the leeks, which are beautifully mild and ideally complement the flavor of the fish. This combination achieves perfection when vegetables of the best quality are used.

1. Finely chop and blanch the whites of leek. Cut the pikeperch fillets into 4 equal portions of about 5 oz/150 g each, leaving the skin on. Salt and pepper the fish, pan-fry in olive oil until golden brown and finish cooking in the oven.

2. Finely slice the mushrooms and sauté in butter with the chopped shallots. Add a pinch of salt.

Carp Roe and Leeks

3. Drain the soft roe on paper towels and dredge in flour. Fry them in a little oil in a nonstick pan until golden brown, turning them carefully.

4. Drizzle the plates with the clarified butter, mixed with the juice of ½ lemon and the veal stock. Arrange the mushrooms, pikeperch and leek in the center and surround with the soft roe.

Preparation time: 40 minutes
Cooking time: 40 minutes
Difficulty: ★

Serves 4

10½ oz/300 g salted salmon
10 potatoes
2 onions
3 eggs

1⅔ cup/400 ml milk
3½ tbsp/50 g butter
3½ oz/100 g dill
salt and freshly ground pepper

The *Vasa*, the superb flagship of the 17th-century Swedish fleet, named after Sweden's ruling dynasty of the time, went down with all hands on its maiden voyage. Wonderfully preserved by the salt water, it was refloated in the 1960s and turned into a museum, where Örjan Klein opened his restaurant "K.B." – the perfect "laboratory" for both traditional and haute cuisine, as this salmon and potato gratin so eloquently demonstrates.

Scandinavian salmon is among the best in the world, and this is hardly surprising when one thinks of the ice-cold waters of Sweden and Norway. Salmon abound here, and it is easy to find good specimens 9–13 lb/4–6 kg. Pink salmon is primarily Norwegian, while the white-fleshed salmon is found in the Baltic.

Once you have chosen your salmon and cut it into thin slices, it only remains to assemble a *gratin*, quite soft and not too thick. If too thick, it would take too long to cook, which would dry out the potatoes, whose primary task is to moderate the temperature around the fish.

Although savory rather than sweet, this pudding can be served at the end of a meal. Some melted butter should be passed around separately for each guest to "customize" the top layer of potatoes in terms of flavor and texture.

1. Gently sauté the finely sliced onions in some butter for a few minutes until soft and reduced in volume. Boil the potatoes whole in their skins, then peel and cut into slices. Cut the salmon into slices.

2. Butter a gratin dish and cover the bottom with a layer of potatoes. Top with half of the onions, dill weed and salmon. Repeat the layering process, finishing with a layer of potatoes.

Salmon Pudding

3. Whisk together the eggs and milk and pour over the pudding. Grind some pepper over the top.

4. Dot the top with butter and bake for 20 minutes at 375–400 °F/190–200 °C. Remove from the oven and garnish with melted butter and chopped dill.

Skate Wing Fried in Sesame

Preparation time: 20 minutes
Cooking time: 40 minutes
Difficulty: ★★

Serves 4

1¼ lb/600 g skate wings
40 leaves flat-leaf parsley
½ white cabbage
1 ginger root
¼ cup/60 ml sesame oil
peanut oil for deep-frying
pinch of sea salt
freshly ground white pepper

For the sauce:
⅓ cup/80 ml concentrated fish stock
2 tbsp/30 ml soy sauce
¼ cup/60 ml maple syrup
2 tbsp/30 ml red-wine vinegar
4 cups/1 l grapeseed oil

For years the soybean has been increasingly popular in European and American cooking, appearing in appetizers, entrées and even desserts in the form of texturized vegetable protein, tofu, soy sauce, and even the beans themselves. Soybeans are low in fat and high in protein, and the subtle flavoring properties of soy sauce are prized by gourmets.

Japanese soy sauce or *shoyu* is a highly savory condiment made from crushed soybeans and wheat that are fermented for several months in salt water. The sauce for this dish can be prepared the day before, so that you can devote yourself entirely to the skate the following day.

Skate is best in winter, a season that suits this large, flat-bodied creature that can reach several yards in length, and that moves along in a fascinating gentle wavelike motion. A voracious carnivore, it possesses small, sharp teeth capable of causing great damage.

If you are not buying your skate already filleted, carefully wash the fish before preparing it, as it can sometimes smell of ammonia. The fillets are always taken from the thickest part. Since they are fragile, they should be monitored closely as they cook. Handle them as little as possible, as they fall to shreds with disconcerting ease.

1. Prepare the sauce by mixing together the fish stock, soy sauce, maple syrup and red-wine vinegar. Reduce to a syrupy consistency. Whisk in the grapeseed oil and keep warm.

2. Wash the cabbage leaves; slice coarsely and wilt in a little butter. Stir with a fork on which you have speared the peeled ginger.

Oil with Soy Sauce

3. Clean, skin, trim and fillet the skate wing. Season with salt and fry in very hot sesame oil.

4. Deep-fry the parsley leaves in peanut oil. Just before serving, arrange the skate wing, cabbage and fried parsley on the plates. Spoon some sauce to the side as a finishing touch.

Sea Urchins with

Preparation time: 20 minutes
Cooking time: 15 minutes
Difficulty: ☆

Serves 4

12 sea urchins
3 tbsp each celery root, carrot and leek, cut into tiny dice
1 shallot, chopped

1 tsp tomato paste
juice of 1 lemon
6½ tbsp/100 ml fish stock
1 tbsp Noilly Prat (dry French vermouth)
1¼ cup/300 ml cream
salt and freshly ground pepper

You would be hard pressed to find a less appealing looking creature than the sea urchin. In France, most of these echinoderms come from Erquy in Brittany. There are also good quality ones from Ireland. In certain parts of the world – Sicily for example – there are varieties of this creature that are not edible.

Fresh sea urchins taste best between November and March. Choose rather large specimens, with firm prickles and a generally robust appearance.

The only edible part of the sea urchin is its coral, the five crimson or orange-colored little "tongues." It is essential that they be cleaned carefully in cool water.

The same is true for their shells, which will be later filled with the cream sauce. Since the coral has a very strong iodine taste, we recommend that you use fish stock in the accompaniment, the subtlety of which is capable of taming this wild flavor. For the same reason, mild-tasting vegetables are used, cut into tiny dice and flavored with vermouth. The mixture of vegetables given here, incidentally, is just a suggestion and can equally well be replaced by other varieties, such as asparagus.

An ideal cream sauce implies a perfect blending of all of the constituent flavors. This can only be achieved with a long cooking time of up to 3 hours.

1. With a pair of scissors, cut a circular opening into the slightly concave side of the sea urchins. Pour their juices through a fine sieve into a bowl. Scoop out the crimson coral with a teaspoon and rinse in cold water. Carefully wash out the shells, turn upside down to drain, and reserve.

2. Transfer the sea urchin juices to a saucepan with the diced vegetables, chopped shallot, tomato paste, fish stock and Noilly Prat and reduce by half.

a Vegetable Cream

3. Add the cream and simmer for 10-15 minutes to allow all the flavors to blend. Correct the seasoning and add the juice of ½ lemon.

4. Place the corals in the shells and heat under the broiler. Fill the shells with the vegetable cream and serve at once.

Pan-fried Mackerel Fillets

Preparation time:	40 minutes
Cooking time:	10 minutes
Difficulty:	★

Serves 4

Two 10½ oz/300 g mackerel
3½ oz/100 g peas
½ large cucumber

2 onions
juice of 1 lemon
2 tbsp aquavit
3½ tbsp/50 ml olive oil
1 bunch of dill
freshly ground pepper
1 tbsp salt

In Denmark, it is not enough to be an accomplished chef, capable of preparing all of the various ingredients in a recipe according to the rule book. The Danes place equal emphasis on the art of food presentation and table decoration, and in this they excel. These details, characterized by harmony and good taste, are of the utmost importance for our chef, Erwin Lauterbach.

Next in importance is the absolute freshness of the mackerel, whose spindle-shaped bodies and shiny, silvery, striped skin are easy to recognize at fish counters. Mackerel pass close to the Danish coasts twice yearly, in spring and fall, in the course of their migrations, traveling through the seas in huge schools from which miraculous harvests are made. Their flesh is very firm and a bit on the fatty side: this can be balanced by judiciously chosen vegetables, or with a shot of brandy or spirits – here, flavored with caraway.

Aquavit, the potato-and-caraway drink traditional in Denmark and other Scandanavian countries, not only lends a lovely color to the sauce, but also is an effective aid to digestion.

We recommend vegetables such as onions and cucumbers in a dressing, or celery, and potatoes.

1. Fillet and bone the mackerel. Leaving the skin on, cut the fillets into 2 in/5 cm pieces.

2. Halve the cucumber lengthwise and scoop out the seeds, then cut into ¼ in/5 mm thick slices. Place in a sieve over a bowl and sprinkle with salt. Weight for at least 1 hour to eliminate excess juices.

with Salted Cucumber

3. Cut up the onions, pod the peas, strip the dill from its stalks and put the stalks to one side. Sweat the onions in olive oil without allowing them to color. Add a little water and the dill. Braise, covered, then reduce, mixing in the peas and cucumber last. When the vegetables are cooked, remove the dill and add the aquavit, lemon juice and oil, to create a dressing.

4. Heat some oil in a nonstick pan and brown the mackerel fillets on the skin side. Divide the dressed onion-cucumber mixture among the plates, placing the pieces of mackerel on top. Garnish with sprigs of dill and spoon some peas in the center.

Broiled Gilt-head Sea Bream

Preparation time: 1 hour 30 minutes
Cooking time: 2 hours
Difficulty: ★

Serves 4

Two 14 oz/400 g gilt-head sea breams
4 purple artichokes
scant 9 oz/250 g fennel
scant 9 oz/250 g tomatoes
2 cloves garlic

2 anchovy fillets
¾ cup/70 g white bread crumbs
¾ cup/200 ml extra-virgin olive oil
1 cup/250 ml white wine
1⅔ cup/400 ml water
½ bunch of flat-leaf parsley
2 tsp/10 g coriander seed
2 bay leaves
1 sprig of thyme
salt and freshly ground white pepper

The gilt-head sea bream is the pearl of the sea breams. Caught on the high seas by pelagic trawlers, it can be recognized by the golden half-moon between its eyes. Its delicate, fine, supple flesh makes this large, 12–20 in/30–50 cm fish one of the best eating fish of the Mediterranean, with the added advantages of having few bones and being quite easy to prepare.

Our chef recommends patting the sea bream dry, brushing it with olive oil and broiling it before finishing it off in the oven, taking care not to overcook it as this might toughen its flesh. The fish is served with a light vegetable sauce. This may be prepared the day before and whisked with the oil just before serving; in fact, advance preparation makes the sauce even more interesting, giving the flavors time to meld with one another.

The purple artichoke, which is well known in the south of France, is eaten both raw and cooked. Cooked in a covered pot, purple artichokes stay supple and firm, and their hearts are ideal for filling with a stuffing of tomatoes seasoned with thyme, garlic and bay leaf. Don't forget the olive oil, whose fine flavor is absorbed by the artichokes and whose subtle nuances contribute to the success of this delicious summer dish, which should be served piping hot.

1. Peel and seed the tomatoes, then blend to a purée. simmer with the finely sliced fennel, pepper, coriander, white wine and 1⅔ cup/400 ml water for 2 hours.

2. Purée the mixture, then reduce and whisk in the olive oil. Trim the artichokes, removing the hairy choke, then cut them in half.

with Greek Vegetable *Jus*

3. Cook the artichokes in a covered pot with the thyme, bay leaves and garlic in a little olive oil. Mix the bread crumbs with the parsley, a little garlic and the chopped anchovy fillets.

4. Heat the artichokes in some olive oil and fill with the breadcrumb stuffing. Broil the sea bream fillets and finish in the oven until just cooked. Arrange the sauce and the stuffed artichoke hearts on the plates. Place a fish fillet on top of the sauce and garnish with some flat-leaf parsley.

Roast Herbed Salmon

Preparation time: 30 minutes
Cooking time: 20 minutes
Difficulty: ★★

Serves 4

2¼ lb/1 kg salmon
½ celery root
1 potato
1 oz/30 g chopped truffle

¼ cup/60 g butter
¾ cup/200 ml cream
⅔ cup/150 ml beef stock
⅔ cup/150 ml reduced brown veal stock
⅔ cup/150 ml olive oil
flour (for dusting)
¾ oz/20 g chives
pinch grated nutmeg
2 tsp/10 g coarse sea salt
salt and freshly ground black pepper

Celery is edible in its enirety: ribs, leaves, seeds and root are all rich in vitamins and minerals, and are known for their calming effect.

Celery root, or celeriac, is a thick, knobby ball that feels quite heavy for its size. Any specimens sounding hollow when tapped should not be used. In this recipe, it is combined with potatoes to make a fine, creamy, not too thick purée. The butter and cream should not be added until the last minute.

And now to the salmon. Choose a piece cut from a fish weighing 8¾–11 lb/4–5 kg, which will yield thick, meaty fillets. Monitor the cooking process very carefully: if cooked at too high a temperature, the fish will dry out and the dish will be spoiled. Three to four minutes cooking time on the skin side is sufficient, followed by a few seconds on the other side, just enough to color it. Between the skin and the flesh of the salmon lies a layer of fat: in this recipe it is removed.

The flavor of this dish is further enhanced by sprinkling the plate with chives that have been heated in butter. Choose the fine-bladed variety if possible, and chop the chives at the last moment before cooking, to retain the most intense flavor.

1. Peel the celery root and potato. Cut into chunks and cook in boiling salted water for 20 minutes. Drain and press through a sieve or put through a food mill.

2. Reheat the celery root and potato purée, adding 8 tsp/40 g butter, the cream, nutmeg, salt and pepper. Mix and keep warm. Bone and trim the salmon. Cut 4 good rectangles from the fillets and dust the skin side with flour.

with a Périgord-style *Jus*

3. Sweat the chopped truffle in butter. Deglaze with the truffle juice from the can. Add the veal stock and reduce slightly. Whisk in the butter. Keep warm. Cook the salmon pieces on the skin side for 3–4 minutes in hot oil: turn and fry for just a few seconds on the other side. Keep warm.

4. Lift the skin from the salmon and remove the layer of fat. Sprinkle on a few grains of coarse sea salt and some chives that have been warmed in butter. Replace the skin. Spoon a circle of celeriac purée onto the plates and top with the salmon, skin-side up. Pour the sauce around the purée.

Preparation time: 40 minutes
Cooking time: 30 minutes
Difficulty: ★★

Serves 4

14 oz/400 g monkfish
14 oz/400 g skate
14 oz/400 g conger eel
14 oz/400 g eel

14 oz/400 g squid (or cuttlefish)
14 oz/400 g onions
1¾ lb/800 g ripe tomatoes
1¾ lb/800 g potatoes
3 cloves garlic
2 green bell peppers
1 small chile
1 bunch of parsley
1 bay leaf
¾ cup/200 ml white wine
¾ cup 200 ml olive oil

Caldeirada à portuguesa is the name given in Portugal to this fish soup, of which there are almost as many versions as there are towns claiming its invention. From the Costa Verde in the North to the tip of the Algarve in the South, it is prepared with the most varied sauces, which are more or less hot with chile, and a variety of ingredients such as pasta or potatoes. In spite of this diversity, however, the basis of the dish always remains the same: it is always a soup made from a wide variety of fish.

If you were a stickler for tradition, you would slice the fish in pieces, bones and all. Our chef departs from custom here, and recommends removing the bones in order to spare your guests this unpleasant chore. Depending on what is available at the fish market, you can prepare this dish with sea bream, red mullet, John Dory or any other flavorful fish – as well as with shrimp, clams and other seafood. Moreover, it is also possible to make this soup with just one type of fish – grouper, for example. We should also mention the *caldeirada* from Aveiro on the west coast of Portugal, which combines both ocean fish and freshwater fish.

By alternating layers of fish and vegetables, you ensure that the flavor of each penetrates the other as the *caldeirada* cooks. In addition, the vegetables trap the heat, so the fish remains firmer. It is essential to the success of the dish that your dinner guests be offered sufficient quantities of strongly seasoned broth (*caldo*).

1. Clean the fish. Cut into pieces and season.

2. Slice the onions into thin rings. Slice the garlic thinly. Peel and seed the tomatoes and cut into rounds. Peel the potatoes and cut into ⅜ in/1 cm thick slices. Halve and slice the green bell peppers. Place the vegetables in separate small bowls.

'Bouillabaisse"

3. Starting with the vegetables, alternate layers of vegetables and fish in a pot until you have used up all the ingredients, seasoning as you go. Add the parsley, bay leaf and a crushed chile.

4. Pour over the white wine and the olive oil. Season, and cook, covered, over low heat for about 30 minutes. Serve in the same pot if possible.

Lemon Sole with Celery

Preparation time: 45 minutes
Cooking time: 15 minutes
Difficulty: ★

Serves 4

Four 10½ oz/300 g lemon sole
2 ribs celery
2 tomatoes
6½ tbsp/100 g butter
1 cup/250 ml fish stock
a little white wine

10 saffron threads
a little lemon juice
tarragon, thyme
salt and freshly ground white pepper

For the celery root mousse:
¼ celery root
3½ tbsp/50 g butter
2 tbsp/30 ml cream
salt and freshly ground white pepper

Dieter Müller is always on the search for something new. Here, he recommends recreating the scales of a fish with overlapping slices of celery, whose shape makes it well suited for this purpose. For the fish, he has chosen lemon sole, which has thicker fillets than Dover sole.

Lemon sole is easy to recognize by its brown spots, which distinguish it from other varieties of flatfish, which tend toward pinkish-gray. The fillets are well-sutied to poaching. If they are too thin, fold them over. If lemon sole is not available, Müller suggests fillets of brill or turbot, or as a freshwater alternative, pikeperch.

Two varieties of celery serve as a garnish: the celery root is made into a light mousse, which acts as a base for the scales, and the scales themselves are made from celery ribs blanched in boiling water. As soon as the celery "scales" are in position, Dieter Müller suggests that you may want to fix them in place with a second layer of celery mousse.

For the saffron sauce, use only high-quality threads, rather than the powdered form of this precious spice.

1. Cook the celery root in boiling salted water. Process to a purée, transfer to a saucepan and stir over medium heat to dry the purée. Add the butter and the stiffly beaten cream and set aside. Thinly slice the celery ribs on a slight diagonal. Blanch briefly in boiling salted water and refresh immediately.

2. Fillet the fish and season with salt and lemon juice. Spread a thin layer of celery root mousse on the fillets and top with overlapping pieces of celery to form "scales."

on a Saffron-tomato *Fumet*

3. Prepare the sauce: Stir the saffron threads into the fish stock. Reduce by half, whisk in the butter and add the peeled, diced tomatoes and the chopped herbs. Season to taste with salt and freshly ground pepper.

4. Place the fish fillets in an ovenproof dish and pour in the white wine and fish stock. Bake for about 8 minutes in a 375 °F/190 °C oven. Ladle some sauce onto the warmed plates and top with the fillets. This dish may be served with fresh noodles, buttered spinach or boiled potatoes.

Baby Squid and Octopus

Preparation time: 50 minutes
Cooking time: 40 minutes
Difficulty: ★

Serves 4

10½ oz/300 g baby squid or cuttlefish
10½ oz/300 g tiny baby octopuses
(approximately ¾–1¼ in/2–3 cm long)
1 slice of fatty serrano ham
7 oz/200 g white kidney beans (ganxet beans)

1 red bell pepper
1 green bell pepper
1 yellow bell pepper
1 carrot
1 tomato
1 onion
3 cloves garlic
flat-leaf parsley
thyme
a little olive oil
salt and freshly ground pepper

The finest Catalan dishes owe a great debt to the *ganxet* or white kidney bean: small, flat, and easy-to-cook with a creamy consistency, it lends depth, body and flavor to cream soups and broths alike. In one famous recipe, *butifarra con judías*, the beans are sautéed in rendered ham fat and served with a large sausage. This filling winter dish inspired Jean-Louis Neichel to create a recipe that brings together the flavors of the land and sea.

There is virtually no difference between the small squid anbd the small octopus, bith of which are known by different names in the various regions where they are caught. They are simply diminutive members of a family that contains some real monsters, a number of which can grow to even more than 6 ft/2 m in length.

The tiny squid and octopus should be deep-fried without being washed first, exactly as is done for the famous tapas, dispensed by the thousand in the bars along the Ramblas in Barcelona.The small octopus, which is somewhat rarer than other varieties, may be a bit more expensive, but boasts a creamier consistency.

The flavor of the typically Sopanish serrrano ham really enriches this dish.

1. Peel, core and seed the 3 bell peppers and cut into strips. Gently sauté the finely sliced onion, peppers, thyme and a crushed clove of garlic in some olive oil for 15 minutes. Cook the white beans in unsalted water for 40 minutes.

2. Sauté the squid and the octopus in separate pans with an unpeeled, crushed clove of garlic in some hot olive oil.

with White Kidney Beans

3. Remove the beans from their cooking water. Cut the serrano ham into small pieces. Peel and carefully seed the tomato and cut into small dice. Sauté all the ingredients in olive oil.

4. Place a spoonful of the mixed peppers and a spoonful of beans on each plate. Top with the squid and octopus and garnish with a little chopped parsley.

Pan-fried Pikeperch with Bone

Preparation time: 30 minutes
Cooking time: 1 hour
Difficulty: ★

Serves 4

1 large pikeperch (3¼ lb/1½ kg)
16 pieces of beef marrow bone, 1½ in/4 cm long
4 shallots
1 clove garlic
1 bouquet garni
1¾ oz/50 g smoked bacon

2 cups/500 ml red gigondas wine
1 cup/250 ml veal stock
6½ tbsp/100 ml olive oil
3½ tbsp/50 g butter
chervil leaves
sea salt
freshly ground pepper

For the onion–black currant marmalade:
1 onion
1 tbsp black currant preserves
6½ tbsp/100 ml wine vinegar
¾ cup/200 ml red wine
2 tsp/10 g sugar

Since eastern France is landlocked, it is primarily river fish that are eaten in this region. The lack of coastline also explains the *marinière de poisson* traditional to this area, prepared with carp, catfish and gudgeon, and seasoned with white wine and onions. This recipe is based on the same principle, but contains only one type of fish, chosen for its delicacy: the pikeperch or zander.

The best pikeperch is fished in the spring, when the water level of streams and rivers sinks. After you have filleted the fish, pan-fry it over moderate heat, taking care not to overcook it. Thicker fillets may need to be finished in the oven.

The beef marrow should remain in the bone until you are ready to prepare it, so it does not dry out. It should be soaked for at least 24 hours in ice-cold water, so refrigerate it and change the water at regular intervals. After removing the marrow from the bones, you should then poach it for a few minutes.

The wine sauce is similar to the base of a *matelote* or eel stew. Gigondas is a powerful red wine from the Rhône valley whose alcohol content is somewhat above average and thus stands up well to the brisk reduction that is essential before the veal stock is added. Finally, the sweetish, slightly tart black currant preserves contrast marvelously with the somewhat more pungent sauce.

1. Scale the pikeperch. Divide into fillets of about 5 oz/150 g and remove all bones. Lightly fry the smoked bacon in a pan until the fat runs. Chop the shallots and clove of garlic and sauté until golden. Pour off the fat and moisten the contents of the pan with the gigondas. Reduce to a syrupy consistency. Prepare the onion-black currant marmalade by sweating the onions and adding all the other ingredients. Stew, covered, over low heat for 40 minutes.

2. Add the veal stock and bouquet garni. Reduce, adjust seasoning and pass through a fine strainer. Set aside in a hot-water bath to keep warm. At the last minute, whisk in 3½ tbsp/50 g butter.

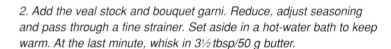

Marrow and Gigondas Sauce

3. Poach the beef marrow for a few minutes in salted water at 195 °F/90 °C. Pour a few drops of olive oil into a nonstick pan. Sauté the fish fillets until golden on both sides, removing as soon as they are just done.

4. Drain the bone marrow and place around the pikeperch fillets. Pour the very hot gigondas sauce all around. Sprinkle a little sea salt on the marrow. Make the onion and black currant marmelade by sweating the onions and adding all the other ingredients. Stew, covered, over low heat for 40 minutes.

Braised Monkfish

Preparation time: 55 minutes
Cooking time: 35 minutes
Difficulty: ★★★

Serves 4

One 3¼ lb/1½ kg monkfish tail

1 generous lb/500 g snow peas
12 pearl onions

2 lemons
6⅔ tbsp/50 g flour
10½ oz/300g unsliced white sandwich bread
3½ tbsp/50 ml white wine
2 cups/500 ml heavy cream
13 tbsp/200 g butter
salt, freshly ground pepper and sugar

Though the head of the monkfish is generally reckoned to be too hideous to display at the fish counter, it has an exquisite-tasting tail, meaty and delicious. It spends most of its time perched on the rocks, waiting for its prey. This it attracts with a sort of "fishing rod" located on its head that terminates in a fleshy "bait" – hence its other name, "anglerfish."

The monkfish tail consists of fine, firm flesh that is completely free of bones, apart from the central bone. Just be sure to remove all of the membrane under the skin so that this does not shrink and toughen while the fish is cooking. Provided that you follow this advice, the monkfish will delight your dinner guests with its tender, tasty white flesh.

We recommend snow peas as an accompaniment for the monkfish. Unlike other varieties of peas, which must be shelled, snow peas have small, thin edible pods with immature seeds, which are always eaten whole (hence their French name, *mangetout* ("eat-all"). Watch them carefully as they cook, because they should be served *al dente*.

The julienne of lemon zest must be blanched long enough to rid it of any bitterness. The crunchy white-bread *croûtons* should serve as a contrast to the soft fish: prepare them at the last moment, making sure they do not absorb too much melted butter.

1. Fillet the fish and remove all the membranes. Cut the zest of 2 lemons into thin julienne; blanch for 5 minutes and drain. Trim and blanch the snow peas.

2. Cut the fish fillets into 12 chunks. Dredge the fish in seasoned flour and pan-fry in ¼ cup/60 g hot butter. Pour off the fat. Quickly sauté the snow peas in ¼ cup/60 g butter.

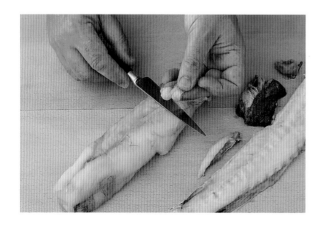

with Snow Peas

3. Deglaze the pan with the white wine and add the cream. Simmer for about 5 minutes. Cut off the crusts of the bread, slice and cut into heart-shaped pieces and brown in butter. Glaze the pearl onions by cooking in butter with a little water and sugar.

4. Put the sauce through a fine strainer and whisk in the remaining butter. Arrange the snow peas in fan shapes on each plate. Place the monkfish in the center and mask with the sauce. Garnish with the glazed onions, the bread hearts and the julienne of lemon.

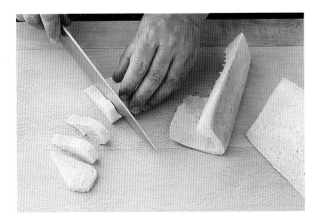

Turbot and Anise Potatoes

Preparation time: 1 hour
Cooking time: 30 minutes
Difficulty: ★★

Serves 4

One 4½ lb/2 kg turbot
2 tsp/10 g black peppercorns
2 tsp/10 g mustard seeds
2 tsp/10 g juniper berries
a few drops olive oil
2 lemons
sea salt

For the anise potatoes:
10½ oz/300 g potatoes
cumin seed

a little olive oil
a little anise-flavored vinegar
salt, freshly ground pepper

For the white sauce:
6½ tbsp/100 g homemade mayonnaise
6 ½ tbsp/100 ml heavy cream
salt and freshly ground pepper
vinegar

For the green sauce:
2 shallots, 2 bunches of basil
1 bunch of chervil
1 bunch of flat-leaf parsley
2 tsp pine nuts
6½ tbsp/100 ml olive oil
a few drops of red-wine vinegar
salt and freshly ground pepper

A member of the flatfish family, turbot is found in cold waters such as the English Channel and the Atlantic. Long prized for its fine flesh, the turbot is so delicate that it usually requires an accompaniment that will enhance, not mask, its flavor. Look for a large European turbot, which should yield good fillets without too much waste.

The fillets are smoked using a method similar to that passed down by the indigenous peoples of the Caribbean and Oceania. This is one of the first methods successfully used by humans to preserve perishable meat and fish.

For this recipe, Horst Petermann strongly recommends the Charlotte potato, a small winter variety with a fine, very smooth skin. Its firm, yellow flesh lends itself well to the creation of a light, soft purée, particularly if you are able to buy the early, shorter potatoes, which are preferable to the longer variety intended for storage. Although relatively new, Charlottes are gaining an ever-growing following among both producers and consumers. Yukon golds are a good alternative.

It is the herbs and other seasonings that make this subtle dish really shine, provided these are prepared properly and used in the quantities stated. Once cooked, the turbot should be served immediately, accompanied by a few flavorful greens such as radicchio, arugula or dandelion.

1. Fillet the turbot. Separately crush the peppercorns, juniper berries and mustard seeds in a mortar with a pestle, then mix together. Add grated lemon peel, a little lemon juice and the olive oil and stir together to make a marinade.

2. For the white sauce, make a mayonnaise with an egg yolk, mustard, salt and vinegar. Add the same quantity of heavy cream to the mixture. For the green sauce, make a dressing by blending together the olive oil and vinegar, then add the basil, chervil, parsley, finely minced shallots and the pine nuts.

with two Sauces

3. Season the fish with sea salt and brush with the marinade prepared in step 1. Wash the potatoes and cook them in their skins in boiling salted water to which some cumin seeds have been added. Cut the potatoes into small rounds and season with anise-flavored vinegar and olive oil.

4. Smoke the fish quickly over high heat in a stovetop smoker. Finish by sautéing in a nonstick pan in some oil. Arrange the potatoes in a semicircle in the center of the plates. Pour over the white sauce. Top with a chunk of fish. Pour the green sauce over and garnish with the salad leaves.

Langoustine, Shellfish

Preparation time: 1 hour
Cooking time: 30 minutes
Difficulty: ✷✷

Serves 4

One 7 oz/200 g red mullet
1 sea bass
4 langoustines (size 18/24)
7 oz/200 g mussels
7 oz/200 g cockles
white part of 1 leek

1 tomato
½ medium carrot
4 cloves garlic
4 shallots
1 tbsp tomato paste
1 tbsp ground turmeric
1¼ cups/300 ml white wine
3½ tbsp/50 ml olive oil
flat-leaf parsley
salt
croûtons
rouille
freshly ground pepper

The combination of shellfish and crustaceans is always a winner. This soup draws its inspiration from traditional fish soups and celebrates fish, mussels, cockles and langoustines with equal enthusiasm. This choice is not meant to be proscriptive, and you could equally well include some clams, or replace the langoustines with shrimp or lobster.

There is one cardinal requirement for preserving the tender flesh and special aroma and flavor of the langoustines: a short cooking time. For this reason, Roland Pierroz has opted for steaming, which treats them with the necessary respect and allows the cook to monitor progress. Another useful tip to ensure success: before cooking, cover the langoustines with ice cubes and refrigerate; this will keep them fresh and firm up their flesh.

The mussels used in this recipe should be shiny, moist, and live. Any mussels that are open before cooking should be discarded, to avoid the risk of food poisoning. The freshness of the shellfish is obviously the best guarantee of quality for your soup.

The subsequent steps yield a beautifully smooth soup sufficiently concentrated by reduction, but not overly strong. Garlic, shallot and turmeric subtly enhance the flavor. Turmeric, incidentally, belongs to the ginger family. A traditional ingredient in curries and other Indian dishes, it is seldom available fresh, but is usually bought in dried, powdered form.

1. Shell the lagoustines. Refrigerate the tails, together with the pieces of fish. Set aside the shells for garnish. In separate covered pots, steam the mussels and cockles with ⅓ cup plus 1½ tbsp/100 ml white wine and half of the chopped shallots until they open. Drain, and strain the cooking liquid.

2. Finely chop 2 shallots. Peel and crush the garlic. Finely slice the white of leek and the half carrot. Heat the oil in a saucepan and sweat all the ingredients together with the tomato paste, stirring constantly. Add ⅓ cup plus 1½ tbsp/100 ml white wine, the shellfish cooking liquid, turmeric, and 4 cups/1 liter water and continue cooking.

3. Bring to a boil and simmer for 20 minutes, uncovered. Press through a strainer and reduce the liquid to 2¾–3½ cups/600–700 ml. Season and reserve. Cut the tomatoes into small cubes for a garnish.

4. Bring some water to a boil in a steamer, and steam the langoustines and the fish pieces for 2 minutes. Steam the shellfish for 30 seconds to reheat. Ladle the soup and the fish into shallow bowls. Garnish with tomatoes and parsley, croûtons and rouille.

Roast Turbot Fillet with

Preparation time: 45 minutes
Cooking time: 10 minutes
Difficulty: ★

Serves 4

One 4½ lb/2 kg turbot
1½ lb/650 g miniature squid
2 red bell peppers

2 tomatoes
juice of 1 lemon
½ head of garlic
7 tsp/35 g butter
¾ cup/200 ml olive oil
½ bunch flat-leaf parsley
salt
freshly ground pepper

This recipe brings together a number of quintessentially Mediterranean products: bell peppers, garlic, squid, and, of course, olive oil. Our chefs have chosen Italian olive oil, whose fruity flavor harmonizes marvelously with the fish, provided it is used with discretion.

Baby squid are particularly prized in Spain, and are available all year round. The squid are first pan-fried in smoking-hot oil until they brown: their juices will caramelize, producing a crisp coating that intensifies their flavor. The squid will shrink as they are frying. Once they are the size of garlic cloves, the red bell pepper, garlic and parsley should be added to the pan. Leave the garlic cloves whole and unpeeled, so that they hold their shape when cooked and look more attractive on the plate. None of these ingredients are particularly robust and care should be taken not to overcook them; try to use a nonstick pan.

The Pourcel brothers are great fans of "noble" Mediterranean fish. Here, they have opted for turbot, but you could substitute Dover sole or sea bass in this recipe. Remember that turbot is a very fragile fish, and should be cooked gently to avoid a disappointing taste and texture.

To give this dish an even stronger Mediterranean bias, other herbs, such as thyme or basil may be used.

1. Break up the garlic into individual cloves. Place the unpeeled cloves in a small saucepan with ⅓ cup plus 1½ tbsp/100 ml water and ¾ cup/200 ml oil and simmer until the cloves are tender inside and yield easily to thumb pressure.

2. Peel the bell peppers and cut into rings. Peel and seed the tomatoes and cut into small dice. Reserve. Sort through the squid; clean and wash thoroughly. Coarsely chop the parsley. Remove the ink sacks from the squid and drain the squid on paper towels.

Pan-fried Baby Squid

3. Pour some olive oil into a pan and sauté the squid over high heat. Halfway through the cooking, add the red bell pepper and a little butter. Fry until the mixture is nicely colored. Add the parsley leaves and the cooked garlic cloves. Season and remove from the pan.

4. Fillet and skin the turbot and cut into 5½ oz/160 g portions. Pan-fry the fillets and season. Add the diced tomato and lemon juice to the squid, along with ¾ cup/200 ml of the oil in which the garlic was simmered. Arrange this mixture on plates and top with the turbot. Pour over the squid cooking juices.

Deep-fried Hake with

Preparation time: 45 minutes
Cooking time: 10 minutes
Difficulty: ☆

Serves 4

1¾ lb/800 g hake fillet
4 tbsp all-purpose flour
1 tbsp cream
1 tbsp egg white

For the garnish:
4½ oz/125 g mushrooms
¼ Savoy cabbage

½ tsp finely chopped garlic
½ tsp finely chopped fresh ginger root
1 tbsp vegetable oil

For the dressing:
½ oz/15 g fresh ginger root
2 tbsp wine vinegar
1 tbsp mushroom-flavored soy sauce or dark soy sauce
1 tbsp chile sauce
2 tbsp vegetable oil
1 tbsp Asian sesame oil
½ bunch of cilantro
salt and freshly ground white pepper

Like whiting and herring, hake is a common fish of the North Atlantic and the Irish Sea, so it is hardly surprising that it once occupied a special place in the cuisine of the British Isles.

Try to buy fillets from a hake weighing 6½–8¾ lb/3–4 kg. A larger fish would be difficult to cook evenly, and the flavor of smaller fillets would be overpowered by the crispy skin during cooking.

The garnish consists of vegetables that are especially popular in Ireland: Savoy cabbage and cultivated mushrooms. Although local tastes do not run to cèpes or porcini, Paul Rankin still thrills at the memory of picking an incredible 66 lb/30 kg of cèpes there in just two hours.

Other green vegetables such as Swiss chard or spinach would also go well here.

The use of ginger in this vegetable accompaniment may come as something of a surprise. Measure the chopped ginger exactly, as its strong taste can eclipse the more subtle flavors of the other ingredients. Combine it sparingly with the soy and chile sauces and the sesame oil to add lightness to the dish.

Other spices may be used to flavor the dressing: cayenne pepper, black and white sesame seeds, garlic powder or curry powder. Use them with discretion, because it is really the fish that has the starring role in this recipe, and its delicate flavor should remain recognizable.

1. First, prepare the dressing. Put the ginger, cilantro, wine vinegar, soy and chile sauces into a small bowl, season with salt and pepper and whisk until the salt has dissolved. Add the vegetable and sesame oils in a thin stream, whisking constantly. Adjust the seasoning.

2. Shred the cabbage and blanch in boiling salted water for 1 minute; drain and refresh in cold water. Heat 1 tbsp oil in a pan, add the garlic and ginger and stir-fry over high heat. Add the cabbage and the sliced mushrooms and cook for 1 minute. Season with salt and pepper, remove from the heat and keep warm.

Sesame-ginger Dressing

3. Cut the hake fillets into 5 oz/150 g pieces and score the skin decoratively. Mix together the cream and egg white in a shallow bowl. Coat the fish with this mixture, then dredge with flour.

4. Heat the oil to 350 °F/180 °C. Add the fish and fry for 3 minutes on each side. Drain on paper towels. Divide the vegetables among 4 warm serving plates, top with the fish and pour the dressing around.

Sautéed Langoustines with

Preparation time: 30 minutes
Cooking time: 3 minutes
Difficulty: ★

Serves 4

24 langoustines
2 zucchini
8 cloves garlic
pinch of thyme
1 tsp/5 g chopped chives
1 tbsp/15 g butter
salt and freshly ground pepper

For the stock:
the langoustine heads
1 onion
1 medium carrot
1 bouquet garni
1 tbsp/15 g butter

For the marinade:
2 pinches of Madras curry powder
3½ tbsp/50 ml olive oil

Curry powder is not a single spice, but a mixture of various ones chosen according to the meat, fish or vegetable it will be used to season. It can consist of cardamom, turmeric, cumin, mustard seed, cloves and a good dose of cayenne pepper, ground together into a fine orange-yellow powder.

The proportions of the spices in curry powders vary a great deal, so you should give some thought as to which curry powder to use for a particular dish. This is particuarly important when preparing *desmoiselles*, as langoustines are called in Cherbourg. Jean-Claude Rigollet recommends the subtle but strong Madras curry powder.

Langoustines should really only be cooked live. If this is not possible, make sure that they are absolutely fresh and translucent. There should be 8–10 langoustines to the pound/15–20 langoustines to the kilo to yield the right size of tail.

Zucchini, with their delicate flesh and subtle taste, make a suitable accompaniment for these different nuances of flavor. A dish like this, however, seems to cry out for yet another piquant element. Our chef has therefore hit on a garlic *jus* whose potent aroma and flavor are unleashed by pounding the cloves in a mortar. Just follow the instructions, and you'll have no trouble in creating this light, aromatic dish.

1. Separate the langoustine heads from the tails. Dice the onion and carrot and gently brown them in butter with the langoustine heads. Pour in enough water to cover, add the bouquet garni and reduce by a quarter. Pass through a fine strainer and keep warm.

2. Meanwhile, shell the raw langoustine tails. Wash the first zucchini and cut into thin strips. Roll each langoustine in a zucchini strip and fasten with a toothpick.

Curry and Garlic Juices

3. Lightly salt and pepper these kebabs. Marinate for 15 minutes in olive oil and Madras curry powder. Lightly sauté the crushed garlic cloves in 1 tbsp butter and moisten with the langoustine stock. Cook this garlic jus over low heat for 10 minutes.

4. Cut the second zucchini into fine julienne and sauté together with the thyme in some olive oil. Heat a little olive oil in another pan and sauté the langoustine tails over high heat. Place a mound of zucchini in the center of each plate and surround with the langoustine kebabs. Pour over some garlic jus and sprinkle with chives.

Bourride with Dover Sole

Preparation time: 1 hour
Cooking time: 2 hours
Difficulty: ★★

Serves 4

3¼ lb/1½ kg Dover sole fillets
12 langoustines

For the Dover sole and langoustine stock:
heads and bones of the Dover sole
heads and bones of the langoustines
1 onion, 1 carrot and 1 leek
½ fennel bulb
1 rib celery
1 bulb garlic
3½ tbsp/50 g butter
3½ tbsp/50 ml olive oil

For the sauce:
2 cloves garlic, 6½ tbsp/100 g butter
3½ tbsp/50 ml cream
3½ tbsp/50 ml olive oil

For the vegetables:
7 oz/200 g carrots, celery, zucchini
14 oz/400 g potatoes

For the honey caramel:
4 tsp/20 g honey
8 tsp/40 g butter
4 tsp/20 ml sherry vinegar

For the garnish:
chives
chervil leaves

Despite hailing from the Ardèche in southern France, Michel Rochedy wasn't always a devotee of olive oil. This recipe, however, would convert all but the most hardened skeptics. Used in conjunction with the butter that subtly underscores the sweetness of the langoustines, olive oil makes its mark in this recipe, adding a distinctly Mediterranean flavor.

As ever, the success of this dish is dependent upon the quality of the ingredients used. Rochedy always prepares this bourride with freshly landed Dover sole, and with langoustines from the bassin d'Arcachon, which he rates highly. He strongly recommends that if you are not planning to cook them immediately, you separate the langoustine heads from the tails, wrap the latter in plastic

wrap and place them in the freezer for up to 3 days.

To caramelize the langoustine tails, melt the butter very slowly in a nonstick pan, then raise the heat to high and sear the crustaceans. The process is quickly finished off by adding the honey and deglazing the pan with sherry vinegar.

The Dover soles are done in no time at all. They should be cooked until barely done, so their flesh will stay nice and tender. Special care should be taken in preparing the stock, which has the task of setting off the individual components of this dish to best effect without overpowering them. Don't forget the garlic, which lends this dish a genuinely Provençal touch.

1. Fillet the Dover soles and shell the langoustines. Melt the olive oil and butter in a pan and gently brown the shells and fish bones together with the finely cut-up stock ingredients. Pour in enough water to half-cover and cook over low heat for 2 hours. Strain. Cut the carrot, celery and zucchini into sticks. Peel the potatoes and trim into olive shapes. Cook the vegetables separately and keep warm.

2. Place the sole fillets in a buttered dish and season. Moisten with half the stock and poach the fish (it should be just barely done).

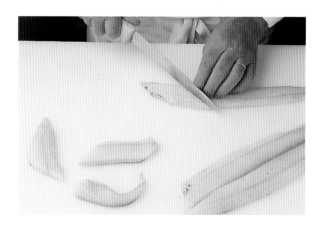

3. Prepare the sauce: Reduce the remaining stock by half, then add 2 garlic cloves and the cream. Boil for 1 minute, then whisk in the butter, followed by the olive oil. Purée and strain the sauce. Correct seasoning.

4. Pan-fry the langoustine tails in butter until they are golden. Add the honey and deglaze with 1 tbsp sherry vinegar. Serve the soles and langoustines in shallow bowls, adding the vegetables. Pour over the sauce and garnish with a few chives and chervil leaves.

Gurnard with Cumin

Preparation time: 15 minutes
Cooking time: 8 minutes
Difficulty: ★

Serves 4

One 4½ lb/2 kg red gurnard
4 artichokes
1 large zucchini
a little extra-virgin olive oil
salt and ground cumin

For the parsley sauce:
2 cups/500 ml extra-virgin olive oil
a few sprigs of flat-leaf parsley

The gurnard, or sea robin, which makes a grunting noise when landed, is one of the 8–10 varieties in the *Triglidae* family (so called because of the triangular shape of its members). The most common variety is the pink-bellied red gurnard, whose ease of preparation makes it a boon to cooks. It can also be prepared Catalan-style, accompanied by a *sofrito* of garlic, onions and tomatoes.

The recipe presented here by Santi Santamaria is so simple: The fish is grilled and finished in the oven, and the artichokes are sautéed. The most unusual thing about the dish is the light sprinkling of cumin powder over the fish fillets. According to Spanish tradition, it is the Moors who, occupying portions of the Iberian peninsula until its reconquest at the end of the 14th century, were responsible for introducing this distinctive-tasting spice to Europe. Frequently found in Indian, North African and Latin American cuisine, cumin seed is less commonly used to season fish dishes. Its relative, caraway, is very popular throughout the Netherlands, the German-speaking countries and Scandinavia.

Cumin is quite a pungent-tasting spice, and should be used sparingly so as not to mask the true flavor of the fish. Sprinkle it over the fillets just before they are done to impart a subtle flavor. Extra parsley may be added to the sauce to give it a brighter color; substitute tarragon if you prefer.

1. Clean the fish and cut into four 9 oz/250 g portions. Trim the artichokes and cook in water acidulated with lemon juice until al dente. Drain upside down. Cut the artichoke hearts into small pieces and sauté in olive oil until golden brown.

2. To make the sauce, strip the parsley leaves from their stalks, then wash the leaves and spin dry. Transfer to a blender and purée to an emulsion with 2 cups/500 ml olive oil.

and Artichokes

3. Salt the fish fillets, sear on a hot grill and transfer to the oven for 8 minutes. Sprinkle with the ground cumin just before they are done.

4. Thinly cut the zucchini on the diagonal. Just before serving, dip in a light batter and deep-fry in hot oil until golden brown. Arrange several pieces of artichoke and a fish fillet on each plate and pour the parsley sauce around. Garnish with fried zucchini slices.

Sea Bream with Lime

Preparation time: 15 minutes
Cooking time: 4–6 minutes, according to fillet thickness
Difficulty: ★

Serves 4

Four 9 oz/250 g sea bream fillets
20 cherry tomatoes
2 medium zucchini
capers

3½ tbsp/50 ml extra-virgin olive oil
2 tbsp butter
1 sprig of rosemary, chopped
1 clove garlic
1 lime
1 lemon
dried oregano and fresh mint
salt
freshly ground pepper

The best recipes aren't necessarily those with the most ingredients. Rather, it is the judicious combination of a few top-quality raw materials that creates the really memorable dishes. This is why Nadia Santini has decided on a simple accompaniment to the sea bream.

Highly rated by the Roman epicure Apicius, who devoted numerous recipes to it, sea bream abounds in the Mediterranean, and is prized by gourmets of this region for its delicate white flesh and distinctive flavor. It should be remembered, though, that this is a very fragile fish, which requires careful cooking to preserve its fine flavor and keep it intact.

Capers, a quintessentially southern European seasoning, harmonize beautifully with sea bream, as with most white fish. If possible, use capers that have been preserved in salt rather than vinegar, to avoid a clash of tastes with the butter in which the fish is browned. A little chopped fresh rosemary sprinkled on top of the fillets as they cook will pleasantly bridge the gap between the delicacy of the fish and the tartness of the capers.

Like other citrus fruits, limes are richj in vitamin C. Choose small firm ones for optimum freshness and tang. The cherry tomatoes lend a bright flavor as well as color to the dish. There are red, yellow and orange varieties available.

If your fishmonger cannot get sea bream for you, this dish could also be made with another variety of white fish, such as a sea bass.

1. Cut off the very top of each cherry tomato. Sprinkle the tomatoes with some oregano and salt and drizzle with a little olive oil. Place in the oven for 5 minutes.

2. Cut the zucchini lengthwise into thin slices and sauté in olive oil until golden brown. Roll up each slice and place a mint leaf on top of each. Keep warm.

Zest and Capers

3. Melt a little butter in a nonstick pan. Add the chopped rosemary, grated lemon zest, garlic, capers and fish fillets. Season with salt and pepper.

4. Turn the fish and cook for 3 minutes on the other side. Place a fillet in the center of each plate, arranging 5 cherry tomatoes and a few zucchini rolls around it. Top the fish with a few strips of lime zest and some capers.

Salt Cod with Cilantro

Preparation time: 15 minutes
Cooking time: 45 minutes
Difficulty: ★★

Serves 4

Four 10½ oz/300 g slices salt cod (desalted
for 48 hours)
7 oz/200 g small potatoes
2 tbsp/30 g butter
2½ cups/600 ml olive oil
1 cup/250 ml milk
6½ tbsp/100 g coarse salt
salt and freshly ground pepper

For the vegetable topping:
2 cloves garlic
2 small onions
3 ripe tomatoes
1 bunch of cilantro
1 bunch of flat-leaf parsley
salt and freshly ground pepper

No one knows who first thought of preserving cod in salt, although the matter has been hotly disputed for centuries. The Portuguese and Spanish winegrowers certainly began to make use of this method a very long time ago, drying and salting this fish for later use.

Your first task will be to acquire the salt cod most suited for this recipe. Although, generally speaking, it is customary to serve modest-sized portions of this fish, this recipe requires as large a piece as possible, since the thicker it is the better it will taste. The Portuguese have literally hundreds of different ways to cook salt cod, and this is one of the more substantial ones.

How to explain the manner in which the Portuguese deal with the *a murro* (literally, "punched") potato? First, it is baked in coarse salt. Then, however, the cook deals it a vicious blow with the fist as soon as it emerges from the oven. Choose small varieties of potato such as "Charlotte" or "Roseval," which will stand up best to this heavy-handed treatment.

The vegetable and herb topping, which should taste strongly of garlic and cilantro, will enhance the flavor of the fish admirably, provided that the ingredients are measured carefully rather than being thrown together in random quantities.

1. Soak the cod for 48 hours to remove excess salt, changing the water several times during this period. Pat the fish dry and place in a high-sided dish. Pour the milk over and set aside for 1 hour.

2. Remove the fish from the milk and pat dry with a cloth. Place the olive oil and the fish in an ovenproof dish. Bake the potatoes at 400 °F/200 °C for 30 minutes on a bed of coarse salt. Remove from the oven, brush off the salt and punch each potato flat with a single blow.

and *a Murro* Potatoes

3. To make the vegetable topping, chop the garlic, cilantro, parsley, onion and tomatoes, combine in a bowl and season with salt and pepper.

4. Top the fish with the vegetable mixture and dot with 2–3 tbsp butter. Bake at 400 °F/200 °C for 45 minutes. Place a portion of fish in the center of each plate and surround with the potatoes.

Fillet of Dover Sole

Preparation time: 30 minutes
Cooking time: 35 minutes
Difficulty: ★★

Serves 4

3 Dover soles
10½ oz/300 g littleneck clams
14 oz/200 g pink shrimp
3½ oz/100 g rice
⅔ cup/150 ml *crème fraîche*

For the sauce:
1 onion
1 tomato
3½ oz/100 g small gray shrimp
3½ tbsp/50 g butter
salt and freshly ground pepper

Like everyone else, the fish-loving Portuguese consider Dover sole to be a prime-quality food. Here Maria Santos Gomes suggests a simple and delicious preparation that will delight both you and your dinner guests.

Dover-sole fillet has quite a supple texture, making it suitable for certain treatments that other more fragile fish would not withstand. According to Santos Gomes, sea bass falls into the same category. Once you have rolled up each fillet around its shrimp filling and secured it with a toothpick, you have excellent *paupiettes* that will stand up successfully to cooking without losing taste or texture.

The proper cohesion between these *paupiettes* and their accompanying sauce is achieved by the little gray shrimp. The sauce should be left to simmer for quite a while, because its success hinges on the various flavors melding properly. So take your time, and only add the *crème fraîche* at the last moment.

Purists might insist that Dover sole deserves to be paired with finer shellfish than the ones suggested here. Lobster and langoustines would be fine in this dish, provided that the sauce is not so highly seasoned as to mask their flavor.

1. First, prepare the sauce: Finely cut up the onion and sauté until golden. Add the quartered tomatoes, followed by the gray shrimp. Cover and sweat for 15 minutes.

2. Wash the clams in 3–4 changes of water. Place in a pot with water to cover, bring to a boil, and cook over high heat until they open. Strain the cooking water into the pan with the shrimp sauce. Bring the sauce to a boil, then purée in a blender and strain.

with Shellfish Sauce

3. Shell the pink shrimp. Fillet the soles and season. Top the fillets with the shrimp and roll up, fastening with a toothpick.

4. Place the paupiettes in a braising pan. Add the sauce, the crème fraîche and the clams, and simmer over low heat for 10 minutes. Arrange the fish rolls and clams on plates and pour over the sauce. Serve with rice separately.

Grouper with Naoussa

Preparation time: *1 hour*
Cooking time: *15 minutes*
Difficulty: ★★

Serves 4

4 medium eggplants
2¼ lb/1 kg grouper
5 oz/150 g each zucchini and potatoes
3 oz/80 g carrots
3 oz/80 g red bell pepper
4 tomatoes

2 cloves garlic
a little olive oil
oil for deep-frying
salt and freshly ground pepper
dill tips for garnishing

For the sauce:
¾ cup/200 ml *Naoussa boutari* (Greek red wine)
¾ cup/200 ml fish stock
a little butter

If you are not yet familiar with Naoussa wine, then it is time that you got to know this red nectar. The powerful flavor of this wine, particularly if it has been allowed to age, makes it ideal for this recipe, in which the fish is prepared *matelote* style (stewed in wine with onions). Note the Franco-Greek character of this dish, with the typically Greek stuffed eggplants on the one hand, and a very Gallic red-wine sauce on the other.

The grouper is known for abundant flesh that makes excellent eating. Grouper yields good fillets, and the bouquet of the red wine makes up for any imperfections, succeeding in conjunction with the eggplant in harmoniously melding all of the individual flavors.

To keep the eggplant "boats" nice and firm, the hollowed-out eggplant halves should be strewn with coarse salt and left to degorge overnight, then deep-fried. The boats will be filled with a mixture of finely diced vegetables and new potatoes.

The grouper can quite happily be replaced by a sea bass – or even milk-fed lamb, so highly prized by Greek gourmets.

1. Hollow out the eggplants, leaving a ⅛ in/½ cm thickness of flesh for the "boat." Deep-fry in plenty of olive oil and place on a grill upside down to drain.

2. Wash, scale and fillet the grouper, then remove all remaining bones. Cut the fillets into large cubes and sauté briefly in olive oil. Season.

Wine in Eggplant Boats

3. Deglaze the pan with some red wine and cook for about 10 minutes. For the sauce, reduce the wine and fish stock by one third, strain and whisk in some butter. Cut all of the vegetables into coarse cubes and blanch separately.

4. Sauté the vegetables in butter. Fill the eggplants alternately with fish and vegetables, pour the sauce over and garnish with vegetable cubes and dill sprigs.

Monkfish in a Shellfish

Preparation time: 2 hours
Cooking time: 30 minutes
Difficulty: ★★★

Serves 4

One 3¼ lb/1½ kg monkfish tail
1¾ oz/50 g pikeperch fillet
14 oz/400 g cultivated mussels
14 oz/400 g littleneck clams
½ egg white
4 tsp/20 ml heavy cream
1 cup/250 g butter
1 loaf white bread (unsliced)
¼ cup/60 ml olive oil
2 cloves garlic
1 large bunch of tarragon

1 bunch of flat-leaf parsley
1 sprig of thyme and rosemary
salt, freshly ground pepper, lemon

For the *mirepoix*:
2 shallots, garlic, ¼ leek
½ fennel bulb, 2 ribs celery
zest of 1 orange; 1 tomato
6½ tbsp/100 ml white wine,
2 tsp/10 ml pastis

For the carrot sauce:
generous 1 lb/500 g carrots
a little sugar
6½ tbsp/100 ml cream
6½ tbsp/100 ml chicken stock
cilantro, tarragon
8 tsp/40 g butter
orange zest

For the tarragon *coulis*:
2 tbsp/30 g butter
3½ tbsp/50 ml shellfish stock

Fritz Schilling admits to a weakness for the Mediterranean, where light and *joie de vivre* are so eloquently reflected in the colors, aromas and flavors of the cuisine. In this dish with Mediterranean overtones, the sweet carrot, the crisp crust and the tender monkfish flesh are placed on a bed of flavorful sauce that discreetly enhances the fish.

The monkfish crust is made from unsliced white bread with its crusts removed. Slightly stale (2-day-old) bread is best, as it is easier to cut into thin slices that do not fall apart. The size of these slices will obviously determine the cut of the monkfish fillet, which must usually be squeezed into shape before it can be rolled up like a cigarette. (The monkfish is supple enough to permit this treatment.) Mollusks are used for the stuffing; they are more varied-tasting, chewier and less expensive than crustaceans.

The carrot sauce should have the purity and uniformity of the light in the Mediterranean. The lightly caramelized carrots develop a subtle complexity of flavor. Puréed, they yield a bright, vivid liquid with a denser, sweeter taste. Once the sauce has been seasoned with cilantro, tarragon and orange zest, then carefully strained, this dish hands you sunshine on a plate.

1. To prepare the sauce, slice one carrot into fine julienne and deep-fry. Cook the remaining carrots in a covered pot over low heat with butter, salt, sugar and chicken stock. Add the cilantro, tarragon and orange zest. Set aside 4 carrots in a little of their cooking liquid. Add the cream to the remaining carrots, then purée the mixture and strain.

2. For the tarragon coulis, purée ⅓ of the parsley and ⅔ of the tarragon in a little water. Strain into a pot and bring to a boil. Cook the shellfish with the diced vegetables until they open. Drain, reserving the cooking liquor. Thicken the liquor with a beurre manié. Add to the coulis, whisk in 4 tsp/20 g butter and season.

Crust with Carrot Sauce

3. Make a classic mousse with the pikeperch fillet. Set aside a few shellfish for the garnish, then shell and coarsely chop the rest and mix with the pikeperch mousse. Trim the crusts from the bread, then cut into ⅛ in/3 mm thick slices and lay on top of some plastic wrap.

4. Spread the slices of bread with the mousse, top with the monkfish fillets, season, and roll up tightly using the plastic wrap. Remove the wrap, then brown the fillets in oil with a little butter, garlic and thyme for 8–10 minutes. Spoon some sauce slightly off-center on the plates and decorate with a spiral of tarragon coulis. Place the monkfish fillets on top and garnish with the shellfish and the carrots.

Dover Sole Shamrock

Preparation time: 45 minutes
Cooking time: 10 minutes
Difficulty: ✫

Serves 4

4 Dover soles
7 oz/200 g spinach
1 medium carrot
2 leeks
1 celery root
3 ribs celery
4 cups/1 l fish stock
salt and freshly ground pepper

For the salmon mousse:
7 oz/200 g fresh salmon

1 egg white
1 cup/250 ml cream
salt and freshly ground pepper

For the cod mousse:
3½ oz/100 g fresh cod
½ egg white
2 cups/500 ml cream
salt and freshly ground pepper

For the dressing:
3 tbsp syrupy reduced lobster stock
6½ tbsp/100 ml tarragon vinegar
¾ cup/200 ml olive oil
1 tbsp chopped chives
1 tbsp chopped chervil

Dover sole is becoming increasingly rare, and you may have to fall back on a fish with a less illustrious pedigree for this recipe. The explanation for this is simple: the soles are caught by trawlers in the North Sea and the English Channel using deep-sea dragnets, and overfishing is threatening the species' very survival. If you do not wish to be an accessory to the decline of the Dover sole, you could used turbot, sea bass, cod or halibut fillets.

This dish was created when the *Queen Elizabeth 2* put in at Cork, on the occasion of the Irish Prime Minister's lunch aboard the luxury liner. It contains a strongly symbolic component, consisting of green spinach, white fillet of Dover sole and orange salmon, in honor of the Irish flag: a harmonious composition arranged in the shape of a shamrock, that quintessentially Irish emblem.

The two different mousses may be prepared in advance, though the dish must be cooked just before serving. Let the fish rest for a few minutes, which makes slicing a good deal easier. If you'd like to chance your luck, there's nothing to stop you from adding a fourth leaf to the clover.

1. Fillet the soles. Flatten the fillets slightly with the blade of a knife, place them on a work surface covered with plastic wrap and season. Prepare the salmon mousse and spread this on the fillets, applying the mixture somewhat more thickly in the center. Wilt the spinach in oil and purée it with a pat of butter.

2. Prepare the cod mousse, blend with the spinach purée and spread on the fillets over the salmon mousse. Roll up the fillets lengthwise using the plastic wrap. Poach the fish roll for 10–12 minutes in fish stock, or steam for 8 minutes.

with Crunchy Vegetables

3. Cut the vegetables into fine julienne and sweat in a little butter. Season. Make the dressing by whisking together all the ingredients.

4. Cut the fish on the diagonal into 12 slices. Arrange on the plates with the vegetable garnish and pour the dressing all around.

Pineapple Tart with

Preparation time: *1 hour*
Cooking time: *20 minutes*
Difficulty: ✶✶

Serves 4

12 oz/350 g fresh pineapple
9 oz/250 g live crayfish
¾ oz/20 g yarrow, chopped
⅓ cup/80 g butter

1¾ oz/50 g puff pastry
2 cups/500 ml French sauternes
6½ tbsp/100 ml Swiss pine liqueur
a little olive oil
salt and freshly ground pepper

Pine liqueur, much prized in Switzerland and served after dinner, is virtually unknown outside that country. In this dish it lends an unexpected, slightly bitter touch that contrasts nicely with the sweet flavor of the pineapple.

This recipe will delight sweet-and-sour enthusiasts, particularly with its combination of pineapple and crayfish. For the record, let it be mentioned that Roger Souvereyns originally prepared this dish with foie gras in place of the crustaceans.

It is not always easy to buy live crayfish. Try to buy red-clawed crayfish, as they are more flavorful. The only trick in preparing them is removing the intestine, which may be done by twisting and pulling the center fin of the tail.

The pineapple should be fragrant and heavy for its size. The outer flesh of the fruit should then be finely diced (the core is generally too woody). The "eyes" and skin should be carefully removed before simmering the pineapple cubes for a couple of hours in a good sauternes and pine liqueur to preserve them. While not the most inexpensive of wines, sauternes' viscosity and sweet richness make it the perfect foil for the slightly tart fruit.

This dish might well be your first introduction to yarrow, an edible plant prized for its bitter aftertaste that has been almost forgotten in the kitchen. Its highly indented leaves have earned its most common species the name "milfoil" ("thousand leaves").

1. Peel the pineapple and remove the "eyes." Cut the flesh into small even dice.

2. Preserve the pineapple cubes by simmering for about 2 hours in sauternes and pine liqueur. Roll out the puff pastry on a baking sheet to a thickness of scant ⅛ in/2 mm and bake at 350 °F/180 °C until golden brown.

Crayfish and Pine Liqueur

3. Toss the live crayfish for 2 minutes in hot olive oil in a covered pan. Remove from the pan, cool and shell.

4. Using a pastry cutter, cut circles out of the baked pastry. Place 1 on each plate and top with the preserved pineapple. Heat the chopped yarrow in the butter, add the crayfish tails, season, and carefully turn in the butter. Place the crayfish next to the pineapple tart and pour over a little butter.

Grouper with

Prepartion time: 25 minutes
Cooking time: 20 minutes
Difficulty: ✳

Serves 4

1¼ lb/600 g thick grouper fillet
generous 5 oz/150 g small fresh cèpes or
porcini
1¾ oz/50 g leaf spinach
1 onion, chopped

7 oz/200 g carrots, julienned
chervil
2 tsp/10 ml cognac
3½ tbsp/50 ml white wine
6½ tbsp/100 ml olive oil
salt and freshly ground pepper

Fortunate in having an almost year-round supply of various members of the cèpe family, Pedro Subijana freely admits to being crazy about these wild mushrooms–understandable considering their fine flavors. In this recipe the mushrooms are flambéed in cognac, which might shock some purists. But far from masking the flavor of these mushrooms, alcohol actually enhances it. In France, in particular, the cèpe (*Boletus edulis*), with its thick stalk and brown cap is highly appreciated for its dense, tasty flesh.

Spinach has been grown in Spain at least since the 6th century. Choose small, delicate leaves, and sauté them quickly. Their fresh taste will lighten the dish.

Grouper is a great classic of Spanish cuisine, especially the Basque variety from the *Cernidae* family, found in both the Atlantic and the Mediterranean. Grouper can grow to over 3 ft/1 m in length, and is particular sought after by fisherman.Once its considerable resistance has been overcome, it offers copious, firm flesh that can be broiled or grilled.

For this recipe, Pedro Subijana recommends cooking the fish on one side only. You will therefore need a very fresh fillet that has not been skinned. The skin should be scored lattice-fashion before the fish is cooked, so that the heat can penetrate the fillet more effectively.

1. Clean the mushrooms and separate the stalks from the caps. Reserve a few nice caps for later use. Heat some olive oil in a pan and gently sauté half of the chopped onion and the cèpes until they color slightly. Flambé with cognac, deglaze with white wine and add water to cover. Simmer over low heat for 15 minutes.

2. Purée the mixture in a food processor or blender, then press through a sieve. Add a little olive oil to lift the flavor and keep warm in a double boiler.

Spinach and Cèpes

3. Sauté the spinach in some olive oil and remove from the pan. Thinly slice the reserved cèpe caps and sauté in the same oil. Finely chop the remaining ½ onion and sweat in another pan without allowing it to color; spoon this mixture over the mushroom slices. Deep-fry the julienned carrot.

4. Clean and fillet the grouper, but do not skin. Season with salt and pepper and pan-fry over high heat, skin-side down, for about 4 minutes. Do not turn the fish. Just before serving, finish by crisping the skin under the broiler. Serve on a bed of spinach and cèpes, garnished with the sauce and some chervil.

Brill and Langoustines

Preparation time: 45 minutes
Cooking time: 15 minutes
Difficulty: ✶

Serves 4

4 brill fillets (generous 5 oz/150 g each)
1 dozen 2¾ oz/80 g langoustines
generous 1 lb/500 g spinach
1 dozen asparagus tips
1 clove garlic
6½ tbsp/100 g butter

For the chive-cream sauce:
⅔ cup/150 ml *crème fraîche*
½ lemon
½ bunch of chives
salt and freshly ground pepper

For the dressing:
3½ tbsp/50 ml olive oil
juice of 1 lemon
2 oz/60 g shallots, chopped
1 tbsp chopped chives
3½ oz/100 g tomatoes, diced
1¾ oz/50 g black trumpet mushrooms
crushed coriander seed
salt and freshly ground pepper

On hot days in the summertime, light dishes with little or no sauce are generally preferred. Brill, with its exquisite, very firm, snow-white flesh is ideal choice for an entrée. It can tolerate only gentle and quick cooking, such as steaming or baking *en papillote* (in a foil or waxed-paper parcel).

For this recipe, you will need fillets from a brill weighing 6½–8¾ lb/3–4 kg to combine to best effect with the langoustines and spinach. The langoustines should also be fairly large; they will be pan-fried in olive oil before being combined with the bright-green spinach. The flavors of the crustacean and the vegetable complement each other beautifully. The medium-size spinach leaves should be stripped off their stalks before they are used.

As for the asparagus, the spears should be stiff and "snappy," since their flavor is dependent chiefly on their freshness. The grayish mushrooms with their earthy aroma will lend this dish a woodsy flavor.

The chive-cream sauce, a light, moderately lemony confection, should be prepared only at the very last minute and the chives added just before serving. Its consistency must be thick enough to coat the fish fillets without running all over the plate.

1. Strip the spinach leaves from their stalks, wash in several changes of water and sauté with a clove of garlic. Gently sauté the mushrooms in butter. Shell the langoustines and pan-fry the tails in butter. Snap off the woody ends of the asparagus, peel if necessary, then wash them and cook until crisp-tender in boiling salted water. Drain.

2. Bring some water to a boil in a steamer. Place the brill fillets on a piece of aluminum foil in the upper part of the steamer. Cover and steam for 2–3 minutes.

with Chives

3. Reduce the crème fraîche in a saucepan. Season with salt and pepper, then add the juice of ½ lemon and ½ bunch of finely chopped chives. Prepare the dressing by combining the ingredients in a bowl.

4. Arrange a mound of spinach and 3 asparagus spears on each plate. Top with a brill fillet, coated in chive-cream sauce. Place the langoustines and mushrooms between the asparagus spears and spoon over some dressing.

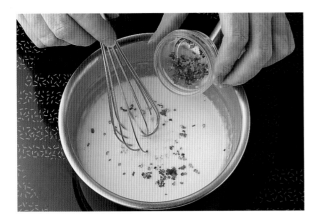

Brandade of Cod

Preparation time: 1 hour
Cooking time: 1 hour
Difficulty: ★★

Serves 4

One 5½ lb/2½ kg fresh cod
2¼ lb/1 kg potatoes
3 cloves garlic
1 bunch of flat-leaf parsley

4 slices of good white bread
1⅔ cups/400 ml veal stock
¾ cup/200 ml olive oil
¾ cup/200 ml cream
6½ tbsp/100 g butter
coarse salt
salt and freshly ground pepper

Brandade de morue is a Provençal dish whose name comes from *brandad*, "something stirred." Originally a very simple dish of salt cod, potatoes and oil, it has "stirred" the imaginations of numerous cooks, who have enriched it with new ingredients. Today it consists of cod emulsified in olive oil and milk, with garlic often added to intensify the flavor.

In this recipe, the brandade is bound with meat juices and is served alongside a pan-fried fillet of fresh cod. You will need a piece of fresh (as opposed to salt) cod that feels good and firm to the touch, sporting a shiny silver skin with mother-of-pearl glints.

The fish is "marinated" in coarse sea salt. Follow the natural shape of the fillets when salting them, and adjust the length of marinating time according to the thickness of the fish. It is then rinsed and marinated in oil to keep it tender. These tasks, which may seem tedious, can be done in advance.

Olives, chives and chopped parsley are appropriate garnishes for this economical and delicious dish, not only underscoring the individual flavors, but adding a vivid touch of Mediterranean color.

1. Fillet the cod. Liberally strew both sides of the fillets with coarse salt and let stand for 20 minutes. Rinse off the salt, pat the fish dry and cut four 4½ oz/120 g portions. Rub with olive oil and set aside. Reserve the remaining cod for the brandade.

2. Peel the garlic and preserve by simmering very gently for 1 hour in olive oil. Wash the potatoes and bake them in their skins. Trim the crusts from the bread, then cut the bread into cubes and deep-fry. Reduce the veal stock to 4 tbsp and whisk in the butter.

with Garlic Oil

3. Coarsely cube the remaining cod and poach in water until just cooked. Drain, removing skin and bones. Pound or blend to a purée in a mortar or food processor. Peel the potatoes and add while still hot to the fish purée. Gradually add the lukewarm olive oil and the cream, stirring constantly. Correct the seasoning.

4. Pan-fry the cod fillets in some olive oil for 4 minutes on each side. Place a dollop of brandade on each plate, arranging a piece of cod next to it and garnishing with a few croûtons and the preserved garlic cloves. Add a spoonful of meat juices and decorate with a few parsley leaves. Serve piping hot.

Monkfish "Tournedos" Threaded

Preparation time: 1 hour
Cooking time: 30 minutes
Difficulty: ★★

Serves 4

2¼ lb/1 kg monkfish tail
4 small fresh sardines
4 anchovy fillets in oil

2 shallots
3 large leeks
2 cloves garlic
¾ cup/200 ml red wine
¾ cup/200 ml red-wine vinegar
4 tbsp/50 g tomato paste
1 bouquet garni
a little white wine
a little stock
6½ tbsp/100 g butter
salt and freshly ground pepper

The monkfish boasts lean, exceptionally fine flesh that is completely free from bones (bar the central one), and can be prepared in 1,001 different ways. For this recipe, 4 "tournedos" should be cut from the head end of the fillet.

To thread the "tournedos" with the anchovy fillets, you can make things easier for yourself by cutting the anchovies on the diagonal and freezing them. A larding needle will also be a help.

Sardines are slender silver-blue fish with semi-fatty flesh. They should be bought absolutely fresh and preferably ungutted. According to Dominique Toulousy, the small, very tasty Mediterranean sardines are the best. They are caught at night by the light if the *lamparo*, a large lantern that lights up schools of fish. It is tempting to assume that sardines originally came from the similar sounding Sardinia, but this is not the case: the main exporters of sardines are the Portuguese as well as the Italians.

The vinegar should be measured sparingly and reduced carefully. Its strong flavor is meant to enhance rather than mask the flavors of the other ingredients. Used too liberally, its acidity could spoil the dish beyond redemption. If you feel that the leek accompaniment is not enough on its own, our chef suggests an orange-flavored onion compote, which would harmonize superbly with the monkfish.

1. Cut 4 medallions from the monkfish tail. Wash the leeks carefully. Cut the white part into ⅜ in/1 cm thick rings. Place the anchovy fillets in the freezer to firm them up.

2. Using a larding needle, thread the monkfish with the anchovies. Proceed exactly as if you were larding meat.

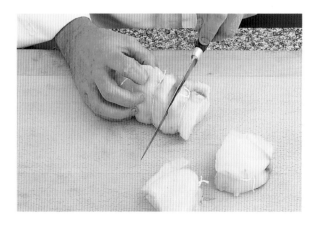

with Anchovies in Verjuice

3. Grind or finely chop the sardines, including their heads and bones. Sweat in a saucepan with the chopped shallots, the bouquet garni and the chopped garlic. Add the tomato paste and the vinegar. Reduce until all of the liquid has evaporated. Add the red wine and reduce by half. Strain and correct the seasoning.

4. Gently sweat the leek rings in a covered saucepan in some butter. Add a little white wine and stock and cook over low heat until soft. Pan-fry the monkfish "tournedos" until golden brown. Place one in the center of each plate, pour some sauce all around and garnish with the leek rings.

Gilt-head Sea Bream in a

Preparation time: 45 minutes
Cooking time: 35 minutes
Difficulty: ★

Serves 4

Two 1¾ lb/800 g gilt-head sea breams
1 bulb of fennel
7 oz/200 g chanterelles
1 red bell pepper
4 roasted tomatoes
1 bunch of dill

1 bunch of cilantro
3½ tbsp/50 g butter
2 orange leaves
1 sprig of lemon balm
3½ tbsp/50 ml olive oil

2 cups/500 ml langoustine stock
a little honey
1 piece fresh ginger root
3½ tbsp/50 g butter
salt and freshly ground pepper

Spices have been traded in the port city of Rouen for centuries. Add to this Gilles Tournadre's innate curiosity, coupled with the chance to sample an impressive array of dishes cooked for him by a Chinese colleague, and you can see how this herb *jus* came into being. In it, sweet and sour tastes combine to season the highly esteemed gilt-head sea bream, recognizable by the golden crescent between its eyes. Low in fat, this fish is at its peak in spring.

Our chef, however, is fairly easygoing and would happily use other sea breams, provided they were absolutely fresh.

In fact you could even use porgy or red mullet, or fall back on John Dory in a pinch.

Whatever fish you decide on, Tournadre recommends that you braise it gently so that it will absorb the sauce well. Make sure to use the herbs and spices in balance, so that their strength doesn't mask the flavor of the fish, and their interplay does not leave unpleasant aftertastes.

Gilles Tournadre had his dinner guests' health in mind when he created this dish containing ginger, lemon balm and ornage blossom, all known for their medicinal virtues.

1. Prepare the vegetables, herbs and spices. Clean, scale and fillet the sea bream, reserving the bones and trimmings.

2. Combine the langoustine stock in a saucepan with all of the herbs, spices and honey. Simmer gently for 15 minutes. Bring the mixture to a boil and reduce by a third. Blend, strain and whisk in the butter.

Herb *Jus* with Chanterelles

3. Cut the sea-bream fillets into large pieces and cook quickly in olive oil.

4. Finely slice the fennel and red bell pepper and sauté all of the vegetables and the chanterelles in butter. Spoon the vegetables into the center of 4 deep plates and sprinkle with chopped dill. Place the fish fillets all around. Pour over the jus and sprinkle with cilantro.

Preparation time: 1 hour 30 minutes
Cooking time: 20 minutes
Difficulty: ★★

Serves 4

4 small arctic char
8 spinach hearts
1 handful of spinach leaves
1 onion, 1 medium carrot
1 rib celery
1 tbsp capers, chopped
3½ oz/100 g tuna in oil
⅓ cup plus 1½ tbsp/100 ml *crème fraîche*
olive oil
dry vermouth

vegetable stock, to taste
salt, pepper, paprika

For the oil sauce (prepare the day before):
salmon caviar
black olive paste
1 bay leaf
1 tsp chopped chervil
1 basil leaf
pink peppercorns
extra-virgin olive oil (to taste)
salt and freshly ground pepper

To garnish:
chervil
basil leaves

Salmerino di fontanta (brook trout) and *salmerino alpino* (arctic char or salmon trout) are both highly esteemed fish, though very different in size. While the brook trout is nearly 40 in/1 m long and tips the scales at about 17½ lb/ 8 kg, the arctic char is just half that size and seldom exceeds 6½ lb/3 kg in weight. Both species live in the cold waters of alpine lakes, home also to the freshwater herring, one of the substitutes suggested by Luisa Valazza. Related to the salmon, brook trout and arctic char are very firm-fleshed fish and thus well-suited to rolling up around a filling.

Luisa Valazza recommends a modest-sized arctic char, between 14–16 in/35–40 cm in length, which will not be too fatty. If you can find no char, you may substitute trout, perch, or other freshwater fish.

The tuna filling is the dominant element in this dish, the oil sauce serving merely to set it off to good advantage. This recipe draws its inspiration from the Piedmontese *vitello tonnato*, thinly sliced poached veal served cold with a tuna and mayonnaise sauce. The stuffing prepared here by Luisa Valazza is considerably lighter than the traditional tuna sauce.

The oil sauce is very subtly seasoned, mainly thanks to the pink peppercorns with their surprising aroma. The black olive paste is what is left of the olives after pressing.

1. Prepare the oil sauce a day in advance: mix all the ingredients together in a bowl and refrigerate overnight.

2. Fillet the fish and remove remaining bones. Prepare a mousse by blending the surplus flesh with salt, pepper, the crème fraîche, a handful of lightly blanched spinach leaves and a shot of dry vermouth.

Arctic Char

3. To prepare the vegetable and tuna fish sauce, lightly sauté the vegetables in olive oil, then add the tuna and capers. Braise lightly and moisten with the vegetable stock. Simmer briefly, then whip vigorously and keep warm. Blanch the spinach hearts.

4. Spread the fillets with the stuffing. Roll up the fillets and secure with a toothpick. Poach in vegetable stock for 8 minutes. Place 2 spinach hearts on each plate, and two spoonfuls of vegetable-tuna fish sauce to the side. Top with the fish roulades, and pour over a little oil sauce. Garnish with the chervil and basil leaves.

Scallops on a Bed o

Preparation time: 20 minutes
Cooking time: 10 minutes
Difficulty: ★★

Serves 4

16 sea scallops
generous 1 lb/500 g Belgian endive
2 green apples
1 onion

1 beet
scant ½ oz/10 g curry powder
4 tsp/20 ml heavy cream
10 tbsp/150 g butter
3½ tbsp/50 ml green-apple juice
2 cups/500 ml peanut oil
2½ tbsp/40 ml olive oil
salt and freshly ground pepper

Geert Van Hecke, who hails from Bruges, is naturally crazy about *witloof*, the Flemish name for Belgian endive, which literally translates as "white leaf." This vegetable is none other than the shoot of the chicory plant, blanched by forcing in the dark. It made its first appearance in Belgium in 1850, having being grown inadvertently in the Botanical Gardens of Brussels. Since then, its season has been substantially extended by the development of early and late varieties. This vegetable is 95% water and therefore virtually calorie-free.

Look for white, firm specimens when buying. Discard any withered leaves, and rinse in plenty of water before cutting the vegetable into julienne (thin strips).

The pilgrimage routes of Saint James also lead through Belgium, and numerous pilgrims from this area have set off towards Santiago de Compostela with their famous scallop shells, which originally served as water ladles and later became their badge of identification. Paradoxically, you should if possible choose live scallops that haven't traveled far. Failing live scallops, you should buy dry packed scallops. The meat of this bivalve mollusk is extremely fragile and should therefore be cooked quickly, for no more than about 10 seconds on each side.

Go easy with the curry powder, as too much of its assertive taste could ruin this dish, which should be very subtly flavored. Serve the scallops piping hot.

1. Wash the scallops under running water, dry and refrigerate until needed. Peel the beet and cut into julienne. Deep-fry for several minutes in hot peanut oil.

2. Cook down the chopped onions and add 1 tsp curry powder. Moisten with 3½ tbsp/50 ml green-apple juice. Reduce by half and stir in the cream. Cook for 5 minutes over medium-high heat. Strain and whisk in the butter.

Belgian Endive and Apple

3. Clean and trim the Belgian endive, cut into julienne and gently sauté in butter for 2–3 minutes. Season with salt and pepper. Shave the unpeeled green apples into thin slices on a vegetable mandoline or with a knife, and set aside.

4. Season the scallops with salt and pepper, then sauté quickly in hot olive oil. Arrange the Belgian endive on a bed of green-apple slices. Top with a circle of overlapping scallops. Spoon the sauce all around and crown the scallops with the fried beet julienne.

Baked Brill with

Preparation time: 20 minutes
Cooking time: 25 minutes
Difficulty: ★★★

Serves 4

One 3¼ lb/1½ kg brill
2 small zucchini
3½ oz/100 g spinach
1¾ oz/50 g potatoes
7 oz/200 g celery root

6½ tbsp/100 ml fish stock
3½ tbsp/50 ml dry white wine
⅓ cup/80 g butter
2 black olives
salt and freshly ground pepper

For the fish filling:
7 oz/200 g whiting
1 egg white
¾ cup/200 ml cream
salt and freshly ground pepper

The inspiration for this marvelous baked brill came to Freddy Van Decasserie from a trip to Japan. Brill is similar to turbot, but is more economical.

The composition of fillings must be geared to the variety of fish they are to stuff. Whiting or other lean fish goes well with brill. The fish should be seasoned with salt and pepper before the cream is worked in, since salt absorbs moisture and helps to thicken the stuffing. Either black pepper or a little cayenne pepper may be used here.

The zucchini "scales" require some explanation. Freddy Van Decasserie recommends small zucchini, which should

be cut into thin, even slices and placed overlapping on the fillet. Begin at the tip of the fish and work your way down to the bottom, laying the scales always from left to right, row by row.

For the remaining accompaniment choose firm celery root, which should feel heavy for its size. Peel it thickly and sprinkle the flesh with lemon juice, so that it doesn't discolor. Here, the potato helps bind the celery root purée.

Finally, the fillet is placed on the sauce, which you have emulsified just beforehand for a creamier consistency. The plates should be decorated with olives, capers and whelks.

1. Prepare the fish stuffing: Finely dice the well-chilled whiting and place in a food processor together with the egg white. With the motor running, add the salt and pepper. As soon as the mixture is smooth, add ¾ cup/200 ml ice-cold cream. Process for a total of 1 minute and push the mixture through a fine sieve.

2. Fillet the brill, season lightly and spread the fillets with the fish stuffing. Slice the zucchini thinly or shave on a mandoline. Sauté briefly in oil and place in overlapping rows on the fish fillets to resemble scales. Moisten with white wine and fish stock. Bake for 10 minutes at 350 °F/180 °C. Season with salt and pepper.

Zucchini "Scales"

3. Poach 7 oz/200 g celery root with 1¾ oz/50 g potatoes over high heat for 15–20 minutes. Purée everything and season with salt and pepper. Fill a piping bag with the puréed celery root and pipe onto the plates in the shape of the brill.

4. Strip the spinach leaves from their stalks. Blanch the leaves, refresh in cold water and press through a sieve. Reduce the liquid in which the fish fillets were cooked to the proper consistency. Remove from the heat and whisk in the butter. Whisk until the mixture is completely cool. Add 1 tbsp spinach purée and allow to dissolve over low heat before emulsifying with a hand-held blender. Strain the mixture and pour inside the piped celery root purée. Place a fillet of brill in the center and serve.

Pandora with an Oyster-

Preparation time: 15 minutes
Cooking time: 1 hour 30 minutes
Difficulty: ★★

Serves 4

10½ oz/300 g pandora fillets
3½ oz/100 g fresh morels
7 oz/200 g oyster mushrooms or chanterelles,
according to season
1 clove garlic
1¾ oz/50 g shallots
1 piece of pork rind

2 eggs
¾ oz/20 g fresh ginger root
1 tbsp diced carrot, onion and celery
1 sprig of thyme
7 oz/200 g chervil
1 bay leaf
6½ tbsp/100 ml *crème fraîche*
¾ cup/200 ml olive oil
salt and freshly ground white pepper

For garnish:
peeled, diced tomato
parsley

This recipe delicately brings together the fruits of the earth and sea while respecting their contrasts and individual flavors. First, we have that highly prized wild woodland mushroom, the morel. Gianfranco Vissani believes that France has the best morels, expecially the conical variety, to whose delicacy and flavor he sings his praises. He combines them here with shallots to provide his dinner guests, and yours, with a gustatory jolt and to keep their taste buds on the alert. He is also full of praise for the cultivated mushroom, and reminds us that it it is the Tuscans to whom we owe the principles of growing mushrooms in layers.

Oyster mushrooms are used in the savory molded custard or *timbale* that accompanies the pandora, a typically Mediterranean fish that is similar to sea bream. Its somewhat lackluster flavor can be perked up with the addition of some fresh ginger. Be sure not to overdo it with this piquant rhizome, because its flavor can be overpowering. The ginger and the shallot, the two strongest-tasting ingredients in this dish, should be measured very carefully.

Care should be taken not to overcook the pandora, or its fragile, delicate flesh could wind up tasting insipid and mushy.

1. Skin the fillets and cut into 2½ oz/75 g pieces. Sauté the oyster mushrooms in olive oil with the thyme and the whole garlic clove.

2. Purée the oyster mushrooms in a blender with the eggs, the chopped chervil, half of the crème fraîche, and salt and pepper. Butter the dariole molds and fill with the custard mixture. Bake in a water bath for 40 minutes at 325 °F/160 °C.

mushroom *Timbale* and Morels

3. Heat some olive oil in a sauté pan and sweat the chopped shallots, the finely diced pork rind, a tablespoonful of finely diced carrot, onion and celery, the bay leaf and thyme. Add a quarter of the morels, the finely sliced ginger, and the cabbage, blanched and cut into thin strips. Moisten with fish stock and add the remaining crème fraîche. Reduce, blend to a purée and press through a fine-mesh strainer.

4. Sauté the remaining morels and the rest of the coarsely chopped, blanched cabbage leaves in butter. Pan-fry the fish fillets. Pour the sauce onto the plates and unmold the mushroom timbale in the center. Arrange the pandora fillets around it, alternating with the morels and cabbage leaves. Garnish with the peeled, diced tomato and sprigs of parsley.

Salmon in a Spinacl

Preparation time: 20 minutes
Cooking time: 20 minutes
Difficulty: ★★

Serves 4

1 salmon (or 14 oz/400 g fillet)
3½ oz/100 g pike fillet
¾ oz/20 g caviar
32 large spinach leaves
1 shallot

1 egg
13 tbsp/200 g butter
6½ tbsp/100 ml heavy cream
6½ tbsp/100 ml whipped cream
2 cups/500 ml white wine
2 cups/500 ml fish stock
3½ tbsp/50 ml Noilly Prat (French dry vermouth)
freshly ground nutmeg
salt, freshly ground pepper

People should stop thinking of salmon as an "anywhere, anytime" food: it is suffering from overexposure and consumers are tiring of it. And that is hardly fair, for this choice fish merits the most sophisticated of preparations. In Scotland and Norway, salmon is farmed on a large scale. Of course there is also wild salmon, which offers delicious, fine flesh.

Scottish salmon has been awarded the French *label rouge* seal of quality, which is not given lightly. Therefore, if it is available, be sure to give it the starring role in this dish.

Whatever salmon you use, it should be absolutely fresh of course. It should be cut carefully into equal-sized portions

of 3½ oz/100 g. Larger pieces might lead to an imbalance with the other ingredients of this dish, according to Heinz Winkler.

Note that the cooking method employed in this recipe preserves the delicate color of the salmon, which contrasts beautifully with its cloak of bright green.

The spinach cloak is lined with a contrasting white fish mousse. Stem and blanch the spinach leaves and dry them in a cloth before spreading with the mousse, topping with the fish and making into little parcels. These should be wrapped tightly, in order to prevent the pike stuffing from leaking out.

1. Cut the well-chilled pike fillet into chunks. Season with salt and chop in the food processor. Add the egg, and gradually incorporate the heavy cream. Season with pepper and freshly ground nutmeg and push through a sieve. Lastly, gently fold in the whipped cream.

2. Fillet the salmon and cut into four cutlets about ⅜ in/1 cm thick and 3½ oz/100 g in weight. Blanch the spinach leaves, spread out over a cloth into 8 small rectangles and dry.

Cloak with Caviar Cream

3. Spread each spinach rectangle with a ⅜ in/1 cm layer of fish mousse. Top with a well-seasoned salmon cutlet and envelop with the spinach. Place the salmon parcel in a gratin dish with a little fish stock and cook for 6 minutes in a preheated 400 °F/200 °C oven. Remove and drain on paper towels.

4. To prepare the sauce, bring the white wine, Noilly Prat and chopped shallots to a boil in a saucepan. Add the fish stock. Reduce by two thirds, whisk in the butter and simmer for 6 minutes. Blend and correct the seasoning. Add the caviar at the last minute, taking care not to boil any further. Serve the salmon on heated plates, garnished with the sauce and a few sprigs of chervil.

Chartreuse of Scallops

Preparation time: *1 hour*
Cooking time: *20 minutes*
Difficulty: ★★

Serves 4

16 large sea scallops
12 cultivated mussels, 12 clams
1½ oz/40 g caviar, 8 cabbage leaves
2 tbsp/30 g butter

For the mussels:
¾ oz/20g each shallot, leek and celery
1 clove garlic, 3 peppercorns
1⅔ cup/400 ml water, ½ cup/125 ml white wine
4 tsp/20 ml olive oil
2 saffron threads
1 pinch of coarse sea salt

For the *nage*:
½ cup/125 ml stock from the mussels and scallop beards ("frills") or trimmings
2 oz/60 g carrots

2 oz/60 g snow peas
2 oz/60 g leek
1 shallot
1 bunch of cilantro
½ cup/125 ml dry wine
4 tbsp/20 ml Noilly Prat (French dry vermouth)
¼ cup/60 g butter
cayenne pepper

For the filling:
3½ oz/100 g langoustines
½ egg white
6½ tbsp/100 ml cream
1 tbsp whipped cream
salt and freshly ground pepper, cayenne pepper

Although cilantro looks something like flat-leaf parsley, its flavor is a good deal more pungent. It should therefore be used in moderation, lest it spoil the dish it is intended to enhance.

A *nage* (French for "swimming") is a court-bouillon in which the shellfish take their last dip. This is transformed into a sauce by reducing it and adding fine flavors. The latter are provided by the cilantro and the scallop beards – which are removed from the white meat when the shells are opened – as well as by the distinctively flavored cultivated mussels.

Incidentally, French cultivated mussels are known as *moules de bouchot*, *bouchot* signifying the stakes and wickerwork to which the mollusks attach themselves via a sticky substance that they secrete. This has led in the west of the country to the term *boucholeur* or *bouchoteur* for the mussel grower, rather than the *myticulteur* (*Mytilidae* is the marine mussel family) prevalent in other parts of France.

Harald Wohlfahrt recommends scallops from Scotland or Ireland, but those from Brittany (especially Baie de Saint-Brieuc) are also good.

1. Lightly sauté the diced vegetables and season with salt and pepper. Add the mussels and clams and sauté lightly. Add the white wine and water. Cook the mollusks until they open, then shell them and set aside. Clean the scallops, pull off and reserve their beards and shell them. Dry the white meat on paper towels. Cook the beards in the shellfish cooking liquor for 15–20 minutes, then strain.

2. Salt and pepper the cooked, chilled langoustine tails. Purée finely, then add the egg white, followed by the cream, which should be incorporated bit by bit. Press the mixture through a sieve and fold in the whipped cream. Correct the seasoning. Blanch and refresh the cabbage leaves and drain on paper towels. Butter 4 ramekins, line with the cabbage leaves and refrigerate.

n a Vegetable *Nage*

3. Using a piping bag, fill the ramekins with the langoustine stuffing. Quarter the scallops, season with salt and pepper and place on top of the stuffing. Tuck in the cabbage-leaf overhang to seal and steam for 6 minutes at 400 °F/200 °C. Cut the vegetables for the nage into fine julienne. Blanch each type separately and refresh in ice water.

4. Reduce the shellfish cooking liquid to a coating consistency. Add the wine and Noilly Prat and whisk in the cold diced butter. Add the vegetables, mussels and clams, and reheat gently. Arrange the cabbage-shellfish molds in the center of each plate. Surround with the vegetables, mussels and clams and pour over the nage. Top each chartreuse with a small mound of caviar and garnish with a few cilantro leaves.

Bacalao a

Preparation time: 1 hour
Cooking time: 20 minutes
Difficulty: ★★

Serves 4

Four 9 oz/250 g pieces of salt cod (soaked
for 48 hours to remove excess salt)
1¾ lbs/800 g red onions
6 cloves garlic

6 dried red bell peppers
1 ham bone
olive oil
salt and freshly ground pepper

Salt cod is not only esteemed in Portugal, but also right along the eastern coastline of the Atlantic and the coast of the English Channel up to the North Sea, where the Norwegians are particulary fond of it. It is hardly surprising, therefore, that this Biscayan-style salt-cod recipe from the Spanish Basque country, the promised land of fish and crustaceans, is extremely common in those regions. Morevover, the Spanish claim that the process for salting the cod catch to preserve it traveled from their country to Norway.

The sauce *a la vizcaína* is a Basque recipe from the province of Vizcaya, and is made with the red or pink onions well known in most Mediterranean countries. These onions contain little sugar, giving the sauce a robust taste. If you want to give the sauce more body and creaminess, you can enrich the mixture with a piece of thick, fatty pork rind or, as here, a ham bone simmered with garlic and onion.

The advantage of a sauce like this is that it can be made all year round, and can also be enriched according to taste with the most varied vegetables, especially potatoes.

1. Desalt the cod 48 hours in advance. In a high-sided frying pan, gently brown the very finely sliced onions, the ham bone and half of the garlic. Cook slowly. Remove the bone.

2. Blanch the red bell peppers 3 times. Peel and seed them and add the flesh to the onions, sautéing gently for 3–4 minutes. Purée the mixture in a blender or food processor, then add the remaining garlic and correct the seasoning. (If the cod is still too salty, bring the water to a boil and blanch it twice).

a Vizcaína

3. Pour some olive oil into a nonstick skillet and pan-fry the pieces of cod over a high heat for 7 minutes. Turn and cook for a further 5 minutes.

4. Cover the bottom of an earthenware casserole with the sauce and arrange the pieces of cod on top. Simmer for a few minutes over low heat. Serve piping hot.

Meat & Poultry

Preparation time: 1 hour
Cooking time: 10 minutes
Difficulty: ★

Serves 4

20 quails' thighs (or 5 quail, quartered)
10 asparagus stalks
32 mild garlic cloves
24 small potatoes
4 different salad greens
chives

7½ tbsp/100 g flour
1 tbsp ginger
¾ cup/200 ml sunflower oil
sherry vinegar
1 tbsp soy sauce
olive oil
salt and pepper

For the soy sauce:
3 tbsp soy sauce
3 tbsp stock
5 tsp/25 g butter

The hunting season gives the people of Catalonia, in northeastern Spain, many opportunities to try out their skills, for there is no lack of game in the countryside. Quail is constantly turning up in old recipes, and here Fernando Adría adapts an old recipe for new tastes. Farm-raised quail can be obtained all year round. Their flavor is not as strong as that of wild quail, but it goes very well with the other ingredients in this recipe.

The quail has a very delicate flavor and so you must be sure not to overwhelm it with other flavors. You should be careful when removing the thighs from the birds, so

as to leave the bone attached to the thigh. This process will take some time, because you should allow 5 thighs per person. As an alternative, you may use 5 quail, quartered.

Our kitchen chef recommends that, contrary to general culinary rules, you can use any kind of meat stock or poultry stock to give the sauce a fine consistency.

The quality of the accompaniments should match that of the birds. Garlic, potatoes and mixed salad greens complement the quail and make for a delicious meal.

1. Remove quails' thighs, leaving the meat on the bone. Prepare the asparagus, using only the tips. Peel and slice the potatoes. Peel the garlic cloves.

2. Dust the quails' thighs with flour. Heat the sunflower oil to 320 °F/160 °C, and fry the thighs until crisp. Drain on paper towels. Broil the asparagus and garlic as close to the heat source as possible. Cook the potatoes over low heat in olive oil and season with salt and pepper. Half a minute before removing them from the heat, add a tbsp of soy sauce.

Soy Sauce

3. To make the sauce, add the stock to the soy sauce. Over low heat, reduce to 4 tbsp and add the butter. Dip the quails' thighs in the sauce. Make a salad dressing with olive oil, vinegar and salt.

4. Arrange 8 garlic cloves around each plate, place the asparagus, cut in half lengthwise, on top, and place a quail's thigh on top of each arrangement. In the center of the dish, pile the cooked potato slices into a pyramid and top with the ginger. Pour some sauce on top of everything. Decorate with whole chives and serve the dressed salad separately.

Stuffed Chicken

Preparation time: 1 hour
Cooking time: 2½ hours
Difficulty: ★★★

Serves 4

1 free-range chicken (3⅓ lb/1½ kg)
6 ripe tomatoes
2 thick slices of Bayonne ham

7 oz/200 g mild green chile or green bell pepper
3 garlic cloves
4½ tbsp/70 ml white Irouléguy (Basque) wine or other dry white wine
butter
2 tbsp/30 ml water
olive oil

This is a very special, sophisticated version of the famous chicken à la basquaise, in which the golden-skinned and nicely browned bird is served with traditional ingredients: tomatoes, peppers, garlic and Bayonne ham.

A perfect chicken from a Basque farm is the best suited for this dish. But failing that, any good free-range chicken will serve the purpose very nicely, as long as it is plump and tender. The bird must be carefully boned so that it can be stuffed afterwards. This preserves the delicate flavor and allows the aromas of the other ingredients to penetrate the meat. In order to prevent the chicken browning unevenly, it should be carefully trussed and you should make sure that the flesh is covered all over by skin.

The roulades of chicken are roasted in the oven until golden, so the skin becomes nicely crisp. If the oven is too hot, the meat may dry out. Test to see if it is done by pressing lightly on the flesh with your finger. If you feel a slight resistance, the chicken is cooked.

Firmin Arrambide recommends replacing the chicken with a guinea-fowl if you prefer, and the Bayonne ham with finely sliced prosciutto.

1. Bone the chicken and set aside the heart and liver. Remove and reserve all the bones. The bird should be divided in half. Peel the tomatoes and seed them. Season with salt and pepper, pour olive oil over them and let them cook in a 140 °F/60 °C oven for about 2 hours.

2. Sauté the peppers and ham until brown. Set aside. Peel and slice the garlic, and brown in the pan until golden-brown; do the same with the heart and liver. Distribute the ham, peppers, garlic, heart and liver in the centers of both chicken halves.

à la Basquaise

3. Roll up the chicken halves and truss as for a roast. Season and brown in a braising pan with the crushed bones.

4. Put the chicken roulades into the preheated oven for 12 minutes. Remove them and keep hot. Skim off the fat in the pan, deglaze with the white wine, and reduce with half a glass of water and a walnut-sized piece of butter. Sieve the juices and keep hot. Cut the roulades into thick slices. Arrange on each plate with the cooked tomatoes and pour the juices over them.

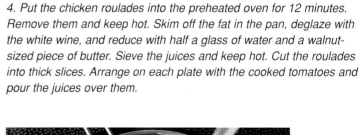

Tournedos

Preparation time: 10 minutes
Cooking time: 10 minutes
Difficulty: ✶

Serves 4

1 bunch white radishes
basic white sauce

veal stock
horseradish, freshly grated
1 bunch of chives
12 red radishes
1¾ lb/800 g beef tenderloin
10½ oz/300 g bacon slices
butter, peanut oil
salt and pepper

Prized since prehistoric times, beef has formed the basis of the most distinguished dishes throughout the centuries. Fresh beef can be recognized by its strong red color and firm texture. Very pale meat is the sign of a young, immature animal, and very dark color indicates that the meat is from an older animal.

The tournedos is cut from the fillet and should be about ¾ in/2 cm thick and particularly juicy. Cuts of meat "à la tournedos" are cut in the same way but do not come from the tenderloin. The tournedos are quickly cooked in butter and served, according to taste, medium or rare.

The sauce should be kept warm until served. Horseradish and chives are added at the end, after which the sauce should not be stirred again, otherwise the chives may blacken and lose their flavor.

This irresistible tournedos, flavored with horseradish, can be served with turnips instead of white radishes.

1. Peel the white radishes and slice finely, then brown them in butter. They should color slightly on both sides. Add the white sauce and simmer for 4–5 minutes over low heat.

2. Thicken the veal stock to the consistency of a sauce and add the horseradish. Season and then sprinkle the finely chopped chives on top.

with Radishes

3. Cut the red radishes into thin strips and deep-fry in hot peanut oil. Drain on paper towels and set aside.

4. Cut the tenderloin into 4 steaks of equal thickness. Wrap a strip of bacon around each steak. Fry in butter on both sides for 5 minutes and season with salt and pepper. Arrange the radish slices in a circle and place the tournedos in the middle. Garnish with the deep-fried radish and decorate with a border of the sauce.

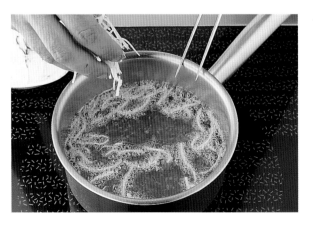

Lamb Tenderloin

Preparation time: 2 hours
Cooking time: 1½ hours
Difficulty: ★★★

Serves 4

1 rack of lamb, weighing 2½ lb/1.2 kg
10½ oz/300 g spinach
5 oz/140 g pork caul

For the stuffing:
2 tbsp finely chopped fresh herbs (tarragon,
chervil, chives)
2 eggs
5 tbsp crème fraîche
salt and pepper

For the garnish:
2 potatoes
4 shallots
1 red bell pepper
1 green bell pepper
4 onions
1 garlic clove
3 cups/200 g finely chopped mushrooms
6½ tbspi/100 g butter

For the sauce:
lamb bones and trimmings
1 bouquet garni
green leaves of 1 leek
tarragon, garlic

There was a time when lamb was eaten primarily at Easter, but nowadays you can enjoy this delicious meat from December to July. You can easily assess the freshness of the meat from its color and brightness. Choose a prime rack of lamb for this dish. After you cook the lamb, it should rest for about 10 minutes so it becomes tender and juicy. This resting period is absolutely necessary to allow the full flavor of the lamb to develop.

There are many ways of using herbs, and they give the lamb a very special flavor. Chopped chervil, chives and tarragon are used to create an herb crust, in which the lamb is snugly wrapped.

The garnish consists of small potato ravioli filled with duxelles, made from finely chopped mushrooms, onions and shallots, which are gently sautéed until the liquid they contain has evaporated. This preparation reminds us of the Marquis d'Uxelles, a gourmet who is no longer well known. His personal chef, the still-famous La Varenne, dedicated this mushroom preparation to him.

To make the ravioli, it is important to use very thin potato slices. The best way to achieve the thinness required to keep them from falling apart is to use a mandoline, or, if you don't have one, a swivel-bladed vegetable peeler.

1. Bone the rack of lamb. Set aside the two tenderloins and prepare a stock with the bones and the other sauce ingredients, except for the tarragon. Prepare the stuffing with the fresh herbs and season it. To make the duxelles, chop the mushrooms and shallots together until very fine. Gently sauté them in butter until all the liquid they give off has evaporated. Set aside.

2. Blanch the spinach and spread it out on a kitchen towel. Sauté the lamb fillets over high heat for 1 minute on each side, then wipe off the fat with paper towels. Cover the fillets with the herb stuffing and wrap first in spinach leaves, then in the pork caul (if you can't find pork caul, brush with olive oil). Set aside to cool.

n an Herb Crust

3. Slice the potatoes very thinly and form them into small ravioli with the duxelles. Sauté the ravioli in clarified butter. Reduce the lamb juices and allow the fresh tarragon to infuse in them. Mix and stir in the butter used to sauté the ravioli.

4. Cook the fillets for 10 minutes in a preheated 355 °F/180 °C oven (basting from time to time if pork caul has not been used). Cut lids off the top of each onion, and hollow out the rest. Braise the bell peppers with the onion scraps. Braise the onion cases and fill with the onion and pepper mixture. After allowing the lamb fillets to rest for 10 minutes in the warm oven, cut into slices and arrange on a serving dish with the vegetables. Decorate it with some of the sauce.

Braised Oxtail with

Preparation time: 1 hour 15 minutes
Cooking time: 3 hours
Difficulty: ★★

Serves 4

4½ lb/2 kg oxtail
3½ oz/100 g salt pork
7 oz/200 g carrots
2 onions
9 oz/250 g celery
1 head of garlic
¼ cup/75 g tomato paste
¾ cup/100 g flour

8 cups/2 l veal or beef stock
4 cups/1 l Burgundy wine
salt and pepper

For the bouquet garni:
1 bay leaf
2 sprigs of thyme
8 sprigs of parsley

For the garnish of spring vegetables
carrots, turnips
pearl onions
new potatoes
peas, beans

Beef is still considered a major delicacy in the British Isles, where Hereford cattle and the Scottish Aberdeen Angus, famous for its protein-rich meat, are only two of the many breeds raised.

For this English oxtail stew you should use the upper, more fleshy parts of the oxtail. The oxtail must be fresh and include firm, red meat. The layer of white fat should only be partially removed, to prevent the meat from drying out. This dish can also be prepared using other cuts of stewing beef.

The garnish should consist of the earliest of spring vegetables, but you can also add chestnuts that have been marinated with the oxtail – their consistency is similar to that of the meat.

Four days are required to make a good oxtail stew, including the day on which the dish is eaten. Marinate it for two days in a robust wine such as a Côtes-du-Rhône, cook it on the third day and simply reheat it on the fourth; this can only improve its flavor.

1. Cut the vegetables (carrots, onions, celery) into large pieces. Bone the oxtail, cut it into large pieces and mix with the vegetables. Add the stock for the marinade, the bouquet garni, the tomato paste, and the garlic. Place in the refrigerator to marinate for at least 48 hours. Drain the oxtail, reserving the vegetables and the marinade, and season and brown on all sides.

2. In a deep pan, braise the vegetables used in the marinade with the salt pork. Add the marinated oxtail. Toast the flour lightly in the oven and stir it carefully into the marinade. Pour it into the pan, bring to a boil, cover and braise in a 350 °F/180 °C oven for about three hours.

Spring Vegetables

3. *Prepare the spring vegetables for the garnish (carrots, turnips, small onions and potatoes, peas and beans). Cook each vegetable separately in boiling salted water.*

4. *After braising, remove the pieces of oxtail from the pan; do not cut them any smaller. Place them in a deep bowl. Add all the vegetables for the garnish. Reduce the Burgundy and add to the braising liquid. Strain and pour over the meat and vegetables. Serve hot.*

Bresse Chicken er

Preparation time: *1 hour 15 minutes*
Cooking time: *45 minutes*
Difficulty: ★★

Serves 4

4 skinless, boneless chicken breasts or
2 chickens, about 3½ lbs/1.5 kg
6 oz/160 g Gruyère cheese
1 generous lb/500 g leaf spinach
4 slices of cooked ham
7 oz/200 g puff pastry

1 egg for brushing on
salt and pepper

For the cream sauce:
9 oz/250 g fresh morels
6½ tbsp/100 ml white wine
2 cups/500 ml heavy cream
5½ tbsp/80 g butter
3 egg yolks
juice of ½ lemon
7 tbsp/50 g chopped tarragon
salt and pepper

This chicken en croûte was prepared by Paul Bocuse in 1993 on the occasion of an assembly of the "Meilleurs Ouvrieres de France" at his restaurant in Collonges-au-Mont-d'Or, near Lyon. It was in that year that Christian Bouvarel was admitted to this highly selective club. This represented a high point in Bouvarel's career, but not its end, for a distinction such as this brings many obligations with it. Our chef places particular value on this recipe because a typical product of his region, the Bresse chicken, is shown to its best advantage.

Bresse chickens are free-range and corn-fed; they have as much freedom to roam as they need, quite in contrast to those unfortunate battery chickens with which our super-markets are flooded. Other excellent free-range and organic chickens are widely available.

One would not have to make such a fuss about the poultry if the other ingredients were not also of outstanding quality. So seek out a first-class ham and an aromatic cheese. If you prefer a more strongly flavored cheese than Gruyère, Christian Bouvarel recommends Comté from the French Alps. Stuff the chicken breast with the cheese before closing the pastry envelope in order to prevent the cheese from leaking out. The spinach should be very fresh; it can, if necessary, be replaced with curly kale, which goes equally well with chicken, because it does not over-power its flavor.

1. Bone the chicken and remove the breasts, cut part way into them lengthwise, and fill with the grated Gruyère. Season with salt and pepper, then seal.

2. Remove the stalks from the spinach, wash thoroughly in cold water and blanch in boiling salted water. Wrap each chicken breast in spinach, and then in a slice of ham.

croûte with Morels

3. Roll out the puff pastry and cut into 4 pieces. Take each chicken breast and wrap in pastry, forming a turnover. Let rest for 30 minutes in the refrigerator, brush with egg and bake in a 375 °F/190 °C oven for 20–30 minutes.

4. Braise the morels in butter and season with salt and pepper. Deglaze with the wine. Add 1 cup/250 ml heavy cream. Cook for 4–5 minutes; mix the egg yolks with the rest of the cream, the lemon juice and the tarragon. Pour over the morels. Stir very gently to bind the sauce. Reduce without allowing the sauce to boil. When it is nice and creamy, remove from the heat and pour into a sauce boat.

Preparation time: 1 hour
Cooking time: 30 minutes
Difficulty: ✫

Serves 4

1lb 5 oz/600 g T-bone veal chops
(loin and fillet)
¾ cup/200 ml chicken stock
¾ cup/200 ml dry white wine
peanut oil
6½ tbsp/100 g butter
salt and freshly ground pepper

For the sweet and sour onions:
14 oz/400 g pearl onions
1¾ oz/50 g raisins
2 tbsp/15 g sugar
2 tbsp/15 g flour
6½ tbsp/100 ml extra virgin olive oil
6½ tbsp/100 ml vinegar

For the chicken stock
2 chicken carcasses
2 carrots
2 turnips
1 leek
salt and freshly ground pepper

Throughout Lombardy, and above all in Milan, veal cooked in its own fat has been familiar since the Renaissance.

Take care to buy milk-fed veal, because it is particularly delicate. Try to remove as much fat as possible from both the loin and the tenderloin, because the sauce will have a better flavor. The cooking process is divided into two stages, both of which should be watched carefully. First, brown the meat quickly on top of the stove so that it takes on some color, but do not let it acquire a crust. Then braise it in the oven, making sure it stays pink on the inside. Cut the meat into slices and serve it as soon as it comes out of the oven.

You should allow a day for the preparation of the chicken stock, because it is best when cooked very slowly over low heat. If it is refrigerated overnight, it acquires a more delicate and fuller flavor.

The sweet and sour onions were long ago adopted from the cuisine of the Austrian empire, formerly a neighbor of Lombardy. The Milanese enriched the recipe with raisins and it is now a popular side dish.

1. The day before you plan to serve the veal, blanch the chicken carcasses, drain and rinse in cold water. Cover with 2 cups/500 ml of water seasoned with salt and pepper. Bring to a boil and skim off the foam. Add the vegetables and allow to simmer for five hours. Strain and refrigerate. Cut the veal into slices.

2. Brown the chops in 3½ tbsp/50 g of butter and a little oil, so they color nicely without burning. Meanwhile, prepare the sweet and sour onions: prepare a roux with oil, sugar and flour, then add the vinegar. Blanch the onions in boiling salted water and drain. Stir the onions and raisins into the roux and cook for 6 minutes.

à la Milanaise

3. Pour the chicken stock and wine over the veal, bring to boil and braise for 15 minutes in a 350 °F/180 °C oven. Remove the meat and keep warm until you are ready to slice it.

4. Reduce the cooking juices by one third. Remove from the heat and whisk in 3½ tbsp/50 g of butter, cubed. Strain and keep warm. Put a little sauce on a plate and place the sliced meat on top. Serve the onions separately and pass the rest of the sauce in a sauce boat.

Fillet of Beef with

Preparation time: 40 minutes
Cooking time: 15 minutes
Difficulty: ★★

Serves 4

4 filets mignons, about 5¼ oz/150 g each
6 oz/160 g raw duck fois gras
¾ oz/20 g truffles, sliced
7 oz/200 g pork caul

1 small leek, 1 small celery stalk, 1 small
carrot, cut into narrow strips
¾ cup/200 ml vegetable stock
¾ cup/200 ml veal stock
8 oz/240 g fresh narrow tagliatelle
6½ tbsp/100 ml heavy cream
6½ tbsp/100 g butter
grated Parmesan
12 sprigs of chervil
salt and pepper
coarse salt

Beef remains indispensable in gastronomy, and its best cut, the fillet, has been an essential culinary delight since the Middle Ages. For this recipe, our chef uses meat from a Belgian breed of cattle, but you can choose from a number of other high-quality breeds. Try to find well-aged prime beef for this luxurious dish.

The preparation of the steaks, cut into three across the grain, takes a little time. A good appearance can be achieved by wrapping the prepared steaks in aluminum foil, and leaving them to cool for a good hour. The caul, which is used after this step, is a fine membrane with fatty veins, which is soaked for a few hours in salted water to soften the texture of the caul and thus make preparation easier. If it is unavailable, brush the meat with olive oil before cooking.

For a well-flavored sauce, our chef recommends preparing a good quality, full-flavored veal stock. The steaks should be served very hot.

1. Season the steaks with salt and pepper and sear on both sides in a walnut-sized pat of butter. Let cool. Cut the fois gras into thin slices, season with salt and pepper, and brown quickly in a nonstick pan. Cut the steaks into 3 across the grain.

2. Cover each slice of fillet with fois gras slices and truffles, stack together like a layer cake, wrap in foil and set aside to cool for 1 hour. Cook the tagliatelle in boiling salted water for 3–4 minutes. Reduce the cream with the vegetable mixture. When the noodles are cooked, strain and add to the sauce.

Duck Foie Gras and Truffles

3. Soak the pork caul in salted water for 3–4 hours. When the fillet slices are quite firm, remove from the foil and wrap in the pork caul. Brown the meat on both sides for 4 minutes, then remove the fat from the pan. Add the two kinds of stock, reduce, season to taste and set aside.

4. Cut each steak into two or three pieces, place on a dish and scatter coarse salt on top. Form the tagliatelle into nests with a fork and place next to the fillets; garnish with chervil leaves. Then serve with the hot sauce and grated Parmesan.

Navarin of Lambs' Sweetbreads

Preparation time: 45 minutes
Cooking time: 1 hour
Difficulty: ☆

Serves 4

1 generous lb/500 g lambs' sweetbreads
9 oz/250 g lamb's tongues
1 bouquet garni
boiled potatoes
2 tomatoes
9 oz/250 g button mushrooms

¾ cup/200 ml white veal stock
2 cups/500 ml lamb stock with tomato
¾ cup/200 ml ruby port wine
1 tsp turtle soup seasoning (basil, marjoram, chervil, savory, and fennel)
1 tsp arrowroot
1 lemon
½ tsp dried herbs
1 pinch of cayenne pepper
1 bunch of tarragon
salt and pepper

Jan Buytaert has preserved only the basic principle of this traditional dish. The lambs' tongues and sweetbreads must be absolutely fresh. Everyone knows what a tongue is; but sweetbreads are the thymus gland and pancreas. The thymus is found at the base of the neck of the immature animal, and is part of the immune system. The tongues and sweetbreads must be soaked in cold water for several hours before preparation; they must then be blanched and the veins and membranes should be removed.

The lamb stock should be enriched with ripe tomatoes, so that it acquires a reddish color. Arrowroot is preferable to potato or corn starch as a thickener, because it is less glutinous. If you are not familiar with it, this recipe offers a good opportunity to discover its qualities.

Do not hesitate to eat this dish if reheated even several days later – it can only improve the flavor.

1. Blanch the sweetbreads and tongues. Cool in a bowl of cold water and remove the outer membranes and veins from the sweetbreads. Trim the bones from the base of the tongues. Cook in the white veal stock with the bouquet garni.

2. Skin the tongues and cut each into 4 pieces. Cut the sweetbreads into large pieces. Peel, seed and dice the tomatoes. Brown the mushrooms in butter.

3. Combine the veal and lamb stocks and reduce by two-thirds. Season the resulting sauce with a pinch of salt, a hint of cayenne pepper, the turtle soup seasoning, the port, the dried herbs and the juice of the lemon. Thicken slightly with arrowroot. Strain.

4. Add the browned mushrooms to the sauce, the diced tomato; and the tarragon leaves. Then add the pieces of sweetbread and tongue. Cook over low heat for 10 minutes and serve with boiled potatoes.

Calves' Liver with

Preparation time: 20 minutes
Cooking time: 20 minutes
Difficulty: ✴

Serves 4

2 generous lbs/1 kg calves' liver
3½ tbsp/50 g butter
flour

For the ginger and soy sauce:
2 medium/40 g shallots
3 tbsp/50 g fresh ginger root
10 tbsp/150 g butter

2 cups/500 ml veal stock
4 tsp/20 ml soy sauce

For the garnish:
2 generous lbs/1 kg small potatoes
5 tbsp/75 g goose or duck fat
1 garlic clove
1 sprig of thyme
1 bay leaf
chives

For the shallots:
9 oz/250 g shallots
½ cup/125 g butter

The use of soy sauce and ginger in this calves' liver recipe bears witness to Jacques Cagna's interest in Japan. During his frequent stays there he has developed a taste for these important Japanese seasonings and enjoys introducing them into French cuisine.

This is by no means an obvious combination, and the very salty soy sauce must be used with care if it is not to overpower the taste of the meat. Cagna first tried this recipe with eel, with little success; it was only when he tried it with calves' liver, with its more delicate flesh and a less distinctive taste, that he achieved a breakthrough. Use only very fresh liver. Remove the outer skin and the veins

before coating in flour and browning nicely on both sides, so that it becomes slightly crisp.

In this dish, Cagna uses grenaille, a small variety of potato that is grown in western France, especially on the island of Noirmoutier. These potatoes are always planted by hand and carefully checked at harvest time, which ensures consistent quality. They are easy to prepare and are favorites at Jacque Cagna's Paris restaurant, where they are also served with veal cutlets and with snails.

Calves' sweetbreads can be prepared in the same way; if you don't like ginger, you can substitute braised shallots.

1. For the ginger and soy sauce, sweat the chopped shallots and the ginger in butter. Deglaze with the veal stock and soy sauce. Simmer over low heat for 30 minutes, then whisk in the butter.

2. Wash the potatoes. Line a pan with aluminum foil, and add the unpeeled potatoes, the melted goose fat, the garlic clove, the thyme and the bay leaf; cover and cook for 1 hour in a 375 °F/190 °C oven.

Ginger and Soy Sauce

3. If you have bought your liver in 1 piece, skin it and cut into ½ in/1 cm slices. Season and brown in butter in a skillet. Finely chop the shallots and cook slowly in butter until quite soft.

4. Cut each slice of liver into five thin slices, and arrange on a warmed dish, covering with the shallots. Arrange the potatoes around them and add the ginger and soy sauce. Sprinkle with chopped chives.

Medallions of Angus Beef

Preparation time: 45 minutes
Cooking time: 15 minutes
Difficulty: ★★

Serves 4

8 filets mignon, each 1 in/2 cm thick
5¼ oz/150 g cèpes or porcini
5¼ oz/150 g chanterelles
3½ tbsp/50 ml olive oil
salt and pepper

For the sauce:
⅔ cup/150 ml Drambuie
⅔ cup/150 ml beef stock
3½ tbsp/50 g butter
¾ cup/75 g brunoise (finely diced carrots, celery and onions)
thyme
1 bay leaf
½ tsp/1 g black peppercorns

Only a Scottish chef can pay proper homage to the Aberdeen Angus. This breed can be found far beyond the borders of Scotland and ranks with whisky and Mary, Queen of Scots as one of Scotland's finest exports. As its name indicates, this breed originates in the Aberdeen region and has now spread throughout the world, to Argentina and the United States, where the craft of cattle-breeding is well understood. On their home ground, Aberdeen Angus are subject to strict quality control.

After slaughter, each carcass is hung for over a month, which intensifies the natural flavor of the meat. There is no need to prepare a highly flavored accompaniment. Complicated sauces, such as are normally inflicted on beef, become redundant. This treatment also tenderizes the meat and greatly reduces the cooking time.

Here, Stewart Cameron serves Angus beef with braised cèpes and chanterelles, which come from the same soil that nourishes the cattle. This combination is far from accidental. But, of course, you can replace these mushrooms with others of your choice.

1. Trim the tenderloin (if purchased in 1 piece) and cut into medallions about 1 in/2 cm thick. Season to taste.

2. Wash the cèpes and chanterelles and slice thinly.

with Cèpes and Chanterelles

3. Braise the diced vegetables with the bay leaf, thyme and pepper in 5 tsp/25 g of butter over low heat; add the Drambuie and flambé. Add the beef stock, reduce by two-thirds, and strain. Whisk in the remaining butter.

4. Heat the olive oil in a pan, then brown the medallions to the desired doneness. Braise the mushrooms in the same pan. Place a medallion in the center of each of 4 plates, the mushrooms on top, and another medallion on top of them. Pour the butter sauce over before serving.

Braised Rabbit with

Preparation time: 45 minutes
Cooking time: 35 minutes
Difficulty: ★★

Serves 4

2 saddles of rabbit
1 shallot
5 black olives
5 green olives

6½ tbsp/100 ml dry white wine
1 sprig of wild fennel or fennel top
meat stock
4 tbsp/60 g butter
3 tbsp/20 g grated Parmesan
salt

For the *garganelli* noodles:
¾ cup plus 1 tbsp/400g flour
4 eggs

The province of Romagna, now Emilia-Romagna, is the birthplace of the pasta called *garganelli*. They are traditionally served with chicken stock (in earlier times with a meat stew with tomatoes), and in summer, particularly by families with modest means, simply with zucchini.

The preparation of this pasta includes the use of a *pettine*, a wooden board over which parallel threads are stretched, on which the *garganelli* are rolled. This gives them their distinctive ridged appearance. Don't worry if you don't succeed the first time you try to make them; our chef admits that there is a certain knack to it, but assures us that one can quickly acquire the necessary expertise. Once you have got the knack you will make this pasta over and over again.

Here, the *garganelli* are eaten with rabbit stewed with white wine and shallots. For this dish Marco Cavallucci uses the excellent rabbit from Liguria, near the Gulf of Genoa. You should choose young rabbits, with little fat—preferably not frozen rabbit parts. The fennel gives the rabbit a special flavor.

1. Bone the saddles of rabbit; dice the meat from one of them, and roast the other whole for about 20 minutes at 355 °F/180 °C (the inside should remain pink). Chop the shallot and braise in a pan with butter, add the diced rabbit and season with salt.

2. Pit the olives, chop and add to the diced rabbit. Add the wine and reduce until thickened, then add the chopped fennel and cook for 10 minutes. Add a little meat stock if necessary.

Garganelli al Pettine

3. Make a pasta dough with the flour and eggs, form into a ball and let it rest for an hour. Then roll out thinly, cut it into 2 in/5 cm squares, roll these around a thin stick and over the pettine or a ridged board, to form the garganelli. Cook in salted water and drain.

4. Cut the roast saddle of rabbit into thin slices. Add the garganelli with the Parmesan to the braised rabbit. Serve hot, garnishing each portion with a few slices of roast rabbit and sprigs of fennel.

Medallions of Vea

Preparation time: 45 minutes
Cooking time: 10 minutes
Difficulty: ★★

Serves 4

4 medallions milk-fed veal tenderloin, each
1½ inch/4 cm thick
4 oz/120 g small chanterelles
4 large slices of beef marrow
1 orange
1 lemon
1 tbsp/15 g granulated sugar

1 sprig of marjoram
salt from Guérande (or other sea salt)
crushed black pepper
salt and ground pepper

For the brunoise:
3½ oz/100 g carrots
3½ oz/100 g small green zucchini
1¾ oz/50 g celery
1¾ oz/50 g white onions
⅔ cup sauce from a traditional osso buco
3½ tbsp/50 g butter
extra virgin olive oil

First prepare an osso buco with marjoram, and keep the juices from this dish. Then you can use them to season the tenderloin of milk-fed calf in this recipe.

The small tenderloin, as its name suggests, is one of the tenderest parts of the animal. It is easy to prepare and retains its delicious flavor throughout the cooking process. To preserve the pale color of the flesh, you can sprinkle lemon juice all over it before cooking. It must remain tender, forming a pleasant contrast to the crisp dried peel of the citrus fruits. In this traditional combination, the delicate apricot flavor of the chanterelles underlines that of the veal, whose juices have been strengthened by the slices of marrow. The vegetables, diced small and carefully arran-

ged on the dish, add a further touch of sophistication.

Marjoram is found throughout the Mediterranean area: Italians like to use it in particular to flavor the *piccata*, a small veal cutlet fried in butter. Greeks use it with grilled goat's meat. In Hungary it is often added to the famous goulash. In France it is one of the traditional herbs of Provence.

Instead of the tenderloin, you could also use boned loin chops for this dish, but they sometimes turn out to be too firm.

1. Cut the orange and lemon zest into thin strips, blanch and then put in a pan to simmer over low heat with some water and the sugar. Then strain and place on a plate to dry.

2. Braise the brunoise of vegetables in oil and butter, making sure that the vegetables stay crisp.

with Marjoram

3. Brown the medallions of veal in oil in a pan to give them a good color, then lower the heat and cook until just done. Briefly boil the chanterelles, strain and then brown. Poach the slices of marrow in salted water.

4. Using a ring 4 ½ in/10 cm in diameter, arrange circles of vegetable brunoise in the center of each plate. Place a veal medallion and a slice of marrow on top, and season with some sea salt and crushed pepper. Arrange the chanterelles around them, pour the osso buco juices over them and garnish with some additional vegetables, orange and lemon peel and marjoram leaves.

Provençal Rib Steak

Preparation time: 45 minutes
Cooking time: 30 minutes
Difficulty: ★★

Serves 4

1 thick rib steak, about 2.2 lbs/1 kg

For the sauce:
10½ oz/300 g firm tomatoes
2 sprigs of tarragon
2 pinches of chopped garlic
¼ cup/60 ml white wine
¼ cup/60 ml olive oil
1¼ cups/300 ml beef stock
10½ oz/300 g butter

For the garnish:
14 oz/400 g new potatoes
8 small artichokes
8 small spring onions
8 small garlic cloves, peeled
7 oz/200 g small zucchini
4 oz/120 g olives
⅓ cup/80 g butter
2 sprigs fresh of thyme
2 sprigs fresh of rosemary
2 fresh bay leaves

To be added at the end of cooking:
¾ cup/180 ml water
2 tbsp/30 ml olive oil
10 basil leaves, finely chopped
salt and pepper

Beef remains the most popular of meats, and there are many breeds of cattle that produce a high quality of beef. For this recipe, choose a prime rib steak and pan fry it gently, after removing the sinews and excess fat. Some fat, however, should remain, because it is the mixture of fat and lean that provides the flavor. Make a very light beef stock for the sauce with the trimmings, adding an onion, thyme, bay leaf and a little water. Strain the stock before using.

The cooking of the beef must be very even, over low heat. The heat must penetrate right through the meat, without burning the surface. Leave the rib bone intact, as this will intensify the wonderful flavor.

Spring vegetables give the dish a contrasting note of freshness. Braise them in a skillet to preserve all their flavor and crispness. Tiny artichokes are eaten raw in southern Europe; they only need to be warmed up.

1. Trim the rib steak, scraping the meat away from the end of the rib, and removing the small bones. Cut the trimmings into small pieces and prepare a stock with them.

2. Wash the potatoes but do not peel them. Trim the artichokes and cut them into slices; peel the spring onions and the garlic cloves. Blanch the olives twice and cut the zucchini into slices 1 inch/2 cm thick. Cook each vegetable separately in salted water, then braise the vegetables in butter for about 15 minutes in a covered nonstick pan.

with Spring Vegetables

3. Season the braised vegetables with thyme, rosemary and bay leaves. Just before serving, add the water, olive oil and chopped basil. Stir vigorously so that all the vegetables are covered by the sauce and remove from the heat immediately.

4. Season the beef with salt and pepper, pan fry for 15 minutes in oil, turning several times. Keep warm on a plate covered with aluminum foil. Deglaze the pan with white wine and add the meat stock and other sauce ingredients. Bring to boil and stir in 2 tbsp/30 ml of oil. Place the beef and vegetables on a warm plate and pour the sauce over.

Stuffed Lamb in a

Preparation time: 20 minutes
Cooking time: 20 minutes
Difficulty: ★★

Serves 4

2 pieces lamb loin roast, about 2.2 lb/1 kg each

10½ oz/300 g foie gras
1¾ oz/50 g truffles
4 russet or other starchy potatoes
16 green asparagus spears
peanut oil
salt and pepper

Jean Crotet uses lamb from Sisteron or the Limousin, a region distinguished for the quality of its pasture land and its small family farms. This meat is particularly tender, rich in flavor and very low in fat.

You should choose only A-grade foie gras, which should maintain its firmness during cooking. As an alternative to truffles, you could substitute dried morels.

Do not wash the shredded potatoes shred, or they will lose their starch, which holds together the mantle of potatoes during cooking.

Our chef recommends asparagus with this dish, to emphasize its springlike character.

1. Bone the lamb, keeping the bones and skin for the stock. Butterfly and season the meat. Trim the asparagus and cook in salted water. Refresh, drain and cut into 3½ in/8 cm lengths, then set aside.

2. Slice half the truffles, keeping the rest for the sauce. Line each piece of lamb with the sliced truffles, and put a thumb-sized piece of foie gras in the middle and fold the meat over the stuffing. Peel the potatoes and shred them with a grater or cut into fine julienne. Season with salt and pepper.

Potato Crust with Truffles

3. Wrap the lamb in the potato julienne. Finely chop the rest of the truffles and add the sauce previously prepared with the bones and trimmings. Strain the sauce before using.

4. Brown the lamb in oil on both sides for a total of about 12 minutes, then finish cooking in the oven at 320 °F/160 °C for 4–5 minutes. Cut each piece in half and place on warmed plates. Garnish with warm asparagus spears and the truffle sauce.

Veal Cutle

Preparation time: 45 minutes
Cooking time: 15 minutes
Difficulty: ★★

Serves 4

3½ lb/1½ kg loin of veal, cut into ¾ in/1.5 cm slices
4 tomatoes
2 carrots
3 fennel
8 mild onions
1 celery rib
flat-leaf parsley
butter

olive oil
sugar
thyme
garlic
salt and pepper

For the veal stock:
veal trimmings and bones
1 tomato
2 onions
1 bouquet garni
4 cups/1 l white stock
1 lemon
1 orange
butter

Very tender milk-fed veal is delivered to Michel Del Burgo from local breeders (from the Carcassonne and Limoux regions), whose quality he respects. Everything that comes from the Aude calf is good: loin, fillet, knuckle, the offal – everything.

Here our chef presents a personal variation on the "osso buco" theme, a classic Italian recipe for veal shank. The originality consists in preparing a veal cutlet in the same way. Thus it is cut from the loin and carefully boned—preferably by your butcher. Make sure that some fat is retained around the meat, which will form a crisp and tasty crust after cooking. Ask your butcher for the bones, to use when making the stock.

The cutlet is first browned in a skillet, with a suitable garnish of small vegetables to give flavor to the oil and butter. When it is well browned, the cooking is completed in the oven at low heat, after the aromatic garnish has been prepared. The meat must be frequently basted during cooking, so that it does not dry out.

The fennel should be quartered carefully so it does not fall apart. Michel Del Burgo suggests artichokes as a possible alternative to the fennel, and any other tender cut of veal instead of the cutlet.

1. Peel and quarter the tomatoes. Remove the seeds and place the quarters on a baking sheet lined with lightly oiled waxed paper, then sprinkle with sugar, salt and pepper, brush with oil and sprinkle with thyme. Place a slice of garlic on each piece of tomato. Let the tomatoes dry out for 2½ hours in the oven at 210 °F/100 °C.

2. Prepare the veal cutlets: brown them in a pan in some butter and olive oil, together with a garnish of chopped onions, carrots and garlic. Then transfer to the oven and cook for 15 minutes at 320–340 °F/160–170 °C. Prepare a fine dice of lemon and orange zest, and set aside.

'Osso Buco"

3. For the veal stock, brown the trimmings and bones and add the fresh tomato, onions and bouquet garni. Skim the fat from the pan and add some water. Reduce until it is thickened, then add the white stock. Simmer for 3 hours, and strain. Finally, add the butter and, at the last moment, the diced lemon and orange zest.

4. Prepare the rest of the onions and the fennel pieces, add the chopped celery, and braise everything in a pan, then add the dried tomatoes and finely chopped parsley. Cut the cutlets into slices and arrange attractively on each plate with the braised vegetables.

Saddle of Lamb

Preparation time: 1 hour
Cooking time: 45 minutes
Difficulty: ★★★

Serves 4

2½ lb/1 kg loin roasts of lamb
6 sheets/120 g filo pastry
3½ oz/100 g button mushrooms
5 oz/140 g chanterelles
9 tbsp/140 g butter
1 cup/240 ml olive oil
8 basil leaves
1½ oz/40 g cinnamon
⅓ oz/10 g nutmeg
chives

⅓ oz/10 g ground cloves
1½ oz/40 g poppy seeds
white pepper
salt and pepper

For the lamb stock:
lamb bones from the loin roast
1 onion
carrots
shallots
garlic
onions
thyme and bay leaves
2½ tbsp/40 ml sherry vinegar
6½ tbsp/100 ml port

There are some chefs who from time to time like to give their guests a little surprise, as in this recipe, in which the lamb, stuffed with mushrooms, is hidden within a crisp pastry covering.

For this recipe our chef prefers the delicate milk-fed lamb of Pauillac, which comes from a region already blessed with famous wines: Château-Lafite and Mouton-Rothschild.

The art of this recipe lies in the choice and quantity of the herbs and spices: one should be able to taste them without their overwhelming the flavor of the lamb. The poppy seeds in which you roll the pastry will stick to it and enclose it with a dark, crisp layer full of flavor.

Our chef tells us that he has also prepared fish (monkfish or salmon) in the same way, using well-seasoned button mushrooms instead of chanterelles.

1. Bone and trim the lamb, reserving the bones to prepare the stock from them. Dice the chanterelles if large.

2. Braise the button mushrooms in butter and season them. Using a sharpening steel or thin-bladed knife, make a hole through the center of each boneless loin and stuff with the mushrooms. Brown the lamb in the olive oil, cook until nearly done, and season with the cinnamon, pepper, nutmeg and cloves. Set aside.

n Spiced Pastry

3. For the stock, brown the bones and trimmings with the aromatic ingredients. Skim off the fat, add the sherry vinegar and port, and simmer for 1 hour. Strain and keep warm. Brown the chanterelles in butter.

4. Brush the pastry with melted butter, using three layers, one on top of the other. Wrap the lamb with the basil leaves in the pastry and put in a 400 °F/200 °C oven for 5 minutes to brown the pastry. Then roll in the poppy seeds (if necessary, brush the pastry with honey first) and cut into thick slices. Place slices of lamb with a little bouquet of chanterelles on each plate, and garnish with chives.

Preparation time: *45 minutes*
Cooking time: *25 minutes*
Difficulty: ✻

Serves 4

2 chickens, about 2 generous lb/1 kg each (or use capon, turkey, guinea fowl or duck)
14 oz/400 g hop shoots

juice of 1 lemon
2 shallots
parsley, chervil
6½ tbsp/100 g butter
6½ tbsp/100 ml Scotch whisky
¾ cup/200 ml white wine
¾ cup/200 ml chicken stock
2 cups/500 ml heavy cream
salt and pepper

Which kind of poultry to use for this recipe is left to your discretion: chicken, capon, turkey, guinea fowl or duck are all equally suitable. The Belgians are proud of their spectacular presentations of poultry, as in the famous "Coucou de Malines" and "waterzooi," which are actually much more lavish recipes than this one.

The preparation of the chicken legs is not very difficult, but the skin must be carefully cut so as to insert the bone as shown. The rest is easy.

The young shoots of the hop plant are very popular in Belgium and can be found on the menus of many restaurants there. Their season is very brief – from mid-March to the end of April. This climbing plant is grown for brewing beer, and can reach a height of 16 feet/5 m. Medicinal properties were attributed to hops in the 15th century, and in the 16th century it was believed to be an aphrodisiac. Today there is a great interest in Europe in this Belgian speciality, which many compare with asparagus. Before sautéing them in butter, the hops should be briefly blanched.

1. Cut each bird into four parts – two breasts and wings and two legs. Bone each piece so that only the meat, the skin and one bone (the wing and drumstick bones) remain.

2. Wrap the meat in its own skin, cutting a little hole in the skin so as to insert the bone in order to close up the pockets.

with Hop Shoots

3. Brown the chicken pockets with the shallots and parsley. Lower the heat and cook, covered, for 5 minutes. Deglaze with whisky and reduce. Add the white wine, reduce again, then add the chicken stock and bring to a boil. Remove the chicken pockets and keep warm. Reduce the remaining liquid and add the cream.

4. Reduce further, until a creamy consistency has been achieved, and season. Add the butter and strain through a fine sieve. Blanch the hop shoots with the lemon juice and then cook gently in butter. Place a quarter of them on each plate with a chicken pocket beside them and spread sauce all around. Garnish with chervil.

Lacquered Leg of Suckling

Preparation time: 20 minutes
Cooking time: 1 hour 30 minutes
Difficulty: ✴✴

Serves 4

1 leg of suckling pig with rind, about 1 kg
¾ cup plus 1 tbsp/200 g sugar
1 tbsp/10 g each lemon thyme, marjoram, rosemary
1 tbsp/22 g honey
1¼ cup/300 ml freshly squeezed orange juice
2¾ oz/80 g shallots, chopped
1 tsp black pepper, ground
white pepper, ground
salt

For the sauerkraut:
14 oz/400 g raw sauerkraut
1 oz/30 g smoked bacon, in 2 pieces
1 potato
3½ oz/100 g onions
½ apple
¾ cup/200 ml white wine
3½ tbsp/50 ml apple cider
6½ tbsp/100 ml stock
1 tbsp peppercorns
1 clove
1 bay leaf
1 juniper berry
5 white peppercorns
salt, sugar and freshly ground white pepper

At Lothar Eiermann's restaurant, the white wine used for this dish is Verrenberger Riesling, one of the best produced in Baden-Württemberg, from the nearby estates of Prince von Hohenlohe. You will probably find it more practical to use a more modest Riesling for the preparation of the suckling pig, but if you can, end the meal with a glass of something closer to "the nectar of Verrenberg."

The first layer of glaze is applied 30 minutes after the start of cooking – on no account earlier. The further layers are applied at regular intervals. Keep basting the meat with its own fat as well, so it does not dry out.

The most important ingredient for the glaze is the honey. Use a flavorful variety and do so sparingly, as its strong flavor might otherwise upset the balance of this dish. Prepare the sauerkraut according to the rules: use goose fat and flavor it with juniper and beer or white wine – or, if you like, with champagne.

1. Score the rind of the pork and brown on all sides in a very hot pan. Roast in a 355 °F/180 °C oven for 30 minutes, skin side down.

2. For the glaze, reduce the orange juice, sugar, honey, shallots and seasoning to a syrup. Remove the meat from the oven and let cool. Glaze with the syrup and return to the oven. Reduce the temperature to 325 °F/160 °C and roast for 1 hour more, basting with the glaze 2 or 3 times during cooking.

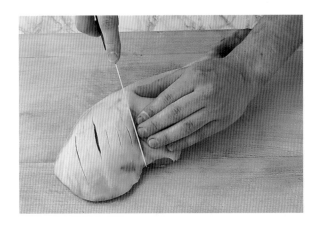

Pig with Sauerkraut

3. Rinse the sauerkraut in cold water and squeeze it dry. Place the herbs and spices in a sachet. Braise the onions and smoked bacon, but do not allow to brown. Add the sliced apple, wine, apple cider and stock. Add the sauerkraut, herbs and spice sachet, and cook for 1½ hours.

4. Grate the potato finely. Remove the bacon and the sachet from the pan and add the potato. Adjust the seasoning. Carve the meat and serve with the sauerkraut.

Muscovy Duckling with

Preparation time: 25 minutes
Cooking time: 45 minutes
Difficulty: ★

Serves 4

2 small Muscovy ducklings
2 fresh figs
2 lemons
2 potatoes
olive oil
13 tbsp/200 g butter
2 sprigs of tarragon

salt and pepper

For the duck stock:
the duckling carcasses
3½ tbsp/50 ml dry white wine
3½ tbsp/50 ml cognac
¾ cup/200 ml veal stock

For the caramel:
½ cup plus 2 tbsp/150 g sugar
3½ tbsp/50 ml red wine vinegar
1 tbsp/22 g honey

Duck meat is tender and tasty, and offers a whole range of different flavors. Jean Fleury favors the Challans duck, which is subject to strict quality controls. The birds are fed grain and each has 8 square feet/2.5 square meters of space. They are slaughtered at 11 weeks, when their flesh has reached a certain maturity. A small duck, such as a muscovy duck, may be substituted.

Duck is suitable for a number of delicious dishes. Black olives go well with it, as do mint, bitter oranges, black currants, cherries, and sauces using port or other richly flavored wines. For this dish, our chef, following tradition, recommends fresh figs, dry white wine and good cognac, to which a savory veal stock is added.

The fig, so often mentioned in the Bible, has maintained its popularity to the present day. Jean Fleury also likes to use figs with guinea fowl.

The preparation of the potatoes is not difficult. The paper-thin slices of potato become almost transparent when sautéed, so that the tarragon leaves will show through. Be careful with the quantities of vinegar and honey, which can dominate the flavor of the dish if too much of either is used.

1. Prepare the ducks for roasting and roast in a 400 °F/205 °C oven for 25–30 minutes; the flesh should remain pink. Remove the breast and legs, and roast the legs until cooked through. For the stock, break up the carcasses and braise, then add the white wine, cognac and finally the veal stock. Cook for about 15 minutes, then strain.

2. Meanwhile, prepare a light-colored caramel with the sugar. Add the red wine vinegar and honey and bring to a boil. Mix with the duck stock, bring back to a boil, simmer briefly and strain. Skim the fat from the surface, add the zest of the lemon and the butter, and season.

Lemon and Honey Sauce

3. Wash and peel the potatoes. Cut them into very thin slices with a mandoline and place a few tarragon leaves on half of the slices. Cover with the remaining potato slices. Roast the figs in the oven with some butter.

4. Brown the potato slices in a nonstick pan with some butter. On each plate place a duck leg, some slices of duck breast, and 4–5 potato slices. Pour over the lemon-and-honey sauce and garnish with a julienne of blanched lemon zest.

Stuffed Pig Tails

Preparation time: 30 minutes
Cooking time: 2 hours
Difficulty: ★★★

Serves 4

8 pigs' tails, lightly salted
2.2 lb/1 kg white beans and string beans, cut, salted and preserved in clay pots (see description below)

7 oz/200 g lean pork
3½ oz/100 g veal
2½ oz/70 g foie gras
6½ tbsp/100 g butter
6½ tbsp/100 ml heavy cream
1 tbsp/15 ml white wine
1 tbsp shallots
nutmeg
salt and pepper
white stock

These preserved beans – a reminder of the days when the Netherlands were governed by Spain – are prepared in the autumn and eaten throughout the winter. After being washed and cut, the beans are layered in a clay pot so that the firmest ones are at the bottom. Then they are covered with salt up to the rim of the pot, before being pressed under a weighted plate. To prepare for eating, they must be rinsed several times and then boiled for 15 minutes.

Before you start to prepare the salted pigs' tails, they must be soaked for 24 hours to get rid of the salt, and then conscientiously cleaned. They should be cooked in barely simmering water and finally refreshed in cold water, which will make them easier to bone. If you do not intend to eat them right away, you can keep the boned tails in the refrigerator for some time.

In any case, the success of this dish depends on the stuffing. Choose only the best quality ingredients. To poach the pigs' tails we recommend wrapping each piece in aluminum foil, then in cheesecloth.

1. Soak the tails for 24 hours. Simmer for 1½–2 hours, drain and allow to cool in cold water until luke-warm. Prepare the stuffing: chop finely the meat of 4 of the pigs' tails, braise the shallots and add the white wine. Add all other ingredients except the beans and butter to the meat, mix carefully and season.

2. Bone the remaining tails: cut open lengthwise, remove the bones and stuff with the prepared filling.

with Preserved Beans

3. Put the tails back together in pairs, the thick end of one with the thin end of the other; wrap in foil, roll up like a sausage and fasten. Rinse the cut beans 2–3 times under running water and soak. Cook in boiling water for about 15 minutes, then prepare both kinds of beans as usual.

4. Poach the stuffed tails in white stock for about 30 minutes. They can then be browned in a pan. Mix the two kinds of beans and add butter. Place on 4 warm plates. Cut the stuffed tails in slices and place them on the plates near the beans. Use the thickened veal stock as a sauce.

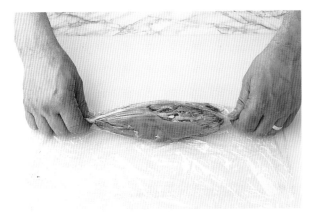

Fillet of Veal with

Preparation time: 1 hour
Cooking time: 20 minutes
Difficulty: ★★★

Serves 4

1 generous lb/500 g veal tenderloin
1 young cabbage
1 bunch young carrots
1 bunch scallions
1 bunch turnips

3½ oz/100 g green beans
9 oz/250 g green asparagus
1¼ cup/300 g butter
¾ cup/200 ml white chicken stock
1 bunch chives
salt and pepper

For the vegetable sauce:
brown truffle sauce
red, green and yellow bell peppers

The meat of the calf has been appreciated at least since antiquity. When Moses received the Ten Commandments on Mount Sinai, the Hebrews constructed a golden calf. A fatted calf was slaughtered to celebrate the return of the prodigal son.

All parts of the calf can be eaten: the glands, the offal and, of course, the meat itself all provide the ingredients for innumerable dishes for the gourmet. Different cuts of veal appear in braised veal shanks, in ragouts and fricassees. It is eaten with particular relish in France, which maintains its position as the greatest producer of veal in Europe.

After some difficult years, the breeders succeeded in regaining the confidence of the French consumer, and now more than 8 lb/4 kg of veal is consumed per person per year in France.

For this dish of veal tenderloin *à la ficelle* (tied with string and poached), which is based on an old household recipe, our chef recommends veal from the Limousin, which is now protected by a seal of quality, from calves reared only on milk. Its flesh is a shining pale pink, very firm and with white fat.

1. Remove the sinews and fat from the veal, season and tie up. Blanch the cabbage leaves, pat dry and place on aluminum foil.

2. Cut the vegetables (carrots, scallions, turnips, asparagus, and green beans) into small pieces and blanch in boiling salted water. Place in rows on each cabbage leaf. Mix the chives with the melted butter and pour over the vegetables. Fold up the foil and roll into a roulade.

Chartreuse of Vegetables

3. Poach the veal tenderloin for about 8 minutes in the chicken stock, then remove and keep cool.

4. Reduce the stock by half, then add butter. Add the brown vegetable sauce (the peppers mixed with the truffle sauce). Season to taste, cut the tenderloins into slices, place on the plates and pour the sauce over. Reheat the chartreuses by steaming, then place one on each plate.

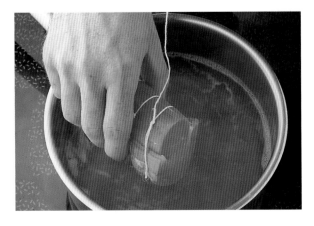

Pork Tenderloin with

Preparation time: 50 minutes
Cooking time: 30 minutes
Difficulty: ☆

Serves 4

2 pork tenderloins, about 28 oz/800 g
2 tbsp/30 g butter
1 medium onion, chopped
stock
4 cardamom seeds 2 cloves
1 pinch of curry powder
1 pinch of caraway seed
2 pinches of paprika
1 pinch of cinnamon
1½ cups/200 g couscous

1 tbsp/15 ml tomato paste
10 small mint leaves
6½ tbsp/100 ml cream
3½ tbsp/50 ml olive oil

For the preserved fruit:
juice of 1 lemon and 1 lime
2 dried figs
3 dried apricots
2 prunes
10 roasted peanuts
5 roasted almonds

Coconut and curry sauce:
(see basic recipes p. 800)

Philippe Groult created this dish on a business trip to Tunisia, where he discovered a veritable garden of Eden, and was inspired by the many unfamiliar spices he found there.

When choosing the couscous, the size of the grains is irrelevant; what is important is its quality and its preparation in olive oil.

The peanuts, almonds and, if you like, chickpeas and pine nuts are fried in the pan. In summer you can also use fresh almonds. Similarly, the dried fruit can be replaced with fresh fruit in summer. For soaking the fruits, the lemon and lime juices play important roles. The lemon counteracts any excessive sweetness in the fruit and the lime enriches it with a subtle note.

The medallion is cut from the top of the tenderloin and is roasted to remain pink in the center. In this recipe, the pork and vegetables form a well-balanced relationship.

1. Soak the figs, apricots, prunes, peanuts and almonds for 10 minutes in the juice of 1 lemon and 1 lime.

2. Briefly toast the couscous in a pan with olive oil, then add the stock with tomato paste. Boil the cream with the crushed spices and add to the couscous with two thirds of the soaked fruits. Remove from the heat and set aside to plump.

Coconut-Curry Sauce

3. Trim the pork and season with salt and pepper; braise it with a chopped onion in a little butter and 2 tsp oil, leaving the meat just barely pink inside, and keep warm on a plate. Add 2 tbsp/30 ml of water to the meat juices and set aside. Cut the pork into 12 medallions.

4. For the coconut and curry sauce: braise the onion, apple and banana in olive oil, add curry powder, coconut milk and chicken stock, bring to a boil, and simmer for 3 minutes. Purée, strain and add the butter. On each plate, place 3 tbsp of couscous in 3 piles, place a medallion of pork on top of each, pour the roasting juices on top and the curry sauce around, and garnish with a piece of coconut and a mint leaf.

Mallard with Figs

Preparation time: 1 hour 30 minutes
Cooking time: 1 hour 30 minutes
Difficulty: ★★

Serves 4

2 mallard or other wild ducks
7 tbsp/150 g honey
2 garlic cloves
4 tbsp/30 g Szechuan pepper
4 tbsp/30 g coriander
1 tbsp/10 g caraway seed
4 cardamom seeds
1 tbsp/15 ml soy sauce

2 tbsp/30 ml sherry
salt

For the red cabbage with figs:
1 red cabbage
8 dried figs
2 large onions
1 fresh ginger root
⅔ cup/150 ml red wine
½ cup/120 ml port
6½ tbsp/100 ml olive oil
2 tbsp/30 ml vinegar
1 pinch of sugar
salt

The imaginations of Europe's best chefs have in recent years been stimulated by the flavors of Asian spices and their potential for combination. Here, the mallard, the most widely distributed breed of wild duck in Europe, is enhanced in a wondrous manner by these spices. If you are unable to obtain a true mallard, you can use other varieties of wild duck.

Red cabbage tastes best in the autumn and winter. A medium-sized head of red cabbage is just right for this recipe. Remove the largest leaves and the stalk, before chopping the cabbage finely and marinating. It should marinate overnight, which will make the cabbage more digestible. Don't use too much sherry: it has a powerful taste which should not be allowed to dominate the flavor of the cabbage. Measure out the Szechwan pepper with care as well.

This recipe is a variation on the Alsatian tradition of serving roast goose at Christmas with red cabbage or sauerkraut. The Auberge de l'Ill, which was established 100 years ago, successfully practices the fine art of variation, and this dish would be a suitable one for a festive occasion.

1. The day before, marinate the cabbage: cut out the stalk, quarter the cabbage and cut in thin strips, season with salt, sugar and vinegar, and let stand overnight.

2. The next day, braise the finely chopped onions in the olive oil. Then add the marinated red cabbage and the diced figs. Add the red wine, port and 3 slices of ginger. Braise gently in a 300 °F/150 °C for 1 to 1½ hours. Season to taste.

and Red Cabbage

3. In a clean coffee grinder, grind the Szechwan pepper, coriander, caraway and cardamom very finely. Mix the spices with the honey, soy sauce, sherry and garlic. Season the mallards inside and out with salt.

4. Prepare and truss the ducks and paint them with the spiced honey. Roast them in a 425 °F/220 °C oven for 20 minutes, then set aside to rest for about 15 minutes. Before serving, give them another coating of spiced honey, and reheat in the oven. Serve with the braised red cabbage.

Squab and Foie Gras

Preparation time: 1 hour 30 minutes
Cooking time: 35 minutes
Difficulty: ★★★

Serves 4

4 squab, about 1 generous lb/500 g each
8 slices raw foie gras
8 slices truffle
16 spinach leaves
2½ lb/1.2 kg puff pastry
(see basic recipes p. 803)
8 Belgian endive
8 carrots

1 egg yolk
clarified butter
salt and pepper

For the stuffing:
7 oz/200 g lean pork
5¼ oz/150 g fatty pork
3½ oz/100 g pork fat
1¾ oz/50 g ham
1 small truffle, chopped
6½ tbsp/100 ml truffle juice
2 cups/500 ml port
salt and pepper

The truffle was once the subject of a superstition: the places where truffles grew were supposed to be avoided at night, as unholy powers were attributed to them, unless one took care to make the sign of the cross on each occasion. Later the fine flavor of this noble fungus was acknowledged and it became known as the "black diamond." A truffle takes several years to reach maturity. The black truffle is the ideal accompaniment for game birds: in this recipe it adds refinement to a squab in a puff pastry crust.

As the preparation of the stuffing is quite a lengthy process,

it is best to make it the day before, which also gives it a finer flavor. If making your own puff pastry intimidates you, by all means substitute frozen all-butter pastry.

Glazing the carrots is not difficult: after cutting them into attractive shapes, give them 10 minutes in a hot pan with a little water, some butter and a pinch of sugar. They should stay crisp, which will also give them a better appearance.

1. Remove the breasts from the squab, and skin them. Bone the thighs, leaving a small length of drumstick intact. Heat clarified butter in a hot pan, and brown the seasoned squab breasts and slices of foie gras.

2. Place 1 slice of truffle on each squab breast and top with a slice of foie gras. Let rest for 30 minutes. Prepare a stuffing from the ingredients listed. Blanch and refresh the spinach leaves. Spread the spinach leaves and the boned squab thighs with stuffing, and wrap the squab breasts and foie gras in the spinach leaves. Brown the stuffed squab thighs for 10 minutes.

Tourte with Truffles

3. Roll out the pastry. With a pastry cutter, cut out one small and one somewhat larger circle from the pastry. Paint the edges with egg yolk. Place the spinach-wrapped squab on the smaller circle, them cover with the larger. Wash the endive and slice diagonally. Braise the endive and glaze the carrots.

4. Close up the pastry edges with a fork, then paint with egg yolk. Set aside to rest for 15 minutes, then bake in a 425 °F/225 °C oven for 10–15 minutes. Let rest for 1 minute and then cut in half. Serve hot with the endive and carrots.

Preparation time: 1 hour 40 minutes
Cooking time: 1 hour 30 minutes
Difficulty: ★★★

Serves 4

2 pheasants
8 Savoy cabbage leaves
⅔ cup/200 g lentils
4 black salsify
8 shallots
1 lemon
parsley
¾ cup/200 ml duck fat
3½ tbsp/50 g butter
salt and pepper

For the Hochepot potatoes:
1 generous lb/500 g potatoes
1 carrot, sliced
½ onion, sliced

1 sprig of rosemary
10 tbsp/150 g melted butter

For the port wine sauce:
the pheasant carcasses
2 celery ribs
1 carrot
1 onion
1 garlic clove
1 bay leaf
1 sprig of thyme
6 peppercorns
¾ cup/200 ml port
¾ cup/200 ml veal stock
2 cups/500 ml white chicken stock
3½ tbsp/50 g butter
salt and pepper

Hochepot is originally a Flemish recipe; here Paul Heathcote introduces a variation using pheasant. Choose a hen pheasant, which has a more refined flavor than the male and does not have to be hung for as long, only a couple of days. If you are unable to obtain a hen pheasant, you could substitute another tender game bird, such as young partridges, grouse, or squabs.

The potato dish suggested here as an accompaniment is prepared in a traditional way. Use a "Pommes Anna" dish, a heavy, deep, straight-sided dish with a lid.

Experts are unable to agree over the origin of the word "hochepot." Some believe that it comes from the verb *hocher*, to shake, and reflects a need to shake the container, but this is not done in any of the recipes in which this term is used. We might conclude that the original dish, whose recipe has apparently been lost, was perhaps a kind of beef stew, which was cooked without water and could not be prepared without an energetic intervention on the part of the cook. On the other hand, it could just be a corruption of "hot pot," which brings us back to Paul Heathcote's Lancashire.

1. Prepare the pheasants if necessary. Remove the breasts and brown on both sides for 7–8 minutes until golden brown. Peel the shallots and braise in duck fat, season and set aside. Wash and blanch the Savoy cabbage leaves.

2. Peel and quarter the salsify and brown in butter until golden brown. Season with salt, pepper, lemon juice, and chopped parsley. Cook the lentils.

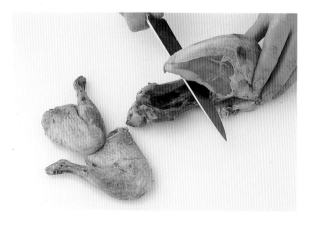

Hochepot Potatoes

3. Season the ingredients for the hochepot, line a buttered Pommes Anna mold or cake pan with a thick layer of potato slices, then fill it with the rest of the potatoes, the carrots, and the onions. Bake for 1 hour in the oven until it is cooked through and nicely colored on top.

4. For the sauce, brown the pheasant bones and the vegetables with the seasoning, deglaze with the port and reduce by half. Add the chicken stock, reduce by half again, finally adding the veal stock, deglaze for a few minutes, and strain. Bring to a boil, skim off the fat and impurities and reduce until it has the consistency of a sauce. Serve on warm plates.

Pickled Goose

Preparation time: 1 hour
Cooking time: 1 hour 20 minutes
Difficulty: ★★

Serves 4

1 goose, 8–9 lb/4 kg
10½ oz/300 g raw foie gras
16 turnips
16 carrots
1 rutabaga

1 onion
2 apples (such as Golden Delicious)
1¾ oz/50 g dried figs
⅔ cup/200 g green lentils
cloves, cardamom, nutmeg, aniseed, coriander
8 cups/2 l chicken stock
6½ tbsp/100 g butter
truffle juice (optional)
⅔ cup/200 g coarse salt
salt and pepper

Because of the severe climate and long winter, the nearer one gets to the Arctic Circle, the more important it becomes to make sure that foodstuffs can be preserved, because it is very difficult to obtain fresh food. For this reason, Norwegians preserve both fish and meat in coarse, iodine-rich sea salt.

The goose, with its thick layer of fat, is well suited to this treatment. But you should realize that salt makes the flesh firmer, and the meat must be rinsed several times after removing it from the brine. Then it should be coo-

ked over low heat in well seasoned stock. Eyvind Hellstrom recommends a traditional Norwegian accompaniment based on rutabagas and young turnips, cut into large pieces. Season this with spices such as cardamom and ground nutmeg. If you wish to give a southern accent to this Nordic dish, you can add thyme, rosemary or parsley.

In the spring you can change the accompaniment to fresh, crisp vegetables, cut small, such as carrots, new potatoes, and green beans.

1. Remove the liver from the goose. Place the goose in the coarse salt and leave it 24 hours. Next day, rinse several times in water. Remove the breasts carefully; cut them open and stuff with a mixture of foie gras, apples, diced dried figs, and the seasoning.

2. Wrap the roulade in cheesecloth and tie securely. Cut the vegetables into attractive shapes and rinse the lentils several times.

Breast with Lentils

3. Poach the roulade for about 1 hour in chicken stock, adding the lentils for the last 20 minutes. Cook the vegetables separately in boiling salted water.

4. Finally brown the roulade in a pan, skin side down. Slice it and place the slices on a bed of the lentils. Arrange the vegetables around the lentils and pour some melted butter, or truffle juice, over them.

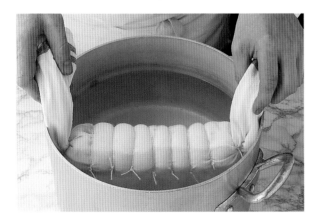

Roulade of Beef with Raisins

Preparation time: 30 minutes
Cooking time: 5 minutes
Difficulty: ★★

Serves 4

3⅓ lb/1.2 kg sirloin steak
4 tbsp/30 g raisins
4 tbsp/30 g pine nuts
parsley
garlic

For the tomato sauce:
6 tomatoes
1 garlic clove
2 cups/500 ml olive oil

For the garnish:
3 tbsp/20 g raisins
3 tbsp/20 g pine nuts
some young chicory leaves
1¼ cup/300 ml oil
garlic

Alfonso Iaccarino's restaurant is called Don Alfonso in memory of his grandfather, to whom this recipe is also dedicated.

Up to the beginning of the 20th century in southern Italy, meat was eaten only on Sundays, because the dry climate precluded the development of pasture land, and the region was thus not suited for the rearing of cattle. Meat was simply grilled or fried and served with raisins and pine nuts. In the evening the meat juices served as a sauce for pasta.

Today, it is easy to obtain meat of excellent quality, and this method of preparation has been greatly refined. Use sirloin steak for preference; it is tender and juicy and will be even more tasty if you beat it flat.

Our chef likes to use very bright red tomatoes, which form the most important part of the accompaniment for this dish. They are puréed and seasoned with garlic. Braise the raisins with chicory leaves, whose bitter flavor forms a subtle contrast to the sweetness of the raisins.

1. Pound the slices of sirloin flat on a sheet of plastic wrap. Toast the pine nuts over moderate heat.

2. Lay on each piece of meat a few pine nuts and raisins, and some chopped garlic and parsley. Form a roulade and fasten with a skewer. For the tomato sauce, braise the garlic in olive oil. Remove the garlic, and add the peeled, seeded and diced tomatoes. Cook for a good 5–10 minutes.

Pine Nuts and Tomato Sauce

3. Brown the roulades on all sides in olive oil in a nonstick pan. When it is half cooked, add the tomato sauce. Simmer for 5 minutes.

4. Blanch the chicory leaves and brown over high heat with the pine nuts, raisins and garlic. Pour the sauce onto each of 4 plates, add the pine nuts, chicory leaves and raisins, and finally the meat, cut in half diagonally

Preparation time: 1 hour
Cooking time: 20 minutes
Difficulty: ★★★

Serves 4

1 guinea fowl

For the liver ravioli:
¾ cup/100 g flour
3½ tbsp/50 ml water
liver of the guinea fowl
1 tsp/5 ml Chinese black bean sauce
chopped parsley
salt

For the guinea fowl and noodle nests:
guinea fowl thigh meat

3½ oz/100 g fresh Chinese egg noodles
1 tsp seeded chopped chile
1 tbsp/15 ml sesame oil
fresh coriander leaves

1 tbsp scallions
salt and pepper

For the guinea fowl breasts:
2 guinea fowl breasts (with skin)
5½ oz/150 g fresh Chinese egg noodles
½ red pepper
4 baby corn cobs
8 dried shiitake mushrooms
2 Chinese cabbage leaves
3½ tbsp/50 ml cooking juices from meat

For the marinade:
fresh coriander leaves
1 garlic clove
1 tsp ground ginger
1 tbsp/15 ml oyster sauce

Despite its frightful screeching, the guinea fowl has made itself welcome in the farmyard as well as at the most distinguished tables since the 17th century. The guinea fowl is not very large, but one weighing 2–3 lb/1–1½ kg is plenty for 4 people.

Typically, André Jaeger, has recommended an exotic variation on the guinea fowl, for which he uses ingredients that are comparatively unfamiliar in most of Europe. The breasts have to be removed, the skin and sinews carefully trimmed from the thighs and the fat removed. The breasts are marinated for 24 hours with finely chopped coriander leaves (which are also known as cilantro and Chinese parsley). This seasoning with its sophisticated aroma gives an extra nuance to the flesh of the guinea fowl. Brown the breasts very briefly in hot oil, to give them a nice color while preserving their tenderness.

This method can also be used for many other kinds of poultry, as long as their flavor goes well with the Asian spices.

1. Remove the breasts with their skin and place in the marinade for 24 hours. Remove the thighs; bone and remove sinews and fat. Soak the dried mushrooms in water. Chop the liver finely, and mix with the black bean sauce and parsley. For the pastry, pour 3½ tbsp/50 ml of boiling water over the flour and add a pinch of salt; make this into a smooth paste and set aside to rest.

2. Roll out the pastry and cut out circles 3 ½ in/8 cm in diameter. On each circle, place a teaspoonful of the liver stuffing, then close the edges by pinching together. Brown these dumplings in oil, then add ½ in/1 cm water. Cover and complete the cooking by steaming.

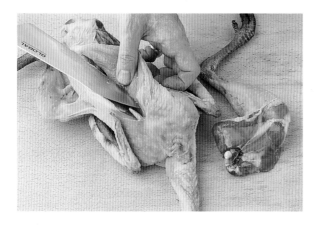

à l'Asiatique

3. Cut the thigh meat into pieces, then chop the scallions and chile finely and mix with the other ingredients. Roll some uncooked noodles around 1 tbsp of this mixture, forming a nest. Brown in hot oil and keep warm.

4. Peel the red pepper and cut into thin strips. Cut the Chinese cabbage into ¼ in/1 cm strips. Cook the mushrooms in the water in which they were soaked. Braise the pepper and cabbage strips, mushrooms, and halved baby corn lightly. Boil and refresh the noodles, brown the guinea fowl breasts in hot oil and set aside to rest. Slice the breasts and serve with the noodles, garnished with oyster sauce and the meat stock.

Braised Calf's Cheek

Preparation time: 20 minutes
Cooking time: 2 hours
Difficulty: ★★

Serves 4

8 calves' cheeks
1 green cabbage
¾ cup/100 g Puy lentils
4 carrots
2 shallots
½ head of garlic

2 onions
½ bay leaf
1 sprig of thyme
2 tbsp/30 g goose fat
2 tbsp/30 g butter
2 cups/500 ml dry white wine
4 cups/1 l veal stock
wine vinegar
3½ tbsp/50 ml olive oil
1 bunch of parsley
salt and pepper

Calf's cheek, with its pale pink flesh, is very suitable for braising. It is tender and should be simmered slowly over low heat, and should be turned at intervals to ensure even cooking. Once the meat is cooked it can be kept for 3 days. It will have even more flavor if prepared in advance and reheated before serving.

Wash and blanch a sufficient amount of cabbage leaves large enough to wrap a calf's cheek in. Make sure that the leaves don't tear, as they will have to contain some sauce as well.

The green Puy lentil, which carries a governmental seal of quality, is a true delicacy. The lentils should be well soaked in cold water before cooking. As they give off a lot of impurities while cooking, the pot should be skimmed several times. All in all, it takes some time to prepare this delicious autumn dish.

1. Brown the calves' cheeks in goose fat, beginning with the fatty side. Then add the garlic with a mirepoix of onions and 2 carrots. Add the veal stock and white wine, season with salt and pepper, cover, and braise for about 2 hours in a 300 °F/150 °C oven.

2. Wash the cabbage, then blanch in salted water. Refresh and drain. Put the lentils in a pan and cover with cold water. Chop the rest of the carrots finely and add to the pan. Add the thyme and bay leaf and simmer for 20–25 minutes over low heat.

with Lentil Vinaigrette

3. After braising the cheeks, remove from the pan, then strain the juices and reduce to the desired consistency. Wrap each cheek with some sauce in a cabbage leaf. Then wrap in aluminum foil, and reheat by steaming before serving.

4. Prepare a vinaigrette with wine vinegar, olive oil, salt and pepper. Drain the lentils and mix with the shallots and chopped parsley. Stir in the vinaigrette. Place a mound of lentils on each plate and place on top a braised calf's cheek, drizzled with butter. Pour the sauce around and serve.

Preparation time: 1 hour
Cooking time: 1 hour
Difficulty: ✲

Serves 4

1⅓ lb/600 g beef tenderloin, in 1 piece
14 oz/400 g potatoes
7 oz/200 g turnips
3½ oz/100 g white of leek
7 oz/200 g Savoy cabbage
3½ oz/100 g carrots
1 onion
3 tbsp/50 g grated horseradish

1 cup/250 ml white wine (such as Alsatian Riesling)
3 cups/750 ml white stock
salt and pepper

For the marinade:
1 cup/250 ml white wine (such as Alsatian Riesling)
2 carrots
2 onions
garlic cloves
1 bouquet garni
peppercorns

During the 19th century, housewives from Alsace prepared the traditional version of this country recipe in the morning using 3 kinds of meat – lamb, beef and pork, which had been marinated overnight in white wine. The vegetables were added in the morning and the mixture taken to the baker, who would cook it in a cool oven from 10 a.m. until noon, so it would be ready for the midday meal for the entire family.

Here Émile Jung suggests preparing beef tenderloin in this way. The meat must be marinated overnight. In the morning, simmer the vegetables until tender (you can also add celery to those listed). The young white turnips, which are rich in vitamins and minerals, are very appropriate. The "baeckeoffe" should be braised over low heat, and the meat must remain pink in the center.

The regional characteristics of this dish include the use of grated horseradish. This large root from the Cruciferae family has a very pronounced flavor and should be grated at the last possible moment, so that the essential oils, similar to those of mustard, do not dissipate. In France, horseradish is sometimes known as "German mustard," a justifiable term considering the extent to which it is used in German cuisine.

1. Marinate the meat overnight with the sliced onions, the halved garlic cloves, the diagonally cut carrots, the bouquet garni and a few white peppercorns, and a cup of white wine.

2. Slice the potatoes, leek, turnips, carrots, and onion, blanch the Savoy cabbage and cut into thin strips. Cook all the vegetables in a braising pan with the white stock and the white wine for 30 minutes.

Beef Tenderloin

3. Add the vegetables to the beef, cover and cook for 30 minutes. Remove the meat and set aside to rest for 10 minutes, then cut into 8 slices. Arrange the vegetables on the plates, alternating according to type and color.

4. Using a ladle, form the cabbage into mounds and place on the plates. Reduce the cooking juices and pour on top of the vegetables. Place two slices of beef on top of the vegetables on each plate. Season with coarse salt and garnish with horseradish before serving.

Suckling Pig

Preparation time: 2 hours
Cooking time: 15 minutes
Difficulty: ☆

Serves 4

1¾ lb/800 g rack of suckling pig
7 oz/200 g pork loin
7 oz/200 g pork caul (if available)
⅔ cup/200 g potato purée
1 generous lb/500 g potatoes

1 Savoy cabbage
finely diced celery, carrot, onion and leek
1 cup/250 ml chicken stock
1 cup/250 g butter
4 tsp/20 ml beer
2 cups/500 ml cream
1 egg white
thyme
rosemary
salt and pepper

It is probably no surprise that the combination of suckling pig and beer is widely popular in Germany, and it gives sparkle to many a festive occasion.

Experience has shown Dieter Kaufmann that a suckling pig of 6 to 8 lb/3 to 4 kg, which can be cooked in one piece, is the best to use. The most delicious part is the saddle, and it is even better when prepared a few days in advance. To give the meat a good color, it should be cooked slowly; allow a good 2 hours for a whole suckling pig, less if you are cooking only the saddle. If you are unable to get suckling pig, you can use the same method with pork tenderloin or spring lamb.

Dieter Kaufmann uses Altbier from Düsseldorf, a light brown beer with a low alcohol content that goes well with the other ingredients. This beer is a good match for the potato dumplings.

If you cannot obtain pork caul, brush the cabbage-wrapped pork with olive oil and baste during cooking.

Your guests will rave about this combination of suckling pig and beer.

1. Remove the skin and fat from the pork and French the ribs. Finely grind the pork and work in the cream and egg white and 1 tbsp of diced vegetables browned in butter. Season the stuffing to taste. Blanch and dry the cabbage, and remove the veins from the leaves.

2. Season the rack of pork and spread with stuffing. Cut the remaining cabbage into thin strips, blanch and braise in butter. Prepare the potato purée.

n Beer Sauce

3. Wrap the rack in the cabbage leaves and then in the pork caul (if used). Brown in an ovenproof skillet, then roast for 6–7 minutes in a 430 °F/220 °C oven.

4. Brown the bones and skin of the rack with the rest of the diced vegetables. Deglaze with beer. Add a ladleful of chicken stock, reduce, then stir in some butter. Put some sauce on each plate, then arrange a portion of potato purée and the cabbage on the plate alongside the meat.

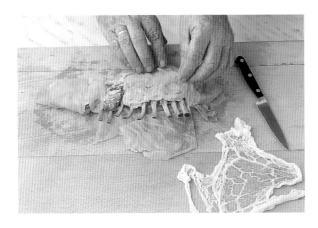

Loin of Lamb with

Preparation time: *1 hour 15 minutes*
Cooking time: *1 hour 15 minutes*
Difficulty: ★★★

Serves 4

2 loin roasts of lamb
4 dates
8 Belgian endive
8 shallots

1 tbsp mustard
4 cups/1 l lamb stock
¼ cup/60 ml red wine vinegar
2 cups/500 ml port
fresh mint leaves
4 star anise
1 tbsp sugar
1 tbsp butter
salt and pepper

The combination of lamb and dried fruit is a favorite one in Morocco, and in Europe, lamb is often spiced "in the traditional manner" with coarse mustard. Here both traditions are united.

The boned loin, which is stuffed and rolled, should first be browned for about 10 minutes to render the fat. The main cooking is then done in the oven on a small bed of potato. Don't forget to allow the meat to rest a little after cooking, in order to regain all its tenderness.

The date originally came from North Africa and the Middle East. It contains phosphorus and calcium, and its use in gastronomy is no longer confined to desserts. According to legend, the date grove of Marrakech grew up from the date pits that the workers discarded while building the royal city.

1. Bone the lamb and trim excess fat. Remove the flaps of meat from the sides and trim excess fat from them. Lightly pound the flaps to produce thin slices. Pit and purée the dates and mix with the mustard.

2. Spread the date and mustard mixture over the flaps of meat. Wrap a piece of loin and a piece of tenderloin in each flap, then tie into cylinders.

Dates and Mustard Seeds

3. Braise the finely chopped shallots, deglaze with the red wine vinegar and reduce until the liquid has disappeared. Deglaze again with the port and reduce again. Add the lamb stock, star anise and some mint leaves. Simmer, strain and keep warm.

4. Separate the endive leaves and blanch. Braise them in butter and sugar over moderate heat until golden. Brown the lamb and cook until medium-rare. Let the meat rest, then cut into 1 in/2 cm thick slices. Put some sauce on each of the plates and arrange 4 lamb slices and some endive on them.

Preparation time: 45 minutes
Cooking time: 25 minutes
Difficulty: ★★

Serves 4

1 chicken, about 4½ lb/2 kg
1¾ oz/50 g fresh chanterelles
½ cup/50 g corn kernels
12 baby leeks

6½ tbsp/100g butter
2 cups/500 ml onion juice, made by juicing
5 medium onions
6½ tbsp/100 ml chicken stock
chives
salt and pepper

For the syrup:
2 tbsp/25 g sugar
3½ tbsp/50 ml water

For a long time the flesh of poultry was considered to be lean, and so people were occasionally allowed to eat it on fasting days, when meat was normally forbidden.

Following the basic revolution in taste that occurred during the Renaissance, poultry came into its own in gastronomy. Highly regarded birds include the poulard, a chicken 7–8 months old that has not yet laid any eggs and is especially fattened to produce a very delicate flesh. Bresse poultry is of particularly high quality: each bird has plenty of room in which to wander, and is fed on maize and milk.

The stuffed chicken rolls can be prepared in advance, so the meat will absorb the flavor of the stuffing ingredients. Because of their thickness, the chicken thighs should be steamed for 10 minutes in advance before they are cooked with the wings.

Corn goes excellently with chicken and is thus an ideal accompaniment. Onions are a basic cooking ingredient whose character is well suited to making stock for a sauce.

For a slightly sharper taste, in the hunting season you can substitute pheasant for Bresse chicken.

1. Prepare the chicken: remove and bone the breasts, wings and thighs. With a meat mallet, lightly pound the chicken pieces until flat. Cook the leeks in salted water. Lightly cook the corn in butter and set aside.

2. Finely chop the chicken breast meat and the mushrooms. Season and prepare as stuffing. Stuff the thighs and wings with this mixture, roll up and tie. Wrap in aluminum foil and refrigerate.

Caramelized Onion Sauce

3. Reduce the onion juice by half. Prepare a light caramel with sugar and water. Add the onion juice and simmer for 15 minutes, or until reduced to about ½ cup/125 ml. Whisk in the butter and chicken stock, then season to taste.

4. Steam the thighs for 10 minutes, basting frequently, then brown in a skillet with the wings. Divide the thighs in half, and slice the wings. Garnish with corn, small pieces of leek, chives and sauce.

Roast Breast of Vea

Preparation time: 1 hour
Cooking time: 1 hour 30 minutes
Difficulty: ★★

Serves 4

3⅓ lb/1½ kg boned breast of veal
1 bouquet garni
1 small onion stuffed with a clove
1 sprig of parsley
celery leaves
salt and pepper

For the baked apples:
3 apples
1 onion, chopped

¼ celeriac
¾ cup/200 ml veal stock
1 tsp ground mustard seeds
1 tbsp/15 ml vinegar
1 tsp Dijon mustard
1 tsp curry powder
2 tbsp/30 g butter
chives

For the beet salad:
2 raw, medium-sized beets
1 garlic clove
1 chopped shallot
5 tbsp/75 ml salad oil
juice of ½ lemon
salt and white pepper

Breast of veal is a somewhat neglected cut in the United States, but it is one of the most economical cuts of veal and is delicious and succulent if prepared carefully.

The accompaniments for this recipe are in accordance with Danish tradition, according to which potatoes are often served with apples. Choose new potatoes or a variety such as Yukon gold, which will go superbly with this mustard-scented roast.

Celeriac, also known as celery root, is also wonderful with apples and with the flavor of curry. The beet salad, also a Scandinavian specialty, completes this dish – with its profusion of root vegetables – to perfection.

1. Cover the meat with water, add salt, and simmer with the vegetables, skimming off the froth from time to time.

2. After 1½ hours, remove the meat, season lightly with salt, cover with a sheet of plastic wrap and press under a heavy object, such as a baking sheet weighted with a couple of cans of tomatoes. Strain the stock and reduce until the required consistency is obtained. Cut the beets into thin slices and marinate with oil, lemon juice, garlic, chopped shallots and pepper.

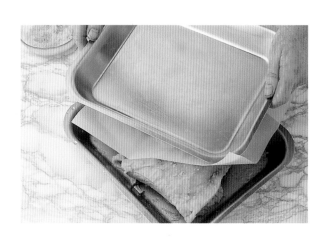

with Apples and Beets

3. Cut the unpeeled apples and the peeled celeriac into 2 in/5 mm cubes. Braise the onions in butter with the curry powder and mustard seed. Deglaze with vinegar and mustard. Add some of the cooking stock, reduce and strain. Whisk in the butter and set aside.

4. Reheat the meat in a little of the stock, then slice. Sauté the celeriac and apple cubes over high heat, mix with the sauce and season. Serve the beet salad separately.

Chicken with Artichokes

Preparation time: 30 minutes
Cooking time: 15 minutes
Difficulty: ★

Serves 4

4 chicken breasts with the 1st joint of the wings
4 small artichokes

2 fennel bulbs
4 sun-dried tomatoes
¾ cup/200 ml olive oil
4 tsp/20 ml balsamic vinegar
4 sprigs of rosemary
parsley leaves
salt and pepper

In Italy the art of drying tomatoes is passed on from generation to generation. First the halved tomatoes are dried in the sun on long strings, then they are steeped in olive oil with herbs.

For this recipe, use tomatoes, fennel and artichokes that are as fresh as you can get them. If possible, you should use the small purple artichokes of Southern Europe. They can be eaten raw or cooked.

The chicken breasts should come from good-quality poultry; preferably free-range and organically raised. It is worth it to seek out a good chicken supplier.

Balsamic vinegar from Modena, matured for many years in a succession of barrels, is an excellent product, whose inimitable flavor will enrich your dish. Rosemary has a typically robust Mediterranean character, and should therefore be used with discretion.

1. Chop the fennel, artichokes and dried tomatoes. Braise in a ceramic casserole with olive oil and rosemary, but do not brown.

2. Season the chicken breasts and add to the vegetables. Add a little water. Bring to a boil, cover the pot and place in a 430 °F/220 °C oven for 6–7 minutes.

3. Remove the chicken breasts and cut into thin slices. Completely reduce the cooking liquid over medium heat.

4. Add the parsley to the vegetables and deglaze with balsamic vinegar. Arrange the vegetables in the center of the serving dish and place the chicken breast on top. Pour some oil over it and garnish with rosemary.

Suckling Pig in a Mantle o

Preparation time:	1 hour
Cooking time:	45 minutes
Difficulty:	★★

Serves 4

6½ lb/3 kg loin of suckling pig, with kidney
1 banana
½ lemon
2 apples (such as Golden Delicious)
¾ oz/20 g fresh cranberries

2 sheets of filo pastry
¾ cup/200 ml grapeseed oil
⅔ cup/150 ml olive oil
⅔ cup/150 ml pork stock (prepared from the bones)

¾ cup/200 ml veal stock
1 tbsp/20 g honey
4 tsp/20 g sugar

butter
salt and pepper

For the stuffing:
the pig's kidney
½ cup/50 g bread crumbs
1 tbsp/10 g green peppercorns
1 tbsp/10 g chopped parsley

For the spicy sauce:
6 tbsp/40 g spices (curry powder, cinnamon, caraway, coriander and ginger)
⅔ cup/150 ml pork stock (prepared from the bones)
¾ cup/200 ml veal stock

The suckling pig has white and remarkably tender flesh. An animal 4–8 weeks old is just right for this dish, whose apparently complicated preparation should not put you off. The suckling pig has been appreciated since the Middle Ages and provides the most delicious meals. Even its skin – cut into thin strips and browned – is tasty.

Boning the pork is challenging but not impossible; if it frightens you, have your butcher do it. Brush olive oil onto the skin before putting the meat in the oven, and regularly baste the meat with its own juices, to make its skin crisper. Before serving, allow the meat to rest for a few minutes so that it will be juicier.

The stuffing can be seasoned either: dried green peppercorns, which have to be soaked before use, or with brined green peppercorns, which should be first rinsed in cold water.

For the fruit accompaniment, you might consider replacing the apples and bananas with a few thin slices of pineapple.

1. Bone the pork, leaving the eye of the loin and belly flaps intact. Reserve the kidneys, and use the bones and trimmings to prepare the stock.

2. Cut the banana in 2 in/4 cm long strips. Marinate for at least 30 minutes in grapeseed oil with a little lemon juice. Quarter each sheet of filo pastry and wrap around the banana strips. Dice the apples, add sugar and lemon juice, and caramelize lightly in butter.

Honey with a Spicy Sauce

3. Stuff the pork with a mixture of pepper, bread crumbs, chopped parsley and kidney; roll up and truss. Rub the skin with butter and olive oil and roast for 45 minutes in the oven. Then remove the string. Brush with honey and allow to caramelize lightly on the top rack of the oven.

4. Pour off the fat from the roasting pan. Add the spices, deglaze with the pork and veal stocks, and reduce. Strain and then whisk in the butter. Brown the pastry-wrapped bananas in butter. Cut the pork into ¼ in/½ cm thick slices, and arrange on each plate 2–3 slices of pork, 2 banana strips, 2 tbsp/30 ml apples and some cranberries. Pour sauce on top.

Preparation time: 1 hour
Cooking time: 2 hours
Difficulty: ★★

Serves 4

3⅓ lb/1½ kg tripe
2 eggs
3½ tbsp/100 g flour
2 cups/200 g bread crumbs

For the sauce:
remainder of the tripe
pork rind, cut in pieces
1 shallot

2 tomatoes
1 onion
1 carrot
½ celeriac
½ leek
7 oz/200 g potatoes
3½ tbsp/50 g butter
4 gherkins
1 tsp/5 ml tomato paste
2 cups/500 ml chicken stock
6½ tbsp/100 ml Madeira
1 cup/250 ml dry white wine
2 cloves
thyme, bay leaf, parsley
salt and pepper

This traditional dish is known as "Kuddelfleck" in Luxembourg. For this recipe Léa Linster recommends the upper part of the stomach, which you should be able to buy cooked. It needs to be cooked for a further 2 hours and then cut into small pieces, covered with bread crumbs and fried. If the tripe has not been blanched beforehand, simply allow twice as long for the preparation.

Choose tripe of good quality, which will stay tender. The slices must be cut absolutely straight.

The sauce can be prepared according to your own taste. Our chef uses white wine and Madeira; these produce a brown sauce with an exquisite flavor, which will flavor the potatoes, which should be of a floury variety.

This dish is recommended for a winter meal, which is when it used to be prepared before the invention of the refrigerator. When the cattle were slaughtered, the parts that would deteriorate the soonest were eaten first.

1. For the sauce, brown the skin of the tripe; the pork rind; diced carrots, onions and celeriac; and thyme and bay leaf. Deglaze with the wine and Madeira, and reduce. Add the chicken stock and tomato paste and reduce until thickened. Strain and whisk in the butter.

2. Cook the tripe with soup vegetables in water for 2 hours. Strain, let cool, and cut into diamond shapes. Coat in flour, egg yolk and, finally, bread crumbs. Dice the gherkins and the peeled and seeded tomatoes.

Luxembourgeoise

3. Brown the tripe in butter over medium heat until golden.

4. Boil the potatoes in salted water, then pass through a potato ricer. Finally add the gherkin and tomato dice to the sauce, season and let cool. On each plate, put 2 pieces of tripe, some potato and a big spoonful of sauce. Garnish with a few parsley leaves that have been braised in butter.

Roast Shoulder of Lamb

Preparation time: 30 minutes
Cooking time: 16 minutes
Difficulty: ★★

Serves 4

1 shoulder of lamb, about 3⅓ lb/1½ kg
40 carrots with greens
1 large potato

10½ oz/300 g flat-leaf parsley
3 tbsp/30 g coriander
3 tbsp/30 g basil
3 tbsp/30 g chervil
5 tbsp/70 g butter
1¼ cups/300 ml lamb stock
2 tbsp honey
olive oil
salt and pepper

Potatoes cut into rose shapes are a true family tradition in the French department of Savoie, where they are often served with coffee.

In the 19th century, about 100 years after their introduction into Central Europe, these potatoes fried in pork fat were a luxury item at festive dinners, where even their skins were greatly prized. These "potato roses" not only add a Savoyard note to this dish but form a very original garnish.

Lamb is considered a symbol of purity, and for centuries it has been associated with a series of mystical traditions; in the three great monotheistic religions – Judaism,

Christianity and Islam – it is traditionally part of the most important religious feasts of each year.

Young lamb is best suited for this. The flesh should be firm and glossy, yet feel tender. The shoulder is a very tender joint with a small amount of fat. It is easy to prepare, and better value than the leg or rib. Make sure that that it has some time to rest after cooking, before it is carved.

To achieve a balance between the various flavors, it is best to use fresh herbs, which have a fuller flavor, and add cayenne pepper if you want to give a Mediterranean flavor to your dish.

1. Place the shoulder of lamb on your work surface and trim off the superfluous fat. Remove the stalks from the herbs, wash them, and cook for 5 minutes in boiling salted water. Drain well, purée and pass through a fine sieve. Peel the carrots, leaving 1 in/2 cm of the greens attached, cook for 5–6 minutes in salted water, and refresh in ice cold water.

2. Reduce the lamb stock, stir in butter and add the herb purée, then season and keep warm. Heat some olive oil in a pan. Season the lamb with salt and pepper, brown, then roast for 16 minutes in a 390 °F/200 °C oven, turning it after the first 8 minutes. Set aside to rest on a rack covered with aluminum foil.

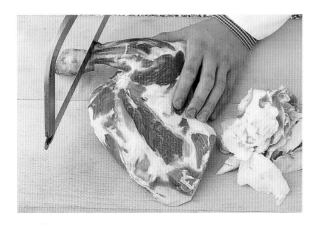

with Potato Roses

3. Put 2 tbsp of honey in a pan and heat until golden brown. Add the carrots and some butter and season. Place the shoulder of lamb in the center of the serving dish with the carrots at the side. Pour some of the herb sauce on top and serve the rest in a sauce-boat.

4. Peel a large potato, and cut into a long, thin strip. Roll up this strip into a rose shape. Plunge into oil heated to 354 °F/179 °C. Remove when browned and drain on paper towels to remove the excess oil; season with salt and serve with the lamb.

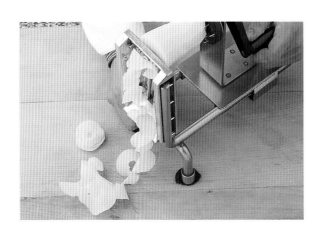

Portuguese

Preparation time: *1 hour*
Cooking time: *50 minutes*
Difficulty: ✭✭

Serves 4

1 kid, about 6½ lb/3 kg
8 small onions
24 small potatoes
2 garlic cloves
olive oil
salt and pepper

To pour on:
3½ tbsp/50 ml vinho verde (Portuguese white wine)
¾ cup/200 ml water

For the paprika paste:
2 garlic cloves
1 tsp ground sweet paprika
6½ tbsp/100 ml brandy or cognac
6½ tbsp/100 ml olive oil
1 bay leaf
parsley

For the chopped spinach:
1 generous lb/500 g spinach
3 garlic cloves
1 tsp flour
3½ tbsp/50 ml olive oil
vinegar

In the flat regions of Portugal, lamb is the meat of choice, while in the mountainous areas of the North, it is kid. In the villages of the Sao Jao Porto area, the Portuguese white wine Vinho Verde is served with roast kid. But the most distinguished type of preparation is found in the university city of Coimbra, where the shanks are used in the famous dish "chanfana de cabro." If the characteristic flavor of kid is too strong for you, you can replace it with a milk-fed lamb.

Roast the meat very slowly, at a moderate heat. Stay near the oven for the whole time and – most important – do not forget to "give the dish a chill" about every 15 minutes.

(This is an expression used in northern Portugal, which refers to the rush of air caused every time you open the oven door to baste the meat.)

This Portuguese-style kid, with a crisp golden-brown skin, has a very special flavor, which comes from the paprika and brandy mixture with which you have marinated the meat.

The dish can be served with a medley of small spring vegetables, as one does with navarin of lamb, instead of the garlicky spinach recommended here by our chef.

1. Remove sinews and fat from the kid, quarter it and cut out the leg, loin, saddle and shoulder.

2. Chop the garlic finely, mix with the paprika, brandy and olive oil, add parsley and bay leaf, and stir until creamy. Prepare the potatoes and onions for the accompaniment. Peel them and place in a baking pan. Add chopped garlic, olive oil, salt and pepper. Bake in a 350 °F/ 180 °C oven for 20 minutes.

Roast Kid

3. Spread the paprika mixture over the meat and refrigerate for about 1 hour. Roast the kid in a 320 °F/160 °C oven. Every 15 minutes, baste with a mixture of white wine and water. Remove from oven, deglaze with some water, and strain.

4. Cook the spinach in bubbling salted water, refresh, strain and chop. Shortly before serving, braise the garlic in olive oil and add the chopped spinach. Dust with the flour, stir, add a little vinegar and serve hot. On each plate arrange one slice of each cut of the meat, add the vegetables and pour sauce on top.

Crèpinette of Venison

Preparation time: *2 hours*
Cooking time: *30 minutes*
Difficulty: ★★

Serves 4

3½ oz/100 g venison
1 oz/30 g goose liver
¾ oz/20 g each bacon, morels, shiitake
mushrooms and chanterelles
2½ tbsp/40 ml cream
2 tsp/10 ml port
thyme, rosemary, salt and pepper

For the red cabbage:
1 red cabbage
2 apples (such as Golden Delicious)
2 shallots, 1 chile

4 tsp/20 g butter
2 cloves
2 cups/500 ml red wine
4 juniper berries
sugar, salt, white peppercorns

For the gingerbread sauce:
1¾ oz/50 g gingerbread
2 cups/500 ml venison stock
1 cup/250 ml red wine
2½ tbsp/40 ml port
6 juniper berries, thyme

For the crèpinettes:
4 medallions of venison, about 3½ oz/100 g
each
pork caul
peanut oil. salt and pepper

For the spinach spätzle:
3½ oz/100 g young spinach
⅓ cup/160 g flour
3 eggs
1 tbsp water, salt

For a successful sauce, use unsweetened or only slightly sweetened gingerbread.

Venison takes center stage in this recipe; during the hunting season it is almost always to be found on restaurant menus. The flesh of a young deer should be cooked when quite fresh; it does not need to be hung and certainly not to be marinated. Take a saddle of venison from which you cut out the tenderloins. With the skin, fat, cream and spicy mushrooms you can prepare a firm, tasty stuffing that is wrapped up in pork caul (if you can't obtain this, brush the meat with oil and baste). You can replace the venison with rabbit or young pigeon, if you prefer.

"Spätzle" can be made in various colors. For this recipe they are colored green with spinach.

1. Chop the mushrooms finely, dice the liver and brown together. Dice the venison and bacon, season and purée in a food processor. Add the liver, port, juniper berries, rosemary, thyme, and cream. Brown the venison tenderloins on both sides and immediately transfer to a cool place. Place a medallion of venison on each piece of caul, spread stuffing on top to a thickness of ¾ in/2 cm, and roll up.

2. For the gingerbread sauce, mix the venison stock, port, red wine, thyme, juniper berries and the crushed gingerbread. Reduce by half. Strain. Return to the heat and reduce to a syrupy consistency. Blanch the large leaves of red cabbage and put aside for the roulade.

with Gingerbread Sauce

3. Cut the cabbage heart into thin strips. Peel the apples, cut into thin slices and mix with the cloves, chile, juniper berries, wine and cabbage. Marinate for 48 hours. Braise the shallots in butter, add the marinated red cabbage and 1 tbsp of sugar, season with salt, cover and braise in the oven for 25–30 minutes. Roll up in the cabbage leaves.

4. Cook the spinach in salted water, refresh and squeeze out excess liquid. Purée, and add the flour, eggs, and 1 tbsp water. Knead the mixture thoroughly in a bowl. Form into "spätzle" and poach in plenty of boiling salted water. Refresh and reheat in the pan with some butter. Arrange on the plates with the venison and sauce.

Catalan Cockerel with

Preparation time: 1 hour 15 minutes
Cooking time: 1 hour 10 minutes
Difficulty: ★★

Serves 4

1 cockerel with comb
8 fresh sea-cucumbers
4 shrimp heads
8 whole shrimp
2 sea urchins
1 large potato
½ tbsp red bell pepper, roasted, peeled, and diced
6½ tbsp/100 ml white wine
1 cup/250 ml chicken stock

3½ tbsp/50 ml heavy cream
olive oil
1 tomato

For the braised vegetables and herbs:
1 tomato
1 onion
1 leek
1 celery rib
1 garlic clove
bay leaf, thyme
pinch of saffron threads

Recommended accompaniment:
4½ oz/120 g fresh pasta

This new example of an eternal triangle combines poultry, shellfish and a very unusual type of seafood. This is a sea cucumber, an echinoderm from the depths of the sea, almost cylindrical in shape. It is native to all the oceans, but is eaten mainly in Asia and the Pacific area, where it is often sold dried. It should be browned very briskly with garlic to prevent its juices from escaping.

No praise can be too high for Catalan poultry. Our chef uses the sturdy prizewinning cockerels from Prat, near Barcelona. The color and texture of the cockscomb gives

the dish an unusual twist. A Chinatown market can supply you with a locally raised equivalent.

The shrimp are served in Catalan style, that is, the tails peeled but complete with their heads.

The preparation times for the ingredients are all different, and you must be very careful to observe them: 1 hour for the cockerel, but only one minute for the shrimp. Finally, the sea urchins' strong flavor of iodine will enrich this delicious poultry dish with a whiff of the sea.

1. Cut the cockerel into 8–10 parts. Cut the cockscomb into 4 pieces. Brown the vegetables and herbs in a braising pan big enough to hold the cockerel as well. Remove the vegetables and set aside.

2. Brown the cockerel pieces in olive oil, then put the vegetables and cockscomb back in the pan with the saffron.

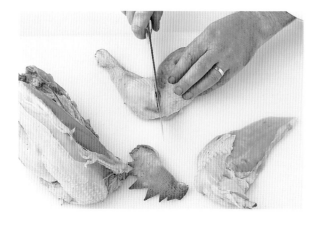

Sea Cucumber and Shrimp

3. Deglaze with white wine and reduce by half. Add the stock, the tomato and the shrimp heads. Cover and simmer for about 1 hour.

4. Brown the sea cucumbers 5 minutes before serving. At the last minute, add the whole shrimp (with tails peeled), the sea urchins and the chopped red pepper. For the sauce, reduce the stock, strain, and add salt, white pepper and heavy cream. Serve with fresh pasta.

Guinea Fowl with

Preparation time: 2 hours
Cooking time: 15 minutes
Difficulty: ★★

Serves 4

1 guinea fowl
4 small turnips with greens
1 shallot
1 pork caul
2 slices white bread, soaked in milk
2 eggs
10 tbsp/150 g butter

1 tbsp/15 ml oil
salt and pepper

For the finely diced vegetables:
3 carrots
1 fennel bulb
3 celery ribs

For the brown stock:
carcass of the guinea fowl
diced carrots, onions, and celery
salt and pepper

The French name for the guinea fowl is *pintade*, the painted one, because of its speckled plumage. Its delicate flesh can be prepared in many different ways. A guinea fowl can be recognized from quite a long distance away because of its very loud screeching.

Our chef raves about the tiny spring vegetables from his native Nantes region. He especially recommends the tur-

nips, which should be used in this recipe along with their greens. As with many other baby vegetables, the turnips only need to be scrubbed, not peeled.

If you use the pork caul, don't forget to soak it before use, to remove all impurities. Then the guinea fowl fillets can be wrapped in it and browned in the pan, turning frequently.

1. Bone the guinea fowl. For the stuffing, finely chop the thigh meat and the white bread which has been soaked in milk. Finely chop the carrots, fennel and 1 celery rib. Braise these vegetables in butter with the chopped shallot, season with salt and pepper. Add the eggs and mix.

2. Make a brown stock with the guinea fowl carcass, 1 carrot, 1 celery rib and 1 finely diced onion. When it is ready, strain and reduce. Season with salt and pepper. Cut each guinea fowl breast into 16 thin scaloppini; gently pound them flat.

Spring Vegetables

3. With a pastry bag, pipe 1 tsp of stuffing onto each guinea fowl scaloppini and wrap in a piece of the softened pork caul, making small parcels.

4. Cut the remaining celery rib into 32 small sticks. Boil in salted water and set aside. Steam the turnips. Brown the stuffed guinea fowl parcels in a little oil and butter, turning frequently. Put some sauce on each plate, place a turnip in the center, drizzling some melted butter on top to make it shine. Arrange guinea fowl parcels and celery sticks alternately in a circle around the turnip.

Salad of Venison with

Preparation time: 45 minutes
Cooking time: 50 minutes
Difficulty: ★★

Serves 4

1¾ lb/800 g loin of venison
2 kohlrabi (or turnips)
3½ tbsp/50 g butter
1 tbsp/20 ml balsamic vinegar
1 tbsp/20 ml hazelnut oil
7 tbsp/50 g hazelnuts, shelled
¾ cup/75 g seasonal salad greens
1 bunch of thyme
parsley
salt and freshly ground pepper

To poach the truffle:
1 truffle (1¾ oz/50 g)
3½ tbsp/50 ml red wine
3½ tbsp/50 ml chicken stock

For the game stock:
3½ oz/100 g carrots and celery
2 shallots
¾ oz/20 g mushrooms
6 juniper berries, chopped
6 black peppercorns
½ bay leaf
6½ tbsp/100 ml robust red wine
¾ cup/200 ml Madeira
¾ cup/200 ml cognac
6½ tbsp/100 ml reduced game stock

Little distinction is made in the kitchen between the red deer and the roe deer, although they are easily distinguished when seen in the wild. The roe deer is generally considered the most appealing of forest animals. Their flavor is best at 10–12 months old. In Europe, they are usually eaten during the hunting season, from September to December.

Horst Petermann, who lives near the Black Forest, benefits from the Swiss privilege of hunting during the summer too. The flesh of the young roe deer, which is a beautiful dark red in color, can be marinated for a day or two in crushed juniper berries and some olive oil.

This makes it more tender and gives it a slightly peppery note.

The accompaniment of truffle and kohlrabi has a powerful flavor, which superbly complements the taste of game. Take a fresh, firm truffle, which can be peeled if you prefer, but should not be washed. Kohlrabi is very popular in Eastern Europe, and may have a green or purplish skin. You can use turnips instead if you like.

If you want to try this recipe outside of the deer-hunting season, our chef recommends using a bird such as squab or guinea fowl.

1 Bone and trim the venison, and refrigerate until ½ hour before needed. Chop up the bones for the stock.

2. For the game stock, brown the bones and trimmings in a pan and add the finely chopped vegetables and the mushrooms. Flambé with cognac, deglaze with Madeira and wine; add the herbs and spices and the game stock. Simmer for 45 minutes over low heat; strain and carefully remove the fat.

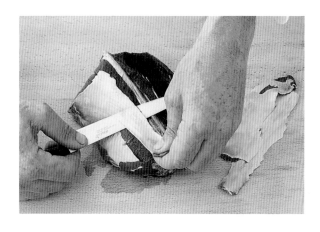

Truffles and Kohlrabi

3. Brown the venison in butter for 5 minutes; it should remain underdone. Keep warm. Poach the truffle in stock and red wine, and cut into thin strips. Peel the kohlrabi and cook in salted water, leaving them crisp, and then cut into thin strips.

4. For the vinaigrette, put the truffle juice in the pan in which the venison fillets were browned. Reduce by half; add the hazelnut oil and the vinegar. Put the truffle and kohlrabi strips in a salad bowl. Chop the hazelnuts, brown in butter and place on top, covering with the vinaigrette. Garnish the venison with thyme and parsley and serve with the salad.

Loin of Rabbit with

Preparation time: 1 hour
Cooking time: 1 hour
Difficulty: ★★

Serves 4

2 saddles of rabbit
1 cup/250 g Puy lentils
3 large carrots
1 leek, white part only
2 shallots
1 bouquet garni
6 tbsp/90 g butter

2 tbsp cream
flat-leaf parsley
salt and freshly ground pepper

For the sauce:
12 oz/350 g rabbit bones
1 onion
1 carrot
1 garlic clove
1 tbsp tomato paste
1¼ cups/300 ml white wine
1¼ cups/300 ml water
oil

Rabbit has the reputation of being dry, but in fact it can be nice and juicy, as long as it is browned gently in plenty of butter, and turned from time to time.

Apart from the preparation of the rabbit you should also take great care with the sauce. It must be well reduced to be successful. It should have a robust taste – if it is too bland, add some herbs to enhance the flavor.

The green Puy lentil is one of the best types of lentil, grown in the volcanic region of Velay in France, and rich in iron and vitamins. In this recipe, the lentils should not be cooked to the *al dente* stage, but until they have opened and become quite soft. They will form a fine contrast to the other vegetables, the carrots and leek, which should remain crisp and crunchy.

1. Cut the white part of the leek into ½ in/1 cm wide strips. Cook in salted water, refresh and drain. Peel the carrots, dice one and cut the other into balls, and boil in salted water. Chop the shallots finely.

2. Remove any fat and sinews from the rabbit saddles and cut the meat into chunks. For the sauce, cut up the bones and the forelegs of the rabbits. Brown in oil. Finely chop the onion and carrots, and add the garlic. Brown while stirring continuously; pour off the fat and return to the heat. Deglaze with white wine and add water and the tomato paste.

Lentils and Carrots

3. Simmer for 30 minutes over low heat. Braise the chopped shallots, then add the carrots, the cooked lentils, 2 tbsp cream, 2 tbsp rabbit stock, and 2 tbsp/30 g of butter. Simmer very lightly until thickened, and season to taste.

4. Season the rabbit pieces and fry lightly in butter, turning continually so that they do not become brown; cook for 6 minutes over a low heat. Sauté the carrot balls and the leek strips in butter. Allow the rest of the rabbit stock to boil for 1 minute over high heat, then whisk in 8 tsp/40 g of butter. Season to taste and garnish with parsley.

Pork Tenderloin with Boulangère

Preparation time: 1 hour 30 minutes
Cooking time: 1 hour
Difficulty: ★★

Serves 4

1 pork tenderloin, about 1¼ lb/600 g
1⅓ oz/40 g smoked bacon
6½ tbsp/100 g brown pork stock
tomatoes
1⅓ oz/40 g lemon zest, chopped
garlic, sage
flat-leaf parsley
olive oil
salt and pepper

For the garnish:
6 very small artichokes
1 generous lb/500 g potatoes
1 lemon
2 tbsp tomato paste
5¼ oz/150 g small onions
3½ tbsp/50 g butter
1 cup/250 ml white chicken stock
olive oil
garlic
bouquet garni
saffron
parsley
salt and pepper

This recipe almost amounts to a family reunion, as pork, potatoes, and sage often meet in the same recipe.

The pork in this recipe could be replaced by a veal tenderloin. The dish acquires its full flavor from the addition of chicken stock with herbs and spices. Those suggested here – garlic, saffron and a bouquet garni – can be replaced by others if you desire.

The combination of meat, potatoes, tomatoes and artichokes is a particularly attractive one, and the strong flavor of Provençal sage goes superbly with pork and veal.

In this recipe Stephane Raimbault uses the Provençal artichokes known as *poivrade*, which are frequently eaten raw. In Provence, artichokes are also used as a kind of barometer. They are hung on a door and one can tell from the opening and closing of the leaves whether there will be sunshine or rain.

1. Finely chop the onions and braise in butter. Finely chop the potatoes and mix with the onions. Place in an ovenproof dish rubbed with garlic. The layer of potato and onion should be ¾ in/1½ cm thick. Cover with the chicken stock in which garlic, a bouquet garni and saffron have previously been infused. Bake in a 390 °F/220 °C oven. Sprinkle with chopped parsley before serving.

2. Prepare the artichokes and cook in salted water with some lemon juice. Slice and brown in olive oil and butter, then add with the tomato paste.

Potatoes and Artichokes

3. Remove fat and sinews from the pork and truss. Season and brown with the bacon, garlic, herbs and the peeled, seeded and finely diced tomatoes. When cooked, keep warm for 10 minutes. Meanwhile, deglaze the pan with the pork stock, strain and add the chopped lemon peel, the chopped sage, and the olive oil.

4. Place a metal ring in the center of the plate, and layer inside it first some artichokes, then overlapping pork slices, and finally the boulangère potatoes, from which you have cut a circle of the same size with a similar ring. Pour the sauce around and serve.

Preparation time: 20 minutes
Cooking time: 1 hour 30 minutes
Difficulty: ✭

Serves 4

3⅓ lb/1½ kg lamb (shoulder or neck)
8 oz/225 g potatoes

8 oz/225 g carrots
8 oz/225 g leeks
8 oz/225 g small onions
2 sprigs of thyme
1 bunch of fresh parsley
1 cup/250 ml heavy cream
1 tsp/5 g butter
salt and pepper

Lamb is now used for this traditional Irish dish, which was formerly based on mutton. It used to be a meal for poor people; it was prepared in one big pot and combined with various vegetables according to the taste and pocket of the housewife.

The best meat comes from lambs that are more than 5 months old and that already have a distinctive taste. The shoulder and neck, right next to the bone, have a particularly good flavor and can stand long cooking.

Potatoes grow successfully in both quality and quantity in Irish soil. Potatoes were grown there for the first time as early as the 16th century, from New World seedlings plundered from captured Spanish ships, and it is now a staple.

The French sometimes describe the leek as "poor man's asparagus." It has, however, made itself welcome in the kitchens of great chefs, and lends its subtle taste to this stew, just right for serving on cold winter evenings.

1. Prepare the lamb and cut into large cubes, discarding the thin layer of fat around the meat. Put the meat in a large pan with water and a little salt. Bring to a boil, skim off the scum and fat from the surface, and simmer for 30 minutes.

2. Peel the potatoes and cut into large pieces. Put half of them in the pan and simmer for another 30 minutes, then stir vigorously so that the potatoes disintegrate.

Stew

3. Add the rest of the potatoes and the other vegetables, and simmer for a further 30 minutes, until the meat and potatoes are thoroughly cooked.

4. Heat the heavy cream with the butter, and add, with the chopped parsley and thyme. Heat briefly and serve.

Tenderloin of Beef with

Preparation time: 30 minutes
Cooking time: 10 minutes
Difficulty: ★★

Serves 4

4 beef tenderloin steaks, about 6 oz/170 g each
8 slices marrow bone slices (1½ in/3 cm long,
2¾ in/6 cm in diameter)
3½ tbsp/50 g butter
3½ tbsp/50 ml oil
allspice

For the sauce:
3 cups/750 ml red wine
1 carrot
1 onion
4 shallots
3½ tbsp/50 g flour
⅓ cup/80 g butter
1 bay leaf

1 sprig of thyme
pepper

For the potato rosettes:
7 oz/200 g potatoes
6½ tbsp/100 g melted butter
salt

For the potato purée with truffles:
7 oz/200 g potatoes
4½ tbsp/70 ml cream
3½ tbsp/50 g butter
2 tbsp/30 ml milk
½ oz/10 g truffle
3½ tbsp/50 g butter for the sauce
salt and pepper

The flesh of Charolais cattle is irresistible; it is one of the best meats in the world. Our chef, who comes from the Ardèche region, adores it and has created a suitable recipe, which also includes bone marrow. Charolais cattle are known for their huge size. The tenderloins from these animals can weigh up to 8¾ lb/4 kg. Here, the seasoned steaks are pan-fried, initially over high heat, then over low heat. The meat must be browned evenly on all sides and repeatedly basted with its own juices during cooking.

Allspice is a dried, red-brown berry that comes mainly from Jamaica. For the sauce, use a red wine rich in tannin. With this feast of flavors, you might be worried that the delicate taste of the bone-marrow will be overwhelmed. In fact its chief role in this recipe is to provide a little variation in texture.

1. Braise the finely chopped onion, carrot, and shallots in butter. Add thyme, bay leaf, and pepper, dust with flour, allow to cook for 2 minutes and add the red wine. Simmer, gradually reducing to ¾ cup/200 ml.

2. Wash and peel all the potatoes (14 oz/400 g altogether). Boil half of them and prepare a purèe with the cream, butter, milk, and finely chopped truffles. Cut the remaining potatoes into thin slices.

Allspice and Bone-marrow

3. For the potato rosettes, arrange the raw potato slices in a buttered nonstick pan in a rosette shape, and brown in melted butter. Season the steaks with salt and allspice, and cook in butter and oil.

4. Soak 4 of the marrow-bone slices in cool water and remove the marrow from each. Gently cook in butter. Poach the remaining pieces of marrow bone. Place the steaks on the marrow bones, and top with the potato rosettes and pieces of marrow. Serve with the potato purée. Finally, pour on the sauce. Garnish with thyme and bay leaves.

Saddle of Rabbi

Preparation time: 15 minutes
Cooking time: 20 minutes
Difficulty: ★

Serves 4

4 saddles of rabbit, with kidneys
1 generous lb/500 g rhubarb

20 scallions
10 tbsp/150 g butter
6½ tbsp/100 ml stock made from the rabbit bones and trimmings
sherry vinegar
oil
confectioners' sugar
salt and pepper

The rabbits for this recipe should weigh about 3⅓ lb/1.5 kg; one that is too young will not have developed enough flavor, even if its flesh is firm and white.

The rhubarb compote may perhaps confuse people used to seeing rhubarb only in desserts. It is true that the red stalks of this plant are used mostly for desserts, but they have been used in medicine for their astringent, stimulating and laxative effects. Also, Joël Roy believes that rhubarb goes extremely well with white fish (such as pike and turbot), and tender, delicate meats. The stems should be firm and crisp and not too fibrous; yielding a nice smooth compote with a subtle flavor.

This dish is best prepared in spring, when the rhubarb is still young.

1. Bone the saddles of rabbit, each yielding 2 loins and 2 tenderloins. Make a stock with the bones and trimmings.

2. Peel the rhubarb and cut in pieces. Peel the scallions and cook for 5 minutes in a mixture of butter, salt and a little water.

with Rhubarb

3. Braise the rhubarb with a nice piece of butter, some confectioners' sugar and salt, until it is soft. Crush with a fork.

4. Season the rabbit with salt and pepper and brown the loins for 5 minutes in butter and oil. Add the tenderloins, cook for 2 minutes, then add the kidneys and cook for 1 minute more. Reduce the rabbit stock and stir in butter. Add a few dashes of sherry vinegar before serving.

Preparation time: 30 minutes
Cooking time: 50 minutes
Difficulty: ★★★

Serves 4

4 young partridges
10½ oz/300 g turnips
8 shallots
1 pork caul (see note on page 32)
5 tsp/25 g butter
6½ tbsp/100 ml olive oil
parsley

For the game butter:
heart and liver of partridge
1 shallot, chopped

butter
curry powder
salt and pepper

For the marinade:
1 cup/250 ml white wine
4 cups/1 l olive oil
2 cups/500 ml sherry vinegar
1 cup/250 ml water
2 tsp/10 g salt
1½ tsp/5 g peppercorns

For the sauce:
the partridge carcasses, chopped
2½ oz/75 g leek
3 tbsp/25 g chopped parsley
1 onion
3½ oz/100 g turnips
4 cups/1 l water or chicken stock
1 cup/250 ml white wine
salt and pepper

As soon as the hunting season begins, the partridge, and particularly the red variety, becomes a favorite meal for Spaniards. Young partridge can be found from the beginning of the hunting season up to 11 November.

Despite his Catalonian origins, Santi Santamaria prefers the Scottish partridge, which has a distinctive gamy taste (they are imported to the United States). This recipe is inspired by a very old traditional method of preparation, the Spanish marinade called *escabèche*. A special taste is given to the partridge by a new element, turnips. Buy very hard, absolutely fresh and unblemished turnips.

Santamaria is actually not a lover of pork caul and uses it only when absolutely necessary. It contains a great deal of fat, which affects the other ingredients.

1. Prepare the partridges; remove the breasts (both sides in 1 piece) and legs, bone the legs. For the game butter, soak the livers and hearts in water overnight. Drain, dry and trim; brown in a small saucepan with the chopped shallot. Strain and mix with the butter. Finally, season with curry powder, salt and pepper.

2. Take the ingredients for the marinade, the unpeeled shallots, the turnips and the partridge legs and simmer them for 40 minutes over low heat. Drain well. Braise the turnips for a little longer, then keep warm. For the sauce, crush the carcasses and brown them in oil with the onion, some parsley, 2½ oz/75 g of leek and 3½ oz/100 g of turnips. Deglaze with wine and water or chicken stock, season with salt and pepper and simmer over low heat.

"en Escabèche"

3. Season the inside of the breasts, and spread with the game butter, keeping some of the butter for the sauce. Strain the sauce. Reduce by half and thicken with the rest of the game butter, then strain again.

4. Fold up the pieces of breast and wrap in the pork caul, if used. Spread some butter over it and cook in a 375 °F/190 °C oven for 7 minutes. Season the braised legs with salt and pepper and fry to a golden brown. Remove the pork caul and place the pieces of partridge in the center of each plate. Add the marinated shallots and browned turnips. Pour the sauce on top and serve garnished with parsley.

Chicken and Crab

Preparation time: 15 minutes
Cooking time: 30 minutes
Difficulty: ★★

Serves 4

2 chicken breasts
16 crayfish
5½ oz/150 g pistachio nuts

½ cup/100 g rice
1 egg
¾ cup/200 ml crème fraîche
1 onion
6½ tbsp/100 g butter
6½ tbsp/100 ml ouzo
6½ tbsp/100 ml white wine
bouquet garni
salt and pepper

The island of Aegina, which lies opposite the harbor of Athens, was an important trading center from the 8th to the 5th centuries, B.C., and it is still famous for its pistachios. Many Greek desserts, cakes, stuffings and soups are garnished with pistachio nuts. Pistachios are very nutritious, but fragile to cook with, and should be handled with care. They will make this dish crisper, more colorful and more aromatic.

In our recipe you can put chopped pistachios into the crayfish stock, but make sure that it has stopped boiling. Add them only towards the end and let them infuse for a short time before you strain the stock.

For this recipe you should choose a chicken with tender flesh and not cook it for too long, lest the breasts become tough.

The typically Greek ouzo sauce has a very refreshing effect. Instead of ouzo, you can use aniseed to flavor the sauce. The chicken can be replaced by rabbit, and if desired you can use almonds instead of pistachios.

1. Butterfly the chicken breasts, carefully press them flat, and save the "tenders" and trimmings for the stuffing. Season with salt and pepper, and marinate for 10 minutes in ouzo. Chop the pistachios and set some of them aside.

2. Purée the chicken trimmings in a food processor; add the egg, 6½ tbsp/100 ml crème fraîche and salt and pepper. Divide this paste among the chicken breasts. Wash the crayfish. Prepare a fumet from 8 of the heads, all of the shells and the finely chopped onions.

with Pistachio Sauce

3. Lay a crayfish tail on each chicken breast, and sprinkle with an even layer of chopped pistachios. Roll up, wrap in aluminum foil and poach for 15–20 minutes. Meanwhile, cook the rice and keep it warm.

4. Add the remaining pistachios to the crayfish fumet. Reduce, add crème fraîche, reduce again, add the ouzo, and strain. Brown the remaining crayfish in butter and deglaze with the wine. Place a few slices of stuffed chicken breast on each plate and pour fumet over them. Serve a cone of rice and herbs on each plate.

Pork Tenderloin with Graviera

Preparation time: 45 minutes
Cooking time: 40 minutes
Difficulty: ★★

Serves 4

1¾ lb/800 g pork tenderloin
7 oz/200 g Greek graviera cheese
1 cup/100 g walnuts
⅔ cup/80 g raisins
30 small shallots
8 potatoes
6½ tbsp/100 ml white Samos wine
¼ cup/50 ml olive oil
cinnamon

For the sauce:
2¼ lb/1 kg pork bones
1–2 medium carrots
1 small leek
1 celery rib
1 onion
1 tsp tomato paste
⅔ cup/150 ml red wine
¾ cup/200 ml sweet Samos wine
6½ tsp/100 ml olive oil
bouquet garni
chervil leaves
salt and pepper

The island of Samos is one of the Greek island group in the Aegean called the Sporades. Muscat wine from Samos has been popular in Europe for centuries, and it turns up in this example of modern Greek cuisine, in which Nikolaos Sarantos combines it with pork tenderloin.

The sweetness of the wine balances the tartness of the other ingredients of the sauce. Leave a little fat on the pork tenderloin; when you brown it, it will form a little crust which will become crisper in the oven and will taste delicious.

The combination of Samos wine and pork is rounded off by the graviera, a hard cheese with a fruity taste, usually enjoyed with olives, golden raisins, or currants. It is made from a mixture of sheep's and cows' milk. Its structure is similar to that of Parmesan, and it is easily recognized by its rind. For this recipe it is melted in wine and mixed with dried fruits; this transforms it into an exquisite accompaniment and an exciting new taste. But be careful when browning the stuffed tenderloins not to let the melted cheese escape: tie the meat carefully to prevent this.

1. Melt the cheese in the wine with the raisins and walnuts. Cool and form into a roll, then refrigerate. Butterfly the tenderloin lengthwise, season, sprinkle with a little Samos wine, scatter chopped walnuts and raisins on it, and lay a slice of the cheese mixture on top.

2. Fold and tie up the tenderloin, and brown briskly in a pan with some olive oil. Deglaze with Samos wine and roast for 15 minutes in a 400 °F/200 °C oven. For the sauce, braise the bones with the finely chopped vegetables, deglaze with the red wine, add water and the bouquet garni, and reduce. Strain, add the Samos wine, and simmer for 5–6 minutes.

...and Samos Wine Sauce

3. Braise shallots in oil, pour on some sauce, add cinnamon, and reduce for 20 minutes over a low heat. Boil the potatoes in salted water. Brown them in oil and then add some sauce.

4. Slice the tenderloins. Arrange on each plate with some sauce, some of the braised shallots, garnished with chervil, and some potatoes.

Loin of Venison with

Preparation time: 3 hours
Cooking time: 1 hour 30 minutes
Difficulty: ★★★

Serves 4

2 generous lb/1 kg loin of venison
3½ tbsp/50 g butter
½ apple 10 cranberries

For the black pepper sauce:
venison bones
8¾ oz/250 g mirepoix of vegetables
3½ tbsp/50 ml chicken stock
2 cups/500 ml red Burgundy wine, such as
Crozes Hermitage, 4 tsp/20 g butter
3½ tbsp/50 ml olive oil, rosemary
thyme, black pepper, salt

For the white pepper sauce:
1 tbsp/10 g white pepper, ground
3½ tbsp/50 ml chicken stock
some white wine

4 tsp/20 ml Noilly Prat dry vermouth
⅓ cup/80 ml crème fraîche
2½ tbsp/40 ml heavy cream
1 bay leaf, 1 garlic clove
2 onions, 4 tsp/20 g butter
1 small sprig of thyme, salt

For the celery purée:
1 celeriac, 4 celery ribs
6½ tbsp/100 ml cream
chives, 3½ tbsp/50 g butter, salt

For the potato noodles:
14 oz/400 g potatoes
2 egg yolks, salt, nutmeg
2 tbsp/40 g cornstarch, bread crumbs
chives, 3½ tbsp/50 g butter

Many Germans have made the deer into a sort of cult, whether they themselves go hunting or not. Thus there are many methods of preparation for this exquisite meat. Fritz Schilling himself does not hunt, but he loves venison, of which there is an abundant supply in the Black Forest.

Cook this fine red meat with care, as it must be cooked only briefly over low heat – too much heat and too long a cooking period would make the meat tough. As pepper goes well with venison, Fritz Schilling has created not one, but two sauces – one using black and one using white pepper. They will surely be a success with your guests.

There are various possibilities in the choice of the cuts of meat. Instead of loin, you could use rib, shoulder or leg with equal success. Wild boar or hare can also be prepared in the same way.

1. Bone the loin. For the black pepper sauce, crush the bones, brown with a mirepoix of vegetables, deglaze with wine, reduce, add chicken stock, bring to a boil, strain, whisk in butter, and season to taste. For the white pepper sauce: braise onions with white pepper, add white wine, chicken stock, vermouth and spices. Add crème fraîche and heavy cream, purée in a blender, strain and season to taste.

2. For the celery purée: peel the celery, and cut into 1½ in/3 cm pieces. Blanch in salted water. Make a purée of the celeriac. Stuff the celery with this, and tie 2 pieces together with a chive. Just before serving, reheat in butter. Brown the venison tenderloins in butter for 3 minutes until cooked to rare.

Two Pepper Sauces

3. Potato noodles: boil the potatoes in their skins, peel, rice and stir in egg yolk and cornstarch; season with nutmeg and salt. Roll into thick noodles and cook in salted water. Drain. Toast the bread crumbs briefly in butter, add the noodles and toss them in the bread crumbs.

4. Poach the apple and garnish with cranberries. Pour white pepper sauce on each plate, and pour black pepper sauce around it to form a border. Place 2 slices of venison in the middle, and arrange 1 piece of apple, 1 stuffed piece of celery and 3 potato noodles on each plate.

Mixed Casserole

Preparation time: 30 minutes
Cooking time: 1 hour 45 minutes
Difficulty: ★★★

Serves 4

1 generous lb/500 g rib of pork
1 fresh knuckle
8¾ lb/250 g shoulder of pork
1 generous lb/500 g boneless belly of pork
½ pig's cheek
3½ tbsp/75 g acacia honey
3½ oz/100 g onions

8¾ oz/250 g potatoes
3½ oz/100 g carrots
3½ oz/100 g baby onions
1½ cups/350 ml red wine
¾ cup/200 ml sherry vinegar
2 cups/500 ml peanut oil
1¼ cup/300 ml veal stock
1 tbsp/5 g each oregano, ground thyme, savory, sage, ground coriander and ground nutmeg
½ bunch of chives
salt and pepper

Throughout France, the slaughtering of a pig always used to be carried out in combination with festivals and festive meals. Christmas above all offered an opportunity to eat plentifully of those parts of the pig that could not easily be preserved, and that were therefore enjoyed in the form of pies, blood sausages, and other sausages. This custom is still not totally obsolete, and butchers who know how to make use of practically every part of the pig are still much sought after.

Here Jean & Jean-Yves Schillinger introduce a very nutritious dish that can be enjoyed on long winter evenings. You can tell from the firmness and color of the flesh whether it is fresh and of good quality. Be careful to observe the various cooking times for the individual cuts, and put them into the pan one after the other – first the shoulder, then the other pieces 10 minutes later. You can use a needle to see whether the meat is cooked – you should feel only a slight resistance when inserting the needle. Don't forget to let the meat rest for a little while before serving. With this rustic dish you should serve a suitable accompaniment, such as sautéed potatoes.

1. Trim excess fat from all the meat, and brown well in peanut oil. Take the meat out of the pan, pour off the fat and braise the finely chopped vegetables with all the herbs and spices.

2. Add the acacia honey and heat for 2 minutes, then deglaze with sherry vinegar. Return the meat to the pan and add veal stock, red wine and water to cover. Bring to a boil, then put in the oven at 400 °F/200 °C for 1 hour 45 minutes, uncovered.

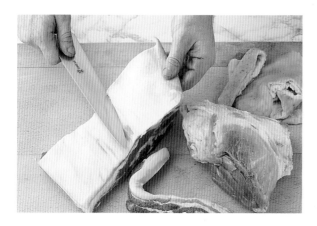

3. Remove all the meat and reduce the stock to the desired consistency. Season to taste. When it has cooled, cut the meat into chunks of equal thickness. Reheat in the sauce before serving.

4. Lightly brown the pearl onions, trim the potatoes to an attractive shape and brown in the pan. Arrange the meat and vegetables in soup dishes and pour sauce over. Scatter finely chopped chives on top.

Leg of Venison with

Preparation time: 45 minutes
Cooking time: 30 minutes
Difficulty: ✮

Serves 4

2⅔ lb/1.2 kg leg of venison
1 oz/25 g truffles, cut into strips
1 tsp/5 g truffles, chopped
1¾ oz/50 g black olives, halved and pitted

1½ oz/40 g walnut halves
5½ oz/150 g perciatelle pasta
½ cup/120 g butter
2 tbsp/30 g clarified butter
¾ cup/200 ml heavy cream
2 tsp/10 ml port
3½ tbsp/50 ml stock
3 tsp olive oil
1 pinch of nutmeg
salt and pepper

Venison is particularly popular in the Belgian province of Limburg, which was formerly considered the Cinderella of the kingdom. Roger Souvereyns seasons this very delicate meat with black olives, which go extremely well with this dish.

The tenderest venison comes from a young male animal. Do not marinate it, but allow it to "mature" for a few days if purchased very fresh. The meat should remain pink inside but well browned on the outside. This can be done by browning it first in a pan and then transferring to the oven – cooked this way, it will remain juicy.

Keep strictly to the quantities and proportions of olives and truffles, as otherwise the flavor of the venison could be affected. Slightly bitter Italian olives go very well with this festive dish. You should use black truffles (*Tuber melanosporum*) such as those from the Périgord region of France; these are gathered at the end of February.

The macaroni represents a break by Roger Souvereyns from traditional accompaniments. Make sure that you cook it *al dente* so it will form a contrast to the delicate meat.

1. Prepare the leg of venison; remove all but the thigh bone, trim sinews, and lard with truffles and black olives. Tie with string and season.

2. Brown in a mixture of whole and clarified butter, and then roast for 20 minutes at 355 °F/180 °C, basting frequently. Meanwhile, cook the macaroni in briskly boiling salted water, then refresh. Quickly brown the nuts in clarified butter and drain on paper towels.

Truffles and Black Olives

3. Reduce the cream with the chopped truffle until it thickens; season to taste and add a pinch of nutmeg. Remove the venison from the oven and allow to rest on a plate covered with aluminum foil.

4. Remove fat from the roasting pan, flambé with port, add the stock and reduce by half. Beat in olive oil using a hand-held mixer, and keep warm. Arrange the macaroni on the plate, pour the truffle cream on top, and brown using a salamander or under the broiler.

Quail with Eggplan

Preparation time: 35 minutes
Cooking time: 20 minutes
Difficulty: ★★★

Serves 4

8 quails
2 large eggplants
2 small eggplants
1 zucchini
2 red (bell) peppers
12 cherry tomatoes
2 heads of garlic
1 onion
1 egg
3½ tbsp/50 g flour
7 tbsp/50 g ground almonds

½ cup/100 g bread crumbs
6½ tbsp/100 ml olive oil
salt and pepper

For the basil sauce:
2 sprigs of basil
5½ oz/150 g shallots
½ cup/125 g butter
⅔ cup/150 ml heavy cream
2 tbsp/30 ml white wine

For the white stock:
the quail carcasses
1 each onion, carrot, leek
1 celery rib
1 bouquet garni

Émile Tabourdiau loves the innumerable colors, fragrances and flavors of Provence and here he invites you to unite them in one dish. He created this recipe for a Provençal week at the Hotel Bristol in Paris.

Choose firm, fresh eggplants with smooth and shiny skins. You need large eggplants for the stuffing and smaller ones, which contain less water, to line the mold.

Choose large quails, because they will be easier to bone. Do not fry the breaded quail legs for too long, or they may become dry. Instead of quail, you could substitute a boned rack of lamb.

The basil sauce is typically Provençal and is made from blanched leaves.

1. Thinly slice the small eggplants and brown them. Place ring molds on a baking sheet. Slice the zucchini and braise. Cut circles out of the red pepper and braise in olive oil. Halve the large eggplants, and cook for 15–20 minutes in the oven with some olive oil. Mix their flesh with the chopped and fried onion and some garlic. Prepare a white stock with the quail carcasses and the vegetables

2. Bone the quails, leaving the upper thighs whole and season. Dredge the legs in flour, dip in egg and ground almonds, and deep-fry in hot oil.

and Basil Sauce

3. Braise the chopped shallots in butter, add the white wine and the stock, and reduce. Add the cream and the blanched basil, mix for a couple of minutes and strain. Braise 12 unpeeled garlic cloves in butter. Braise 12 cherry tomatoes. Brown the quail breasts, leaving them pink inside.

4. Line ring molds with the eggplant slices. Put in a layer of stuffing, add 2 quail breasts, fill with more stuffing. Top with rounds of zucchini and bell pepper. Bake at 375 °F/190 °C for 7 minutes. Pour the basil sauce onto the plates and unmold an eggplant charlotte onto each plate. Place the quail legs near the rim of the plate and alternate the garlic cloves and cherry tomatoes in a circle around the plate.

Saddle of Hare

Preparation time: 1 hour
Cooking time: 3 hours
Difficulty: ★★

Serves 4

1 saddle of hare, about 600–1¾ lb/800 g
8 cups/2 l robust red wine
4 carrots
4 celery ribs
3 onions
4 tomatoes
5 cloves

cinnamon
6 juniper berries
bay leaves
basil
1 tsp cocoa powder
oil
butter
salt and pepper

For the tomato compote:
2 generous lb/1 kg green tomatoes
3 lemons
1⅔ cup/400 g sugar

Because this recipe includes a double marinade, you must plan to make it well ahead of the time you want to serve it: 32 hours for the tomato compote and 24 hours for the hare marinade.

The mixture of tomatoes, sugar and lemon zest must be stirred every 2–3 hours during the whole period of marination. The green tomatoes will absorb some water, but will still stay crisp. If you cannot get green tomatoes, you could substitute a typically North Italian accompaniment, the piquant *mostarda di frutti* (fruits preserved in mustard syrup), which is produced in Cremona.

The hare should be marinated in a good red wine. The roasting of the hare must be carefully monitored, as the meat can become tough if it is cooked for too long. Venison can be prepared in the same way.

The originality of this dish lies in its use of Oriental spices, and reminds us of the Venetian merchants who conducted an intensive trade in spices in the days of Marco Polo. These spices, formerly weighed against gold, were the focus of lively competition between the chefs of the great houses of the nobility, and still play an important role in Italian cuisne.

1. Place the hare in a large dish with the celery, 2 carrots, 2 onions, 2 tomatoes, cloves, cinnamon, juniper berries, bay leaves and basil, and season with salt and pepper. Pour on 8 cups/2 l of red wine, and marinate for 24 hours.

2. Remove the hare and strain the marinade, discarding the solids and reserving the liquid. Chop the rest of the raw vegetables. Heat oil and butter in a large skillet, add the chopped vegetables and cook for 5 minutes.

with Tomato Compote

3. Add the hare and brown on both sides. Pour on the wine from the marinade, and simmer for 3 hours. Season to taste and add 1 tsp of cocoa powder.

4. For the compote, place the green tomatoes with the sugar and the grated and caramelized lemon peel in a large pan, and bring to boil. Leave to macerate for about 32 hours, until a compote is produced. Cut the saddle of hare into smaller pieces and serve with the vegetables and 1 tbsp of the compote for each person.

Roast Lamb

Preparation time: 1 hour 30 minutes
Cooking time: 30 minutes
Difficulty: ★★★

Serves 4

1 loin roast of lamb, about 3⅓ lb/1½ kg
2 lamb kidneys
2 zucchini
2 tomatoes
1 head of garlic

1 bunch of parsley
1 bunch of thyme
3½ tbsp/50 g tapenade
(see basic recipes p. 805)
1 tsp tomato paste
6½ tbsp/100 g butter
4 cups/1 l white wine
1 cup/250 ml olive oil
salt and pepper

The word tapenade comes from the Provençal (*tapeno* and contains, in addition, black olives, garlic and anchovies and olive oil. Tapenade is served with salads, fish and meat dishes. Since the ingredients keep well, it can be prepared in advance. In an airtight container in a cool place it will keep for up to 3 months.

When the lamb has been stuffed with the kidneys, it must be tied up carefully, so it is evenly shaped. This should be done working inward, from the edges to the middle. You can certainly prepare the meat in advance.

1. Season the whole kidneys, and brown for 5 minutes over high heat. Then pierce them so that the excess moisture can escape, halve, and slice. Bone the lamb and butterfly open.

2. Stuff the two sides of the loin with the kidneys. With the bones, prepare a lamb stock, while allowing the white wine to reduce. Carefully roll and tie the meat. Peel, seed and dice the tomatoes, then add to the tapenade with the olive oil and tomato paste.

with Tapenade

3. Cut the zucchini into long strips, then blanch for a few minutes. Refresh and drain. Season the lamb stock to taste and add the finely chopped basil, thyme and parsley.

4. Roast the lamb for 20 minutes with garlic, then allow to rest. Pour some sauce onto each plate. Cut the meat into eight slices and place 2 slices on each plate. Arrange the finely chopped tomatoes and the zucchini braised in butter around the plates. Garnish with tapenade.

Preparation time: *2 hours*
Cooking time: *2 hours 15 minutes*
Difficulty: ★

Serves 4

1⅓ lb/600 g white beans
4 pieces confit of duck
4 smoked sausages

4 Toulouse sausages
6½ tbsp/100 g duck fat
3½ oz/100 g fresh pork rind
7 oz/200 g unsmoked bacon
¾ cup/200 ml duck stock
1 carrot
1 onion
10 garlic cloves
2 bunches of thyme and bay leaves
salt and pepper

This is the most famous dish in the cuisine of southwestern France. The word *cassoulet* comes from *cassole*, the earthenware pot in which its preparation is completed. Many variations of this dish are known. One is a simple combination of beans and meat, the cassoulet of the poor; the second is a more refined version with confit of duck and partridge; the third, still more sophisticated, variation also contains pork rind and sausages, which make the dish particularly juicy. This last variation is presented here.

The white beans should be soaked in cold water for 12 hours. The women chefs of the great Toulouse tradition, Dominique Toulousy's aunts and grandmothers, knew that the secret of cassoulet is the long preparation time.

Meat and vegetables are equally important in this dish, and you should follow our chef's instructions precisely. The vegetables for the mirepoix, for example, must be chopped very finely. Otherwise, you just need some patience and should keep to the traditional method – try, for instance, to use an earthenware pot.

Cassoulet is a complete meal in itself, needing no appetizer, and rich desserts are best avoided. If you follow it with a light green salad, your guests will be well satisfied. Cassoulet can be enjoyed all year round.

1. Soak the white beans in cold water for 12 hours. Then blanch the beans and the bacon, cut into large dice. Refresh. Dice the carrot and onion.

2. In a deep pan, braise the diced vegetables with the duck fat. Add the pork rind, bacon, white beans and duck stock. Add thyme, bay leaves and the chopped garlic, and simmer for 90 minutes.

Cassoulet

3. Meanwhile, brown the confit of duck in a pan until golden brown. Add the sausages, brown, and set aside.

4. Put the beans and all the meats into an earthenware casserole. Season to taste and bake for 45 minutes in a 400–450 °F/210–240 °C. Serve hot.

Duck Legs with

Preparation time: 1 hour 30 minutes
Cooking time: 40 minutes
Difficulty: ★★

Serves 4

4 boned duck legs
4 slices of cooked ham
meat trimmed from the top of the thighs
fresh pistachios
1 egg yolk
dry white bread
butter

2 sage leaves
parsley
salt and pepper to taste

For the sauce:
4 ladlefuls brown duck stock
½ cup/125 ml white wine
2 tsp balsamic vinegar
1 carrot
1 onion
1 celery rib
some butter

In Piedmont the duck is very popular, and forms the basis of innumerable recipes, in which the breast plays a leading part. But to depart from the beaten track, Luisa Valazza here suggests stuffing the duck's legs. A certain skill in needlework could stand you in good stead when closing up the legs, but don't worry, it is not that difficult.

A duck of 5½ lb/2½ kg will have nice meaty legs. If you like, you can enrich the stuffing with a noble specialty of Piedmont, the white truffle.

If you have time, chop the meat with a knife rather than using a food processor, which produces a uniform but too fine result.

To close the legs after stuffing, you must sew them up with kitchen thread. You can do all this in advance, browning only just before serving. You can check the progress of roasting in the oven with a needle: if the escaping juices run clear, the meat is cooked through. Let it rest for about 10 minutes in a warm place before serving.

1. To make the stuffing, briskly brown the duck meat in butter with sage and the ham cut in strips. Chop in a food processor or with a knife.

2. Mix in a bowl the egg yolk, bread crumbs (soaked in milk and then squeezed to remove excess milk), parsley, pistachios and the duck meat and ham. Season to taste.

Balsamic Vinegar

3. Stuff the boned duck legs and pull the skin over the opening, then sew up with kitchen thread. Put in a pan, brown on all sides, pour off fat, and deglaze with white wine and balsamic vinegar for the sauce.

4. Add the finely chopped vegetables, brown until golden, and add the duck stock. Place in the oven for 30 minutes. Remove the legs and keep warm. Reduce the meat juices until they thicken, add butter and salt. Strain. Remove the thread from the legs. Cut into slices and arrange on plates in a fan shape. Pour sauce over, and garnish with vegetables.

Preparation time: *30 minutes*
Cooking time: *30 minutes*
Difficulty: ★

Serves 4

1 chicken, about 4½ lb/2 kg
1¼ cup/300 ml heavy cream
10 tbsp/150 g butter
nutmeg
salt, coarse and fine
freshly ground black pepper

For the chicken:
1 leek
1 onion stuck with cloves
2 carrots
white celery
parsley
garlic
thyme
bay leaf

For the garnish:
white part of leek
1 carrot
7 oz/200 g celery root

The people of Belgium have such a devotion to eating good food that in the Middle Ages many streets were named after foods. Even today, towns and villages have retained this tradition, so that tourists are in danger of confusing street names with restaurant menus. The dish called waterzooi is to Belgium what bouillabaisse is to Marseilles, and our chef is particularly fond of it.

This dish is of Flemish origin (the name "waterzooi" is connected to the city of Ghent) and was originally prepared with fish. Eventually, however, chicken came to be preferred.

Do not forget that this dish is supposed to be light, so you should not overdo the heavy cream that is added to the soup. Serve the dish hot and do not keep it any longer than 48 hours – that is, if any is left over.

1. First remove the legs from the chicken and cut them in half, then remove the breasts. Cover the legs and breasts with salted water, bring to a boil, then drain the meat.

2. Finely chop the parsley and set aside. Simmer the chicken, together with the other ingredients, for about 30 minutes over low heat. Remove the chicken from the pan, skin and bone it, then cut into large pieces.

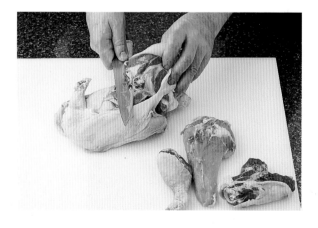

3. Cut the carrots, leek and celery into julienne strips, and cook separately in salted water. Refresh. Strain the water in which the chicken was boiled, and remove the fat.

4. Add the heavy cream, the chicken pieces, and the julienne of vegetables. Heat gently, stir in the butter, and season to taste with nutmeg, salt, and pepper. Serve in warm soup plates, garnished with the parsley leaves.

Preparation time: 1 hour 30 minutes
Cooking time: 7 hours
Difficulty: ★★

Serves 4

3⅓ lb/1½ kg beef cheek
1 duck foie gras
2 pork cauls (see note on page 428)
5 carrots
2 shallots
1 onion studded with cloves
diced carrots and onions
2 garlic cloves

1 bouquet garni
8 cups/2 l Burgundy or other dry red wine
10 cups/2½ l veal stock
oil
coarse salt
salt and pepper

For the purée:
3⅓ lb/1½ kg potatoes
13 tbsp/200 g butter
4 cups/1 l milk
7 oz/200 g smoked bacon
salt and pepper

Here Gérard Vié is making an allusion to the classic *grande cuisine* dish, hare "à la royale", for which he has created a variation using beef. Since game is not available all year round, a substitute needs to be found, and in this case it is beef cheek, which is delicate and meltingly tender.

The preparation is somewhat tedious, and so you should start a couple of days in advance. Prepare the stock two days ahead, and be careful in measuring out the seasoning, since an excessively strong stock could overpower the fla-

vor of the meat. Take the opportunity to stew other cuts of beef along with the cheek, because you can use then later for salads or pies.

The fondants are wrapped in pork caul, which you should first soak in cold water. When you shape the fondants in a ladle or small bowl, press the meat a little, because beef cheek contains gelatin, and the fondants will hold together better if their structure is uniform. The meat should braise slowly in the oven – this was one of the secrets of chefs of the old school.

1. Trim the rind from the beef cheek. Boil the rind with 2 carrots, the onion studded with cloves and the bouquet garni for 2 hours in 8 cups/2 l of salted water. Boil the potatoes, drain, purée and stir in butter and milk. Dice the bacon finely and fry without additional fat and add to the purée.

2. Season the beef cheek and brown in oil, chop the remaining vegetables coarsely, add to the meat and brown. Add wine and veal stock, reserving ⅔ cup/150 ml of each. Cook in a covered pan for 4 hours over low heat. Dice the meat. Reduce the cooking liquid until the consistency of a sauce. Strain.

Burgundy and Potato Purée

3. Slice the foie gras and brown. Line a medium-sized ladle or small bowl with pork caul, half-fill with diced meat, add a slice of foie gras, and fill with more diced meat. Press well, then close up the pork caul. Repeat for 3 more portions.

4. Put the diced carrots and onions in a baking dish, then lay the fondants on top, and add ⅔ cup/150 ml stock and ⅔ cup/150 ml wine. Cook for 40 minutes at 320 °F/160 °C, basting frequently. Place a fondant in the center of each plate, adding a mound of potato purée on each side. Add sauce and serve.

Rack of Lamb

Preparation time: 1 hour
Cooking time: 4 hours
Difficulty: ★★

Serves 4

2 racks of lamb, about 1¾ lb/800 g each
11 oz/300 g lamb shoulder
2 eggplants
1 large tomato, diced
2 pearl onions
2 garlic cloves
1 celery rib
1 sprig of thyme

1 bay leaf
1 sprig of rosemary
1 bunch of chives
1 bunch of flat-leaf parsley
1 egg
1 cup/250 ml white veal stock
6½ tbsp/100 ml olive oil
¾ cup/200 ml white wine
1 stick of cinnamon
5 cloves
10 juniper berries
40 white and black peppercorns
salt

Innumerable ways of preparing lamb are found on the menus of the great restaurants of Europe. Among the many breeds of lamb available to him, our chef prefers Pauillac lamb, which is slaughtered when it is 65 days old and whose flesh is famous for its tenderness. The leanest ribs are selected for the rack.

Lamb shoulder can be roasted the same way as a leg. Here, however, it is important to stick strictly to the preparation time given (braise for about 3 hours), because only then will it be fork-tender. The exquisite taste of lamb can be underlined by herbs and spices, but should not be disguised by them. So measure them out with care.

For the moussaka you need very fresh eggplants with firm flesh and smooth, glossy skins. The eggplant is an ingredient in countless dishes containing olive oil, such as ratatouille, and it is often combined with tomatoes and zucchini.

1. Braise the shoulder with the onions, garlic, celery, herbs, and spices, adding water and white wine. Cook for 3–4 hours over low heat. Remove the meat and break it up with a fork. Pour the fat from the pan, then reduce the stock to intensify its color and flavor.

2. Cut the 2 eggplants in half lengthwise, place in an ovenproof dish, season with coarse salt, and roast at 300 °F/150 °C on the middle rack of the oven for 40 minutes. Sauté the diced tomatoes briskly in olive oil. Mix the flesh of the eggplants with the lamb shoulder. Add the egg, chives, and chopped parsley.

with Spicy Sauce

3. Line small molds with the eggplant skins and fill with the eggplant mixture. Then bake at 340 °F/170 °C on the middle rack of the oven for 20 minutes.

4. Brown the racks of lamb on all sides in hot oil and continue to cook until medium-rare. Let rest for 5 minutes, then cut in half. Put a stuffed eggplant skin in the center of each plate, place the pieces of lamb on top, and pour the sauce around.

Preparation time: 30 minutes
Cooking time: 3 hours 30 minutes
Difficulty: ★★

Serves 4

2 calves' tails
1 eggplant
2 small zucchini
1 red (bell) pepper
5 celery ribs
3 carrots

finely diced celery, carrot, onion
1 generous lb/500 g peeled tomatoes
1 tsp pine nuts
4 garlic cloves
20 purple basil leaves
3 bay leaves
1 tsp cocoa powder
12 cups/3 l meat stock, unsalted
6½ tbsp/100 ml white wine
extra virgin olive oil
salt and pepper

This recipe would be entirely Roman if it were not for the typically Sicilian *caponata* that goes with it. Once beef and veal were reserved for the wealthy, so it was very rare in the region around Rome. The slaughterhouse workers (*vaccinari*) of Rome were paid in *naturalia*, that is, the less sought-after parts of the animals, such as the tripe, ears or tails. This historical circumstance explains the Italian name of this dish, *coda alla vaccinara*.

The calves' tails should not be boned before cooking, because they would lose some of their flavor. It is impor-

tant that it should cook for a long time over very low heat. This gives you time to prepare the *caponata* with the care it deserves. This is a sophisticated medley of flavors and colors, combining zucchini, peppers and pine nuts. The vegetables must be cut into very small dice.

The celery enhances this dish with its delicate but crisp freshness. Take care that the stems are firm and glossy, with healthy-looking leaves. The powerful taste of basil will be enough on its own with no further herbs and spices.

1. Cut the calves' tails in 1³/₄ in/3½ cm pieces. Put the finely diced vegetables, the 2 unpeeled garlic cloves and the bay leaves in a deep pan with some olive oil. Braise over low heat. Add the meat and brown, still over low heat, for about 20 minutes. Add white wine and reduce completely.

2. Sprinkle with cocoa powder, season with salt and pepper and add the stock. Cover and simmer for 3 hours. At the end of this time, add to the meat the peeled, finely chopped tomatoes, 3 carrots and 3 ribs of celery cut into thin strips. Cook for 20 minutes. Remove from the heat and take the meat out of the sauce.

alla Vaccinara

3. Put the celery and carrot strips in a bowl and keep warm. Strain the sauce. Julienne the remaining 2 ribs of celery and braise in a pan in olive oil, finally adding the purple basil leaves. Toast the pine nuts in a pan.

4. For the caponata, dice the eggplant, zucchini and red pepper, and braise for 3 minutes in olive oil, without browning. Place pieces of calves' tail in the center of each plate, pour on sauce and garnish with celery and carrot strips. Lay the celery julienne on top of the meat and garnish the plate with caponata and some olive oil.

Beef Tenderloin

Preparation time: 15 minutes
Cooking time: 15 minutes
Difficulty: ★

Serves 4

1 beef tenderloin, about 1⅓ lb/600 g
red wine
1 celery rib
1 shallot
1 bay leaf
thyme
rosemary
5 peppercorns

salt and pepper

For the vegetables:
6 carrots
1 zucchini
15 small onions

For the sauce:
4 cups/1 l red wine
3½ tbsp/100 ml port
1 cup/250 ml veal stock
4 shallots
1 cup plus 3½ tbsp/300 g butter
salt and pepper

This dish is one for connoisseurs who can distinguish Charolais from Angus beef at a glance!

It is a light dish, whose gentle preparation brings out the flavor and character of the meat. It is only for those who like rare beef.

Heinz Winkler refuses to serve a dish unless he knows the ingredients are fresh and from an impeccable source. His passion for the white Charolais breed is a tribute to French cattle breeding.

Nevertheless one cannot deny that the Charolais has formidable competition in the Scottish Angus, a breed of black cattle that are, with justification, the pride of Scotland. Of course, American beef of many breeds, including the Angus, has earned a global reputation for its high quality.

1. For the vegetable stock, peel the shallot, cut into coarse dice and cook with red wine and salt. Add herbs, celery and pepper. Cut the beef into 4 thick slices.

2. Clean the carrots, zucchini and onions. Cut the carrots and zucchini into large olive shapes, and cook separately in salted water with a dash of sugar, until just cooked.

n Red Wine

3. For the sauce, bring the red wine and port to a boil with the chopped shallots, reduce by two thirds, let cool slightly and add the butter in small pieces, stirring constantly. Strain and add the veal stock. Reheat and season to taste.

4. Bring stock, red wine and herbs to the boil. Add the meat slices and simmer, gently, for 8 minutes. Put the sauce on heated plates, with one slice of meat on top, and surround with the garnish of vegetables.

Preparation time: 30 minutes
Cooking time: 45 minutes
Difficulty: ★★★

Serves 4

1 guinea fowl
1 chicken or guinea fowl carcass
salt pork fatback to cover the guinea fowl
4½ lb/2 kg clay (not plastic-based)
1 onion
1 celery rib
2 large potatoes
8¾ oz/250 g leek

12 egg yolks
⅔ cup/150 ml cream
6½ tbsp/100 g butter
3½ oz/100 g puff pastry
3½ tbsp/100 ml truffle juice
3½ tbsp/50 ml chicken roasting juices
1 cup/250 ml chicken stock
2 cups/500 ml white wine
oil
rosemary
tarragon
basil
salt and pepper

For Heinz Winkler, the guinea fowl is typically French, and rosemary has the robust flavor of the Mediterranean south. This, of course, is flattering to French national pride, but it is not quite correct: the guinea fowl is esteemed throughout the Mediterranean, and the method of preparation described here, in a coat of clay, comes from North Africa. In any case, the dish is quite delicious.

Winkler originally tried this recipe with pheasant and chicken, but was disappointed by the results and eventually decided in favor of the guinea fowl, which always remains juicy, tender and full of flavor in its clay covering. The rosemary, for its part, imparts an additional exquisite aroma to the bird.

Place a few sprigs of rosemary inside the guinea fowl, along with some tarragon and a couple of basil leaves. Do not overdo the herbs; the various flavors, of which rosemary is the dominant one, complement each other well, but their combined effect could easily cover up the flavor of the guinea fowl.

Finally, you must transform yourself into a potter, so as to be able to manage the clay. This is not particularly difficult, if enough water is added to make it smooth and easy to spread out. This method ensures even cooking and an intensification of the flavors, and gives you the opportunity for a spectacular presentation for your guests – the breaking of the clay covering with a hammer.

1. Place the clay on a damp kitchen towel, cover with another cloth and roll out. Prepare the sauce: cut up the carcass and brown the bones with the rosemary and the diced onions and celery. Deglaze with white wine, reduce, add chicken stock and juices, reduce again, and strain.

2. Clean the guinea fowl, wash and dry, and season inside and out. Stuff with herbs (basil, tarragon and rosemary), cover with fatback, enclose in the clay and bake for 45 minutes in a 355 °F/180 °C oven. Remove from the oven and allow to rest for 15 minutes.

with Rosemary

3. For the potato-leek tart, peel the potatoes, slice, dab dry and season. Cover the bottom of a pan with oil, heat and add the potatoes in 1 thick layer. Cook until golden brown, turning once. Cut the white of leek diagonally and cook in cream. Add white wine and truffle juice. Season.

4. Place a ¼ in/½ cm thick layer of leek on top of the potatoes. Roll out the puff pastry and cut out circles of the same diameter as the potatoes. Cover the leeks with the pastry, brush with egg yolk and bake for 5–8 minutes in a 430 °F/220 °C oven. Break the clay covering, remove the guinea fowl and cut slices from the breast. Serve on heated plates with the sauce and portions of the quartered potato-leek tart.

Medallions of Wild Hare

Preparation time: 2 hours
Cooking time: 40 minutes
Difficulty: ★★

Serves 4

12 loin medallions of wild hare, 1½ oz/40 g each
1¼ cup/300 ml vegetable oil
salt and ground pepper

For the mushroom crust:
12 small cèpes, caps only
5½ oz/150 g chanterelles
5½ oz/150 g whole cèpes
1 shallot, 3½ tbsp/50 g butter
salt and ground pepper

For the quince compote:
2 large quinces, ¾ cup/200 ml red wine
¾ cup/200 ml port, 1 tbsp sugar
6½ tbsp/100 ml crème de cassis

For the sauce:
bones and trimmings of the hare
5½ oz/150 g carrot, shallot and celery
6½ tbsp/100 ml game stock
3½ tbsp/50 ml Madeira, 3½ tbsp/50 ml port
4 tsp/20 ml cognac
1 cup/250 ml cream, 2 tsp/10 ml gin
rosemary, ½ bay leaf, thyme
4 juniper berries, crushed
salt and ground pepper

For the chartreuse:
2 small carrots
1 celeriac, 3½ oz/100 g thin green beans
2 leaves Savoy cabbage
2 tsp/10 ml truffle juice
2 tsp/10 ml port, 5½ oz/150 g raw foie gras
salt and pepper

The combination of game with sweet and fruity flavors is one of the great traditions of German cuisine. Harald Wohlfahrt proves himself a worthy heir of this tradition in presenting to us here a dish of hare with quinces.

The mushrooms recommended here are chanterelles and cèpes, which are very plentiful in the Black Forest. Try to mold the foot of a cèpe with the finely chopped mushrooms,

on which the cèpe cap will then be placed, to give the impression of a whole cèpe. The quince is a yellow fruit with hard flesh, whose medicinal qualities have long been recognized.

The hare can be replaced by venison in this recipe, and the quince by apples or pears. Cauliflower also goes very well with this dish.

1. For the compote of quince, peel and core the fruit. Poach in red wine, port, sugar and cassis. Leave in the poaching liquid for at least 24 hours. Finally purée the quince pieces in a food processor. Cook the liquid down until it becomes a syrup, then add the quince purée and simmer until it has reached the desired consistency.

2. For the chartreuse, cut carrots, celery and beans into 1¼ x ¼ in/ 3 x ½ cm strips. Blanch and refresh. Cut the foie gras into ¼ in/½ cm thick slices, 2¼ in/5 cm in diameter, and then marinate for 1 hour in salt, port, pepper and truffle juice. Blanch the cabbage. Line the sides of small round baking pans alternately with the vegetable strips, line the bottoms with cabbage, place a slice of foie gras on top, and finish with another layer of cabbage. Heat in the oven for 12 minutes.

with Quince Compote

3. Season the hare medallions with salt and pepper, brown on each side for 2 minutes, and keep warm. Clean the mushrooms well, and cut into small dice. Heat the butter in a pan until foaming, add the shallot, season with salt and pepper and set aside. Prepare the cèpe caps the same way.

4. Add the finely chopped bones and trimmings of the hare to the medallions and brown nicely. Deglaze with port and Madeira, and reduce. Add the game stock and the cream, reduce again, strain, and add cognac and gin. On each medallion, place finely chopped mushrooms and place the cèpe caps on top. Heat through in the oven. Arrange on plates with the quince compote and the sauce.

Variations on Wild Boa

Preparation time: 2 hours 30 minutes
Cooking time: 3 hours 15 minutes
Difficulty: ★★★

Serves 4

2 tenderloins of wild boar, 1 loin of wild boar
1 pork caul (see note on page 428)
4 Savoy cabbage leaves
5½ oz/150 g each chanterelles and cèpes
1 tbsp finely chopped chervil
3½ tbsp/50 g butter
1 shallot 4½ oz/120 g game stuffing
oil, salt and ground pepper

For the sauce:
bones and trimmings of wild boar

5½ oz/150 g carrot, celery and shallot
3½ oz/100 g mushrooms oil
2 tbsp tomato paste 2 cups/500 ml red wine

6½ tbsp/100 ml port
3½ tbsp/50 ml Madeira
10 juniper berries

For the garnish
2 apples (such as Granny Smith)
5½ oz/150 g cèpes
5½ oz/150 g chanterelles
1 tbsp finely chopped chervil
1 chopped shallot, 2 cloves
⅓ cup/80 g butter
1 tsp confectioners' sugar
4 sheets filo pastry
2 thyme leaves 1 bay leaf
6½ tbsp/100 ml heavy cream
¾ cup/200 ml white wine
salt and ground pepper

At Harald Wohlfahrt's restaurant, the Schwarzwald-stube, on the edge of the Black Forest, the visitor has the opportunity to become acquainted with the wealth of game in the region. The wild boar must take first place here; all hunters have an equal admiration for it and the recipes in which it features are delicious.

The young boar follows the sow with the rest of the litter, and communicates with his family by grunting. It should be no more than 6 months old when bought. At this age its flesh has practically no fat, and should be cut up carefully. It is suitable for the simplest as well as the most complicated methods of preparation.

Here our chef recommends the use of the loin, which is generally regarded as the finest cut, and whose slightly sweet taste distinguishes it from the powerful flavors of other types of game.

Accompanied, according to season, by red or green cabbage and wild mushrooms (Harald Wohlfahrt is especially fond of *trompettes de la mort*), young boar is a great success at the table. The delicious caramelized apples are in accordance with the German tradition of combining game with fruit. If you cannot get wild boar, you can prepare venison in the same way.

1. For the sauce, chop up the bones and brown them with the mirepoix of vegetables. Deglaze with wine, port and Madeira, add tomato paste and the seasonings. Reduce, add water, and simmer for about 3 hours. Strain. For the garnish, peel and quarter the apples. Caramelize the butter and sugar, and add the white wine and the apples.

2. Cut 4 medallions from the loin, cover with slices of cèpes and wrap in a pork caul, or brush all over with oil. Dice the rest of the cèpes and the chanterelles, and brown briskly with the shallot and chervil. Mix with the game stuffing. Make little baskets with sheets of filo pastry 6 in/15 cm in diameter with the help of a champagne cork.

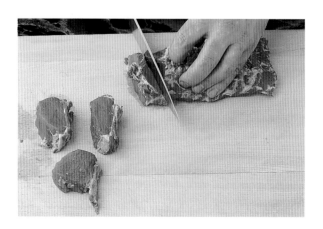

with Pepper Sauce

3. Clean the mushrooms for the garnish, and cut in thin slices. Braise the chopped shallot and mushrooms, and season to taste with cream and chervil. Blanch the savoy cabbage, refresh, dry, press flat and spread a fine layer of stuffing on each leaf. Season the tenderloins with salt and pepper, wrap in cabbage leaves and then in pork caul (if used).

4. Put both meats in a 430 °F/220 °C oven for 3–8 minutes, according to size, then allow to rest. Add the roasting juices to the sauce and reduce to the desired consistency. Finally, add pepper and stir in butter; season to taste. Fill the little pastry baskets with mushrooms and serve with the caramelized apples, the meat and the sauce.

Saddle of Venison

Preparation time: *15 minutes*
Cooking time: *2 hours*
Difficulty: ✳✳

Serves 4

1¾ lb/800 g loin of venison, boned
¼ cup pine nuts
4 cups/1 l red wine
½ cup marsala
¼ cup cognac
4 cups/1 l stock
2 cups/500 ml peanut oil
1 tbsp flour
1 tbsp sugar

For the polenta:
1¼ lb/500 g corn meal
1 tbsp olive oil
4 cups/1 l water
salt

For the marinade:
4 cups/1 l red wine
1 onion
2 carrots
2 celery ribs
3 bay leaves
rosemary
20 juniper berries
10 cloves
½ stick cinnamon

Armando Zanetti himself is fond of hunting small game, but here he gives us his method of preparing venison. As a chef he has often had the opportunity to do so, as many of his customers own hunting grounds. Venison is one of the noblest meats; its qualities are best realized when it is cooked rare. Our chef recommends using the meat of a young animal. The description "Monviso" recalls the forests of that name, where venison is traditionally prepared in this way.

The marinade contains many of the spices which Marco Polo claimed to have brought back from India. That tireless traveler, or others who followed him, exercised a permanent influence on European cuisine. Be careful with the quantities, to avoid making the marinade too robust. By the way, Armando Zanetti would not forgive you if you did not use a tannin-rich wine, such as a good Bordeaux.

Now we come to the polenta, which is prepared in many ways in northern Italy. Resist the temptation to use instant polenta. Just before serving, the little polenta triangles should be reheated under the broiler.

1. A day ahead, marinate the saddle of venison in 4 cups/1 l of red wine. Add the finely chopped vegetables and the marinade herbs and spices. Next day, take out the meat and strain the marinade.

2. For the polenta, bring water to a boil with salt and oil. Slowly sprinkle in the corn meal, constantly stirring with a whisk. Cook for about 45 minutes over low heat, stirring constantly.

Monviso

3. In a pan, brown the marinade vegetables in oil. In another pan, briskly brown the loin of venison for a few minutes in a little oil, and then remove. Put the venison in the pan with the vegetables, and dust with flour. Add sugar, and flambé with cognac and marsala.

4. Add 4 cups/1 l red wine and reduce. Slowly add the stock and gently simmer for 1 hour. Remove the venison and strain the sauce. Slice the meat and serve with the polenta, which has been cut into triangles and reheated under the broiler. Garnish with a few pine nuts.

Preparation time: 1 hour 30 minutes
Cooling time: 24 hours
Cooking time: 2 hours
Difficulty: ★★

Serves 4

6 pigs' feet
12 dried red peppers
3 onions

1 leek
1 head of garlic
parsley
bay leaf
2 cups/200 g bread crumbs
flour
2 eggs
1 cup/250 ml olive oil
salt and white pepper

In Spanish the front extremities of the pig are called "hands," while we say "feet" for both front and back. For this recipe you should use *manitas*, that is, "little hands," as the Spanish call them.

The saying "with the swine, everything's fine" describes the special quality of the pig, all parts of which are eaten. However, pigs' feet demand quite special attention. First they must be carefully cleaned and then cooked for a long time. Afterwards they must be boned, scraping off all the gelatin in the process. Finally, the sliced meat must be coated twice in flour and egg, so that the coating stands up well to deep-frying. Inciden-

tally the gelatin will be better if the pigs' feet are prepared the day before. The dried red peppers, frequently used in Spanish and Basque cuisine, have been grown since the 16th century, when Christopher Columbus brought them to Europe. Today Spain leads the world in their production. They are harvested from April to October, and after being dried can be used throughout the following year.

As an accompaniment, lentils, beans and chick peas are equally suitable. If you prefer, you can use calves' feet instead, but use the cheeks as well, as they have a higher gelatin content than the feet.

1. Cook the pigs' feet in unsalted water, together with the garlic, leek, onions, bay leaf and white pepper. Bone the cooked pigs' feet and chop finely. Season, pack into a terrine and refrigerate for 24 hours.

2. For the sauce, blanch the dried peppers three times. Scrape out the flesh. In another pan, reduce by three quarters the cooking water from the pigs' feet with the flesh of the dried peppers. Season to taste, purée and strain the sauce.

Pimento Sauce

3. Next day, take the terrine out of the refrigerator and cut the gelled meat carefully into ½ in/1 cm thick slices.

4. Coat the slices in flour, egg and then bread crumbs mixed with chopped parsley. Deep-fry in hot oil. Arrange on plates with the sauce.

Desserts

Coconut and Chocolate

Preparation time: 2 hours
Cooking time: 30 minutes
Difficulty: ★★★

Serves 4

For the caramelized bananas:
1 banana
6¹/₂ tbsp / 100 g sugar

For the curry jelly:
1¹/₂ sheets of gelatin
1 cup / 250 ml water
a pinch of curry
2 tbsp / 30 g sugar

For the cylinders:
chocolate
grated coconut

For the chocolate sauce:
³/₄ cup / 200 ml each sugar, coconut water
3¹/₂ oz / 100 g each cocoa butter, chocolate

For the curry mousse:
1 cup / 250 ml cream
4 egg yolks
2¹/₂ tbsp / 40 g sugar
a pinch of curry

Coconut and curry, this combination of such very different flavors, is now broadly accepted by chefs.

The Indians have been masters of the combination of coconut and curry in all imaginable variations for centuries, as proven by the menus in the best Indian restaurants.

There one finds curry, or "cary" as the mixture of spices is known in India, equally often in sweet and savory recipes. It can be bought as a powder or paste. When selecting curry, the mixture should at the very least contain turmeric, ginger, cumin, coriander, and pimento. The spices need to be well-balanced so that no one flavor stands out. This fine balance is all the more important for the success of this particular recipe, as the flavor of both the mousse and the jelly depend on it.

Originally the dish was meant to be a savory one with only curry and coconut water. There is something quite bold about the idea of transforming it into a dessert by combining it with chocolate, and our chef may well have broken out in a cold sweat when he first served it to an illustrious group of top international chefs. However, he passed this test with style, and is now willing to reveal that for this recipe to succeed it is absolutely essential to use chocolate with a very high level of cocoa (at least 70%).

This recipe is a good example of the increasing importance of spices in the preparation of desserts: cinnamon, poppy, nutmeg, and star anise are by now popular ingredients in fine pastries and desserts, and gourmets consider them to be tasteful in the truest sense of the word.

1. Peel the banana, cut it into large pieces and caramelize with the sugar for 5 minutes. For the curry jelly, dissolve the gelatin in cold water. Bring the water, curry, and sugar to a boil. Remove from heat, stir in the gelatin and allow to cool.

2. To make the cylinders, warm the chocolate. Using a plastic strip and adhesive tape, form a chocolate cylinder measuring 3¹/₂ × 2 in / 8 x 4 cm. Place this on the plate, fill with grated coconut and cover well with a lid of chocolate. For the chocolate sauce, boil the sugar, coconut water, and cocoa butter, then add the chocolate.

Dessert with Curry

3. To make the curry mousse, bring the cream to a boil in a pan. In a bowl, beat the egg yolks with the sugar until the mixture is foamy and add the hot cream. Pour everything back into the pan and cook like a custard (see basic recipes p. 800). Pour into a bowl and add the curry powder. Refrigerate for one day, then beat again with a mixer.

4. Arrange some pieces of banana at the edge of each plate, add the curry jelly and curry mousse and decorate it with a little chocolate sauce. Garnish with mint leaves.

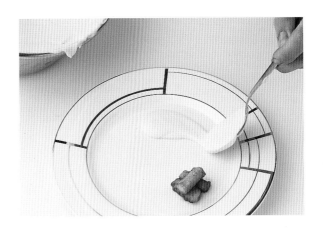

Preparation time: 1 hour
Cooking time: 1 hour
Difficulty: ★★

Serves 6

9 oz / 250 g puff pastry
(see basic recipes p. 803)

For the creamy rice pudding:
6 tbsp / 85 g short grain rice
3/4 cup / 190 ml milk
3/4 cup / 190 ml crème fraîche
peel of 1 untreated lemon
2 tsp sugar
1/2 cinnamon stick

For the rice pudding mousse:
11 1/2 oz / 335 g rice pudding
2 egg yolks

3 1/2 sheets of gelatin
5 oz / 135 g meringue
(see basic recipes p. 802)
3/4 cup / 200 ml cream

For the glazed cherries:
juice of 3 lemons
5 tbsp / 85 ml water
thyme
4 1/2 tbsp / 70 g sugar
3 oz / 85 g cherries, stoned

For the apple sorbet:
1 lb 7 oz / 660 g apples (e.g. Rennets)
1 cup / 250 ml syrup (3/4 cup / 170 ml water,
1/3 cup / 80 g sugar)
juice of 3 lemons

Next to wheat, the most familiar grain is rice, which is prepared in countless fashions throughout the world. It fulfills many functions, being a cleaning product (rice powder), the basic material used in the production of sculptures and white earthenware, and above all an essential basic foodstuff. It has been known in Spain since the 7th century, when it was introduced by the Moors who conquered the country. The long presence of the Arabs, until the 15th century, made rice a permanent part of the traditional cuisine of the Iberian peninsula. From there rice appears to have spread to northern Italy to the Po plain, so we can indirectly thank the Moors for dishes such as the generally popular risotto.

Here, Hilario Arbelaitz tempts us with a classically prepared, European-style creamy rice pudding. Genuine rice pudding is made with short grain rather than long grain rice; it soon cooks and expands in the milk, producing an even mass that is firm enough to be spread between sheets of pastry without oozing away.

To add to people's enjoyment of this dessert, something refreshing should be served as a contrast to the sweetness of the rice pudding. For this purpose, our chef recommends an apple sorbet made with sweetish-sour apples, which has precisely the desired effect.

1. For the creamy rice pudding, combine the rice, milk, crème fraîche, lemon peel, sugar, and cinnamon stick in a pan. Cook over a low heat until the mixtures thickens to a creamy consistency.

2. For the rice pudding mousse, mix the creamy rice pudding, egg yolks, and the gelatin (that has been soaked in water). Add the meringue and, as the final step, fold in the cream, which has been whipped to a stiff consistency.

Creamy Rice Pudding

3. Roll out the puff pastry as thinly as possible and cut out rounds with a diameter of 4¹/₂ in / 10 cm. Place the rounds in an oven preheated to 300 °F / 150 °C and bake until golden brown. Place one thin round on a plate and put a spoonful of rice pudding mousse onto it. Repeat three times, finishing with a piece of pastry.

4. For the glazed cherries, boil the lemon juice, water, thyme, and sugar for 2 minutes. Add the cherries and cook at 185 °F / 85 °C in a double boiler for 30 minutes. To make the apple sorbet, chop the apples in a juice extractor, then pour the sugar syrup and lemon juice into the apple puree. Thoroughly mix everything in a ice cream machine. Place sorbet on the plates next to the pastry and garnish with the cherries.

Preparation time: 1 hour
Cooking time: 2 hours
Difficulty: ★★

Serves 4

For the Italian meringue:
5 tbsp / 75 g sugar
2 egg whites, lightly beaten

For the parfait:
5 tbsp / 75 g sugar
4 egg yolks, beaten
coffee extract
2 cups / 500 ml cream, whipped

For the baked meringue:
2 egg whites
¼ cup / 60 g sugar
1 tsp freeze-dried coffee

For the sauce:
5 tbsp / 75 g sugar
4 egg yolks
rum
2 cups / 500 ml cream, whipped

confectioners' sugar for dusting

One could eat this delicious dessert at any time of day for the sheer pleasure of it. The preparation does, however, require a degree of effort and care.

Meringue is a devilish invention that, according to some sources, was imported from Poland in the 18th century by Stanislas Leczinsky, the father-in-law of King Louis XV. There are three different sorts of meringue: piped, baked, and the smoother Italian meringue, which is made with lightly beaten egg white. It is important to add the boiled sugar syrup last and at the prescribed temperature. The same is true of the parfait; the sugar must reach a temperature of 250 °F / 118 °C before it is poured over the egg yolks. The mixture then has to be beaten continuously close to the edge of the bowl until it cools.

Generally, the dessert is composed of three layers and is served on a plate with sauce. In this case our chef has enriched the sauce with cream. In contrast to the other ingredients, which can be kept for a day, the sauce has to be prepared on the day of serving.

The last step is to beat the egg whites until they are so stiff that the dessert will not collapse, but not so stiff that the parfait's texture becomes grainy.

After baking, the dessert is served immediately. One can add another flavor to this dessert by using high-quality chocolate, if desired, without altering the recipe in the process.

1. To make the Italian meringue, cook the sugar with water at 250 °F / 118 °C. Add to 2 egg whites that have been lightly beaten, and beat continuously until completely cooled. Next, prepare the parfait. Again, heat the sugar with water to 250 °F / 118 °C, and this time pour onto the 4 beaten egg yolks. Beat until cooled.

2. Combine the parfait with the Italian meringue and add the coffee extract. Finally, fold in the whipped cream. Pour onto a baking tray with a high edge and place in the freezer.

Coffee Parfait

3. For the baked meringue, beat the egg whites and sugar until they are stiff, then mix in the freeze-dried coffee. Spread the stiff egg whites onto a sheet of baking paper to a thickness of ¹/₂ in / 1 cm and steam at 175 °F / 80 °C for 2 minutes. For the sauce, heat the sugar to 250 °F / 118 °C, then carefully add the 4 egg yolks. Beat until the mixture has cooled, then stir in the rum and cream.

4. For each portion, cut out 2 circles of meringue and 1 circle of parfait with a diameter of ca. 3 in / 6.5 cm. Place some sauce on each plate and glaze. Layer a slice of meringue, a slice of coffee parfait and another meringue slice. Place on top of the sauce. Sprinkle with confectioners' sugar. Glaze again.

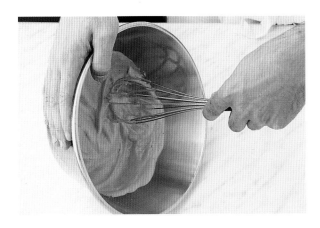

Zabaglione with Dessert Wine

Preparation time: 1 hour 15 minutes
Cooking time: 30 minutes
Difficulty: ★★

Serves 4

For the zabaglione:
8 egg yolks
4 tbsp superfine sugar
³/₄ cup / 200 ml dessert wine from Liguria (or another dessert wine)

For the fried dough:
4 cups / 500 g flour
3¹/₂ tbsp / 50 g soft butter
3 eggs
6¹/₂ tbsp / 100 g superfine sugar
6¹/₂ tbsp / 100 g confectioners' sugar
3 tbsp cognac
a pinch of salt
6 cups / 1¹/₂ l oil for deep-frying
grated peel of 1 untreated lemon

Ligurian cuisine is characterized by simplicity, but it would be a great mistake to think that it is too humble to be interesting. Even though this region in northwestern Italy has a very dry climate, its difficult location between the Alps and the Mediterranean does not prevent certain varieties of vegetables and fruit being cultivated here, as they are protected from the winds from the north and east. Wines cultivated in this region are the perfect accompaniment to a gastronomy with refined taste.

After the harvest in the latter part of September, grapes that have spent the whole summer soaking up southern European sunshine are hung for a few weeks in the open air. A unique dessert wine is created from these grapes, which is used in diverse recipes and here gives its special character to the zabaglione.

It is said that the Ligurian zabaglione was invented during the carnival season, the raucous pre-Lenten festivities celebrated in parts of Europe. The chefs must have kept their cool during the celebration, or they might not have had much success preparing the delicate wine cream in a double boiler. The chemical reaction created by the use of a copper bowl gives the egg yolks a better consistency for the dessert.

The dough can only be prepared using soft butter, to ensure an even texture. It should be left to rest for several hours before continuing or, if desired, it can be prepared the previous day. The dough strips must be narrow enough to be knotted before being deep-fried.

This dessert can be eaten hot or cold. In the unlikely event that there should be some left over, the knots can be kept in an airtight container.

1. For the zabaglione, place the egg yolks and sugar in a copper bowl. Beat for 5 minutes with a whisk. Add the wine. Place the bowl in a double boiler and stir over low heat until the mixture has a thick, creamy consistency. Keep lukewarm.

2. To make the dough, mound the flour on a work surface. Make a well in the middle and place all the other ingredients in it; then mix everything thoroughly until a smooth dough forms. Wrap in plastic wrap and allow to rest for several hours.

and Fried Dough Knots

3. Roll the dough out to a thickness of $^1/_2$ in / 1 cm, and use a serrated pastry cutter to cut the dough into 5 x 1 in / 10 x 2 cm strips. Knot each of them once.

4. Deep-fry the knotted strips in boiling oil. Drain thoroughly and dust with confectioners' sugar. Serve warm or cold with the zabaglione.

Preparation time: 2 hours
Cooking time: 30 minutes
Difficulty: ★★★

Serves 4

For the milk & white chocolate mousses:
3¹/₂ oz / 100 g each milk & white chocolate,
   grated
1 cup / 240 ml cream for each mousse

For the chocolate sorbet:
3¹/₂ oz / 100 g chocolate coating
¹/₃ cup / 35 g cocoa powder
2 tsp / 15 g honey
¹/₂ cup plus 2 tbsp / 150 g sugar
1²/₃ cups / 400 ml water

For the chocolate cake:
3 oz / 85 g bittersweet chocolate
3¹/₂ tbsp / 50 g butter
3 eggs, separated

3 tbsp / 20 g cocoa powder
6¹/₂ tbsp / 100 g sugar

For the bittersweet chocolate mousse:
7 oz / 200 g bittersweet chocolate, grated
1¹/₄ cups / 300 ml each milk, cream
¹/₄ cup / 60 g sugar, 3 egg yolks

To garnish:
3¹/₂ oz / 100 g raspberry sauce
¹/₃ cup / 70 g candied orange peel
²/₃ cup / 70 g grated chocolate
2 tsp coffee extract
a little pistachio or bitter almond extract

9 oz / 250 g custard (see basic recipes p.800)

Though the wide range of ingredients in this recipe may at first seem daunting, the preparation is by no means as difficult as one might suppose. If you follow our chef's instructions step by step, you will certainly succeed in creating an array of desserts of the very highest quality.

When making the mousses, it is essential that the chocolate be at the proper temperature: it must be warm enough for the ingredients to combine, but not hot enough to melt the whipped cream. It is best to prepare the sorbet immediately before serving. Stirring it while it is cold will give it a nice sheen.

When preparing the sponge cake, make sure that the mixture of chocolate and butter is not heated for too long, as this would

impair the flavor of the chocolate. After baking, handle the sponge cake as little as possible, and then very gently.

As soon as the boiling custard has reached the right consistency, it is advisable to dip the bottom of the bowl in cold water to prevent the custard from continuing to cook. It must be beaten thoroughly after cooking and cooling; only then should the custard be divided, one third to be flavored with coffee, and another third with pistachio extract. This method results in three custards with the same consistency, but different colors and flavors, which supplement each other nicely.

When creating this gourmet recipe, Michel Blanchet certainly had chocolate enthusiasts in mind: it is well known that chocolate is useful in alleviating stress and generally lifting spirits.

1. For the milk chocolate mousse, whip the cream until stiff. Melt the milk chocolate in a double boiler, then stir in the whipped cream and leave to cool. Repeat these steps to prepare the white chocolate mousse. For the sorbet bring water, sugar and honey to a boil. Then dissolve the chocolate coating and cocoa powder in it. Leave to cool and blend in an ice cream machine.

2. To make the sponge cake, break the chocolate into pieces and melt in a double boiler with the butter. Beat the egg yolks with half of the sugar until they are light yellow. Add the cocoa. Beat the egg whites with the remaining sugar until stiff. Add the egg yolk mixture and the chocolate mixture to the egg whites. Pour into a springform pan and bake for 6 to 8 minutes at 355 °F / 180 °C.

Variations

3. Make 9 oz / 250 g custard according to the basic recipe. Separate the custard into three portions; flavor one part with coffee and another with pistachio extract. To make the bittersweet chocolate mousse, mix the milk and cream and bring to a boil. Whisk the egg yolks with the sugar until foamy and pour the hot milk mixture over them. Simmer while stirring, then add the grated bittersweet chocolate. Allow to set.

4. Divide the sponge cake horizontally and layer with the milk chocolate mousse. Dust with cocoa powder. Use forms to cut the sponge cake into small pieces. Arrange and decorate the various elements according to taste.

Cherry Trifle

Preparation time: 30 minutes
Cooking time: 15 minutes
Difficulty: ★★

Serves 4

For the sponge cake:
$1/2$ cup plus 2 tbsp / 150 g sugar
5 eggs
$1^1/4$ cups / 150 g flour
$1^1/4$ cups / 450 g sour cherry jam

To soak the sponge cake:
1 tbsp / 15 ml rum
$2^1/2$ tbsp / 35 ml cherry brandy
5 tbsp / 70 ml sugar syrup at 30 °Beaumé

For the pudding:
$1^1/2$ cups / 375 ml milk
2 tbsp / 30 g sugar
4 tsp / 10 g pudding powder
2 egg yolks
1 egg

To garnish:
2 cups / 500 ml cream
$3^1/2$ tbsp / 50 g superfine sugar
almonds, blanched and roasted
pistachios, chopped
raspberry jelly
fresh strawberries

Perfection in cooking is achieved only through attention to detail: who could exemplify this more clearly than the master pastry chefs at the Connaught Hotel in London?

This dessert, made with soaked sponge cake, is a typical English dish. It combines the flavors of rum and cherry brandy, the latter drink being particularly popular with the English upper classes and only mistakable for sherry by the completely uninitiated. As one can well imagine, the two potent alcoholic drinks have to be measured very carefully. The invention of rum, by the way, dates back to the French missionary Jean-Baptiste Labat: he worked in the Antilles in the 18th century and succeeded in producing rum from sugar cane, which at the time was a bone of contention between the French, British, and Dutch. The priest also distinguished himself in battle against the British, which in hindsight is not without a certain irony...

When preparing the sponge cake, one must work with precision during the decisive stage: it must retain its light consistency when mixed with the other ingredients. The sponge cake must be allowed to cool completely before continuing. It can even be prepared a day in advance, so that it is a little firmer. When soaking the cubes of sponge cake, it is important to insure that the liquid is distributed evenly over all the cubes.

The whipped cream used to decorate the trifle must be foamy and light. Our chef says the cream will be even lighter if an egg white is folded in at the last moment. One can use raspberry jam in place of cherry to fill the sponge cake.

1. To make the sponge cake, sprinkle the sugar on a baking tray covered with waxed paper and heat in the oven. Beat the eggs with a mixer until foamy. Add the heated sugar, continuing to stir until the mixture has cooled. Stir in the sifted flour. Pour the mixture into a greased cake pan, and bake at 390 °F / 200 °C until golden brown, then reduce the heat to 320 °F / 160 °C and bake until finished.

2. Allow the sponge cake to cool, cut in half horizontally and fill with cherry jam. Combine the rum, cherry brandy, and syrup. Dice the sponge cake and fill a bowl half full with the cubes (this will be the serving bowl). Pour the alcohol and syrup mixture over the cubes and allow to soak in.

'Wally Ladd"

3. To make the pudding, bring the milk to a boil. Beat the sugar and eggs with a whisk. Stir in the pudding powder (instant pudding mix). While stirring, add a little boiling milk, then pour the mixture into the hot milk and continue cooking as for a custard (see basic recipes). Pour through a pointed sieve and whisk thoroughly again.

4. When the syrup has been thoroughly soaked up by the sponge cake, pour the custard over it. Allow to cool. Garnish with sweetened whipped cream, blanched almonds, pistachios, raspberry jelly, and strawberries.

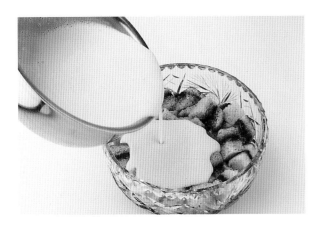

Preparation time: 10 minutes
Cooking time: 5 minutes
Cooling time: 2 hours
Difficulty: ★★

Serves 4

1³/₄ cups / 425 ml heavy cream (48 % fat)
²/₃ cup / 150 ml light whipping cream (40 % fat)
1 vanilla bean
8 egg yolks

¹/₄ cup / 60 g sugar
2 cups wild strawberries
¹/₂ cup plus 1 tbsp / 100 g brown sugar

The desserts that we are familiar with nowadays have been part of our gastronomic culture since about 1850. The term "dessert" is derived from the French word *desservir*, which means "clear (the table)." So a dessert was evidently what was served after the previous meal had been cleared away. In those days, it was customary to prepare the dessert at the head of the table at the beginning of the meal, and the lavish compositions positively enticed people to overindulge. These days top chefs create sweet temptations in more moderate portions: they invite us to indulge without damaging our health.

The pastry chefs at the Connaught Hotel in London, the Power twins, are masters in their field and convincingly demonstrate every day that an exceptional meal may only be followed by an equally exceptional dessert. Our crème brûlée is also based on this maxim.

As the quality of dairy products has improved, keeping cream fresh and storing it is much less of a problem than it used to be, and as a result it is less difficult to work with. However, it is important that the proportions of the different varieties of cream in our recipe are precisely reproduced.

Wild strawberries are extremely well suited to this recipe because of their small size; but other small strawberries could also be used. It is essential that the crème cools down completely before it is glazed, so that the sugar sprinkled over it can be caramelized without re-heating the crème. The contrast between the heat of the Bunsen burner, used in professional kitchens, and the coolness of the crème from below, creates a smooth, shining sugar glaze. Afterwards, the crème must be refrigerated again so that it can set slightly and form a homogeneous whole.

1. Combine the heavy and light creams in a pan with the opened vanilla bean and bring to a boil. Using a whisk, beat the egg yolks and sugar until they are light yellow, then mix in a little of the hot cream. Pour the mixture back into the pan and bring everything to a boil while stirring constantly. Pour through a pointed sieve.

2. Place a layer of wild strawberries in the dessert bowls and hold them in place with some of the crème. Refrigerate the bowls. Also refrigerate the remaining crème, then fill the bowls completely. Refrigerate for 2 to 3 hours.

Brûlée

3. Take the dessert bowls out of the refrigerator, sprinkle on a generous layer of brown sugar and glaze under a hot grill without heating the crème.

4. Finally, heat the glaze with a Bunsen burner, so that it becomes smooth and shiny. Alternatively, the dessert can be briefly re-glazed under a hot grill. Place in the refrigerator again until the glaze has reached the desired firmness. Serve very cold.

Preparation time: 2 hours
Cooling time: 12 hours
Difficulty: ★★

Serves 4

For the Pan di Spagna sponge cake
(see basic recipes p. 805):
4 eggs
$^1/_2$ cups / 125 g sugar
1 cup / 125 g flour

For the ice cream:
$^3/_4$ cup / 180 g sugar
6 egg yolks

1 vanilla bean
2 cups / 500 ml milk
grated peel of 1 untreated lemon

For the cream:
2 egg whites
$^1/_2$ cup / 75 g sugar
4 tbsp candied fruit, soaked in rum
$3^1/_2$ tbsp / 50 ml crème fraîche

For the sauce:
strawberries or similar fruit

To garnish:
seasonal red fruits

On the island of Sicily, a true paradise for gourmets, almost all the fruits one can imagine are grown. Many are preserved by being candied, and thus available for use in refined dishes year-round. It is equally well known that the Sicilians have an exceptional talent for making cakes and desserts, and are internationally admired for specialties such as exquisite cheese-filled cannoli pastries and, of course, the frequently imitated cassata. Cassata has a permanent place on Carlo Brovelli's menus, and the chef has been praised by many a Sicilian who visited him on the mainland and appreciated his consciousness of tradition.

The quantity and variety of crunchy, colorful fruit that make this dessert so special are considered to be a sign of respect for the guests. A cassata is a vital part of any festive occasion or banquet in Sicily.

The preparation of a genuine cassata requires a great deal of time and experience, so the instructions should be followed step by step. Begin your preparations a day in advance, for the ice cream needs to be very firm before the remaining steps are taken to complete the cassatas.

The finished dessert is chilled overnight so that it achieves the required firm consistency.

The name of the sponge cake, *Pan di Spagna* (It. Spanish bread), may be surprising. Actually, numerous Italian desserts are originally derived from bread (pane), and these terms have been retained up to the present day out of respect for the country's traditional cuisine. This is also true of the "Pan di Natale," or Christmas bread, which is traditionally made and served at Christmas.

1. Make the Pan di Spagna sponge cake. Line small hemispherical forms with aluminum foil, then line each mold with a 1 in / 2 cm layer of sponge cake.

2. Mix all the ingredients for the ice cream and prepare in an ice cream machine. Spread a layer of vanilla ice cream onto the sponge cake layer lining the molds and freeze.

Siciliana

3. Beat the egg whites and sugar with a whisk until stiff. Add the rum-soaked candied fruits. Stir the crème fraîche until smooth. Combine both mixtures in one bowl and mix with a spatula for about 10 minutes until it becomes a homogeneous cream.

4. Completely fill the individual molds with the cream and smooth with a knife. Allow to set overnight in the freezer. Turn each mold out onto a plate, garnish with some red fruits and serve with a strawberry sauce made of strained strawberries.

Preparation time: 45 minutes
Cooking time: 18 minutes
Difficulty: ★★

Serves 4

4 apples (Rennets and Granny Smiths)
3¹/₂ tbsp / 50 g butter
3¹/₂ tbsp / 50 g sugar

Puff pastry (see basic recipes p. 803):
4 squares measuring 3 × 3 in / 6 × 6 cm

Apple sorbet (see basic recipes p. 798):
1 cup / 250 ml

For the pastry cream
(see basic recipes p. 802):
3¹/₂ tbsp / 50 ml kirsch
4 tbsp cream, whipped and sweetened

For the apple sauce:
several apples
6¹/₂ tbsp / 100 g sugar
juice of 1 lemon

2 tbsp / 20 g almonds, roasted

Our chef considers this hot and cold dessert the quintessence of his commitment to the preservation of the traditional dishes and produce of Normandy. The apples of Pays d'Auge, the region where the best Calvados is made, are legendary, both the varieties that no longer exist and those that are still cultivated. Michel Bruneau singles out Napoleon apples, which are just the size of a cherry, as those he considers the very best.

In this varied dessert, however, other sorts of apples are used. It is best to use a mixture of apples, such as the tart Granny Smiths which give taste and color to the sorbet, and sweeter Rennets for the sauce. It is precisely this interplay of flavors that make this dessert an unforgettable delight.

Entirely in keeping with Norman tradition, the cream filling is made with dairy cream. Combined with the aroma of cherries, it enriches the entire composition. To make the sorbet, cut the apples into thin slices, place them in the freezer the previous day in order to make the flesh firmer, and then pour very hot syrup over them before placing them in the ice cream machine.

One should be particularly careful when cooking apples that have been cut lengthwise: while the exterior becomes shiny and caramelized in the butter and sugar, the interior should still be crisp and hot.

The finished dessert can also be decorated with caramel lattice made using brown sugar, or, if desired, one can pour some cider or pommeau – a mixture of Calvados and new cider – over it.

1. Prepare the puff pastry, pastry cream and apple sorbet according to the basic recipes. Bake the puff pastry in the oven for 12 minutes. Meanwhile, peel the apples and cut into lengthwise pieces (6 to 8 pieces per person).

2. Cook the apple segments with the butter and sugar in a frying pan for 4 to 5 minutes, or until golden brown. In a mixing bowl, flavor the pastry cream with kirsch and blend in the sweetened whipped cream.

Delight

3. Remove the pieces of puff pastry from the oven and, while they are still warm, fill them with the cream and top with several cooked apple segments. For the apple sauce, place apples in a juicer, then bring the juice to a boil with the sugar and reduce to the desired consistency. Allow to cool, then stir in the lemon juice.

4. Arrange the puff pastry pieces with the apple sorbet on the plates. Scatter the roasted almonds on top, decorate with the apple sauce, and if desired garnish with a perfect strawberry.

Tarte Tatin with Figs

Preparation time: 45 minutes
Cooking time: 15 minutes
Difficulty: ★

Serves 4

6 lb 9 oz / 3 kg fresh figs
6 tbsp acacia honey
1 tbsp pectin
14 oz / 400 g puff pastry
juice of 1 lime
6¹/₂ tbsp / 100 g butter

For the syrup at 30 °Beaumé:
4 cups / 1 kg sugar
4 cups / 1 l water

To garnish:
roasted almonds
red currants

It is not entirely clear whether the Mesdemoiselles Tatin, who were born in the small French town of Neung-sur-Beuvron, invented this small, inverted, intensely sweet cake themselves, or simply brought it home with them from a trip to Provence. If possible, the Tatin should be served lukewarm. Though it is traditionally made with apples, it is certainly no crime to replace the "holy apple" with figs, as they are also highly regarded by gastronomes throughout the world. Indeed, the Hanging Gardens of Babylon, one of the Seven Wonders of the Ancient World, is said to have been mainly populated with fig trees.

It would, of course, be ideal to pluck the figs straight from the tree. They are increasingly available even far from their indigenous areas; in northern Europe one can usually get lovely dark figs with a very red, tasty flesh in the markets. Ripe figs are easy to peel and caramelize with honey. If the figs are very fresh, according to our chef, they should be caramelized the previous evening, placed in the molds and then refrigerated, so that the cake can be completed with the puff pastry at the last minute.

The aroma and color of the acacia honey blends exceptionally well with figs. Alain Burnel favors honey produced in Provence, for he finds it to have a richer taste and a truly astonishing transparency. Rivers of honey with nectar and ambrosia are said to have flown at the banquets of the Olympian Gods. Those lucky enough to be served this lukewarm dessert with vanilla ice cream will surely feel that they have been transported to that very place.

1. Carefully peel the figs. Caramelize half of the honey in a saucepan, then add the figs and pectin, making sure the figs are coated on all sides with the caramelized honey.

2. Place the cooled figs in ovenproof molds. Make sure that the bottom of the dish is completely covered. Cover with a layer of sliced figs.

and Acacia Honey

3. After filling all the molds, cover each with a thin layer of puff pastry and bake for a few minutes in the oven.

4. Pour the remaining honey into a pan, bring to a boil and deglaze with the lime juice. Add the sugar syrup and beat with the butter. Invert the individual cakes onto the center of the plates and glaze with the honey butter. Decorate with a finely sliced fig, and with lukewarm roasted almonds or red currants.

Chocolate Teardrops

Preparation time: 2 hours
Cooking time: 15 minutes
Cooling time: 3 hours
Difficulty: ★★★

Serves 4

For the chocolate teardrops:
9 oz / 250 g bittersweet chocolate coating

For the pear mousse:
4 sheets of gelatin
6¹/₂ tbsp / 100 g sugar
1 cup / 250 ml cream, whipped
9 oz / 250 g pear puree
3¹/₂ tbsp / 50 ml pear schnapps

For the caramel sauce:
¹/₂ cup / 125 g sugar
2 tbsp / 30 g butter
1 cup / 250 ml cream
¹/₂ cup / 125 ml milk
1 tsp vanilla sugar
5 egg yolks
3¹/₂ tbsp / 50 ml caramel

For the pear glaze:
6¹/₂ tbsp / 100 ml pear juice
3¹/₂ tbsp / 50 g sugar
1¹/₂ sheets of gelatin

To garnish:
chopped pistachios

These tears are little more than crocodile tears, for there is certainly no reason to cry where such a dessert is concerned! Chocolate, caramel sauce, and pear mousse – elegantly presented so as to be a treat for the eyes as well as the tastebuds.

Pears appear in three different forms in this composition: as a puree, a fruit schnapps for the mousse and a juice for the pear glaze. This is a lovely way of using this fruit, whose praises were sung by Homer and Virgil and of which several thousand varieties now exist. This multitude need not be confusing, for the pears most widely available are perfectly suitable for this recipe. Pear schnapps is produced by fermenting fresh fruit in a sealed container.

Not everyone can prepare chocolate teardrops on their first attempt: they require a little skill, if only to be able to recog-

nize the optimal consistency of melted chocolate needed to form the teardrops. However, with a little practice and perseverance, one can succeed.

It is best to use strips of plastic to shape the teardrops as depicted in the first picture below, and they should then be allowed to set in the refrigerator for several hours. When you are ready to continue, remove the plastic, and if necessary smoothen and straighten the teardrops a bit. Of course, the chocolate used must match the pears in quality, in other words only the finest. It is easier to produce teardrops with high quality chocolate, and the taste makes its own contribution to the effect of the dessert.

1. To make the chocolate teardrops, melt the chocolate coating in a double boiler. Apply a thin layer of chocolate to three plastic strips of different lengths and form teardrop shapes. Allow to set in the refrigerator.

2. For the pear mousse, soak the gelatin in cold water. Mix the sugar and pear puree; bring to a boil until the sugar melts. Add the gelatin and simmer until the mixture is the color of caramel. Allow to cool, then blend in the whipped cream and pear schnapps. Refrigerate the mousse for three hours.

with Pear Mousse

3. To make the sauce, melt the sugar over medium heat, then carefully add half of the cream and the butter. Bring to a boil and simmer until caramel-colored. In another pan bring the remaining cream, milk, and vanilla sugar to a boil. Beat the egg yolks with a little sugar and stir into the mixture. Prepare like a custard (see basic recipes) and pass through a pointed sieve. Add the caramel.

4. Prepare the pear glaze by bringing the sugar and pear juice to a boil, adding the previously soaked gelatin and passing the mixture through a pointed sieve. Fill the teardrops with pear mousse and use a pastry brush to coat them with glaze. Arrange the tears on a plate, pour some caramel sauce next to them and garnish with chopped pistachios.

Preparation time: 1 hour
Cooking time: 1 hour
Difficulty: ★★

Serves 4

For the panna cotta:
3 whole eggs
2 egg yolks
$^1/_2$ cup / 125 g sugar
2 cups / 500 ml crème fraîche
$1^3/_4$ cups / 50 g amaretti biscuits (almond macaroons)

For the caramel:
$^1/_2$ cup plus 2 tbsp / 150 g sugar
1 cup / 250 ml water

For the cake dough:
$^2/_3$ cup / 75 g ground almonds
$^1/_2$ cup plus 2 tbsp / 75 g flour
5 tbsp / 75 g sugar
5 tbsp / 75 g butter
1 pinch of salt

For the zabaglione:
2 tbsp sugar
2 egg yolks
$^3/_4$ cup / 200 ml dry Marsala

To garnish:
vanilla sugar
red fruits
sprigs of mint

Don Pellegrino Artusi, in honor of whom this dessert was invented, was a 19th-century Italian gourmet who collected many traditional recipes. Inspired by Renaissance chefs and the age of the great duchies, his main work, *The Art of Eating Well*, was reprinted 120 times and is still considered the most complete treatment of Italian cuisine. Although Artusi was particularly fond of the Romagna region and Tuscany, he gathered recipes from all over Italy and contributed to making them well known.

Artusi was also the first to prepare zabaglione (wine cream) with Marsala, and suggested using a pure, dry variety of this amazingly light Sicilian dessert wine. Marsala is now produced in a controlled environment, eliminating any unpleasant surprises when drinking it.

Panna cotta is simple to make, as long as one is careful when cooking it. The use of small amaretti biscuits, which are mixed into the cream, provides the almond flavor and macaroon-like consistency. They should be used in preference to gelatin. The difficulty is only to resist the temptation to eat these delicious cookies before adding them to the panna cotta.

In addition, our chef recommends that the almond cake be prepared like a dry sponge cake, which makes it possible to use it as a sort of edible spoon for the zabaglione.

1. To make the panna cotta, whisk the eggs, egg yolks, and sugar, then add the crème fraîche. Mix thoroughly, pass through a sieve and add the crumbled amaretti biscuits.

2. For the caramel, dissolve the sugar in boiling water until it turns brown. Coat the bottom of an ovenproof dish with a little caramel, add the panna cotta cream and bake in the oven for 45 minutes at 265 °F / 130 °C in a water bath. Allow to cool.

Zabaglione à la Artusi

3. Prepare the almond cake by combining all the cake ingredients and roll out the dough to form a ¹/₂ in / 1 cm thick circle. Bake for 10 minutes at approximately 340 °F / 170 °C.

4. To make the zabaglione, mix the sugar into the egg yolks, beat in a double boiler with a whisk and add the Marsala. Place the panna cotta, cut into teardrop shapes, onto plates and cover with the caramel. Arrange wedges of cake dusted with vanilla sugar next to them and pour on some zabaglione. Garnish with fruits and a sprig of mint.

Citrus Fruit Terrine with

Preparation time: 45 minutes
Cooking time: 15 minutes
Cooling time: 2 hours
Difficulty: ★★

Serves 4

$^2/_3$ cup / 150 ml orange juice
$3^1/_2$ tbsp / 50 ml grapefruit juice
6 tbsp / 90 g sugar
8 sheets of gelatin
$^1/_2$ vanilla bean
a little freshly ground pepper
fresh mint, shredded
$^2/_3$ cup / 150 ml muscatel

6 oranges
2 grapefruit

For the tea sauce:
4 tea bags
2 cups / 500 ml water
$^1/_2$ cup / 125 g sugar
4 sheets of gelatin

For the glazed orange peel:
2 tbsp grenadine
1 tbsp water
$3^1/_2$ tbsp / 50 g sugar
peel of 1 untreated orange

Playing with the flavor and appearance of fruit is a pleasure known since classical times. The development of certain products has made it possible to create stylish fruit terrines whose composition flatters the gourmet's tastebuds.

It is citrus fruits that have inspired our chef to create this dessert, more precisely the orange and the grapefruit, which are similar to each other in appearance and taste. The orange is a winter fruit, and we have the seafarer Vasco da Gama (1469–1524) to thank for its introduction to Europe. The grapefruit was cultivated from the pomelo or shaddock, native to warmer regions of North America, and was not exported to Europe from Florida until the 19th century. By now, so many different varieties exist that they can be classified both by their country of origin and their color, so one has to compare the various types of oranges and grapefruit and decide which complement each other best. Blood oranges, however, should be avoided, as their coloring is too intense. Whichever you select, please make sure that all the seeds have been carefully removed. It can be quite unpleasant to bite down on a seed when enjoying a refreshing slice of citrus fruit terrine.

The jelly that forms the basis of this recipe contains muscatel, or more precisely muscatel from Rivesaltes, if the choice were left to our chef. This is a fine, highly aromatic wine that has been produced in Roussillon for centuries. Its intoxicating aroma provides an excellent contrast to the English tea sauce.

1. Slightly warm the orange juice and grapefruit juice. Add the sugar, soaked gelatin and the pulp of the vanilla bean to the juices. Add a little pepper and the shredded mint. Heat everything at a low temperature, then allow to cool. Stir in the muscatel.

2. Peel the oranges and grapefruit, and cut out segments without seeds or skin. Cut the peel of one orange into thin strips.

Muscatel and Tea Sauce

3. Use a ladle to pour a layer of the orange and grapefruit jelly into a rectangular baking dish, and allow to set in the refrigerator for about 15 minutes. To make the tea sauce, bring 2 cups / 500 ml of water to a boil, then add the sugar, tea bags, and soaked gelatin. Allow to steep until completely cooled. Remove the teabags and pass through a pointed sieve.

4. Once the jelly has set, place a layer of fruits flat onto it. Cover with another layer of jelly and again allow to set in the refrigerator. Continue this process until all the ingredients have been used. Bring the water to a boil with the sugar and grenadine, and glaze the orange peel in the resulting syrup. Simmer for 10 minutes. Serve the terrine in slices. Garnish with the tea sauce and orange peel.

Delicate Apple Cake

Preparation time: 1 hour
Cooking time: 20 minutes
Difficulty: ★★

Serves 4

2 apples (e.g. Granny Smiths)
pieces of butter
superfine sugar

For the puff pastry
(see basic recipes p. 803):
4 cups / 500 g flour

3 tsp / 15 g salt
1 cup / 250 ml water
2 cups / 500 g butter

For the tarragon sorbet:
$1^3/_4$ cups / 100 g tarragon
3 cups / 750 ml milk
$6^1/_2$ tbsp / 100 g sugar
$2^1/_2$ tbsp / 60 g dextrose

Had a piece of nearby tarragon not accidentally fallen into a pan of cooking apples, our chef might never have had the idea to combine the two. After adding more tarragon (this time intentionally) and measuring it more precisely, one must admit that he has created an exquisitely light and refined dessert.

According to Jean Crotet, the most suitable apples for this dessert are Rennets, small yellow apples with red spots whose firm, crunchy flesh is sweet and aromatic. Alternatively, one could use the sour Granny Smiths, with light-green skins and white flesh. One should choose whichever variety one likes best and cut the apples into strips as thin as the cake base. This results in an interesting contrast between the soft pieces of fruit and the crunchy pastry.

It is very unusual to use tarragon in a sorbet. For this purpose, it is recommended that one use only fresh leaves with a strong aniseed smell, which is brought out further by simmering in sweetened milk. It is advisable to prepare the sorbet a few hours ahead of time and serve it with the hot cake as soon as the latter has finished baking.

This sweet, invigorating dessert inevitably reminds one of that old English saying, "An apple a day keeps the doctor away."

1. Make the puff pastry according to the basic recipe, allowing the mixture of water, salt, and flour to stand for 1 hour. Fold the puff pastry six times. Roll out a dough $^1/_8$ in / 2 mm thick. Trace and cut out a circle with a diameter of 9 in / 20 cm. Place on a baking sheet.

2. Peel and core the apples and cut into very thin slices.

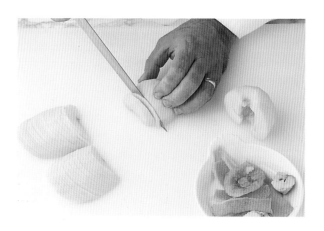

with Tarragon Sorbet

3. Arrange the apples on the dough base. Place some small pieces of butter on the apples and sprinkle with superfine sugar, which will caramelize the apples. Bake for about 15 minutes at 355 °F / 180 °C.

4. To make the sorbet, bring all the ingredients to a boil and add the washed and chopped fresh tarragon. Allow to seep for 1 hour. Pass through a pointed sieve and pour into a ice cream machine. Prepare the sorbet ahead of time so it can be served with the cake hot out of the oven.

Peach Soup

Preparation time: 30 minutes
Difficulty: ★

Serves 4

4 peaches

For the marinade:
4 cups / 1 l red wine
1¼ cups / 300 ml raspberry sauce
¼ cup / 60 g sugar
lemon juice

For the lemon verbena ice cream:
2 oz / 50 g fresh lemon verbena
1 cup / 250 ml cream
1 cup / 250 ml milk
6 egg yolks
¾ cup plus 1 tbsp / 200 g sugar
peel of 2 untreated limes

To garnish:
½ cup plus 2 tbsp / 100 g raspberries or
    wild strawberries
fresh almonds

Louis XIV had a royal passion for peaches, and his orchards were full of them – over 30 different varieties in the end. Peaches continue to be very popular and the flesh of these tender and juicy summer fruits is one of the great pleasures of summer. Peaches are one of the main products cultivated in the Languedoc-Roussillon region of France, and purists place great value on the quality of fruit from this area.

Our chef has chosen the yellow peach for its flesh, which is firmer and juicier than that of the white peach. Above all he recommends the peaches from the area around Carcassone, though these are not easy to come by. Due to the many vineyards around the medieval city, Michel Del Burgo need not worry about obtaining good quality wines; they flow, so to speak, right up to his doorstep.

The marinade used in this recipe has to be prepared with considerable care, for bruised raspberries should not be used even to prepare a sauce. If fresh raspberries of a suitable quality are not available, an alternative is to buy fruit pulp, which is frequently surprisingly good.

The same is true of the lemon verbena; preferably it should be fresh. But even in its dried form (as sold in herbal shops to make herbal tea) it can be used to produce an ice cream of amazing finesse, which is matched only by thyme and rosemary ice creams, if at all. And on the theme of possible variations, why not use flavorful, tender pears or red plums instead of peaches?

1. Mix the red wine, raspberry sauce, sugar, and lemon juice in a bowl without heating, to make the marinade for the peaches. To make the lemon verbena ice cream, use the ingredients listed above to produce a custard (see basic recipes) and then steep the lemon verbena in it. Glaze the lime peel and dice into small pieces. Add to the custard and thoroughly stir it in an ice cream machine.

2. Clean the peaches, peel them and cut them into eight pieces. Lay the pieces flat on a metal baking sheet.

...with Red Wine

3. Pour the marinade over the peaches and allow to marinate for 2 hours. Peel the fresh almonds and cut them lengthwise.

4. Drain the peach segments, arrange them on a plate in a fan shape and place a ball of ice cream in the center. Pour some of the marinade around them, and garnish with wild strawberries or raspberries and the almonds. Serve cold.

Pancakes

Preparation time: 45 minutes
Cooking time: 25 minutes
Difficulty: ★

Serves 4

For the pancake batter:
(see basic recipes p. 802)
1 cup / 125 g flour
3½ tbsp / 55 g sugar
1 cup plus 2 tbsp / 280 ml milk
4 eggs
1 tbsp / 15 g butter
1 pinch of salt
2 tbsp / 30 ml water

For the orange sauce:
2 tbsp / 30 ml orange juice
2 cups / 500 ml water
¾ cup plus 1 tbsp / 200 g sugar
1½ tbsp / 20 ml Grand Marnier

For the crème Chiboust:
3 untreated oranges
sugar syrup at 30 °Beaumé
butter
¼ cup / 60 ml lemon juice
2½ tbsp / 40 ml heavy cream
3 eggs
1½ tbsp / 20 g superfine sugar
2 tbsp / 15 g pudding mix powder
1 sheet of gelatin

No one knows for sure who Suzette was, but we know some of her professed inventors, including the great master chefs Escoffier and Charpentier. The latter professed to have invented this celebrated orange-flavored dessert in Monte Carlo in honor of the companion of the future King Edward VII of England, giving it her Christian name. The rapid rise of Charpentier, who worked for Queen Victoria and the Rocke-fellers, appears to confirm this version – assuming, of course, that the former heir to the British throne really did escort a young woman named Suzette.

Philippe Dorange prepares the dessert just as his parents, both experienced in gastronomy, taught him. The recipe retains all the basic elements of the classic suzette. Here the mandarin flavor is introduced by Grand Marnier, an orange liqueur based on cognac, which should be used sparingly as it can overpower the flavor of the pancakes if one adds even a few drops too many.

In order to both improve the taste of the pancake batter and make it firmer and smoother, one could add a little condensed milk. There should be a short break between preparing the mixture and making the pancakes to allow the flavors of the ingredients to blend more thoroughly.

The Chiboust cream, also called St. Honoré cream, reminds our Parisian chef of the 19th century, when a gifted pastry chef named Chiboust invented the classic St. Honoré gâteau and named it after the patron saint of pastry chefs; the cream was named after him. Its preparation requires a degree of care, especially when stirring the butter into the cream with a wooden spoon without causing the eggs to collapse. Once that has been done, half an hour in the refrigerator should give this special cream the desired consistency without further ado.

1. Prepare the pancake batter. Let it rest for a short time, and make small pancakes. Using a cookie cutter, cut out circles with a diameter of 3½ in / 8 cm.

2. For the orange sauce, make a caramel using water and sugar, then pour the orange juice into it. Add the Grand Marnier and simmer. Cut the peels of the oranges into thin strips and glaze them in the sugar syrup (30 °Beaumé). Add the butter. To make the Chiboust cream, mix the lemon juice with the juice of the 3 oranges, add the heavy cream and bring to a boil.

Suzette with Orange Sauce

3. Separate the eggs. Beat the egg yolks with the sugar, add the pudding powder, combine with the boiling cream in step 2 and finish like a pastry cream (see basic recipes). Remove from the heat, add the gelatin that has been soaked in cold water, and allow to cool. Beat the egg whites until stiff and fold into the cream.

4. Spread the Chiboust cream onto half of each of the pancakes, and then fold them together. Arrange on a deep plate and bake for 5 minutes at 355 °F / 180 °C. After removing from the oven, pour the orange sauce around the pancakes. Decorate with the glazed orange peel.

Mango Fans with

Preparation time: 30 minutes
Cooking time: 10 minutes
Difficulty: ★

Serves 4

2 ripe mangoes
10 passion fruit
sugar

For the vanilla ice cream:
1 vanilla bean
³/₄ cup / 200 ml milk
3¹/₂ tbsp / 50 g sugar
2 egg yolks
1²/₃ cups / 400 ml crème fraîche

Slices of baked puff pastry
(see basic recipes p. 803)

To garnish:
4 sprigs of mint
confectioners' sugar

With this recipe, Claude Dupont is attempting to lure us into an imaginary "Garden of Earthly Delights." The fruit of the mango tree comes from India, though they can also be found in Africa and America. Passion fruit is grown mainly in Latin American (Brazil and Venezuela) and in the warmer regions of the United States (Florida and Hawaii).

There is nothing coincidental about the combination of mango and passion fruit: it is a successful balance of two fruits whose flavors complement without overpowering each other. However, both fruits should be at their very best. The mangoes must be just ripe and not too soft to the touch; it does not matter what color the skin is. Choose heavy fruits with a smooth skin. Avoid fruits with black spots on the skin, as these

are signs of overripe fruit with fibrous flesh. The mango has a large, flattened stone that is somewhat difficult to remove. One is left with about two-thirds of the fruit that can be used for the fans.

The passion fruit, with its brownish skin tinged with violet, makes a somewhat weatherworn impression. Its sour flesh is exceptionally well suited to making a fruit sauce, including all the fruit's little black seeds.

This tasty dessert is extremely rich in vitamins and, for that reason, need not deter those on a diet or watching their weight. Perhaps this recipe will inspire you to become creative and discover other ways to prepare and enjoy these two tropical fruits.

1. Peel the mangoes and remove the stones. To make the vanilla ice cream, pour the milk into a pan with the vanilla bean, bring to a boil and remove from the heat. In a mixing bowl, beat the sugar and egg yolks with a whisk, and pour the hot milk onto them. Combine thoroughly and allow to cool. Mix in the crème fraîche and stir in an ice cream machine until cold. Freeze.

2. Cut the four mango halves into thin segments, so that they can be arranged in a fan shape. Dust the mango fans with confectioners' sugar and heat slightly under a hot grill.

Vanilla Ice Cream

3. Halve the passion fruits and scoop out all the flesh. Puree in a blender and pass the resulting fruit sauce through a sieve, then add sugar to taste.

4. Place a mango fan on each plate. Pour some fruit sauce over each fan. Arrange two balls of vanilla ice cream on crispy slices of puff pastry. Garnish with a sprig of mint dusted with confectioners' sugar.

Swabian Gugelhupf

Preparation time: 30 minutes
Cooling time: 12 hours
Difficulty: ★★

Serves 4

2 tbsp / 20 g raisins
3¹/₂ tbsp / 50 ml rum
3 egg yolks
4¹/₂ tbsp / 70 g sugar
grated peel of 1 untreated orange
2¹/₂ tbsp / 40 ml Grand Marnier

5 tsp / 25 ml cream
³/₄ oz / 20 g chocolate
1¹/₄ cups/300 ml cream, whipped

To garnish:
various fruits
mint leaves

There are almost as many varieties of gugelhupf as there are different ways of writing it in the German-speaking world: Kugelhopf, Kougelhof, Guggelhopf, etc. The Alsatians, old masters in this field, make it using yeast dough with raisins and almonds, and always bake it in the traditional gugelhupf tin with a large cylindrical opening in the middle. Lothar Eiermann, who comes from Swabia in Germany, swears by his regional black-and-white variation of the dessert. He has, however, added other gugelhupf variations to his repertoire over the years, including some savory ones with goose livers or salmon.

In this variation consisting entirely of ice cream, which is of course kept in the freezer, it is especially important to use the right quantity of sugar. Since the raisins also contains sugar, it might be necessary to reduce the amount slightly. One should also be careful with the egg yolks, which are rich in carbohydrates. In the first stage of the work, the egg yolks and sugar must be beaten until they form an even, foamy mixture, for this is decisive in creating an ice cream cake with a light texture. It is obvious that everything needs to be prepared beforehand, as the ice cream needs at least 12 hours to set in the freezer.

Even after this period of time, it is possible that the mixture will still be soft and the ice cream will not be hard enough to turn out of the mold. This is usually the case when too much sugar has been added despite our chef's warning. If that should happen, do not say you were not warned ...

This excellent and very fresh dessert can be served with whipped cream, raisins, almond cookies or other dry cookies, according to taste.

1. Soak the raisins in the rum for 12 hours or longer. Beat the egg yolks and sugar until foamy, then add the drained raisins, orange peel and Grand Marnier.

2. Heat the cream and chocolate together and bring to a boil, then let cool. Combine one-third of the egg mixture with the chocolate sauce.

with Fruit

3. Fill a gugelhupf mold, or bundt pan, with alternating layers of the "white" and "black" mixtures.

4. Use a fork to create a marble effect, then freeze the gugelhupf for 12 hours. Decorate with fresh seasonal fruits and sprigs of mint and serve.

Preparation time: 20 minutes
Cooking time: 3 minutes
Difficulty: ★★

Serves 4

2 mangoes
2 kiwis
12 strawberries

For the almond cream:
2 cups / 250 g finely ground almonds
1 cup / 250 g sugar
1 cup / 250 g butter
6¹/₂ tbsp / 100 ml rum
3 eggs

For the ice cream:
12 egg yolks
1¹/₄ cups / 300 g sugar
2 cups / 500 ml milk
2 cups / 500 ml almond milk
1 cup /250 ml cream

For the pastry cream:
(see basic recipes p. 802)
2 cups / 500 ml milk
6 egg yolks
¹/₂ cup / 125 g sugar
6¹/₂ tbsp / 50 g flour
1 vanilla bean

Do fruits such as kiwis, mangoes and strawberries actually go with an almond cream? It will be very difficult for gourmets to resist this enjoyable and tasty combination on their plates.

Once known only as an exotic fruit, the kiwi is now cultivated in more northern latitudes as well. Italy is the leading producer and exporter in Europe. Kiwis can be integrated into many dishes, and in addition to their high levels of vitamin C, they are also very low in calories. They also keep well, another point in favor of this fresh, invigorating fruit.

The fleshy, juicy mango was introduced to Europe by the Portuguese, who discovered it growing in Brazil. Both sweet and rich in vitamins, the mango traditionally has been used in the preparation of chutneys or spicy dishes such as Indian curries. Just like kiwi, the mango contains very few calories and is a favorite among dieters.

The almond cream derives its delicate flavor from the addition of powdered almonds, and is complemented by the almond milk in the ice cream.

1. To make the almond cream, mix the ground almonds, sugar, and softened butter in a mixing bowl. Add the eggs and rum and beat thoroughly with a whisk.

2. To make the ice cream, beat the egg yolks and sugar until foamy. Bring the milk to a boil and carefully mix with the egg yolk and sugar mixture. Add the almond milk and cream. Pour everything into the ice cream machine. Peel the kiwis and mangoes and cut into thin slices. Also slice the strawberries.

3. Make the pastry cream according to the basic recipe, and combine it with the prepared almond cream.

4. Spread some almond cream onto the center of each plate and decoratively arrange the fruit on it. Place under a hot grill for a few minutes and serve with a scoop of ice cream.

Blancmange with

Preparation time: 1 hour
Cooking time: 20 minutes
Cooling time: 30 minutes
Difficulty: ★★

Serves 4

5¼ oz / 150 g white chocolate

For the almond mousse:
½ cup / 80 g confectioners' sugar
1 cup / 250 ml milk
3½ tbsp / 50 g sugar
3 egg yolks
3 sheets of gelatin
1 cup / 250 ml cream, whipped
½ cup / 50 g ground almonds

2 bitter almonds, ground
bitter almond extract

For the almond sponge cake:
1 egg yolk
1 egg
6 tbsp / 60 g confectioners' sugar
½ cup / 60 g ground almonds
7 tbsp / 50 g flour
2½ tbsp / 40 g sugar
2 egg whites

For the kirsch syrup:
2½ tbsp / 40 ml kirsch
6½ tbsp / 100 ml sugar syrup (60 °Beaumé)
2½ tbsp / 40 ml mineral water

Blancmange was originally completely white. It was made using almond milk and thickened with jelly, which was occasionally flavored. Constant Fonk has enriched his modern version of blancmange with a gold leaf decoration, quite in the style of the Venetians, whose merchant ships brought spices and silks from the Far East to Europe in the 15th century. The Dutch, so history tells us, were keen to emulate them and in the following century founded the Dutch colonial empire. This led to the incorporation of herbs and a range of spices in Dutch gastronomy from an early stage.

The almonds in this recipe have to be ground extremely finely so that the ingredients combine completely and form a light, airy mousse. The bitter almonds and bitter almond extract have to be measured carefully, as they otherwise might spoil the flavor of the entire dish. But it is precisely this combination of the two most important types of almond that make it a classic in haute cuisine.

It is unusual that one's very first attempt to make a complete chocolate ruffle is successful. Even the majority of professional chefs admit that their own efforts only led to failure at first. So you must have a little patience! One more tip about the white chocolate ruffles: briefly placing the baking sheet in the refrigerator will give the chocolate a firmer consistency and make it easier to form complete ruffles.

When making the kirsch syrup, please do not experiment or use inexpensive substitute ingredients: use only genuine kirsch.

1. For the almond mousse, mix the ground almonds and confectioners' sugar. Bring the milk to a boil with half of the sugar. Beat the egg yolks and the remaining sugar until foamy. Pour the boiling milk onto the eggs. Cook like a custard (see basic recipes), then add the soaked gelatin. Pour over the almond mixture and allow to cool. Add the stiffly whipped cream and blend carefully.

2. Pour a thin layer of melted white chocolate onto a warmed baking tray. As soon as it is firm, use a metal spatula to create chocolate ruffles.

White Chocolate Ruffle

3. To make the sponge cake, combine the egg yolk and whole egg with the confectioners' sugar. Add the ground almonds and flour. Finally, fold in the egg whites, which have been whipped until stiff with the sugar. Pour the mixture onto a baking sheet lined with baking paper and bake for about 10 minutes at 355 °F / 180 °C. Cool, then cut with a cookie cutter.

4. Prepare a mold with a diameter of 8 in / 18 cm and height of 1 3/4 in / 3.5 cm or 4 individual molds with a diameter of 2 3/4 in / 6 cm and height of 2 in / 4 cm. Line the bottom with almond sponge cake and soak with the kirsch syrup. Fill each mold with almond mousse right to the top and allow to set in the refrigerator. Turn out onto a dessert plate and decorate with the chocolate ruffles. If desired, garnish with gold leaf.

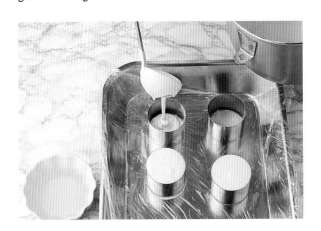

Preparation time: 2 hours
Cooking time: 20 minutes
Difficulty: ★★★

Serves 4

1 cup / 100 g shelled walnuts
¹/₂ cup / 50 g cocoa powder

For the chocolate sponge cake:
6 eggs
¹/₂ cup plus 2 tbsp / 150 g superfine sugar
¹/₄ cup / 30 g cocoa
³/₄ cup plus 1 tbsp / 100 g flour

For the praline mixture:
6 oz / 175 g bittersweet chocolate coating

³/₄ cup / 200 ml cream
7 tsp / 35 g butter

For the pastry cream with coffee
pastry cream (see basic recipes p. 802)
a little instant coffee
³/₄ cup / 200 ml cream, whipped

For the coffee custard
(see basic recipes p. 800):
2 cups / 500 ml milk
6 egg yolks
1¹/₂ oz / 40 g coffee beans
6¹/₂ tbsp / 100 g sugar

chocolate coating, melted

Opinions are divided as to when exactly cocoa was introduced to France from America. Some think it was Queen Anna of Austria, daughter of the Spanish king, who introduced it at court in 1615. Others believe it was Alphonse de Richelieu, archbishop of Lyon and brother of the priest, who used the cocoa bean after 1661 to "calm the humors of his spleen" at the advice of a Spanish monk. Once condemned by theologians, frequently made out to be the root of all evil, chocolate is now a much-revered candy of the very best quality and the object of devotion.

This dessert, in which chocolate and coffee are combined, can only be made using products of an exceptional quality. A dark bittersweet chocolate with a pure cocoa content of at least 60 to 70 % should be used. The best coffee is surely that from Colombia, which is both milder and more acidic, and this is particularly true of the Supreme variety. It is frequently used as an instant coffee, as its dry essence does not alter the consistency of the cream. For a lighter pastry cream, a little whipped cream can be added to the ingredients.

The walnuts give this dessert a delightfully crunchy touch. After shelling, they are chopped and refrigerated. Varieties with nuts that are easy to remove from the shell are particularly suitable.

This exceptional dessert sweetens the days in Drouant, where members of the Academie Goncourt have been received since 1914, and some of them positively lust for chocolate ...

1. To make the chocolate sponge cake, beat the eggs and sugar with an electric mixer in a double boiler for 7 to 8 minutes in order to produce an even batter. Mix in the cocoa and flour using a skimmer. Pour onto a baking sheet lined with baking paper and bake for 8 to 10 minutes at 355 °F / 180 °C.

2. For the praline mixture, cut up the chocolate coating, add the boiling cream, stir with a spatula, add the butter and reduce, stirring occasionally, until thick.

with Walnuts

3. Prepare the pastry cream and, towards the end of the cooking process, add the instant coffee. Allow to cool and blend in the very stiffly whipped cream. To make the coffee custard, boil the crushed coffee beans in the milk, allow to steep for 10 minutes, then continue as described in the basic recipe. Pass through a sieve and refrigerate.

4. Cut the sponge cake using round cookie cutters with a diameter of 3^1/$_2$ in / 7 cm and a height of 2 in / 4 cm. Spread the praline mixture on the sides and then alternate layers of pastry cream and walnuts. Finish with a piece of sponge cake. Cover with chocolate coating and arrange on a plate with the custard.

Preparation time: 1 hour
Cooking time: 20 minutes
Cooling time: 2 hours
Difficulty: ★★

Serves 4

4 cups / 1 l water
2 cups / 500 g sugar
4 peaches
2 vanilla beans

For the pistachio ice cream:
2 cups / 500 ml milk
2 cups / 500 ml cream

1 vanilla bean
1 cup / 250 g sugar
10 egg yolks
bitter almond extract
2 cups / 250 g pistachios, shelled and crushed

For the champagne zabaglione:
8 egg yolks
1 cup / 250 g sugar
1²/₃ cups / 400 ml champagne
6¹/₂ tbsp / 100 ml cream

To garnish:
whipped cream

From June until September, the peach is the quintessential summer fruit. Its tender, juicy flesh can be enjoyed in a number of ways: as it is, with or without the downy skin that adds so much to the charm of the peach. Originally from China, where it is a symbol of both fertility and immortality, the peach reached the western world via Persia. That is also the source of the Latin name, *persicum* or *persica*. Whether yellow or white (the latter is famed for its aroma), peaches should be peeled at the last minute because they oxidize very quickly, and they should be handled carefully, as they bruise easily.

Great care and attention is needed in preparing the zabaglione: the mixture must be beaten continuously with a whisk while it is being heated and cooled. This produces a thick consistency, even though the final effect of this cream, which is whipped with champagne, is very light.

Our chef recommends serving a flavorful ice cream with vanilla, bitter almonds, and pistachios with this dessert. Bitter almond extract is usually so concentrated that just a few drops are enough. The high fat and sugar content of the pistachios ensures an intense flavor. In order to achieve the optimal flavor, as Marc Haeberlin does, use pistachios from the Mediterranean region. The dessert should be served very cold with a glass of champagne or Gewürztraminer wine (a very sweet wine from Alsace).

1. To make the ice cream, boil the milk and cream with the vanilla bean and half of the sugar. Beat the egg yolks with the remaining sugar and pour the hot milk over them. Return to the stove and simmer over a low heat. Remove from the heat and add a few drops of bitter almond extract. Stir in the ice cream maker and add the shelled, crushed pistachios at the last minute.

2. To prepare the peaches, bring the water and sugar to a boil with the vanilla beans. Wash the peaches and place in the syrup without peeling. Poach at a low temperature for 15 to 20 minutes. Test with the tip of a knife to check their tenderness. Allow to cool in the syrup.

'Haeberlin"

3. To make the zabaglione, beat the egg yolks and sugar until foamy. Add the champagne and the cream. Whisk at a low temperature in a double boiler until the mixture thickens. Remove the frothy wine cream from the heat.

4. Place the hot pan in a bowl with ice cubes and continue to beat with the whisk until cool. Peel the cooled peaches. Arrange a peach and a ball of pistachio ice cream in a large deep plate. Cover with zabaglione and garnish with whipped cream.

Preparation time:	*20 minutes*
Cooking time:	*30 minutes*
Cooling time:	*overnight*
Difficulty:	★

Serves 4

For the chocolate mousse:
5 egg yolks
½ cup / 125 g sugar
3½ oz / 100 g bittersweet chocolate
3½ tbsp / 50 g butter
1 sheet of gelatin
1½ cups / 350 ml heavy cream
2 egg whites
7 tbsp / 50 g chopped walnuts
7 tbsp / 50 g chopped hazelnuts

For the green coffee sauce:
2 cups / 500 ml milk
⅓ cup / 50 g green coffee beans
4 egg yolks
6½ tbsp / 100 g sugar

For the chocolate crêpes:
6 tbsp / 40 g cocoa powder
1 cup / 250 ml milk
2 eggs
¾ cup / 100 g flour
1 pinch each of salt and sugar

To garnish:
grated chocolate

It is already unusual to make crêpes out of a chocolate dough. But the most uncommon aspect of this exquisite and simple recipe is that the crêpes are folded into cannelloni shapes, filled with a creamy chocolate mousse and served with an exceptional sauce made with green coffee. This sauce's finesse guarantees that the dessert will be a success. All it requires is a little planning and organizational skills.

The mousse should be prepared using quality chocolate with a high cocoa content. Since there is no arguing with personal preferences, milk or white chocolate could be used instead of bittersweet, always assuming that the chocolate is fresh and shiny and has a good consistency. The chocolate must melt in the mouth and form a thick, creamy mass when heated.

If you are decidedly passionate about chocolate, you might wish to join one of the discriminating and elite clubs of chocolate-tasters, whose festive gatherings are evidently an outstanding cure for every type of stress. And to think that not all too long ago cocoa was quite unfairly accused of causing a plethora of bad side effects ...

Green coffee consists of shelled, sorted beans that have not been roasted, and which produce an unusually intense aroma. They are not so readily available, but turn the coffee sauce into something that even experts will find unforgettable, and your guests are also sure to enjoy. If you wash and freeze the green coffee beans after using them for the infusion, you will be able to use them again.

1. To make the mousse, whisk three egg yolks and the sugar to produce a glistening, foamy mixture in a double boiler. Melt the chocolate and butter in another double boiler. Add 2 egg yolks and the soaked gelatin to the chocolate. Combine the two mixtures. Fold in the heavy cream, the stiffly beaten egg whites and half of the chopped nuts. Refrigerate overnight.

2. Infuse the milk with the green coffee beans for 20 minutes. Beat the egg yolks and sugar until foamy and add the boiling hot milk. Beat over low heat until the sauce starts to thicken. Pour through a pointed sieve and allow to cool for 1 hour.

Mousse Cannelloni

3. Prepare the crêpe dough using the given ingredients and allow to rest for a short time. Make the crêpes one after the other in a very hot pan, frying each side for 2 minutes. Place on a plate and let cool for 1 hour.

4. Fill the crêpes with the chocolate mousse, sprinkle them with the remaining chopped nuts, and roll them up. Before serving refrigerate for 3 to 4 hours. Arrange two "cannelloni" on each plate in a V-shape. Pour the coffee sauce in between the crêpes and sprinkle them with dark and white chocolate flakes.

Almond Waffles

Preparation time: 1 hour
Cooking time: 20 minutes
Difficulty: ★

Serves 4

30 small strawberries

For the waffle dough:
1 cup / 250 g sugar
6¹/₂ tbsp / 100 ml water
7 tbsp / 50 g flaked almonds

For the caramelized almonds:
15 blanched whole almonds
¹/₃ cup / 50 g confectioners' sugar
olive oil
confectioners' sugar to garnish

For the almond cream:
³/₄ cup / 190 ml cream, whipped
a little almond oil
sugar to taste

For the strawberry sauce:
9 oz / 250 g strawberries
6¹/₂ tbsp / 100 g sugar

This crunchy delight for the tastebuds, which looks pretty and is simple to prepare, requires only a little patience and above all small, ripe strawberries. It is important that they are small and rounded in flavor. Supposedly, strawberries were so fashionable in 18th-century France that even baths were decorated with them, which is less surprising if one considers that the French word for strawberry, *fraise*, is derived from the Latin word *fragrare*, which means "to smell good."

Fresh strawberries must be red and shiny, not soft to the touch, and have a firm stem. It is best to remove the stems after the fruits have been washed so they do not fill with water.

The waffles are ready to be removed from the oven when they start to vibrate gently. The almond mixture for the waffles can be prepared the previous day and kept in the refrigerator overnight. This gives one more time to attend to the final preparations without distraction, and perhaps even devote a little time to the life and achievements of Marshall Plessis-Praslin (1598–1675), who was an ardent defender of royal power during the Fronde revolts and was victorious at Turenne Rethel (1650). Roasted almonds are supposed to have been invented in his kitchens, and in French they are called *praline*, a term derived from his name. They are the original form of the sweets that we now know as pralines.

These waffles can, of course, be prepared with other flavors: instead of using strawberries and almonds, one might, for example, use raspberries and hazelnuts, oranges and pistachios or other similar combinations.

1. To make the waffle dough, boil the sugar and water until they take on a golden color, then allow to become hard. Once the caramel is firm, combine it and the blanched almonds in a blender and blend to produce a fine powder. Store in an airtight container in the freezer until needed.

2. To caramelize the almonds, pour olive oil into a hot pan and sprinkle in the confectioners' sugar. Once the mixture is well browned, sauté the whole almonds until they are coated with caramel. Then roll them in additional confectioners' sugar. Set aside. Add the almond extract to the cream and beat until stiff. Add sugar to taste. Set aside.

with Strawberries

3. Place molds with a 4¹/₂ in / 10 cm diameter on a non-stick baking tray and sprinkle in a layer of the caramel powder. Remove the molds and bake the waffles in the oven for approximately 2 minutes. Allow to cool until they are only lukewarm, remove from the baking tray and allow to rest on a plate. One needs three waffles per serving.

4. To make the strawberry sauce, boil the strawberries and sugar with a little water for 8 minutes, and then pass through a pointed sieve. Pour a little sauce onto the plate, then use a pastry bag to alternate mounds of almond cream and strawberries around the edge of four of the waffles. Place waffles on top of the cream and strawberries and repeat. Garnish with the caramelized almonds.

Preparation time: 20 minutes
Cooking time: 30 minutes
Difficulty: ✭

Serves 4

2 lb 3 oz / 1 kg fresh rhubarb
1 cup / 250 g sugar
1¼ cups / 300 ml water
9 oz / 250 g strawberries
3½ oz / 100 g wild strawberries
2 vanilla beans
1 tbsp cornstarch

For the vanilla ice cream
(see basic recipes p. 806):
2 cups / 500 ml milk
6 egg yolks
6½ tbsp / 100 g sugar
2 vanilla beans

This rhubarb-based dessert combines tradition, freshness, and lightness with a somewhat unusual ingredient. The rhubarb plant consists mainly of decorative leaves, and has fibrous red and green stems that are used in numerous desserts, cakes, and compotes. Rhubarb is also known as a plant with medical and astringent properties.

The main problem in using rhubarb is its sourness, which can be reduced by marinating it in sugar for several hours or blanching it briefly in boiling water. Whichever method one chooses, one should use firm, thick stems with intense coloring, and check for an intense aroma when sliced. In this recipe, the rhubarb is cooked together with strawberries for about half an hour.

Unfortunately, wild strawberries do not keep very long and there is nothing one can do to alter this. Our chef claims to have found a variety that is still fresh the day after being picked, but they are not widely available. One should use the freshest berries possible.

Eyvind Hellstrøm feels that the soup is perfect without any other additions, and does not require spices such as cinnamon and ginger such as the English, for example, like to add. It can be prepared at any time of year, served cold in summer and hot in winter.

1. Coarsely dice 1 lb 12 oz / 800 g of the rhubarb and simmer with the sugar, water, and strawberries for 20 to 30 minutes. Pass through a pointed sieve.

2. Bring the resulting liquid to a boil again, spoon off the foam and add the vanilla beans. Reduce slightly and add the cornstarch.

Soup "Bagatelle"

3. Dice the remaining 7 oz / 200 g rhubarb finely. Prepare the vanilla ice cream according to the basic recipe.

4. Briefly brown the diced rhubarb in a pan with some additional sugar, and then add to the rhubarb soup. Pour a little rhubarb soup into each bowl, place a spoon of vanilla ice cream in the middle and arrange the wild strawberries around it. Serve either cold or hot, according to the time of year.

Orange Jelly with

Preparation time: 15 minutes
Cooking time: 30 minutes
Cooling time: 1 hour
Difficulty: ★

Serves 4

3 untreated lemons
juice of 2 oranges
2¼ cups / 550 g sugar
2 sheets of gelatin

This very simple and heavenly light dessert, shining with the light of the Mediterranean sun, is a worthy conclusion to a special meal. It can be prepared effortlessly at any time of year, keeps well, and seduces the diner with its freshness and finesse, which are combined with an exceptionally high vitamin content. Oranges contain not only vitamin C, but are also very high in calcium and magnesium, and contribute to one's well-being in many different ways. Originally grown in Southeast Asia, Liguria in Italy is the first place this fruit was cultivated in Europe. Today the United States is the world's leading producer of oranges.

For this dessert, the first step is to squeeze orange juice using juicy fruits of a very high quality. The navel orange, given that name by the British because it has a "navel," the Valencia orange or the blood orange with its red flesh would all be sure to make this dessert a success. The oranges should not be squeezed until the last minute, so that the utmost flavor is retained and any oxidization is minimized.

Since the Middle Ages, lemons have also been cultivated in Italy. As this recipe uses only lemon peel, one should choose untreated fruits that are sufficiently large and firm. In addition, it is recommended to wash them in warm water and brush the peels thoroughly before grating.

This delicious, refreshing citrus fruit jelly, in which the fruits can be cut according to one's own imagination (giving the dish a personal decorative touch), is also easy to digest. Try serving it with a glass of Grand Marnier – its amber color and superb taste provide a masterly finishing touch.

1. Peel and thinly slice the lemon rinds. Wash the lemon peel in 2 cups / 500 ml cold water. Repeat five or six times. Bring 2 cups / 500 ml water to a boil with 2 cups / 500 g of the sugar and the lemon rind, and simmer for an hour over low heat.

2. Meanwhile, in another pan, carefully reduce the orange juice with the remaining sugar and ⅔ cup / 150 ml water for half an hour.

Marinated Lemon Peel

3. Dissolve the sheets of gelatin in cold water, then add them to the reduced and slightly cooled fruit juice. Pour into a dish and refrigerate.

4. Cut various shapes out of the set jelly. Place on serving plates and garnish with the reduced lemon peel.

Preparation time: 2 hours
Cooking time: 20 minutes
Cooling time: 30 minutes
Difficulty: ★★★

Serves 4

For the sponge cake dough:
3 eggs
5 tsp / 25 ml water
2 tbsp / 15 g cocoa
1/2 cup / 130 g sugar
1 cup / 130 g flour
1 tsp / 3 g baking powder
coffee liqueur (Kahlua)

For the mocha cream:
5 tbsp / 70 ml pastry cream (see basic

recipes p. 802)
1/2 tsp / 2 g gelatin
2 tbsp / 30 ml strong coffee (espresso)
3/4 cup / 200 ml crème fraîche
bittersweet chocolate

For the light chocolate sauce:
9 oz / 250 g white chocolate coating
1/2 cup / 125 ml heavy cream
4 tsp / 20 ml water

For the dark chocolate sauce:
9 oz / 250 g bittersweet chocolate coating
1/2 cup / 125 ml heavy cream
4 tsp / 20 ml water

For the caramelized nuts:
almonds, cashews, pistachios, sugar, oil

For the peppermint ice cream:
vanilla ice cream (see basic recipes p. 806)
a little melted chocolate
3/4 cup / 200 ml peppermint liqueur

This outstanding dessert originally derived its name from Queen Charlotte, the wife of King George III of England. Ever since, the charlotte has been enjoyed in countless permutations of cake-lined, cream-filled delicacies according to country and era, and charlotte russe is still one of the favorite versions. It is best to prepare the charlotte early and refrigerate it until it is served; this gives it a firmer consistency and lets the sponge cake gradually absorb the flavor of the filling. As sponge cake can absorb an enormous quantity of liquid, the charlotte should be covered while it is in the refrigerator so that it does not pick up any other flavors.

Mocha is a type of coffee with a very mild aroma, which produces an extremely oily drink. For that reason it is best suited to making espresso, which is used to make the cream filling for the charlotte. The flavour is enhanced by the coffee liqueur

(Kahlua) with which the sponge cake is drenched. Mocha beans first appeared in Yemen in the 6th century, and their name is derived from the Yemen port of Mokka.

In this recipe our chef has created an imaginative combination of two ingredients that are extremely well-suited to each other: coffee and chocolate. Chocolate appears in various nuances of flavor in the sponge cake and sauces, which contrast and yet complement each other. The two sauces must have the same consistency and must not be allowed to simmer when heated, as this would cause them to lose their sheen. The sauces should not be poured onto the plates until immediately before serving the dessert, as they might otherwise set and detract from the quality of the presentation. This dessert will be an absolute success and is guaranteed to be irresistible accompanied by a glass of dessert wine.

1. To make the sponge cake, beat the eggs, water, sugar, flour and baking powder until fluffy. Separate the mixture into two halves and mix the cocoa into one half. Line a baking tray with baking paper. Using two pastry bags, pipe alternating strips of the two mixtures. Bake at 430 °F / 220 °C.

2. Line the sides and bottoms of individual molds with the sponge cake. Soak the sponge cake with coffee liqueur. Beat the pastry cream. Dissolve the gelatin in cold water, pour into the espresso and mix with the pastry cream. Stir the crème fraîche until creamy, then carefully fold it into the mocha coffee cream.

Ice Cream and Nuts

3. Caramelize the nuts in sugar and place on an oiled plate. Prepare the light chocolate sauce by heating the heavy cream and water, adding the chopped chocolate coating, and stirring over low heat until a smooth sauce is produced. Make the dark chocolate sauce in the same way. Fill the charlottes completely with mocha coffee cream and smooth off the excess. Refrigerate.

4. Prepare the vanilla ice cream and divide into two bowls. To make the peppermint ice cream, add the peppermint liqueur to one bowl of ice cream; stir until cold in an ice cream maker and, shortly before finishing, add a thin stream of liquid chocolate. Pour the two sauces onto the dessert plates, place a charlotte in the center of each, and arrange the ice cream and caramelized nuts decoratively around them.

Preparation time: 45 minutes
Cooling time: 2 hours
Difficulty: ★★

Serves 4

3 egg yolks
3 1/2 tbsp / 50 g sugar
1 cup / 250 ml cream
1 3/4 oz / 50 g printen or other spiced cookies,
    chopped
3 1/2 tbsp / 50 ml rum

For the spiced oranges:
3 large oranges
3 1/2 tbsp / 50 g sugar
6 1/2 tbsp / 100 ml orange juice
1 whole clove
cinnamon, vanilla, star anise, cardamom

For the caramel:
2 tbsp dextrose
1/2 cup / 120 g sugar
3 tbsp / 40 ml water

"Good Christmas printen are baked at Easter," states our chef like a shot, eager to revive this old gourmet tradition. Printen, a variation of the cookies spiced with cinnamon and cloves that are beloved throughout northern Europe, derive their name from *printen*, "to press," because they are made with specially carved rolling pins that literally press the dough into various shapes.

This parfait, which has a firmer consistency than usual that suits the oranges well, is a true symphony of spices and astonishing tastes. The ingredients should be chosen carefully.

Star anise should not be confused with aniseed, which is used in many other desserts and dry cakes. The fruit of this bush, native to Vietnam, contains an intensely aromatic extract that has a soothing effect on the digestive system. Cardamom is the name given to fruits and brown seeds derived from several Indian plants that have a distinctive, peppery flavor. In India these are combined to make a spice that is used in many curries and rice dishes. In European recipes cardamom is mainly used for baking, especially spiced bread. Due to its intense flavor, it should be added carefully.

Cinnamon is the dried inner bark of the cinnamon tree. It can be obtained as a whole piece of curled bark (cinnamon stick) or in a ground form. Here, too, it is important to be careful with the quantity, as too much can destroy the flavor of the dessert.

1. Whisk the egg yolks in a double boiler with the sugar. Allow to cool, stirring constantly, and add the liquid cream. Add the chopped printen cookies and the rum, pour into a bowl, and place in the freezer.

2. For the spiced oranges, peel the oranges and divide them into segments. Use the sugar to make a dry caramel, then carefully and gradually add the orange juice to it. Add the spices and orange segments. Bring to a boil and allow to cool in an uncovered bowl.

Parfait

3. In a small pan, make a brown caramel out of the sugar, dextrose, and water. Coat the outside of a ladle with oil and pour fine strands of the caramel over it to form a cage. Allow to cool and remove from the ladle. Repeat, making one caramel cage per serving.

4. Remove the parfait from the freezer and divide into portions. Place a slice of the parfait onto the center of each plate, cover with a caramel cage and arrange some spiced oranges around it.

Pears with Cranberries

Preparation time: 1 hour
Cooking time: 40 minutes
Difficulty: ★★

Serves 4

1 lb / 500 g cranberries
6$^{1}/_{2}$ tbsp / 100 ml water
1$^{1}/_{3}$ cups / 200 g confectioners' sugar
1 cinnamon stick
5 pears (with stems)

For the vanilla sauce:
$^{3}/_{4}$ cup / 200 ml milk
6$^{1}/_{2}$ tbsp / 100 ml cream
1 vanilla bean
1 egg yolk
2 tbsp confectioners' sugar

Örjan Klein, who presents us here with a Swedish dessert, is very enthusiastic about traditional dishes using the produce of his native country. This dish is a further example of his culinary skill, and it calls to mind two memories for Örjan Klein: the orchard full of pear trees around his country house in Nølgarder, and the cranberries from Småland, where he was born. This delight for the taste buds used to be served on Sundays, and he had many opportunities to enjoy it as a child.

The pears should be very flavorful and cook well. Of the numerous varieties available, several will be suitable for this recipe. They need only be peeled shortly before adding them to the stewed cranberries, whose sour taste will permeate the pears.

The small, red cranberries are often served as an accompaniment to game, which in Sweden includes reindeer and elk, and feature in a whole variety of recipes. Whole berries keep for an astonishingly long time. In this recipe, their sour taste combines with the gentle flavor of vanilla, which moderates the acidity of the berries somewhat. Cranberries grow not only in North America, but throughout Sweden as well, which certainly contributes to their popularity in that country. It would be difficult to replace them in this recipe, except perhaps with a red wine syrup flavored with cinnamon.

1. Reserve some of the cranberries for garnishing. Puree the rest in a blender. Cook the puree in a saucepan for 15 minutes with the water, sugar, and cinnamon.

2. Peel the pears without removing their stems, set them into the saucepan with the puree mixture and continue to simmer for 20 minutes.

and Vanilla Sauce

3. Remove the pears and place them in a deep bowl. Pass the puree through a sieve and pour the resulting liquid over the pears. Refrigerate for a few days.

4. To make the vanilla sauce, mix the milk and cream and bring them to a boil with the opened vanilla bean. Whisk the egg yolk and sugar, then pour onto the vanilla milk, stirring continuously until slightly thickened. Pass the sauce through a pointed sieve and allow to cool. Pour the sauce onto plates, place a pear on each one, and garnish with cranberries.

Grapefruit Gratin with

Preparation time: *30 minutes*
Cooking time: *5 minutes*
Difficulty: ☆

Serves 4

2 grapefruit
some almonds, colored pink and roasted
2¹/₂ tbsp / 40 ml cream

For the zabaglione:
6 egg yolks
¹/₂ cup / 125 ml sugar syrup at 30 °Beaumé
3¹/₂ tbsp / 50 ml grapefruit juice
¹/₂ cup / 125 ml cream

The brilliant 17th-century French military leader, Marshall César de Plessis-Praslin, surely could not have guessed that three hundred years after his death his name would become synonymous with exquisite sweets. It was actually one of his cooks, rather than Plessis-Praslin himself, who had the idea to make roasted almonds (*praline* in French).

Almonds can be bought flavored or colored. For example, pink ones are popular in the Auvergne or Bourbonnais for decorating brioches, giving them a bit of color and taste. They can always be found at fairs, and are sometimes even replaced by peanuts, which is a less expensive, though much less tasty option.

The tart or even slightly bitter taste of grapefruit, with its yellow, pink or red flesh, provides a strong contrast to the almonds. Pink grapefruit would be attractive in this dessert because of the complementary colors. The grapefruit is a descendant of the sweet orange, which is called *pompelmoes* in Dutch, and is very rich in vitamins A and C. It should be prepared at the last minute in order to retain its freshness and vitamins. That is true for the segments, which are arranged on the serving plates, and the juice, which is used in the zabaglione.

The zabaglione, the only part of this recipe that can be a little difficult to create, is prepared at a temperature no greater than 160 °F / 70 °C. One starts with low heat and increases it slightly once the zabaglione starts to thicken. The whipped cream is not added until the mixture has cooled, as the heat would otherwise make it collapse. A sorbet made of passion fruit, or grapefruit if one uses a different fruit for the gratin, would be an excellent accompaniment to this dessert.

1. *To make the zabaglione, mix the slightly beaten egg yolks with the syrup. Stir in the grapefruit juice, heat until it thickens slightly, and then allow to cool.*

2. *Peel the grapefruit and remove the skin. Remove the seeds, together with any small pieces of skin that could leave a bitter taste.*

Roasted Almonds

3. Whip the cream until stiff and combine with the cooled zabaglione, stirring carefully.

4. Pour some zabaglione onto each plate and arrange grapefruit segments on it in the form of a rosette. Sprinkle on the crushed pink almonds, then place under a hot grill for a few minutes. Serve with a passion fruit sorbet.

Preparation time: 20 minutes
Cooking time: 10 minutes
Cooling time: 30 minutes
Difficulty: ✶

Serves 4

40 sour cherries
10 slices of phyllo pastry
a little confectioners' sugar
clarifed butter

For the ganache filling:
6¹/₂ tbsp / 100 ml cream
3¹/₂ oz / 100 g chocolate coating

4 tsp / 20 g butter
1 tbsp / 20 g dextrose
1 egg

For the syrup at 15 °Beaumé:
2 cups/500 ml water
2³/₄ cups/700 g sugar

For the orange marmalade:
2 oranges
a dash of Grand Marnier
a dash of orange juice

A light dessert can be satisfying both for those who are watching their figures and for gourmets. This dessert, composed of fruits full of character such as cherries and oranges, the former in a light pastry and the latter as a marmalade, is an excellent example.

The sour cherry, with its firm, lightly sweet flesh, is harvested in July and August. It is frequently sold in stores in the form of preserves, syrup or fruit schnapps. Of course, cherries can also be eaten raw, but keep in mind that they keep for only a few days. In order to help sweet tooths control their natural appetite for sweet morsels – who can withstand a bowl full of cherries? – Jacques Lameloise has prepared these little pastries, in which the sour cherries are strictly counted out, nestled in a chocolate filling and wrapped in a crisp pastry. There should be a balance between the flavors of the fruit and the chocolate, so that neither detracts from the individual taste of the other.

The chocolate filling must be quite thick. If it is prepared a day in advance, it will have a more even consistency and be easier to work with. The origin of the name *ganache* (French for "fool") for this tasty combination of chocolate and cream – a term normally reserved for the old fools in slapstick farces – remains mysterious.

Oranges, in this case used to make a marmalade, are always well received when combined with chocolate. Oranges with a thin peel should be used, and their flavor is enhanced by the Grand Marnier, which is produced using orange peel marinated in cognac.

1. For the chocolate filling, bring the cream to a boil. Immediately add the chocolate coating and let it melt. Then add the butter, dextrose, and egg, and thoroughly mix everything over a low heat.

2. For the orange marmalade, cut the oranges into slices and cook them for about 10 minutes in the sugar syrup at 15 °Beaumé. Strain. Use a hand blender or food processor to chop them, then add orange juice that has been enriched with a dash of Grand Marnier until the marmalade has the desired consistency.

Chocolate and Oranges

3. Cut the slices of phyllo dough in strips 2 in / 4 cm wide. Using a pastry brush, brush on a little clarified butter, so that the dough becomes saturated with it.

4. Place a little chocolate filling in the center of each strip of dough, then top with two sour cherries. Wrap the dough around the filling like candy wrappers and bake in a 390 °F / 200 °C oven for 5 minutes. Sprinkle the pastries with a little confectioners' sugar and serve with the orange marmalade, adding a little chocolate ice cream if desired.

Rote Grütze

Preparation time: 30 minutes
Cooking time: 25 minutes
Difficulty: ★

Serves 4

3 cups / 750 ml water
1 lb 10 oz / 750 g berries (1 lb 5 oz / 600 g
   red currants, 2¹/₂ oz / 75 g raspberries,
   2¹/₂ oz / 75 g black currants)
1 vanilla bean

³/₄ cup / 180 g sugar
7 tbsp / 50 g cornstarch
7 tbsp / 50 g flaked almonds

To garnish:
7 tbsp / 50 g chopped almonds
whipped cream

Our chef, Erwin Lauterbach, admits that he prepared this delicious dessert in order to round off his contribution to Eurodélices, and that it is more of a family tradition than a gastronomic specialty. Indeed, *rote grütze*, a kind of thickened fruit soup or pudding, is a beloved dessert in many northern European countries. Our chef recalls that it was a great favorite of his and his grandmother often served it to him in bed before he went to sleep.

Countless variations of *rote grütze* exist, all of them delicious, and virtually any combination of ripe red fruits can be used. This recipe calls for a typical summer mixture. As always, the berries should be ripe, fresh, and carefully selected so that no spoiled or bruised fruits are used.

Instead of incorporating other flavors into this dessert, which already has an intense taste, our chef has decided to add only vanilla and chopped almonds, but he readily admits that even this is not necessary if the berries are ripe and flavorful enough. However, it is still customary to decorate all traditional Danish desserts with whipped cream.

The addition of black cherries to this dessert would provide a good opportunity to discover the Danish Cherry Heering, an excellent liqueur that is frequently served with pancakes, but also goes very well with *rote grütze*.

1. Combine the water and berries in a saucepan and bring to a boil. Pass through a pointed sieve into another pan, bring the sauce to a boil again and then simmer carefully.

2. Scrape the pulp out of the vanilla bean and add both the pulp and husk of the bean to the fruit sauce. Add sugar to taste. Let cool.

with Almonds

3. Pour ³⁄₄ cup / 200 ml of the cooled fruit puree into a pan and add the cornstarch. Mix thoroughly with the remaining puree, bring to a boil again and add the flaked almonds.

4. Quickly cool the red jelly by placing the pan in cold water and covering it with a lid. Pour the cold jelly into a serving bowl and garnish with the chopped almonds if desired. Serve with whipped cream.

Grandmother's Egg

Preparation time: 30 minutes
Cooking time: 10 minutes
Difficulty: ★★

Serves 4

4 cups / 1 l whole milk
1 cup / 240 g superfine sugar
2 vanilla beans
8 eggs
1 tsp cornstarch

What would family cooking be without grandmothers? Full of good advice and wisdom based on experiences gathered over the course of decades, every grandmother has her special culinary delights that her family associates with trust and tenderness. Léa Linster also has lovely memories like this and honors her grandmother with a dessert that is a masterly combination of feeling and expertise.

Before she started, our chef's grandmother always "borrowed" the things she needed from her husband, who was a baker. She whipped the egg whites in a copper bowl, using a primitive whisk with a wooden handle and a conical head. It is still best to whip the eggs by hand for this recipe, and it is essential to use only very fresh eggs. They must be whipped until they are very stiff, so that they do not lose their shape while cooking.

Most people will already be familiar with low-quality desserts made with beaten egg whites. This is partly due to the use of electric mixers, and is also a sign that the beaten egg whites were not used quickly enough. They should, therefore, be whisked at the very last minute and the egg white dumplings poached as soon as they have the right consistency.

It is important to add a small spoonful of cornstarch to the custard in order for it to thicken. If the mixture seems too thick when it is finished, one can always add a little cold cream and stir it again. In keeping with tradition, only real vanilla should be used, rather than artificial flavors.

1. Put the milk and 6¹/₂ tbsp / 100 g of the sugar and the halved vanilla beans into a pan and bring to a boil. Separate the eggs and beat the egg whites, preferably by hand, with 3¹/₂ tbsp / 50 g of sugar in a copper bowl until stiff.

2. Using two tablespoons, shape the stiffly beaten egg whites into dumplings and carefully poach them in the hot milk for 3 minutes on each side. Make sure that the milk does not boil again. Drain the dumplings.

White Dumplings

3. Whisk the egg yolks with the remaining sugar and add a teaspoon of cornstarch. Pass the milk through a pointed sieve, pour onto the egg yolks and prepare like a custard (see basic recipes). Allow to cool.

4. Pour a ladle of the custard into small dessert bowls and place two egg white dumplings on top. Serve immediately.

Quark Desser

Preparation time: 20 minutes
Cooking time: 10 minutes
Difficulty: ★

Serves 8

For the quark:
1¼ cups / 300 g quark
6 tbsp / 95 g sugar
2 sheets of gelatin
½ cup / 130 ml cream, whipped

For the sweet pastry:
½ cup / 60 g flour
3½ tbsp / 50 g slightly salted butter

1 egg yolk
3 tbsp / 40 g sugar
a pinch of salt
⅕ oz / 5 g dried yeast
15 almonds, finely ground

For the raspberry sauce:
2 cups / 500 ml raspberry puree
½ cup / 125 ml sugar syrup at 30 °Beaumé
confectioners' sugar

1 lb / 500 g raspberries

In this simple, light, and enticing dessert, which can be prepared at any time of year, quark is harmoniously combined with red berries, which are rich in vitamin C. Quark is a very mild, smooth, unripened cheese popular in several European countries, which has a consistency something like sour cream.

The natural fat content of quark makes it an ideal companion for fruits, as it moderates their acidity. Served with a dry cake, such as these cookies made from sweet pastry, the result is a delicious contrast of soft quark and crunchy dough. All this contributes to the perfect balance of this composition.

The red berry sauce, which can be made using red currants, blackberries or a combination of berries instead of raspberries, is passed through a sieve in order to remove the small seeds, hairs, and stems that one could not otherwise neatly remove from the berries. If desired, this dessert can be prepared using figs or quinces, and a sauce made with apples would be marvelous with them.

1. Mix the quark with the sugar and beat until foamy. Add the dissolved gelatin, then fold in the whipped cream.

2. Line the molds with a spoonful of the quark mixture. Place three raspberries in each mold, then fill them with quark. Refrigerate.

with Raspberries

3. For the cookie dough, combine the flour and butter. Mix the remaining ingredients together, than add the flour and butter mixture. Roll out the dough and cut out cookies in the shape of glasses, then make eye-shaped holes in half of the cookies. Bake for 10 minutes at 355 °F / 180 °C. Place cookies with eye-shaped holes on top of plain cookies and dust with confectioners' sugar.

4. Using the raspberry puree and sugar syrup, make the raspberry sauce. Arrange the raspberries in the shape of a bunch of grapes on the plates, and pour the sauce onto the bottom of the plate. Decorate with some thinned quark. Turn the quark balls out of the molds onto the plates. Pour a little red sauce into the holes in the cookies.

Preparation time: 45 minutes
Cooking time: 45 minutes
Difficulty: ★

Serves 6

1 cup / 250 g sugar
6 eggs, separated
2 cups / 250 g crushed walnuts
1 tsp breadcrumbs

For the egg cream:
10 egg yolks
6¹/₂ tbsp / 100 g sugar
1 cinnamon stick
6¹/₂ tbsp / 100 ml water

For the roasted walnuts:
6¹/₂ tbsp / 100 g sugar
a little lemon juice
7 tbsp / 40 g shelled walnuts

For the sweetened whipped cream:
2 cups / 500 ml cream
¹/₃ cup / 80 g superfine sugar

In order to avert the sin of gluttony, Portuguese desserts implore religion, saints, and the almighty divinity for aid with dishes such as "nuns' stomachs," "heavenly bacon," or, as in this case, "Madonna" walnut tree. Throughout Portugal there are 200 different terms of this sort. This tradition is not so very astonishing in a country densely populated with abbeys and monasteries, which played a major role in the development of agriculture and livestock breeding until the 17th century.

In this quite unusual recipe, two very monastic products are contrasted: the egg (which can be prepared in thousands of ways, both sweet and savory) and the walnut from Cascais, close to Lisbon. As usual, whole walnuts do not betray the quality of the nut they conceal. They must be shelled to ascertain whether they are rancid or too dry. Caution is advised when selecting the nuts, as a single bad nut can destroy the entire dessert.

Cinnamon is used for the egg cream in this cake, though it should be added in moderation. This element we owe to the Portuguese seafarer Vasco da Gama, the courageous discoverer of far-off places, who brought substances back to Europe that had never been seen before.

There is a large spectrum of Portuguese delicacies, all of which in principal should be preceded by a prayer ...

1. To make the egg cream, pass the egg yolks through a fine sieve. In a pan, make a syrup from the sugar, cinnamon stick, and water. Allow to cool. Remove the cinnamon stick. Add the egg yolks. Rapidly whisk over low heat with a wooden spatula or spoon so that the eggs become creamy. Do not boil!

2. Grease a cake pan with a diameter of 10 in / 22 cm and a height of 2 ¾ in / 6 cm, and line it with greased baking paper. Prepare the cake. In a mixing bowl, stir the egg yolks and sugar until creamy, then add the crushed nuts and breadcrumbs. Whisk the egg whites and add. Fill the pan and bake for 30 minutes at 320 °F / 160 °C.

Walnut Tree

3. For the roasted nuts, cook the sugar and several drops of lemon juice in a pan and add the shelled walnuts. Once the caramel is brown, pour the mixture into an oiled bowl. Allow to cool, and divide it into two halves. Crush one portion with a rolling pin, and grind the other half in a blender.

4. Take the cake out of the oven and turn it out of the pan. Allow to cool on a rack and then cut through once horizontally. Mix the crushed, roasted nuts with the egg cream, and spread this on the bottom layer of the cake. Replace the top half and cover the top and sides with the cream that has been whipped until stiff with the sugar. Sprinkle the cake with the ground nuts.

Preparation time: 2 hours
Cooling time: 2 hours
Difficulty: ★★★

Serves 4

For the white chocolate mousse:
3 sheets of gelatin
3¹/₂ oz / 100 g white chocolate coating
1 egg
2 egg yolks
4 tsp / 20 ml white rum
1 cup / 250 ml cream, whipped

For the passion fruit mousse:
1¹/₄ cups / 300 g passion fruit flesh
2¹/₂ tbsp / 40 ml Cointreau
4 sheets of gelatin

2 egg whites
1 cup / 250 g sugar
1¹/₃ cups / 330 ml cream, whipped

For the moscato jelly:
1¹/₂ cups / 350 ml moscato or muscatel wine
3¹/₂ tbsp / 50 g sugar
3 sheets of gelatin

For the Cointreau ice cream:
4 cups / 1 l milk
4 cups / 1 l cream
1 vanilla bean
20 egg yolks
1¹/₂ cups plus 2 tbsp / 400 g sugar
1¹/₃ cups / 300 ml Cointreau

To garnish:
1 baby pineapple
mint, bittersweet chocolate

Thanks to Dieter Müller, white chocolate has become better known in Germany and this recipe promises to make further converts: in an exotically colored dessert, the sweet melting sensation of chocolate is combined with the tart taste of passion fruit. One can accurately speak of a passion when it comes to our chef's innovative use of first-class produce from distant countries to conjure up repeatedly new color and taste combinations.

As the combination of white chocolate and passion fruit mousse does not produce any particularly great contrast in color, our delicate Charlotte is served in a fine dark chocolate cage, which serves as a kind of lace border. It would be unforgivable to do without the baby pineapple – a product of the island of Réunion: a few slices of it, cut wafer-thin and arranged on the plates in fan shapes, round off the decoration

of the dessert. Connoisseurs value this little pineapple above all for its concentrated flavor, which lends this recipe a considerable part of its effect. However, a large pineapple can be used if the smaller ones are not available.

According to our chef, a key element for the success of this dessert is the correct consistency of the chocolate mousse, which is prepared entirely without sugar; before freezing it must be almost liquid. In the end it will have a soft consistency that harmonizes marvellously with the creamy Cointreau ice cream with which it is served. The orange liqueur, which is produced using a combination of bitter oranges from the Antilles and mild oranges from the Mediterranean, is shown off to advantage here. Its alcohol content of 40% adds a welcome flavor to the charlotte.

1. Melt the bittersweet chocolate in a double boiler. Using a pastry bag, pipe a net of diagonal lines onto strips of waxed paper. Allow to harden, then carefully peel off the paper. For the white chocolate mousse, dissolve the gelatin in cold water. Melt the white chocolate in a double boiler. Add the egg, egg yolks, gelatin, rum, and cream and combine well. Pour the mousse into individual molds with a diameter of 3¹/₂ in / 8 cm to a depth of 1 in / 2 cm and freeze.

2. Heat part of the passion fruit flesh, then add the Cointreau and gelatin that has been dissolved in the liqueur. Combine everything with the remaining passion fruit flesh. Make a meringue: whisk the egg whites until very stiff, add the melted sugar and allow to cool. Combine with the fruit mixture and whipped cream. Pour 1 in / 2 cm of the passion fruit mousse onto the chocolate mousse in the molds and freeze.

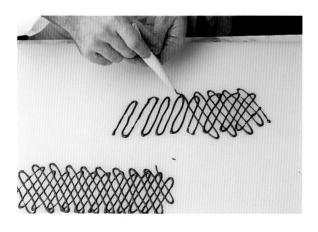

Chocolate Charlotte

3. To make the jelly, heat the moscato, then remove it from the heat and add the sugar and dissolved gelatin. Allow to cool. Cover the top of the charlottes with the jelly. For the Cointreau ice cream, bring the milk, cream, and pulp of the vanilla bean to a boil. Whisk the egg yolks and sugar, then add the hot milk mixture and reduce while stirring. Allow the ice cream to cool, stir in the Cointreau, and let it harden in an ice cream maker.

4. Arrange thin slices of pineapple on four plates. Place a charlotte in the center of each and surround with a chocolate cage. Garnish with finely chopped mint leaves. Serve with a ball of Cointreau ice cream and a chocolate stick made of rolled up bittersweet chocolate.

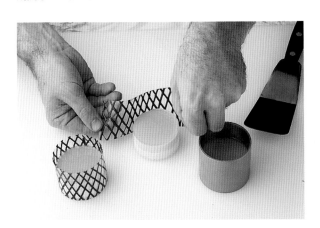

Quince Sorbet with

Preparation time: 40 minutes
Cooking time: 25 minutes
Difficulty: ★★

Serves 4

1 lb / 500 g quinces
a sprig of rosemary
sugar
1 untreated lemon
10½ oz / 300 g rhubarb
1 glass quince liqueur
sugar syrup

For the fruit sauce:
7 oz / 200 g black currants or blueberries
1 tsp cassis (black currant liqueur)

For the spice cookies
(see basic recipes p. 805)

To garnish:
sprigs of rosemary
several whole berries

This recipe would not exist if it were not for the fertile quince tree in Jean-Louis Neichel's garden. The quince, a curious little yellow fruit (*Cydonia vulgaris* in Latin), has more to offer than its unassuming appearance might lead one to suspect at first sight. Quinces cannot be eaten raw; they have to be turned into jelly, pastries or syrup. Some methods of preparation have justifiably gained a certain degree of fame, such as the quince preserves from Orléans, a jam made using quinces and bitter orange, which was highly regarded by Louis XIV and remains popular throughout the world.

Quinces are categorized according to their shape either as apple quinces, with a tart flavor, or as milder pear quinces. In some Jewish communities whole cloves are stuck into quinces on New Year's Day. They are passed around during prayer so that they can fill the room with their pleasant fragrance.

Quinces have to be cooked carefully, and much longer than apples; this is best done in a pot with a closed lid so that the cooking juices do not evaporate. This yields a delicious amber-colored compote that can easily be turned into a sorbet.

Our chef loves rhubarb mainly because of its connections with Alsace; in central Europe (Germany and Switzerland), it is very highly valued. It is harvested twice a year, and because of its digestibility is suitable for many recipes.

1. Peel the quinces, cut them into pieces and cover with water. Cook for 15 minutes at a low temperature with a sprig of rosemary, some sugar, the lemon peel, and some of the lemon juice. Cut the fruit into small pieces in the liquid.

2. Peel the rhubarb and cut it into small pieces. Cook it in a little water until it is reduced to the consistency of a compote, adding sugar to taste.

Rhubarb Compote

3. Cook the black currants or blueberries briefly with a little sugar. Mix and pass through a pointed sieve. Add a few drops of cassis and a little lemon juice to the sauce. Put the quince puree and the glass of quince liqueur into an ice cream maker. Add a little sugar syrup and mix everything thoroughly, then put in the freezer.

4. Prepare the cookie dough, spread it on a baking sheet in very thin circles and sprinkle on spices. Bake for a few minutes. In deep plates, arrange some of the rhubarb compote on one side and a scoop of the quince sorbet on the other. Pour a little fruit sauce in the center and garnish the dessert with some whole berries and a sprig of rosemary.

Ice Cream

Preparation time: 20 minutes
Cooking time: 10 minutes
Difficulty: ✶

Serves 4

4 apples (Golden Delicious)
4 tbsp / 60 ml butter
4 tbsp / 60 ml superfine sugar
2 tbsp / 30 ml brown rum

For the vanilla ice cream:
2 cups/500 ml milk
6 egg yolks
¹/₂ cup/125 g sugar
1 Bourbon vanilla bean

The apple is probably the oldest and most widespread pomaceous fruit. Though most people are familiar only with the thirty-odd kinds that are widely available in grocery stores, there are in reality more than a thousand different variations of this quintessential fruit, and still others have unfortunately disappeared. Just reciting their names stimulates the imagination with their echoes of country life: Ontario, Clochard, McIntosh, Winesap, Rome Beauty ...

The Golden Delicious apple is a relative newcomer: it was first discovered in the USA in 1912. The color of this apple, which is available all year round, varies from an even green to yellow depending on its ripeness. It has a fine, juicy sweet flesh, which achieves a melting consistency when cooked. For this recipe one should use large, thoroughly ripe and intensely flavored

fruits. By the way, the peel contains a large part of the apple's vitamin C, so it should not generally be removed.

The caramel is made with equal parts of butter and sugar and should be light; a dark caramel would taste bitter. But the most outstanding element of this dessert is the harmonious combination of softly cooked apples and vanilla. The origins of vanilla date back to the pre-Columbian Aztec civilizations. The beans of this tropical orchid plant should be soft and fleshy and have a very intense fragrance. The fame of vanilla led to its being very desirable for a long time, so that a variety of alternatives were invented. For our recipe, however, only Bourbon vanilla is good enough. Our chef, Pierre Orsi, has named the dessert after his wife as a small token of his esteem for her.

1. Peel and core the apples, then cut them into slices ¹/₄ in / 0.5 cm thick. For the ice cream, bring the milk to a boil. Whisk the egg yolks with the sugar until foamy. Scrape out the vanilla pulp and add to the milk. Pour the vanilla milk onto the frothy eggs and stir in. Simmer for 3 minutes at 195 °F / 90 °C, then cool and allow to harden in an ice cream maker.

2. Heat the butter and the sugar in a non-stick pan and cook until the mixture forms a light caramel.

'Geneviève''

3. Add the apple slices to the pan with the caramel, and brown evenly all around over a high heat.

4. Once the apples are soft, add the rum, flambé them and remove from the heat. Put a large ball of vanilla ice cream into each dessert bowl. Arrange the apples around the edges and serve immediately.

Sweet Chestnut Desser

Preparation time: 45 minutes
Cooking time: 15 minutes
Difficulty: ✶

Serves 4

9 oz / 250 g chestnut puree, unsweetened
³/₄ cup / 120 g confectioners' sugar
9 oz / 250 g bittersweet chocolate coating
5 tbsp / 70 g butter

For the hazelnut custard:
(see basic recipes p. 800)
4 eggs
¹/₄ cup / 40 g confectioners' sugar
1 cup / 250 ml milk
²/₃ cup / 100 g hazelnuts, shelled and finely
 chopped
2¹/₂ tbsp / 50 g pureed almonds

The sweet chestnut (not to be confused with the inedible horse chestnut) was for a long time an essential source of nourishment for poor people in the Mediterranean countries. Whether served as a soup or puree, chestnuts are an extremely good source of energy. Unshelled nuts, which can be gathered during October and November, should have a smooth, shiny, round shell.

Underneath the shell one finds a fibrous skin, which is easily removed if the chestnuts are briefly dipped into boiling water. To make a puree, the chestnuts are cooked in milk at a low temperature for about 40 minutes, without adding sugar. If the puree will be kept for a few days, one should avoid oxidization

by adding a slice of lemon before mashing them, and refrigerate the mixture in an airtight container. Unsweetened chestnut puree is also available in grocery stores.

The hazel tree produces oval-shaped nuts in a very hard shell. Our ancestors thought they had magical and medicinal properties. Nowadays, crunchy hazelnuts are valued mainly for their abundance of roughage and fats, and their fine taste adds a pleasant flavor to the custard. The third nut flavor is also added to the custard, in the form of almond butter or pureed almonds, not to be confused with almond paste, available at natural foods stores.

1. Mix the chestnut puree with the confectioners' sugar. Melt the chocolate coating in a double boiler and stir in the butter.

2. Combine the chestnut puree and the melted chocolate. In order to produce a soft, light mixture, beat thoroughly with a whisk.

with Hazelnut Sauce

3. Pour the mixture into a rectangular pan and freeze for 48 hours. Using the eggs and sugar, prepare a custard according to the basic recipe. Then add the milk, to which the shelled and finely chopped hazelnuts have previously been added, and cook over low heat until thick.

4. After preparing the custard, dissolve the almond puree in it. Before serving, turn out the dessert and cut into slices like a cake. Serve with the hazelnut custard.

Melon Sorbe

Preparation time: 1 hour
Difficulty: ★

Serves 4

2 melons, each 2 lb 3 oz / 1 kg
1 $^2/_3$ cups / 250 g confectioners' sugar
juice of $^1/_2$ lemon
1 lb / 500 g strawberries

For the sauce:
9 oz / 250 g strawberries
3 tbsp / 30 g confectioners' sugar
juice of 1 lemon
1 glass vodka

To garnish:
peppermint leaves

One fine day the Chinese discovered that a mixture of milk, water, and fruit gained a very special consistency when it was frozen. Frozen desserts and sorbets have been a success ever since. It is recommended that a sorbet be prepared at the last minute and that an alcoholic flavoring that complements the fruit be poured over the sorbet after it is frozen. In this case, a muscatel would be the ideal finishing touch for the melon. However, it is not necessary to add alcohol. In this recipe, only the strawberry sauce contains alcohol in the form of vodka.

As is the case with all summer fruits, melons used in a dessert should always be ripe and aromatic. There are a number of varieties, and cantaloupe melons in particular have a very delicate flesh. For our chef, it is impossible to talk about melons without thinking of the small Provençal town of Cavaillon in France, where they are cultivated. In summer, the air there is thick with the scent of melons.

The strawberry sauce requires very ripe berries, whose stems are easily removed, to produce the most intense color and flavor. The strawberries used for garnishing, in contrast, should be firmer and a little less ripe, so that they are easier to cut. Strawberries do not keep for long, so they cannot be bought in large quantities or ahead of time.

For the finishing touch, Paul Pauvert recommends decorating the two-fruit composition with peppermint leaves, whose refined flavor lends a slightly piquant contrast to the sweetness of the melon sorbet.

1. Quarter one melon, remove the seeds and cut the flesh into cubes. Puree in a blender. Combine the melon puree with the confectioners' sugar and lemon juice. Prepare the sorbet in an ice cream maker.

2. Halve the second melon. Remove the seeds and scoop large balls out of the flesh.

with Strawberries

3. Carefully wash the strawberries with the stems on. Halve them and arrange on the serving plates with the cut side facing upwards, alternating with balls of melon.

4. To make the sauce, wash the strawberries and pass them through a sieve. Add the sifted confectioners' sugar, lemon juice, and vodka. Pour the sauce onto the plates and arrange a ball of sorbet in the center.

Preparation time: 2 hours
Cooking time: 6 minutes
Cooling time: 5 hours
Difficulty: ★★★

Serves 8

For the brittle:
3¹/₂ tbsp / 50 g sugar
2 tsp / 10 ml water
²/₃ cup / 100 g almonds
²/₃ cup / 100 g hazelnuts

For the nougat:
meringue (see basic recipes p. 802)
2 cups / 500 ml cream, whipped
6 tbsp / 75 g each raisins, dried apricots
2 tbsp / 25 g maraschino cherries
2 tbsp / 25 g candied orange peel
¹/₄ cup / 40 g pistachios

For the cigarette batter:
(see basic recipes p. 799)
sesame, saffron

For the spice mixture:
1 tsp / 2 g ground licorice
1 tsp / 2 g ground vanilla
1 tsp / 2 g ground pepper
2 tsp / 4 g ground cinnamon
1 whole clove
2¹/₂ tbsp / 10 g instant coffee

For the sauce:
4¹/₂ tbsp / 100 g honey
1 vanilla bean
6¹/₂ tbsp / 100 ml lemon juice
3 tbsp / 30 g peel of untreated oranges
pistachios

Our chef, born in the Vendée region of France, was inspired in his creation of this recipe by his travels to Asia. During his time there, in addition to living for a while in Japan, he retraced Marco Polo's journey along the dangerous "spice route." It was here that he gathered aromas and adapted the various flavors that give his nougat its special quality, so suited to the European palate. The spices should be selected with great care; their scent is less important than their actual taste.

The mixture of spices must be balanced, for the entire dessert can be ruined by imprecise measuring or poor ingredients. It has been said before but bears repeating: excessive use of spices is the enemy of all good cooking.

Two points are very important when preparing this complex recipe:

– All the basic components, such as the brittle and the fruit and spice mixtures should be prepared in advance.
– The light, sensitive ingredients – the meringue and the whipped cream – should be folded in very carefully so that they do not collapse.

In honor of his present home, Stéphane Raimbault uses this opportunity to incorporate the Midi region's sweet almonds, rich in calcium and magnesium, into his dessert. Along with other various delicacies and dried fruits, nougat is one of the famous "thirteen desserts" served on Christmas Eve in Provence.

1. To make the brittle, boil the sugar and water at 230 °F / 116 °C to produce a syrup. Add the blanched almonds and hazelnuts and caramelize them. Allow to cool, then crush. Make the meringue according to the basic recipe. Combine the fruits, then add the fruit mixture to the whipped cream.

2. Fold the meringue into the whipped cream, then add the crushed brittle as well. Turn the nougat into a bowl and freeze for 5 hours. Prepare the cigarette batter according to the basic recipe, incorporating the spice mixture listed above.

a "Spice Route"

3. Using a triangular stencil, spread the batter onto a non-stick greased baking tray. Sprinkle lavishly with sesame and saffron. Bake for a few minutes at 355 °F / 180 °C.

4. To make the sauce, bring the honey to a boil with the opened and scraped out vanilla bean. Remove from the heat and add the lemon juice and other ingredients. Allow to cool. Place a thick slice of nougat on each plate. Lean three spiced triangles against it and pour some of the sauce around the base. Garnish with mint.

Warm Charlotte

Preparation time: 40 minutes
Cooking time: 40 minutes
Difficulty: ★

Serves 4

1 lb / 500 g cooking apples
6–8 tbsp sugar
13 tbsp / 200 g soft butter

grated peel and juice of
 $^1/_2$ untreated lemon
$^1/_2$ loaf white loaf bread

For the molds:
butter
3 tbsp sugar

The archetypal British apple, the Bramley, could be a cross between the Rennet and the Golden Delicious apple. Because of its acidic taste, it is better for cooking than for eating raw. When cooked, it does not fall apart and develops an extremely fine flavor. In our recipe, it forms the basis for a traditional, economical, and easily prepared dessert. If you are not able to find Bramley apples, substitute other cooking apples. Whichever variety you choose, the apples must be cooked in an uncovered pan so that the liquid can steam off, resulting in a smooth, thick compote that still contains a few firm pieces of fruit.

The firmness of the charlotte is produced by the slices of white bread with which the molds, preferably metal ones, are lined.

The molds have to be thoroughly sugared on the inside, so that a crisp brown crust can form. The most suitable bread is a firm white sandwich loaf, or a yeast bread made with egg and milk. It is vital that the slices of bread overlap along the edges so that the fruit filling does not leak out. After baking, this bread casing produces a firm, golden brown crust, so that the charlottes do not collapse when turned out of the molds.

Serve the dessert warm rather than hot, with custard, a caramel sauce or simple whipped cream. Your guests will love this warm sweet. And, to be completely British, indulge yourself and your guests with a cup of first-class tea!

1. Peel the apples and core them. Cut the flesh into coarse cubes and cook with the sugar, butter, lemon juice, and peel over a moderate heat to produce a thick compote. If necessary, add a little more sugar. Preheat the oven to 390 °F / 200 °C.

2. Cut the crusts off the white bread. Cut the bread into slices $^1/_4$ in / 0.5 cm thick and use a pastry brush to spread butter on them. Cut out round slices of bread with the same diameter as the molds for the lids, and several strips about $1^3/_4$ in / 3.5 cm wide for the edges.

with Bramley Apples

3. Brush the molds with butter, sugar them and line them with the strips of bread: the strips should overlap, so that the compote cannot seep out during baking. The bread should stand about ¹/₄ in/0.5 cm over the top edge of the molds.

4. Fill each mold seven-eighths-full with warm apple compote and firmly close with a bread lid. Bake the charlottes for 10 minutes at 390 °F / 200 °C, then reduce the oven temperature to 320 °F / 160 °C and bake for another 20 to 30 minutes. As soon as the bread is firm and golden brown, take out and serve warm.

Crêpe Pouches with

Preparation time:	1 hour
Cooking time:	15 minutes
Difficulty:	★

Serves 4

4 Williams pears
a little lemon juice
1 tbsp flower honey
1 vanilla bean
7 oz / 200 g raspberries
mint leaves

For the crêpe mixture:
1 cup / 125 g flour
3 eggs
1 cup / 250 ml milk
3½ tbsp / 50 g butter

The pear has been known since classical times, and countless varieties have been bred through the centuries. Ever since it was first bred 180 years ago by an Englishman of the same name, the Williams pear has experienced ongoing popularity. Due to its fine flavor and melting consistency, it is the summer pear *par excellence*, frequently preferred over other equally good pears like the Louis Bonne and Bosc varieties. It is probably only surpassed by the Vereins-Dechants, the "queen of pears," which has a harmonious, voluptuous form raved about by gourmets.

Carmelizing the pears presents no problem at all; simply warm the pears in honey, the "sweet dew" whose flavor sent the Hebrews into raptures. Jean-Claude Rigollet recommends using a honey made with flowers, or perhaps an acacia honey whose fine flavor goes equally well with the pears.

The crêpe mixture has to be carefully stirred by hand so that no lumps form. If necessary, one could always pour the mixture through a fine sieve. Either way, it should be completely smooth and homogeneous. If the milk is poured into the flour and egg mixture gradually and mixed in immediately, the batter should be successful. The mixture is then normally set aside for a few hours before being used to make the crêpes, which improves its consistency due to the gluten in the flour.

1. Prepare the crêpe mixture. Mix the flour and eggs. Gradually add the milk as well as the melted and lightly browned butter and stir in. Allow the mixture to rest.

2. Meanwhile, peel the pears and drizzle lemon juice onto them. Quarter and core them and cut into small pieces. Make the crêpes, one for each serving.

Caramelized Pears

3. Heat the pear pieces with the honey in a pan. Arrange some of the pears in the center of each of the four thin crêpes.

4. Gather the sides of the crêpes to form little pouches and tie with a vanilla bean that has been cut lengthways into four strips. Retain several choice raspberries for garnishing, and prepare a sauce with the rest. Cover the plates with raspberry sauce, place the crêpe pouches on top and garnish with whole raspberries and mint leaves.

Hot Pineapple or

Preparation time: 15 minutes
Cooking time: 5 minutes
Difficulty: ★★

Serves 4

1 pineapple
3¹/₂ tbsp / 50 g butter
4 cups / 1 kg sugar
2 cups / 500 ml water
3¹/₂ tbsp / 50 ml brown rum

For the pineapple sauce:
1 medium-sized pineapple
1 tbsp sugar
1 cup / 250 m white rum
ice cubes

For the sorbet:
2 cups / 500 ml pineapple juice
6¹/₂ tbsp / 100 ml white rum
2¹/₄ oz / 70 g ice cubes

To garnish:
3 tbsp / 20 g blanched almonds

The idea for making this "hot and cold" pineapple dessert, an homage to the juicy fruit found almost everywhere in the Antilles, came to our chef during a family holiday on Puerto Rico. Though he admits that preparing savory dishes is his main preference, he worked almost unceasingly at this recipe once he returned to Spain. After a few trials, a result emerged that was completely satisfactory to him. Very likely, you will be as excited as our chef.

Pineapple originally grew in Central and South America, where Europeans discovered it in the 16th century in Brazil. It was first cultivated in France during the reign of Louis XV, but the European climate is not entirely suitable for this bromeliad, which grows so luxuriantly in the tropics; Hawaii is the leading producer of pineapple today.

Before harvesting, pineapples should be grown to a decent size and ripened in their country of origin. Santi Santamaria considers the small pineapples from the island of Réunion to be less suitable: while they have a more intense flavor, they are difficult to work with. It should be easy to remove the individual leaves of the rosette, a sign that the fruit is ripe.

If you carefully follow the instructions in the recipe, you will create a dense composition of flavors that may awaken a forgotten memory, especially if you sniff your fingertips, which will smell of the fruit. The most important ingredient in this delightfully light dessert is its scent (as suggested by the fruit's name in German, *Ananas*, which derives from the Guaraní word for "scent," *ana*). It provides a virtuoso conclusion to a meal with friends or family.

1. Peel a pineapple and quarter it. Cut the flesh from one quarter pineapple into small cubes. Slice the remaining pineapple lengthwise. Discard the peels.

2. To make the pineapple sauce, chop the flesh of the medium-sized pineapple in a blender. Pass through a fine sieve and add the sugar together with the white rum and ice cubes. Mix everything thoroughly and stir in the small pineapple cubes. Refrigerate. For the sorbet, mix all the ingredients in a blender and prepare in an ice cream maker.

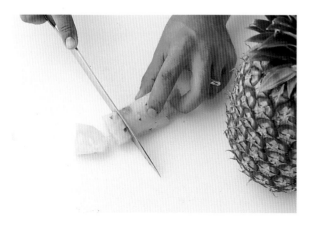

a Piña Colada Sorbet

3. In a pan, heat the butter and slightly brown the pineapple slices in it.

4. Add the sugar, water, and brown rum and reduce the syrup until it starts to caramelize. Arrange a pineapple slice in each bowl on a pool of pineapple sauce, garnish with the almonds, pour syrup over it and serve with a ball of sorbet.

Hot Chocolate Pudding

Preparation time: 30 minutes
Cooking time: 15 minutes
Difficulty: ★★

Serves 6

3¹/₂ tbsp / 50 g butter
1¹/₂ oz / 45 g bittersweet chocolate
1 egg
2 egg yolks
3 tbsp / 25 g flour

¹/₂ cup / 75 g confectioners' sugar
1 cup / 250 ml milk
1 cup / 250 ml crème fraîche
12 oz / 350 g white chocolate, coarsely
   chopped

The whole Santin family helped to perfect this delightful dessert, an example of the superlative confection-making skills of the Italians. Note that the choice of ingredients produces a marvelous harmony of black and white, a classic color combination, pleasing to the eye.

If you prefer the pudding to have a somewhat more bitter flavor, use chocolate with a higher cocoa content. Experts consider the criollo beans from Venezuela to have the best flavor, but they are rare. However, excellent varieties of chocolate with a high cocoa content (70 % or higher) are available in stores, and these guarantee quite a fine flavor. Bringing all the ingredients to room temperature before preparing this dessert will help ensure its success.

Great care must be taken in choosing the white chocolate for the sauce. This ingredient is very sensitive, and unfortunately there are a few varieties of poor quality. It is best to store it in a cool, dry place. Chocolate can sometimes seem to "sweat," when the cocoa butter forms little pearls and crystallizes on the surface. This is a sign that it has been stored in an unsuitable place and should be kept in a cooler one.

This chocolate duet not only contains many nutrients, it also offers a balance between the delicate aromas. It provides the perfect excuse to quote Chateaubriand, who felt that "taste is the common sense of genius."

1. In the top half of a double boiler (85 °F / 30 °C), melt the butter and bittersweet chocolate. Beat the eggs until they are an even pale yellow. Add the flour and sugar and mix well until the dough has a thicker consistency.

2. Carefully pour in the melted chocolate and butter, stirring constantly.

with White Chocolate Sauce

3. Bring the milk and creme fraîche to a boil and pour over the coarsely chopped white chocolate. Cover and allow the chocolate to melt for a few minutes.

4. Grease four molds (3 in / 7 cm diameter, $2^3/_4$ in / 6 cm height) with butter and dust with confectioners' sugar. Fill them with the bittersweet chocolate mixture and bake for 10 minutes at 355 °F / 180 °C. After taking them out of the oven, slide the puddings out onto plates and pour the white chocolate sauce around them.

Preparation time: 2 hours 30 minutes
Cooking time: 1 hour
Cooling time: 4 hours
Difficulty: ★★

Serves 4

For the cocoa meringue:
1 egg white (40 g)
3 tbsp / 40 g sugar
1 tbsp / 10 g cocoa powder
2¹⁄₂ tbsp / 25 g confectioners' sugar

For the chocolate mousse:
5¹⁄₄ oz / 150 g bittersweet chocolate
²⁄₃ cup / 150 ml crème fraîche

For the banana mousse:
3¹⁄₂ oz / 100 g banana
1 tbsp / 15 g sugar
1 tsp lemon juice
1 tsp / 3 g ground gelatin
6¹⁄₂ tbsp / 100 ml crème fraîche

During his honeymoon in the Antilles, Maurizio Santin, our chef's son, became enchanted with a combination of rum, chocolate mousse, and banana sorbet. He returned determined to combine these three elements, producing a special harmony, a taste rich in exotic aromas.

Bananas are native to the Antilles, and bittersweet chocolate is its ideal companion here, especially chocolate with a high cocoa content (about 70 %). However, it must be treated with care: the melted chocolate should be lukewarm when mixed with the crème fraîche. The mousse should be prepared without interruption and filled into the molds immediately.

The meringue should be made light; it is better to apply it in a thin layer so that the baking time remains short. After half the baking time has elapsed, opening the oven door a bit to let air in will make the meringue a little more crisp.

One tip (according to our chef, the key to success): Start by preparing the meringue, then make the chocolate mousse followed by the banana mousse, and finish with a chocolate sauce or custard with vanilla and rum flavoring.

1. Prepare the cocoa meringue by beating the egg white and then carefully folding in the sugar and cocoa. Spread the mixture onto a baking tray to a height of 1 in / 2 cm and bake at 210 °F / 100 °C for 45 minutes.

2. For the chocolate mousse, melt the chocolate in a double boiler, allow to cool and carefully fold in the crème fraîche, which has been stirred until creamy. Cut the baked meringue into circles with a diameter a little smaller than the cutters used in step 4.

Bananas and Chocolate

3. To make the banana mousse, mash up the bananas and mix with the sugar and lemon juice. Add the gelatin, which has been dissolved in a teaspoon of water. Stir the crème fraîche until creamy and mix into the banana mixture.

4. Cover a baking tray with plastic wrap and place on it four round cookie cutters with a diameter of 3¹/₂ in / 8 cm and height of 2 in / 4.5 cm. Place a slice of meringue in each cutter. Spread some chocolate mousse on it, then top with another slice of meringue. Finish with a layer of banana mousse. Refrigerate for about 4 hours. Place on dessert plates and decorate with a border of chocolate sauce.

Brittle Cake

Preparation time: 20 minutes
Cooking time: 10 minutes
Cooling time: 6 hours
Difficulty: ★

Serves 4

1 cup of coffee
6½ tbsp / 100 ml milk
10 ladyfingers
1¼ cups / 300 ml cream
3½ tbsp / 50 g sugar
1¾ oz / 50 g macaroons, crushed
3½ oz / 100 g shortbread, crumbled

For the almond brittle:
3½ tbsp / 50 g sugar
⅔ cup / 100 g almonds

For the zabaglione:
2 egg yolks
2 tsp sugar
2 tsp white dessert wine

The name of this dessert in Italian is *torta di cantucci*, which translates as "almond brittle torte." But words and names cannot do justice to this delicacy; one should instead concentrate fully on its preparation.

Very fresh almonds with a pronounced flavor are needed for the brittle. For the greatest possible freshness, look for nuts still in the shell. Almonds are grown in warm climates throughout the world, including South Africa, Australia, Asia, the Mediterranean region, and, of course, California. They are chockfull of nutrients, including protein, calcium, magnesium, and potassium.

The consistency of the almond brittle, which is rich in fat, provides a delightful contrast with the soft ladyfingers. In order

for it to be firm enough, the cake must be refrigerated for at least 6 hours.

A second contrast is not evident until the very last minute, when the cold cake is served with the warm zabaglione. To give it the perfect finishing touch, it is important to serve this dessert with a truly first-class, dessert wine. Likewise, the coffee used to soak the ladyfingers must be of a high quality – if possible, a very good arabica. All these pieces of advice may seem superfluous, but once you have experienced this extraordinary cake, it becomes clear that it is worth every bit of extra effort.

1. To make the brittle, heat the sugar in a small pan without adding water. Add the almonds and stir until they are thoroughly coated. Turn the brittle onto an oiled tray. Allow to cool, then crush.

2. Combine the coffee and milk. Place the ladyfingers on a tray so that they form a square. Spoon the milk and coffee mixture over the ladyfingers to soak them. Press firmly with your fingers so that the liquid is better absorbed. Beat the cream and sugar until stiff.

with Coffee

3. Spread the whipped cream over the ladyfingers . Make the zabaglione in a double boiler using the ingredients listed above.

4. Spread half of the zabaglione over the cake. Cover it with alternating layers of macaroons, shortbread, and crushed brittle; repeat all three layers. Refrigerate for 6 hours. After taking out of the refrigerator, cut into four pieces and serve with the remaining warmed zabaglione.

Encharcada

Preparation time: 20 minutes
Cooking time: 3 minutes
Difficulty: ★

Serves 4

15 egg yolks
1 small cinnamon stick
2 cups / 500 g sugar
2 cups / 500 ml water

For seasoning:
ground cinnamon

The Convent, or rather the *Conventual*, is a restaurant set up in a former monastery by Maria Santos Gomes, who seeks to transform the necessary act of eating into an exquisite pleasure for her guests. The nuns who lived in these places are worthy predecessors for Maria Santos Gomes, because the majority of the desserts now traditional in Portugal were invented by their religious orders in the 17th and 18th centuries.

The Portuguese specialty introduced here, *encharcada*, is a dessert in which eggs play the central role. It is vital that they be completely fresh, so be sure to check the laying and use-by dates before you purchase them. Only the egg yolk is used in this dish. Though egg yolk has been much maligned because of

its relatively high concentration of cholesterol and calories (75 of the 90 calories in a 2 oz / 60 g egg), it is still an excellent source of protein, iron, and vitamins A and D. A fresh yolk retains its shape when separated: if it splits, has dark spots or flattens out, it is probably not completely fresh.

We can thank the Portuguese *conquistadors* for cinnamon. They brought the spice, actually the peeled bark of the cinnamon tree, from India. It is difficult to imagine Portuguese cooking without it. So if you finish the dessert off by seasoning it – in moderation, of course – with cinnamon, this will be a well-deserved homage to the bold discoverers of foreign territories.

1. Mix the sugar, water and cinnamon stick in a pot on the stove and simmer until small bubbles start to appear. Beat the egg yolks. As soon as the syrup is ready, remove the cinnamon stick and pass the egg yolks through a sieve into the hot syrup.

2. Over a constant low heat, allow to simmer and as it does so carefully stir with a wooden spatula or spoon from time to time.

3. Allow the encharcada to continue simmering, and use a wooden spatula or spoon to scrape the outer edge of the mass toward the middle of the pan, so that no crust forms. Remove the mixture from the heat as soon as the eggs are cooked, but a little syrup still remains.

4. Pour the encharcada onto plates, season with cinnamon and briefly grill in a hot oven until golden yellow.

Preparation time: 30 minutes
Cooking time: 10 minutes
Difficulty: ★

Serves 4

3 cups / 750 ml cream
6 eggs, separated
1 cup / 250 g sugar
6¹/₂ tbsp / 100 ml mastic liqueur
3 tbsp / 20 g mastic powder

1 lb / 500 g kataifi dough (available in Greek
and Turkish stores)

For the sauce:
³/₄ cup / 200 ml milk
3¹/₂ tbsp / 50 g sugar
4 egg yolks
1 cinnamon stick
¹/₂ cup / 80 g light and dark raisins

Even Victor Hugo found worthy of a vivid poem the destruction wrought on the Aegean island of Chios in the 19th century during the battle for Greek independence. Afterward, Chios became famous for its mastic, a resin obtained from the gum mastic tree. The trees are grown on plantations on the island, and are tapped once a year in August and September. The resin itself is a clear yellow glass-like substance, which is washed and sold in crystalline form.

Mastic finds the most varied uses, from industrial adhesives to varnishes to medicines. Small packages of the crystals are sold as chewing gum in Greece. Pounded into a powder, it is a uniquely Greek flavoring commonly used in baking, as well as other sweets including puddings and ice creams. Naturally,

there is also a liqueur made from the mastic tree, called *Mastiha* or *Mastika*. Although the taste is delicate, use it carefully, as too much of it can ruin any dessert.

Another Greek specialty – sheets of kataifi dough – is used mainly for preparing small tarts filled with dried fruit. The combination of ingredients for these tarts differs according to the region and its indigenous products.

Make sure that the kataifi dough is not allowed to soak up any moisture – this will make it soft, and it will taste doughy and be unpalatably sticky. Pay particular attention to this tip if you intend to store the sheets for a few days. It is best to serve the dessert fresh.

1. Whip the cream. Beat the egg yolks with 6¹/₂ tbsp / 100 g of the sugar until foamy. Using the egg whites and remaining sugar prepare a meringue (see basic recipes p. 802). Gently combine the whipped cream, egg yolks, and meringue, then blend in the mastic liqueur and powder. Refrigerate for a few hours.

2. Plait braids out of the kataifi dough. Place the braids on a greased baking tray and bake them until golden yellow.

Mousse

3. For the sauce, heat the milk with half of the sugar. Mix the egg yolks with the remaining sugar, stir in the hot milk, then return to the stovetop and heat to about 175 °F / 80 °C. Add the cinnamon.

4. Form "nests" out of the braided dough and fill the center with some raisins. Place a scoop of the mastic mousse in each nest and pour some sauce around the dessert. Garnish with the remaining raisins.

Preparation time: 15 minutes
Cooking time: 6 minutes
Cooling time 24 hours
Difficulty: ✮

Serves 4

To garnish:
red berries
4 sprigs of mint
4 tbsp cream, whipped
confectioners' sugar
red fruit sauce

¹/₃ cup / 80 g butter
2 oz / 60 g sweet apples, chopped
3¹/₂ oz / 100 g each strawberries, raspberries,
  blackberries, and blueberries
sugar
6 sheets gelatin
12 slices of white loaf bread or yeast bread

The way our chefs prepare summer berries here is similar to a charlotte (named after the wife of the British King George III) or even the typical British pudding, a method of preparation particularly suited to fruits too ripe to be used in a fruit salad. Here they are wrapped in a coating of sliced white bread that, as long as you use firm bread cut into thin slices, forms a tasty "container" for the fruit. Sliced white bread is a traditional, extremely common food in Great Britain; it is eaten at every meal from breakfast to dinner, including the inevitable afternoon tea, which is served with a variety of sandwiches.

Take care in selecting the fruits; they should be very ripe but not too badly bruised and certainly not spoiled. It is also important that the bread casing is pressed firmly into the molds

so that none of the fruit compote can escape, or the bread casing will not be firm enough. The choice of molds is also important – if they are too high, too much compote will fit inside and the dessert will fall apart when turned onto serving plates. If the molds are too small, though, there will be too much bread in proportion to fruit. In order to make it easier to turn the dessert out of the molds, you can put a layer of plastic wrap between the bread and the sides of the molds.

It is recommended that an apple be added to the berry compote, because its sweetness counterbalances the slight acidity of the berries. Its consistency also makes the compote a little firmer. Bramley, Cox's Orange Pippin or Golden Delicious would all work well.

1. Melt the butter in a saucepan over low heat. Add the chopped apple and stew for 1 minute. Add the berries, sugar to taste, and a half glass of water. Bring everything to a boil, then remove from the heat and add the sheets of gelatin.

2. Brush oil into four molds with a height and diameter of 2³/₄ in / 6 cm, or line them with plastic wrap. Cut the crusts off the sliced bread and cut the bread into strips. Use it to line the forms.

with Summer Fruits

3. Carefully close any gaps between the bread strips. Pour the fruit compote into the bread-lined molds, soaking the bread thoroughly.

4. Finish the compote off with a round slice of bread on top. Allow to infuse in the refrigerator for 24 hours. Invert onto plates and pour a red fruit sauce over the dessert. Garnish with fresh berries, whipped cream, and sprigs of mint.

Puff Pastry Pouches with

Preparation time: 30 minutes
Cooking time: 15 minutes
Difficulty: ★★

Serves 4

puff pastry (see basic recipes p. 803)
confectioners' sugar
2 cups / 500 ml sour sheep's milk
5 tsp / 25 g sugar
1 sheet of gelatin

For the caramelized apples:
4 small apples (e.g. Rennets), peeled and
  quartered
butter

3¹/₂ tbsp / 50 g sugar
3¹/₂ tbsp / 50 ml water
2 tbsp / 30 ml Sagardoz (apple schnapps)

For the apple sauce:
7 oz / 200 g apple flesh, chopped
¹/₂ cup / 125 ml water
3 tbsp / 40 g sugar
juice of 1 lemon
1 cinnamon stick
2 tbsp / 30 ml Sagardoz

To garnish:
red berries

Soured sheep's milk (*mamía* in Spanish) is a traditional Spanish dessert prepared with Sagardoz, a spirit made with apples.

It is not particularly complicated to use soured sheep's milk as long as you make sure to remove the whey produced by the process. You should beat it with sugar, add a sheet of gelatin, and allow it to curdle again. Too much gelatin, however, will give the soured sheep's milk a too-firm, tough consistency. If the necessary utensils are available, you can follow the traditional method of burning off the top layer of the soured sheep's milk with a hot piece of iron.

The only addition to this main ingredient are apples of the *Errecilla* variety, which used to be plentiful in the countryside of Spain. Farmers stored them bedded in sand and straw so that

a supply was available year round. *Errecilla* apples have been almost totally forgotten today, though Pedro Subijana still has a few of these special apple trees in his orchard and is making every effort to restore them to their former glory. But you can quite happily use different kinds of apples, such as Rennets.

Sagardoz, an apple schnapps produced during the distillation of cider, is an extremely tasty spirit. It flows like water, and not just during the Txox competitions between cider makers. During the entire competition, the most exciting dishes are available for sampling: beef ribs, cod omelette and, of course, soured sheep's milk with nuts. The Sagardoz adds a very special delicacy to this dessert. Our chef even had the honor of serving King Juan Carlos and his wife, Queen Sophie, in person.

1. Roll out the puff pastry to a thickness of ¹/₄ in / 0.5 cm. Cut eight triangles measuring 6 ³/₄ in / 15 cm × 6 ³/₄ in / 15 cm × 2 ¹/₂ in / 6 cm out of the puff pastry and bake. Remove the pastry from the oven, dust the triangles with confectioners' sugar and put them back in the oven to caramelize. Allow to cool.

2. Beat the sour sheep's milk and mix in the sugar and gelatin, which has been soaked in water. Do not stir again. Place a layer of the sour sheep's milk mixture between two puff pastry triangles.

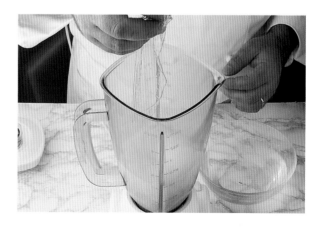

Mamía and Sagardoz

3. Peel, quarter, and core 4 apples. Brown them until golden brown in a saucepan with melted butter. Caramelize the apples in the sugar, then carefully and gradually add the water and boil until the caramel dissolves. Stir in the apple schnapps and allow to cool in the pan.

4. For the sauce, bring the chopped apple to a boil in the water with the sugar, lemon juice, and cinnamon. Mash and pass through a pointed sieve. Stir in the apple schnapps. Pour a ladle of apple sauce in the center of each plate, place a puff pastry pouch on top, and arrange the apple pieces with the caramel sauce around the edge.

Pineapple with Saffron

Preparation time: 35 minutes
Cooking time: 25 minutes
Difficulty: ★★

Serves 4

1 large pineapple
light sugar syrup
saffron butter

For the coconut cookies:
$^1/_3$ cup / 80 g sugar
$^3/_4$ cup / 70 g shredded coconut
3 tbsp / 20 g flour
2 large egg whites
4 tsp / 20 g butter, melted

For the coconut cream:
$^1/_2$ cup / 125 ml milk
$^1/_2$ cup / 125 ml coconut milk
1 vanilla bean; 3 eggs
$3^1/_2$ tbsp / 50 g sugar

4 tsp / 20 ml Grand Marnier
3 tbsp / 25 g flour
$3^1/_2$ tbsp / 50 ml cream

For the sauce:
$1^3/_4$ oz / 50 g fresh root ginger
$3^1/_2$ tbsp / 50 ml fresh pineapple juice
Grand Marnier

For the syrup:
$^1/_2$ cup plus 3 tbsp / 150 g dextrose
$5^1/_4$ oz / 150 g fondant
$6^1/_2$ tbsp / 100 g butter
a pinch of ground saffron
$^1/_3$ cup / 50 g almonds, colored pink and
  roasted

The visible refinement and variety of exotic flavors in this recipe will transform the end of your meal into a culinary journey through sunny realms.

As in most European languages, the German word for pineapple, *Ananas*, is derived from the Guaraní word, *ana-ana*, which means "scent of scents." The English name refers to its resemblance to a pine cone. Pineapples have long been a symbol of hospitality. Native to South and Central America, pineapples are now grown in Hawaii and Florida as well, though our chef prefers fruits from Martinique or the Ivory Coast, and are available year-round. They should be quite heavy and have a good amber color, a firm peel with flat "eyes" and leaves that can be detached readily.

The greatest difficulty in this dessert is preparing the syrup. The dextrose and fondant must, with a little skill, be reduced until they have formed a dense mixture that must nonetheless remain smooth and fluid enough not to form lumps. The ideal temperature for the syrup from which the spun sugar is made is 320–340 °F / 160–170 °C.

The combination of steamed pineapple and saffron, which produces decorative red spots of color on the flesh even when used very moderately, creates a dish that is a true delight for the eyes and the taste buds.

The coconut cookies are a traditional accompaniment. As soon as they take on their characteristic curved shape, they should be stored in a cool, dry place so that they do not flatten out again.

1. Peel the pineapple, leaving it whole. Cut horizontally into 12 even pieces of approximately the same thickness and cut out the woody section in the middle of each slice. To make the coconut cookies, combine the ingredients listed above, drop small amounts of the mixture onto a baking tray lined with baking paper and bake at 465 °F / 240 °C.

2. Steam the pineapple slices for about 5 minutes in a light sugar syrup, then cool and drain. Retain the syrup. Steam the pineapple slices again, this time in a pan with saffron butter.

3. For the coconut cream, bring the milk and coconut milk to a boil with the vanilla bean, then set aside and allow to infuse. Beat the eggs and sugar slightly, then add the Grand Marnier and flour. Combine with the milk mixture and bring everything to a boil. Allow to cool and finally stir in the cream carefully with a whisk. Spread the coconut cream onto the pineapple slices and layer on top of each other.

4. To make the sauce, simmer the chopped ginger in the pineapple syrup retained in step 2. As soon as a caramel has been formed, remove from the heat and deglaze with the pineapple juice. Flavor the sauce with a little Grand Marnier. Combine the ingredients for the syrup and use it to "spin" fine threads of sugar. Garnish the dessert with the spun sugar and scatter pieces of almond on top.

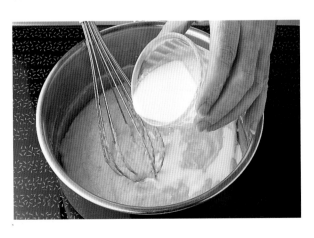

Tortelloni with Cream

Preparation time: 1 hour
Cooking time: 25 minutes
Difficulty: ★★

Serves 4

2 lb 3 oz / 1 kg lard (for deep-fat frying)
confectioners' sugar

For the dough:
4 cups / 500 g flour
3 eggs
3 tsp light oil
3 tsp grappa
3 tsp sugar

For the cream:
2 cups / 500 ml milk
4 vanilla beans
6 egg yolks
1 cup / 250 g sugar
1/2 cup plus 2 tbsp / 80 g flour

For the coffee sauce:
3/4 cup / 200 g sugar
6 1/2 tbsp / 100 ml water
6 cups espresso coffee

Not everyone knows that the fresh pasta frequently served as an appetizer in Italian restaurants can also be served as a dessert. This recipe is certain to astonish those not in on the secret. The preparation of the dough pouches (tortellos) differs in no way from the preparation of the usual Italian noodles. Like many pasta dishes, this dessert also combines economy and tradition.

Three elements typical of Italian cuisine are noticeable in this delicacy. Lard, which is frequently used for sponge cakes and pastries, produces an even dough. Grappa, a marc originally produced using the Nebbiolo grape from the Barolo (Piedmont) region, gives the dough its malleability and minimizes the taste of the fat used for frying. It is frequently used to make

pastries but can also be drunk as a *digestif* with friends. And finally coffee, to which Italians have become addicted, even though the Finns and other northern peoples consume the largest quantities. The quality of the Italian roasting houses should not be underrated, however, and neither should the coffee specialties, such as espresso and cappuccino, prepared throughout the peninsula.

Romano Tamani is willing at least to tolerate the thought that one might wish to serve this dessert with a bittersweet chocolate sauce made from a caramel base. For the coffee sauce, an *arabica* mixture from a good source should be chosen, from Ethiopia or Kenya for instance. Its fine flavor will emphasize the charm of this dessert all the more.

1. Mound the flour on a flat work surface and place the other ingredients for the dough in a well in the center. Mix by hand until the dough is even. Roll it out and cut out squares with sides 2 1/2 in / 5 cm long.

2. For the cream, bring the milk to a boil with the vanilla beans. Beat the egg yolks and sugar for 10 minutes in another pan. Carefully add the flour to the egg yolks, stir into the milk, bring to a boil and simmer gently for another 3 minutes. Allow to cool on the stove. Fill the squares with the cream, and fold the edges over and press the unfilled ends together to form a circle.

...and Coffee Sauce

3. Heat the lard in a large, tall pot. Once the fat is hot enough, deep-fry the tortelloni until golden brown. Drain and dust with the confectioners' sugar.

4. To make the sauce, dissolve the sugar in the water in a saucepan. Add the coffee and caramelize the mixture. Refrigerate for a few minutes. Cover a deep plate with the coffee sauce and arrange the tortelloni on top.

Creamy Rice with

Preparation time: 1 hour
Cooking time: 1 hour
Difficulty: ★★

Serves 4

1 pineapple
8 dates
butter

For the creamy rice pudding:
6 tbsp / 80 g rice
1²⁄₃ cups / 400 ml milk
1 vanilla bean
3¹⁄₂ tbsp / 50 g superfine sugar
2 egg yolks
6¹⁄₂ tbsp / 100 ml heavy cream

For the syrup:
1 cup / 250 g sugar
1 cup / 250 ml water
1 vanilla bean
a little brown rum

For generations, medicinal and purifying properties have been attributed to rice. There are thousands of varieties of rice, but it is enough to name the three main types: short grain, medium grain and long grain rice. It is also fascinating to realise just how extremely widespread rice is, in all countries worldwide, and that it connects gourmets everywhere.

Our chef, who has settled in St. Tropez, considers long grain rice most suitable for this dessert, and he draws his inspiration from the creamy rice pudding traditional in many European countries for generations. To start with, the rice has boiled in water, which softens the surface of the grains somewhat. After draining it, cook the rice in the vanilla milk in the usual way until it is ready. The most difficult aspect is probably to achieve a creamy consistency while definitely retaining the distinct flavor of rice.

Our chef has an interesting method of cooking the rice pudding: the mixture is placed in a casserole dish and the lid is sealed to the pan with a dough made of water and flour. This ensures that the cooking process is hermetic, so that all the flavor and various aromas of the rice are retained.

The consistency and delicacy of this unusual dessert will delight anyone who tries it; on top of everything else, it is also very healthy.

1. Wash the rice in water; drain. Cover it with water in a pot and bring to a rolling boil. Drain again. Bring the milk to a boil. Add the rice and the slit vanilla bean. Simmer over a low heat for 25 minutes without stirring.

2. Peel the fresh pineapple and cut into eight slices. Using a corer, remove the hard flesh in the center. Retain the peel. Using the sugar, water, and vanilla bean, prepare a syrup. Poach the pineapple and dates in the syrup; drain.

Pineapple and Dates

3. Poach the pineapple peels in the same syrup. Add the rum. Blend and pass through a pointed sieve. Once the rice has finished cooking, add the sugar, the egg yolks, and the heavy cream.

4. Place the rice into a casserole dish. Seal the lid as described above and cook at 275 °F / 140 °C for 15 minutes. Slightly brown the pineapple and dates in butter. Arrange both on a plate and cover with the rum mixture. Serve the rice separately.

Almond Crêpes with

Preparation time:	30 minutes
Cooking time:	10 minutes
Difficulty:	★★★

Serves 4

2 tsp / 10 g butter

For the crêpe mixture:
$^1/_3$ cup / 45 g flour
4 tsp / 20 g sugar
5 egg yolks
a pinch of salt

$^3/_4$ cup / 200 ml milk
3 tbsp / 50 g almond paste (or crushed almonds)

For the zabaglione:
6 egg yolks
3 tbsp sugar
$^3/_4$ cup / 200 ml champagne

To garnish:
10$^1/_2$ oz / 300 g raspberries
3 tbsp / 30 g confectioners' sugar

In this zabaglione, the qualities of the egg are exploited to their fullest. The egg contains important nutrients – protein, fat, and vitamins – and, thanks to its consistency, is able to unite ingredients as apparently incompatible as butter and water. Yolks are also brushed on cakes and cookies to give them a pleasing golden-brown glaze; they are also responsible for the thick, creamy consistency of custard.

The eggs are beaten with a whisk in this zabaglione and warmed slightly to give them volume. Add the egg yolks one at a time and whisk until foamy. To do this, stir the whisk in a figure of eight, using an absolutely regular stroke.

But other techniques can be used as well. For example, the cream can be whisked at room temperature to begin with and then stirred over a low heat, with white wine or Marsala, until finished. In this recipe, José Tourneur uses champagne, but this is only a suggestion.

Whatever utensils you use to prepare the zabaglione, make sure that they are absolutely free of dirt or grease; the mixing bowl, for example, should be thoroughly rinsed beforehand, ideally with a mix of water and vinegar, and dried with a clean towel.

All precautions aside, luck does play a part in making this sensitive cream. Do not despair if you do not succeed at first! Even the best chefs have experienced such disappointments.

1. To make the crêpe batter, beat the flour, sugar, and egg yolks with a whisk until they form a shiny, foamy mixture; add a pinch of salt. Stir the milk in gradually so that the batter remains smooth. Stir in the almond paste and allow to rest for 30 minutes.

2. Make golden-brown crêpes and keep them warm. Set aside several choice raspberries for garnishing and make a raspberry sauce with the rest. To do so, puree the raspberries with the confectioners' sugar and pass through a sieve.

Zabaglione and Raspberries

3. Begin the zabaglione by beating the egg yolks in a pan at room temperature. Gently heat the foamy eggs over a low heat, then beat in the sugar. Finally, add the champagne and whisk continuously to produce a thick, foamy cream.

4. Place the crêpes on the plates, pour a portion of zabaglione in the center and fold each crêpe once so that the zabaglione runs out a little at the sides. Arrange the raspberries around the edge of the plates and dust the crêpes with confectioners' sugar.

Preparation time: 30 minutes
Cooling time: 4 hours
Difficulty: ☆

Serves 4

5 egg yolks
⅓ cup / 50 g confectioners' sugar
1 lb / 500 g mascarpone cheese
5 tsp Cognac
24 firm ladyfingers
4 cups very strong coffee
3 tsp cocoa powder

You would think that tiramisù is so well known outside Italy these days that there is no need to publish the recipe. You might also believe, like Luisa Valazza, that it is important for exactly that reason to look toward tradition and do away with the recipes that call just about any dessert a tiramisù.

Ideally, one should use savory Italian ingredients such as ladyfingers from Savoy (which has been part of France only since 1860), mascarpone, and certain varieties of coffee. Tiramisù was originally prepared using leftovers, which explains the use of coffee for soaking what was probably stale sponge cake. It appears to have originated in Lombardy, and can now be found on the menus of the most exclusive restaurants. The special feature of this dessert is the sweet/bitter contrasts among the sponge cake, cocoa, and coffee. Between the layers is mascarpone, a creamy, soft cheese with a high fat content and a mild, cream-like flavor.

The ladyfingers should have a texture that enables them to soak up the liquid well without completely disintegrating. Our chef recommends serving the dessert with maraschino, a liqueur made from wild cherries grown near Trieste.

1. To make the mascarpone cream, beat the egg yolks and confectioners' sugar in a bowl until creamy. Add the mascarpone and Cognac and beat for a few minutes.

2. Soak the ladyfingers in the coffee and set aside until needed.

3. In an attractive dish or individual forms, alternate layers of mascarpone cream, the coffee-soaked ladyfingers, and cocoa powder.

4. Finish with a layer of mascarpone. Refrigerate for 4 hours. Before serving sprinkle confectioners' sugar and sifted cocoa on top.

Preparation time: *20 minutes*
Cooking time: *10 minutes*
Difficulty: ★★

Serves 4

20 prunes
7 oz / 200 g marzipan
2 cups / 500 ml whole milk
8 egg yolks
1½ cups / 225 g confectioners' sugar

3½ oz / 100 g lebkuchen
3½ oz / 100 g spekulatius (spiced cookies)
6½ tbsp / 100 ml cream
6½ tbsp / 100 ml dark beer (preferably Belgian
    beer from Leffe)
6½ tbsp / 100 ml cream, whipped

Marzipan, traditional in certain regions of France, Italy, and central Europe, is made of crushed almonds, sugar, and egg whites. It is used to make small cakes and pastries that are sometimes glazed or made into pralines like those available in Belgium over the New Year. In Austria, marzipan is used at Easter to make eleven balls that decorate a cake made with dried fruits, representing the eleven apostles left after Judas betrayed Christ. In southern Italy, among other places, marzipan is used to make small figures that look like fruits, vegetables, even animals and people.

Prunes are dried plums that have retained their consistency, juice, and softness. They are best kept in an airtight container in a cool place, as they quickly dry out and become tough.

Belgians are particularly fond of spekulatius, a dry cookie flavored with cinnamon and cloves, but it is also very popular in other countries.

Despite the decline of so many Belgian breweries – of the 3,200 in existence at the beginning of the century, only about a hundred still survive – the incomparable Leffe Abbey still continues the centuries-old tradition of monks brewing beer. Particularly popular is the fine, delicious Radieuse, and their dark beer has a somewhat more bitter flavor that is valued highly by experts. Try to resist the temptation to add more beer than is called for, because it easily overpowers the flavor of the dessert.

1. Stone the prunes. Roll out the marzipan and cut pieces 1½ in / 3 cm long. Place the marzipan pieces inside the prunes.

2. Heat the milk. Whisk 6 egg yolks with ¾ cup plus 1 tbsp / 125 g confectioners' sugar. Pour the hot milk onto the egg yolks and continue stirring at 175 °F / 80 °C until the mixture has a creamy consistency. Pass the custard through a pointed sieve.

Marzipan and Beer

3. Add the crumbled lebkuchen and crushed spekulatius cookies to the custard. Add the cream and stir thoroughly in an ice cream maker.

4. Combine the two remaining egg yolks and $2/3$ cup / 100 g confectioners' sugar. Add the beer and whisk until foamy. Blend in the whipped cream. Arrange the prunes on deep plates. Pour the beer mixture over them and glaze under a hot grill. Serve with the ice cream and, optionally, petits fours.

Chocolate Souffle

Preparation time: 20 minutes
Cooking time: 15 minutes
Difficulty: ★★

Serves 4

4³/₄ oz / 130 g bittersweet chocolate
4 tsp / 10 g cocoa powder
¹/₄ cup / 60 ml green walnut liqueur
2 eggs, separated
¹/₃ cup / 50 g confectioners' sugar
4 tsp / 20 g superfine sugar

For the pastry cream:
1 cup / 250 ml milk
¹/₂ vanilla bean
2 egg yolks
3 tbsp / 40 g sugar
3 tbsp / 20 g flour
2 tbsp / 15 g cornstarch

Christopher Columbus brought chocolate to Europe from a place he mistakenly believed to be India, where the cocoa bean was apparently used as a unit of currency by the natives. Chocolate has been popular ever since it was first introduced to the French court by Queen Anne, the wife of Louis XIII, and countless recipes have been developed using pure, bitter, hard chocolate that melts in the mouth. This is the very chocolate that our chef has selected for his soufflé, prepared with all the expertise customary in Belgium. The exceptional quality of Belgian chocolate has made it one of the country's most widely exported products.

Apart from the beaten egg whites, which should be folded in at the last minute, all the ingredients for the soufflé can be pre-pared in advance. Carefully watch the baking time and serve the soufflé as soon it is ready, to avoid any danger of collapse. For the same reason, this dessert cannot be kept or reheated.

The green walnut is a liqueur with a flavor sure to surprise those who have not experienced it. If necessary, it can be replaced by Banyuls, a Catalan dessert wine that has been produced since the 13th century using black Grenache grapes, which are exposed to 325 days of sun every year.

Even though the preparation is a little risky, the triumphant moment when this soufflé is served makes it all worthwhile.

1. To make the pastry cream, bring the milk to a boil with the halved vanilla bean. In another bowl, beat the egg yolks with the sugar, then add the flour, cornstarch, and hot milk. Return everything to the pan and stir constantly until the cream briefly boils. Remove from the heat. In a double boiler, melt the chocolate, then stir in the lukewarm pastry cream, cocoa powder, and one-third of the walnut liqueur.

2. Remove from the heat and stir in the egg yolks. Whisk the egg whites until very stiff; add the confectioners' sugar while continuing to beat.

with Walnut Liqueur

3. Fold the beaten egg whites into the chocolate mixture and carefully blend with a wooden spatula or spoon. Grease four ovenproof soufflé dishes and sprinkle them with superfine sugar.

4. Pour the chocolate mixture into the dishes and sprinkle some sugar on top. Place halved walnut or egg shells with the open sides facing upward in the center, and bake for 12 minutes at 430 °F / 220 °C. Remove from the oven, pour the remaining liqueur into the shells, flambé, and serve immediately.

Apple Jelly

Preparation time: 30 minutes
Cooking time: 15 minutes
Cooling time: 2 hours
Difficulty: ★★

Serves 4

4 apples (Granny Smiths)
3 sheets of gelatin
1²/₃ cups / 400 ml juice from green apples
1 pinch of cinnamon

For the sorbet:
4 cups / 1 l apple juice
6¹/₂ tbsp / 100 g sugar
5 tbsp / 50 g dextrose

For the zabaglione:
3 egg yolks
6¹/₂ tbsp / 100 g sugar
6¹/₂ tbsp / 100 ml juice from green apples
²/₃ cup / 150 ml hard cider (slight alcohol content)
²/₃ cup / 150 ml Calvados
4 tsp / 20 ml cream, whipped

For as long as humanity has known the meaning of despair – surely since the beginning of time – we have also known sugar's capacities to restore morale and vitality. But it was not until the 18th century that dessert became a fixed part of a meal. Nowadays, a wide range of sweets tempts us.

The apple is the quintessential fruit and, in this recipe, appears in three different forms: as a jelly, a sorbet, and as Calvados in the zabaglione. The zabaglione will certainly be the most difficult part of the recipe, as some skill is required to prepare it. The challenge is to prevent the eggs from becoming too firm and impairing the smooth texture, while still cooking them so that the cream as a whole does not collapse. The degree to which you achieve this balance will determine the success of the entire recipe. The typical Normandy combination of cider and Calvados gives the zabaglione a distinct apple flavor.

Green Granny Smith apples are used for the zabaglione and jelly because they are one of the varieties of apples best able to withstand cooking without becoming mushy or flavorless.

Our chef, eager to simplify the preparation of his recipe, suggests preparing the jelly and sorbet a day in advance. Aside from the fact that this allows you to devote your entire attention to the zabaglione, the consistency of the jelly and sorbet actually benefit from the extra resting time. Be careful with the amount of cinnamon – too much could ruin the flavor of the dessert.

1. Mix the ingredients for the sorbet and place in the freezer. Peel the apples and dice them. Soak the gelatin in cold water for 5 minutes. Bring the apple juice to a boil with the cinnamon.

2. Add the diced apples to the hot apple juice, then add the gelatin. Stir carefully, remove from the heat and allow to cool until the mixture is lukewarm.

...ith Calvados

3. Spoon equal amounts of the apple jelly into four deep dishes. Allow to set in the refrigerator for about 2 hours.

4. For the zabaglione, whisk the egg yolks and sugar and gently heat them. Add the apple juice, then the cider. Remove from the heat and continue to beat the cream with a whisk as it cools. Stir in the Calvados and whipped cream. Cover the apple jelly with some zabaglione. Sprinkle with superfine sugar and brown briefly. Serve with the sorbet.

Preparation time: 3 hours
Cooking time: 1 hour
Cooling time: 12 hours
Difficulty: ★★★

Serves 8–10

For the caramel cream:
6¹/₂ tbsp / 100 g (ml) each sugar and cream

For the caramel sauce:
6¹/₂ tbsp / 100 g sugar; 2 tbsp / 30 ml water

For the custard:
6¹/₂ tbsp / 100 ml milk; 4 tsp / 20 g sugar
2 egg yolks; ¹/₂ vanilla bean

For the nougat parfait:
2 egg whites, 6 tbsp / 90 g sugar
³/₄ cup / 170 ml cream, whipped
1¹/₄ cups / 150 g caramelized nuts

For the apple cake:
³/₄ cup / 300 g apple sauce
¹/₃ cup / 80 g butter; 1 egg

For the baked caramel custard:
1 cup / 250 ml milk; 1 egg plus 1 egg yolk
3¹/₂ tbsp each: cream and sugar
1 vanilla bean

For the caramel flan:
sponge cake (see basic recipes p. 805)
1 egg yolk; ¹/₄ cup / 60 ml cream
1 sheet of gelatin
¹/₃ cup / 80 ml caramel cream
2 egg whites; 2 tbsp / 30 g sugar
¹/₄ cup / 60 ml cream, whipped

There is surely something for everyone in this stunning array of sweets: cake, nougat parfait, caramel flan, and ice cream. A selection like this requires high-quality ingredients, and that is just what Jean-Pierre Vigato makes sure he has on hand when he begins.

Nuts with intense flavor for the nougat, apples for the apple sauce – all must withstand Vigato's scrutiny. Choose good cooking apples, the Golden Delicious for example, or another to your own taste. The vanilla beans used to refine the flavor of both the custard and the caramel custard should be tender and fleshy.

Though caramel is prepared in myriad ways all over the world, little is known about the origins of the name itself. It first appeared in Spain in the 16th century, a term derived from the Latin word for cane sugar, *cannamella*. The word "caramelized" means that something has the color or flavor of caramel.

But how to celebrate this balance of flavors and consistencies – melting and crunchy, lukewarm and cold, sweet and bitter? Such contrasts, perfectly managed by an experienced and talented chef, lead to a dessert that will surely leave a lasting impression on everyone fortunate enough to partake of it.

1. Prepare the caramel cream by caramelizing the sugar in a pan without water, then carefully and gradually adding the cream to it. Make the caramel sauce in the same way adding the water in place of cream. Prepare a custard (see basic recipes) with the above ingredients. To make the caramel ice cream, combine the custard and caramel cream. Allow to set in an ice cream maker.

2. Make the nougat parfait a day in advance: begin with a meringue made from the egg whites and sugar (see basic recipes). Allow to cool, then fold in the whipped cream. Blend in a mixture of chopped and caramelized nuts. Freeze.

Feast

3. For the apple cake, start by making a greatly reduced apple sauce. Beat in the egg and butter. Spoon the mixture into a greased and sugared cake pan and bake for 1 hour at 340 °F / 170 °C in a water bath. Prepare the baked caramel custard using the ingredients given and bake in a water bath for 30 minutes. Allow the cake and baked custard to cool. Pour the caramel sauce onto the baked custard.

4. To make the caramel flan, whisk the egg yolk with the cream. Pass through a pointed sieve. Stir in the dissolved gelatin, $^1/_3$ cup / 80 ml caramel cream and a meringue (see basic recipes) made with the egg whites, sugar, and whipped cream. Pour into a pan that has been thinly lined with sponge cake and allow to set. Arrange everything on plates with caramel cages, if desired.

Parfait with Madeira

Preparation time: 20 minutes
Cooking time: 10 minutes
Cooling time: 3 hours
Difficulty: ★★

Serves 4

For the parfait:
³/₄ cup / 200 g sugar
6 egg yolks
6¹/₂ tbsp / 100 ml Madeira
2 cups / 500 ml cream

For the blueberry sauce:
6¹/₂ tbsp / 100 g sugar
6¹/₂ tbsp / 100 ml water
Peels of an untreated lemon and orange
3¹/₂ oz / 100 g blueberries
juice of 1 lemon

Whether served as the centerpiece of a family celebration, to mark the close of a contract or to reflect the sweetness of a tryst, this dessert is always an uplifting moment and needs to be treated accordingly.

Keep precisely to the recommended ingredients of the parfait and their quantities, and allow it to freeze for at least 3 hours. This is the only way to insure the dessert has a light consistency and can be turned out of the mold later without falling apart. This dangerous enterprise can be simplified somewhat by dipping the base of the molds in hot water first, but do not do this until the very last minute.

The sauce can be made using other fruits, or even a mixture of them if you would like to add a personal touch by varying the colors and flavors of the dessert. For example, the blueberry sauce could be accompanied by a sour cherry sauce or a sauce from any other berries (strawberries, raspberries, red currants or black currants). Before serving, it is important to pass every fruit sauce through a fine pointed sieve to remove the berries' small seeds and other bits. You could even use a chocolate sauce, whose dark color would produce the same visual contrast with the light color of the parfait.

Depending on your taste, the parfait itself can be flavored using spirits other than the Madeira – a clear fruit schnapps, for instance, which will give it more bite and firmness, or perhaps a fine Cognac or old Armagnac.

1. To make the parfait, place the sugar and egg yolks in the top of a double boiler and beat until the mixture is even and foamy.

2. Over moderate heat, add the Madeira and continue to beat until a creamy mixture has been produced. Remove from the heat and allow to cool while continuing to beat with a whisk.

and Blueberry Sauce

3. Whip the cream until stiff. Carefully fold in the completely cooled Madeira mixture. Fill individual molds with the parfait mixture and freeze for at least 3 hours.

4. Prepare a syrup using the sugar, water, and orange and lemon peel. Bring to a boil, then remove from the heat and let steep until completely cooled. Pass through a pointed sieve. Add the blueberries to the syrup and cook for 4 to 5 minutes. Allow to cool completely, then add the lemon juice, mix the sauce in a blender and again pass it through a pointed sieve. Serve the parfaits on a bed of sauce, garnished with whole blueberries.

Quark Omelette with Pears

Preparation time: 1 hour
Cooking time: 30 minutes
Difficulty: ★★

Serves 4

2 large pears

For the marinade:
2 tbsp / 30 g sugar
1 cup / 250 ml red wine
$^1/_2$ cup / 125 ml port
1 whole clove
1 small cinnamon stick
1 piece of ginger

For the ice cream:
1 cup / 250 ml each milk, cream

6 egg yolks, $^1/_3$ cup / 75 g sugar
$4^1/_2$ oz / 125 g white chocolate coating, melted

For the quark omelette:
$5^1/_4$ oz / 150 g quark

3 eggs, separated
3 tbsp flour
1 pinch of salt
1 vanilla bean
grated peel of 1 untreated lemon

For the sauce:
4 egg yolks
$3^1/_2$ tbsp / 50 g sugar
$^1/_2$ cup / 125 ml milk
$^1/_2$ cup / 125 ml cream
1 vanilla bean

To garnish:
1 tbsp raspberry sauce
1 tbsp mango sauce
4 sprigs of mint

The expertise of the chef at the Schwarzwaldstube ranges from exquisite appetizers to delicious desserts. This small restaurant, opened in 1984, has earned a good reputation through the excellent recipes and its welcoming atmosphere, and this quark omelette certainly does nothing to dispel that. It is also a worthy tribute to Germany's superb and manifold dairy products.

Harald Wohlfahrt suggests using Williams pears, but other varieties are also delicious. For the accompaniment, our chef sticks to old traditions: the quark, ice cream, sauce, and carefully selected spices (increasingly popular since the Middle Ages) combine to provide wonderful taste and texture experiences.

Cinnamon, which comes from Sri Lanka, gives the liquid in which the pears are prepared a touch of bittersweetness. Use cinnamon sticks to achieve a more intense flavor than ground cinnamon. Cinnamon is used in many meat dishes in northern Africa and the Middle East, though in the west it is found primarily in desserts. Cloves can also be used, though without onions as is so often the case in European broths; for example, they are used by the Japanese to flavor their famous sushi.

1. For the marinade, caramelize the sugar in a pan, then carefully and gradually add the red wine and port. Add the whole clove, cinnamon stick, and ginger and cook over a low heat until reduced by half. Peel the pears and add them to the pan. Bring the marinade briefly to a boil, then remove from the heat and let stand for 4 to 5 hours.

2. To make the ice cream, boil the milk and cream. Beat the egg yolks and sugar, then add the hot milk and beat with a whisk in a double boiler until creamy. Pass through a pointed sieve. Add the chocolate coating and whisk thoroughly. Allow to set in an ice cream maker. For the omelette, combine the quark, egg yolks, flour, salt, vanilla bean and grated lemon peel in a mixing bowl.

and Chocolate Ice Cream

3. Beat the egg whites until stiff and gradually add to the quark mixture. Prepare the vanilla sauce by beating the egg yolks with the sugar, adding the boiling milk and cream mixture and the vanilla bean and stirring in a double boiler until the sauce thickens. Allow to cool.

4. Fill the quark mixture into four greased and floured forms. Cut the pears into thin slices and arrange on top of the quark mixture in the shape of a rosette. Bake for 15 to 20 minutes at 355 °F / 180 °C. After baking, sprinkle sugar over the pears and caramelized under a grill. Pour some sauce onto the serving plates, turn the omelettes out of the forms onto it, garnish with the remaining pears and the mango and raspberry sauces and add a spoonful of ice cream.

Preparation time: 20 minutes
Cooling time: 12 hours
Difficulty: ★

Serves 4

$^1/_2$ oz / 12 g ground gelatin
1$^1/_4$ cups / 300 ml milk
1 tbsp almond milk
$^1/_2$ cup / 125 g sugar
1$^1/_4$ cups / 300 ml cream

1 lb / 500 g raspberries, blueberries, wild strawberries or red currants

A traditional dish from the Piedmont region, *panna cotta* (Italian for "cooked cream") may have originated during the reign of Charles Albert, King of Sardinia and Piedmont (1798–1849), who was forced to abdicate after being defeated by Austria. The dessert is prepared using milk, almond milk, and gelatin. In order to assure the success of the dessert, either use cream with a fat content between 30% and 35%; or add more gelatin. The cream must then be slowly warmed over a moderate heat, so that it does not turn yellow.

Armando Zanetti has no interest in forcing the use of almond milk on anyone, especially since it puts some people off with its distinctive, unusual aroma. Since it is not a decisive ingredient in this dessert, it can simply be omitted. Other flavors, such as melted chocolate or vanilla, will also produce a delicious result. The preparation of this *panna cotta* is quite straightforward, requiring no further elaboration.

The subtle grace of this dessert supports northern Italy's generations-old claim of being able to compete with the south when it comes to pastry and ice cream-making. While it cannot be compared with a Sicilian cassata or other familiar southern Italian desserts, the eye-catching forest berries add their own acidic flavor to this presentation, and its simple elegance is an irresistible temptation.

1. Soak the gelatin in cold water. Bring the milk and almond milk to a boil with the sugar, and then stir in the soaked gelatin. Add the cream and slowly whip with a whisk.

2. Pour the panna cotta mixture into ovenproof dishes with a height of 2$^3/_4$ in/6 cm to 3$^1/_2$ in / 8 cm. Refrigerate for at least 12 hours.

Forest Berries

3. Carefully turn the chilled panna cotta out of the dishes. Wash the berries briefly (do not soak them). Do not remove the stems from the strawberries.

4. Place a panna cotta on the center of each dessert plate, and arrange the various colored berries in circles around it. Serve with a red berry sauce and garnish with mint leaves.

Filled Pastry Rolls

Preparation time: 30 minutes
Cooking time: 45 minutes
Difficulty: ★★

Serves 4

For the short pastry:
6 cups / 750 g flour
3 eggs
3¹/₂ tbsp / 50 g sugar
3¹/₂ tbsp / 50 ml Cognac
2 cups / 500 g butter
grated peel of 1 untreated lemon

For the walnut cream:
8 cups / 2 l milk
1 cinnamon stick
2¹/₂ cups / 250 g shelled walnuts
1 cup / 250 g sugar
4 tsp / 10 g flour

confectioners' sugar for dusting

The unusual word in our recipe title is the Basque term for the walnut cream described below, an expression of our chef's attachment to his native region. The walnut, a classic autumn nut, is held in particularly high regard in southwestern and northern Spain. The best nuts are those harvested in November or December, the small ones in particular, with their more concentrated flavor. Fresh walnuts keep for about two weeks after ripening but then quickly turn rancid. If dried nuts are used, remove the bitter skin around the kernels by soaking the nuts in salt water for three days.

Do not chop the nuts in an electric blender, because this tends to pulverize them and give them an oily consistency. Instead, use a chopping knife, or better still, crush the nuts with a pestle and mortar. That way, the consistency of the nuts will remain intact. Set aside some nuts for garnishing and caramelize them; this allows the nuts to form a crunchy contrast with the delicate cream.

As odd as this may sound, a small quantity of water in which a cod has been soaked is traditionally added to the nut cream. In that way, the bounties of land and ocean unite to form a stunning combination of flavors. Unfortunately, this ancient tradition has been all but forgotten because most people today have difficulty imagining that the intensive flavor of cod could go with the sweetness of such a dessert.

If the walnut cream does not appeal to you, the rolls could also be filled with a pastry cream flavored to your own taste, or with a creamy rice pudding.

1. To make the short pastry, mound the flour on a work surface, make a hollow in the middle and put the eggs, sugar, Cognac, grated lemon peel, and softened butter into it. Knead by hand to form a dough. Shape the pastry into a ball and refrigerate.

2. Roll out the pastry and, using a pastry wheel, cut out strips of pastry 3 in / 7 cm wide and 9 in / 20 cm long. Roll these onto metal tubes with a diameter of 1¹/₂ in / 3 cm and bake at 375 °F / 190 °C. Alternatively, the rolls can also be deep-fried.

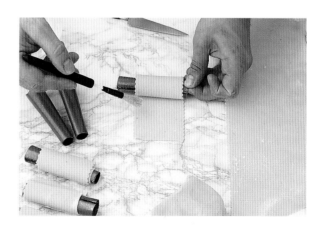

'Intxaursaltza'

3. Prepare the cream: bring half of the milk to a boil with the cinnamon stick; stir in the crushed or chopped nuts (see text above) and the sugar and simmer. Add the second liter of milk to the simmering mixture in two or three portions. Continue cooking until the liquid has reduced to the consistency of a caramel. Refrigerate. Fill the baked rolls with the cream using a pastry bag.

4. Before serving, dust the pastry rolls with confectioners' sugar and briefly glaze with a salamander or under a hot grill. Arrange on a plate, decorate with caramelized nuts, and serve cold or warm.

Pastries

Preparation time: 45 minutes
Cooking time: 30 minutes
Difficulty: ★★★

Serves 8

Viennese sponge cake, short pastry, marzipan
mixture: (see basic recipes p. 806, 804, 802)

For the Riesling cream:
3¹/₂ tbsp / 50 ml Riesling wine
3¹/₂ tbsp / 50 g superfine sugar
3 egg yolks
3 sheets of gelatin
4 tsp / 20 ml pear schnapps
³/₄ cup / 175 ml cream, whipped

For the topping:
3 Williams pears

For the syrup:
2 tbsp / 30 g superfine sugar
²/₃ cup / 150 ml Riesling wine
juice of ¹/₂ lemon

For the coating:
1 oz / 25 g milk chocolate, melted

For the jelly:
2 tbsp / 30 g superfine sugar
³/₄ cup / 200 ml pear juice
1 tbsp agar

For the apricot glaze:
1 tbsp / 25 g apricot jam

Adolf Andersen has a few things in common with his name-sake Hans Christian Andersen, creator of "The Little Mermaid." Both are certainly inventive and have an extremely deft touch when it comes to making their ideas manifest. And, just as the author made the imaginary seem real, Adolf Andersen feels it is important to preserve the natural flavor and quality of the ingredients he uses, making the real seem heavenly.

Once upon a time, there was a gentle little fruit from England, soon available all over Europe and much in demand because it stayed firm when cooked and went very well with alcohol. It was the Williams pear. In this recipe, it is paired with a marzipan mixture, which must be very fresh and tender even though it consists almost entirely of marzipan and contains neither sugar nor eggs.

The marzipan mixture is easy to work with. Like the Riesling cream, it is important to infuse it with air, but neither mixture should be stirred too long or it will collapse when baked or cooked.

In this recipe, Adolf Andersen replaces gelatin with agar, a gelling agent produced from a certain marine algae, which produces a somewhat jelly-like result when cooked. In the Far East, especially in Japan, agar is very widely used. You will be pleased with the result; in a way, it provides the final touch for the Riesling Fairy Tale, just like that old ending, "and they lived happily ever after ..."

1. To make the Riesling cream, bring the wine and sugar to a boil, then whisk with the egg yolks until foamy; remove from the heat and continue to beat. Before the foamy mixture has completely cooled, add the gelatin, which has been soaked in water and carefully drained. Allow to cool. Add the pear schnapps and carefully fold in the stiffly whipped cream. Prepare the Viennese sponge cake and the short pastry.

2. Place the marzipan mixture in a pastry bag with a large tip and pipe rings with a diameter of 12 in / 26 cm onto baking paper. The mixture must be quite stiff or it will lose shape and flatten during baking. Bake for 12–15 minutes at 320 °F / 160 °C until golden brown. Peel the pears, quarter them and add to the boiling syrup. Remove from the heat. Allow the pears to cool in the syrup until they are soft but still firm. Drain and rinse with cold water.

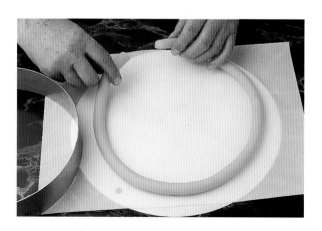

Fairy Tale

3. Cut out a short pastry base with a diameter of 12 in / 26 cm, prick several times with a fork and bake for 20 minutes at 320 °F / 160 °C. Spread the melted milk chocolate on it, and place three macaroon rings on top. Halve the Viennese sponge cake, and cut one of the sponge cake bases in half again. Place the thickest layer of sponge cake inside the rings and cover with Riesling cream (leave 1/2 in/1 cm free around the edge); repeat. Cover with the last base, and garnish with Riesling cream.

4. To make the jelly, add the sugar and agar to the pear juice, and boil for three minutes while stirring constantly. Cut the pear quarters into thin slices and arrange on the cake in the form of a fan. Cover with the jelly and refrigerate for two hours. Before serving, brush the macaroon sides with the hot apricot jam.

Raspberry

Preparation time: 1 hour
Cooking time: 30 minutes
Difficulty: ☆

Serves 8

Viennese sponge cake, short pastry:
  (see basic recipes p. 806, 804)

For the raspberry cream:
1²/₃ cups / 400 ml cream
¹/₂ cup, 1 tbsp / 140 g sugar
1 tsp freshly squeezed lemon juice
6 sheets of gelatin
10¹/₂ oz / 300 g raspberries

For the coating:
1³/₄ oz / 50 g milk chocolate, melted

To garnish:
small raspberries
³/₄ cup / 200 ml cream
2 tsp sugar
1 sheet of gelatin

Raspberries, already familiar in ancient times, were known as the "bush of Ida" (after the mountain of that name on the island of Crete, where they originated). In northern Europe, they are used relatively rarely for cakes. But this recipe, which brings out the full velvety flavor of the raspberries, is sure to go down well anywhere.

When you prepare the raspberry cream, there are a few things you can do to preserve both the bright color and high vitamin content of the raspberries. Use only unblemished raspberries, preferably without washing them, and dab them clean using paper towels. The cream can also be prepared when raspberries are in season and kept in the freezer for a real treat in winter.

Raspberries should not be stirred too long or too vigorously if their flavor is to be fully retained. Adolf Andersen sticks to the principles of his grandfather, also a pastry chef. In his view, it is better to use more raspberries than cream and to use as little sugar as possible. If you keep to these guidelines, you will not be disappointed.

This cake is a little like a fruit mousse and can be made in many other flavor varieties. In the Andersen *konditorei* (pastry shop) it was long made using strawberries. If you use generous amounts of wild strawberries, the results will be difficult to surpass.

1. Make the Viennese sponge cake according to the basic recipe, folding the flour into the foamy egg mixture as shown below. After it has thoroughly cooled (and preferably rested overnight), slice the sponge cake horizontally into two layers. Prepare the short pastry and roll it out to a thickness of ¹/₄ in / 3 mm. Cut out a base with a diameter of 13 in / 28 cm, prick several times with a fork and bake for 20 minutes at 320 °F / 160 °C.

2. To make the raspberry cream, beat the cream until stiff. Coarsely puree the raspberries with the sugar and lemon juice. Dissolve the soaked and thoroughly drained gelatin in a double boiler, and add to the raspberry puree. Fold in a quarter of the whipped cream to blend, then fold in the remaining cream.

Cream Torte

3. For the garnish, whip the cream until stiff, add the sugar and stiffen with the dissolved gelatin. Place the short pastry in a cake ring and coat it with melted milk chocolate. Place a $^1/_2$ in / 1 cm thick layer of Viennese sponge cake on top. Cover with half of the raspberry cream, and top with a second, slightly smaller sponge cake layer. Cover with the remaining raspberry cream, leaving a $^1/_4$ in / 5 mm space around the edge. Fill the cake ring with whipped cream. Refrigerate for three hours.

4. Remove the cake ring from the torte. Garnish the top by piping dollops of cream around the perimeter of the torte, and place a raspberry on top of each.

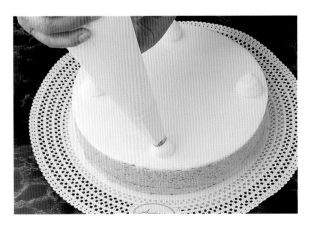

Preparation time: 1 hour 30 minutes
Cooking time: 1 hour 30 minutes
Difficulty: ★★★

Serves 8

For the chocolate glaze:
3¹/₂ oz / 100 g milk chocolate coating
4 tsp / 20 ml sugar syrup
4 tbsp condensed milk
1 tbsp / 20 g honey
Caracas sponge cake, Sacher sponge cake,
Baumkuchen
(see basic recipes p. 799, 804, 798)

Cream for garnishing:
6¹/₂ tbsp / 100 g butter

4¹/₂ tbsp / 50 g confectioners' sugar
1 egg
¹/₂ oz / 15 g bittersweet chocolate

For the ganache:
7 oz / 200 g bittersweet chocolate
1¹/₄ cups / 300 ml cream
6¹/₂ tbsp / 100 g butter
³/₄ cup / 200 g sugar
2 egg yolks
4¹/₂ tbsp / 70 ml lemon juice, freshly squeezed

For the coating:
2¹/₂ oz / 75 g bittersweet chocolate

For the marzipan topping:
5¹/₄ oz / 150 g marzipan
3 tbsp / 30 g confectioners' sugar

In the Middle Ages the Hanseatic League was a powerful association of more than one hundred and fifty north German towns that banded together to promote their trade interests. Hamburg, along with Bremen and Lübeck, was one of its most important members and to this day retains a special administrative status derived from its role as a Hansastadt. Hamburg is now one of three German cities that is also a state (something like Washington D.C.) and, uniquely, is ruled by a senate; hence this cake is also called "Senator's Torte."

Hansa torte is a rich combination of several elements. It is filled with ganache, which does not achieve its full effect until it is combined with certain types of sponge cake; for example, the Caracas sponge cake, made using marzipan and a praline

paste, and the *baumkuchen*, which is composed of a number of different layers. The latter is a German specialty found throughout Germany around Christmas. It is baked in a cylindrical form and then sliced horizontally, just as tree trunks are. A certain degree of skill is required to make it. One could also substitute chocolate-covered sponge cake or ladyfingers for the *baumkuchen*. Surprisingly, a variation on the *baumkuchen* is even found in the Pyrenees, perhaps a legacy of the Visigoths on one of their numerous raids.

But there can be no compromising with the ganache, which must be smooth and creamy, not too firm. Using a marzipan made with Italian almonds, which have a higher moisture content, makes the marzipan smoother.

1. To make the chocolate glazing, melt the milk chocolate coating in a double boiler with the sugar syrup (30 °Beaumé), honey and condensed milk, heating it to 100–105 °F / 38–40 °C. Bake the Caracas and Sacher sponge bases. For the garnishing cream, melt the chocolate in a double boiler, and beat the egg and confectioners' sugar until foamy. Cream the butter, then fold in the cooled beaten egg mixture and melted chocolate.

2. Begin the ganache a day in advance by bringing the cream to a boil with the butter and sugar. Set aside. The following day, whisk the egg yolks with part of the cream, then mix everything together and heat until the cream starts to thicken. Remove from the heat, fold in the finely chopped chocolate and the freshly squeezed lemon juice. Refrigerate until needed.

Torte

3. On a cake plate, place the Caracas sponge base inside a cake ring and cover with a quarter of the ganache. Place the Sacher sponge cake on top, centered, and surround with halved baumkuchen rings. Cover with the remaining ganache cream. Press down firmly to eliminate air pockets, and smooth off the surface. Refrigerate for two hours. Invert onto a cake lid, and spread melted chocolate onto the base. Allow to set, then invert again onto a cooling rack.

4. Roll out the marzipan and cover the cake with it. Reheat the chocolate glaze, pour onto the center of the cake and smooth over the top and sides with a spatula. Allow to cool. Pipe chocolate flowers onto waxed paper. Using the garnishing cream, make small balls of the size of a quail's egg and arrange around the sides of the top. Finally place a chocolate flower on top of each dollop of cream.

Preparation time: 30 minutes
Cooking time: 1 hour 30 minutes
Difficulty: ★

Serves 8

Sacher sponge cake: (see basic recipes p. 804)

For the chocolate glaze:
1³/₄ oz / 50 g milk chocolate
¹/₂ tbsp / 10 ml liquid honey
2 tbsp / 30 ml condensed milk

Sixteen-year-old Franz Sacher, employed by Prince Metternich, invented Sachertorte in 1832. Without it, where would Viennese baking be now? The fact that it started a quarrel between the two most famous Viennese *konditoreien* (pastry shops), Demel and the Sacher Hotel, attests to the symbolism and importance of this delicacy, valued by a select clientele far beyond the borders of Austria.

Adolf Andersen, who has his own version of Sachertorte, remembers when even the Dresden *konditoreien* once tried to lay claim to the Sachertorte. Andersen's cake is based on what information has leaked about the secret original recipe, apparently strictly guarded, and offers many opportunities for exchanging tips and tricks.

The Sacher mixture will only succeed if certain conditions are met: it must contain plenty of butter and chocolate, and the ingredients should have the same temperature. It should not be stirred too vigorously and must be baked at an even temperature. Since it contains only a little flour, it looks more like a soft chocolate mixture than a sponge cake. Before serving, you might like to garnish the Sachertorte with a cream topping.

The honey glaze, a feature exclusive to German varieties, adds a final touch to the general appearance of the cake. Sachertorte must be prepared well in advance; the glaze must have time to set so that the cake does not collapse when it is cut.

1. Prepare the Sacher sponge cake, following the procedure given in the basic recipes, folding the beaten egg yolk and slightly cooled melted chocolate into the batter as shown below. Bake the sponge mixture in a greased cake pan with a diameter of 12 in / 26 cm for 90 minutes at 275 °F / 140 °C.

2. Allow the sponge to cool in the cake pan. Turn it out onto a cooling rack, cover and allow to rest overnight. To make the chocolate glaze, melt the milk chocolate in a double boiler, allow it to cool a little, add the honey and slightly warmed condensed milk, and stir until smooth.

3. Level out any unevenness in the sponge cake with a serrated knife. Retain the sponge cake that you cut off, and sift it to make sponge cake crumbs. Spread the chocolate glaze over the top and sides of the sponge cake.

4. Finally, press the sifted sponge cake crumbs against the sides of the torte. Before serving, refrigerate for 45 minutes.

Preparation time: 30 minutes
Cooking time: 40 minutes
Difficulty: ★★★

Serves 12

For the baba dough:
¹/₂ cup / 125 ml milk
¹/₂ oz / 15 g bakers' yeast
1¹/₂ cups / 200 g flour
5 tsp / 25 g sugar
3 egg yolks
1 pinch of salt
a pinch of vanilla powder
grated peel of ¹/₂ lemon

6¹/₂ tbsp / 100 g butter, melted
6 tbsp / 80 g currants

For the syrup:
1 cup / 250 g superfine sugar
2 cups / 500 ml orange juice
1 cup / 250 ml brown rum
grated peel of ¹/₂ orange

For the glaze:
9 oz / 250 g fondant

To garnish:
Morello cherries
angelica

In Polish, the word *baba* is a childish variation of *babka* – a fat, old woman, whose appearance this traditional yeast cake is probably supposed to resemble. We probably have the Polish king and later Duke of Lorraine, Stanislaus Leszcynski, to thank for the baba's migration to France; he named it after Ali Baba, his favorite hero from *A Thousand and One Nights*. Then again, people in Austria are firmly convinced that the baba originated in Bohemia. Whatever the case, it is not easy to make an excellent baba, for they require concentrated attention. The same is due the ingredients: finely sifted flour, fresh yeast and only brown rum for soaking.

All the ingredients should be at room temperature, except for the milk, which should be a little warmer (95 °F / 35 °C). The

dough should be neither too firm nor too runny; experience will teach you to recognize the right consistency. A pastry bag is used to pipe the dough into greased ramekins or other forms that have been sprinkled with sugar. The forms should only be filled two-thirds full since the babas will rise considerably during baking.

After they are baked the babas are placed upside down; the pressure exerted by the forms produces their bulbous appearance. Do be aware that these seemingly innocent cakes pack quite a punch: the currants are marinated in rum, and the babas themselves are drenched in rum syrup after they have cooled.

1. To make the dough, gently warm a third of the milk and dissolve the yeast in it. Add a quarter of the flour, blend, and leave the mixture to prove in a warm place. Thoroughly mix the remaining flour, sugar, egg yolks, salt, vanilla powder, grated lemon peel, and remaining milk with the dough hook of an electric mixer. Add the yeast mixture, and finally, the lukewarm butter and currants.

2. Place the dough in a large bowl, cover with a cloth and allow to rise at room temperature until it has doubled in size. Grease the ramekins with butter, sprinkle with sugar, and fill two-thirds full with the mixture. Leave to rise again, then bake for 20 minutes at 390 °F / 200 °C.

au Rhum

3. Turn the babas out of the forms. To make the syrup, combine the orange juice, rum, sugar, and grated orange peel into a saucepan and bring to a boil. Allow to cool a little. Prick the babas around the sides with a fork so that they better absorb the liquid. Fill the baba forms half-full with syrup and soak the babas in them.

4. Allow the babas to drain on a cooling rack. Heat the fondant in a saucepan and glaze the babas with it. Arrange on a plate and garnish with morello cherries and angelica.

Preparation time: 30 minutes
Cooking time: 20 minutes
Difficulty: ★

Serves 6

Vanilla sugar:
2 vanilla beans
2 tbsp / 20 g confectioners' sugar

For the kipferl dough:
13 tbsp / 200 g butter
¼ cup / 60 g superfine sugar

1½ cups / 180 g flour
⅔ cup / 100 g hazelnuts, very finely ground
3½ tbsp / 50 ml rum

For dusting:
confectioners' sugar

Crème Anglaise:
(see basic recipes p. 800)

During the wars between the Turks and the Austrian-German Empire the symbol of the Turkish crescent made its way to Austria. Crescents, or croissants as they are often called today, were allegedly invented by an Austrian baker after the peace treaty at Passarowitz (1718), which led to the final retreat of the Turkish invaders. The influence of Turkey on 18th-century Austria is obvious, as in the famous Turkish March, the Rondo alla turca in Mozart's 11th Sonata (KV 331).

Two different sorts of crescents exist in Austria, where they are called *kipferl* – one firmer and one somewhat softer. The one in this recipe is usually served with tea in the Demel *konditorei*.

For this recipe, the hazelnuts should be freshly roasted and then ground. After kneading the *kipferl* dough, leave it to rest

in the refrigerator and then continue working it with your hands in the traditional manner, just as the bakers of old used to. The crescents can be fairly thick; thinner *kipferl* tend to burn easily when baked. Leave enough space between the crescents on the baking tray so that there will be no problem separating them after baking.

Sugar is used twice in this recipe – first to make the dough sweet, though it is used in moderation, and then to garnish the *kipferl* and round off their flavor. This is the source of the unique *kipferl* taste.

1. To make the vanilla sugar, slit the vanilla beans lengthwise. Scrape out the vanilla pulp using a knife and mix it with the confectioners' sugar.

2. To make the kipferl dough, cream the butter with the vanilla sugar and superfine sugar until light and almost foamy with a mixer. Add the flour, finely ground hazelnuts and rum, and knead everything thoroughly.

Kipferl

3. Form the dough into several rolls, and allow to rest overnight in the refrigerator.

4. Cut each dough roll into pieces 1 in / 2 cm long and shape them into crescents. Place them on a baking sheet and bake for about ten minutes at 410 °F / 210 °C. Allow to cool, then dust them with confectioners' sugar. Serve with Crème Anglaise.

Preparation time: 30 minutes
Cooking time: 15 minutes
Difficulty: ★★

Makes 25

For the cookie dough:
1¹/₂ cup, 2 tbsp / 400 g butter
2 cups / 300 g confectioners' sugar
3 eggs
5¹/₄ cups / 650 g flour

For the pistachio mixture:
7 oz / 200 g marzipan
rum
³/₄ oz / 20 g pistachio paste
¹/₃ cup / 40 g pistachios, chopped

For the coating:
9 oz / 250 g chocolate coating

The name given to these irresistible cookies might call to mind the composer, Wolfgang Amadeus Mozart, especially since the *Mozartkugeln* chocolates named after him are available throughout Austria (and increasingly in gourmet stores in North America).

Although the two confections share several flavors in common – chocolate, pistachio, and marzipan – Franz Augustin says that he did not invent these cookies in memory of Mozart. He was simply fascinated by the color contrast among the green marzipan, dark brown chocolate, and light cookies.

For the dough to achieve the correct consistency, it is important for all the ingredients, especially the butter and egg yolks,

to be used chilled. The recipe was designed to be made with Lübeck marzipan, if possible, and definitely choose a raw marzipan (rather than ready-to-eat) that can absorb more sugar. Instead of chocolate coating, which needs to be melted at a high temperature, one can use liquid chocolate to accent the layered cookies.

One decorative possibility is to use a fluted rolling pin to roll out the dough, giving it a decorative pattern that will be retained during baking if the dough is refrigerated beforehand. The cookies' grooved appearance is sure to please your guests.

1. To make the dough, cream the butter and confectioners' sugar until light, add the eggs and mix everything thoroughly. Add the sifted flour and knead to a smooth dough. Allow the dough to rest in a cool place for about an hour and then roll out to a thickness of ¹/₄ in / 3 mm.

2. Using round, smooth cookie cutters, cut out circles with a diameter of 2 in / 4 cm, place on a baking tray and bake for 15 minutes at 390 °F / 200 °C.

Cookies

3. After baking, allow the cookies to cool on a cooling rack. To make the pistachio mixture, stir the marzipan and rum until smooth with a stiff whisk, then add the pistachio paste and chopped pistachios. Garnish half of the cookies with the pistachio mixture, and then top with the remaining cookies.

4. Melt the chocolate coating in the top of a double boiler. Use a wooden spoon or spatula to cover half of one side of every cookie sandwich with the chocolate coating, being careful not to let any of the glaze run down to the bottom side. Serve 4–5 cookies per person.

Preparation time: 20 minutes
Cooking time: 40 minutes
Difficulty: ★

Makes 16

2²/₃ cups / 400 g sweet almonds, blanched and ground
1¹/₂ cups, 2 tbsp / 400 g sugar
1 tbsp / 10 g bitter almonds, ground

3 large egg whites
1 tsp grated lemon peel
5 egg yolks
6 eggs
¹/₂ cup / 120 g sugar
1 cup, 2 tbsp / 140 g maizena
9 tbsp / 140 g butter, melted

For sprinkling in the forms:
sponge cake crumbs

According to at least one source, Madeleine Paumier was a chef working for Madame Perrotin de Barmond when she invented the cakes bearing her Christian name, but that is all we know about these two ladies. Madeleines have been around since the Middle Ages, and several French towns have laid claim to being their original home, including Commercy in Lorraine (this version of the story was supported by Stanislaus Leszczynsky in the 18th century), Illiers-Combray near Chartres, and Saint-Yrieix in Limousin.

Several precautions are necessary when making these dry, shell-shaped cakes, particularly with the almonds, which need to be ground twice into a fine almond flour.

Blanched almonds from Spain (Marcona), Italy (Avola) or Provence (Aï) work well. The process of grinding the almonds twice is intended to release the almond oil and produce a dry flour, but overdoing the grinding can have fatal consequences during baking. Find the middle ground and allow the almonds to rest a few minutes after grinding, so that they again become a little softer.

That middle ground is important during baking as well, for the Madeleines must not darken too much. The oven temperature must be low enough for them to develop a lovely golden-yellow color, but high enough for the crust not to become too thick. After baking, they can be stored under a layer of plastic wrap for a few days.

1. Grind the sweet almonds, sugar, and bitter almonds twice in a blender, or finely grind with a handmill.

2. Place the almond flour into a bowl. Stir in the egg whites and grated lemon peel, and combine everything thoroughly.

Madeleines

3. Add the egg yolks and whole eggs one at a time, beating to combine after each addition. Stir the mixture to produce a smooth dough. Finally, fold in the sugar, maizena, and the melted butter.

4. Grease the fluted baking forms with butter, and sprinkle sifted sponge cake crumbs into them. Pour the mixture into the forms (approximately 3^1/$_2$ oz / 100 g per tin). Bake for 40 minutes at 340 °F / 170 °C. Allow to cool before serving.

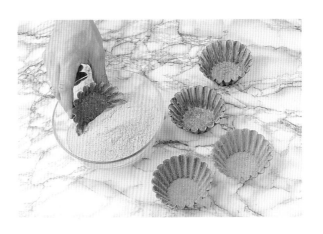

Preparation time: 2 hours
Cooking time: 10 minutes
Difficulty: ★★

Serves 8

biscuit natur, cigarette pastry:
   (see basic recipes p. 798, 799)

For the biscuit spécial:
2 cups / 225 g almonds, very finely ground
1 1/2 cups / 225 g confectioners' sugar
1/2 cup / 60 g flour
4 eggs
3 tbsp / 45 g butter
2 tbsp / 30 g sugar
6 egg whites
yellow food coloring

For the lime mousse:
1/2 cup, 1 tbsp / 130 ml lime juice
1 tbsp / 15 ml lime juice concentrate
3 tbsp / 45 g sugar
grated peel of 1 lemon

2 egg yolks
7 sheets of gelatin
1 3/4 cups / 450 ml whipping cream

For the Italian meringue:
4 egg whites
3/4 cup / 180 g sugar
3 tbsp / 45 ml water

For the syrup for soaking:
3 1/2 tbsp / 50 ml lemon or lime juice
5 tsp / 25 ml sugar syrup

To garnish:
red currants
cake glaze: green/yellow and clear

Few citrus fruits are more adaptable than lemons and limes. They have a remarkably powerful flavor, lots of vitamin C, and the extraordinary ability to ripen artificially. While lemons originated in southeast Asia and are now grown in tropical regions around the world, limes are indigenous to North and Central America and remain somewhat exotic in European countries. This light, tart, mousse-filled dessert brings out all of its virtues.

Created by Eric Baumann, this torte is rather unusual by Swiss standards, where lemons are well-known, but their green cousin from Mexico, the lime, is quite rare. About the size of a largish walnut, they are decidedly smaller than the lemon. They are a little more difficult to work with – their tough rind is hard to grate – but the strong flavor they lend to the cream makes them the most important element of the torte.

The custard that is the basis for the lime mousse is best prepared a day in advance so that it has time to cool thoroughly before the Italian meringue is folded in, very gently so that it does not collapse. Allow enough time to assemble the torte so you do not have to rush the job.

The same is true of the *biscuit*; much of this can be made in advance and kept under a sheet of plastic wrap. Beginners should start with a smaller sponge cake and not attempt to make larger ones until they feel comfortable with the procedure.

1. Prepare the cigarette pastry, then the biscuit spécial as described in the basic recipes but using the amounts given above; color the biscuit spécial mixture a pleasing yellow. Pipe a thin layer of it onto a sheet of plastic, use a cake comb to draw lines through it, then freeze. After it has set, spread a layer of cigarette pastry on top and bake for 6–7 minutes at 430 °F / 220 °C.

2. Make a lime custard by bringing the lime juice, lime juice concentrate, sugar, and lemon peel to a boil. Beat the egg yolks with a whisk until foamy, combine with the lime mixture and thicken like a custard. Remove from the heat and add the gelatin, which has been soaked in cold water; cool. To make the syrup for soaking, mix the sugar syrup and lemon or lime juice. Prepare the biscuit according to the basic recipe and slice into two layers.

Torte

3. To prepare the meringue, dissolve two-thirds of the sugar in the water and bring to 250 °F / 121 °C. Slowly pour this syrup over the egg whites, which have been beaten until stiff with the remaining sugar. Continue to beat until completely cooled. For the lime mousse, combine the meringue with the lime custard, and finally fold in the whipped cream. Line a cake ring with a strip of baking paper and a strip of the biscuit spécial, leaving about $^1/_2$ in / 1 cm free at the top.

4. Place a biscuit natur base in the cake ring, and fill the ring two-thirds full with the lime mousse. Place the second sponge layer on top, soak it with the syrup and fill the ring with the remaining mousse. Freeze for four hours. Coat the top of the torte with the green/yellow cake glaze, then top with a thin layer of clear glaze. Serve well-chilled.

Preparation time: 1 hour 30 minutes
Cooking time: 40 minutes
Difficulty: ★★

Serves 8

génoise, biscuit spécial, clear cake glaze:
  (see basic recipes p. 801, 798, 800)

For the chocolate mousse:
3 egg yolks
6½ tbsp / 100 ml sugar syrup
7 oz / 190 g milk chocolate coating
1½ cups / 375 ml whipping cream

For the caramel mousse:
3 egg yolks
¼ cup / 55 ml sugar syrup

3½ sheets of gelatin
1¼ cups / 300 ml whipping cream

For the caramel:
7 tbsp / 115 g sugar
3½ tbsp / 50 ml glucose
1 tbsp / 15 g butter
¾ cup / 165 ml crème fraîche (35% fat)

For the caramel syrup:
a little liquid caramel
a little water

To garnish:
caramel glaze
clear cake glaze
chocolate decorations

So far, there have been three generations of the Baumann family adding to the fame of Swiss pastry chefs in Lausanne, Biel, and Zurich, and they have always adhered to strict quality criteria for their products. This has led to a firmly-rooted family tradition that is founded on extensive expertise, yet has remained open to new ideas all along.

It is in this spirit that Eric Baumann, who continues this family tradition, has been searching for a way to produce a caramel with an intense flavor, in which the sweet and bitter notes balance each other. Experiences have taught him that the best method is to heat the purest English sugar until it has a strong color, but is not too dark, which signals that the caramel has become bitter.

So that the caramel flavor is not overpowered, the milk chocolate used in this recipe must not be too sweet. When using chocolate, keep in mind its characteristic qualities such as flavor, melting properties, and consistency.

There is a certain element of risk when mixing the chocolate coating with the beaten eggs. To reduce this risk, make sure the temperature is not too high and thoroughly combine the chocolate with the cream until the mixture is smooth. Then there should be no problem folding it into the beaten egg mixture. Instead of caramel, hazelnuts, almonds or coffee could also be used to make the torte.

1. To make the chocolate mousse, beat the egg yolks with the sugar syrup in a double boiler until it becomes a firm foamy mixture. Remove from the double boiler and continue to beat until completely cooled. Reduce the hot chocolate coating with a little water until it has a creamy consistency, then fold it into the cold beaten egg mixture. Fold in the whipped cream. Using a pastry bag, pipe 1 in / 2 cm of the mousse into cake rings and freeze.

2. To make the caramel mousse, prepare the egg yolks and sugar syrup as above. Caramelize the sugar until it is fairly brown and dissolve the glucose in it. In another pan, bring the crème fraîche to a boil; add the butter and boiling crème fraîche to the sugars. Heat everything to 215 °F / 103 °C, then allow to cool.

3. Combine the caramel with the cooled egg yolk mixture. Heat the gelatin (previously soaked in cold water) with a little sugar syrup and add to the caramel. Finally, fold in the whipped cream. Line a cake ring with a strip of baking paper three-quarters the height of the ring, then line the cake ring with a strip of biscuit spécial of the same width.

4. Place a ¹/₂ in / 1 cm thick layer of génoise in the cake ring and soak it with caramel syrup. Fill the ring two-thirds full with caramel mousse. Place the set chocolate mousse on top, then completely fill the ring with caramel mousse. Refrigerate for four hours. Marble the top of the torte with caramel glaze and clear cake glaze, and decorate with chocolate decorations. Serve well chilled.

Preparation time: 1 hour 30 minutes
Cooking time: 40 minutes
Difficulty: ★★

Serves 8

génoise, Japonaise sponge cake:
  (see basic recipes p. 801)

For the kirsch buttercream:
$^1/_2$ cup / 120 ml milk
$^1/_2$ cup / 120 g sugar
$1^1/_2$ vanilla beans
5 egg yolks
$1^2/_3$ cups / 400 g butter
6 tbsp / 90 ml kirsch, 100% proof
1–2 drops red food coloring

For the Italian meringue:
1 large egg white
6 tbsp / 90 g sugar
2 tbsp / 30 ml water

For the syrup for soaking:
$^2/_3$ cup / 150 ml kirsch, 100% proof
$6^1/_2$ tbsp / 100 ml sugar syrup

To garnish:
flaked almonds, roasted
confectioners' sugar
ground pistachios
Morello cherries marinated in kirsch

The canton of Zug, near Zurich, used to be ruled by the Hapsburg dynasty, and in 1352 it joined the Swiss Confederation, a mutual defense league. Because of the complicated proceedings of the Middle Ages, however, Zug was not incorporated until 1415, when it was finally granted the same rights as the other Swiss cantons. Eric Baumann pays his respects to the culinary traditions of this canton, famous for its *Zuger Pfefferkuchen* (gingerbread), with a kirsch torte.

This versatile fruit schnapps, used to flavor the buttercream in this recipe, can also serve as an excellent complement to chocolate and a variety of fruits. The buttercream is also given a slightly reddish tint to serve as a visual reminder of cherries, though the cherries used to produce kirsch have a very dark juice.

For decorating the cake, Eric Baumann principally uses the type of fruit from which the fruit schnapps used for soaking the sponge cake is made. For this torte, though, he is willing to make an exception and would even accept pineapple as a garnish. He, personally, prefers to decorate the Zug Cherry Torte with Morello cherries, so that it does not pretend to be something it is not. The cherries should have been marinated in kirsch for two months.

Less experienced bakers need to take special care to grease the baking paper thoroughly before spreading the Japonaise sponge mixture on to it. Bake the sponge cake very slowly at a stable temperature so that it bakes evenly, and then keep it in an airtight container.

1. To make the buttercream, bring the milk to a boil with half the sugar and the content of the vanilla beans. Whisk the egg yolks and remaining sugar until foamy. Stir in some hot milk; pour back into the saucepan and thicken at 180 °F / 82 °C like a custard. Let cool. For the meringue, beat the egg whites with 2 tsp / 10 g sugar until stiff. Heat the water and remaining sugar to 250 °F / 121 °C and pour onto the egg whites while beating. Cream the butter, combine with the custard, and fold in the meringue.

2. Finally, tint 1 lb / 450 g of the buttercream red and flavor it with kirsch. Make the Japonaise sponge cake according to the basic recipe. Use a round stencil to spread the mixture on to greased baking paper and bake for 10–12 minutes at 300 °F / 150 °C. Then prepare the génoise, also according to the basic recipe, and turn into a baking paper-lined cake pan of the same diameter as the stencil used for the Japonaise sponge cake. Bake for 20 minutes at 340 °F / 170 °C.

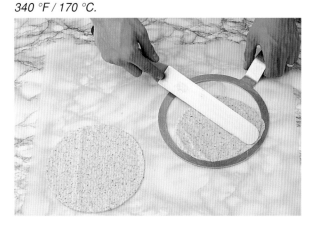

Cherry Torte

3. To make the syrup for soaking, mix the kirsch with the sugar syrup. Spread a thin layer of kirsch buttercream on to one of the Japonaise sponge layers, place the kirsch syrup-drenched génoise on top, spread it generously with kirsch buttercream and cover with the second layer of Japonaise sponge cake.

4. Spread the remaining kirsch buttercream on the top and sides of the cake, and press roasted flaked almonds on to the sides. Dust the top with confectioners' sugar and garnish with chopped pistachios and cherries marinated in kirsch. Refrigerate for about four hours before serving.

Preparation time: 40 minutes
Cooking time: 40 minutes
Difficulty: ★

Serves 8

génoise, Charlotte cream:
  (see basic recipes p. 801, 799)

For the passion fruit cream:
7 oz / 200 g Charlotte cream
2 cups / 500 ml whipping cream
6$^1/_2$ tbsp / 100 g passion fruit extract
$^2/_3$ cup / 100 g confectioners' sugar

For the syrup for soaking:
4 tsp / 20 g passion fruit extract
$^1/_3$ cup / 80 ml sugar syrup

To garnish:
3 kiwis
1$^1/_2$ cups / 200 g flaked almonds, roasted
1$^1/_4$ cups / 300 ml whipping cream

Clear cake glaze: (see basic recipes p. 800)

Eric Baumann is quite a fan of some of the exotic fruits increasingly available in our grocery stores. In the following unique and delicious recipe, he uses kiwis and passion fruit, after several experiments convinced him that the flavors of the two fruits complement each other very well.

The best kiwis, also known as Chinese gooseberries, are definitely those grown in New Zealand, where the Hayward variety is cultivated. For some years now this fruit has received the highest praise, for it is full of vitamins and apparently covers our daily requirement of vitamin C, despite being very low in calories. Use ripe kiwis that are still firm and do not give when pressed.

The passion fruit (or granadilla) is not always easy to use. Here it appears in the form of an extract, which preserves the full

impact of its flavor without adding enough liquid to the cream to distort its consistency. Using ripe, wrinkled fruits, start by deseeding the flesh, then reduce it with added water and pass it through a sieve. The juice thus produced is reduced a second time. The resulting fruit extract keeps well in the freezer.

The whipped cream should have a fat content of 35% and be very cold. Whip it until stiff, with a twentieth of its weight in sugar. Begin by whipping only 80% of the cream; adding the remaining 20% toward the end of the process. When making the Charlotte cream, it should not be overheated (180 °F / 82 °C at the most) before the gelatin is folded in.

1. Make the génoise and Charlotte cream according to the basic recipes. Slice the génoise horizontally into two layers. For the passion fruit cream, reheat the Charlotte cream slightly and add the confectioners' sugar and passion fruit extract (see text above). Combine everything thoroughly, then carefully fold in the whipped cream.

2. For the syrup to soak, stir the extract into the sugar syrup. Line a cake ring with a strip of baking paper. Place a $^1/_2$ in / 1 cm thick layer of génoise inside, soak it with passion fruit syrup and fill the ring two-thirds full with passion fruit cream. Place a second layer of génoise on top, soak and cover with the remaining cream. Refrigerate for four hours.

Passion Fruit Cream

3. Remove the cake ring and the baking paper. Spread a thin layer of whipped cream on the top and sides of the cake. Arrange slices of kiwi on the top, leaving a 1 in / 2 cm border free around the outside; cover the kiwi slices with clear cake glaze.

4. Roast the flaked almonds using a salamander and decorate the edge of the cake with them. Pipe a whipped cream garland along the edge of the top. Serve well chilled.

Preparation time: 30 minutes
Cooking time: 20 minutes
Difficulty: ★

Serves 8

génoise, pastry cream, buttercream:
   (see basic recipes p. 801, 802, 799)
³/₄ cup / 150 g candied fruits, diced
3¹/₂ tbsp / 50 ml kirsch

For the syrup for soaking:
(see basic recipes p. 805)
6¹/₂ tbsp / 100 ml water
6¹/₂ tbsp / 100 g superfine sugar
6¹/₂ tbsp / 100 ml kirsch

To garnish:
marzipan

For the egg white icing:
1 egg white
confectioners' sugar
juice of 1 lemon

Because it combines several elements fundamental to pastry-baking, this torte is a classic and was long seen as a way of testing bakers who wanted to prove that they knew their trade. Maybe this is why it is called Ambassadeur. Maurice and Jean-Jacques Bernachon have fastidiously held to the principles by which it is made, and it is still much requested by their customers in Lyon.

To achieve such expertise in baking, the production of the génoise – made with only the best butter and eggs – must be perfectly mastered. The classic pastry cream, made with whole milk, very fresh egg yolks, and particularly aromatic vanilla, and using traditional copper implements, also has to be just so.

Kirsch is distilled from deep black cherries, producing a clear schnapps; a well-known example is that produced by the Fougerolles community in the Franche Comté region of France. The exquisite aroma of the distilled kirsch gives the pastry cream a delicate touch and gives the "ambassador" a special flavor, sure to be appreciated by diplomats all over the world.

In order to harmonize with this composition, the marzipan needs to be very homogeneous, so knead it carefully with the balls of your hands until it reaches the desired consistency. Before rolling it out, lightly dust the working surface and the rolling pin with confectioners' sugar so that the marzipan does not stick to them.

1. Prepare the simple génoise a day in advance, and slice it horizontally into three equally thick layers. Make both the pastry cream and the syrup for soaking using the basic recipe as a guide with the ingredients listed above. Marinate the diced candied fruits in kirsch. Place a layer of sponge cake on a cake lid and soak it with a third of the kirsch syrup.

2. Pipe a ¹/₂ in / 1 cm thick layer of pastry cream onto the sponge cake base, then sprinkle with half of the (drained) candied fruits. Place the second sponge layer on top, soak with another third of the kirsch syrup, pipe more pastry cream onto the sponge cake and sprinkle with the rest of the candied fruits. Top with the third sponge cake layer and soak with the remaining kirsch syrup.

3. Spread buttercream on the sides and top of the torte and refrigerate for one hour. To make the egg white icing, place the egg white in a bowl and use a wooden spatula to stir in the sifted confectioners' sugar gradually until the mixture has a creamy consistency. Finally add the lemon juice. Cover with a damp cloth.

4. Roll out the marzipan with a rolling pin to a thickness of about ¹/₄ in / 4 mm and cover the torte with it. Trim the excess and finally decorate the torte's surface with the egg white icing, placing a marzipan rose in the center.

Preparation time: 1 hour 15 minutes
Cooking time: 15 minutes
Difficulty: ⋆⋆

Serves 8

simple génoise, ganache, pastry cream:
(see basic recipes p. 804, 801, 802)

For the syrup for soaking:
(see basic recipes p. 805)
6¹/₂ tbsp / 100 ml rum
6¹/₂ tbsp / 100 ml water
6¹/₂ tbsp / 100 g superfine sugar

To garnish:
chocolate rolls and flakes

In France, the traditional Christmas dinner is somehow incomplete without this wonderful dessert. Whether made with sweet chestnuts, meringue, chocolate, Grand Marnier or some other creative variation, the chocolate *bûche de noël* (Yule log) is elemental to Christmas. The Bernachons have made it their task to continue this unshakable tradition. A time-consuming procedure, the creation of a *bûche de noël* is best carried out over the three or four days before Christmas.

The génoise should be spread very thinly on to a baking sheet and then baked immediately so that it remains soft. Rolling the sponge cake is easier if you spread some pastry cream or gan-

ache on to it; this produces a slight condensation, making the sponge cake softer. The Bernachon pâtisserie uses an exclusive mixture of twelve varieties of cocoa for the ganache, one of them the much sought-after Chuao, named after a town in the mountains of Venezuela. Touton, a French company, is the sole European importer of this exceptional cocoa.

The effect achieved with a well-chilled *bûche de noël* is a natural result of its combination of fine flavors: génoise, ganache and old rum make this festive dessert unforgettable. Serve it with vanilla ice cream or a delicious crème anglaise.

1. Make the génoise and ganache a day in advance according to the basic recipes. Prepare a classic pastry cream and syrup for soaking, again following those instructions. When you are ready to assemble the cake, heat a third of the ganache in a double boiler, stirring constantly, until it softens and then combine it with the pastry cream. Spread this mixture onto the sponge cake, which has been cut into a rectangular shape.

2. Carefully roll up the sponge cake covered with cream, using a knife or spatula to roll it evenly. Wrap the sponge cake roll firmly in plastic wrap and refrigerate for at least one hour.

3. Cut off the ends of the sponge cake roll at an angle with a knife that has been dipped in hot water. Place these pieces on the top of the log to form decorative knotholes.

4. Using a pastry bag with a star-shaped tip, garnish the log all over with the remaining ganache and decorate to taste with chocolate flakes and rolls, meringue mushrooms, or other decorations.

Preparation time: 45 minutes
Cooking time: 25 minutes
Difficulty: ★★★

Serves 8

For the génoise:
6 eggs
1/2 cup, 3 tbsp / 170 g superfine sugar
a little honey
1 1/2 cups / 200 g flour, sifted
1/2 cup / 120 g best-quality butter

For the ganache:
1 cup / 250 ml crème fraîche with a high fat
  content

12 oz / 375 g Avellino bar chocolate
3 1/2 oz / 100 g baking chocolate

For the marinated cherries:
10 Montmorency cherries
1/2 cup / 120 ml cherry brandy

To garnish:
7 oz / 200 g bittersweet chocolate
candied violets
cocoa

This génoise enhanced with refined flavors is a variation of the classic Montmorency Cherry Torte created for the occasion of Maurice Bernachon's old friend Paul Bocuse receiving the Cross of the Legion of Honor, and in honor of Valéry Giscard d'Estaing, the French president at the time. The cake has been known by several names, including Valéry Torte, Anne Aymone Torte and finally, especially for this volume, Elysée Torte. The Elysée ganache consists of cream, chocolate, nut nougat, and very finely chopped brandy-marinated cherries, and the sponge cake is soaked with cherry brandy (like a Montmorency Cherry Torte).

The most distinctive feature of this torte is, however, its decoration, a delicate structure of chocolate flakes that has to be made on a marble slab using a handmill.

Because of the artistic arrangement of chocolate flakes on the top of the cake, it is particularly difficult to cut the cake into many or very thin slices. The record for this is held by the Hermès company with a cake made for a reception of about 500 people in Lyon. Very creative means of transportation had to be arranged for that cake!

When the topic of this torte comes up, Maurice Bernachon never misses the chance to quote one of his customers, who said, "This is a cake you eat twice, the first time with your eyes …" Bernachon was very moved by this at the time and still considers it his nicest compliment.

1. Marinate the cherries in the brandy. For the ganache, bring the crème fraîche to a boil in a saucepan, break the chocolate into small pieces and stir it in. Remove from heat and whisk until smooth. Cover and allow to cool in a refrigerator for at least 12 hours. Then reheat the ganache in a double boiler, stirring constantly, until it softens. Reserve 1/4 of it for covering the cake. Add the drained and finely chopped cherries to the remaining ganache.

2. For the génoise, combine the eggs with the sugar and honey in a double boiler and gently warm. Remove from the heat and continue to beat with a mixer until the mixture hangs down in long ribbons. Fold in the flour and melted butter. Pour into a round cake pan with high sides and bake for 20 minutes at 390 °F / 200 °C. Cut the sponge cake horizontally into three layers. Place one layer on a cake lid, soak with cherry brandy and spread with ganache.

Torte

3. Place the second sponge cake layer on top and again soak with brandy and cover with ganache. Top with the third génoise layer, soak with the remaining cherry brandy, and refrigerate for one hour. Use the reserved ganache to cover the top and sides, smoothing with a spatula.

4. Melt the bittersweet chocolate in a double boiler at 85 °F / 31 °C, spread on to a marble slab and allow to cool. Form rolls, arrange them on top of the cake and dust with cocoa. Serve the torte with crème anglaise or pistachio ice cream, according to taste.

Preparation time: 45 minutes
Cooking time: 20 minutes
Difficulty: ★

Serves 8

simple génoise: (see basic recipes p. 804)

For the buttercream:
(see basic recipes p. 799)
5 tbsp / 75 g butter
1/2 cup, 2 tbsp / 150 g superfine sugar
4 egg yolks
6 1/2 tbsp / 50 g flour
1 vanilla bean

2 1/2 cups / 600 ml whole milk
2 pinches of salt

For the syrup for soaking:
(see basic recipes p. 805)
6 1/2 tbsp / 100 ml kirsch
6 1/2 tbsp / 100 ml water
6 1/2 tbsp / 100 g sugar

For the filling:
2 lb 3 oz / 1 kg strawberries

To garnish:
9 oz / 250 g marzipan
confectioners' sugar

Strawberry cakes are usually available only in spring and early summer, when strawberries are nice and ripe and their flavor has had the chance to develop fully through exposure to sunshine. Gourmets must respect the cycle of the seasons and adjust the pleasures of the palate around the rhythms of nature.

The more aromatic, small, dark red strawberries are best suited for this recipe. Raspberries or wild strawberries could be used instead, as long as they are available in sufficient quantity. Generally, large berries are not suited to this recipe, because you need aromatic berries that are fully ripe but not too soft.

Washing strawberries in a lot of water impairs their flavor, so it is better to wipe them carefully with damp paper towels, especially if there is still some soil on them.

The génoise will be more velvety if it is made with a little honey; the cake will then require a bit less sugar, and also keep longer.

If you decide to make a raspberry cake, replace the kirsch with the best raspberry schnapps you can find. Its delicate bouquet will give the sponge cake a distinctive flavor.

1. Bake the génoise a day ahead. Slice it horizontally into two equal layers. Make the buttercream and syrup for soaking according to the basic recipes, but with the ingredients listed above. Take the stems off the strawberries and wipe them clean. Place a layer of génoise on a cake lid, soak with the kirsch syrup, and spread a 1/2 in / 1 cm layer of buttercream on it. Arrange the strawberries on top, placing a ring of strawberries of equal size around the edge.

2. Cover the strawberries with the remaining buttercream and smooth off the top.

Torte

3. Place the second sponge cake layer on top of the strawberries and buttercream, and soak with the remaining kirsch syrup. Refrigerate for one hour or longer.

4. Roll out the marzipan mixture with a rolling pin to a thickness of $1/8$ in / 2 mm, cut a zigzag pattern along the edge, and place it on top of the cake. Dust the torte lightly with confectioners' sugar and use a salamander or hot iron to burn a pattern into the marzipan. Decorate to taste with a marzipan rose or strawberries.

Preparation time: 30 minutes
Cooking time: 20 minutes
Difficulty: ★

Serves 8

simple génoise:
(see basic recipes p. 804)

For the pastry cream:
2¹/₂ cups / 600 ml milk
1 vanilla bean
1 pinch of salt
4 egg yolks
¹/₂ cup, 2 tbsp / 150 g superfine sugar
6¹/₂ tbsp / 50 g flour

For the syrup for soaking:
(see basic recipes p. 805)
6¹/₂ tbsp / 100 ml Grand Marnier
6¹/₂ tbsp / 100 g superfine sugar
6¹/₂ tbsp / 100 ml water

For the filling:
9 oz / 250 g buttercream (see basic recipes p. 79)
¹/₂ cup / 100 g candied orange peel marinated in
   Grand Marnier
9 oz / 250 g orange-colored marzipan

For the egg white icing:
1 egg white
confectioners' sugar
juice of 1 lemon

For almost fifty years now, Maurice Bernachon has made a Grand Marnier *cordon rouge* (red label) torte with chocolate or ganache, paying tribute to the fine flavor and consistent quality of the well-known liqueur in this and many other creations. Grand Marnier is made by marinating the peels of bitter Antillian oranges in high-quality cognac that has been matured in old oak barrels.

This Grand Marnier torte contains candied orange peel, which our fastidious pastry chefs make themselves from Spanish navel oranges. The peels of the untreated oranges are first blanched, then marinated in large copper pans and flavored with vanilla. But that is not all: as soon as the orange peels are

saturated with sugar syrup, they are preserved in stoneware jars and finally marinated again in Grand Marnier for six weeks before use.

The marzipan (ideally made using the Spanish Avola almond) has to withstand quite a bit in this recipe; it needs to be kneaded very thoroughly before it is rolled out and draped over the torte.

The egg white icing can be replaced by other toppings, such as a layer of ganache with some elegantly arranged peach slices. Their color and shine would also enhance the total effect of the Grand Marnier torte beautifully.

1. Make the génoise a day in advance. For the pastry cream, bring 2 cups / 500 ml of milk to a boil with the slit vanilla bean and salt. Whisk the egg yolks and sugar in a bowl until foamy, then fold in the flour. Add the remaining milk, cold (to prevent lumps), then stir in the boiled milk. Pour everything into a saucepan, return to a boil and simmer while stirring with a whisk for three minutes. Allow to cool and refrigerate.

2. Prepare the syrup for soaking according to the basic recipe. Cut the génoise horizontally into three equally thick layers. Place one layer on a cake lid and soak it with a third of the Grand Marnier syrup. Pipe a ¹/₂–1 in / 1–2 cm thick layer of pastry cream on the génoise and sprinkle some marinated orange peel over it. Repeat with the second layer of génoise.

Torte

3. Place the third sponge layer on top, soak it and spread buttercream all over the sides and top of the torte. Refrigerate for one hour. Roll out the marzipan out with a rolling pin to a thickness of ¹/₈ in / 2 mm, cover the torte with it and trim the excess.

4. To make the egg white icing, put the egg white in a bowl and gradually stir in the sifted confectioners' sugar with a wooden spatula until the mixture has a creamy consistency. Add a dash of lemon juice. Cover with a damp cloth. Decorate the cake with the egg white icing and garnish with a candied orange peel and marzipan leaves.

Preparation time: 2 hours
Cooking time: 25 minutes
Difficulty: ★★★

Serves 8

génoise, rum syrup for soaking, sweet pastry:
  (see basic recipes p. 801, 805)

For the buttercream:
3 eggs
6¹/₂ tbsp / 100 g superfine sugar
5 tsp / 25 ml water
1 cup / 250 g butter
grated peel of 1 lemon

For the marzipan topping:
9 oz / 250 g marzipan
4 egg yolks
1 egg
sugar syrup

For the cigarette pastry:
6¹/₂ tbsp / 100 g butter
²/₃ cup / 100 g confectioners' sugar
3 egg whites
³/₄ cup, 1 tbsp / 100 g sifted flour
cocoa powder

During the France of the Belle Epoque, the *canotier*, a flat, round straw hat, became the symbol of carefree days outdoors; it was a great favorite of the Impressionists. Here, Christian Cottard presents us with a new variation on the torte of the same name.

You need plenty of excellent quality butter for the sweet pastry, and since it must not be kneaded too vigorously, use flour that is not too sticky. Almonds can also be added to the dough, along with a little baking powder to keep it light; almonds absorb excess fat and give the dough a fine flavor. Make sure the oven temperature is not too high.

Cigarette pastry makes an excellent lining, but it has to be used immediately after baking, while it is still hot, because it dries out when cooled. Its texture makes it particularly suited for garnishing, and it is often used for just that purpose.

Recall Maurice Chevalier, who has made the *canotier* known throughout the world, and listen to one of his unforgettable *chansons* while serving Le Canotier with ice cream or chilled fruit on a summer's afternoon. Relive the charm of a past era.

1. Bake the génoise 1–2 days in advance. For the buttercream, whisk the eggs until foamy. Heat the water and sugar to 250 °F / 121 °C and slowly pour the syrup over the eggs; beating continuously until completely cooled. Cream the butter, then fold it into the egg mixture with the grated lemon peel. Make the rum syrup for soaking. Slice the génoise into three layers, soak them with syrup, spread buttercream on two of them, and sandwich them together.

2. Cover the top and sides of the torte with the remaining buttercream and refrigerate. Prepare the sweet pastry according to the basic recipe. After the dough has rested, roll it out evenly and bake; then cut out a round pastry base with the same diameter as the torte. To make the marzipan topping, beat the marzipan until smooth with the egg yolks, then add the whole egg.

3. Using a pastry bag with a flat, ribbed tip, pipe a woven network of marzipan strips onto the torte. Allow to dry overnight in a cool place (but not in the refrigerator). Bake briefly (five minutes or less) at 430 °F / 220 °C. After baking, brush the surface with sugar syrup and place on top of the sweet pastry base.

4. For the cigarette pastry, cream the butter, add the confectioners' sugar, and continue beating with a whisk. Gradually add the egg whites and finally fold in the flour. Pipe the mixture on to a tray lined with baking paper. Use a stencil to make strips of dough and freeze. Spread a thin layer of cigarette pastry mixed with cocoa on to the tray to produce a pattern. Bake at 430 °F / 220 °C. After baking, quickly wrap the pastry around the torte.

Puff Pastry Cake

Preparation time: 2 hours
Cooking time: 30 minutes
Difficulty: ★★★

Serves 8

For the puff pastry:
(see basic recipes p. 803)
8¹/₃ cups / 1 kg flour
2 tbsp / 30 g salt
2 cups / 500 ml water
4 cups / 1 kg butter
superfine sugar

For the pastry cream:
(see basic recipes p. 802)
1 cup / 250 ml milk
2 egg yolks
3¹/₂ tbsp / 50 g sugar
3¹/₂ tbsp / 50 ml whipping cream
5 tbsp / 50 g confectioners' sugar

For the light cream:
2 oz / 350 g pastry cream
2³/₄ cups / 700 ml whipping cream
6 sheets of gelatin
¹/₂ cup / 70 g confectioners' sugar

To garnish:
confectioners' sugar

To say that this mille-feuille consists of precisely 1,000 layers, as the French word for puff pastry suggests, is the same as saying a millipede actually has 1,000 feet. The term dates back to the Renaissance, when the first experiments were performed on the composition of puff pastry, which had been brought by the Crusaders back from the Middle East. It is still used widely today – in croissants, for example, since the 18th-century retreat of the Turks after their defeat at Vienna, and in puff pastry turnovers.

A genuine mille-feuille pastry, such as the one required for the palmiers that ring the side of this spectacular torte, needs to be folded and turned six times; first four normal turns, for which one must allow approximately two hours, and then another two turns in which superfine sugar is generously added to the pastry.

Christian Cottard insists that the butter used for the puff pastry be very fresh and of the best quality; it is wrapped in a simple flour and water dough and it is the butter alone that makes the pastry exquisite. If you are curious about the precise number of layers, a brief calculation certifies that puff pastry that has been folded and turned six times contains 729 layers of butter and 730 layers of flour and water dough; hence the melting, pure taste of butter!

The fruit of all these efforts is a great puff pastry classic, frequently used to gauge young bakers' abilities and one of the most famous gifts of this vocation in which patience and creativity work in concert with a love of flavors.

1. Make a classic puff pastry (without sugar), roll it out ¹/₈ in / 2 mm thick and allow to rest for two hours. Cut into strips 9 in / 20 cm long and ¹/₂ in / 1 cm wide. Use them to weave the lid, and rest for one hour. Bake for 20 minutes in a hot oven, turning it over and dusting it with confectioners' sugar after ten minutes. The lid must be baked thoroughly and have a caramelized sheen. Make two puff pastry bases with the same diameter as the cake ring being used.

2. For the palmiers, prepare a normal puff pastry and make four normal turns; during the two final turns generously incorporate superfine sugar into the pastry. Roll it out to a thickness of ¹/₂–1 in / 1–2 cm and cut into strips 2¹/₂ in / 5 cm wide. Refrigerate until firm, but no longer. Cut the strips into pieces ¹/₂ in / 1 cm wide, place on a baking sheet next to each other and bake. Line a cake ring with the palmiers while they are still hot.

with a Woven Lid

3. To make the light cream, start by preparing a pastry cream (see basic recipes for method). Allow to cool. Whip the cream with the confectioners' sugar until stiff; soak the gelatin in cold water. Heat a little pastry cream and fold in the gelatin. Add the remaining pastry cream, beat until smooth with a whisk, and carefully fold in the whipped cream.

4. Assemble the mille-feuille by alternating the puff pastry bases with a layer of light cream piped from a pastry bag with a round, $^1/_2$ in / 10 mm-wide tip. Finally, place the woven puff pastry lid on top. Refrigerate for about three hours before serving.

Preparation time: 1 hour 30 minutes
Cooking time: 20 minutes
Difficulty: ★★

Serves 8

For the Italian meringue:
(see basic recipes p. 801)
2 large egg whites
¹/₂ cup / 125 g superfine sugar
¹/₄ cup / 60 ml water

For the coconut mousse:
¹/₂ cup / 125 ml cream
9 oz / 250 g coconut meat, grated
4 sheets of gelatin
2¹/₂ tbsp / 35 ml sugar cane rum

For the succès sponge cake:
2 large egg whites
¹/₂ cup, 2 tbsp / 150 g superfine sugar
1 tbsp / 10 g cornstarch
¹/₃ cup / 50 g almonds, very finely ground
7¹/₂ tbsp / 50 g pecan nuts, chopped

For the caramelized bananas:
2 tbsp / 30 g superfine sugar
2 tbsp / 30 g butter
2 bananas, sliced

To garnish:
bittersweet chocolate coating

Prized by pastry chefs, coconut is used to make pastries like coconut macaroons as well as this coconut mousse paillote, which has the shape of a straw hat. The coconut meat available in stores is of a good quality, but you can also puree copra, the dried coconut meat containing milk.

The liquid ingredients have to be added to the meringue mixture very slowly so that the mousse becomes light but not runny. Fold the whipped cream in at the end.

As soon as these first steps have been completed, you can devote all your attention to the paillote. Use bittersweet choco-late coating of about 70% cocoa; its slightly bitter taste will contrast with the sweet flavor of the coconut mousse and the succès sponge cake, which provide the base for the mousse. The "chocolate roof" may look rather complicated, but you will get the hang of it quickly and undoubtedly take pride in your architectural abilities.

One final word about pecans, which originated in North America: An easily digested dried fruit that does not spoil, they are very difficult to shell. They can replaced with ordinary walnuts, but these will be a little less exotic.

1. To make the coconut mousse, first prepare an Italian meringue according to the basic recipe, but using the amounts given above. Beat the cream until stiff and warm the coconut meat slightly. Soak the gelatin in cold water and dissolve it in the heated rum. Fold it into the meringue with the coconut meat, then gently blend in the whipped cream.

2. For the succès sponge cake, whisk the egg whites and beat with some of the sugar until stiff, then add the cornstarch. Combine the remaining sugar with the ground almonds and chopped pecans, and fold into the beaten egg whites. Using a pastry bag with a round hole (¹/₂–³/₄ in / 12–14 mm), pipe the mixture on to baking paper and bake at 430 °F / 220 °C. Caramelize the sugar and butter in a saucepan. Brown the banana slices in it and then set aside.

Coco-Créole

3. Make a Chinese hat using a sheet of plastic and invert it on a cake ring to keep it level. Place an equally large but lower ring inside the hat to form the base for the paillote.

4. Fill the hat with coconut mousse, arrange the banana slices on top and cover with the sponge cake base. Freeze for at least 12 hours. Remove the plastic hat and cake ring, and use a pastry bag to garnish the mousse with melted chocolate in the shape of a straw hat.

Preparation time: 3 hours
Cooking time: 20 minutes
Difficulty: ★★

Serves 8

clear cake glaze: (see basic recipes p. 800)

For the apricot puree:
7 oz / 200 g apricots
8 tsp / 40 g sugar
1/2 vanilla bean
water

For the dacquoise:
2 egg whites
1/2 cup, 2 tbsp / 150 g sugar

1/2 cup, 1 tbsp / 100 g unblanched almonds, very finely ground
4 tsp / 10 g cornstarch

For the apricot mousse:
3 1/2 oz / 100 g Italian meringue:
  (see basic recipes p. 801)
3/4 cup / 200 g apricot puree
2 tsp / 10 ml Amaretto
6 1/2 tbsp / 100 ml whipping cream
2 sheets of gelatin

For the Bavarian cream:
2 1/2 tbsp / 30 g very finely ground almonds,
  roasted
3/4 cup / 200 ml milk
3 egg yolks
3 1/2 tbsp / 50 g sugar
3 sheets of gelatin
3/4 cup / 200 ml whipping cream

For the Roussillon Torte, Christian Cottard prefers fully ripened apricots from the Roussillon region of France; they have a nice velvety red color, "a color that excuses nothing," as the famous French author Victor Hugo once said. The name of this fruit is derived from the Arabic *al-barqúq*, or its Catalan derivative *abercoc*.

Choose apricots that have small spots, but no bruises. The very simple apricot puree consists only of superfine sugar, apricots, and a vanilla bean. Steam the apricots for about twenty minutes to allow the puree to reach the right consistency and preserve its tartness. It would be unfair to Christian Cottard to use a ready-made product here.

If the cake is to be a success, its surface must be completely smooth. To ensure this, assemble it upside down and remember that it will shrink a little in the refrigerator. Bavarian creams, and parfaits in general, tend to do so.

Christian Cottard advises making the roasted almond Bavarian cream a day in advance. Use almonds with a very high fat content that are aromatic and develop their full flavor when eaten. The dash of Amaretto (an Italian liqueur made with almonds and apricots) accentuates the harmony of almonds with apricots. One final tip: place the various mixtures in the cake ring without delay, and refrigerate the finished cake as soon as possible.

1. For the puree, place the halved apricots in a saucepan with the sugar, vanilla, and a little water and steam for 20 minutes. Allow to cool. To make the dacquoise, beat the egg whites with 3 1/2 tbsp / 50 g sugar until stiff. Combine the ground almonds, cornstarch, and remaining sugar and carefully fold into the egg whites. Use a pastry bag with a round 1/2–3/4 in / 12–14 mm tip to pipe circles of the sponge mixture on to baking paper and bake at 430 °F / 220 °C.

2. To make the apricot mousse, prepare an Italian meringue according to the basic recipe, and whip the cream until stiff. Soak the gelatin in cold water, dissolve it in Amaretto and warm. Carefully combine the meringue, apricot puree, Amaretto and whipped cream.

Torte

3. Roast the ground almonds for the Bavarian cream in the oven, add them to the boiling milk, then remove from heat. Cover with plastic wrap and leave to infuse; do not strain. Beat the egg yolks and sugar until the mixture is foamy and falls from the whisk in smooth ribbons. Add the almond milk; thicken like a custard, and then add the soaked gelatin. Allow to cool and then fold in the whipped cream.

4. Assemble the torte upside down. Cover a cake round with plastic wrap and place a 8 x 2 in / 18 x 4 cm cake ring on it. Pour in the apricot mousse and top with a layer of dacquoise. Spoon in the Bavarian cream and cover with a second layer of sponge cake. Refrigerate. Turn out of the ring, cover with clear cake glaze and garnish with almond halves.

Preparation time: 2 hours 30 minutes
Cooking time: 30 minutes
Difficulty: ★★★

Serves 8

pastry cream, Italian meringue, choux pastry,
 puff pastry:
  (see basic recipes p. 802, 801, 799, 803)

For the Chiboust cream:
1 cup / 250 ml milk
1–2 egg yolks
3$^1/_2$ tbsp / 50 g sugar

3$^1/_2$ tbsp / 25 g flour
3–4 egg whites
$^3/_4$ cup / 200 ml sugar syrup
5$^1/_2$ sheets of gelatin

For the caramel glaze for the cream puffs:
$^3/_4$ cup, 1 tbsp / 200 g sugar
$^1/_4$ cup / 60 ml glucose
4$^1/_2$ tbsp / 70 ml water

Both the famous Saint-Honoré and the Chiboust cream, which is its signature, were created in the previous century in a *pâtisserie* in Paris. The cake was named after St. Honoré, the patron saint of bakers, and the cream bears the name of the pastry chef who invented it, Chiboust. His name is frequently misspelled, which is not exactly an homage to the artist. To this day the cake is an excellent exercise in stylistic composition for all pastry chefs, as it contains two "pillars" of the art of baking, puff pastry and choux pastry.

Given the size of the cake, Christian Cottard is happy to make use of leftover puff pastry. It may not be balled together or shaped, and must contain butter. One could even use deep-frozen puff pastry as long as it contains no stabilizers.

The oblong cream puffs that garnish the cake are an elegant variation of classic choux pastry. Make sure they dry thoroughly during baking, giving off plenty of steam.

While some pastry chefs might fill the Saint-Honoré with whipped cream for the sake of simplicity, doing so diminishes its character; the Chiboust cream filling, also known as Saint-Honoré cream, is its hallmark.

1. For the Chiboust cream, make a pastry cream using the milk, egg yolks, sugar, and flour, and make an Italian meringue with the egg whites and sugar syrup (see basic recipes for procedure). Soak the gelatin in water, then fold it into the warm pastry cream. Carefully combine the pastry cream and meringue while both are still warm. Prepare the puff pastry, roll it out, and cut out a round base with a diameter of 8 in/18 cm. Refrigerate and leave to rest for two hours.

2. Follow the basic recipe to make the choux pastry. Fill it into a pastry bag with a medium round tip (no. 6) and pipe a ring of choux pastry around the puff pastry base, then bake it for 20 minutes at 430 °F / 220 °C. Pipe oblong cream puffs (of choux pastry) onto a baking sheet and bake for 20 minutes at 430 °F / 220 °C. Make the caramel and glaze them with it.

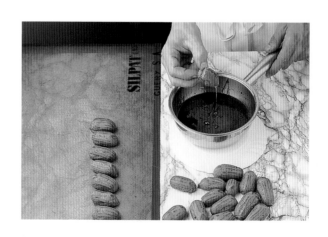

Torte

3. Place the puff pastry base on a cake round and, using a pastry bag with a triangular tip, pipe the Chiboust cream onto it. Lightly brown the surface with a salamander, or in the oven.

4. Halve the cream puffs. Use the remaining caramel to affix the lower halves of the cream puffs to the choux pastry ring of the Saint-Honoré. Use a pastry bag with a wave-shaped tip to garnish them with Chiboust cream and place the glazed upper halves on top. Serve immediately.

Preparation time: 1 hour 30 minutes
Cooking time: 30 minutes
Difficulty: ★★

Serves 8

For the chocolate sponge cake:
6 eggs
3/4 cup / 180 g sugar
3/4 cup, 1 tbsp / 110 g flour
1/4 cup / 35 g cornstarch
1/4 cup / 30 g cocoa powder

striped Joconde sponge cake, clear cake
   glaze (see basic recipes p. 805, 800)

For the chocolate mousse:
5 egg yolks
2/3 cup / 150 ml sugar syrup
11 1/2 oz / 330 g baking chocolate, melted
2 cups, 3 tbsp / 540 ml whipping cream

For the bavarois:
1 cup / 250 ml milk
1/4 oz / 8 g tea (Earl Grey)
4 egg yolks
3 1/2 tbsp / 50 g sugar
5 sheets of gelatin
1 cup / 250 ml whipping cream

In a Zeebrugge inn where he was asked to sample several refined teas, Lucas Devriese decided to create a dessert that would show off tea to its full advantage, once and for all. Tea is said to be the oldest drink in the world. The tea bush, probably native to China originally, is cultivated in many places around the world with varying success according to altitude and climate, and many countries actively trade in tea. The inhabitants of the English colonies brought tea to Europe in about the 17th century, where myriad varieties remain popular to this day.

Among these is Earl Grey tea, which derives its particular flavor from essence of bergamot, a substance won from the peel of small bergamot oranges. Its name is attributed to the resourcefulness of the fourth Earl Grey (1812–1898), governor of Australia and later of New Zealand.

The preparation of the bavarois (Bavarian cream) needs to move rapidly, because tea stays fresh for little longer than 24 hours, particularly when it is infused in milk (the best way to develop its full aroma). This means that the tea can be made at most a day in advance, shortly before you begin making the mousse.

One last note: unsweetened cocoa works better for making the chocolate sponge cake than does sweetened cocoa.

1. To make the chocolate sponge cake, beat the eggs with the sugar until the mixture drops off the beaters in smooth ribbons. Sift the flour with the cornstarch and cocoa powder, and carefully fold into the eggs with a wooden spatula. Use a pastry bag to pipe the sponge mixture onto a baking sheet lined with baking paper and bake for 25 minutes at 355 °F / 180 °C. Prepare the striped Joconde sponge cake according to the basic recipe and bake.

2. To make the chocolate mousse, whisk the egg yolks and pour the lukewarm sugar syrup over them while continuing to beat. Heat the mixture to 195 °F / 90 °C in a double boiler. Once it starts to thicken, pour into a mixer and continue to beat at high speed until completely cooled. Stir in the melted chocolate and then gently fold in the whipped cream.

nd Chocolate

3. For the bavarois, bring the milk to a boil with the tea, cover, and allow to infuse for up to 24 hours. Pour through a sieve. Beat the egg yolks and sugar thoroughly, then add the milk. Pour the mixture into a saucepan and thicken at 185 °F / 85 °C. When the desired consistency has been reached, remove from heat. When just lukewarm, add the soaked gelatin and, finally, fold in the whipped cream.

4. To assemble the torte, line the sides of the mold with a narrow strip of striped Joconde sponge cake. Slice the chocolate sponge into two layers, place one in the mold, and fill halfway with chocolate mousse. Top with the second sponge layer and pipe the bavarois onto it. Refrigerate for three hours. Garnish the top with cocoa and cover with a clear cake glaze.

Puff Pastry Torte with Chibous

Preparation time: *2 hours*
Cooking time: *30 minutes*
Difficulty: ★★★

Serves 8

puff pastry, Italian meringue:
(see basic recipes p. 803, 801)

For the Chiboust cream:
1¹/₂ cups / 375 ml milk
6 egg yolks
5 tbsp / 75 g sugar
6 tbsp / 40 g powdered cream
1 vanilla bean
5 sheets of gelatin

For the crème anglaise:
1 cup / 250 ml milk
2 cups / 500 ml crème fraîche

13 tbsp / 190 g butter
6 eggs
2 tbsp / 30 ml Calvados

For the caramelized apples:
8 apples (Jonagold)
2 cups / 500 g sugar
1 cup / 250 g butter

For the filling and garnish:
1 cup / 200 g sultanas, marinated in Calvados
shelled walnuts
superfine sugar

The Jonagold apple, a cross of the Jonathan and Golden Delicious varieties, is widely available in Belgium and neighboring countries. Its skin is bright yellow with blushes of elegant orange-red, and its crunchy flesh has a pleasant tartness that is retained even when the apple is cooked. It works well for this dessert, because the individual slices become tender and almost transparent when caramelized, but do not collapse into puree. In Belgium, the Jonagold is highly valued as a national product. It comes as no surprise, then, that Lucas Devriese also recommends it.

For this version of Chiboust cream, which immortalizes the name of the famous pastry chef who invented the classic Saint-Honoré cake, powdered cream is used. One could also use dried milk or cornstarch, as long as they are sifted to ensure a homogeneous cream that is easy to work with.

Lucas Devriese recommends making the base out of puff pastry that has been folded and turned five times and allowed to rest for one and a half hours in the refrigerator between each turn. This extra time and effort is definitely worthwhile, because it makes the finished pastry extremely light and yet well able to carry the other parts of the dessert.

1. For the Chiboust cream, prepare the Italian meringue according to the basic recipe. Bring the milk to a boil with the vanilla and half the sugar. Whisk the egg yolks, remaining sugar, and powdered cream until pale yellow. Pour a little hot milk into the egg yolks, blend, then return everything to the pan and continue stirring until thickened. When the mixture has cooled to 140 °F / 60 °C blend in the soaked gelatin, then fold into the Italian meringue.

2. For the crème anglaise, bring the milk and crème fraîche to a boil. Beat the butter with the eggs. Pour a little hot milk onto the butter mixture, stir and return to the saucepan. Heat, stirring continuously, until the crème anglaise thickens. Add the Calvados and set the crème anglaise aside. Peel, core and slice the apples. Caramelize the sugar without adding water until it is light brown, then carefully add the butter. Place the apple slices in the caramel and steam over low heat for 30 minutes, then drain.

Cream and Apples

3. Make the puff pastry and use it to line a springform pan to a height of 1 in / 2 cm. Fill the shell with dried lentils or baking beans so it does not dry out, and bake blind. Allow to cool. Place a 2 in / 4 cm wide strip of doubled waxed paper or baking paper around the puff pastry base to form a collar. Pour in the créme anglaise, then top it with the caramelized apples, marinated sultanas, and a handful of shelled walnuts.

4. Finally, spoon in a layer of Chiboust cream to fill the collar. Dust the top with superfine sugar and caramelize with a salamander. Garnish with shelled walnuts.

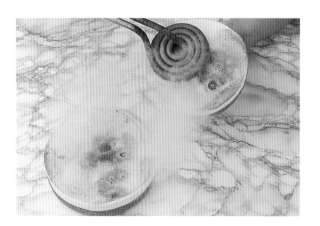

Preparation time: 1 hour
Cooking time: 30 minutes
Difficulty: ★★

Serves 8

Duchess sponge cake: (see basic recipes p. 800)

For the crème anglaise with white wine:
1½ cups / 375 ml white wine
1⅔ cups / 400 g sugar
14 egg yolks
juice of 1 lemon

For the white wine mousse:
15 oz / 420 g crème anglaise with white wine

3⅔ cups / 820 ml whipping cream
9 sheets of gelatin

For the syrup for soaking:
15 oz / 420 g crème anglaise with white wine
5 tbsp / 75 ml sugar syrup

To garnish:
fresh fruits of the season, e.g. blueberries,
   red currants, blackberries, raspberries,
   strawberries, apples, star fruit, limes

Clear cake glaze: (see basic recipes p. 800)

These days there are fewer genuine duchesses, but the number of inanimate objects holding this title have grown. In Belgium, duchesse describes a type of daybed and a pear (Duchess d'Angoulême), and in France it names a fabric. And then there are a few famous dishes like duchess potatoes (creamed with egg and butter, piped into shapes and baked) and duchess sponge cake, used in this recipe, that attest to this phenomenon.

As long as one follows these instructions, preparing and baking this pastry should be fairly straightforward. Actually, the end result depends mainly on the quality of the white wine used to flavor the crème anglaise, which is used both in the mousse and the syrup for soaking the sponge cake.

The mousse with which Lucas Devriese covers the sponge cake is composed mainly of crème anglaise. Choose one of the lovely golden yellow wines made only with light grapes. Lucas Devriese, a great fan of wines from the Champagne region, prefers Chardonnay for the custard because he feels its bouquet offers the best complement. Whichever wine you select, be sure to prepare the crème anglaise rapidly and then use it right away.

In this case, a great deal of experimentation is to be discouraged. If you had thought to flavor the crème anglaise with cinnamon, you need not go to the trouble. Lucas Devriese himself tried this and bitterly regretted it.

1. To make the crème anglaise, bring a little white wine, the lemon juice, and half the sugar to a boil in a saucepan. Beat the egg yolks with the remaining sugar until foamy in a bowl. Add the remaining white wine to the eggs, pour them into the saucepan with the hot wine syrup, and thicken at 185 °F / 85 °C. Allow to cool. To make the white wine mousse, mix 15 oz / 420 g of the white wine custard with the dissolved gelatin and whipped cream.

2. Prepare the duchess sponge cake according to the basic recipe. Use a pastry bag to pipe it on to a baking sheet lined with baking paper and bake. To make the syrup for soaking, combine the white wine crème anglaise and sugar syrup. Slice the duchess sponge cake horizontally into two layers. Place one layer in a cake ring and soak with syrup.

Duchess

3. Pipe a generous layer of the white wine mousse on top of the sponge base. Arrange the raspberries on the mousse and top with the second sponge layer. Fill the cake ring with mousse. Refrigerate for two hours.

4. Take the torte out of the cake ring, and spread the remaining mousse on the sides of the cake. Cover with clear cake glaze and garnish with fresh fruits of the season.

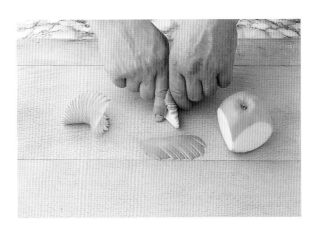

Preparation time: 45 minutes
Cooking time: 25 minutes
Difficulty: ★

Serves 8

7 oz / 200 g Morello cherries

For the chocolate sponge cake:
(see basic recipes p. 805
"sponge cake dough")
7 eggs
$^3/_4$ cup, 1 tbsp / 200 g sugar
1 cup / 130 g flour
$^1/_3$ cup / 45 g cornstarch
$^1/_4$ cup / 30 g cocoa powder

For the chocolate mousse:
5 egg yolks
$^2/_3$ cup / 150 ml sugar syrup
12 oz / 330 g chocolate, melted
2$^1/_4$ cups / 540 ml cream, whipped

For the whipped cream:
3 cups / 750 ml whipping cream
$^3/_4$ cup / 120 g confectioners' sugar

For the chocolate leaves:
9 oz / 250 g milk chocolate coating

Because the Black Forest in southwestern Germany is renowned for the cherries that grow in its orchards, which are used to distill a very pure fruit schnapps, its name graces this classic of the baker's trade. The Black Forest Torte is easy to make and shows off the exquisite flavor of Morello cherries to full advantage.

The various types of cherries fall into two categories: sweet and sour. Sweet cherries range in color from reddish-yellow (Bigarreau cherries, used to distill kirsch) to the dark red, almost purple Black Tartarian and Bing varieties. More acidic, sour cherries are generally smaller and include Belle de Choisy, Montmorency, and Morello. Accordingly, cherry trees are divided into sweet cherry and sour cherry trees.

The Black Forest Torte is one of Lucas Devriese's favorites, and he takes particular care in preparing it. Morello cherries, best marinated in kirsch beforehand, are an excellent complement to bittersweet chocolate, whose intense flavor is pleasantly tempered by whipped cream.

Some skill and experience are required to turn a plain block of chocolate into the garnish for the cake. When the chocolate coating has been tempered and spread thinly on a slab, use one hand to warm it slightly so that it softens, and guide the spatula with the other hand. To produce large chocolate leaves, you will have to work rapidly.

1. Make the chocolate sponge cake according to the basic recipe "sponge cake dough", but using the ingredients listed above. Pipe the mixture on to a baking sheet and bake. When completely cooled, slice the sponge through twice. For the chocolate mousse, beat the egg yolks with the syrup, then stir in the melted chocolate. When this has cooled, fold in the whipped cream. Place one sponge base in a cake ring and garnish with Morello cherries.

2. Whip the cream with the confectioners' sugar, and pipe a layer of whipped cream to cover the cherries. Place the second sponge layer in the cake ring and cover with chocolate mousse. Again garnish with Morello cherries, top with the third sponge cake layer, and pipe whipped cream onto it. Refrigerate for two hours.

Torte

3. Melt the milk chocolate coating in a double boiler and spread thinly on to a slightly warmed slab. Refrigerate for 30 minutes and then bring back to room temperature. Using a metal spatula, draw up large flakes. Take the cake out of the cake ring.

4. Completely cover the cake with the individually shaped chocolate flakes. Dust with cocoa and confectioners' sugar.

Preparation time: 1 hour
Cooking time: 8 minutes
Difficulty: ★★★

Serves 8

Duchess sponge cake:
  (see basic recipes p. 800)

For the Italian meringue:
8 egg whites
2 cups / 500 g superfine sugar

For the quark cream:
5 egg yolks
3¹/₂ tbsp / 50 ml water

³/₄ cup, 1 tbsp / 200 g sugar
1 lb 5 oz / 600 g quark
2²/₃ cups / 640 ml whipping cream
6 sheets of gelatin

For the syrup for soaking:
6¹/₂ tbsp / 100 g sugar
³/₄ cup / 200 ml water
¹/₃ cup / 80 ml kirsch

To garnish:
2 pint baskets of raspberries

Lucas Devriese did not mean to be provocative in naming this dessert after Europe's highest mountain. Despite the fact that they live in Belgium, which Jacques Brel described in song as *le plat pays* (the flat country), when Devriese's wife Hilde first tasted it, she was reminded of a mountain. In any case, this exquisite creation's elegance and flavor certainly more than live up to the name.

The various elements of this dessert should be prepared in one day, and since the dessert must be frozen for a while after the first layer of cream is applied, one must be careful to allow sufficient time to assemble it. For that reason, choose quark with a firm consistency and a medium fat content (20% to a maximum of 30%) so that it does not collapse later.

If you start by beating the egg yolks alone and then add the sugar, the cream will be lighter. If necessary, replace the quark with crème fraîche, but make sure that its distinctive taste is retained. All ingredients must be at room temperature when they are mixed for the dessert to succeed.

The cream will not keep for longer than three days and calls for high quality ingredients. If you like, you can flavor it; raspberry puree would be one obvious choice.

1. Prepare the duchess sponge cake and spread it on to a baking sheet lined with baking paper (allow 1 lb 5 oz / 600 g sponge mixture for a 18 x 27 in / 40 x 60 cm baking tray). Bake for six minutes at 480 °F / 250 °C. Let cool on a cooling rack. To make the meringue, beat the egg whites and sugar in a mixing bowl over a source of heat until they have a firm consistency, then continue to beat with an electric mixer until completely cooled.

2. For the quark cream, beat the egg yolk until foamy. Heat the sugar and water, slowly pour the syrup over the egg yolks while beating at the highest speed. Allow to cool a little and add the dissolved gelatin. Once the mixture has completely cooled, rapidly fold in the quark and whipped cream. Follow the basic recipe for the kirsch syrup for soaking.

3. To assemble the dessert, slice the duchess sponge cake horizontally to make two layers. Place one layer on a cake round, soak with kirsch syrup and spread it with quark cream. Soak the second layer and place it on the cream. Freeze for one hour. Once the dessert is cold, cut out tartlets using a round cookie cutter (2³/₄ in / 6 cm diameter).

4. Place each tartlet on to a somewhat larger base to make it easier to apply the meringue with a pastry bag. Put the tartlets in the oven until the meringue is golden grown, then place on dessert plates and fill the center with fresh raspberries.

La Feuillantine

Preparation time: *1 hour*
Cooking time: *1 hour 30 minutes*
Difficulty: ★★

Serves 8

makes 2 cakes measuring 7 in / 16 cm

For the Japonaise sponge cake:
1²/₃ cups / 400 g sugar
8 egg whites
6¹/₂ tbsp / 100 ml water
1 cup / 130 g hazelnuts, very finely ground

For the chocolate wafers:
14 oz / 400 g bittersweet chocolate coating

For the honey mixture:
2¹/₂ oz / 75 g white chocolate coating
²/₃ cup / 150 ml crème fraîche
3 tbsp / 60 g honey
1 sheet of gelatin
vanilla sugar
1¹/₂ cups / 350 ml whipping cream

To garnish:
1 honey praline
confectioners' sugar

Anyone familiar with Victor Hugo's works may well wonder why the Florentine, a puff pastry cake popular in the 17th century, is now called a Feuillantine. There is a cloister by the same name, the Feuillantines in the Fauburg Saint-Victor region, which long served as a prison for ladies of the oldest profession, but any surmised connection between the two would be purely speculative.

At first, this composition contained only bittersweet chocolate. Then a young pastry chef named Laurent Buet added a honey mixture, for which high-quality honey is used – that found in the Swiss Jura, for example, and preferably pine honey. It is a good idea to prepare the honey mixture a day in advance so that it develops a uniform consistency.

Philippe Guignard also recommends making the vanilla sugar yourself, using the finest superfine sugar and first-class vanilla beans that have been ripened over a long period of time in drying chambers.

The crème fraîche should be beaten neither too long nor too briefly. At one extreme it tastes too much like milk, and at the other it becomes too firm and loses its characteristic flavor. The hazelnuts give the Japonaise sponge cake a firmer consistency and will absorb some of the sugar, so they are preferable to almonds. This base is actually a meringue base similar to the French succès sponge cake. Philippe Guignard normally uses a pastry bag to pipe it directly onto a baking sheet, which makes it lighter when baked.

1. For the Japonaise sponge cake, whisk the egg whites until stiff with one-quarter of the sugar. Heat the water and remaining sugar to 250 °F / 121 °C, then slowly pour onto the beaten egg whites, beating continuously until cooled. Fold in ¹/₂ cup / 50 g finely ground hazelnuts. Pipe the mixture in a spiral onto a tray lined with baking paper, sprinkle the rest of the hazelnuts onto the sponge mixture, and bake for 60–90 minutes at 320 °F / 160 °C.

2. To make the chocolate wafers, melt the bittersweet chocolate coating, spread it thinly onto a tray lined with waxed paper, and allow it to cool for at least one hour. Before the mixture is completely hard, cut out two round wafers the same size as the Japonaise sponge base. Cut each wafer into eight triangles.

au Miel

3. Prepare the honey mixture a day in advance: melt the white chocolate coating in a double boiler. Heat the crème fraîche and stir into the chocolate coating. Add the honey, dissolved gelatin and vanilla sugar. Allow the mixture to cool and set aside until needed. The following day, whip the cream until stiff and fold into the honey mixture.

4. Melt a little bittersweet chocolate coating, spread it on the Japonaise sponge base, and use a pastry bag to pipe the honey mixture onto it. Place one of the chocolate wafers (divided into triangles) on top, pipe more of the honey mixture onto it and cover with another chocolate wafer. Dust with confectioners' sugar and garnish with the honey praline.

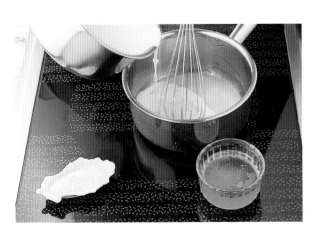

Preparation time: 1 hour
Cooking time: 35–40 minutes
Difficulty: ★★

Serves 8

vanilla cream, puff pastry:
  (see basic recipes p. 806, 803)

$^1/_2$ fresh pineapple
2 tbsp / 30 g butter
sugar
cinnamon
1 tbsp rum

For the almond cream:
$^1/_2$ cup / 125 g butter
$^3/_4$ cup, 1 tbsp / 125 g blanched almonds,
  ground
$^2/_3$ cup / 100 g confectioners' sugar
$^1/_3$ cup / 40 g cornstarch
3 small eggs
5 tsp / 25 ml rum
12 oz / 350 g vanilla cream

To garnish:
2 egg yolks
1 pinch of salt
sugar

Though it may be surprising to find a specialty that made the French town of Pithiviers famous in Switzerland, fans of Three Kings' Cake, or *Dreikönigskuchen* in German, should only be pleased. This torte is so-called because it is traditionally enjoyed on Epiphany, the day when the arrival of the three wise men in Bethlehem after Jesus's birth is celebrated. Consisting of almond cream and puff pastry and enhanced by the fresh flavor of pineapple, it is delicious all year around and is not particularly difficult to make.

The choice of almonds is an important consideration. Most suitable are medium-sized blanched almonds like the Spanish Marcona or Californian Thomson. Mix the ingredients for the almond cream very gently and carefully – they should be neither beaten nor stirred until foamy. Round off the cream's flavor with brown Jamaican rum, a vital ingredient of the Pithiviers Torte.

Start by making a light puff pastry that contains only pure butter (82% fat). The Swiss have a great deal of experience making puff pastry, and one pastry they make with it is *Waadter Cremehörnchen* (Waadt cream horns). They know how important it is to bake puff pastry at precisely the right temperature and use only the freshest ingredients. In this case, the pastry should be made three days in advance and folded and turned twice each day, leaving it to rest for 24 hours each time.

A Pithiviers has to be baked slowly so that it bakes all the way through and has a tender consistency. The top is slightly caramelized, which not only enhances its appearance but also further accentuates the flavor of the puff pastry.

1. Prepare the puff pastry and 12 oz / 350 g of vanilla cream according to the basic recipes. To make the almond cream, beat the butter with the ground almonds, confectioners' sugar, and cornstarch, then add the eggs one at a time and stir until smooth. Add the rum and finally blend in the vanilla cream.

2. Peel a fresh pineapple, dice the flesh finely and brown half of it in butter. After one minute dust lightly with sugar and cinnamon. After another two minutes, add 1 tbsp / 15 ml rum, reduce and then allow to cool. Whisk the egg yolks for the egg wash with the salt and sugar.

Torte

3. Roll out the puff pastry and cut out two circles, one slightly larger than the other. Place the smaller layer onto a cake plate. Brush a 1/2 in / 1 cm wide path around the edge with the whisked egg yolk, and spread almond cream in the middle. Arrange the diced pineapple on top of the cream. Cover with the larger circle of puff pastry, pressing the edges together.

4. Brush the top of the Pithiviers with egg yolk and make rosette-shaped marking with a knife (be careful not to cut all the way through the pastry). Slit the edge at even intervals and push in the dough to make a border of half moon shapes. Allow to rest for 20 minutes, then bake for 35–40 minutes at 430 °F / 220 °C. Dust the cake with confectioners' sugar before the last five minutes, and put back in the oven to caramelize. Serve lukewarm.

Preparation time: 30 minutes
Cooking time: 20 minutes
Difficulty: ★★

Serves 12

For the dough:
1³/₄ oz / 50 g yeast
3¹/₂ tbsp / 50 ml milk
4¹/₂ cups / 550 g flour
3¹/₂ tbsp / 50 g sugar
5 eggs
2 tsp / 10 g salt
grated peel of 1 lemon
13 tbsp / 200 g butter

For the filling:
2 cups / 500 ml cream
³/₄ cup / 100 g flour
³/₄ cup, 1 tbsp / 200 g sugar
1 pinch salt
pulp of 1 vanilla bean

To glaze:
1 egg yolk, lightly beaten

Philippe Guignard shows his true colors as a champion of the Swiss canton of Waadt by presenting us with one of the oldest recipes from this region: a dessert that tastes sweet, though it may not appear to be at first.

Guignard is a master of this yeast dough delicacy, which can be prepared in myriad variations, as long as it contains a delicious cream with a 33% fat content. Heavy cream can also be used, if you prefer the taste. In Switzerland, the cream tastes strongly of the alpine pastures where the dairy cows graze, and this takes some getting used to. Be careful not to beat the cream for too long or too vigorously. Otherwise, it may turn into butter when baked.

Preparing the dough demands concentrated attention. It is kneaded for quite a while, like a brioche dough, so that the gluten in the flour makes it soft and elastic. If you have time to make it a day in advance and refrigerate it overnight, the butter will nearly retain its original consistency, and the dough will be firmer and easier to work with. Brushing the edges with egg yolk twice gives the dough color and added suppleness.

When this pastry is baked, two contrasting effects result: the melting and liquefaction of the filling, and the rising of the dough, which keeps the filling from seeping out.

1. To make the dough, dissolve the yeast in the milk. Using the dough hook of an electric mixer, knead the flour with the sugar and dissolved yeast. Add the eggs, salt, and grated lemon peel. Knead for 7–8 minutes, then add the butter to the dough in small pieces. It is best to make the dough a day in advance and allow it to rest in the refrigerator overnight.

2. Grease a flat pie pan with butter. Roll out the dough and line the pan with it. Allow it to rise in a warm place for one hour. Brush the edges with egg yolk twice, and prick the base with a fork. Using a pastry wheel, cut off the surplus dough.

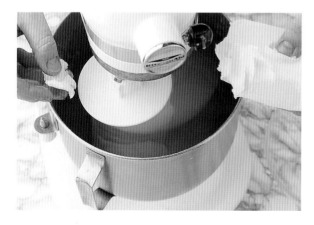

Cream Flan

3. For the filling, beat the cream until stiff. In another bowl, mix the flour with the sugar, a pinch of salt, and a little vanilla pulp.

4. Cover the dough with this mixture of dry ingredients. Use a pastry bag to pipe the whipping cream on top of it and dust the surface with superfine sugar. Bake for 15–20 minutes at 445 °F / 230 °C. Allow to cool before serving.

Orange and Almond

Preparation time: 45 minutes
Cooking time: 45-50 minutes
Difficulty: ★★

Serves 8

puff pastry, vanilla cream:
  (see basic recipes p. 803, 806)

1 lb / 500 g puff pastry
6 oranges

For the almond cream:
$^1/_2$ cup / 125 g butter
1 cup, 3 tbsp / 125 g almonds, very finely
  ground

$^2/_3$ cup / 100 g confectioners' sugar
2 tbsp / 15 g cornstarch
1 pinch of salt
2 small eggs
1 tbsp / 15 ml Grand Marnier (or rum)
$4^1/_2$ oz / 125 g vanilla cream

For the coating:
oranges
apricot jelly

To garnish:
half-candied orange peel
grenadine

You can never be too careful with fruit that has a very thick peel. Once, because Philippe Guignard failed to take this into consideration, he was very disappointed in an orange cake he made, and resolved to create a dessert that satisfied him. The result is this delicious tart incorporating a thoroughly baked puff pastry shell, almond cream, and a coating of thinly sliced oranges.

Take care when baking the puff pastry. Put the pastry into a hot, pre-heated oven, and then reduce the temperature quickly to allow the inner layers to rise nicely as well as the outer ones. If the pastry is not baked through properly, the edges will be a nice, golden yellow, but the tart's flavor will not be optimal.

In this recipe, the choice of oranges plays an important role. Guignard recommends Minneola oranges from Israel, a medium sized variety with a relatively thin skin. Marinate the peel in grenadine overnight or longer, so that it takes on a delicate purple-red color. This half-candied orange peel is both soft and crunchy. Though it does taste delicious, its main purpose is to lend a decorative effect.

For the almond cream, use Marcona almonds. Grind them yourself, adding a dash of Grand Marnier to intensify their flavor. A very fruity Chardonnay or a good Riesling goes well with this pastry.

1. Make the puff pastry and vanilla cream according to the basic recipes. Line a cake ring with puff pastry, and allow to rest in the refrigerator for one hour. For the almond cream, cream the butter, then stir in the ground almonds, confectioners' sugar, cornstarch, and salt. Add the eggs one at a time and beat the mixture with a whisk until it is smooth and light. Blend in the Grand Marnier and, finally, the vanilla cream.

2. Pipe a thin layer of almond cream onto the puff pastry base. Cut the orange peel into thin strips. Blanch the strips, lightly candy them in grenadine syrup for 7–8 minutes, and leave in the syrup to cool overnight.

Cream Tart

3. Using a pastry jagger, trim the excess paste at the height of the almond cream. Halve the oranges and cut them into very thin slices.

4. Cover the surface evenly with orange slices, sprinkle a little superfine sugar on top and bake for 45–50 minutes at 355 °F / 180 °C. Coat with the apricot jelly flavored with oranges. Before serving, garnish the center of the tart with the candied orange peel.

Preparation time: 1 hour
Cooking time: 8–10 minutes
Difficulty: ★★★

Serves 8

For the biscuit roulade:
15 egg yolks
1/2 cup / 120 g sugar
2/3 cup / 80 g flour
grated peel of 1 lemon
6 egg whites
1 pinch of salt

For the pineapple mousse:
Vanilla custard:
1 cup / 250 ml milk
3 1/2 tbsp / 50 g sugar
1/2 vanilla bean
1 egg yolk

1/4 cup / 25 g powdered cream, heated
3 sheets of gelatin
2 tsp / 10 ml kirsch
2 tsp / 10 ml rum
1 lb / 500 g diced pineapple
1 2/3 cups / 400 ml whipping cream

For the coating:
4 1/2 tbsp / 100 g apricot jam

To garnish:
pistachios
1 pineapple slice

Tourte is the Swiss term for desserts consisting of a sponge cake base topped with a flavored cream. Philippe Guignard named this classic recipe Tourte royale (Royal Cake), and he feels that it is unforgettably good. In this recipe, he strives to bring out the character of pineapple, particularly pineapples grown on the island of Réunion, which are highly valued for their consistency and flavor.

We can thank the Swedish botanist Olaf Bromel for discovering bromeline, an enzyme in pineapple and other bromeliads that gives the ripe fruit its singular flavor and also stimulates the digestive system.

The Tourte royale hinges on the clever combination of pineapple and custard; because it contains whipped cream, the resulting cream is very light, but also nutritious and rich in flavor. Blend the two mixtures carefully. The cream can also be flavored with rum and kirsch.

Take some pains when making the biscuit roulade, a popular sponge cake frequently used as a base for tortes. It is manageable and, thanks to the jam spread on it, delicious; bake it rapidly at a very high temperature so that it does not dry out. After it is baked and cooled, roll it up immediately. Spread the jam thinly so that it does not seep out.

1. To make the biscuit roulade, beat the egg yolks with 1/4 cup / 65 g sugar until the mixture falls from the whisk in long ribbons, then fold in the sifted flour and grated lemon peel. Whisk the egg whites, salt and the remaining sugar until foamy. Carefully combine the two mixtures. Spread the sponge cake mixture onto a tray lined with baking paper.

2. Bake the biscuit roulade at 480 °F / 250 °C, making sure that it stays soft; after baking carefully sprinkle it with sugar. As soon as it has cooled, spread the biscuit with a thin layer of apricot jam. Wrap it up very tightly in plastic wrap and refrigerate for three hours.

Cake

3. To make the vanilla custard, heat the milk with the sugar and slit vanilla bean. Whisk the powdered cream with the egg yolk and add a little hot milk. Return everything to the saucepan with the hot milk, bring to a boil and allow to cool. Add the gelatin dissolved in cold water, kirsch, rum, and diced pineapple, then carefully fold in the whipped cream.

4. Place a cake ring on baking paper. Line the base and sides with thin, uniformly sliced rounds of biscuit roulade. Fill with the pineapple mousse, cover with more slices of biscuit roulade and allow to set in the refrigerator. Turn out onto a serving dish and cover with apricot jam. Garnish the center of the cake with a rosette of whipped cream, a pineapple slice and halved pistachios. Refrigerate for one hour before serving.

Preparation time: 1 hour
Cooking time: 20 minutes
Difficulty: ✫

Makes 30

For the choux pastry:
1/2 cup / 125 ml water
1/2 cup / 125 g butter
2 tbsp sugar
vanilla sugar
1 pinch of salt
1 cup / 125 g flour
2 eggs
6 egg yolks

For the pastry cream:
1 cup / 250 ml cream
2 egg yolks
8 tsp / 40 g sugar
1 tbsp / 15 g vanilla sugar
2 tbsp / 15 g cornstarch

For the vanilla cream:
2 1/2 cups / 600 ml cream
10 1/2 oz / 300 g pastry cream

For dusting:
confectioners' sugar

Throughout Europe there are a fabulous variety of *beignet* specialties, delightful hand-size pastries, and they have different names depending on the language spoken where they are made. In France they are called *bugnes*, *frivoles*, *oreillettes* or *guenilles*; in Spain, *churros*; in Italy, *cannoli*; and in Greece, *loukoumade*. Diverse ingredients are used for these pastries, and there are all manner of traditions and occasions for which they are made, from birthdays and public holidays throughout the year to religious feasts in honor of patron saints, and more.

These cream puffs are made using choux pastry, cooked on the stove top and then cooled before the eggs are added (hence its German name, *Brandteig*, which means burnt). But this recipe is for a regional Austrian specialty and, of course, there are other ways to make it.

Homemade vanilla sugar gives a more satisfying flavor and, in the long run, is the most economical use of vanilla beans. To make it, store sugar with dried vanilla beans in an airtight container, occasionally adding new beans to strengthen the flavor. Sugar flavored in this way is used for both the choux pastry and the vanilla cream.

When making the cream puff pastry, you will first make a sort of syrup that softens the dough and causes it to give off steam while baking, which is essential because that is what makes the dough rise. The puffs must be baked in an oven that closes properly and can reach a very high temperature. During baking, do not open the oven door for any reason.

1. To make the choux pastry, combine the water, butter, sugar, vanilla sugar, and salt in a saucepan and bring to a boil. Add the flour and stir the pastry vigorously with a wooden spatula until it is smooth and comes away from the sides of the pan. Remove from the heat and cool slightly. Add the eggs one by one and beat thoroughly after each one.

2. For the pastry cream, heat the cream in a saucepan. Beat the egg yolks with the sugar and vanilla sugar in a bowl until they are creamy and almost white. Add the cornstarch, and slowly pour the boiled cream over the mixture. Pour everything back into the saucepan, bring to a boil, then pour into another pan and allow to cool.

Cream Puffs

3. Using a pastry bag with a star-shaped tip, pipe cream puffs the size of small cream rosettes onto a tray and bake until golden brown. Start by baking for ten minutes at 390 °F / 200 °C, then continue at 355 °F / 180 °C so that they dry thoroughly. To make the vanilla cream, stiffly whip the cream and fold it into 10$\frac{1}{2}$ oz / 300 g of the pastry cream.

4. Carefully halve the cream puffs horizontally. Use a pastry bag with a star-shaped tip to fill them with vanilla cream, then replace the pastry "lids" and dust with confectioners' sugar. Arrange three on each plate.

Preparation time: 1 hour
Cooking time: 20 minutes
Difficulty: ★★

Makes 20

For the dough:
¹/₃ cup / 80 ml milk
6¹/₂ tbsp / 100 g butter
1 pinch of salt
5 tsp / 25 g sugar
¹/₂ oz / 15 g yeast
2 tsp / 10 g vanilla sugar
2 cups / 250 g flour
juice of ¹/₂ lemon

For the nut filling:
1 cup / 150 g walnuts, shelled and halved
³/₄ cup / 180 ml milk
3¹/₂ tbsp / 50 g sugar
2 tsp / 10 g vanilla sugar
1 cinnamon stick
4 tsp / 20 ml rum
2 eggs
3¹/₂ oz / 100 g nougat
4¹/₂ oz / 130 g sponge cake crumbs
mint leaves

For the egg wash:
1 egg

In 1683, a vast army of 200,000 Turks besieged Vienna in the largest Turkish attack in the country's history. It finally took an enormous mobilization of the Christian world, with the active assistance of the Polish king and the duke of Lorraine, to force the retreat of the Grand Vizier Kara Mustapha's troops. This historic threat is remembered in this pastry shaped like the Turkish crescent; it became an icon of Vienna's skill in baking and is known the world over as a typically Viennese pastry.

Many variations of this *Nußßbeugel* (Austrian for nut crescent) are available in Vienna, all having in common that they are invariably served with coffee in the Sacher Hotel, whether *Schwarzer Kaffee* (espresso), *Kapuziner* (with whipped cream) or *Franziskaner* (with grated chocolate).

The walnut tree is the best-known member of the *Juglandaceae* family (a term that really melts in the mouth). Use only fresh walnuts for the filling, and shell them yourself to make sure that the texture and flavor are perfect. Walnuts, even those of high quality, quickly become rancid, and the flavor of the shelled nuts frequently sold in plastic bags leaves much to be desired.

Italian and Greek walnuts can be recommended, as are French walnuts from the Périgord and Dauphiné regions. If no first-class walnuts are available, another delicious alternative would be a poppy seed filling.

1. Knead together all the ingredients for the dough thoroughly with the kneading attachment of an electric mixer. Shape the dough into a long roll and allow to rest in the refrigerator for one hour.

2. Cut the dough roll into slices of about 1 oz / 25 g each. Shape these into balls and use a rolling pin to roll them out to a slightly oval shape. Refrigerate the rolled-out ovals.

Crescents

3. To make the nut filling, chop the nuts finely. Bring the milk to a boil with the sugar, vanilla sugar, cinnamon, and rum. In another pan, combine the slightly beaten eggs, nougat, sponge cake crumbs and mint leaves, pour the hot milk over them, add the chopped walnuts and heat for 2–3 minutes. Pour the mixture into another bowl and allow to cool.

4. Using a pastry bag, pipe a little walnut paste onto each oval piece of dough, roll them up and bend slightly into a crescent shape. Place the crescents on a baking sheet, brush with whisked egg, and bake for 20 minutes at 355 °F / 180 °C. Serve warm.

Quark Ravioli witl

Preparation time: 45 minutes
Cooking time: 10 minutes
Difficulty: ★

Serves 4

For the quark dough:
1¼ cups / 140 g flour
1 pinch of salt
1 tsp vanilla sugar
1 egg
9 oz / 250 g quark
5 tbsp / 70 g butter

For the quark filling:
9 oz / 250 g quark
⅓ cup / 50 g confectioners' sugar

1 tsp / 5 g vanilla sugar
2 egg yolks
4 tsp / 10 g cornstarch
juice of ½ lemon
¼ cup / 50 g raisins
2 tsp / 10 ml rum

For the butter crumbs:
10 tbsp / 150 g butter
¾ cup / 100 g dry bread crumbs

For the rösti:
fresh or canned apricots (depending on the
    season)
clarified butter
confectioners' sugar

Some truly surprising experiences can occur in famous Austrian cafés. For example, while these turnovers are called ravioli in Vienna (probably due to the influence of nearby Italy), they are a typically Austrian specialty, if only because of their quark filling.

Austrians clearly think of ravioli as something quite different from the usual square affairs. Here, a round piece of dough is folded in the middle, giving the turnovers a half-moon shape – possibly yet another nod to the Turkish crescent.

Once this understanding of ravioli has been explained, it is a logical conclusion that the manner and composition of the fill-

ing are varied and allow for some inventive departures; whether sweet, savory, filled with fruit or other refreshing flavors, anything goes in giving the ravioli tastes that are both delicious and diverse. In this instance we concerned with the sweet version.

The ravioli are combined with a type of *rösti*, though in this case we are talking not about the familiar Swiss specialty, potato pancakes fried in a pan, but about apricot *rösti*, ideally made using very fleshy apricots. The apricots are caramelized in a pan with butter and sugar to give them an acidic flavor that is a beguiling flavor contrast to the ravioli.

1. To make the quark dough, combine the flour, salt, vanilla sugar, egg, butter, and quark in a bowl, mix everything thoroughly and then allow to rest for 20 minutes.

2. Marinate the raisins for the filling in the rum. Combine all the ingredients for the filling, except the raisins and rum, in a bowl and stir until the mixture is smooth. Then fold in the drained raisins.

Apricot Rösti

3. Roll out the quark dough thinly using a rolling pin. Cut out circles with a diameter of 2³/₄ in / 6 cm, put some quark cream in the center of each circle, and fold them together like turnovers. Press the edges together firmly with your fingers. For the butter crumbs, melt the butter in a saucepan, then stir in the bread crumbs to coat them evenly and brown them slightly.

4. Poach the ravioli for 8–10 minutes in boiling water, then drain. Place each ravioli in the buttered bread crumbs and coat both sides. For the rösti, cut the apricots into thin slices and caramelize in a pan with clarified butter and confectioners' sugar. Arrange three ravioli with apricot rösti on each plate, and dust with confectioners' sugar.

Quark Strudel with

Preparation time: 30 minutes
Cooking time: 1 hour
Difficulty: ★★

Serves 8

For the strudel dough:
2 cups / 250 g flour
2 tbsp / 30 ml oil
²/₃ cup / 150 ml water
a pinch of salt

For the filling:
6¹/₂ tbsp / 100 g butter, softened
3¹/₂ tbsp / 50 g each confectioners' sugar, sugar
1 tsp vanilla sugar
a pinch of salt
peel and juice of ¹/₂ lemon

4 eggs, separated
1 lb / 440 g quark
1 cup / 250 ml sour cream
¹/₂ cup / 60 g flour

¹/₄ cup / 50 g raisins marinated in 2 tsp / 10 ml rum

For the vanilla sauce:
2 cups / 500 ml milk
2 tbsp / 10 g each powdered cream, vanilla sugar
1 vanilla bean
6 egg yolks
¹/₃ cup / 80 g sugar
4 tsp / 20 ml rum

For the egg milk:
1 cup / 250 ml milk
2 tbsp / 30 g sugar
2 eggs

For dusting:
confectioners' sugar

The word strudel has, since the beginning of the 18th century, described a pastry rolled into a spiral shape. It probably derives from the verb *studan*, which, among other things, means "to wring out a cloth" or "rapidly turn in a circle." The latter refers to the spiraling movement of draining water as it forms a funnel. Perhaps another of its meanings, "to burn with passion," was coined to describe strudel's true fans …

During the 19th century, the citizens of Vienna made Sunday excursions into the Wienerwald, the Viennese forest, where they made a permanent institution of frequenting the cafés and eating strudel. This tradition lives on, and the Sacher Hotel continues to make and serve strudel.

All stages of work in making the strudel can take place the same day. No great instruction is necessary as to how to make the dough, except that rolling it out requires some skill; the dough has to be rolled out thin enough that, on a marble slab, the very veins of the marble can be seen through it.

When preparing the strudel filling, adhere strictly to the recommended ratio of sour cream to quark, and make sure the raisins are thoroughly marinated in rum before use. Once the filling is spread on the dough, roll it up tightly before baking. This is why, although it is wafer-thin, the dough must remain very pliable.

1. To make the strudel dough, knead the flour with the oil, water, and salt using the dough hook of an electric mixer. Shape the dough into a ball, brush its surface with oil and allow it to rest for one hour.

2. For the filling, beat the softened butter with the confectioners' sugar, vanilla sugar, salt, lemon peel, and lemon juice. Gradually add the egg yolks, quark, and sour cream. Beat the egg whites until stiff with the sugar, then fold them into the filling mixture. Finally, blend in the flour and the raisins marinated in rum.

Vanilla Sauce

3. Roll out the dough paper-thin on a floured pastry cloth, spread the filling over half its surface, and use the cloth to roll it up. To make the vanilla sauce, bring the milk, powdered cream, and vanilla bean to a boil in a saucepan. Using a whisk, beat the egg yolks with the sugar and vanilla sugar until foamy. Stir in a little hot milk, pour everything into the saucepan with the milk, and thicken over a gentle heat. Pass through a sieve and add the rum.

4. Prepare the egg milk in the same way: boil the milk, whisk the eggs and sugar together, then combine and thicken. Grease a rectangular baking form with butter, place the strudel in it and bake for 15 minutes at 355 °F / 180 °C. Pour the egg milk over it and bake for another 45 minutes. Finally, dust with confectioners' sugar and serve while still lukewarm with vanilla sauce.

Preparation time: 1 hour
Cooking time: 20 minutes
Difficulty: ★★

Serves 12

striped Joconde sponge cake:
(see basic recipes)

For the milk chocolate ganache:
1 lb / 500 g milk chocolate
¹/₂ cup / 125 ml unsweetened condensed milk

For the Duchess sponge cake:
9 eggs
3 egg yolks
1 cup / 250 g sugar
2 cups / 250 g flour

3¹/₂ tbsp / 50 g butter

For the sweet chestnut cream:
4¹/₂ oz / 125 g canned glazed sweet chestnuts
2 tsp / 10 ml brown rum
1 cup / 250 ml crème frâiche

For the rum syrup:
(see basic recipes p. 805)
³/₄ cup / 200 ml water
6¹/₂ tbsp / 100 g sugar
²/₃ cup / 150 ml rum

To garnish:
phyllo pastry
glazed sweet chestnuts

The use of glazed sweet chestnuts has long been tradition in Belgian pastry-making, and the Nihoul family has close to 100 years of experience in this field. Christian Nihoul's grandfather created *Dijonnaises*, a meringue garnished with whipped cream and chopped sweet chestnuts. The *Merveilleux* (French for "marvel") is another Belgian variation of this delicacy that includes chocolate cream. Whichever he is making, Christian Nihoul always chooses his basic ingredients with the greatest of care.

In just the last few generations, a fundamental change has taken place. Rather than preparing each element of their recipes themselves, pastry chefs can now buy their ground nuts, fondant, nougat, marzipan, and so forth from wholesalers;

however, their standards for quality remain as strict as always. The chopped sweet chestnuts, even if they do not look particularly promising, must likewise be first class.

A puree of glazed sweet chestnuts, combined with a dash of brown rum and unsweetened whipped cream, form an ideal topping for this torte, without any need for additional sugar.

For the ganache, choose a chocolate with a high milk content and very little sugar, such as that made by Belgian manufacturers. The Sweet Chestnut Torte is a very rich dessert, and is particularly popular during the cold winter months. Christian Nihoul tells us that it has also been a favorite in the Japanese branches of his *pâtisserie* for several years.

1. Make the ganache a day in advance by melting the chocolate, bringing the condensed milk to a boil and stirring it into the chocolate. Refrigerate until needed. To prepare the sponge cake, beat the eggs, egg yolks, and sugar with a mixer over low heat. Remove from heat and beat until cooled. Use a skimmer to add the sifted flour and warm melted butter. Pipe the sponge cake mixture onto a baking sheet and bake for 20 minutes at 355 °F / 180 °C.

2. To make the sweet chestnut cream, puree a can of chopped sweet chestnuts, including the syrup, in a blender and stir in the rum. Refrigerate. Whip the cream until stiff and fold it into the sweet chestnut puree. Make the rum syrup according to the basic recipe.

Chestnut Torte

3. Cut the sponge cake into three layers with the same diameter as a cake ring. Fill the ring with alternating layers of sponge cake (each soaked with rum syrup) and sweet chestnut mousse. Refrigerate the torte for 24 hours. Warm the ganache in a double boiler and use it to evenly coat the top and sides of the torte.

4. Place a strip of striped Joconde sponge cake around the outside of the torte. Cut chestnut leaves out of the phyllo pastry and brown them in the oven. Garnish the cake with the chestnut leaves and a few whole glazed sweet chestnuts.

Preparation time: 1 hour
Cooking time: 20 minutes
Difficulty: ★★

Serves 12

For the Montmorency sponge cake:
12 oz / 375 g marzipan
4 eggs
¹/₃ cup / 40 g flour
8 egg whites
8 tsp / 40 g sugar
8 tsp / 40 g butter, melted

For the pastry cream:
2 cups / 500 ml milk

¹/₄ cup / 60 g sugar
5 egg yolks
¹/₃ cup / 40 g cornstarch

For the coffee cream:
2 sheets of gelatin
2 cups / 500 ml cream, stiffly whipped
2 cups / 500 ml pastry cream
3¹/₂ tbsp / 50 ml coffee extract

To garnish:
white chocolate
milk chocolate
cocoa

There are many legends concerning the origins of coffee, one being that it was a gift from the ancient gods to the pitiable mortals. A similar legend originates in Yemen, where trade flourishes between the small harbor town of Mocha and Ethiopian coffee farmers – those in the small kingdom of Kaffa, to be more precise, from whose name the word "coffee" is thought to be derived.

Of the hundreds of species of coffee plants, Arabica and Robusta are the two varieties of beans most widely available on the market. Robusta is a hearty variety with a straightforward flavor, while the more sensitive Arabica grows at higher altitudes and yields coffee with more subtle nuances of flavor.

When making the pastry cream, omit the vanilla bean that would ordinarily be used, for its flavor would clash with that of the coffee. For this recipe, Christian Nihoul recommends using the high-quality Trablit coffee extract, which gives the pastry cream an exquisitely intense flavor. Some brave souls may prefer to make the coffee extract themselves. To do so, pour boiling coffee, complete with the coffee grounds, onto melted sugar. Be aware that the gases and steam released in the process will send glowing particles shooting in all directions! If you are not particularly enamored of volcanoes, you will probably prefer to stick to the more peaceful Trablit.

Use particular care when preparing the Montmorency sponge cake. Do not expect to find the cherries of the same name in it; the sponge cake's name derives from the Duke of Montmorency-Laval, foreign minister to King Louis XVIII.

1. To make the Montmorency sponge cake, beat the marzipan and whole eggs until smooth, then fold in the flour. Whip the egg whites and sugar until stiff, fold them into the marzipan mixture and finally blend in the warm melted butter. Spread the mixture onto a baking sheet and bake at 355 °F / 180 °C. When the sponge cake has cooled, cut out three round layers with the same diameter as a cake ring.

2. For the pastry cream, bring the milk to a boil with some of the sugar. Beat the egg yolks with the remaining sugar until they are creamy and white, then add the cornstarch. Stir a little hot milk into the egg yolks, pour the mixture into the pan with the milk, and return to a boil. Allow to cool. For the coffee cream, add the soaked gelatin together with the stiffly whipped, sweetened cream to 2 cups / 500 ml of the pastry cream. Flavor with coffee extract.

Cream Torte

3. To assemble the torte, using a cake ring if desired, alternate layers of Montmorency sponge cake and coffee cream, using a pastry bag to pipe the cream onto the sponge cake. Refrigerate.

4. Use white chocolate and milk chocolate to form a striped band, and place this around the torte. Form milk and white chocolate rolls and garnish the cake with them. Dust the top with cocoa.

Wedding Cake

Preparation time: 1 hour
Cooking time: 20 minutes
Difficulty: ★★

Serves 12

For the sponge cake:
3 1/2 oz / 100 g marzipan
9 eggs
5 egg yolks
1 cup / 250 g sugar
2 1/2 cups / 315 g flour
6 1/2 tbsp / 100 g butter, melted

For the syrup for soaking:
(see basic recipes p. 805)
6 1/2 tbsp / 100 g sugar

3/4 cup / 200 ml water
2/3 cup / 150 ml Cointreau

For the filling:
whipping cream

For the buttercream:
3 cups / 750 kg butter
1 lb 9 oz / 750 g Italian meringue
   (see basic recipes p. 801)

To garnish:
fresh fruit (pineapple, raspberries,
   strawberries, grapes)
confectioners' sugar

Goodwill alone is not enough here; acquaintance with two people determined to say "I do" is vital to the successful presentation of this cake. Although the statistics might lead one to think otherwise, this particular species is far from extinct.

Christian Nihoul assures us that this wedding cake is as easy to make as any cream-filled sponge cake. The purpose of the cream decoration is to conceal what lies beneath it, and the artistic pattern created with the aid of a pastry bag gives it an extraordinary look befitting such an important occasion. Bakers generally use fondant glazes or very smooth coatings of white marzipan to give wedding cakes their immaculate, virgin-white appearance, but Christian Nihoul has found an

alternative considerably lower in sugar, not to mention much easier to cut. A wedding cake is usually not cut until toward the end of the wedding meal, by the bride and groom themselves, and the general commotion makes it a challenge to concentrate on the task. If you like, add further decorations to the cake, perhaps a pair of turtle doves out of porcelain or sponge cake.

Many variations are possible with the syrup used for soaking the sponge cake layers, as long as the flavor of the syrup and the fruits used to garnish the finished cake complement each other. Possibilities include kirsch and red berries, Grand Marnier and oranges, or even pieces of pineapple, banana, or other exotic fruits.

1. To make the sponge cake, beat the marzipan, eggs, egg yolks, and sugar over an electric source of heat until smooth. Stir in the flour and melted butter. Spread on a baking sheet and bake for 20 minutes at 340 °F / 170 °C. When the sponge cake is cool, cut out three round layers with the diameter of the cake ring. Prepare the syrup according to the basic recipe. Place one of the layers in the cake ring, soak it with Cointreau syrup, spread it with whipped cream and garnish with fresh fruit.

2. Place the second sponge cake layer on top, drench it with the syrup, spread it with whipped cream and arrange fresh fruit on it, then cover with the third sponge cake layer. Prepare the Italian meringue according to the basic recipe.

with Fresh Fruits

3. To make the buttercream, cream the butter for several minutes until it is light and fluffy, then combine it with an equal amount of Italian meringue. Spread some of this in a dome shape on the cake.

4. Fill a pastry bag with the remaining buttercream and, using a flat, waved tip, pipe a lattice pattern onto the cake. Garnish with fresh fruit before presenting.

Preparation time: 1 hour 30 minutes
Cooking time: 15–20 minutes
Difficulty: ★★

Serves 12

For the chocolate sponge cake:
5 eggs
1 egg yolk
1/2 cup plus 1 tbsp / 135 g sugar
3/4 cup / 90 g flour
1/3 cup / 40 g cornstarch
3 1/2 tbsp / 25 g cocoa powder

For the basic cream:
1/2 cup / 125 g sugar
5 tsp / 25 ml water
5 egg yolks

For the chocolate mousse:
4 1/2 oz / 125 g chocolate coating, very bitter
2 oz / 60 g basic cream
2 sheets of gelatin
2 cups / 500 ml whipping cream
10 egg whites
3 1/2 tbsp / 50 g sugar

For the ganache coating:
1 lb / 500 g bittersweet chocolate
1 1/2 cups / 350 ml unsweetened condensed milk

To garnish:
chocolate wafers and truffles

Christian Nihoul introduced this recipe at Expo '92 in Seville, aiming it at fans dedicated to extra-bitter chocolate – not sour, but with a flavor definitely more intense than regular bittersweet chocolate. The chocolate used for this cake produces a long, intense aftertaste. It should be used fresh and not melted until just before it is used. Christian Nihoul cautions us to heat it gradually and carefully; it does not tolerate sudden changes of temperature. A night in an electric oven at 100–120 °F / 40–50 °C will give it the right consistency.

Some of chocolate's ingredients react in different ways to changes in temperature. As is sometimes the case with the chocolate sauce for the classic poire Hélène dessert, too-rapid heating can cause it to separate into its original components.

To simplify the preparation of the Seville Torte, make the sponge cake and ganache a day in advance, and refrigerate them separately. Wait until the last possible minute to coat the torte with the ganache.

Using condensed milk in the ganache makes it softer and much shinier than that made in the usual way, and thus perfectly suited for use as a chocolate coating or glaze.

1. Prepare the chocolate sponge cake by beating the egg yolks and eggs in a copper bowl until the mixture falls from the spoon in long ribbons. Sift the flour with the cornstarch and cocoa, and use a wooden spatula to fold it into the eggs. Pour the mixture into a greased and floured springform pan 1 1/2 in / 3 cm high. Bake for 15–20 minutes at 355 °F / 180 °C.

2. To make the basic cream, proceed as for an Italian meringue. While the sugar and water are heating to 250 °F / 121 °C, beat the egg yolks in a food processor until they are creamy and white. Beating at low speed, slowly pour the hot sugar syrup onto the egg yolks. Stir continuously until the mixture has cooled completely. Measure 2 oz / 60 g of the cream for use in the chocolate mousse.

Torte

3. For the chocolate mousse, melt the chocolate coating and combine it with the basic cream. Soak the gelatin in cold water, drain, dissolve and add it to the chocolate cream. Whip the cream until stiff, and beat the egg whites and sugar until stiff. Carefully blend the three mixtures. To make the ganache, melt the chocolate and, in a separate pan, bring the condensed milk to a boil. Combine the two, cool, and put in the freezer until needed.

4. Place a ¹/₂ in / 1 cm-thick layer of chocolate sponge cake inside a cake ring and coat it with chocolate mousse. Place a second sponge cake layer, soaked with a little sugar syrup, on top and fill the ring with the remaining mousse. Allow to set in the refrigerator. Heat the cake ring briefly to release the torte, and refrigerate it. Warm the ganache in a double boiler and cover the torte with it. Garnish with chocolate wafers and truffles.

Preparation time: 20 minutes
Cooking time: 2 hours
Difficulty: ★

Serves 10

For the meringue:
3 egg whites
6¹/₂ tbsp / 100 g superfine sugar
¹/₂ cup plus 2 tbsp / 100 g confectioners' sugar
 ground vanilla pulp (optional)

For the Gianduja cream:
1³/₄ oz / 50 g hazelnut paste
1³/₄ oz / 50 g chocolate coating
2¹/₂ tbsp / 20 g bitter cocoa

¹/₃ cup / 50 g roasted hazelnuts
2¹/₂ cups / 600 ml whipping cream

To garnish:
cocoa powder
roasted chopped almonds

Gianduia or Gianduja is a particularly smooth type of chocolate, a fine paste made of chocolate and hazelnuts. It is also the term for a traditional Piemontese mask. Piemonte (or Piedmont), in northern Italy, is home to wonderful hazelnuts like Avellinos or the round Piedmont hazelnuts. Naturally, the cakes and tarts typical to this region, which usually contain hazelnuts, are also referred to as gianduja.

Flavio Perbellini recommends using small, fragrant hazelnuts, which should be thoroughly roasted before being mixed into the cream. The cream itself is very mild and contains no sugar. It is bound with chocolate coating, which must contain at least 60% cocoa.

When preparing the gianduja cream, proceed delicately. Fold the whipped cream in very carefully to prevent the cream from collapsing and becoming too soft. The meringue also must be made with care and dried in a very low oven, so that steam does not develop – can even be left to dry overnight.

To give the meringue a significantly better consistency, use egg whites that have been stored for about 15 days at 40 °F / 4 °C. This should not cause any problems and is of no concern health-wise. As a finishing touch, the torte is topped with a decorative dusting of cocoa powder, applied with the aid of a stencil.

1. To make the meringue, beat the egg whites and superfine sugar in a bowl until stiff. Using a small skimmer, fold in the sifted confectioners' sugar and a little ground vanilla pulp, if desired. Retain a quarter of the meringue for spreading on the torte.

2. Grease a baking sheet with butter and dust it with flour (or line it with waxed paper). Pipe two round meringue layers with a diameter of 9 in / 20 cm onto it. Bake the meringues for two hours at 250 °F / 120 °C (or overnight at a lower temperature).

with Gianduja Cream

3. To make the Gianduja cream, melt the hazelnut paste, the chocolate coating, and bitter cocoa in a double boiler. Add the crushed roasted hazelnuts. Allow the mixture to cool, then fold in the stiffly whipped cream.

4. To assemble the cake, place one of the meringue bases on a cake round, spread it with Gianduja cream, then place the second meringue layer on top. Spread the remaining meringue all over the torte. Use a stencil to sift a cocoa powder pattern onto the top and press chopped roasted almonds into the sides.

Panettone

Preparation time: 3 hours
Cooking time: 1 hour 5 minutes
Difficulty: ★★★

Serves 30

1 oz / 30 g fresh compressed yeast
1 oz / 30 g brewer's yeast
4$\frac{1}{2}$ tbsp / 70 ml milk
8 cups / 1 kg gluten rich flour
10 eggs

2 cups / 500 g butter
1$\frac{2}{3}$ cups / 400 g sugar
2 tsp / 10 g salt
vanilla extract
lemon extract
orange extract
1$\frac{1}{2}$ cups / 300 g raisins
$\frac{3}{4}$ cup / 140 g candied orange peel
$\frac{3}{4}$ cup / 140 g candied lemon peel

In Milan, they say that *panettone*, now known and highly regarded throughout the world, was invented by a poor Milanese baker who made his fortune baking it. The exact combination of ingredients in panettone vary from town to town: the Veronese, for example, make it using a yeast starter specially enriched with brewer's yeast, a method of preparation completely foreign to the Milanese. The Perbellini family, with four generations of pastry chefs, has kept its *panettone* recipe a secret since 1852. Here Flavio Perbellini presents a popular recipe for this yeast cake, originally baked at Christmas time.

In accordance with tradition, this *panettone* contains both dried and candied fruits. You should not use too much of either, for dried fruits soak up the cake's moisture, and candied fruits may make it overly sweet, impairing its distinctive delicate flavor. The Venetian version of *panettone*, interestingly, includes a fairly intense orange essence instead of candied fruits.

To help the dough rise perfectly, Perbellini incorporates a bit of dough reserved from a previous baking into the yeast starter; he and his forefathers have kept their starter in continuous use in this fashion for thirty years already, carefully stored wrapped in a thick cloth. This, combined with baking the dough wrapped in the famous Pizotino baking paper (much more practical than a metal cake ring), keeps the *panettone* in line with the best gastronomic tradition.

1. Dissolve the fresh compressed yeast and combine it with the brewer's yeast, milk and 1 cup plus 2 tbsp / 140 g flour. Allow the dough to rise at 85 °F / 30 °C until it has doubled in size.

2. To the dough produced in step one, which should weigh approximately 9$\frac{1}{2}$ oz / 270 g, add 2 cups plus 6 tbsp / 300 g flour, 3 eggs, 3$\frac{1}{2}$ tbsp / 50 g butter and 3$\frac{1}{2}$ tbsp / 50 g sugar, and knead thoroughly. Allow the dough to prove until it has doubled in size again.

3. To the dough that now weighs approximately 1 lb 13 oz / 820 g, add 4½ cups / 560 g flour, 7 eggs, 1 cup plus 7 tbsp / 350 g sugar, 1 cup plus 13 tbsp / 450 g butter, salt, one drop each of vanilla, lemon, and orange extract, and knead until the dough is smooth.

4. Add the finely diced candied fruits (orange and lemon peel) and the raisins and work them into the dough. Divide it into portions weighing 2 pounds / 1 kg each, shape them into balls and then place them inside paper baking forms. Allow the dough to rise for ten hours at 75 °F / 24 °C until they have doubled in size, and then bake for 65 minutes at 350 °F / 175 °C.

Preparation time: 25 minutes
Cooking time: 30 minutes
Difficulty: ★★

Serves 10

For the Savoy sponge cake:
4 eggs
2 egg yolks
1/2 cup / 125 g sugar
3/4 cup / 90 g flour

For the tiramisu cream:
7 egg yolks
1 cup / 150 g confectioners' sugar
14 oz / 400 g mascarpone cheese

8 egg whites
1 cup / 250 g sugar

For the coffee syrup:
1/2 cup / 30 g instant coffee
1 2/3 cups / 400 ml water
3/4 cup plus 1 tbsp / 200 g sugar

For the roasted flaked almonds:
2 cups / 300 g flaked almonds
a pinch of ground vanilla
orange petal water
sugar syrup (30 °Beaumé)

To garnish:
confectioners' sugar

Tiramisu Bianco, a very rich dessert, has three components – mascarpone cheese, coffee, and the Savoy sponge cake. It is popular throughout Italy, especially in Verona where it is prized for its distinctive coffee flavor (very strong, very Italian) and creaminess. This classic, fortifying egg dessert also has a devoted following outside Italy. Flavio Perbellini, in his determination to maintain superb quality, continues to use an old family recipe.

The Savoy sponge cake (the dukes of Savoy later became the kings of Italy) differs from the classic Genoese sponge cake, or génoise, in that it contains more egg yolk and less egg white and flour. It should not be confused with the Savoy gâteau, which is made in a completely different way.

The choice of the mascarpone, which should be fresh, mild and creamy, almost like a very high-fat cream, plays a decisive role in the flavor of the dessert. Mascarpone is now available all year round, rather than just in winter as used to be the case; there is even a pasteurized version that keeps well for a few days in the refrigerator. Be sure the mascarpone used for this tiramisu has no trace of bitterness.

If the tiramisu is not sweet enough for your taste, a light, frothy zabaglione is a wonderful accompaniment to this dessert.

1. Prepare the Savoy sponge cake with the ingredients given above, using the basic recipe for génoise as a guide, and pour the mixture into a greased and floured 9 in / 20 cm cake pan. Bake for 30 minutes at 390 °F / 200 °C. Allow the cake to cool and then slice it horizontally into three layers. To make the tiramisu cream, vigorously whisk the egg yolks and confectioners' sugar until the mixture is thick and foamy, then add the mascarpone. Finally, beat the egg whites until stiff with the sugar.

2. Carefully fold the mascarpone and egg mixture into the very stiffly beaten egg whites. For the coffee syrup, bring the sugar and water to a boil. Remove from the heat and stir in the instant coffee powder.

Bianco

3. Place a layer of Savoy sponge cake on a cake round, soak it with coffee syrup and spread it with tiramisu cream. Place the second layer on top, soak it with coffee syrup and cover it with a layer of tiramisu cream. Top it with the third layer of sponge cake, and cover it with the remaining cream.

4. Spread out the flaked almonds on a tray and drizzle over them a mixture of orange petal water and sugar syrup (which has been flavored with a pinch of ground vanilla). Roast the nuts in the oven or with a salamander. Sprinkle them all over the cake and dust with confectioners' sugar. Refrigerate.

Preparation time: *25 minutes*
Cooking time: *40 minutes*
Difficulty: ★★

Serves 10

pastry cream, génoise:
  (see basic recipes p. 802, 801)

For the maraschino cream:
10¹/₂ oz / 300 g pastry cream
1 tbsp / 15 ml Maraschino liqueur

For the almond paste:
3¹/₃ cups / 500 g blanched almonds
1³/₄ cups plus 2 tbsp / 450 g sugar
3¹/₂ tbsp / 50 g invert sugar
1 egg white
grated orange peel

For the syrup for soaking:
6¹/₂ tbsp / 100 g superfine sugar
6¹/₂ tbsp / 100 ml water
3 tbsp / 45 ml maraschino liqueur

To glaze:
sugar syrup (30 °Beaumé)
or clear cake glaze (see basic recipes p. 800)

The recipe for this almond cake is familiar to all Italian pastry chefs, who make it with varying degrees of success. Flavio Perbellini prepares this *torta delizia* in accordance with long Perbellini family tradition, using pastry cream and a génoise soaked with maraschino liqueur. Maraschino liqueur, which originated in the region around Zara (now Zadar) in Dalmatia, is made from a fruit schnapps distilled exclusively from wild Marasca cherries, a sour cherry also native to this area.

Marasca cherries are also used for other desserts, such as ice cream – like Amarena cherries, they go very well with vanilla. Flavio Perbellini also notes the Amarcine, a dessert made of Marasca cherries, which are steamed in sugar with cloves, cinnamon, and a concentrated syrup.

There are several types of almonds you could choose from, but Flavio Perbellini names the Sicilian Marri as most suitable for this recipe. The almond paste must be very fine, so use an almond mill or food processor for grinding the almonds. If neither is available, crush the almonds with a mortar in a wooden pestle, which is time-consuming, but the results are worth the extra effort.

In the unlikely event that some of the cake is left over, it will keep at room temperature for two days or, if need be, for five to six days in the refrigerator.

1. Prepare a classic pastry cream according to the basic recipe, allow it to cool and flavor it with maraschino liqueur. Make the génoise, again following the basic recipe, and pour it into a greased and floured cake pan with a diameter of 9 in / 20 cm. Bake for 30 minutes at 390 °F / 200 °C, and after it has cooled slice it through horizontally.

2. To make the almond paste, grind the blanched almonds with the sugar and invert sugar in a food processor and mix thoroughly, then add the egg white and grated orange peel. Follow the basic recipe for the syrup for soaking.

Cake

3. To assemble the cake, place a layer of génoise on a cake round, soak it with maraschino syrup and spread pastry cream on it, then place the second génoise layer on top.

4. Using a pastry bag with a flat, ribbed tip, decorate the top of the cake with woven strips of almond paste. Put in the oven for 8–10 minutes at 480 °F / 250 °C until the surface has browned slightly. Remove it from the oven and coat the cake with clear glaze or sugar syrup.

Preparation time: 1 hour
Cooking time: 30 minutes
Difficulty: ★★★

Serves 10

génoise, pastry cream, Italian meringue:
  (see basic recipes p. 801, 802)

For the pistachio cream:
5¼ oz / 150 g pastry cream
4½ oz / 125 g Italian meringue
1 oz / 30 g pistachio paste

For the rum cream:
5¼ oz / 150 g pastry cream
4½ oz / 125 g Italian meringue
3½ tbsp / 50 ml rum

For soaking the génoise:
3½ tbsp / 50 ml rum
3½ tbsp / 50 ml Alchermes
3½ tbsp / 50 ml Marsala

The typically Italian dessert Zuppa inglese was actually created by Neapolitan pastry chefs and has nothing to do with England, in spite of its somewhat misleading name. Zuppa inglese does not mean English soup (*minestra* is the Italian word for soup), but would be better translated as English pudding, and thus perhaps derives its name from the well-known British fondness for puddings of all sorts.

Keen observers cannot fail to notice that the three colors of the Italian flag are used here. As in the Torta Italiana, three spirits are used – brown rum, Marsala – and Alchermes. Other combinations are also possible, however; for example, the Marsala can be replaced by Madeira or port, and the Alchermes by Grand Marnier.

The hallmark of the Zuppa inglese is that each of the three génoise layers is soaked in a different spirit, and three different creams (actually two creams and an Italian meringue) are also spread between those layers. You can further refine the creams with the addition of chopped hazelnuts, bits of chocolate or marinated fruits, but be careful not to overdo it.

One final point worthy of note is the Italian meringue, which should not be prepared until you are ready to use it, as the cake's final touch. Flavio Perbellini insists that it must be absolutely smooth, without any lumps. Browning the torte slightly with a Bunsen burner makes the presentation even more elegant.

1. Prepare the pastry cream and Italian meringue according to the basic recipes. Follow the basic recipe for the génoise, pour into a greased and floured cake pan with a diameter of 9 in / 20 cm, and bake for 30 minutes at 390 °F / 200 °C. Allow the génoise to cool and then slice it into three layers. To make the pistachio cream, mix the pastry cream with the Italian meringue and pistachio paste.

2. To make the rum cream, again combine pastry cream and Italian meringue, replacing the pistachio paste with the rum.

Inglese

3. To assemble the torte, place a layer of génoise onto a cake round, soak it with Alchermes and cover it with rum cream. Place the second layer on top, soak it with rum and spread pistachio cream on it. Put the third layer on top and soak it with Marsala.

4. Spread Italian meringue on the top of the torte, smooth the surface and use a pastry bag to apply a meringue decoration. Then garnish with fresh fruits and refrigerate the torte until served.

Preparation time: 45 minutes
Cooking time: 1 hour 30 minutes
Difficulty: ★★

Serves 8

For the chocolate sponge cake:
5 eggs
¼ cup / 60 g sugar
6½ tbsp / 50 g flour
1 oz / 30 g stabilizer
⅓ cup / 80 g butter
5¼ oz / 150 g milk chocolate coating, melted

For the mousse Jivara:
2½ tbsp / 40 ml sugar syrup
4 egg yolks
¼ cup / 60 g sugar

1¾ cups / 420 ml cream
7 oz / 200 g milk chocolate coating, melted

For the ganache with forest berries:
1¼ cups / 200 g forest berries
2¼ oz / 70 g bittersweet chocolate coating
8 tsp / 40 g sugar
1½ sheets of gelatin

For the crème brûlée:
1 cup / 250 ml cream
3½ tbsp / 50 g sugar
4 egg yolks
½ vanilla bean

To garnish:
chocolate discs

The derivation of this specialty's name, also the name of the *pâtisserie* owned by Bernard Proot, is not exactly clear. In Spanish, it means "belonging to the King," but its meaning contains another small spin, a discreet homage to the former owner of the shop, Adèle Reymacckers, who was more than happy to go along with this word play.

As far as the preparation of the torte bearing the name is concerned, the mousse Jivara is best made a day in advance. Be sure to fold the stiffly whipped cream into the caramel and chocolate mixture at exactly the right moment; to ensure that the cream does not collapse, this mixture should be only lukewarm. The mousse develops the flavor of milk chocolate with a slightly fruity aftertaste.

For the ganache, select only fully ripe, aromatic berries of the highest quality. Even though they will not function as garnish, do not use any bruised or damaged berries, which would impair the flavor of the whole. Gourmets prefer to use bittersweet chocolate with a cocoa content of 50% to 55% for the ganache. Use it sparingly so that the taste of the berries is neither overpowered nor adulterated.

Garnish this dessert in whatever way you like. Use your imagination, and perhaps the inspiration of a special occasion, to create decorations worthy of this torte's royal name.

1. To make the sponge cake, beat the eggs and sugar until foamy, then add the flour and stabilizer. Melt and combine the butter and chocolate coating. Use a pastry bag to pipe two spirals onto a baking tray, and bake for 40 minutes at 210 °F / 100 °C. For the mousse Jivara, whisk the egg yolks, pour the hot sugar syrup onto them and beat until cooled. Caramelize the sugar and carefully add ¼ cup / 60 ml cream. Whip the remaining cream. Pour the melted chocolate coating onto the egg yolk mixture, add the caramel, and fold in the stiffly whipped cream.

2. Prepare the ganache with forest berries by melting the chocolate coating. Boil the berries with the sugar, allow them to cool slightly, then add the soaked gelatin and the melted chocolate coating. To make the crème brûlée, mix all the ingredients without heating them. Pass the mixture through a sieve, pour into large, flat Flexipan tins and bake for 50 minutes at 210 °F / 100 °C.

3. After it has cooled, spread a thin layer of the ganache with forest berries onto the crème brûlée, and place in the freezer.

4. To assemble the torte line a cake ring with a strip of baking paper and spoon in some mousse Jivara. Top it with a layer of chocolate sponge cake, then a slice of frozen crème brûlée. Fill the cake ring with the remaining mousse and finish off with the second layer of sponge cake. Then turn out the torte and remove the baking paper. Garnish the top of the cake, and arrange a border of chocolate wafers around the outer edge.

Preparation time: 40 minutes
Cooking time: 5 minutes
Difficulty: ★★

Serves 8

For the Joconde sponge cake:
2 egg whites
2 tbsp sugar

Almond and sugar mixture:
1/3 cup / 80 g sugar
1/2 cup / 80 g finely ground almonds
6 eggs
3 tbsp / 25 g flour
1 oz / 25 g praline
1 oz / 25 g mocha coating
 melted butter

For the orange mousse:
5 egg yolks
1/2 cup / 120 ml sugar syrup (35 °Beaumé)
6 oz / 175 g orange chocolate
4 1/2 oz / 125 g bittersweet chocolate coating
3 1/2 oz / 100 g sweet almond praline
1 3/4 cups / 450 ml whipping cream, unsweetened

For the chocolate mousse with almond milk:
2/3 cup / 150 ml almond milk
4 egg yolks
4 oz / 120 g bittersweet chocolate coating
5 1/4 oz / 150 g mocha coating
2 cups / 500 ml unsweetened whipping cream

For the cocoa glaze:
3/4 cup plus 3 tbsp / 225 g sugar
3/4 cup / 180 ml water
2/3 cup / 150 ml cream
3/4 cup / 75 g cocoa
4 sheets of gelatin
 clear cake glaze

To garnish:
white chocolate coating
marbled chocolate

It was for this recipe that Gunther Van Essche, Bernard Proot's brilliant assistant, was named best pastry chef in Belgium of 1995 and awarded the Prosper Montagné Prize, the most respected in Belgium. So translate the "Victoria" in the name of this torte as "victory." Other interpretations, such as it being a reference to the indefatigable English queen, do not merit serious consideration.

The Victoria Torte is an imaginative variation of two mousses with similar, yet distinctive flavors. Gunther Van Essche contends that for this recipe, only chocolate with a 50% cocoa content will meet the most discerning standards. It is used as bittersweet chocolate coating in both the orange and almond milk mousses. Both should be light and have a melt-in-the-mouth consistency. To achieve this, along with a perfect visual effect, combine the ingredients with great care.

If you prefer to make the orange chocolate yourself, you can prepare a concentrated infusion that is flavored with orange peel and then mixed with the mousse. So that the cocoa glaze has a nice sheen, use very finely ground cocoa.

1. To make the Joconde sponge cake, beat the eggs until foamy with 1 tbsp / 5 g sugar, and beat the egg whites and remaining sugar until stiff. Combine both mixtures. Blend the flour with the almond and sugar mixture, and fold the dry ingredients into the eggs. Stir in the melted chocolate and praline, and finally add the melted butter. Pipe spirals with a diameter of 10 in / 22 cm onto a tray and bake for five minutes at 445 °F / 230 °C. When cool, slice through horizontally.

2. For the orange mousse, warm the egg yolks and sugar syrup in a double boiler and beat until cool. Melt the orange chocolate and chocolate coating, stir in the praline, and add to the egg yolks. Cool slightly, then carefully fold the mixture into the whipped cream. Place a layer of Joconde sponge cake in a cake ring 1 in / 2 cm high. Fill the ring with mousse and place it in the freezer. Prepare the marbled chocolate for the garnish.

Torte

3. To make the chocolate mousse, beat the almond milk and egg yolks in a double boiler. Add the melted chocolate and mocha coatings and carefully fold in the whipped cream. Line a 11 in / 24 cm cake ring, 2 in / 4 cm high, with a strip of baking paper and spread some chocolate mousse in it. Place the frozen orange mousse in the ring, centered, and cover it with the remaining chocolate mousse. Top it with a layer of Joconde sponge cake and freeze.

4. Prepare the cocoa glaze by combining all the ingredients, except the gelatin, in a saucepan and heating to 150 °F / 65 °C. Allow to cool, then dissolve the soaked gelatin in it. Thicken with clear cake glaze until it reaches the desired consistency. Remove the torte from the ring. Spread cocoa glaze over its entire surface, and line the edge with chocolate wafers. Use a tiny paper pastry bag to apply a garnish of white chocolate and decorate with marbled chocolate.

Preparation time: 1 hour 30 minutes
Cooking time: 15 minutes
Difficulty: ★

Serves 8

For the dacquoise sponge cake:
20 egg whites
1 cup / 250 g superfine sugar

Almond and sugar mixture:
³/₄ cup plus 3 tbsp / 225 g sugar
1¹/₄ cup / 225 g finely ground almonds
³/₄ cup / 100 g flour
3¹/₂ tbsp / 50 ml cream
¹/₂ cup / 45 g chocolate flakes

macadamia nuts
confectioners' sugar

For the crème anglaise:
1¹/₂ cups / 330 ml milk
7¹/₂ tbsp / 110 g sugar
5 egg yolks

For the chocolate mousse:
1 lb / 500 g crème anglaise
1 lb / 450 g bittersweet chocolate coating
2¹/₂ cups / 600 ml whipping cream

The Macadamia Torte is not, as you might think, an homage to city life or the tarmac (also called "macadam") that paves our cities, immortalizing the name of its inventor, the Scottish engineer J. McAdam. "Macadamia" refers to a type of nut native to Australia that is named for the Australian chemist and naturalist John Macadam.

The macadamia, or Queensland nut, has a taste reminiscent of coconut and is the fruit of a tropical evergreen, a member of the *Proteaceae* family. It should not be confused with the Brazil nut (*Lecythidaceae*) or pecan nut (*Juglandaceae*).

Use very fresh egg whites for the dacquoise sponge cake to ensure that the dessert will have the proper consistency and not collapse. Beyond this, one important thing to keep in mind is to see that the ingredients for the mousse are the correct temperature when combined, which is no more difficult than the preparation of a traditional crème anglaise. Wait to fold in the whipped cream until the mousse has cooled.

When assembling the torte, refrigerate it for a short time after each stage of the work. This allows the various components to achieve the right consistency, and the cake will have the necessary firmness. The chocolate mousse could be replaced with buttercream, though this will not set as firmly.

1. To make the dacquoise sponge cake, beat 15 of the egg whites with the sugar until stiff. Beat the remaining egg whites and blend into them the almond and sugar mixture, flour, cream, and chocolate flakes. Fold the two mixtures together. Place two 1 in / 2 cm high cake rings on a tray lined with baking paper and fill them with the dacquoise mixture. Remove the cake rings, sprinkle macadamia nuts onto the sponge cakes, dust with confectioners' sugar and bake for 15 minutes at 340 °F / 170 °C.

2. To make the chocolate mousse, start by making a crème anglaise: bring the milk to a boil, and beat the egg yolks and sugar until foamy. Combine the egg yolk mixture with the milk and thicken. Stir the chocolate coating into the crème anglaise while still warm. Allow to cool, then fold in the stiffly whipped cream.

Torte

3. Using a pastry bag with a round tip, pipe the chocolate mousse onto one of the sponge cake layers in the form of lamellas.

4. Place the second sponge cake layer on top. Refrigerate the dessert for two hours. Before serving, dust with confectioners' sugar.

Preparation time: 1 hour 30 minutes
Cooking time: 20 minutes
Difficulty: ★★

Serves 8

striped Joconde sponge cake, Duchess
  sponge cake, Italian meringue:
  (see basic recipes p. 805, 800, 801)

For the passion fruit mousse:
1 lb / 500 g passion fruit flesh
3 cups / 750 ml whipping cream
4 sheets of gelatin
7 oz / 200 g Italian meringue

For the syrup for soaking:
(see basic recipes p. 805)
12 oz / 375 g passion fruit flesh
6½ tbsp / 100 ml sugar syrup
2½ tbsp / 40 ml kirsch

For the raspberry jam:
6¼ cups / 1 kg raspberries
4 cups / 1 kg sugar
¾ oz / 20 g pectin

To garnish:
seasonal fruits
passion fruit jelly

The homely fruits of the passion flower, fresh and ripe, can be recognized by their wrinkled, dull, grey-brown peel. Once you get past these first impressions, you will discover a delicate flavor inside. Bernard Proot's clever use of them enhances this flavor even further and will be a true treat for your taste buds. But there are a few things to keep in mind as you prepare this experience.

For example, add the passion fruit very gradually and carefully to the whipped cream. The part of the fruit used is the flesh, or, more precisely, the fleshy aril covering the seeds. Pass the flesh through a sieve to filter out seeds.

The recent growth in demand for passion fruit is not surprising, for it is rich in vitamins, minerals, and other nutrients. By now it is, along with pineapples, the most popular exotic fruit. In this recipe, passion fruit harmonizes beautifully with the raspberry jam spread on the second sponge cake layer.

Assemble the cake from the bottom up to give the mousse a completely smooth surface and help the jelly adhere to it better. The sponge cake layers must be soaked carefully and evenly with the passion fruit punch. Proot suggests using a spray bottle or baby bottle to distribute the liquid evenly over the entire surface of the sponge cake.

1. Prepare the striped Joconde and Duchess sponge cakes according to the basic recipes. Line a cake ring with a strip of the Joconde sponge cake. To make the passion fruit mousse, gently combine the stiffly whipped cream with the passion fruit flesh. Fold the dissolved gelatin into the Italian meringue while it is still slightly warm. Allow to cool and then combine the meringue with the passion fruit whipped cream.

2. Follow the basic recipe for the syrup for soaking. Place a layer of Duchess sponge cake in the cake ring, soak it with passion fruit syrup and cover with a layer of mousse. To make the raspberry jam, heat the raspberries, sugar, and pectin over low heat until the mixture has a syrupy consistency. Remove from the heat and allow to cool.

Fruit Torte

3. Spread the raspberry jam onto the second Duchess sponge cake and place it in the cake ring on top of the passion fruit mousse.

4. Fill the cake ring with the remaining mousse and carefully smooth the surface. Freeze for four hours. Cover the top of the cake with passion fruit jelly and garnish with seasonal fruits.

Preparation time: *1 hour 30 minutes*
Cooking time: *15 minutes*
Difficulty: ★★★

Makes 12

biscuit (see basic recipes p. 798)

For the Chiboust cream with champagne:
$^3/_4$ cup / 190 ml champagne
6 tbsp / 90 ml mandarin juice
$^1/_4$ cup / 60 ml cream
6 egg yolks
1 oz / 30 g pudding powder
5 sheets of gelatin
2 tbsp / 30 ml Napoléon mandarin liqueur
6 egg whites
$^3/_4$ cup plus 3 tbsp / 225 g sugar

For the mandarin mousse with almond milk:
2 egg yolks
$^1/_2$ cup / 120 ml almond milk
2 egg whites
6 tbsp / 90 g sugar
6 sheets of gelatin
1 cup plus 3 tbsp / 280 ml cream
$^3/_4$ cup / 190 ml mandarin juice
2 tbsp / 30 ml Napoléon mandarin liqueur

For the mandarin jelly:
$6^1/_2$ tbsp / 100 ml mandarin concentrate
$1^1/_4$ cups / 300 ml water

For the wood-grain chocolate wafers:
white chocolate ganache
(see basic recipes p. 806)
chocolate liqueur

This royal composition, created by Bernard Proot, does credit to its name. Contributing elements include its exquisite ingredients; its effective, truly regal presentation; and the renown of the champagne that enhances the Chiboust cream. The refreshing tartness of mandarins, used both as a juice and as a liqueur, predominates the dessert's flavor.

Developed in the mid-19th century by a Belgian, the Napoléon mandarin liqueur is made from Sicilian mandarin oranges marinated in Cognac. Today, the Belgian Georgy Fourcroy, who also awards the annual Prix Mandarine Napoléon to the world's best pastry chefs, is responsible for the continuing high quality of this liqueur.

Creating the chocolate wafers with the distinctive appearance of wood grain can be difficult. First, a fine layer of dark chocolate liqueur, or cocoa mass (left over when cocoa butter is removed from cocoa beans), is spread with a cake comb to yield the wood grain effect. Then it sets in the freezer before a thin coating of white ganache is smoothed over it.

The various components of the cream and mousse should be combined with particular care. With the Chiboust cream, especially, it is important to be aware of the temperature of the different elements when combining them. One final tip: color of the mandarins can be intensified by the addition of a little orange jelly.

1. To make the wood-grain wafers to garnish, prepare the white chocolate ganache according to the basic recipe. Spread the chocolate liqueur thinly over plastic wrap using a cake comb to yield a wood-grain effect. Freeze. When set, smooth white chocolate ganache over it. Refrigerate and allow to set. Follow the basic recipes for the biscuit.

2. For the Chiboust cream, bring the champagne, mandarin juice and cream to a boil. Beat the egg yolks until they are light yellow and slightly thick, then stir in the pudding powder and add to the champagne mixture. Return to a boil, stirring constantly. Remove from the heat and cool slightly, then add the soaked gelatin and the mandarin liqueur. Use the egg whites and sugar to make an Italian meringue, beating until cooled. Combine the two mixtures. Freeze the Chiboust cream in small Flexipan tins for 1–2 hours.

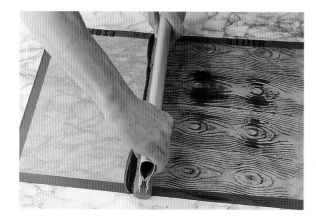

Royal

3. Make the mandarin mousse by beating the egg yolks in a double boiler with 3 tbsp / 45 ml almond milk. Again use the egg whites and sugar to prepare an Italian meringue, then fold the soaked gelatin into it. Whip the cream until stiff and then blend in the remaining almond milk, the mandarin juice and mandarin liqueur. Combine the egg yolk, whipped cream and meringue mixtures.

4. To assemble the Royals, divide the mandarin mousse between individual forms similar to those shown below. Press frozen portions of Chiboust cream into the mousse. Cover with circles of biscuit, and refrigerate for 1¹/₂ hours. Turn the desserts out of the forms and cover them with mandarin jelly. Decorate each with wood-grain chocolate wafers and garnish with Cape gooseberries dusted with confectioners' sugar.

Preparation time: 1 hour
Cooking time: 20 minutes
Difficulty: ★★

Serves 8

striped Joconde sponge cake, Duchess
  sponge cake, Italian meringue
  (see basic recipes p. 805, 800, 801)

For the rhubarb mousse:
$^3/_4$ cup / 170 ml whipping cream
9 oz / 250 g pureed rhubarb
1 oz / 30 g pureed strawberries
4 sheets of gelatin
$4^1/_2$ oz / 125 g Italian meringue

For the strawberry mousse:
$^3/_4$ cup / 170 ml whipping cream
9 oz / 250 g pureed strawberries
juice of $^1/_2$ lemon

6 sheets of gelatin
6 oz / 170 g Italian meringue

For the syrup for soaking:
(see basic recipes p. 805)
9 oz / 250 g pureed strawberries
$6^1/_2$ tbsp / 100 ml strawberry liqueur
$^3/_4$ cup / 200 ml sugar syrup

For the strawberry jelly:
9 oz / 250 g pureed strawberries
1 cup / 250 g sugar
1 tsp / 2 g pectin

To garnish:
wild strawberries
mint leaves

Just as Venice holds an air of mystery, its past an enduring presence in the buildings lining the canals, the outer appearance of this torte, which is known as Le Venise, conceals its true flavors beneath a topping of wild strawberries. Only after his guests have begun to eat it does Bernard Proot tell them, with mischievous glee, that they have been enjoying rhubarb mousse. Due to its beneficial effect on the digestive system, rhubarb has been used medicinally and therefore does not have a terribly exciting reputation in Belgium.

Rhubarb is best eaten in season, usually from May to July but sometimes as late as October. The rhubarb stalks should be nice and red, firm and crunchy. This member of the buckwheat family also freezes well, and is excellent for making purees and jams.

Rhubarb, highly regarded in the United States and England but (according to Proot) misjudged by many in Belgium, cannot really be replaced by any other fruit. If you must, you could try using limes, as long as they are very aromatic; but the results may be disappointing.

The step-by-step assembly of the cake, from the Duchess sponge cake right through to the meringue, should be done as a continuous process. The cake is placed in the freezer periodically so that its components become firm.

Strawberries, by the way, are well-loved in Belgium. The Belgian-cultivated Elsanta variety has a pleasing shape; the ripe berries have an intense flavor and are marvelously fragrant.

1. Follow the basic recipes for the Duchess and striped Joconde sponge cakes. For the rhubarb mousse, mix the whipped cream with the pureed rhubarb and strawberries. Dissolve the gelatin, which has been soaked in cold water, and fold it into the Italian meringue. Combine with the rhubarb and strawberry whipped cream. Prepare the strawberry mousse in the same way.

2. To make the syrup for soaking, bring the sugar syrup and pureed strawberries to a boil, allow to cool, then stir in the strawberry liqueur. Line a cake ring with a strip of the striped Joconde sponge cake, then place a layer of Duchess sponge cake inside. Fill the ring half way with rhubarb mousse.

Rhubarb Torte

3. Top the mousse with a layer of Duchess sponge cake soaked with strawberry syrup, arrange wild strawberries on it. Fill the cake ring with strawberry mousse and smooth the surface. Freeze for about four hours. To make the strawberry jelly bring the pureed strawberries to a boil with the sugar. Remove from the heat, add the pectin and allow to cool.

4. Pipe a garnish of Italian meringue around the perimeter of the torte using a pastry bag with a special Saint-Honoré tip. Brown the meringue with a salamander. Cover the center of the torte with the strawberry jelly and garnish with whole, perfect wild strawberries and mint leaves.

Preparation time: 2 hours 15 minutes
Cooking time: 30 minutes
Difficulty: ★★★

Serves 8

For the coffee and caramel cream:
1 cup / 250 g superfine sugar
2 cups / 500 ml cream
4 tsp / 5 g instant coffee
6 egg yolks
6 sheets of gelatin
3 cups / 750 ml whipping cream

For the wafer base:
10¹/₂ oz / 300 g Jijona nougat, liquid
7 oz / 200 g milk chocolate coating

3¹/₂ tbsp / 50 g butter
4 oz / 120 g crisp wafers, crushed

For the hazelnut sponge cake:
7 egg whites
5 tbsp / 75 g sugar
3¹/₂ cups / 375 g roasted hazelnuts, ground

Clear cake glaze:
(see basic recipes p. 800)

To garnish:
seasonal red fruits
chocolate lattice

What distinguishes this cake is its crispy wafer base, whose rough texture resembles honeycomb. Its uneven surface could be smoothed over with a thin layer of sugar, cream, jam or other sweet substances of creamy, soft texture that would complement the crunchy base.

Francisco Torreblanca's impetus for this dessert arose when he was eating an ice cream containing chocolate flakes. The contrast inspired him to create this crunchy wafer base, enhanced with butter and milk chocolate coating, and then frozen until it achieves the right consistency.

The torte is filled with a coffee and caramel cream. Begin by making a light, dry caramel. The cream itself must be prepared

with great care and not allowed to boil. Use a particularly mild variety of coffee to flavor it, either very finely ground Colombia beans or highest quality instant coffee. Too intense a coffee flavor will overpower the taste of the caramel.

For the hazelnut sponge cake, Francisco Torreblanca prefers to use the delicious Spanish hazelnuts from Tarragona, but you can also substitute pistachios or walnuts. These are ground complete with their peel and stirred right into the sponge cake mixture.

1. To make the coffee and caramel cream, caramelize the sugar in a saucepan without added liquid. Heat the cream and carefully combine the caramel with the hot cream and instant coffee. Whisk the egg yolks, then combine the two mixtures and thicken like a custard to 185 °F / 85 °C. Add the gelatin, which has been soaked in cold water. Allow to cool and finally fold in the whipped cream.

2. For the wafer base, melt the chocolate coating and combine it with the nougat. Cream the butter and add the chocolate mixture to it. Carefully fold in the crumbled wafers. Pour the mixture to a depth of ¹/₄ in / ¹/₂ cm into a cake ring with a diameter of 7 in / 16 cm. Freeze for four hours.

Caramel Torte

3. Prepare the hazelnut sponge cake: beat the egg whites and sugar until stiff, then gently fold in the ground hazelnuts. Pipe two spirals with a diameter of 7 in/16 cm onto a tray lined with baking paper and bake for 30 minutes at 340 °F / 170 °C. Place a 8 in / 18 cm cake ring that is 1³/₄ in / 3¹/₂ cm high on a cake round and set a sponge cake base inside it. Top with a layer of cream, and then the chilled wafer base. Spread more cream on the wafer base, then place the second sponge cake layer on it and again spread with cream. Freeze.

4. Marble the top surface of the torte with melted caramel, remove it from the cake ring, and cover it with clear cake glaze. Garnish with seasonal fruits and decorate the perimeter with a chocolate lattice.

Preparation time: 2 hours
Cooking time: 20 minutes
Difficulty: ★★★

Serves 8

shortbread: (see basic recipes p. 804)

For the pastry cream:
1 cup / 250 ml milk
6 egg yolks
6 tbsp / 90 g sugar
4 tbsp / 30 g cornstarch

For the saffron cream:
 pastry cream
10 saffron threads
3 sheets of gelatin

For the Italian meringue:
5 tsp / 25 ml water
1/2 cup / 115 g sugar
2 egg whites

To garnish:
10 1/2 oz / 300 g apricots
seasonal fruits
chocolate decorations (optional)
Serve with a passion fruit or apricot coulis

The tender hands of the fetching Dulcinéa del Toboso, Don Quixote's beloved, very likely often helped in the harvest of saffron in La Mancha, the adventure playground of bold, wind-mill-tilting heroes in the work of 17th century Spanish author Miguel de Cervantes. Now as then, saffron stigmata are still gathered by hand in the early morning before sunrise, each flower yielding just three threads, just before the purple blossoms of this member of the crocus family close. Francisco Torreblanca uses this understandably expensive spice for his Dulcinéa torte, which he named after the heroine in Cervantes' novel.

Saffron gives food a rich color and distinctive flavor, and should therefore always be used sparingly. It is available either as a powder or as whole stigmas, called threads. The powdered form loses its flavor quickly and threads are definitely preferable.

Before adding the saffron threads to the cream, they can be lightly toasted with a salamander. The slight heat highlights the unique flavor of saffron, a spice that is surprising over and over again, and is certainly not commonplace in a pastry such as this. Since it keeps well in the refrigerator, the saffron cream can be prepared a day in advance.

For the cake to be worthy of its name, decorate it in a manner befitting its class, crowning it with a wreath of ripe, fleshy, golden orange apricots and serve it with an apricot or passion fruit coulis.

1. Follow the basic recipe for the shortbread dough, then refrigerate. Roll it out evently and use it to line a greased springform pan with a diameter of 8 in / 18 cm. Bake it blind for 15 minutes at 355 °F / 180 °C.

2. To make the pastry cream, bring the milk to a boil. Meanwhile beat the egg yolks and sugar, and add the cornstarch. Stir some of the hot milk into the egg yolks, return to the pan with the hot milk and cook for two minutes, stirring continuously so it does not stick to the pan. To make the saffron cream, add the saffron threads and the soaked and wrung-out gelatin to the pastry cream.

Dulcinéa

3. For the Italian meringue, boil the water and 6 tbsp / 90 g sugar to 250 °F / 121 °C. Beat the egg whites with 5 tsp / 25 g sugar until stiff, then slowly pour the hot sugar syrup onto them while stirring. Continue beating at a medium speed until the mixture is completely cooled. Carefully combine the saffron cream and Italian meringue. Pour the mixture into a cake ring with a diameter of 7 in / 16 cm and freeze for four hours.

4. Remove the frozen saffron cream from the freezer and place it on the shortbread base. Caramelize the middle of the frozen saffron cream with a salamander. Cut the apricots into segments, sprinkle with sugar and caramelize with the salamander. Ring the torte with apricot segments and garnish the center with seasonal fruits or chocolate decorations.

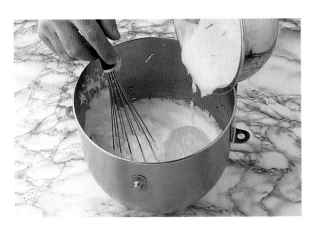

Preparation time: 1 hour 30 minutes
Cooking time: 10 minutes
Difficulty: ★★

Serves 8

For the cinnamon and almond sponge cake:
6 eggs
1 cup / 250 g sugar
1²/₃ cups / 250 g almonds, very finely ground
1 tsp cinnamon

For the apple jelly:
4 cups / 1 l apple juice, made from apple peel
4 cups / 1 kg sugar
³/₄ oz / 20 g pectin
10 sheets of gelatin

For the muscatel jelly:
3 cups / 1 kg apple jelly
³/₄ cup / 200 ml muscatel wine (Moscatel)
¹/₂ cup / 125 ml glucose syrup

For the vanilla cream:
1 vanilla bean
1 cup / 250 ml milk
5 egg yolks
6¹/₂ tbsp / 100 g sugar
9 oz / 250 g white chocolate coating
4 sheets of gelatin
2¹/₂ cups / 600 ml whipping cream

For the white cake glaze:
1¹/₂ cups / 500 g muscatel jelly
11¹/₂ oz / 325 g white chocolate coating

To serve:
cherry coulis

Because of cinnamon's powerful aroma, it should always be used sparingly. Around Valencia, however, a type of intensely flavored cinnamon milk granité (*granizado*) is traditionally enjoyed during the first balmy days of summer. In Francisco Torreblanca's recipe for cinnamon, finding just the right balance between cinnamon and almonds is the key element.

It is best to make the apple jelly for this cake yourself. Place apple peels into a mixture of water and pectin, bring them to a boil, add the glucose and gelatin and freeze the mixture for a while to let it set. This method yields a natural, slightly tart jelly that keeps well.

Moscatel, a muscatel wine from the Jávea region near Alicante, is prized by gourmets for its honey-like aftertaste and gives the jelly an extra, pleasing nuance of flavor. Once you have become adept in making the jelly, you can also flavor it with other muscatels, a Sauternes or champagne.

The first step in preparing the vanilla cream is to allow a carefully scraped-out vanilla bean to infuse in milk for 24 hours. When thickening, the cream should be heated no higher than 185 °F / 85 °C. It will keep for three to four days in the refrigerator and can even be frozen.

1. To prepare the sponge cake, separate the eggs; beat the egg whites and sugar until stiff, then add the lightly whisked egg yolks, ground almonds, and cinnamon. Spread this mixture onto a tray lined with baking paper and bake for seven minutes at 445 °F / 230 °C. To make the apple jelly, boil the apple peels and cores in water, then strain. Add an equal amount of sugar to the resulting juice and bring to a boil. Add the pectin and gelatin, and pass through a sieve.

2. Combine 3 cups / 1 kg of the apple jelly with the wine and glucose, and heat gently to make the muscatel jelly. For the vanilla cream, infuse the vanilla bean in the milk for 24 hours, then bring to a boil. Whisk the egg yolks with the sugar, add to the vanilla milk and thicken like a custard. Add the chopped white chocolate coating and the gelatin, which has been soaked in cold water. Allow to cool and then fold into the stiffly whipped cream.

Torte

3. Assemble the torte from the top down in an 8 in/18 cm cake ring that is 1³/₄ in / 3¹/₂ cm high. Cover a cake round with plastic wrap and place the cake ring on it. Alternate two layers of vanilla cream and two sponge cake layers, beginning with cream. Freeze for about four hours. Make the white cake glaze: heat the muscatel jelly with the white chocolate coating and stir to combine thoroughly.

4. Remove the torte from the freezer, invert it onto a cooling rack, and cover with the white cake glaze. Dry a slit vanilla bean in the oven, dip it in egg white and roll it in sugar, and return it to the oven to crystallize. Edge the cake with chocolate wafers and garnish with the vanilla bean and candied rose petals. Serve with a cherry coulis.

Preparation time: 1 hour 30 minutes
Cooking time: 7 minutes
Difficulty: ★★

Serves 8

For the almond sponge cake:
5 eggs
1 cup / 250 g sugar
1²/₃ cups / 250 g almonds, very finely ground
grated peel of 2 lemons
a little candied ginger

For the lemon cream:
³/₄ cup / 200 ml lemon juice
1²/₃ cups / 400 g sugar

1 cup / 250 g butter
grated peel of 4 lemons
8 eggs

For the lemon syrup:
(see basic recipes p. 805)
1 cup / 250 ml water
¹/₂ cup / 125 g sugar
juice of ¹/₂ lemon

To garnish:
clear cake glaze (see basic recipes p. 800)
white chocolate decoration
seasonal fruits

In the Spanish province of Alicante, many fruits are grown and are quite rightly renowned. Particularly in the lower Segura valley, a truly idyllic stretch of land peppered with vineyards and orchards, grow countless orange, lemon, and apricot trees. Francisco Torreblanca comes from this fruitful region, and pays it homage in the form of this delicious Lemon Torte recipe, which has been made in the Totel *pasteleria* since 1989.

The basis of this torte is an almond sponge cake made using Marcona almonds, a type of almond that has a very high oil content (store them in the refrigerator to prevent them from becoming rancid). The Marcona almond tree bears copious nuts that only ripen late in the season, in October, and must be eaten within a year.

The almonds must be ground until the almond oil seeps out and the almonds form a homogeneous mixture, rendering it unnecessary to add flour to the sponge cake.

A unique detail of this recipe is the contrast between the fairly acidic lemons from Alicante and the intense flavor of the candied ginger – use it sparingly! You may have to use additional sugar to produce a lemon syrup suitable for soaking the cake, especially if the lemons are fresh. Torreblanca serves the cake with *horchata de chufa*, a refreshing drink made by infusing chufa nuts (also called earth almonds or tiger nuts) in water, which is a specialty of the town of Alboraya near Valencia.

1. To make the almond sponge cake, separate the eggs. Beat the egg whites and sugar until stiff, and gradually add the egg yolks, ground almonds, grated lemon peel, and finely chopped candied ginger. Spread the sponge cake mixture onto a tray lined with baking paper and bake for seven minutes at 445 °F / 230 °C.

2. To prepare the lemon cream, bring the lemon juice to a boil with half of the sugar, the butter, and grated lemon peel. Whisk the eggs with the remaining sugar. Combine the two mixtures and continue to cook for 2–3 minutes. Pass through a sieve and allow to cool. To make the lemon syrup, bring the water to a boil with the sugar and juice of half a lemon.

Torte

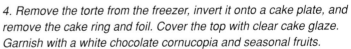

3. Place a cake ring that is 1³/₄ in / 3¹/₂ cm high and 8 in / 18 cm around on a cake round covered with foil, and line it with a 1¹/₂ in / 3 cm-wide strip of sponge cake that has been sprinkled with cocoa powder. Cut out two sponge cake bases. To assemble the torte, pour some of the lemon cream into the cake ring, top it with a sponge cake layer and soak with lemon syrup. Repeat with the remaining cream, sponge cake, and syrup. Freeze for four hours.

4. Remove the torte from the freezer, invert it onto a cake plate, and remove the cake ring and foil. Cover the top with clear cake glaze. Garnish with a white chocolate cornucopia and seasonal fruits.

Preparation time: 1 hour 45 minutes
Cooking time: 20 minutes
Difficulty: ★★

Serves 8

almond sponge cake (see recipe p. 794)

For the Jijona cream:
7 oz / 200 g Jijona nougat
3¹/₂ oz / 100 g milk chocolate coating
1 cup / 250 ml cream
5 sheets of gelatin
2 cups / 500 ml whipping cream

For the caramelized almonds:
¹/₄ cup / 65 g superfine sugar
³/₄ cup plus 2 tbsp / 125 g blanched almonds
1 tbsp / 15 g butter

For the chocolate glaze:
³/₄ cup / 180 ml sugar syrup (30 °Beaumé)
¹/₄ cup / 60 ml glucose syrup
¹/₄ cup / 60 ml cream
¹/₃ cup / 40 g cocoa powder
2 sheets of gelatin

To garnish:
candied cherry leaves
chocolate wafers
chocolate decorations

The town of Jijona, in the province of Alicante, is famed for its raisins and Turrón, a light nougat made with almonds and honey, similar to the Nougat de Montélimar. There is even a *denominación origen*, a government-regulated designation of origins, Turrón de Jijona, which guarantees that only rosemary honey and Marcona almonds (a late-ripening Spanish almond) are used to produce nougat bearing this label.

Marcona almonds should also be used for the caramelized almonds, if possible. They are slowly caramelized once the sugar has turned to caramel, and only then is the butter added. The caramel should remain transparent throughout this process.

The almonds used for the classic almond sponge cake should be lightly roasted. For the sponge cake mixture to have an especially soft texture, you can add a little honey, but it must be heated to 140 °F / 60 °C beforehand. The nougat for the Jijona cream should be passed through a large-meshed sieve so that a few crunchy pieces of nut remain.

The sponge cake also contains cinnamon (for which we can thank the Moors, who ruled Spain in the Middle Ages), though only a very small quantity. For this spice to develop its full flavor, use a cinnamon stick that is grated as needed and then passed through a fine sieve, rather than the powdered form.

1. Prepare the almond sponge cake with cinnamon and lemon according to the recipe on page 794. To make the Jijona cream, pass the Jijona nougat through a large-meshed sieve. Melt the chocolate coating and combine it with the nougat. Bring the cream to a boil and add it to the chocolate-nougat mixture, then the gelatin, which has been soaked in cold water. Allow to cool to 85 °F / 30 °C, then fold in the stiffly whipped cream.

2. For the caramelized almonds, heat the sugar (without liquid) until it melts and caramelizes. Add the blanched almonds and stir to coat them thoroughly, then add the butter. Place the nuts on waxed paper that has been brushed with oil. Retain a few almonds for garnishing the torte, and crush the others.

de Jijona

3. Cover a cake round with plastic and place an 8 in/18 cm cake ring that is 1³/₄ in / 3¹/₂ cm high on it. Cut out two sponge cake bases with the same diameter as the cake ring. Assemble the torte from the top down by alternating two layers of Jijona cream and two sponge cake bases, beginning with the cream. Scatter crushed caramelized almonds on each layer of cream. Freeze for four hours.

4. To make the chocolate glaze, heat the sugar syrup, glucose, cream, and cocoa powder and bring to a boil. Turn off the heat and add the gelatin, which has been soaked in cold water. Cover the torte with the chocolate glaze. Garnish with caramelized almonds, crystallized cherry leaves and fine chocolate rolls, and edge with chocolate wafers.

Basic Recipes

Apple Jelly

Recipe: Cinnamon Torte by Francisco Torreblanca

Ingredients:
5¹/₂ lb / 2¹/₂ kg acidic apples – 4 cups / 1 kg sugar – ³/₄ cup / 200 ml glucose syrup

Method:
Wash the apples and cut them into 6 segments. Put them in a pan and add enough water to cover. Bring to a boil while stirring, and cook until they are tender and falling apart. Strain and press through a cloth to yield about 4 cups / 1 l of juice. Bring the juice to a boil, then add the sugar and glucose. Stirring constantly, reduce to 32 °Beaumé (35 °Beaumé at most). Cool immediately and store in an airtight container.

Apple Sorbet

Recipe: Normandy Delight by Michel Bruneau

Ingredients:
2 apples (Granny Smith) – juice of 1 lemon – freshly ground pepper – 6¹/₂ tbsp/100 ml sugar syrup at 30 °Beaumé (3¹/₂ tbsp/50 g sugar – 3¹/₂ tbsp/50 ml water)

Cooking steps:
Cut the apples into small pieces and place them in the freezer to freeze the skin. Mix with the lemon and pepper in a blender, stir into the syrup and place in an ice cream maker.

Baumkuchen

Recipe: Hansa Torte by Adolf Andersen

Ingredients:
1 cup / 250 g butter – 5 eggs – 1 cup / 250 g sugar – 2 cups / 250 g flour – ¹/₂ vanilla bean – ¹/₄ cup / 35 g chopped roasted almonds – 1 cup / 250 ml rum

Method:
Slowly melt the butter. Meanwhile vigorously beat the eggs and sugar until light yellow. Fold in the flour and mix rapidly. Add the vanilla pulp, almonds, rum, and melted butter. Wrap waxed paper around a cone-shaped wooden roller. Make a wood fire. Fasten the wooden roller onto a spit. Rotate the roller and apply a first layer of batter with a ladle. Bake it by turning the spit constantly, catching any batter that falls off in a bowl. Continue ladling batter onto the roller until it has all been used. Allow the baumkuchen to cool on the spit before removing it.

Biscuit

Recipe: Le Royal by Bernard Proot and Gunther Van Essche

Ingredients:
4 small eggs – ³/₄ cup / 175 g sugar – almond and sugar mixture: ¹/₂ cup plus 2 tbsp / 112 g finely ground almonds and 7¹/₂ tbsp / 112 g sugar – peel of 1 orange – 5 egg whites – 9 tbsp / 75 g flour – ¹/₂ cup plus 1 tbsp / 100 g ground walnuts – 3¹/₂ tbsp / 50 g melted butter

Method:
Whisk the eggs with 3¹/₂ tbsp / 50 g sugar, the almond and sugar mixture and the grated orange peel. In a separate bowl, beat the egg whites and remaining sugar until stiff. Carefully combine both mixtures, then fold in the flour, walnuts, and melted butter. Spread the biscuit mixture onto a tray lined with baking paper and bake for 10 minutes at 355 °F / 180 °C.

Biscuit Natur

Recipe: Lemon-Lime Torte by Eric Baumann

Ingredients:
10 egg yolks – 6¹/₂ tbsp / 100 ml sugar syrup – 5 tbsp / 75 g superfine sugar – 7 egg whites – 3 tbsp / 45 g sugar – 1 cup / 125 g flour

Method:
Whisk the egg yolks with the sugar syrup and superfine sugar. Beat the egg whites and sugar until stiff. Combine the two mixtures; then fold in the sifted flour with a wooden spatula. Spread the sponge cake mixture onto a tray lined with baking paper or in a cake pan and bake for 20 minutes at 430 °F / 220 °C.

Biscuit Spécial

Recipe: Caramel Torte à la Baumann by Eric Baumann

Ingredients:
²/₃ cup plus 2 tbsp / 150 g very finely ground almonds – 1 cup / 150 g confectioners' sugar – ¹/₃ cup / 40 g flour – 4 eggs – 2 tbsp / 30 g butter – 4 egg whites – 4 tsp / 20 g sugar

Method:
Whisk the ground almonds, confectioners' sugar, and flour with half of the eggs. Gradually add the remaining eggs and then the melted butter. Beat the egg whites and sugar until stiff. Carefully combine both mixtures with a wooden spatula. Spread half the sponge mixture onto baking paper and make a pattern with a cake comb; color the other half as desired and proceed as for a striped Joconde sponge cake.

Brioche dough

Recipe: Russian salmon koulibiac by Michel Bourdin

Ingredients:
2 lbs 10 oz / 1.2 kg all-purpose flour – 1¹⁄₂ oz / 40 g sugar – 1 oz / 24 g salt – 10 eggs – 1¹⁄₂ oz / 40 g fresh yeast – ¹⁄₃ cup plus 1¹⁄₂ tbsp / 100 ml milk – 2¹⁄₂ cups / 600 g butter (at room temperature).

Preparation:
Dissolve the yeast in the cold milk. Place the flour, salt, sugar and milk in a mixing bowl, together with the yeast and eggs. Using a dough hook attachment, knead for 10 minutes at medium speed. As soon as the dough is supple and smooth, quickly mix in egg-sized pieces of the softened butter. Knead thoroughly. Turn the dough out into a bowl in which it has room to rise. Cover with a cloth, and allow to rest at room temperature for about 1¹⁄₂ hours. Punch down the dough and refrigerate overnight.

Buttercream

Recipe: L'Ambassadeur by Maurice and Jean-Jacques Bernachons; Grand Marnier Torte by Maurice and Jean-Jacques Bernachons; Wedding Cake with Fresh Fruits by Christian Nihoul

Ingredients:
5 eggs – ³⁄₄ cup plus 1 tbsp / 200 g superfine sugar – a pinch of salt – 2 cups / 500 g butter

Method:
Whisk the eggs, sugar, and salt in a double boiler until frothy. Once they have reached body temperature, remove from the heat and allow to cool while stirring. Cream the butter until it is creamy and white, then gradually add the egg and sugar mixture.

Caracas Sponge Cake

Recipe: Hansa Torte by Adolf Andersen

Ingredients:
2 tbsp / 30 g butter – 3 tbsp flour – 1 oz / 30 g nougat – 1 / 2 cup / 30 g sponge cake crumbs – 3 egg yolks – 1¹⁄₄ oz / 35 g marzipan – 4 tsp / 20 g sugar – a pinch of salt – 4 egg whites – 5 tbsp / 75 g superfine sugar

Method:
Melt the butter and let it cool again. Whisk the egg yolks until frothy with the marzipan, sugar and salt. Beat the egg whites and superfine sugar until stiff. Combine a third of the beaten egg whites with the egg yolk mixture, then fold in the remaining egg whites with a wooden spatula. Fold in the flour, sponge cake crumbs, nougat and finally the melted butter, not stirring longer than necessary. Pour the sponge cake batter into a greased and floured cake pan that has been lined with waxed paper. Bake for 12–15 minutes at 340 °F / 170 °C. Invert onto a cooling rack to cool.

Charlotte Cream

Recipe: Kiwi Torte with Passion Fruit Cream by Eric Baumann

Ingredients:
2 cups / 500 ml milk – ³⁄₄ cup / 180 g sugar – 15 egg yolks – 6¹⁄₂ sheets of gelatin

Method:
Bring the milk to a boil with the sugar. Whisk the egg yolks vigorously, then add them to the milk and thicken while reducing the temperature (to about 180 °F / 82 °C). Fold in the gelatin, which has previously been soaked in cold water. Refrigerate.

Choux Pastry

Recipe: Saint-Honoré by Christian Cottard

Ingredients:
1 cup / 250 ml milk – 6¹⁄₂ tbsp / 100 g butter – 1 tsp / 5 g salt – 1 tsp / 5 g sugar – 1¹⁄₄ cups / 150 g flour – 5 eggs

Method:
Combine the milk, salt, sugar, and small pieces of butter in a saucepan and bring to a boil. Once the butter has melted, add the flour and beat vigorously with a wooden spatula over low heat until the dough is smooth. Continue stirring for 1–2 minutes until the dough separates from the sides of the pan. Once it comes off the spatula easily, remove from the heat. Add the eggs one by one, stirring each one in thoroughly.

Cigarette Batter

Recipes: Lemon Tart by Eric Baumann

Ingredients:
²⁄₃ cup / 160 g butter – 1 cup / 160 g confectioners' sugar – 5 egg whites – 1¹⁄₄ cups / 160 g flour

Method:
Cream the butter, then add the confectioners' sugar and half of the egg whites, followed by half of the flour, whisking continuously. Stir in the remaining egg white and flour.
For chocolate cigarette batter, replace a portion of the flour with cocoa powder; for colored cigarette batter, add food coloring as desired.

Cigarette Pastry

Recipe: Nougat Parfait by Stéphane Raimbault

Ingredients:
13 tbsp / 200 g butter – 1¹⁄₃ cups / 200 g confectioners' sugar – 7 egg whites – 1¹⁄₄ cups / 150 g flour – 1 tsp / 5 ml vanilla extract – 2 tbsp / 20 g pistachios – 1 tbsp / 20 g raisins – ¹⁄₄ cup / 20 g shredded coconut – 2 tbsp / 20 g almonds – 3 tbsp / 20 g flaked almonds

Cooking steps:
Beat the butter until fluffy, then add the confectioners' sugar and in rapid succession the egg whites, flour, and vanilla extract. Spread the mixture evenly onto a non-stick baking tray using a round spatula. Sprinkle it with the pistachios, raisins, shredded coconut, almonds and flaked almonds. Bake for a few minutes at 355 °F/180 °C.

Clear Cake Glaze

Recipes: Caramel Torte à la Baumann and Kiwi Torte with Passion Fruit Cream by Eric Baumann; Roussillon Torte by Christian Cottard; Bavaroise with Tea and Chocolate and White Wine Duchess by Lucas Devriese; Coffee and Caramel Torte and Lemon Torte by Francisco Torreblanca; Almond Cake by Flacio Perbellini

Ingredients:
1³/₄ cups / 450 ml water – 1 cup / 225 ml glucose syrup – ¹/₂ oz / 12 g citric acid – ¹/₂ oz / 12 g pectin – 2¹/₂ cups / 570 g superfine sugar

Method:
Bring the water to a boil with the glucose syrup and citric acid. Remove from the heat and add the pectin and part of the sugar. Allow to cool slightly, then gradually add the remaining sugar, stirring until completely dissolved. Refrigerate until needed.

Coconut and curry sauce

Recipe: Pork tenderloin with coconut and curry sauce by Philippe Groult

Ingredients:
¹/₂ onion – ¹/₂ apple – ¹/₂ banana – 1 coconut – ¹/₃ cup plus 1¹/₂ tbsp / 100 ml chicken stock – 1 tbsp / 15 g Madras curry powder – 3¹/₂ tbsp / 50 ml olive oil – ¹/₄ cup / 60 g butter – salt and pepper

Preparation:
Heat oil in a saucepan, and braise onion, apple and banana in it. Add curry powder. Mix the coconut milk with the chicken stock and boil for 5 minutes. Purée all ingredients in a blender, then strain and stir in butter. Season to taste.

Crème Anglaise

Recipes: Vanilla Kipferl by Franz Augustin

Ingredients:
2 cups / 500 ml milk – ¹/₂ cup plus 2 tbsp / 150 g sugar – 1 vanilla bean – 6 egg yolks

Method:
Bring the milk to a boil with half of the sugar and the slit vanilla bean. Beat the egg yolks and remaining sugar in a bowl until the mixture is light yellow. Stir a little hot milk into the egg yolks, then pour everything into the saucepan and stir with a wooden spoon over low heat. Do not allow to boil! Remove from the heat, and stir continuously until completely cooled. Pass through a sieve.

Crêpe batter

Recipe: Russian salmon koulibiac by Michel Bourdin

Ingredients:
3¹/₂ oz / 100 g all-purpose flour – 2 eggs – 1 cup / 250 ml milk – pinch of salt – 3¹/₂ tbsp / 50 g butter – small bunch of chives

Preparation:
Sieve the flour into a bowl with the pinch of salt. Beat in the whole eggs with a whisk, followed by the milk, a little at a time, until you have a smooth batter. Melt the butter in a crêpe pan and remove from the heat as soon as it turns nut brown in color. Pour the butter into the batter, whisking constantly. Strain. Let stand for 20 minutes before making the crêpes.

Custard

Recipes: Chocolate Variations by Michel Blanchet; Sweet Chestnut Dessert by Georges Paineau

Ingredients:
2 cups / 500 ml milk – 1 vanilla bean – 6 egg yolks – ¹/₂ cup plus 2 tbsp / 150 g sugar

Cooking steps:
Bring the milk to a boil with half of the sugar and the vanilla bean, which has been cut open lengthwise. Thoroughly whisk the egg yolks and remaining sugar until foamy. Add a little hot milk to the egg yolks, then pour everything into the pan with the milk and stir constantly with a wooden spatula or spoon until the desired consistency is reached. Do not allow to boil! Remove from the heat and continue to stir until completely cooled. Pass the custard through a pointed sieve.

Duchess Sponge Cake

Recipes: White Wine Duchess and Montblanc by Lucas Devriese; Passion Fruit Torte, Strawberry and Rhubarb Torte by Bernard Proot and Gunther Van Essche

Ingredients:
4 eggs – 6¹/₂ tbsp / 100 g sugar – ³/₄ cup / 100 g flour – almond and sugar mixture: 1 tbsp / 10 g finely ground almonds and 2 tsp / 10 g sugar

Method:
Beat the egg whites and sugar until stiff. Carefully fold in the sifted flour and almond and sugar mixture. For a 18 x 27 in / 40 x 60 cm baking tray, 600 g of sponge cake mixture is needed. Bake for 6 minutes at 480 °F / 250 °C.

Ganache

Recipe: Bûche de Noël by Maurice and Jean-Jacques Bernachon

Ingredients:
10¹/₂ oz / 300 g cooking or bittersweet chocolate – 1 cup / 250 ml crème fraîche

Method:
Pour the crème fraîche into a saucepan with a thick bottom. Boil for one minute over high heat while stirring with a whisk. Remove from the heat. Break the chocolate into small pieces and add to the hot crème fraîche. Beat the mixture as it cools until it is smooth and homogeneous. Cover and refrigerate for at least 12 hours.

Génoise

Recipe: Duck's Liver Tart with a Confit of Grapes by Dieter Kaufmann

Ingredients:
8 eggs – 1 cup / 250 g sugar – 1 cup / 250 g flour

Preparation:
Whisk eggs and sugar in a bowl in a bain-marie, heating all the while until room temperature. Remove from the heat, continue whisking rigorously at first, then whisk slower until the mixture has cooled. Fold in the flour carefully with a spoon. Fill into buttered and floured spring forms and bake for 30 minutes at 400 °F / 200 °C.

Recipes: Caramel Torte à la Baumann, Zug Cherry Torte and Kiwi Torte with Passion Fruit Cream by Eric Baumann

Ingredients:
6 eggs – 5 egg yolks – 1 cup plus 1 tbsp / 260 g sugar – 2 cups plus 2 tbsp / 260 g flour – ¹/₂ cup/120 g butter

Method:
Beat the eggs, egg yolks and sugar in a double boiler (at 100 °F / 37 °C) until the mixture falls from the whisk or beater in long ribbons. Using a wooden spatula, fold in the sifted flour, and finally add the melted butter. Bake for 20 minutes at 340 °F / 170 °C.

Recipes: Le Canotier by Christian Cottard; Tiramisu Bianco, Almond Cake and Zuppa Inglese by Flavio Perbellini

Ingredients:
4 eggs – ¹/₂ cup / 125 g sugar – 1 cup / 125 g flour

Method:
In a double boiler over lukewarm water, beat the eggs and sugar at a high speed until foamy, then remove from the heat and continue at medium speed until the mixture has cooled and falls from the beaters in long ribbons. Carefully fold in the sifted flour with a skimmer. Pour the génoise batter into a greased and floured cake pan and bake for 30 minutes at 390 °F / 200 °C.

Note: for Le Canotier, replace 5 tsp / 25 g of the sugar with 1 tbsp / 25 g honey and a little ground vanilla.

Hollandaise Sauce

Recipe: Black Salsify with Fresh Walnuts by Philippe Groult

Ingredients:
scant ⁷/₈ cup / 200 g butter – 4 egg yolks – 4 tbs water – salt – pepper – 1 pinch of cayenne pepper – 4 dashes of almond milk

Preparation:
Melt the butter in a saucepan. In a different saucepan, whip egg yolks and water over a low heat until frothy. Remove from the stove and gradually stir in the melted butter. Season with salt, pepper, and cayenne pepper; add four dashes of almond milk.

Italian Meringue

Recipes: La Paillote Coco-Créole, Roussillon Torte and Saint-Honoré by Christian Cottard; Puff Pastry Torte with Chiboust Cream and Apples by Lucas Devriese; Zuppa Inglese by Flavio Perbellini; Passion Fruit Torte, Strawberry and Rhubarb Torte by Bernard Proot and Gunther van Essche

Ingredients:
2 cups / 500 g superfine sugar – 1 cup / 250 ml water – 8 egg whites

Method:
In a copper pan, combine the sugar and water and heat to 250 °F / 121 °C. Meanwhile, in a mixer beat the egg whites until stiff, then slowly pour the boiling sugar syrup between the beaters and the side of the bowl while stirring continuously. Beat for three minutes at high speed, then at medium speed until completely cooled.

Japonaise Sponge Cake

Recipe: Zug Cherry Torte by Eric Baumann

Ingredients:
8 egg whites – ³/₄ cup plus 3 tbsp / 225 g superfine sugar – ¹/₄ cup / 35 g flour – 1¹/₄ cups / 190 g very finely ground hazelnuts

Method:
Beat the egg whites and sugar until stiff. Sift the flour with the ground hazelnuts and use a wooden spatula to carefully fold them into the beaten egg whites. Bake the sponge cake mixture for 10 minutes at 300 °F / 150 °C.

Lobster soup

Recipe: Lobster Gazpacho by Michel Haquin

Ingredients:
2 lobsters, 1 lb / 500 g each – 1 carrot – 1 onion – ¹/₂ cup / 100 ml dry white wine – 2 tbsp / 30 ml cognac – 1 bouquet garni with extra parsley – 1 sprig of thyme – half a bay leaf – pepper and salt – ¹/₄ cup / 50 ml vegetable oil – 1¹/₄ cup / 300 ml veal or fish broth – 1 tbsp / 15 g concentrated tomato paste – ¹/₂ cup / 20 ml cream – ¹/₂ cup / 20 g rice

Preparation:
Separate lobster heads and tails, split the heads lengthwise. Remove sand and place coral in a bowl. Chop carrot and onion and sweat in olive oil. Add lobster meat and cook until the meat has been cooked well and the shell has turned red. Add tomato paste, cognac and white wine and reduce. Cover with broth, bring to a boil and simmer for ten minutes. Remove the lobster. Crush the lobster heads with a mortar and pestle, transfer to the cooking liquid and mix with the cream, the rice (which has been soaked in ¹/₂ cup / 125 ml of cold broth) and the coral. Cook for ten minutes, strain through a fine-meshed sieve and adjust seasoning to taste.

Marzipan Mixture

Recipe: Riesling Fairy Tale by Adolf Andersen

Ingredients:
1 lb / 450 g marzipan – 3 egg yolks – ¹/₂ cup plus 1 tbsp / 90 g confectioners' sugar – grated peel and juice of 1 untreated lemon – a pinch of salt

Method:
Stir the marzipan and egg yolks until smooth. Sift the confectioners' sugar with the lemon peel, then add it to the marzipan with the lemon juice and salt. Combine everything thoroughly.

Mayonnaise

Recipes: Artichoke and Lobster Layers in a Green Sauce by Michel Blanchet; Schrimps and Cooked Dill-vegetables by Erwin Lauterbach

Ingredients (to yield 1¹/₂ cups / 300 g mayonnaise):
2 egg yolks –1 cup / 250 ml peanut oil – 1 tbsp / 15 ml white vinegar – ¹/₂ tbsp / 5 g salt – ground white pepper – 1 tbsp / 5 g mustard

Preparation:
Mix egg yolks, mustard, salt, and pepper in a bowl. Whisking constantly, add oil in a very thin stream. Stir in the vinegar and season to taste.

Meringue

Recipes: Nougat Parfait by Stéphane Raimbault; Puff Pastry with Creamy Rice Pudding by Hilario Arbelaitz

Ingredients:
4¹/₂ tbsp / 100 g pine honey – 1 tbsp / 25 g glucose – ¹/₂ cup / 120 ml water – 3¹/₂ tbsp / 50 g sugar – 4 egg whites – a pinch / 2 g gelatin

Cooking steps:
Place the honey, glucose, water and sugar in a small pan. Reduce at 250 °F/121 °C. Beat the egg whites until stiff, then pour the hot syrup onto them. Beat with an electric mixer at high speed for 4 minutes, then at medium speed until the mixture has completely cooled. Stir in the dissolved gelatin.

Pancake Batter

Recipe: Pancake Ravioli with "Suzette" Orange Butter by Philippe Dorange

Ingredients:
2 cups / 250 g flour – ¹/₃ cup / 80 g sugar – 1 large pinch of salt – 4 eggs – 2 cups / 500 ml milk – 6¹/₂ tbsp / 100 g butter

Cooking steps:
Combine the sifted flour, sugar and salt in a bowl. Stir in the eggs with a whisk and gradually add the milk in order to produce a smooth mixture. Melt the butter in a pan, and once it is brown remove from the heat and add to the batter while stirring. Pass through a pointed sieve. Allow the batter to rest for half an hour before cooking the pancakes.

Pastry Cream

Recipe: "Chocolat-Café" with Walnuts by Louis Grondard

Recipe: Mocha Charlotte with Ice Cream and Nuts by André Jaeger

Recipe: Fruit Gratin with Almonds by Jean Fleury

Ingredients:
4 cups / 1 l milk – 1 vanilla bean (optional) – 10 egg yolks – ³/₄ cup / 200 g sugar – ¹/₂ cup plus 2 tbsp / 80 g cornstarch

Cooking steps:
Bring the milk to boil in a large pan with the vanilla bean, which has been slit lengthwise. In a bowl, beat the egg yolks and sugar until creamy. Add the cornstarch. While stirring, pour the boiling milk onto the egg yolks, then pour everything back into the pan and simmer for 2 minutes while stirring continuously. Make sure the cream does not burn! Pour into a bowl and top with a little butter to prevent a crust from forming.

Recipe: Bûche de Noël and L'Ambassadeur by Maurice and Jean-Jacques Bernachon

Ingredients:
2¹/₂ cups / 600 ml milk – a pinch of salt – 1 vanilla bean – 4 egg yolks – ¹/₂ cup plus 2 tbsp / 150 g superfine sugar – 6¹/₂ tbsp / 50 g flour

Method:

In a saucepan, bring 2 cups / 500 ml of milk to a boil with the salt and vanilla bean, which has been slit lengthwise. Boil for 2 minutes. Vigorously beat the egg yolks and sugar in a bowl. Add the flour, then 6½ tbsp / 100 ml cold milk so that no lumps form. While stirring, pour the boiled milk onto the egg yolk mixture, then pour everything back into the pan and boil for 3 minutes, stirring constantly with a whisk. Allow to cool and refrigerate.

Recipes: Puff Pastry Torte with a Woven Lid and Saint-Honoré by Christian Cottard; Dulcinéa Torte by Francisco Torreblanca

Ingredients:

1 cup / 250 ml milk – 1 vanilla bean – 3 egg yolks – ¼ cup / 65 g superfine sugar – 4 tsp / 10 g flour – 2½ tbsp / 15 g pudding powder – (5 tsp / 25 g butter)

Method:

In a large saucepan, bring the milk to a boil with the vanilla bean, which has been slit lengthwise. Beat the egg yolks and sugar in a bowl until the mixture is light yellow. Sift the flour and pudding powder together, then add to the egg yolks. Stir in the boiling milk. Pour everything into the saucepan and boil for 2 minutes, stirring constantly so the cream does not stick to the bottom of the pan. (When the cream has cooled to 120–130 °F / 50–55 °C, add the butter.)

Note: add the butter to the pastry cream for Christian Cottard's recipes.

Recipes: Almond Cake and Zuppa Inglese by Flavio Perbellini

Ingredients:

1¼ cups / 300 ml milk – 3 egg yolks – 6½ tsp / 95 g sugar – ⅓ cup / 40 g flour – 5 tsp / 13 g cornstarch – confectioners' sugar

Method:

Bring the milk to a boil. Beat the egg yolks and sugar until light yellow. Sift the flour and cornstarch together, then add to the egg yolks. Stir in the boiling milk. Pour everything into the saucepan and boil for 2 minutes, stirring constantly so the cream does not stick to the bottom of the pan. Pour it into a bowl and dust with confectioners' sugar so that no crust forms.

Puff pastry

Recipes: Squab and foie gras tourte with truffles by Michel Haquin; Puff Pastry Tart with Tuna, Tomatoes and Basil by Dominique Le Stanc; Oxtail Soup with Puff Pastry Hat by Roger Jaloux; Normandy Delight by Michel Bruneau; Puff Pastry with Creamy Rice Pudding by Hilario Arbelaitz; Delicate Apple Cake with Tarragon Sorbet by Jean Crotet; Puff Pastry Pouches with Mamia and Sagardoz by Pedro Subijana; Puff Pastry Torte with a Woven Lid and Saint-Honoré by Christian Cottard; Pithiviers Torte, Orange and Almond Cream Tart by Philippe Guignard

Ingredients:

4 cups / 500 g flour – 1 tbsp / 15 g salt – 1 cup / 250 ml water
For turning: 2 cups / 500 g butter

Method:

Sift the flour onto a work surface and make a well in the center. Put the salt and water in it and combine with the flour to make a ball of dough without kneading excessively. Allow to rest in the refrigerator for 20 minutes, then on a marble slab roll out the dough into a narrow rectangle. Place the butter in the middle and fold the dough in thirds over the butter to form a square. Immediately, and gently, roll out to form a long strip of dough, without pressing the butter out at the edges. Fold the ends of the strip in to meet at the center, then fold the dough in half and refrigerate for 20 minutes.

Turning (folding and rolling out): Turn six times (three times two turns) at 20-minute intervals, refrigerating the dough in between.

Recipe: Puff Pastry Torte with Chiboust Cream and Apples by Lucas Devriese

Ingredients:

4⅓ cups / 540 g flour – 1 tbsp / 13 g salt – ¾ cup / 200 ml water
For turning: 13 tbsp / 200 g butter

Method:

See above.

Quince Sorbet

Recipe: Quince Sorbet with Rhubarb Compote by Jean-Louis Neichel

Ingredients:
1 lb / 500 g fresh quinces – water – 1 tsp rosemary, freshly chopped – 2 cups / 500 g sugar – 1 untreated lemon – 1 small glass of quince liqueur

Cooking steps:
Peel the quinces, cut them into pieces and place in a pan. Cover with water and cook for 15 minutes over low heat with the rosemary, sugar, quince liqueur, lemon juice and a piece of lemon peel. Allow to cool, stir again in a blender, and then freeze.

Sacher Sponge Cake

Recipes: Hansa Torte and Sacher Torte by Adolf Andersen

Ingredients:
9 tbsp / 140 g butter – 8 tsp / 40 g superfine sugar – a pinch of salt – pulp of ¹/₂ vanilla bean – 4 egg yolks – 6 oz / 175 g bittersweet chocolate coating, melted – 3 egg whites – ¹/₃ cup / 80 g sugar – ¹/₂ cup plus 1 tbsp / 70 g flour

Method:
Cream the butter with the superfine sugar, salt, and vanilla until fluffy and light. Blend in the egg yolks and the melted and cooled chocolate coating. In a separate bowl, beat the egg whites and sugar until stiff. Add a third to the butter mixture, then fold in the remaining beaten egg whites and the flour.

Sauce américaine

Recipes: Light pike quenelles by Christian Bouvarel; Stuffed velvet swimming crabs with dried tomatoes by Jaques Cagna; Spiny lobster with olives by Jacques Chibois

Ingredients:
2 lobsters (generous 1 lb / 500 g each), 1 carrot, 1 onion, ¹/₃ cup plus 1¹/₂ tbsp / 100 ml dry white wine, 2 tbsp cognac, 3¹/₂ tbsp / 50 ml oil, 2 cups / 500 ml veal or fish stock, 4 tomatoes, 1 tbsp tomato paste, 1 bouquet garni (parsley, thyme, bay leaf, chervil, tarragon), salt, cayenne pepper, 10 tbsp / 150 g butter.

Preparation:
Sever the lobster heads from the tails. Halve the heads lengthwise, and remove and discard the dark intestine running down the body, as well as the stomach that is located at the top of the head. Place the coral in a bowl and mix with 3¹/₂ tbsp / 50 g butter. Finely dice the onion and carrot. Heat the oil in a braising pan to very hot, then put in the lobster pieces and sauté until the shell turns bright red. Add the cognac, the white wine, the tomatoes, peeled, cored and chopped, the bouquet garni, the tomato paste and 2 cups / 500 ml veal or fish stock. Cover the pan and cook for about 20 minutes. Remove the lobster and bind the sauce with the coral butter. Bring to a boil and season with salt and cayenne pepper. Pass through a fine sieve and whisk in 6¹/₂ tbsp / 100 g butter to finish.

Shortbread

Recipe: La Dulcinéa by Francisco Torreblanca

Ingredients:
4 cups / 500 g flour – 1 cup / 250 g butter – 1 tsp / 5 g salt – ³/₄ cup plus 2 tbsp / 125 g confectioners' sugar – ¹/₂ tsp / 2 g emulsifier

Method:
Sift the flour onto a work surface and make a well in the middle. Place the softened butter and the other ingredients into it and knead everything together thoroughly. Refrigerate the dough until needed.

Short Pastry

Recipes: Riesling Fairy Tale, Raspberry Cream Torte by Adolf Andersen

Ingredients:
1 egg yolks – 3 tbsp / 30 g confectioners' sugar – a pinch of salt – ¹/₄ cup / 60 g butter – pulp of ¹/₂ vanilla bean – ³/₄ cup / 90 g flour

Method:
Using the kneading attachment of a mixer, combine all the ingredients except the flour to produce a smooth dough. Gradually add the flour, and knead thoroughly. Wrap the pastry in a cloth and refrigerate until the next day, so that it is easier to work with.

Simple Génoise

Recipes: L'Ambassadeur, Bûche de Noël, Strawberry Torte and Grand Marnier Torte by Maurice and Jean-Jacques Bernachon

Ingredients:
3 eggs – 6 tbsp / 90 g superfine sugar – ³/₄ cup / 90 g flour – 2 tbsp / 30 g butter

Method:
Warm the eggs and sugar in a bowl over a double boiler, then whisk. Remove from the double boiler and continue beating with a mixer until the mixture is light yellow and falls from the beaters in long ribbons. Use a wooden spatula to fold in the flour, then add the hot melted butter. Butter and flour a baking sheet with a high rim, and spread the sponge cake mixture on it 1¹/₂ in / 2–3 cm thick, smoothing the top with a spatula. Bake for 10 minutes at 430 °F / 220 °C in a preheated oven. Make a day in advance.

Spice Cookies

Recipe: Quince Sorbet with Rhubarb Compote by Jean-Louis Neichel

Ingredients:
³/₄ cup / 100 g flaked almonds – ³/₄ cup / 100 g sugar – 3 tbsp / 20 g flour – 2 eggs – spices to taste

Cooking steps:
Mix the almonds, sugar, flour, eggs and spices in a bowl. Allow to rest and infuse for about 2 hours. Spoon the batter onto a greased tray and bake at 465 °F / 240 °C.

Sponge Cake Dough

Recipes: Cassata alla Siciliana by Carlo Brovelli; Caramel Feast by Jean-Pierre Vigato

Ingredients:
1 cup / 250 g sugar – 8 eggs – 2 cups / 250 g flour

Cooking steps:
Whisk the sugar and eggs until foamy over low heat in the top of a double boiler. Remove from the heat when lukewarm. Beat at high speed with an electric mixer. Reduce the speed and continue to stir the mixture as it cools and thickens. Using a skimmer, carefully fold in the sifted flour. Turn into a greased and floured cake pan and bake for about 30 minutes at 390 °F / 200 °C.

Striped Joconde Sponge Cake

Recipes: Bavaroise with Tea and Chocolate by Lucas Devriese; Sweet Chestnut Tarte by Christian Nihoul; Passion Fruit Torte and Strawberry and Rhubarb Torte by Bernard Proot and Gunther Van Essche

Ingredients:
4 small eggs – ¹/₂ cup / 125 g superfine sugar – almond and sugar mixture: ¹/₂ cup plus 2 tbsp / 112 g finely ground almonds and 7¹/₂ tbsp / 112 g sugar – grated peel of 1 orange – 6 egg whites – 3¹/₂ tbsp / 50 g sugar – 9 tbsp / 75 g flour – 3¹/₂ tbsp / 50 g butter

Method:
Beat the eggs with the superfine sugar, almond and sugar mixture and grated orange peel until foamy. Separately, beat the egg whites and sugar until stiff. Combine the two whipped egg mixtures, then carefully fold in the flour and melted butter.

Passion Fruit Torte and Strawberry and Rhubarb Torte: *Use half of the sponge cake batter to spread a thin layer onto a tray lined with baking paper. Draw stripes in it with a cake comb and freeze until set. Flavor and color the remaining batter with strawberry or raspberry jelly and spread it thinly over the frozen sponge cake. Bake for 5 minutes at 390 °F / 200 °C.*

Bavaroise with Tea and Chocolate and Sweet Chestnut Tarte: *Make chocolate Joconde sponge cake by replacing one-third or more of the flour with cocoa powder, then proceed as above.*

Sweet Pastry

Recipe: Le Canotier by Christian Cottard

Ingredients:
1 cup / 250 g butter – 1 cup / 150 g confectioners' sugar – 2 eggs – 2 tbsp / 30 ml crème fraîche – 1¹/₂ tsp / 8 g salt – grated peel of ¹/₂ lemon – 4 cups / 500 g flour – 1³/₄ tsp / 10 g baking powder

Method:
Knead the soft butter with the confectioners' sugar. Add the eggs, crème fraîche, salt, grated lemon peel, and, finally, the flour sifted with the baking powder (if using American double-acting baking powder, use one-third less). Shape the dough into a ball and refrigerate.

Syrup for Soaking

Recipes: L'Ambassadeur, Strawberry Torte, Grand Marnier Torte by Maurice and Jean-Jaques Bernachon

Ingredients:
6¹/₂ tbsp / 100 g superfine sugar – 6¹/₂ tbsp / 100 ml water – 6¹/₂ tbsp / 100 ml liqueur, or fruit puree, depending on recipe

Method:
Boil the water and sugar to make a sugar syrup; cool, then add the liqueur or fruit puree. See individual recipes for exact proportions and ingredients.

Tapenade

Recipe: Roast lamb with tapenade by Laurent Tarridec

Ingredients:
1 oz / 35 g pitted olives – 1 anchovy fillet – 1 finely chopped shallot – a few capers – pepper

Preparation:
Mix all ingredients and finely chop in the food processor.

Vanilla Cream

Recipes: Pithiviers Torte and Orange and Almond Cream Tart by Philippe Guignard

Ingredients:
2 cups / 500 ml milk – 6¹/₂ tbsp / 100 g sugar – 1 vanilla bean – ¹/₂ cup / 55 g cream powder – 1 egg yolk

Method:
Bring the milk to a boil with the sugar and slit vanilla bean. Mix the cream powder and egg yolk. Stir in a little hot milk, pour everything back into the saucepan and bring to a boil. Pour into a bowl and cover with foil until needed.

Vanilla Ice Cream

Recipes: Mocha Charlotte with Ice Cream and Nuts by André Jaeger; Rhubarb Soup "Bagatelle" by Eyvind Hellstrøm

Ingredients:
2 cups / 500 ml milk – ¹/₂ cup plus 2 tbsp / 150 g sugar – 1 vanilla bean, slit lengthwise – 6 egg yolks – 1 cup / 250 ml crème fraîche

Cooking steps:
Combine the milk, half of the sugar and the vanilla bean and bring to a rolling boil. In a bowl, beat the egg yolks and the remaining sugar until creamy. Pour a little hot milk onto the eggs, then return to the pan with the hot milk and continue to cook while stirring continuously with a wooden spatula or spoon. Do not allow to boil! Remove from the heat and continue to stir until completely cooled, then pass through a pointed sieve. Stir in the crème fraîche and place in an ice cream machine to harden.

Viennese Sponge Cake

Recipes: Riesling Fairy Tale, Raspberry Cream Torte by Adolf Andersen

Ingredients:
3¹/₂ tbsp / 50 g butter – 5 eggs – ³/₄ cup / 180 g sugar – a pinch of salt – ³/₄ cup / 100 g flour – ³/₄ cup plus 2 tbsp / 110 g wheat starch

Method:
Melt the butter and allow it to cool again. Beat the eggs, sugar, and salt in a double boiler over low heat until the mixture is frothy and at body temperature (about 95 °F / 36 °C). Remove from the heat and stir constantly until completely cooled. Carefully fold in the flour and wheat starch, then the melted butter. Grease a round 11 in / 24 cm cake pan with butter and line the bottom with baking paper. Pour in the sponge cake batter and bake for 30 minutes at 340 °F / 170 °C. Allow to cool in the cake pan for several hours.

White Champagne Sauce

Recipe: Leipziger Medley with Vegetables by Lothar Eiermann

Ingredients:
scant ⁷/₈ cup / 200 ml veal sweetbread stock – 4 tsp / 20 ml Noilly Prat (vermouth) – 2 tbs / 30 ml champagne – 1 shallot – 4 tsp / 20 g butter – half a bay leaf – salt, pepper – two white peppercorns, crushed – 1 lemon – generous ³/₈ cup / 100 ml crème fraîche – generous ³/₈ cup / 100 ml cream

Preparation:
Reduce the fish stock with the chopped shallot, bay leaf, and salt to half its volume, add the cream and reduce again. Pass through a fine sieve and add vermouth. Bring to a boil again, add crème fraîche, butter, and finally, the champagne. Season to taste.

White Chocolate Ganache

Recipe: Le Royal by Bernard Proot and Gunther van Essche

Ingredients:
4¹/₂ tbsp / 70 ml cream – 4¹/₂ tbsp / 70 ml milk – 5 tbsp / 75 ml glucose syrup – 1 lb 2¹/₂ oz / 525 g white chocolate – 9 tbsp / 135 g butter

Method:
Bring the cream to a boil with the milk and glucose syrup. Remove from the heat and add the white chocolate broken into small pieces and the butter. Mix thoroughly. Allow to cool.

The Chefs

Fernando Adría

born May 14, 1962

Restaurant: **El Bulli**
Address: 30, Apartado de Correos Cala
Montjoi 17480 Rosas, Spain

As a young, talented 21-year-old back in 1983, Fernando Adrìa received two Michelin stars for his culinary achievements in El Bulli, his restaurant on the Costa Brava whose kitchens had previously been run by his friend Jean-Louis Neichel. Awarded 19 points and four red chef's hats by Gault-Millau, Adrìa has also fared well with the Spanish restaurant guides: four stars in Campsa and 9.5/10 in Gourmetour. A winner of the "Spanish national gastronomy award", Fernando Adrìa also received the "European culinary grand prix" in 1994. When his work leaves him time, this chef is a great supporter of the Barcelona soccer team.

Hilario Arbelaitz

born May 27, 1951

Restaurant: **Zuberoa**
Address: Barrio Iturrioz, 8
20180 Oyarzun, Spain

Born in the heart of the Spanish Basque Country, whose gourmet traditions form the emphasis of his cooking, Hilario Arbelaitz began his career in 1970 at Zuberoa, where he became chef in 1982. Since then, he has received numerous French and Spanish awards: two Michelin stars and three red chef's hats and 17 points in Gault-Millau, as well as four Campsa stars. In 1993 he was named "Best Chef in Euzkadi" (the Basque Country), after being named "Best Chef in Spain" in 1991. He brings equal measures of enthusiasm to the Basque game of pelota and family life, and is very interested in the history and future of his profession.

Firmin Arrambide

born September 16, 1946

Restaurant: **Les Pyrénées**
Address: 19, place du Général de Gaulle
64220 Saint-Jean-Pied-de-Port, France

Firmin Arrambide has been at the helm of this restaurant not far from his place of birth since 1986, garnering two Michelin stars and three red chef's hats and 18 points in Gault-Millau for Les Pyrénées. His regionally inspired cuisine won him second place in the 1978 Taittinger awards and carried him to the finals of the Meilleur Ouvrier de France competition in 1982. True to his Basque origins, Arrambide hunts woodpigeon and woodsnipe in the fall, and also loves mountain climbing; occasionally, though, he enjoys simply soaking up the sun by the side of the swimming pool.

Jean Bardet

born September 27, 1941

Restaurant: **Jean Bardet**
Address: 57, rue Groison
37000 Tours, France

Before opening a restaurant in Tours under his own name in 1987, Jean Bardet traversed the whole of Europe, working mainly as a sauce chef at the Savoy in London. A member of Relais et Châteaux, Relais Gourmands and the Auguste Escoffier Foundation, he was awarded four red chef's hats in Gault-Millau (19.5) and two Michelin stars. In 1982 he had the honor of preparing dinner for the heads of state at the Versailles Summit. Jean Bardet is an enthusiastic cigar smoker (American Express awarded him the title of "Greatest Smoker in the World" in 1984) and in the fall indulges his passion for hunting together with friends.

Giuseppina Beglia

born May 16, 1938

Restaurant: **Balzi Rossi**
Address: 2, Via Balzi Rossi
18039 Ventimiglia, Italy

Since 1983 her restaurant has towered over this famous vantage point and the caves of the Balzi Rossi ("red cliffs"), but Giuseppina Beglia herself is just as well known in Italy for the television cookery programs broadcast under her direction between 1985–90. A member of Le Soste, the prestigious Italian restaurant chain, she holds two Michelin stars, three red chef's hats in Gault-Millau (18) and 82/100 in the Italian Gambero Rosso guide. In 1992 she won the first "Golden Key of Gastronomy" to be awarded by Gault-Millau to chefs outside of France. Giuseppina Beglia is very interested the flower arrangements in her restaurant, and loves skiing in the nearby Alps.

Michel Blanchet

June 16, 1949

Restaurant: **Le Tastevin**
Address: 9, avenue Eglé
78600 Maisons-Laffitte, France

After a top-notch training from 1967–71 at *Maxim's*, *Lutétia* and *Ledoyen*, Michel Blanchet took over the reins at *Tastevin* in 1972; today, the restaurant boasts two Michelin stars. Blanchet's talents have more than once carried him through to the final rounds of prestigious awards: the Prosper Montagné prize (1970 and 1972); the Taittinger prize (1974); and the Meilleur Ouvrier de France competition in 1979. Michel Blanchet is a Maître Cuisinier de France and a member of the "Culinary Academy of France". A great lover of nature, he enjoys rambles through the woods – during which he sometimes also collects mushrooms – as well as cycling and hiking.

Michel Bourdin

born June 6, 1942

Restaurant: **The Connaught**
Address: Carlos Place, Mayfair
London W1Y 6AL, England

One of the old and distinguished line of French chefs in Great Britain, Michel Bourdin has been delighting London diners at the *Connaught* since 1975. The recipient of numerous prizes (Prosper Montagné, Taittinger) since training at *Ledoyen* and under Alex Humbert at *Maxim's*, he has been Chairman of the British branch of the "Culinary Academy of France" since 1980. In addition, he is a member of the "100 Club", and like Paul Haeberlin is also an honorary member of the Chefs des Chefs association. His pastry-chef colleagues, the twins Carolyn and Deborah Power, have made the *Connaught* famous for its desserts.

Christian Bouvarel

born April 26, 1954

Restaurant: **Paul Bocuse**
Address: 69660 Collonges-au-Mont-d'Or, France

The youngest chef at *Paul Bocuse* had famous teachers, training under Raymond Thuillier at *Ousteau de Baumanière* in Baux-de-Provence in 1971 and Paul Haeberlin at the *Auberge de l'Ill* in Illhaeusern in 1972 before coming to work at this celebrated restaurant in Collonges in 1975. Three Michelin stars, four red chef's hats in Gault-Millau (19), four stars in the Bottin Gourmand guide: Christian Bouvarel has also naturally played his part in the success story of this restaurant, and was named Meilleur Ouvrier de France in 1993. A native of Lyons, he is an enthusiastic nature-lover and spends his scarce leisure hours preferably mountain climbing.

Carlo Brovelli

born May 23, 1938

Restaurant: **Il Sole di Ranco**
Address: 5, Piazza Venezia
21020 Ranco, Italy

One "sun" – it was only fitting that the Italian restaurant guide Veronelli should pay tribute to this restaurant with the sun in its name by awarding it this distinction. Looking back on a 120-year-old family tradition, *Il Sole di Ranco* is run in a masterly fashion by Carlo Brovelli, who took over the reins in 1968 after training at the college of hotel management in La Stresa. A member of the Le Soste, Relais et Châteaux and Relais Gourmands chains, Brovelli has received many accolades: two Michelin stars, three chef's hats in Gault-Millau (18), 84/100 in the Italian Gambero Rosso. Carlo Brovelli loves cycling and soccer, as well as his favorite sport, hunting.

Jean-Pierre Bruneau

born September 18, 1943

Restaurant: **Bruneau**
Address: 73-75, avenue Broustin
1080 Brussels, Belgium

For a good 20 years now, Jean-Pierre Bruneau has run the restaurant bearing his name which stands in the shadow of the important Koekelberg Basilica in the center of Brussels. The sophisticated creations of this Belgian "Maître Cuisinier" have won him many distinctions: three Michelin stars, four red chef's hats in Gault-Millau, three stars in Bottin Gourmand and 94/100 in the Belgian restaurant guide Henri Lemaire. He is also a member of Traditions et Qualité. Outside of the kitchen, he enjoys hunting and car racing (first hand); in addition, he collects old cars.

Michel Bruneau

born February 11, 1949

Restaurant: **La Bourride**
Address: 15-17, rue du Vaugueux
14000 Caen, France

"Normandy is proud of herself" – this is the motto of Michel Bruneau, who never tires of enumerating the sumptuous produce of the Calvados region on his exhaustive, tempting menu. Starting off his career in the midst of the plantations in Ecrécy, on the banks of the Guigne (1972–82), he then moved to *La Bourride* in Caen, where he has been since 1982. Here he continues to delight gourmets with his inventive cooking, steeped in regional traditions, which has also impressed the critics: two Michelin stars, three red chef's hats in Gault-Millau (18). In his spare time, Michel Bruneau enjoys cooking for friends and playing soccer.

Alain Burnel

born January 26, 1949

Restaurant: **Oustau de Baumanière**
Address: Val d'Enfer
13520 Les Baux-de-Provence, France

Alain Burnel served his apprenticeship in Beaulieu at *La réserve de Beaulieu* (1969–73), in Nantes at *Frantel* under Roger Jaloux, in Marseilles at *Sofitel* and in Saint-Romain de Lerps at the *Château du Besset*, where he served as chef from 1978-82 before taking over the reins from the famous Raymond Thuillier in Baux, whose restaurant is now owned by the Charial family. Alain Burnel has earned two Michelin stars, three white chef's hats in Gault-Millau (18) and is a member of Traditions et Qualité, Relais et Châteaux and Relais Gourmands. In his free time this chef is a keen cyclist, and was even once a participant in the Tour de France.

Jan Buytaert

born October 16, 1946

Restaurant: **De Bellefleur**
Address: 253 Chaussée d'Anvers
2950 Kapellen, Belgium

Despite being a dyed-in-the-wool Belgian who has spent a large part of his career in his native country (first at the *Villa Lorraine* in Brussels from 1973–4), Jan Buytaert worked for two years in the kitchens of *Prés et Sources d'Eugénie* in Eugénie-les-Bains under Michel Guérard (1974–5). In 1975, after this French interlude, he opened his current restaurant, which has earned him two Michelin stars and is one of the best in the region. This Belgian Maître Cuisinier loves gentle activities such as hiking and riding, and also enjoys working in the garden.

Jacques Cagna

born August 24, 1942

Restaurant: **Jacques Cagna**
Address: 14, rue des Grands Augustins
75006 Paris, France

This distinguished chef has worked the most famous restaurants of the French capital (1960 at *Lucas Carton*, 1961 at *Maxim's*, 1964 at *La Ficelle*), and was even Chef to the French National Assembly (1961–62) before opening his own restaurant under his own name in 1975, for which he has received high honors: two Michelin stars, two red chef's hats in Gault-Millau (18) and three stars in Bottin Gourmand. Jacques Cagna is a Knight of the "Mérite nationale des Arts et des Lettres". He knows his way around Asia very well, speaks fluent Japanese and is keen on classical music, opera and jazz.

Stewart Cameron

born September 16, 1945

Restaurant: **Turnberry Hotel & Golf Courses**
Turnberry KA26 9LT, Scotland

Since 1981, the kitchens of the *Turnberry* Hotel – one of only two 5-star Scottish restaurants – have had a real Scot at the helm: Stewart Cameron, who previously worked at *Malmaison*, the restaurant of the *Central Hotel* in Glasgow. This chef is also a member of the "Taste of Scotland" and of the British Branch of the "Culinary Academy of France". In 1986 and 1994 he was privileged to play host in his restaurant to the participants of the British Golf Open. When he gets the chance, Stewart Cameron goes hunting or fishing. A rugby fan (of course!), he is one of the Scottish Fifteen's most faithful supporters.

Mario Cavallucci

born May 20, 1959

Restaurant: **La Frasca**
Address: 38, Via Matteoti
47011 Castrocaro Terme, Italy

Two Michelin stars, 4 chef's hats in Gault-Millau (19), one sun in Veronelli, 89/100 in Gambero Rosso: what more could Mario Cavallucci want? Working in perfect harmony with the restaurant's proprietor and cellarman, Gianfranco Bolognesi, this young, energetic chef has already received many accolades. A member of the Le Soste restaurant chain, he has vigorously supported Italy's great culinary tradition since 1978. This extraordinarily busy chef nevertheless manages to find a little spare time for fishing, reading, seeing the occasional movie, and playing cards, soccer and billiards.

Francis Chauveau

born: September 15, 1947

Restaurant: **La Belle Otéro**
Address: Hôtel Carlton (7th floor)
58, La Croisette
06400 Cannes, France

Although born in Berry in the northwest of France, Francis Chauveau's encounter with Provencal cooking has led to outstanding results, which visitors to the legendary *Palace-Hotel* in Cannes – holder of two Michelin stars – have been enjoying since 1989. Francis Chauveau gained his first experience as a chef in the *Hôtel d'Espagne* in Valencay, continuing his career at the *Auberge de Noves* in 1965. Later, he worked in prestigious restaurants such as the *Auberge du Père Bise, the Réserve de Beaulieu*, the *Terrasse* in the Hotel Juana in Juan-les-Pins, and in the famous restaurant *L'Amandier* in Mougins from 1980–89.

Jacques Chibois

born: July 22, 1952

Restaurant: **La Bastide St-Antoine**
Address: 45, avenue Henri Dunant
06130 Grasse, France

During the course of a career involving many moves, Jacques Chibois has met many famous names in French gastronomy: Jean Delaveyne in Bougival, Louis Outhier in La Napoule, Roger Vergé in Mougins, and the famous pastry chef Gaston Lenôtre. Since 1980 he has repeatedly worked under Michel Guérard, and was awarded two Michelin stars during his time at *Gray d'Albion* in Cannes (1981–95). He opened *La Bastide Saint-Antoine* in Grasse in 1995. In his spare time, Jacques Chibois is an enthusiastic cyclist and nature-lover, as well as a keen hunter and angler.

Serge Courville

born: December 9, 1935

Restaurant: **La Cote 108**
Address: Rue Colonel Vergezac
02190 Berry-au-Bac, France

Serge Courville names his three teachers – Roger Petit, Robert Morizot and Jean-Louis Lelaurain – with warmth. Although not much interested in accolades, he has nevertheless reached the final of numerous culinary competitions (Prosper Montagné prize, 1971; Trophée national de l'Académie Culinaire, 1972; Taitinger prize, 1973). Since 1972, he and his wife have together run *La Cote 108*, which in 1982 received one Michelin star. When not working, Serge Courville enjoys cooking for friends; he is also a passionate reader and cyclist and spends a lot of time in the wilds, fishing or hunting for mushrooms.

Bernard & Jean Cousseau

born September 15, 1917 born May 6, 1949

Restaurant: **Relais de la Poste**
Address: 40140 Magescq, France

Bernard Cousseau embodies the regional gastronomy of Landes. Honorary president of the Maîtres Cuisiniers de France, he serves a fine regional cuisine to his guests at the Relais de la Poste, which openend in 1954 and has been holding two Michelin stars since 1969. On the height of his extraordinary career, the Chef is now an officer of the Mérite Agricole and a Knight of both the Légion d'Honneur and the Palmes académiques. His son Jean has been working with him at the Relais de la Poste since 1970, after an examplary Franco-Hispanic career at the Café de Paris in Biaritz, the Plaza-Athénée in Paris and the Ritz in Madrid.

Richard Coutanceau

born: February 25, 1949

Restaurant: **Richard Coutanceau**
Address: Place de la Concurrence
17000 La Rochelle, France

Richard Coutanceau, whose restaurant boasts a marvelous location in "green Venice" between Marais Poitevin and the Côte Sauvage, started out his career in Paris at *L'Orée du bois* in 1968. He then moved to *La Rochelle* and the *Hôtel de France et d'Angleterre*, where he worked from 1968-82. This native of Charentais has received many distinctions: two stars in Michelin, three stars in Bottin Gourmand and three red chef's hats and 17 points in Gault-Millau. His restaurant belongs to the Relais Gourmands chain, and he is also a member of the "Young Restauranteurs of Europe". Richard Coutanceau is an avid tennis player and a keen fisherman.

Jean Crotet

born: January 26, 1943

Restaurant: **Hostellerie de Levernois**
Address: Route de Combertault
21200 Levernois, France

Amidst a splendid park of Louisiana cedar, willow and ash, through which a small river flows, Jean Crotet offers discerning diners a sophisticated cuisine which has been awarded two Michelin stars and three stars in Bottin Gourmand. He is a Maître Cuisinier de France, as well as a member of Relais et Châteaux and Relais Gourmands chains. In 1988, after working for 15 years at the *Côte d'Or* in Nuits-Saint Georges, he settled down in Levernois, near Beaune. In his spare time Jean Crotet enjoys fishing, flying a helicopter, playing tennis, hunting and gardening.

Michel Del Burgo

born: June 21, 1962

Restaurant: **La Barbacane**
Address: Place de l'Église
11000 Carcassonne-La Cité, France

This young man from the northern province of Picardy has worked in the kitchens of Alain Ducasse in Courchevel, Raymond Thuillier in Baux-de-Provence and Michel Guérard in Eugénie-les-Bains, all in the south of France. After a short stay in the Rhône valley and Avignon (1987-90), Michel Del Burgo was in 1991 appointed chef of *La Barbacane* in the center of Carcassonne by Jean-Michel Signoles. In 1995 he was awarded his second Michelin star, the "Lily of the restaurant trade" and the Gault-Millau "golden key", as well as three red chef's hats and 18 points in the latter guide. Michel Del Burgo rates the cooking of his fellow chefs in the "Land of the Cathars", but is also fond of music, motor sport and hiking.

Joseph Delphin

born: September 4, 1932

Restaurant: **La Châtaigneraie**
Address: 156, route de Carquefou
44240 Sucé-sur-Erdre, France

A Maître Cuisinier de France and member of the "Culinary Academy of France", Joseph Delphin delights gourmets from the Nantes area with his culinary skills. A knight of the Mérite agricole, this chef has also received the Vase de Sèvres award from the French President. His restaurant, *La Châtaigneraie* (one Michelin star), sits right on the banks of the Erdre, and can be reached by road, river or helicopter...You are sure to be won over by the warmth of the welcome from the Delphin family, as Jean-Louis, a member of the "Young Restauranteurs of Europe", works here together with his father.

Philippe Dorange

born: May 27, 1963

Restaurant: **Fouquet's**
Address: 99, avenue des Champs Élysées
75008 Paris, France

Does one actually need to to introduce the legendary *Fouquet's* in these pages? Surely not, nor the prestigious restaurants in which Philippe Dorange has worked in the past: Roger Vergé's *Le Moulin de Mougins* (1977–81), Jacques Maximin's *Negresco* in Nice (1981–88), and lastly *Ledoyen* in Paris, where he was chef from 1988–92. All in all, a fine career path for a young chef whose Mediterranean origins are reflected in his culinary preferences, a fact which is particularly esteemed by his Champs-Élysées clientele. When not in the kitchen, Philippe Dorange likes to box, drive sports cars or play soccer.

Claude and Eric Dupont

born June 7, 1938; April 16, 1966

Restaurant: **Claude Dupont**
46, Avenue Vital Riethuisen
Brussels 1080, Belgium

The Belgian and French gourmet restaurants have positively showered awards on Claude Dupont's cooking: two Michelin stars since 1976, three white chef's hats in Gault-Millau (17). and 92/100 points in the Belgian Henri Lemaire guide. In 1967 he was awarded the Prosper Montagne prize, and in 1973 the Oscar of Gastronomy. In addition, this chef ran the Belgian pavilion at the 1970 World Fair in Osaka. His son was taught by the Brussels master chefs Freddy Van Decasserie, Pierre Wynants, and Willy Vermeulen. Today he works with his father.

Lothar Eiermann

born: March 2, 1945

Restaurant: **Wald- & Schloßhotel Friedrichsruhe**
Address: 74639 Friedrichsruhe, Germany

For over 20 years now Lothar Eiermann has worked at Friedrichsruhe, the summer residence of the Prince von Hohenlohe-Öhringen which belongs to the Relais et Châteaux chain. Before this, he traveled throughout the whole of Europe, working as a chef in Switzerland between 1964-72 in the *Grappe d'Or* in Lausanne and in the Hotel *Victoria* in Glion. He then worked in the *Gleneagles* Hotel in Scotland, traveled south to England, and returned to Scotland, where he managed a hotel from 1972-3. This Bordeaux-wine enthusiast also has a degree in Economics from the University of Heidelberg, and depending on the season, enjoys skiing, cycling or playing tennis.

Jean Fleury

born: April 22, 1948

Restaurant: **Paul Bocuse**
Address: 69660 Collonges-au-Mont-d'Or, France

After a highly promising début in his home town of Bourg-en-Bresse – the chief town of Bresse, a region renowned for its outstanding produce – Jean Fleury achieved fame as a chef in the *Hotel Royal* in Évian (1968–69) and in the Brussels *Hilton* (1971–78). Winner of the Prosper Montagné prize in 1976, he was named Best Chef in Belgium in the same year, and won the Meilleur Ouvrier de France competition in 1979. In 1985 he left the kitchens of the *Arc-en-ciel* in Lyons, following Paul Bocuse to his famous restaurant in Collonges. Jean Fleury loves traveling and hiking and collects antique cookbooks, from which he enjoys drawing inspiration.

Constant Fonk

born: September 1, 1947

Restaurant: **De Oude Rosmolen**
Address: Duinsteeg 1
1621 Hoorn, the Netherlands

Thanks to Constant Fonk, the town of Hoorn in North Holland has had a two-Michelin-starred restaurant since 1990. After his first highly promising steps in the Amsterdam *Hilton* (1965–6), and the *Amstel Hotel* (1966–7), our chef returned to his home town, where in 1967 he began work in *De Oude Rosmolen*, finally taking over the reins of the kitchen in 1976. A lover of fine cuisine and good wines, he especially enjoys partaking of both with like-minded people. As far as sport is concerned, golf is his favorite form of exercise, and makes a change from the kitchen.

Louis Grondard

born: September 20, 1948

Restaurant: **Drouant**
Address: 16-18, rue Gaillon
75002 Paris, France

It is no easy task to have catered for the members of the jury of the prestigious Goncourt literary prize every year since 1990; rather, it requires someone with the skills of this chef, who was named Meilleur Ouvrier de France in 1979. Louis Grondard served his apprenticeship at *Taillevent* and at *Maxim's*, first in Orly, then in Roissy. He then achieved his first successes in the Eiffel Tower restaurant and in the famous *Jules Vernes*, which opened in the Tower in 1983. To quote Michel Tournier, "The stars [two in Michelin] fall as his due from heaven." Louis Grondard has also received three white chef's hats and 17 points in Gault-Millau. He loves literature, music and opera.

Philippe Groult

born: November 17, 1953

Restaurant: **Amphyclès**
Address: 78, avenue des Ternes
75017 Paris, France

A devoted pupil and colleague of Joïl Robuchon at *Jamin* from1974–85, this native Norman now runs his own restaurant, to the satisfaction of diners and critics alike. Named Meilleur Ouvrier de France in 1982, today Philippe Groult has two Michelin stars and three red chef's hats (18) in Gault-Millau. In 1988 he was a contender in the "Culinary Olympics" in Tokyo, and one year later took over the reins in the kitchen at *Amphyclès*. He has been a member of Devoirs Unis since 1978. Philippe Groult is a keen traveler, a connoisseur of the Far East and an enthusiastic martial arts practitioner.

Marc Haeberlin

born: November 28, 1954

Restaurant: **Auberge de L'Ill**
Address: 2, rue de Collonges-au-Mont-d'Or
68970 Illhaeusern, France

This worthy heir to the Haeberlin dynasty will on no account disappoint the gourmets who, once lured by the success of his father Paul, return to this temple of Alsatian cuisine. Three Michelin stars, four red chef's hats (19.5!) in Gault-Millau and four stars in Bottin Gourmand are the impressive distinctions garnered by this former student at the college of hotel management in Illkirch. Completing his training with Paul Bocuse and the Troisgros brothers, he proved his skills in Paris at the *Lasserre* back in 1976. When time allows, Mark Haeberlin occupies himself with painting and cars. In winter he goes downhill-skiing on the slopes of the Vosges.

Michel Haquin

born: September 27, 1940

Restaurant: **Le Trèfle à 4**
Address: 87, avenue de Lac
1332 Genval, Belgium

Not far from Brussels, on the shores of Lake Genval, Michel Haquin successfully pursues a culinary career which began in 1961 in the Belgian capital. There, from 1977–85, he ran a restaurant under his own name. As a Belgian Maître Cuisinier and member of the Culinary Academy of France, this chef was admitted to the Order of the Thirty-three Masterchefs and was awarded the "Oscar of Gastronomy". The guidebooks have showered him with honors: two Michelin stars, three red chef's hats in Bottin Gourmand and 91/100 in the Belgian guide Henri Lemaire. In his leisure time, Michel Haquin enjoys reading and traveling.

Paul Heathcote

born: October 3, 1960

Restaurant: **Paul Heathcote's**
Address: 104 - 106 Higher Road,
Longridge PR3 3 SY, England

This young British chef is very open to culinary influences from the other side of the English Channel. After working with Michel Bourdin at the *Connaught*, he spent two years with Raymond Blanc at the *Manoir au Quatr'Saisons* in Oxfordshire, and worked at the *Broughton Park Hotel* in Preston before finally opening his own restaurant (two Michelin stars) in 1990. In 1994, the Egon Ronay guidebook awarded him the enviable title of "Best Chef of the Year". An enthusiastic sportsman, Paul Heathcote loves soccer, squash and skiing.

Eyvind Hellstrøm

born: December 2, 1948

Restaurant: **Bagatelle**
Address: Bygdøy Allé 3
0257 Oslo, Norway

No other chef in Scandinavia has received as many accolades as Eyvind Hellstrøm. This chef is strongly influenced by French gastronomy, with which he became familiar in the course of his training under famous chefs such as Guy Savoy, Alain Senderens, Bernard Loiseau, and Fredy Girardet. A member of Eurotoques and Traditions et Qualité, Eyvind Hellstrøm was awarded two Michelin stars for his restaurant in 1982. A passionate wine connoisseur and a lover of Burgundies in particular, this chef often visits the wine cellars of Beaune and the surrounding area. He enjoys traveling and skiing, and is a self-confessed fan of the Swedish skier Ingmar Stenmark.

Alfonso Iaccarino

born: January 9, 1947

Restaurant: **Don Alfonso 1890**
Address: Piazza Sant'Agata,
80064 Sant'Agata sui due Golfi, Italy

In 1973, Alfonso Iaccarino named his restaurant, with its marvelous view of the Gulf of Naples and Salerno, after his grandfather. A member of the Le Soste, Relais Gourmands and Traditions et Qualité chains, this chef has garnered numerous honors: two Michelin stars, four chef's hats in Espresso/Gault-Millau, one sun in Veronelli and 92/100 in Gambero Rosso. In 1989 he was awarded the title of "Best Winecellar in Italy" for his collection of noble Italian and French wines. In his private life, Alfonso Iaccarino is a true sportsman and particularly enjoys racing and cycling. He also loves nature, painting and traveling.

André Jaeger

born: February 12, 1947

Restaurant: **Rheinhotel Fischerzunft**
Address: Rheinquai 8,
8200 Schaffhausen, Switzerland

André Jaeger can proudly claim to have successfully inspired Swiss and even European gastronomy with an oriental flavor. His restaurant, which he opened in 1975, boasts two Michelin stars and four red chef's hats in Gault-Millau (19). Named 1995 "Chef of the Year" by Gault-Millau, he was awarded the "Golden Key of Gastronomy" in 1988 and appointed Chairman of the Grandes Tables in Switzerland. He is also a member of Relais et Châteaux and Relais Gourmands. A connoisseur of wines from around the world, André Jaeger is also very interested in contemporary art and collects cars.

Roger Jaloux & Christian Bouvarel

born May 20, 1942   born April 26, 1954

Restaurant: **Paul Bocuse**
Address: 69660 Collonges-au-Mont-d'Or, France

As the most loyal among the loyal pupils of Paul Bocuse, Roger Jaloux followed his mentor into the latter's famous restaurant in 1965. It was here that he prepared for competition for prestigious title of Meilleur Ouvrier de France, which he won in 1976. In his spare time, Roger Jaloux enjoys artistic activities and numerous sports. Christian Bouvarel, the youngest Chef at the Restaurant Paul Bocuse, had famous teachers: Raymond Thuillier in Baux-de-Provence in 1971 and Paul Haeberlin at the Auberge de l'Ill in 1972. 3 Michelin stars, 4 red chef's hats in Gault-Millau (19), 4 stars in Bottin Gourmand: Christian Bouvaral naturally contributes to the restaurant's enormous success.

Patrick Jeffroy

born: January 25, 1952

Restaurant: **Patrick Jeffroy**
Address: 11, rue du Bon Voyage
22780 Plounérin, France

A Breton with a penchant for solitude, Patrick Jeffroy settled down in a village in the Côtes-D'Armor département, where he serves innovative, delicious food in his restaurant, established in 1988 and now boasting one Michelin star and three red chef's hats in Gault-Millau (17). The earlier part of his career was spent in Abidjan in the Ivory Coast (1972) and the *Hôtel de l'Europe* in Morlaix back in France (1977–87). Patrick Jeffroy has had his Michelin star since 1984; he is also a Maître Cuisinier de France, and a recipient of the Mandarine Impériale first prize. Outside of working hours, he enjoys going to the theatre and the movies.

Émile Jung

born: April 2, 1941

Restaurant: **Le Crocodile**
Address: 10, rue de l'Outre
67000 Strasbourg, France

Behind the sign of the crocodile - an allusion to Napoleon's Egyptian campaign - can be found Émile Jung's restaurant, highly rated by food lovers and a veritable temple of Alsatian cuisine, boasting no fewer than three Michelin stars, three white chef's hats in Gault-Millau (18) and three stars in Bottin Gourmand. The awards hardly come as a surprise, when one considers that this chef's career took him from *La Mère Guy* in Lyons to *Fouquet's* (1965) and *Ledoyen* (1966) in Paris. Émile Jung is a Maître Cuisinier de France and member of Relais Gourmands and Traditions et Qualité. A passionate enologist, he is particularly well versed in Alsatian wines.

Dieter Kaufmann

born: June 28, 1937

Restaurant: **Zur Traube**
Address: Bahnstraße 47,
41515 Grevenbroich, Germany

Dieter Kaufmann harbors a great love of France, and that country knows how to repay him in kind: with two Michelin stars and four red chef's hats in Gault-Millau (19.5) he figures among the most highly esteemed non-French chefs, and was named Gault-Millau 1994 "Chef of the Year". He is a member of the prestigious Traditions et Qualité, Relais et Châteaux and Relais Gourmands chains. With over 30 000 bottles and some remarkable vintages, his restaurant, which he has run since 1962, boasts what is without a doubt the most important wine cellar in Germany. A bibliophile and polyglot, Dieter Kaufmann is also an enthusiastic traveler.

Örjan Klein

born: May 15, 1945

Restaurant: **K.B.**
Address: Smalandsgatan, 7
11146 Stockholm, Sweden

At the pinnacle of a career based largely in the Swedish capital (*Berns* from 1966–7 and *Maxim's* of Stockholm from 1971-9), Örjan Klein joined forces with Ake Hakansson in 1980 to open *K.B.*, which boasts one Michelin star. Named "Chef of the Year" in 1993, Örjan Klein is also a Nordfishing Trondheim and Swedish Academy of Gastronomy gold-medallist (1976 and 1983, respectively). A nature lover, our chef enjoys gardening and hiking. He also writes (cook)books and keeps fit by playing tennis and skiing.

Robert Kranenborg

born: October 12, 1950

Restaurant: **La Rive/Hotel Amstel Inter-Continental**
Address: Prof. Tulpplein, 1
1018 GX Amsterdam, the Netherlands

One doesn't become chef of *La Rive* (one Michelin star) – the restaurant of the *Inter-Continental*, the most prestigious hotel in Amsterdam – overnight. In point of fact, Robert Kranenborg had a string of successes as glowing references when he began work there in 1987: *Oustau de Baumanière* in Baux-de-Provence (1972-4), *Le Grand Véfour* in Paris (1975-7) and *La Cravache d'Or* in Brussels (1979-86). In 1994, Robert Kranenborg was named "Chef of the Year". When he is able to escape from the kitchen, he enjoys playing the drums or sports – golf being his favorite.

Étienne Krebs

born: August 15, 1956

Restaurant: **L'Ermitage**
Address: 75, rue du Lac
1815 Clarens-Montreux, Switzerland

As chef-proprietor of a magnificent house on the shores of Lake Geneva, Étienne Krebs is a happy man: a member of the "Young Restauranteurs of Europe" and Grandes Tables Suisses, he boasts one Michelin star and three red chef's hats in Gault-Millau (18), as well as the title of "Chef of the Year" 1995 for French-speaking Switzerland. After training with the greatest Swiss chefs – Fredy Girardet in Crissier and Hans Stucki in Basel – he ran the *Auberge de la Couronne* in Cossonay from 1984–90, before finally opening *L'Ermitage* in Montreux. Étienne Krebs enjoys walking and cycling around the lake, as well as cooking for his family.

Jacques Lameloise

born: April 6, 1947

Restaurant: **Lameloise**
Address: 36, place d'Armes
71150 Chagny, France

The third generation of his family to bear the name, Jacques Lameloise has since 1971 also carried on the tradition of running the family restaurant. Cutting his professional teeth at Ogier's in Pontchartrain, from 1965–9 he worked at the Parisian temples of gastronomy *Lucas Carton*, *Fouquet's*, *Ledoyen* and *Lasserre*, not forgetting the *Savoy* in London. The *Lameloise* can boast three stars in both Michelin and Bottin Gourmand, as well as three red chef's hats in Gault-Millau (18), and is a member of the Relais et Châteaux, Relais Gourmands and Traditions et Qualité chains. Our chef is especially keen on antiques and old cars, and enjoys golfing and skiing.

Erwin Lauterbach

born March 21, 1949

Restaurant: **Saison**
Address: Strandvejen, 203
2900 Hellerup, Denmark

From 1972–3, Erwin Lauterbach served up the cuisine of his native Denmark at the *Maison du Danemark* in Paris – a time of which he has many fond memories. From 1977–81 he cooked in Malmö, Sweden at *Primeur*, after which he returned to Denmark. Opened in 1981, *Saison* boasts one Michelin star. Our chef is also member of the Danish Academy of Gastronomy, and is a virtuoso proponent of Danish culinary traditions. An admirer of naive painting, he is a passionate museum-goer and visitor of exhibitions. Of all the sports, he enjoys playing soccer the most.

Dominique Le Stanc

born December 7, 1958

Restaurant: **Chanteclerc – Hôtel Negresco**
Address: 37, Promenade des Anglais
06000 Nice, France

Some of the biggest names in the world of gastronomy have watched over the early stages of Dominique Le Stanc's career. After serving an apprenticeship with Paul Haeberlin, he worked with Gaston Lenôtre, Alain Senderens and Alain Chapel, and became chef de partie under the latter before putting out his own shingle, first at the *Bristol* in Niederbronn-les-Bains (1982–84) then in Monaco and Èze. A member of the Italian chain Le Soste, he has been head chef of *Negresco* since 1989, earning this celebrated establishment two Michelin stars and three red chef's hats in Gault-Millau (18). A keen athlete, our chef takes part in triathlons and water-skis.

Michel Libotte

born May 1, 1949

Restaurant: **Au Gastronome**
Address: 2, rue de Bouillon
6850 Paliseul, Belgium

Since 1978, Michel Libotte has presided over the kitchens of *Au Gastronome*, rated 94/100 in the Belgian restaurant guide Henri Lemaire. French critics have also been unstinting in their praise, awarding our chef's establishment two Michelin stars and three stars in Bottin Gourmand. Michel Libotte has won the title of "Best Cook in Belgium", and is a member of Eurotoques and the Culinary Academy of France. His restaurant, which lies close to the Franco-Belgian border, serves a highly individual, imaginative cuisine. Michel Libotte collects firearms as a hobby, and keeps fit by swimming and playing tennis regularly.

Léa Linster

born April 27, 1955

Restaurant: **Léa Linster**
Address: 17, route de Luxembourg
5752 Frisange, Luxembourg

Léa Linster is the first, and to date the only woman to receive the highest gastronomic accolade, the Bocuse d'Or, awarded to her in Lyons in 1989 by the Master himself in well-earned recognition of her daily efforts to make the generous cuisine of Luxembourg better known to the dining public. Converting her parents' inn into an haute cuisine restaurant in 1982, this chef received her master craftsman's diploma in 1987. In addition to her obvious enthusiasm for fine cuisine, Léa Lister enjoys walks in the wild and stimulating conversations with diners in her restaurant.

Régis Marcon

born June 14, 1956

Restaurant: **Auberge et Clos des Cimes**
Address: 43290 Saint-Bonnet-le-Froid, France

In 1995, at only 39 years of age, Régis Marcon was awarded the Bocuse d'Or, with his neighbor Michel Troisgros serving as godfather – just one more glowing distinction in a career already crowned with accolades: the Taittinger prize in 1989, the Brillat-Savarin prize in 1992 and several-time finalist in the Meilleur Ouvrier de France competition (1985, 1991, 1993). In 1979 our chef opened a restaurant in his village which has earned him three red chef's hats in Gault-Millau (17), and which was designed to resemble "a cloister bathed in light". Here one recognizes the eye of the painter, which is what Régis Marcon, a great sportsman and medal-winning skier, at one time hoped to become.

Guy Martin

born February 3, 1957

Restaurant: **Le Grand Véfour**
Address: 17, rue de Beaujolais
75001 Paris, France

It would be impossible to summarize Guy Martin's career in just a couple of sentences – two Michelin stars, three white chef's hats in Gault-Millau (18), three stars in the Bottin Gourmand and 18.5/20 in Champérard. This young prodigy of gastronomy studied first with Troisgros, then in his native region, chiefly in Divonne. In 1991 he took over the reins of *Le Grand Véfour*, that jewel among Parisian restaurants at which the litterati of the French metropolis have rubbed shoulders for over 200 years, made famous by Raymond Oliver. Guy Martin remains true to the memory of his mother and to his native region of Savoy, of whose culinary history he is a fervent devotee.

Maria Ligia Medeiros

born August 9, 1946

Restaurant: **Casa de Comida**
Address: 1, Travessa das Amoreiras
1200 Lisbon, Portugal

Since 1978, Maria Ligia Medeiros has run the kitchens of a cozy restaurant owned by Jorge Vales, a former stage actor of the *Casa de Comedia* theater – hence the pun of the restaurant's name (comida = "food"). There, in the heart of the historic Old Town of the capital, she dishes up traditional Portuguese dishes with skill and flair, for which she was awarded a Michelin star several years ago. In addition to haute cuisine, our chef loves classical music and spends a large part of her leisure hours reading.

Dieter Müller

born July 28, 1948

Restaurant: **Dieter Müller**
Address: Lerbacher Weg,
51469 Bergisch Gladbach, Germany

Dieter Müller had already beaten a career path across several countries and continents by the time he settled down in his native Germany in 1992: from 1973 onward he served as head chef of various establishments in Switzerland, Australia (Sydney), Japan and Hawaii, collecting numerous awards along the way, including the title of "Chef of the Year" in the Krug guidebook in 1982 and in Gault-Millau in 1988. Today, he boasts two Michelin stars and four red chef's hats (19.5), as well as a National Gastronomy prize. A member of Relais et Châteaux and Relais Gourmands, his hobbies are photography and collecting old recipes, as well as playing ice hockey and soccer.

Jean-Louis Neichel

born February 17, 1948

Restaurant: **Neichel**
Address: Beltran i Rûzpide, 16 bis
08034 Barcelona, Spain

Thanks to his training under such culinary celebrities as Gaston Lenôtre, Alain Chapel and Georges Blanc, Jean-Louis Neichel is a European chef par excellence. For 10 years he brought his invaluable experience to bear while running *El Bulli* in Rosas, where Fernando Adrìa is now head chef, before opening his own restaurant in Barcelona in 1981, esteemed in particular for its collection of old Armagnacs and Cognacs. Awarded two Michelin stars and 9/10 in Gourmetour, Jean-Louis Neichel is also a member of Relais Gourmands. His leisure hours are devoted to oil painting (landscapes), his family, and sports (tennis, cycling, skiing).

Pierre Orsi

born July 12, 1939

Restaurant: **Pierre Orsi**
Address: 3, place Kléber
69006 Lyons, France

Pierre Orsi's career reads like a dream: named Meilleur Ouvrier de France in 1972, he has worked with the culinary greats of his generation: with Bocuse from 1955–8, then at *Lucas Carton*; with Alex Humbert at *Maxim's*, and at *Lapérouse* in Paris. There followed a stint in the USA from 1967–71, after which he returned to Lyons and put out his shingle at the edge of the Tête d'Or quarter. His superb restaurant, which boasts one Michelin star and three stars in Bottin Gourmand, is a mecca for gourmets. A member of Relais Gourmands and Traditions et Qualité, Pierre Orsi is also interested in table decoration and collects art objects and antiques.

Georges Paineau

born April 16, 1939

Restaurant: **Le Bretagne**
Address: 13, rue Saint-Michel
56230 Questembert, France

Georges Paineau had the unusual good forture to start off his career under Fernand Point at *La Pyramide* in 1960. Since then, he drew ever closer to Brittany, stopping off in La Baule (1962) and Nantes (1963), before settling at *Le Bretagne* in Questembert, close to the Gulf of Morbihan, where he now collects stars (two in Michelin and four in Bottin Gourmand) and Gault-Millau chef's hats (four red, 19 points). Our chef works with his son-in-law, Claude Corlouer. His restaurant, an old coaching inn, is a member of Relais Gourmands and Relais et Châteaux. A gifted painter, Georges Paineau also loves literature and rugby.

Paul Pauvert

born July 25, 1950

Restaurant: **Les Jardins de la Forge**
Address: 1, place des Piliers
49270 Champtoceaux, France

Professionally speaking, Paul Pauvert took his first steps at the *Café de la Paix* in Paris; from 1972-4 he served a stint in the kitchens of the Transatlantic Shipping Company's famous ocean liner *Grasse*, after which he worked at the Hotel *Frantel* in Nantes at the invitation of Roger Jaloux. In 1980 he opened his own restaurant in his home town, on the same spot where his ancestors had once run a forge. The holder of one Michelin star, Paul Pauvert is also a member of the Culinary Academy of France and the "Young Restauranteurs of Europe". The border area between Anjou and Nantes where our chef lives offers ample opportunity for hunting, fishing and riding.

Horst Petermann

born May 18, 1944

Restaurant: **Petermann's Kunststuben**
Address: Seestraße 160,
8700 Küsnacht, Switzerland

After serving his apprenticeship in Hamburg, Horst Petermann continued his career in Switzerland, in Saint Moritz, Lucerne and Geneva. He cooked in the kitchens of Émile Jung at *Le Crocodile* in Strasbourg, and at the Culinary Olympics in Tokyo in 1985, where he figured among the prizewinners. Further accolades received were the "Golden Key of Gastronomy" in 1987, "Chef of the Year" in 1991, four red chef's hats in Gault-Millau (19) and two Michelin stars. The success of his restaurant is also ensured by his master pastrycook, Rico Zandonella. As well as being a keen sportsman, Horst Petermann is passionate about his work.

Roland Pierroz

born August 26, 1942

Restaurant: **Hôtel Rosalp-Restaurant Pierroz**
Address: Route de Médran,
1936 Verbier, Switzerland

Since 1962, Roland Pierroz has worked in this popular winter-sports resort in an equally popular restaurant. The holder of one Michelin star, four red chef's hats and 19 points in Gault-Millau, and three stars in Bottin Gourmand, he was awarded the "Golden Key of Gastronomy" in 1980 and named "Chef of the Year" in 1992. Roland Pierroz trained in Lausanne (Switzerland) and London, and is a member of Relais et Châteaux and Relais Gourmands, as well as vice-chairman of the Grandes Tables Suisses. A native of the Valais, he enjoys hunting and golf.

Jacques and Laurent Pourcel

born September 13, 1964

Restaurant: **Le Jardin des Sens**
Address: 11, avenue Saint Lazare
34000 Montpellier, France

Though specializing in different areas, these inseparable twins underwent the same training, serving apprenticeships with Alain Chapel, Marc Meneau, Pierre Gagnaire, Michel Bras, Michel Trama and Marc Veyrat. Together with their business partner, Olivier Château, they opened the *Jardin des Sens* in a house made of glass and stone in 1988, since when they have collected stars in various guides: two from Michelin and three red chef's hats in Gault-Millau (17). Both chefs are Maîtres Cuisiniers de France and members of Relais Gourmands.

Stéphane Raimbault

born May 17, 1956

Restaurant: **L'Oasis**
Address: rue Honoré Carle,
06210 La Napoule, France

After working for several years in Paris under the watchful eye of Émile Tabourdiau at *La Grande Cascade*, followed by a stint with Gérard Pangaud, Stéphane Raimbault spent nine years in Japan, where he ran the *Rendez-vous* restaurant in the *Hotel Plaza d'Osaka* in Osaka. After returning to France in 1991, he took over *L'Oasis* in La Napoule, with his brother as pastry chef. The recipient of two Michelin stars and three red chef's hats in Gault-Millau (18), he was also a finalist for the title of Meuilleur Ouvrier de France. In addition, he is a Maître Cuisinier de France and a member of Traditions et Qualité.

Paul Rankin

born October 1, 1959

Restaurant: **Roscoff**
Address: 7, Lesley House, Shaftesbury Square, Belfast BT2 7DB, Northern Ireland

Paul Rankin has had an international career, working first in London with Albert Roux in *Le Gavroche*, then in California and Canada. It was not, however, in Canada, but on a cruise in Greece that he got to know his Canadian wife Jeanne, whose skills as pastry chef have delighted diners at *Roscoff* since 1989. Named "Best Restaurant in the United Kingdom" by the Courvoisier guidebook in 1994–5, it is only a wonder that Roscoff has just one Michelin star. Paul Rankin also presents the BBC television program "Gourmet Ireland". Our chef loves traveling and wine, plays soccer and rugby and practices yoga.

Jean-Claude Rigollet

born September 27, 1946

Restaurant: **Au Plaisir Gourmand**
Address: 2, rue Parmentier
37500 Chinon, France

Jean-Claude Rigollet began his career at *Maxim's* under Alex Humbert, then arrived in the Loire valley, working first at *Domaine de la Tortinière* in Montbazon (1971–7), then at the famous *Auberge des Templiers* of the Bézards (1978–82), not far from Montargis. In 1983 he became chef at *Plaisir Gourmand* in Chinon in the Touraine, the home of Rabelais. He received one Michelin star in 1985. Although he comes from the Sologne, Jean-Claude Rigollet also cooks in the style of the Touraine, and his wine cellar is testament to his extensive knowledge of regional wines.

Michel Rochedy

born July 15, 1936

Restaurant: **Le Chabichou**
Address: Quartier Les Chenus,
73120 Courchevel 1850, France

Michel Rochedy received his earliest professional instruction from André Pic, the celebrated chef from Valence, from 1954–6. Originally from the Ardèche, Rochedy arrived in Savoy in 1963 and succumbed to the charms of that region. His restaurant *Chabichou*, which specializes in Savoy cuisine, has earned him two Michelin stars and three red chef's hats in Gault-Millau (17). A Maître Cuisinier de France and member of Eurotoques, he is also the chairman of the tourist information board of Courchevel. In his spare time, Michel Rochedy enjoys art and literature, fishes, and plays soccer and rugby.

Joël Roy

born November 28, 1951

Restaurant: **Le Prieuré**
Address: 3, rue du Prieuré,
54630 Flavigny-sur-Moselle, France

In 1979, while still in the employ of Jacques Maximin at the Hôtel *Negresco* in Nice, Joël Roy won the Meilleur Ouvrier de France competition. Shortly afterwards, he became head chef at the *Frantel* in Nancy. In 1983 he opened *Le Prieuré*, which looks like a modern cloister with its arcades and garden. His one-Michelin-starred establishment is in the Lorraine, a region he loves for its traditions and natural beauty. An expert on fish, he is especially fond of river angling, and also enjoys cycling in his spare time.

Santi Santamaria

born July 26, 1957

Restaurant: **El Racó de Can Fabes**
Address: Carrer Sant Joan, 6
08470 San Celoni, Spain

Since 1981, Santi Santamaria has taken great pleasure in serving specialties from his native Catalonia to his discerning clientele. His restaurant, which is just a stone's throw away from Barcelona, at the foot of Montseny national park, has been awarded three Michelin stars and 8/10 in Gourmetour. In addition, Santi Santamaria is a member of Relais Gourmands and Traditions et Qualité. Our chef also organizes gastronomic seminars, on herbs in the spring and on mushrooms in the fall. These gourmet workshops are always a great success. In his free time, Santi Santamaria enjoys reading.

Ezio Santin

born May 17, 1937

Restaurant: **Antica Osteria del Ponte**
Address: 9, Piazza G. Negri
20080 Cassinetta di Lugagnano, Italy

Ezio Santin's culinary talents have been common knowledge since 1974, when he became chef at the *Antica Osteria del Ponte*. Three Michelin stars, four red chef's hats in Gault-Millau (19.5), one sun in Veronelli and 92/100 in Gambero Rosso: these honors justify the high regard in which he is held by his fellow Italian chefs, who have elected him chairman of Le Soste, an association of the best restaurants in Italy. Ezio Santin enjoys reading in his spare time. An enthusiastic fan of Inter Milan soccer club, he is also interested in modern dance.

Nadia Santini

born July 19, 1954

Restaurant: **Dal Pescatore**
Address: 46013 Runate Canneto sull'Oglio,
Italy

Since 1974 Nadia Santini has presided over the kitchens of *Dal Pescatore*, which was opened in 1920 by her husband's grandfather. The outstanding reputation of this restaurant is impressively documented in both Italian and French restaurant guides: two Michelin stars, four red chef's hats in L'Espresso/Gault-Millau (19), one sun in Veronelli and 94/100 in Gambero Rosso. A member of Le Soste, Relais Gourmands and Traditions et Qualité, she was awarded the prize for the "Best Wine Cellar of the Year" by L'Espresso/Gault-Millau in 1993. Nadia Santini is interested in history, especially the history of the culinary arts, from which she draws inspiration.

Maria Santos Gomes

born August 10, 1962

Restaurant: **Conventual**
Address: Praça das Flores, 45
1200 Lisbon, Portugal

The *Conventual* is located in the historic Old Town of Lisbon, right by the Parliament. There, in 1982, Dina Marquez engaged the young chef Maria Santos Gomes – to the great delight of Lisbon politicians, who dine there regularly. Much of the restaurant's decor comes from the former cloister of Igreja (hence the restaurant's name). Maria Santos Gomes' inventive cuisine has already earned her one Michelin star; in 1993, she won first prize in the "Portuguese Gastronomy Competition", which always takes place in Lisbon. In addition to cooking, she loves literature, going on walks and traveling.

Nikolaos Sarantos

born December 5, 1945

Restaurant: **Hôtel Athenaeum
Inter-Continental**
Address: 89-93, Syngrou Avenue
117 45 Athens, Greece

From 1971–88, Nikolaos Sarantos traveled around the Mediterranean and the Middle East, honing his culinary skills in the various *Hilton* Hotels in Teheran, Athens, Corfu, Kuwait City and Cairo before finally settling down at the *Athenaeum Inter-Continental* in 1988. Nikolaos Sarantos is a member of the jury at international cooking competitions in San Francisco, Copenhagen and Bordeaux. Chairman of the "Chef's Association of Greece", he is also a great sports fan, and a keen tennis, soccer and basketball player.

Fritz Schilling

born June 8, 1951

Restaurant: **Schweizer Stuben**
Address: Geiselbrunnweg 11,
97877 Wertheim, Germany

A chef since 1972, Fritz Schilling opened his restaurant in the Main valley near the romantic little town of Wertheim in 1990. His refined and versatile cuisine, which cultivates the best German gastronomic traditions, has already earned him two Michelin stars and four red chef's hats in Gault-Millau (19.5). A member of Relais et Châteaux and Relais Gourmands, his restaurant is one of the best in Germany. In his spare time, Fritz Schilling loves listening to pop music. A passionate driver, he enjoys playing golf and likes most beach sports.

Jean and Jean-Yves Schillinger

born January 31, 1934   born March 23, 1963
died December 27, 1995

Jean Schillinger was Chairman of Maître Cuisiniers de France and a symbol of Alsatian gastronomy; his restaurant in Colmar (1957–95) boasted two Michelin stars, three red stars in Gault-Millau (17), and three stars in Bottin Gourmand. A Knight of the Ordre de Mérite, he raised the profile of French cuisine throughout the world, from Japan to Brazil and Australia.

His son Jean-Yves belongs to the fourth generation of the restaurant family and has worked all his life in famous restaurants: the Crillon and Jamin in Paris, and La Côte Basque in New York. From 1988 to 1995 he worked in the family-owned restaurant in Colmar.

Rudolf Sodamin and Jonathan Wicks

born April 6, 1958; June 14, 1958

Restaurant: Passenger Ship *Queen Elizabeth II* Home port: Southampton, Great Britain

These two chefs work for the shipping company Cunard Line, which owns several liners apart from the *Queen Elizabeth II*. The Austrian Rudolf Sodamin is chef de cuisine and chief pastry chef. He has attracted the notice of many restaurants in Austria, France, Switzerland, and the United States. In New York he worked in the famous Waldorf Astoria.

Jonathan Wicks has worked in several London restaurants, among them the Mayfair Intercontinental, Grosvenor House in Park Lane, and the *Méridien* in Piccadilly. In 1987 he was appointed chef de cuisine of the *Queen Elizabeth II*.

Roger Souvereyns

born December 2, 1938

Restaurant: **Scholteshof**
Address: Kermstraat, 130
3512 Stevoort-Hasselt, Belgium

Since 1983, Roger Souvereyns has presided over the *Scholteshof*. This 18th-century farmstead has a large vegetable garden which used to be tended by his friend and gardener Clément, and which is the source of the wonderful fresh fruit and vegetables used in his cooking. Roger Souvereyns has two Michelin stars, four red chef's hats in Gault-Millau (19.5), three stars in Bottin Gourmand, and 95/100 in the Belgian restaurant guide Henri Lemaire. A member of Relais et Châteaux, Relais Gourmands and Traditions et Qualité, he is a collector of antiques and old pictures. He also loves opera, and enjoys swimming and cycling.

Pedro Subijana

born November 5, 1948

Restaurant: **Akelaré**
Address: 56, Paseo del Padre Orcolaga
20008 San Sebastian, Spain

Since 1981, Pedro Subijana has had his own restaurant overlooking the Bay of Biscay. Awarded two stars in Michelin and 9/10 in Gourmetour, he was named "Best Cook in Spain" in 1982. Subijana underwent a traditional training at the college of hotel management in Madrid and at Euromar college in Zarauz, and became a cooking teacher in 1970. In 1986 he became Commissioner General of the European Association of Chefs, whose headquarters is in Brussels. He presents food programs on Basque Television and on Tele-Madrid. Pedro Subijana loves music and the movies.

Émile Tabourdiau

born November 25, 1943

Restaurant **Le Bristol**
Address: 112, rue du Faubourg Saint-Honoré
75008 Paris, France

Since 1964, Émile Tabourdiau has worked only in the most famous of restaurants: First at *Ledoyen*, then at *La Grande Cascade*, and finally, since 1980, at *Le Bristol*, located in the immediate vicinity of the Élysée Palace and boasting magnificent large gardens. A former pupil of Auguste Escoffier, Émile Tabourdiau is a member of the "Culinary Academy of France", and was the winner of the Prosper Montagné prize in 1970 as well as Meilleur Ouvrier de France in 1976. He restaurant has one Michelin star. In his spare time he loves painting, and enjoys playing tennis and spending time in his garden.

Romano Tamani

born April 30, 1943

Restaurant: **Ambasciata**
Address: 33, Via Martiri di Belfiore
46026 Quistello, Italy

Romano Tamani is the only one of our top chefs to hold the coveted title of Commendatore della Repubblica Italiana, a distinction conferred on him by his native Italy in 1992. This Lombardian, who learnt his craft in London and Switzerland, is without doubt one of the most skillful representatives of Italian gastronomy to be found. Together, he and his brother Francesco have run the *Ambasciata* since 1978. Accolades include two Michelin stars, three chef's hats in Espresso/Gault-Millau, one Veronelli sun and 90/100 in Gambero Rosso, as well as membership of the prestigious Italian chain Le Soste. It is hardly surprising, therefore, that cooking is Tamani's consuming passion.

Laurent Tarridec

born May 26, 1956

Restaurant: **Le Restaurant du Bistrot des Lices**
Address: Place des Lices,
83990 Saint-Tropez, France

That this Breton, a pupil of Michel Rochedy, could set himself up on the Côte d'Azur of all places, and after only one year (1995) walk off with one Michelin star and three red chef's hats in Gault-Millau (18), is testimony to his extraordinary adaptability. Before this, he honed his skills in Brittany at the *Lion d'Or*, in Paris, and in the Rhone valley at the *Beau Rivage*. Laurent Tarridec is interested in politics, as well as anything related with the sea. He also skis, rides a motorcycle, and, since living in Saint-Tropez, has discovered the game of boules.

Dominique Toulousy

born August 19, 1952

Restaurant: **Les Jardins de l'Opéra**
Address: 1, place du Capitole
31000 Toulouse, France

Dominique Toulousy has only been resident in Toulouse since 1984. Hanging out his shingle on the Place du Capitole, he reaped accolades by the dozen: "Golden Key of Gastronomy" (1986), three red chef's hats in Gault-Millau (18) and two Michelin stars, as well as the title of Meilleur Ouvrier de France (1993). Before this, he had his first successes in Gers, a region known for its generous cuisine. Dominique Toulousy is a member of the "Young Restauranteurs of Europe", the Prosper Montagné association, Eurotoques, and Traditions et Qualité. He enjoys poring over old cookbooks and loves gardening, tennis and swimming.

Gilles Tournadre

born June 29, 1955

Restaurant: **Gill**
Address: 8 & 9, quai de la Bourse
76000 Rouen, France

Even a Norman can occasionally be persuaded to leave his native region in order to learn his craft: Gilles Tournadre started out his career at *Lucas Carton*, followed by the *Auberge des Templiers* of the Bézards and *Taillevent*, before finally winding up – on his own two feet – in Bayeux, and lastly in 1984, back in his home town. His career successes have justified all these changes: the young gastronome can boast two Michelin stars and three red chef's hats (17 points) for his restaurant right near Rouen cathedral. A member of the "Young Restauranteurs of Europe", this enthusiastic sportsman loves judo, golf and motor sports, and is also a passionate conservationist.

José Tourneur

born January 4, 1940

Restaurant: **Des 3 Couleurs**
Address: 453, avenue de Tervuren
1150 Brussels, Belgium

The three colors which José Tourneur chose in 1979 as the logo and name of his restaurant are those of the Belgian national flag. The restaurant, which is wholly dedicated to Belgian cuisine, has one Michelin star and was awarded 88/100 in the Belgian restaurant guide Henri Lemaire. A self-taught cook, Tourneur gained further experience in Brussels and Nice, won the Prosper Montagné prize in 1969, and was chef de cuisine at the Brussels *Carlton* from 1969–79. He is also a member of the "Order of the 33 Masterchefs of Belgium", the "Culinary Academy of France", and the "Vatel Club". His other interests all revolve around the sea: he loves ships, and enjoys fishing and waterskiing.

Luisa Valazza

born December 20, 1950

Restaurant: **Al Sorriso**
Address: Via Roma, 18
28018 Soriso, Italy

Taking their cue from the name of the restaurant which she and her husband Angelo have run since 1981 in their home town in the Piedmont region, the food critics have all "smiled" on Luisa Valazza, awarding Al Sorriso two Michelin stars, four chef's hats in Espresso/Gault-Millau (19.2), one sun in Veronelli and 90/100 in Gambero Rosso. Our chef, who is also a member of the Le Soste chain, remains modest in the midst of this avalanche of praise, carefully cooking the recipes she has amassed since 1971 in the *Europa* in Borgomanero. Luisa Valazza is passionately interested in art, especially painting and literature. A keen museum-goer, she is also an enthusiastic practitioner of winter sports.

Guy Van Cauteren

born May 8, 1950

Restaurant: **T'Laurierblad**
Address: Dorp, 4
9290 Berlare, Belgium

Before opening his restaurant T'Laurierblad ("The Bay leaf") in 1979, Guy Van Cauteren was taught by some of France's most outstanding chefs: Alain Senderens at *Archestrate* in Paris, and the Allégriers at *Lucas Carton* (1972–4). He then spent several years cooking at the French Embassy in Brussels (1974–9). Since then, he has acquired two Michelin stars, three red chef's hats in Gault-Millau (17) and 89/100 in the Belgian restaurant guide Henri Lemaire. In addition, he was the fortunate recipient of the bronze Bocuse in 1993, and holds the title of Maître Cuisinier de Belgique. Guy Van Cauteren collects old books and enjoys traveling. In his spare time, he relaxes by cycling.

Freddy Van Decasserie

born October 10, 1943

Restaurant: **La Villa Lorraine**
Address: 75, avenue du Vivier d'Oie
1180 Brussels, Belgium

Freddy Van Decasserie started off at *La Villa Lorraine* in 1963 as a kitchen boy and worked his way up the hierarchy until finally becoming head chef and the recipient of numerous awards: two Michelin stars, three red chef's hats in Gault-Millau (18), three stars in Bottin Gourmand and 92/100 in Henri Lemaire. He is a Maître Cuisinier de Belgique and a member of the "Culinary Academy of France" and Traditions et Qualité. In his spare time, he stays fit by being a "training partner" to the racing cyclist Eddy Merckx . He also swims and goes to the occasional soccer match.

Geert Van Hecke

born July 20, 1956

Restaurant: **De Karmeliet**
Address: Langestraat, 19
8000 Bruges, Belgium

Geert Van Hecke was introduced to his craft by Freddy Van Decasserie at the *Villa Lorraine* in 1977, then served a stint with Alain Chapel at the famous *Cravache d'Or* in Brussels, finally opening his own restaurant in a renowned historic house in the heart of Bruges, the "Venice of the North". To date, his cooking has earned him two Michelin stars, three stars in the Bottin Gourmand, three red chef's hats in Gault-Millau (18) and 92/100 in Henri Lemaire. A winner of the "Best Chef in Belgium" award, he is also a member of Traditions et Qualité. It was not sheer coincidence which led him to settle in Bruges, a well preserved medieval town and popular tourist destination, as he is interested in art and enjoys visiting museums.

Gérard Vié

born April 11, 1943

Restaurant: **Les Trois Marches (Trianon Palace)**
Address: 1 boulevard de la Reine
78000 Versailles, France

The incomparable chef of the *Trois Marches* (since 1970) started his career at the tender age of 13 at *Lapérouse*. Then followed stints at *Lucas Carton* and the *Plaza-Athénée* in Paris and *Crillon Tower's* in London, as well as three years with the *Compagnie des Wagons-Lits* (1967–70). Today, Gérard Vié can boast two Michelin stars and three red chef's hats (18). Recipient of the "Silver Table" award from Gault-Millau in 1984, he was presented with the "Golden Key of Gastronomy" in 1993. An enthusiastic fan of the theater, opera and movies, he collects paintings and is a Chevalier des Arts et Lettres. He also loves hiking and swimming.

Jean-Pierre Vigato

born March 20, 1952

Restaurant: **Apicius**
Address: 122, avenue de Villiers
75017 Paris, France

Jean Pierre Vigato started off as a cellarman and served an apprenticeship in various restaurants before his first major successes at *Grandgousier* in Paris from 1980–3. In 1984 he set up on his own, opening *Apicius* in his native Paris. The restaurant, named after a famous Roman epicure, was awarded its first Michelin star in 1985, and its second two years later. It also boasts three red chef's hats in Gault-Millau (18). A member of Relais Gourmands, Jean-Pierre Vigato was Gault-Millau "Best Chef of the Year" in 1988, and chef at the French Pavillion at the 1992 World's Fair in Seville, Spain.

Gianfranco Vissani

born November 22, 1951

Restaurant: **Vissani**
Address: 05020 Civitella del Lago, Italy

With a rating of 19.6 and four chef's hats, Gianfranco Vissani got a near-perfect report card from Espresso/Gault-Millau – the best in all of Italy. Two Michelin stars, one Veronelli sun and 87/100 in Gambero Rosso complete the guidebook honors showered on the restaurant run by Vissani since 1980 as a family concern together with his wife, mother, and sister. One of the selling points of his establishment is his own olive oil, an indispensable seasoning in his Mediterranean cooking. In his spare time, this gourmet collects clocks and relaxes by listening to classical music or reading. In addition, he is an unconditional fan of the AC Milan soccer club.

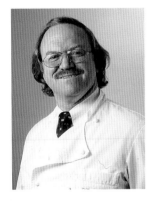

Heinz Winkler

born July 17, 1949

Restaurant: **Residenz Heinz Winkler**
Address: Kirchplatz 1,
83229 Aschau im Chiemgau, Germany

At only 31 years of age, Heinz Winkler already boasted three Michelin stars: how on earth did he do it? Perhaps by training at the *Victoria* in Interlaken, under Paul Bocuse, and at *Tantris* in Munich, before opening the *Residenz Heinz Winkler* in 1991. To crown it all, this gastronome has three white chef's hats (18) and was "Chef of the Year" in 1979 as well as "Restauranteur of the Year" in 1994 in Gault-Millau. Heinz Winkler is a member of Relais et Châteaux, Relais Gourmands, Traditions et Qualité, and the Italian chain Le Soste. He enjoys poring over old cookbooks, playing golf and skiing.

Harald Wohlfahrt

born November 7, 1955

Restaurant: **Schwarzwaldstube**
Address: Tonbachstrasse 237,
72270 Baiersbronn, Germany

Harald Wohlfahrt started work at the *Schwarzwaldstube*, the restaurant of the Hotel *Trauben-Tonbach* in the heart of the Black Forest, in 1976, and has been chef there since 1980. He learned his trade at *Stahlbad* in Baden-Baden and *Tantris* in Munich. Voted "Chef of the Year" in 1991 by Gault-Millau, he currently boasts three Michelin stars and four red chef's hats (19.5). He is also a member of Relais Gourmands and Traditions et Qualité. While his main interests, unsurprisingly, are eating- and cooking traditions, Harald Wohlfahrt is also an outstanding athlete, with swimming, soccer and cycling being his favorite sports.

Armando Zanetti

born December 11, 1926

Restaurant: **Vecchia Lanterna**
Address: Corso Re Umberto, 21
10128 Turin, Italy

A native Venetian, Armando Zanetti ran the *Rosa d'Oro* in Turin from 1955–69 before opening the evocatively named *Vecchia Lanterna* ("Old Lantern") restaurant in the same city in 1970. Today, our chef, who devotes himself chiefly to the traditional cuisine of his native country, proudly boasts two Michelin stars and four chef's hats in Espresso/Gault-Millau (19.2/20). In his spare time, Armando Zanetti tirelessly researches European cuisine of bygone eras. He derives special pleasure from trying new dishes, both his own and those of his fellow chefs.

Alberto Zuluaga

born March 31, 1960

Restaurant: **Lopez de Haro y Club Nautico**
Address: Obispo Orueta, 2
48009 Bilbao, Spain

As a Basque from the Spanish province of Vizcaya on the Bay of Biscay, Alberto Zuluaga is especially proud to be able to exercise his profession in the true capital of his native province. He has been chef of the five-star luxury restaurant *Club Nautico* in the banking district of Bilbao since 1991. Before this, from 1987–91, he cultivated his love of Basque cuisine and culinary traditions at the *Bermeo* in the same city, earning the title of "Best Cook in Euzkadi" (the Basque Country) in 1988. It goes without saying that our chef enjoys playing Basque boules in his spare time, but he also likes car racing. He is also an enthusiastic mushroom hunter when time allows.

The Pastry Chefs

Adolf Andersen

born August 10, 1936

Konditorei Café Confiserie Andersen
Wandsbeker Markstraße 153
D-22041 Hamburg, Germany
Branches: Jungfernstieg 26; Market 16,
Glinde; EKZ Hamburger Straße; Axel-Sprin-
ger-Platz; EKZ Quarree Wandsbek Markt;
Stadtzentrum Schenefeld

Adolf Andersen comes from a family whose
members have been in business as pastry chefs
since 1910; he owns a confectioner's shop with
a number of branches in Hamburg. In his cafés,
visitors can sample his creations based on "old
family recipes, highly modern techniques, and fine discrimination." His personal
style was developed mainly during his apprenticeship in the Voigt confectioner's
shop in Braunschweig. His hobbies are cycling, fishing, and jazz.

Franz Augustin

born April 12, 1954

Demel k.u.k. Hofzuckerbäckerei
Kohlmarkt 14
A-1010 Vienna, Austria

Demel, the court confectioner's – the most
famous of such establishments in the time of the
Austro-Hungarian empire and supplier to the
imperial and royal court – needs no introduction.
Franz Augustin, who received sound training in
the Baumert (1969–74) and Nahodil (1974–89)
confectioneries, has been manager of the
bakery in this renowned establishment since
1994. Besides his great love of classic Viennese delicacies, Franz Augustin is
interested in movies and documentary films. His other hobbies are bowling and
travel.

Eric Baumann

born September 29, 1961

Confiserie Pâtisserie Baumann
Balgriststraße 2
CH-8005 Zürich, Switzerland

Eric Baumann is a perfectionist. He first trained
at the Kaderschule in Zürich (1988–90) and
then worked in notable establishments in Biel,
St. Gall, and Zürich, as well as a period in
Mulhouse with Gérard Bannwarth. Eric
Baumann maintains excellent contacts with
various pastry chefs' associations, such as the
Cercle des Confiseurs, of which he has been a
member since 1993, and the international society *Relais Desserts*, which he
joined in September 1996. In his free time, Eric Baumann enjoys horseback
riding. He also goes jogging twice a week with his fellow-workers.

Jean-Jacques Bernachon

born October 27, 1944

Chocolaterie Pâtisserie Bernachon
42, Cours Franklin Roosevelt
F-69006 Lyon, France

After an apprenticeship in the Pâtisserie
Marchand in Bougoin-Jallieu in the French
département of Isère, Jean-Jacques, the son of
Maurice Bernachon, completed several periods
of practical training in Paris at Suchard, in
Amsterdam at Blooker, and at Basle at the
École La Koba. In 1967–8 he worked for
Bocuse, to whose principles he has remained
faithful ever since. In 1969 he returned to Lyon, to work in his father's
establishment. Jean-Jacques Bernachon enjoys team sports, such as soccer
and rugby, and also plays golf. He is also interested in contemporary art,
reading, and travel.

Maurice Bernachon

born January 10, 1919

Chocolaterie Pâtisserie Bernachon
42, Cours Franklin Roosevelt
F-69006 Lyon, France

The "*roi du chocolat*" (king of chocolate),
Maurice Bernachon, received his training at
Deboges in Pont-de-Bauvoisin and, before the
beginning of World War II, in Lyon at Lauthome
and at Collard. As a result of a war injury, he
returned to Lyon in 1942, and worked at the
Durand establishment. After a brief interlude in
Trévoux, he opened his own confectioner's
shop in Lyon. A close friend and colleague of Paul Bocuse, Maurice Bernachon
has been awarded the Ordre du Mérite Agricole and the Ordre des Arts et
Lettres. His hobbies are flowers, reading, and soccer.

Christian Cottard

born July 17, 1959

Pâtisserie Christian Cottard
49, Rue de la République
F-06600 Antibes, France

Christian Cottard comes from a family of pastry
chefs in Menton. In 1986 and 1989 he reached
the finals for the title of Best Craftsman of
Europe, and in 1989 he became *Champion de
France en Desserts*. In the same year he settled
in Antibes, after demonstrating his abilities at
the Oasis in La Napoule, and the Hôtel de Paris
and the Louis XV in Monaco with Alain
Ducasse. He is "open to all things beautiful" and likes to take part in the
glittering social occasions on the Côte d'Azur. Christian Cottard enjoys skiing
and surfing, is interested in photography, and particularly values family life.

Lucas Devriese

born January 3, 1964

Pâtisserie Lucas
Van Bunnenplein 29
B-8300 Knokke-Heist, Belgium

Lucas Devriese trained with Jeff Damme in Ghent in 1985–9. In 1989, in Knokke – where he had gained his first professional experience with Roelens in the Notre-Dame confectionery – he opened his own establishment on the premises of the butcher's shop formerly owned by his parents-in-law. Today he is a member of the association *Top Desserts*. Lucas Devriese's hobbies are motorcycling and cycling in the nearby park, Het Zwin. He also likes dining out. He never forgets to mention how important his wife Hilde is to him in all his personal and professional enterprises.

Philippe Guignard

born March 13, 1963

Maison Guignard Desserts
Grand-Rue 17-19
CH-1350 Orbe (Canton of Waadt),
Switzerland

Since 1989 Philippe Guignard has managed his own bakery and confectionery, to which he added a café-restaurant in 1992. Meeting his friend Albert Bise, a friend with a passion for gastronomy, was decisive in his choice of career. Together with his head pastry chef, Laurent Buet, Philippe Guignard combines "whatever is good and beautiful and goes well together," and he is proud of the constant encouragement he receives from his customers. Philippe Guignard is a nature-lover, enjoys cycling, plays tennis, and is an active member of the Yverdon football club.

Helmut Lengauer

born February 1, 1961

Hotel Sacher
Philharmonikerstraße 4
A-1010 Vienna, Austria

The genuine Sachertorte is produced in the Hotel Sacher, which is famous far beyond the borders of Austria. This delicious *torte* is named after Metternich's cook Franz Sacher, who created it in the summer of 1815 for the Congress of Vienna. Since 1985 Helmut Lengauer has been head pastry chef at the Hotel Sacher, where he upholds the tradition and renown of this establishment, whose pastries exemplify the European lifestyle. Not surprisingly, Helmut Lengauer is a great lover of classical music. He also loves playing tennis, and in the winter he skis in the mountains.

Christian Nihoul

born October 8, 1946

Gourmand Gaillard
1–7, Rue J. Jourdaens
B-1000 Brussels, Belgium

For 100 years the family Nihoul's confectionery business, which moved into its premises in the Avenue Louise in Brussels, has been a household name, and in particular it enjoys the patronage of the Belgian royal family. Christian Nihoul, who has managed the business since 1964, created a chocolate violin for Queen Fabiola. Moreover, he has set up numerous contacts in other countries (the United States, Korea, the World Exhibition in Seville), and has even opened two branches in Japan. He is a member of the Culinary Academy of France. For a long time Christian Nihoul's hobbies included fencing. He is also interested in Formula 1 racing and comic books.

Flavio Perbellini

born November 8, 1954

Pasticceria Ernesto Perbellini
Via V. Veneto, 46
1-37051 Bovolone (Verona), Italy

The members of the Perbellini family have worked as pastry chefs for five generations – since the foundation of the firm by Luigi Perbellini in 1862. Flavio Perbellini received his training at the Technical Institute in Forli and then completed his practical training in France, at the Lenôtre School and with Taillevent. In 1986 he won a prize at the confectionery competition in Mestre. He carries on the family tradition with his brothers Giovanni Battista and Enzo. Flavio Perbellini loves his native city of Verona. Other interests are figurative painting – Botticelli is his idol – and swimming.

Bernard Proot

born July 30, 1954

Chocolaterie Pâtisserie Del Rey
Appelmanstraat 5
B-2018 Antwerp, Belgium

Bernard Proot gained his first professional experience in the Del Rey confectionery, observed by his employer Marchand, who sent him to Lenôtre for several periods of practical training. To avoid "getting out of practice," he then went to Brussels for two years to work with Paul Wittamer. In 1963 he opened his own *chocolaterie-pâtisserie*, which was extended to include a café. He is a member of *Relais Desserts* and the association *Top Desserts*. "One can always exceed one's limits" is Bernard Proot's motto. He values family life, and enjoys good food and going to the cinema. He also likes squash and basketball, especially when his son Jan is playing.

Francisco Torreblanca

born February 5, 1951

Pasteleria Totel
Gran Avenida 103
E-03600 Elda (Alicante), Spain

Since 1978 Francisco Torreblanca has run the Pasteleria Totel, one of the most famous confectioners in Alicante, a Greek and later Roman colony that once laid the foundation for the prosperity of the kingdom of Valencia. Francisco Torreblanca has received many awards, such as Best Pastrycook in Spain in 1988. In 1990 he was awarded the title of Best Pastrycook in Europe in Madrid. He is a member of *Relais Desserts* and has won a reputation that extends far beyond the borders of Spain. Francisco Torreblanca is very interested in painting and classical music, to which he dedicates much of his spare time.

Gunther Van Essche

born August 11, 1965

Chocolaterie Pâtisserie Del Rey
Appelmanstraat 5
B-2018 Antwerp, Belgium

Bernard Proot's colleague Gunther Van Essche trained with Paul Wittamer in Brussels and then worked in the Pâtisserie Etienne in Ophasselt. In 1994 he received the international prize Mandarine Impériale, and in 1995 the Prosper Montagne, which is awarded to the best pastry chef in Belgium. In the same year he became World Champion Pastry Chef jointly with Rik de Baere and Pierre Marcolini. To achieve all this, is it enough to be a "perfectionist," as he describes himself? Certainly a great deal of talent and the constant ambition to create something new also have something to do with it. Gunther Van Essche devotes his spare time to gardening, fitness training, and ju-jitsu.

Glossary

TO ADD LIQUID: adding liquid such as wine or broth to the contents in the frying pan to loosen them from the base of the pan.

TO ADJUST SEASONING TO TASTE: seasoning a dish towards the end of preparation, or seasoning its components as you complete their preparation, with salt, pepper, spices, or herbs according to taste rather than measurement.

AÏOLI: a Provençal garlic mayonnaise (in French, ail meants garlic) traditionally served with steamed fish, hard-boiled eggs, or vegetables, such as crudités.

AL DENTE: to keep pasta or vegetables from being overcooked, and thus render them too soft to resist slightly a diner's bite, Italians instruct they be cooked "to the tooth."

ALMOND AND SUGAR MIXTURE: Mixture of equal parts (by weight rather than volume) of ground almonds and refined sugar.

AMERICAN SAUCE: a sauce made with roasted root vegetables and crushed lobster shells; the sauce is flambéd with brandy, white wine is added, and it is finally whisked with butter. It is traditionally served with fish and shellfish.

ANGELICA: A herb, related to parsley, with a slightly bitter flavor. The stalk of the angelica plant is usually dried and candied and used as a garnish for tortes or other sweet dishes.

APRICOT GLAZE: Hot, strained apricot jam can be spread onto pastries, either as a glaze or as an isolating layer underneath glazes and cream or fruit fillings.

ASPIC: a flavored jelly, often made from clarified meat juices (but also from vegetables or fish) that sets to form a clear or semi-clear elastic mixture, prepared with pectin or gelatin. Used as a base for molded dishes as well as a garnish – served, for example, as a cubed accompaniment next to a terrine that is based on the same aspic.

BAIN-MARIE: an extremely delicate method of cooking ingredients, such as custards or sauces, that will turn if subjected to a sudden change in temperature. A pot, bowl, or pan of food is placed in a larger pot that is filled with warm water (sometimes boiling, sometimes at a lower temperature); the combination is then cooked in an oven or on the stove. See double boiler.

TO BAKE: To cook food surrounded by the dry heat of an oven.

TO BAKE AU GRATIN: to sprinkle cooked dishes with bread crumbs, cheese, or pats of butter and bake at high heat, allowing a crust to form.

TO BAKE BLIND: To bake a pastry shell without a filling. The bottom should be pricked with a fork to release steam, then covered with waxed or baking paper and filled with dried beans, rice or metal baking beans, which pre-vent the bottom from buckling and the sides from collapsing.

TO BAKE WITH OR WITHOUT STEAM: Most professional ovens, but few home ovens, are outfitted with a special vent that traps moisture in the oven when closed, but allows steam to escape when opened, creating a drier heat similar to home ovens. When a recipe specifies to bake with steam, one can create a similar effect at home by placing a shallow pan filled with water in the oven. To achieve better results when baking in a convection (or fan) oven, which creates a very dry heat, always add a source of moisture.

TO BASTE: to moisten roast meat (such as roast beef, roast duck, suckling pig, roast turkey, etc.) with the meat's own juices to prevent the meat from drying out while in the oven. Basting is also done to encourage skin to become crispy or a crust to build up.

BÉCHAMEL SAUCE: one of the French "mother sauces," made with flour, butter, and milk (the proportions determine its consistency, which may vary), blended into a creamy sauce and served hot.

TO BIND: Adding any of a number of substances, including flour, cornstarch, eggs, egg yolk, gelatin or cream, to a hot liquid in order to make it creamier.

TO BIND IN A ROUX: to bind (or thicken) sauces or bind vegetables together in a heated mixture of equal amounts of flour and butter.

BISCUIT: The French word for sponge cake. In Eurodélices, biscuit designates a classic sponge cake of egg whites and egg yolks, each beaten separately with sugar until light and foamy, then combined and enriched with a small amount of flour, ground nuts and/or baking powder.

TO BLANCH: a technique with two purposes: the first is to cook ingredients, particularly vegetables, in boiling water for just a moment then in cold water to either soften a harsh flavor or scent, or kill germs or enzymes. The second is to pour boiling water over fruit, vegetables, or nuts to facilitate peeling or shelling; alternately, they may be dipped in the boiling water for a moment (as in blanching tomatoes).

TO BLEND: See to fold.

BLINI: the traditional small Russian pancakes made with buckwheat flour, usually served with soured cream, caviar or smoked salmon.

BOUQUET GARNI: a bunch of herbs that are tied together and used for seasoning soups, casseroles, etc. The traditional bundle consists principally of thyme, bay leaf, and parsley, but rosemary, marjoram, lovage, fennel, leek, or celery might also be used, depending on the recipe and the region.

TO BRAISE: a technique (in the oven or on the stove) of cooking vegetables or meat, alt-hough it may also be used with certain kinds of fruit. The ingredients are first browned in butter, oil, or lard, then a small amount of liquid (such as water, broth, stock, or wine) is added, the pan is tightly covered, and the ingredients are slowly cooked. The ingredients thus cook in fat, liquid and vapor, with tender, flavorful results.

TO BREAD: to roll meat, poultry, vegetables, or fish in a mixture of flour, eggs, and bread crumbs, for subsequently frying or deep-frying.

BRITTLE: A mixture of caramelized sugar and nuts, often ground hazelnuts or almonds; crumbled it is a common topping for cakes and desserts, particularly in Europe, where it is called krokant.

BROTH: a spiced cooking broth, which is the result of having cooked meat, fish, or vegetables in water; the cooking ingredients impart their flavor into the water and turn it into stock that can then be used for cooking other ingredients.

TO BROWN: to cook briefly over a high or medium-high heat, usually in a buttered or oiled frying pan on top of the stove. Often used to cook a tender piece of meat or a slice of bacon, or thin slices of vegetables such as potatoes; the method browns the exterior but enables the interior to remain moist.

BRUNOISE: a mélange or mixture of vegetables that have been either shredded, grated, or diced finely, and are then slowly cooked in butter, to be used primarily to flavor sauces or soups.

CAKE GLAZE: Cake glaze is available in most European countries as a ready mix. The commercial mixture is modified starch, the gelling agent carrageenan, with the addition of calcium tartrate. At home one could use 1 heaped tbsp / 15 g of a mixture of cornstarch and ground gelatin or carrageenan and 2 level tbsp / 30 g of sugar, to which 1 cup / 250 ml water (or a little more than 1 cup / 250 ml fruit juice) is gradually added over low heat. Stir continuously until the glaze is smooth, then bring to a boil and thicken. use immediately.

TO CANDY: To immerse, marinate or cook fruits, flowers, peel or seeds (e.g. cherries, ginger, lemon peel, orange peel, violets) in one or more increasingly concentrated sugar syrups and then allow them to air-dry. The sugar crystallizes, forming the typical thick crust.

CARAMEL: Caramel is produced when sugar is melted and heated to 320–350 °F/160–177 °C and becomes light to dark brown. To make caramel candy or sauce, other ingredients like water, cream and butter are added, but one must add liquid carefully and gradually to sugar heated to these temperatures.

TO CARAMELIZE: To melt sugar until it becomes caramel; or to coat with caramelized sugar; or to sprinkle sugar on the surface of a cake or dessert and then apply strong heat briefly until the sugar turns into caramel (for example, a crème brûlée).

CARPACCIO: a classic Italian dish with a legendary history (see carpaccio recipes throughout this volume), in which extremely thin slices of filleted, raw meat (usually beef) are dressed with oil and lemon juice, a mayonnaise or mustard dressing, or with an olive oil vinaigrette, and served as an appetizer. The term has also come to include types of fish and shellfish.

TO CARVE: to slice meat, poultry or fish, or to cut these for presentation, traditionally in front of the dining guests. A large and very sharp knife and a chopping board are required for carving.

CHANTILLY: part of the French culinary vocabulary, meaning dishes (à la chantilly), from sweet puddings to savory appetizers, that are served with or mixed with whipped cream. The dessert Chantilly cream is a sweetened whipped cream, often flavored with a liqueur or vanilla extract.

CHARLOTTE: A charlotte is multi-layered; a form begins with spongecake, finger biscuits (ladyfingers), waffle, or buttered bread base, topped with layers of either a pudding of pureed fruit, or whipped cream or custard.

CHARTREUSE: a pie made with chopped meat, vegetables and bacon, cooked in a bain-marie, and served cold. There is also a liqueur of the same name, that comes in green or yellow varieties and was originally developed by the monks of La Grance Chartreuse in France.

CHOCOLATE COATING: Also known by its French name, couverture, chocolate coating is professional-quality chocolate with a high cocoa butter content (around one-third) that makes it particularly suitable for thin, shiny chocolate glazes. It is available in chocolate shops or gourmet supply stores.

CLARIFIED BUTTER: Butter from which the milk solids and water have been removed, leaving pure butter fat. It has a higher smoking point than whole butter but less butter flavor. To clarify butter, melt it slowly in a double boiler without stirring, then remove and discard the foam on the surface and pour off the clear butter without the solids at the bottom of the pan.

TO CLARIFY: to make a cloudy liquid, such as a soup or sauce, clear by stirring in slightly whisked egg white, carefully heating, cooling, and, finally, straining through a seive or cheesecloth; the egg whites attract the sediment.

TO COAT: In baking, coating generally refers to covering cakes and pastries with a surface layer of chocolate, marzipan or other substance.

COCKLES: molluscs of the family cardium, who have striped and ribbed brown-and-white (to varying degrees) shells. Cockles are at home in the flat coastal waters of the Atlantic and the Mediterranean. Wash thoroughly to clean them of substantial amounts of sand, and serve raw with lemon juice, fried, or steamed.

CONFECTIONERS' SUGAR: American term for icing sugar. Also known as powdered sugar.

CONSOMMÉ: a meat or vegetable broth, cooked and reduced for a long time and finally clarified until it is translucent. Served cold or hot, and often used as the base for a stock or soup.

CORAL: the roe of crustaceans, from lobsters to scallops, so named because, when cooked, it turns a salmon-pink color that resembles the color of some ocean coral; regarded by gourmets as a particular delicacy.

COULIS: A thick sauce consisting of pureed fruit, sometimes with the addition of lemon juice and sugar syrup.

CROUTONS: roasted or toasted diced bread, used to garnish soups, baked dishes or salads; often browned in garlic, herbs, or spices.

CRUDITÉS: a French term for raw vegetables, usually cut into strips, served as an appetizer with dips, a cold dressing, or sauce.

CUSTARD: sauce for puddings made with confectioners' sugar, an egg yolk, milk, and a pinch of salt, rounded off with cream. Often cooked in a bain-marie.

TO DEEP-FRY: to cook (usually until crisp and brown) ingredients, usually vegetables, fish, or meat, by immersing them in extremely hot oil or other fat. The exterior crust formed seals in the food's flavors and moisture.

TO DEGLAZE: To use a liquid such as wine, water, or stock (or fruit juice in sweet recipes) to dissolve food particles and/or caramelized drippings left in a pan after food has been roasted or sautéed in it. The liquid is usually used to make a sauce to serve with the food.

DIJONNAISE: French term for dishes prepared with light Dijon mustard, a special, creamy kind of mustard made with mustard grains soaked in sour, fermented juice of unripe grapes, and hailing originally from Dijon, France.

DOUBLE BOILER: Also called a bain-marie, a double boiler is two pans that nestle into each other. The bottom pan is filled with simmering water and the top pan rests over, but not in, the hot water, providing a gently source of heat to cook delicate foods like custards and sauces, to melt chocolate, and to dissolve gelatin. See also water bath.

EXTRACT: Baking extracts are the concentrated flavors and scents of fruits, plants and spices, which are suspended in "carriers" (usually alcohol or oil). Some of the most commonly used in baking include vanilla, lemon, bitter almond, rum, and arrack.

FLAMBÉ: though often a technique of presentation intended to impart a sense of drama to a dish – the word is French for "flaming" – it may also be a step during the cooking process. Either way, it involves pouring liquor on top of foods most often a dessert (crêpes, crème brûlée still

cooking and lighting the alcohol to better render the food's aroma.

TO FLAVOR: Adding spices, herbs, extracts or alcohol to foods in order to give them a particular taste.

TO FLOUR: Also called dusting, this means coating a greased baking pan with flour, sugar, bread crumbs, sesame seeds, finely ground almonds or other nuts, or another fine substance.

TO FOLD: Also called blending. A means of combining a light, airy mixture (often beaten egg whites) with a second, heavier mixture. With the lighter mixture on top of the heavier one, use a spatula to cut through both, scrape along the bottom of the bowl and then up the side. Rotate the bowl slightly and repeat until the mixtures are thoroughly blended. This should be done very carefully and gently so that the lighter mixture does not collapse and its volume is retained.

FONDANT: A mixture of sugar, water, and cream of tartar cooked until the syrup is reduced, then kneaded and beaten until the mixture can easily be molded. It is used to form decorations, or warmed and used as icing for cakes.

TO FRY BRIEFLY: to fry meat, fish, onions or other ingredients in a little hot fat, just until brown.

GALANTINE: a classic French layered dish, often consisting of a spicy pie that is cooked rolled in cloth or thin strips of meat, or in an appropriate form.

GARNISH: the decoration of a dish, considered a crucial aspect in many cuisines; also used to refer to ingredients added to a soup or sauce, such as cream or chopped onions in soup, or chopped herbs in a sauce.

GAZPACHO: a cold vegetable soup of Spanish origin traditionally made with ripe tomatoes, red peppers, cucumber, olive oil, garlic and bread crust.

GELATIN: A clear and flavorless substance used to jell liquid mixtures. Gelatin is available in 1/4 oz / 7 g envelopes of granules (more common in the United States), or in paper-thin sheets (standard in Europe). Sheet gelatin should be soaked in cold water for 5–10 minutes, then thoroughly wrung out before, like ground gelatin, being dissolved in a small amount of hot liquid (preferably in a double boiler) before use. To jell 2 cups / 500 ml of liquid, one needs 1 envelope or 4 sheets of gelatin.

GÉNOISE: A type of sponge cake in which whole eggs are beaten with sugar until light and foamy before flour, finely ground nuts or other ingredients are folded into them.

TO GLAZE: To spread a thin layer of eggs, jelly or jam, gum arabic or any other kind of coating onto foods to give them a shiny finish.

GLUCOSE: A thickening syrup that is often added to sugar when it is cooked to ensure that the sugar recrystallizes.

TO GREASE: Brushing a thin layer of butter or some other fat onto baking pans so that the finished pastry is easier to remove from the pan.

TO GRILL: a method of cooking that retains a certain freshness in the food, either on wood or charcoal over a grill.

HALF AND HALF: Mixture of equal parts milk and cream, widely available in the United States.

HEAVY CREAM: American term for double cream.

HOISIN SAUCE: a spicy reddish-brown sauce from China made from fermented soy beans, flour, salt, sugar, and raw rice. Its natural coloring lends visual depth to many Chinese dishes.

INSTANT COFFEE: Soluble coffee with a very intense flavor that is manufactured according to a particular process.

ITALIAN MERINGUE: A variation of meringue made by beating egg whites until stiff and then pouring hot sugar syrup over them while beating continuously until the meringue has completely cooled.

JELLY: (also see aspic) clear or semi-clear elastic mixture, prepared with pectin or gelatin; also: meat juices set to form a jelly.

JULIENNE: to cut vegetables (often raw) into thin strips often about matchstick size; some chefs prefer to julienne by hand, some use a slicer.

TO KNEAD: To combine thoroughly and work the components of a dough either manually with both hands or with the dough hook of an electric mixer. Kneading by hand, it can take 15 minutes or longer until a smooth, elastic dough is produced.

LANGOUSTINE: a French term for a crustacean that is wholly different from either a prawn, a crayfish, or a shrimp. Langoustines have pink or pale-red bodies and elongated, but pronounced front claws; their flavor is both sweet and subtle, and lends them well to dishes such as terrines. Unfortunately, langoustines can not survive for too long out of water, and so are often sold cooked in regions far from the coast.

LARD: to lace or wrap lean meat with strips of bacon, truffle slices, or cloves of garlic to prevent it from drying out, and to impart additional flavors.

LIGHT CREAM: American term for single cream.

TO MARINATE: a technique known in virtually every cuisine in which fish, meat, poultry, vegetables, or even fruit are coated with a mixture of, usually, oil, vinegar, and lemon juice flavored with herbs and spices. As the food absorbs the flavors of the marinade, it also tenderizes, thus reducing cooking time, and in some cases even replacing the cooking process. To marinate fruits (especially dried fruits) in alcohol or liqueur until they take on the flavor of the marinating liquid.

MARZIPAN: A paste-like mixture of finely ground almonds, sugar or confectioners' sugar, and often egg whites. Raw marzipan is available ready-made.

MERINGUE: A light mixture consisting of sugar and stiffly beaten egg whites; it can be used as an icing or topping, an element of a mousse or cream, or baked as cookies or bases for tortes. see also Italian meringue.

MOUSSE: a French word for foam. A mousse is an airy yet substantial sweet or savory dish that owes its soft, delicate and fluffy structure to egg whites that have been whisked until stiff, or whipped cream. To further bind a mousse, gelatin may be added as well.

NOUGAT: Called praline in French, nougat is a paste or cream consisting of finely ground roasted nuts (most often hazelnuts or almonds), sugar, and sometimes honey or cocoa. Light nougats, such as Nougat del Montélimar, contain no cocoa solids.

PARFAIT: in French, the word means perfect or complete; a cold dish made with a delicate stuffing, bound with gelatin or egg white, filled into forms and inverted after chilling. A sweet parfait is a chilled pudding, usually composed of ice cream, jelly, egg cream, a lacing of syrup or liqueur, and cream, served in a special high glass.

PERSILLADE: from the French word for parsley; a mixture of finely chopped parsley and garlic or of thin strips of cold beef and vinegar, oil, and plenty of parsley.

PHYLLO DOUGH: a dough made with sticky flour (wheat), water, and oil (fat) that is rolled out paper-thin, cut into slices, brushed with oil, and stacked, often between layers of wax paper. Used frequently in the Near East, Turkey, Greece, Austria, and Hungary. It is similar to puff pastry, which may be used instead.

TO POACH: to cook ingredients by immersing them in a small amount of liquid over low heat, often used for fish or dumplings.

PRALINE: See nougat.

PRAWN: an often-confusing term, sometimes used to describe any large shrimp, or to refer to langoustines (see langoustines), or to refer to freshwater shrimps. However, prawns in the strictest sense of the word are both salt and fresh water dwellers, migrating from one to the other to spawn. They are larger than shrimps and have longer legs and narrower bodies. King prawns may also be marketed as jumbo shrimps, particularly in the United States.

TO PRICK: Making holes in an uncooked dough (such as short pastry) at regular intervals with a fork before baking, so that it does not form blisters while baking.

TO PROVE: See to rise.

PUREE: to work soft ingredients into a smooth and even mixture, usually using either a blender or a food processor.

QUARK: A soft, spreadable, unripened cheese extremely popular in German-speaking countries, quark has a flavor similar to cottage cheese, but with the texture of sour cream. Unlike ricotta, it is unsalted, and is milder and less rich than mascarpone. It is used to make cheesecakes, as a substitute for sour cream, in a number of desserts, or simply spread on bread or eaten with fruit. As a fresh cheese, it is best consumed within a short time of manufacture. It is increasingly available in specialist outlets in the US.

TO REDUCE: to cook a sauce or gravy for so long that its liquid content evaporates, resulting in a distilled, thick, and more intensely aromatic sauce.

TO REFRESH: A means of preventing sensitive foods like custards from continuing to cook while cooling slowly by rinsing or submerging the cooking pot or bowl in cold water in order to lower the temperature rapidly.

RÉMOULADE: a sauce; essentially an herb mayonnaise and mustard blend seasoned with chopped tarragon, chervil, parsley, gherkin pickles, and capers. It is available in some shops as a ready-made product, and often accompanies cold meat, fish, and crustaceans.

RENNET: A small, speckled apple well-suited to cooking and baking, it is beloved by chefs and cooks in Europe but not available in the United States. Pippin or Granny Smith are the closest substitutes.

TO RINSE WITH COLD WATER: a technique used to arrest the cooking process immediately, rather than let a just-cooked ingredient keep cooking in its absorbed heat. Invaluable for keeping vegetables crisp and green, and pasta al dente.

TO RISE: Allowing a yeast dough or yeast mixture to rest covered in a warm place so that it can increase in size.

TO ROAST: often a misunderstood term, to roast something simply means to cook it in the oven uncovered, that is to say in dry heat, until brown and crisp. Nuts and kernels become more aromatic through roasting; tender pieces of meat or vegetables benefit from it as well.

ROYAL ICING: A decorative icing that consists of beaten egg white, sifted confectioners' sugar, and lemon juice.

SABAYON: See zabaglione.

SAFFRON: spice harvested from the stamen of the saffron flower (a kind of purple crocus). As the tiny dust threads containing the saffron powder can only be picked by hand it is the world's most expensive spice. Fortunately, only extremely small amounts are required to add its pungent flavoring or unique yellow color to, for instance, fish and rice dishes, curries and puddings.

SALAMANDER: A hand-held kitchen tool used to grill or brown food.

SAUTÉ: to fry ingredients briefly over direct heat in a little butter or oil until slightly brown.

SCALLOPS: a mollusc with a characteristic flat shell. It moves about with the shell open, using a large muscle; that muscle is the part that is consumed, along with the orange coral. Scallops are usually prepared and served in their shell, and come in two basic types: the small, delicately flavored bay scallop, and the larger, slightly stronger-flavored sea scallop.

TO SCOOP: a technique of scooping out dumplings, balls and similar shapes with a specially fashioned scoop or a spoon, sometimes for further blanching.

TO SCORE: to make incision on both sides of a piece of meat or fish for decorative reasons, also useful for preventing food from splitting and achieving even cooking on all surfaces.

SHRIMP: the most popular crustacean in the United States is actually a grouping of hundreds of sub-species. Essentially, a shrimp is a small crustacean without claws or shears, with slim legs and a large, plump body. The color varies according to species, but most turn orange-red when cooked. Shrimp exist in cold and warm waters and in fresh water as well as in sea water. They form the basis for a variety of dishes in many countries, and range in size from colossal to miniature.

TO SIMMER: to cook ingredients in liquid over a low heat to prevent the liquid from boiling, or to reduce the heat from ingredients that have reached a boil to a slower rate of cooking.

TO SKIM: to remove the fat floating on the surface of a liquid (usually soups or sauces) with a skimming spoon or by straining the liquid; sometimes also used when clarifying sauces or butter.

TO SOAK: To drizzle a mixture of sugar syrup, spirits, fruit juice or other ingredients onto sponge cake bases, pastries, etc. until they are completely drenched. Smaller pastries can also be briefly dipped into the soaking liquid.

SOUFFLÉ: a light, airy dish based on eggs from the French term for inflating. Can be sweet or savory, served hot (which may require some delicate handling) or cold. The airy and fluffy structure is achieved by folding whisked egg whites that are very stiff into a warm sauce or puree. Often cooked in a special round and straight-sided soufflé dish.

TO STEAM: a technique that has gained in popularity in the past decade or two. To steam food is to cook it over vapor rising from boiling stock or liquid, using a steamer equipped with a rack, or in multi-layered metal or bamboo steam pots. Also used to describe the process of cooking ingredients in their own juices, with perhaps a very small amount of liquid or fat added.

STOCK: the juices produced by meat, poultry, vegetables, or fish during cooking, used to form the base of sauces. Can be purchased ready-made, or made far in advance and kept chilled or frozen until ready to use.

TO STRAIN: to pass ingedients (mostly liquid) through a sieve; a technique often used for clarifying sauces and stocks.

STUFFING: a mixture of chopped meat or fish with herbs and spices for filling pies or poultry. Rice, vegetables, rice, bread crumbs, or eggs mixed with meat or entrails are also used for stuffing.

SUGAR SYRUP: A solution of sugar and water that has briefly been boiled, sugar syrup can be made in various concentrations and is used for countless purposes in baking and confection-making. In Eurodélices, the sugar syrup called for is a heavy syrup of equal parts sugar and water, unless otherwise specified. The sugar is heated to a temperature of 212 °F / 100 °C, or to 28 °Beaumé (the equivalent of 30 °Beaumé once cooled). The concentration, or density, of the syrup is measured in degrees Beaumé using a sugar scale, which was invented by the French chemist and engineer, Antoine Beaumé (1728–1804).

TO SWEAT: to cook vegetables, in particular onions, or flour, over a low heat in fat without allowing them to turn brown, but only until they soften and begin to glisten, as if sweating.

TARTARE: traditionally, a dish comprised of raw ground beef prepared with finely chopped onions, gherkins, capers or parsley, pepper and salt; increasingly, chefs are discovering other ingredients to present as tartares, such as fish.

TO TEMPER: A method of preparing chocolate to be used for decorative work or coating by slowly melting chocolate, then allowing it to partially cool, then reheating it very briefly. This complicated process serves the purpose of preventing the cocoa butter contained in the chocolate from crystallizing, which would severely detract from the appearance of the finished product.

TERRINE: a dish made with finely chopped meat, poultry, game, fish, or vegetables (or a combination of any of these), cooked in a deep dish or form with straight walls (also called a terrine, or a terrine form). Terrines are usually served cold, and are often bound in aspic.

TO THICKEN: To slightly thicken liquid mixtures either by stirring in egg yolk and cream, milk or butter; or by cooking a cream or sauce without allowing it to boil, stirring constantly, until it coats a wooden spoon, i.e. reaches a thick but still liquid consistency. Also see reduce.

TRUFFLES: this delicacy actually includes quite a few varieties, the most famous of which is the black truffle. Essentially, a truffle is a large wild edible mushroom with a bulbous stem and a fleshy red-brown cap, but its sublime flavor and the effort involved in harvesting it have helped to make it one of the most luxurious ingredients used in cooking. It is found by truffle dogs or pigs in the fall, under oak and chestnut trees.

TURNING: A particular sequence of folding dough into thirds, rolling it out, and folding it into thirds again when making puff pastry. The more frequently this process is repeated, the more puffy layers the dough has. Flaky puff pastry is folded and turned four to six times, and must be refrigerated between each turn.

VANILLA SUGAR: Sugar infused with the flavor of vanilla bean, or containing some ground vanilla bean. It is easy to produce sugar with the distinctive vanilla fragrance at home by placing one or more vanilla beans in a jar filled with superfine sugar. After a week or two the sugar is permeated with the aroma of vanilla.

VANILLIN SUGAR: Sugar containing vanillin, an artificial vanilla substitute.

VELOUTÉ: another of the "mother sauces" from French cuisine, so named for its velvety consistenty (in French, velours means velvet). This thick, white sauce is made with butter, flour, veal or chicken stock, and seasoned with salt and pepper. Available ready-made.

VINAIGRETTE: a salad dressing based on the perennial combination of vinegar and oil, often laced with herbs, deepened with mustard, and finally seasoned with salt and pepper.

WATER BATH: Similar to a double boiler, foods cooked in a water bath are placed in a larger pan partially filled with water while baked in an oven.

YEAST MIXTURE: Also called yeast starter, a yeast mixture is the first stage in preparing many yeast dough recipes. Generally, it consists of the yeast, a portion of the flour and liquid, and a little sugar. This is worked into a soft dough and allowed to rise in a warm place, covered, until its volume has doubled. It is then kneaded with the other ingredients to form the yeast dough.

ZABAGLIONE: An extremely light, frothy custard consists of egg yolks, sugar and wine or Champagne that are whisked together in the top half of a double boiler. Served hot or cold with puddings, and also called sabayon in France.

Index